SERIES AMERICANA

SERIES AMERICANA

Volume I

Post Depression-Era Regional Literature
1938 – 1980

A Descriptive Bibliography

Including Biographies of the Authors, Illustrators, and Editors

by

CAROL FITZGERALD

Edited by Jean Fitzgerald

OAK KNOLL PRESS
New Castle, Delaware

THE CENTER FOR THE BOOK IN THE LIBRARY OF CONGRESS
Washington, D.C.

2009

First Edition 2009

Published by

Oak Knoll Press
310 Delaware Street
New Castle, DE 19720
www.oakknoll.com

in association with

The Center for the Book
Library of Congress
101 Independence Ave., SE
Washington, DC 20540
www.loc.gov/loc/cfbook

ISBN: 978-1-58456-252-8

Editor: Jean Fitzgerald
Publishing Director: Laura R. Williams
Designer/Typographer: Scott James Vile

∞Printed in the United States of America on acid-free paper meeting the requirements of ANSI/NISO Z39.48−1992 (Permanence of Paper)

Library of Congress Cataloging-in-Publication Data

Fitzgerald, Carol, 1942-
  Series Americana: post Depression-era regional literature, 1938-1980 : a descriptive bibliography, including biographies of the authors, illustrators, and editors / by Carol Fitzgerald ; edited by Jean Fitzgerald. — 1st ed.
    p. cm.
  Includes bibliographical references and index.
  Summary: "A descriptive bibliography of American regional literature in the post Depression era (1938-1980). Includes thirteen "Series Americana," with information on American history, culture, customs, and landscapes. Each section includes a bibliographical description of the first edition, a publishing history, and biographical sketches of editors, authors, and illustrators"—Provided by publisher.
  ISBN 978-1-58456-252-8 (set : hardcover : alk. paper) 1. American literature—20th century—Bio-bibliography. 2. Regionalism in literature—Bio-bibliography. 3. United States—In literature—Bio-bibliography. 4. Series (Publications)—Bio-bibliography. I. Fitzgerald, Jean. II. Title. III. Title: Post Depression-era regional literature, 193

For my husband
Jean

᷍

My sons
John and Jim

᷍

My grandchildren
Sarah, Justin, & Jason

Three Generations of Americans

CONTENTS

VOLUME II

PREFACE

ON Oct. 25, 2007, the Bienes Museum of the Modern Book at the Broward County Library in Fort Lauderdale Florida opened an unusual exhibit of great interest to students of 20th century American history and culture: "Series Americana: An Exhibition of Selected Post Depression-Era Regional Literature from the Collection of Carol Fitzgerald."

The exhibit presented a selection — 78 titles — from 12 series of books, totaling 153 titles, that described American culture and society and the nation's natural resources. The exhibit was unusual not only because of the range of topics covered by the books, including American forts, lakes, seaports, regions, and even murders, but because these 12 series were published, between 1940 and 1980, by no fewer than nine American publishers. Obviously in the decades following the Depression, Americans remained interested in things America; the 12 "series Americana" continued to fill in the national self-portrait that began with the publication of state guide series by the Federal Writers' Project of the WPA (1937–1942), and continued with the Rivers of America series (1937–1974).

The other unusual aspect of the exhibit was that all of the books had been gathered and subsequently described and presented in these two volumes by one individual, Carol Fitzgerald of Fort Lauderdale, Florida, with help from her husband and editor Jean. In fact, Carol added one series to this work after the exhibit closed on Jan. 8, 2008: the 10-volume *American Landmarks* series published by Hastings House between 1938 and 1942.

Thus these two volumes contain thirteen series, containing a total of 163 titles.

This is the second collaborative effort between the Center for the Book and Oak Knoll Press that has brought Carol Fitzgerald's broad perspective as a book collector and her singular skills as a bibliographer, biographer, and publishing historian before the public. In 2001, we copublished her formidable (899 pages in two volumes) and extremely well received *The Rivers of America: A Descriptive Bibliography*, edited by Jean Fitzgerald, which included biographies of all 121 "Rivers" authors, illustrators, and editors. At its heart were complete bibliographical descriptions of the nearly 400 printings of the 65 titles that make up the Rivers of America series.

A stepping stone on the way to the publication was a symposium which, with Carol's help, the Center for the Book and the Library's American Folklife Center hosted at the Library of Congress on April 9–10, 1997. Eleven

Rivers of America authors, illustrators, and editors were able to participate, a major accomplishment considering that this unique series had been launched sixty years earlier. The symposium is described in the *Library of Congress Information Bulletin* for June 9, 1997.

In an act of generosity marking the 25th anniversary of the Center for the Book in 2002, the Fitzgeralds donated their "Rivers of America" archive to the Library of Congress, a collection comprising more than 400 first editions and subsequent printings, related correspondence, audio and video recordings, original art work, and other materials. Today that collection is available to all researchers in the Library's Rare Book and Special Collections Division.

Facilitating projects that demonstrate the key role that books, authors, collectors, and publishers have played-and continue to play-in American life and culture comes naturally to the Center for the Book (www.loc,gov/cf-book.)

Established by Congress in 1977, the center uses the resources and prestige of the Library of Congress to promote books, reading, literacy, and libraries. From the beginning it has been a small, catalytic public-private partnership; the Library of Congress pays its four staff salaries, but all of its publications and program activities are supported by tax-deductible contributions from individuals, corporations, and foundations or, depending on the project, by other government agencies. With its many educational programs that reach readers of all ages, through the key role it plays in the National Book Festival and through its dynamic network of centers in all 50 states and the District of Columbia, the center has developed a nationwide network of organizational partners dedicated to promoting the wonders and benefits of reading.

Shortly after its creation, the center began organizing and hosting events that honored "the book," important individuals in the world of books and reading, and notable book series as well. In addition to the previously described "Rivers of America" symposium and publication, two other publishing history projects may be of interest to readers of the present work.

The fortieth anniversary of the Armed Services Editions, those squat paperbacks distributed by the millions to U.S. servicemen and servicewomen during World War II, was celebrated by the center at the Library of Congress on Feb. 17, 1983. Several people with firsthand experience were brought together with publishers, scholars, collectors, and readers of these popular books. A volume based primarily on the day's events, *Books in Action: The Armed Services Editions,* ed. by John Y. Cole (Washington, 1984), includes a list of the 1,322 titles in the series.

The New Deal Arts projects of the 1930s and early 1940s were discussed at "Amassing American Stuff: the Library of Congress's New Deal Arts Collections," a Center for the Book program on Dec. 8–9, 1994. Twenty-one veterans and observers of the New Deal Arts projects and curators from throughout the Library came together for two days of interviews, reminiscing, and discussion. The Federal Writers' Project (1935–1943) and its publications were one of the featured projects. The program is described in the Feb. 6, 1995 issue of the *Library of Congress Information Bulletin.*

The Center for the Book is delighted to be associated with Series Americana, another important contribution to American cultural and bibliographic studies by Carol Fitzgerald.

JOHN Y. COLE
Director, Center for the Book, Library of Congress
Washington, D.C.
January 2009

FOREWORD

THE term "Series Americana" implies books in series and regionalism. Literary regionalism has been defined as the use of regional characteristics — locale, customs, culture, or speech — that serve to preserve the character of a geographic area and its people. Although regionalism is an element in nearly all literature, since most literature involves a locale or a setting, the term is most often used when the locale is a subject that is itself interesting.

During the Great Depression and continuing well into the decades that followed, American regionalism and regional writing became increasingly popular. While the American Guide Series produced by the Federal Writers' Project created the first credible national self-portrait in print, the popular *Rivers of America* series, planned by Constance Lindsay Skinner and inaugurated in the mid-1930s, established a promising pattern for the many series that followed. Various series of non-fiction books with American themes and settings — "Series Americana" — were planned and published by such newly-formed firms as Hastings House and Duell, Sloan and Pearce and by established companies such as Bobbs-Merrill and Doubleday, Doran.

While I was collecting books in the *Rivers of America* series, I learned of other Series Americana, often because they included books by authors who had also written for the *Rivers* series. Over the years, I have concentrated on thirteen series that I believe provide a valuable, credible self-portrait of America's people, culture, history, and geographic regions. These thirteen series and their publishing histories, authors, editors, and illustrators are the subject of this book.

The series featured in this book were published during the years 1938–1980 and comprise 163 titles and the work of 237 authors and 19 editors, providing a broad representation of the Series Americana published in the post-Depression era and the following decades. There are other non-fiction American series, but, taken together, the thirteen series covered here provide a compelling portrait of America, a unique inward look that encompasses the American people, their history and culture, and the nation's natural treasures — its mountains, plains, lakes, and trails — over a broad sweep of time measured in centuries.

CAROL FITZGERALD
Fort Lauderdale, Florida
April 2009

ACKNOWLEDGMENTS

MY interest in Series Americana evolved during my search for books in the *Rivers of America* series, as I became aware of other Series Americana. As I look back over some five years of writing and research for this book and twenty years of collecting books in series, I realize that I can never adequately thank the scores of people who have helped me along the way, including authors, librarians, book dealers, and friends and family members of authors of books in the series addressed in this book. In particular, I am deeply grateful to Dr. John Y. Cole, Director of the Center for the Book in the Library of Congress, for his unflagging support and encouragement over the nearly twenty years of my writing the present work and my earlier book, *The Rivers of America.*

Although the interviews, telephone conversations, letters, faxes, e-mail messages, press clippings, and reference and archival material that support each title addressed in this book are cited in the related chapter, there are those who deserve special thanks for their contributions to my work.

I shall never forget the friendship and encouragement extended to me by the distinguished author and Kentucky historian, the late Dr. Thomas D. Clark. Dr. Clark wrote a book in the *Rivers* series and a book in the *Regions of America* series.

Two special friends, Dr. Alexander McLeod of Nashville, Tennessee and Nicholas Basbanes, who has written many books about books, book collecting, book collectors, and other elements of the literary world, have for years extended their support and encouragement as I worked on the *Rivers* book and on the present work. I deeply appreciate all they have done for me.

At their home in Ojai, California, the Western author David Lavender and his wife, Muriel, were extraordinarily hospitable, granting unlimited access to David's extensive files; furnishing background information for several series covered in this book, information that was otherwise unavailable from any source; and participating in several personal interviews over a three-day period.

I am grateful for the grant I received from the Book Club of California. The grant supported my travel to California, where I interviewed Richard Dillon, Ferol Egan, and Remi Nadeau, all of whom warmly welcomed my husband, Jean, and me into their homes. The three are authors of books covered in the present work, and they generously provided a wealth of information bearing on their writing and on the publication of a number of the Series Americana addressed in this book.

I am indebted to Stetson Kennedy, who wrote *Palmetto Country* in the *American Folkways* series, for his friendship and encouragement over many years. I thank David Remley, who wrote *Crooked Road* in *The American Trails Series*, for the invaluable information he supplied about the book. Two respected illustrators gave me useful information about their work on books in *The American Trails Series*: Marian Ebert Wolle, illustrator of *Westward Vision*, and Don Almquist, illustrator of *Doomed Road of Empire*. My thanks to both of them.

I express my gratitude and appreciation to the many relatives, family members, and friends of the authors who wrote in the series addressed in this book. Among them are: Paul H. Altrocchi, M.D., son of Julia Altrocchi (*The Spectacular San Franciscans*); Elizabeth Barash, daughter of Alfred Powers (*Redwood Country*); Anna W. Giddings, widow of Theodore Giddings (*The Berkshires*); Richard Hinkle, son of George and Bliss Hinkle, and Christney McGlashan (*Sierra-Nevada Lakes*); Edwin S. James, brother-in-law of Francis Guess (*South Carolina*); Muriel Lavender, widow of David Lavender; Helen Long, daughter-in-law of Haniel Long (*Piñon Country*); Charles J. Patterson, Jr. (*Cleveland Murders*); Norma J. Spurgeon, daughter of Everett Webber (*Escape to Utopia*); Joseph Walton, son of George H. Walton, (*Sentinel of the Plains*); and Albert N. Williams III and Christopher Williams, sons of Albert N. Williams (*Rocky Mountain Country*).

I acknowledge with thanks the special assistance I have received from The Bancroft Library at the University of California, Berkeley; the Broward County (Florida) Main Library; the Columbia University Library; the University of Kentucky Library; The Lilly Library, Indiana University; the Syracuse University Library; and the files and records of the New York State Historical Association. I also extend special thanks to the copyright section of the Library of Congress, whose staff was invariably courteous and efficient in guiding me in the use of their extensive files and records.

Among the many other librarians and libraries across the country who provided information and copies of documents and other records, I am especially grateful to Cindy Adams and Carol Tobin of the University of North Carolina Davis Library; Bradley Block of the Interpretive and Educational Services Program, Custer State Park, South Dakota; Phyllis M. Cohen of the Museum of Fine Arts, Museum of New Mexico, Santa Fe; Lynda Corey Claasen of the Mandeville Special Collections Library, University of California, San Diego.

And Prudence J. Doherty of the Bailey/Howe Library, University of Vermont; Alice S. Diehl of Lebanon Valley College; Wayne Everard of the New Orleans Public Library; Leanne Garland of Lincoln Memorial University; Donald Glassman of the Wollman Library, Barnard College; Daniel D.

Haacker of the Milton Public Library, Milton, Massachusetts; Linda W. Jackson of the museum at Chesterwood, Stockbridge, Massachusetts; Jeff Korman and Mendy Gunter at the Enoch Pratt Free Library, Baltimore, Maryland.

And Valerie-Anne Lutz of the American Philosophical Library, Philadelphia, Pennsylvania; Norma McCallan of the New Mexico State Library; Mary A. Medlicott of Franklin College, Franklin, Indiana; Wilbur E. Meneray of Tulane University Library; Jennifer I. Moore of the American Antiquarian Society, Worcester, Massachusetts; Theresa Regnier of the D. B. Weldon Library, University of Western Ontario; Janice Strickland, Statesboro Regional Library, Statesboro, Georgia; Jacque Roethler of the University of Iowa.

My special thanks to James Findlay and Lillian Perricone at the Bienes Museum of the Modern Book at the Broward County (Florida) Main Library for their professional preparation and presentation of the Series Americana books exhibition 2007–2008, which featured seventy-eight books from my collection.

Among the many book dealers who have assisted me in building my collections of American books in series, my special thanks go to Marc Selvaggio and his late wife, Donnis, of Schoyer's Books, to John Townsend of Town's End Books, Rock Toews of Back Creek Books, and to the late Robert Mattila of Seattle.

Special thanks to my sister, Jeannie Knoepfel and her husband, Hans, for their advice, assistance, and encouragement over the years I have worked on this book.

INTRODUCTION

REGIONALISM, the use of regional characteristics — locale, customs, culture, or speech — whether such use be in literature or in art, serves to preserve the character of a geographic area and its people. Regional literature was already common and widespread in America in the 1930s when many of the series described here were conceived. In 1940, in the foreword and the outline of a course in American regional literature that he taught at the University of Wisconsin, August Derleth (1909–1971) wrote in part:

> From 1920 on, the Regional aspect of American literature is marked. The great and spreading interest in America and the American back- ground stems from a number of well-defined influences: 1) post-War disillusionment — taking the form of an immediate depression early in the 1920's . . . and the current depression begun in October, 1929; 2) the rise of influential men in editorial and critical positions power- ful enough to blast the conventional tradition of American criticism up to that time. . . . It should be made clear, however, that the uncon- scious movement called Regionalism is not an end in itself, but a phase in the development of literature with a national tradition. It should be accepted at once, also, that the [American] regions as roughly defined . . . do not have established borders, but are already in fusion, as in years to come, the regions here set down will be nationally fused. . . . It should be understood also that interest in regional American writing can be extended backward to Colonial times, and does, in fact, begin there; but it was not until after 1900 that the regional writing of today began to grow out of Naturalism or Realism in that important period of American letters.[1]

Regionalism is an element in nearly all literature, since most literature involves a locale or setting. The term, however, is usually applied to writings in which the locale is thought of as a subject interesting in itself.[2] By the summer of 1940, as the Depression wore on, regional books were becoming so popular that bookshops devoted entire window displays to them. In an article headed "Regional Books Respond to Bookshop Promotion" in the August 17, 1940, issue of *Publishers' Weekly*, Helen R. Tiffany, a bookseller in Toledo, Ohio, reported, "We have noticed, as probably everyone else has, an increased demand for books about America, both past and present. It has

1. *American Regional Literature: Towards a Native Rural Culture.* A study of the Literature of Rural Life, based on a course given by August Derleth in 1940 for students in the Farm Folk School — College of Agriculture, University of Wisconsin.
2. Shaw, Harry. *Dictionary of Literary Terms.* McGraw-Hill, 1972, p. 319.

grown gradually from the time when books on local subjects brought a limited response, to the present when we find our most enthusiastic and regular customers among those who buy books about American subjects."

Lewis Gannett's essay, "Reading about America," in the May 3, 1941, issue of *Publishers' Weekly*, began: "From the evergreen land of pointed firs in Maine to the eternal brown of the Mojave Desert, from the immense rain forests of the Northwest Coast to the strange tropical south of Florida, Americans everywhere are looking at their country with new and curious eyes. It is as if we had never seen it before, as if we were Rip Van Winkles rousing from a long sleep, or immigrants ourselves. . . . The new continental consciousness inevitably reflects itself in the books men write and in the books we read."

Later in the essay, Gannett observed, "It is no accident of Depression that we have today in the WPA *American Guides* our first real series of handbooks to the nation. They have not created this new awareness of our history, our folklore, our local byways and beauty spots; they have expressed it with a completeness elsewhere non-existent. The *Guides* have been appearing almost simultaneously with the stately row of *Rivers of America* books which Constance Lindsay Skinner planned and Carl Carmer and Stephen Vincent Benét carry on. . . . The *Seaports of America* series recently inaugurated . . . has the same pride in the past."

In his classic work, *A History of Book Publishing in the United States*, John Tebbel, describing aspects of publishing in the years 1944 and 1945, noted:

> There seemed to be no end to the demand for historical fiction about America, and following Rinehart's lead with its distinguished Rivers of America series, new series were appearing on American states, harbors, lakes, mountains, regions, and other topographical attractions. There was a wide popular audience for all these books.
>
> Many of these productions were legacies from the Depression years, when hundreds of unemployed writers, put to work by the Works Progress Administration, had gathered mountains of historical data of every kind in counties and communities across the country. . . . On these and other optimistic notes, 1944 came to an end — like its predecessor, a remarkable year in many ways. Using 15 percent less paper, publishers had nevertheless contrived to produce more books than in any previous year, mostly by making their volumes thinner and lighter.[3]

American regionalism and regional writing became increasingly popular, and the successful *Rivers of America* series established a promising pattern for the many series that followed. In the late 1930s,"Series Americana,"

3. Tebbel, John. *A History of Book Publishing in the United States* (Bowker) *Volume IV, The Great Change*, 1940-1980, pp. 57–58.

non-fiction books in series with American themes and settings, were being planned by established publishers such as Bobbs-Merrill and Doubleday, Doran, and by such newly-formed houses as Duell, Sloan and Pearce and Hastings House.

The earliest of these series is the *American Landmark Series,* ten volumes of "Camera Impressions" of New England cities and towns published by Hastings House from 1938 to 1942. The series features the work of photographer Samuel Chamberlain. Walter Frese founded Hastings House specifically to publish Chamberlain's work.

The Seaport Series consists of twelve volumes published by Doubleday, Doran (later Doubleday) between 1940 and 1947. There was no general editor of the series. The books were written by established writers and journalists of the day and recount the histories of major seaports in the United States, Canada, and Hawaii. (Canadian subjects appear from time to time in Series Americana, in the *Rivers of America* and the *American Lakes* series, for example.) To Doubleday's credit, the series flourished despite wartime restrictions on paper use and pervasive personnel shortages.

The *American Folkways Series* is perhaps the best-known and most successful of the post-Depression era regional series. Conceived by the three partners of the newly-founded Duell, Sloan & Pearce and edited by Erskine Caldwell, the series was launched in 1940 with the publication of *Desert Country* by Edwin Corle. Caldwell's literary fame, his keen interest in regional life in the United States (which he later described as having completely absorbed him), and his hands-on approach moved him to assemble a group of talented, respected writers for the series. The twenty-eight volumes address folkways in much of the nation; and, for the most part, the books sold well both regionally and nationally. Many of the series authors were well-known to those living in the region addressed, but others, such as Wallace Stegner and Stanley Vestal, had established national literary stature, thus creating a wider market for sales of the books. The *Folkways* series maintained popular appeal for nearly two decades. Its final title was published in 1958.

Vanguard Publishing produced two series: the *American Mountain Series* and the *American Customs Series.* The *Mountain* series, edited by geologist Roderick Peattie and written by scientists and local experts of the day, includes nine volumes published between 1942 and 1952. The books provide detailed, scholarly portraits of the major mountain ranges in the United States. The *Customs* series, published between 1946 and 1949, includes seven titles. The series is light-hearted and includes engaging information and anecdotes that might well have been lost had it not been published.

The American Lakes Series comprises ten volumes relating to major lakes in the United States and Canada published by Bobbs-Merrill and edited by the historian Milo Quaife. The first five volumes in the series cover the five

Great Lakes. Later volumes cover Lake Pontchartrain, Lake Champlain and Lake George, the Great Salt Lake, Lake Okeechobee, and the Sierra-Nevada lakes. The publisher's announcement of the series noted in part that the volumes would be "written for the general reading public by historians of known scholarly standing" and would "provide an accurate history of the role the individual lake played in the settling of its environs, the development of American commerce, and the noble and thrilling role it may have played in the wars of America." While the *Lakes* series fits in well with the regional literature produced at the time, the series itself had a rather short life — from 1944 to 1949.

In 1944, Duell, Sloan & Pearce took regional writing to a new level with the *Regional Murder Series*. Edited by Marie Rodell, at the time the head of the Bloodhound Mysteries department at the firm, each volume is a compilation of non-fictional accounts of murders that occurred in a major American city. Sixty-six crime writers and journalists contributed to the series. The nine volumes were published from 1944 to 1948, and cover murders in New York, Chicago, Denver, San Francisco, Los Angeles, Cleveland, Charleston, Detroit, and Boston. Each book in the series is identified as *A Bloodhound Book*.

In 1947 and 1948, Bobbs-Merrill published three volumes in their *American Trails Series*. Edited by writer and Lincoln historian Jay Monaghan, the series experienced a short life. Fourteen years later, *The American Trails Series* was revived in concept by McGraw-Hill under the general editorship of A.B. Guthrie, Jr., a well-known Western writer. McGraw-Hill published fifteen volumes in their *American Trails Series*, from 1962 to 1977, including histories of the Oregon Trail and the California Spanish Mission Trail, as well as some on trails that were not wholly American, such as the El Dorado Trail and the Siskiyou Trail.

E. P. Dutton's *Society in America Series* covers eight major American cities, Boston, Washington, D.C., Memphis, San Francisco, New Orleans, Cincinnati, Dallas, and Baltimore. The publisher's goal was "to portray the individual characteristics, to underscore the idiosyncrasies, and to trace the growth of sectional societies with special emphasis on local traditions and on the personalities who embodied them." In 1947, Cleveland Amory led off the series with his immensely popular *The Proper Bostonians*. Published in October 1947, the book sold sixty thousand copies by December 1949. The series continued until 1951.

The Mainstream of America Series consists of twenty volumes published by Doubleday & Company between 1953 and 1966. The general editor of the series was Lewis Gannett. The series includes three books by John Dos Passos and works by Irving Stone; David Lavender; C. S. Forester; Harold Lamb;

and Hodding Carter. In announcing the series, Doubleday noted that each volume would present the past "in terms of people and their stories" without "dull dates, dim figures, lists of battles," and vowed that the series would make history "as moving and lively as the finest fiction." The series encompasses a vast range of American history, from the European discovery of America and early exploration to the American Revolution, westward expansion, and industrial development.

In the early 1950s, Hastings House named Henry Alsberg, who had served as national director of the Federal Writers' Project from 1935 to 1938, general editor of the *American Procession Series*. Alsberg had directed Hastings House's production of *The American Guide* (1949), a one-volume, 1,348-page condensation of the Writers' Project guide series. (The book was a Book-of-the-Month Club alternate selection that brought the club its largest-ever dividend.) The publisher described the series as "a new literary series . . . which will center around periods in our history and cultural growth which have not yet been fully explored." Comprising nine titles, the series was published from 1954 to 1964 and includes volumes on the Know-Nothing movement, the communal movement, early Yankee inventors, and the first Western land rush, as well as three volumes by Mari Sandoz covering cattlemen, buffalo hunters, and beaver men.

In the mid-1950s, Harper Bros. hired Carl Carmer, an editor of the *Rivers of America Series*, to oversee their *Regions of America Series*. Carmer, himself a well-known regional writer, signed up other popular regional writers, many of whom, including Marjory Stoneman Douglas and Thomas D. Clark, had contributed volumes to the *Rivers* series. The publisher's detailed description of the *Regions* series noted the principal purpose of each series volume as "to bring to life and tell the story of a particular area; its distinguishing characteristics in people, topography and spirit; its achievements and failures; how it began, where it has gotten to and how; and where it may be going," adding, "History is of course of major importance, but so are personalities, trends, insights." The first of the fourteen volumes in the series, *Virginia: A New Look at the Old Dominion* by Marshall Fishwick, was published in 1959; the last, *California: Land of New Beginnings* by David Lavender, in 1980.

Stewart Holbrook, a widely respected regional writer, conceived and planned the *American Forts Series* in the early 1960s. Although he died before the first volume was published, he had planned eight of the nine books. In his words, it would be "a series of historical works centered around forts in the United States and Canada that were of significant importance to American history." Prentice-Hall published the nine books between 1965 and 1973. Like many other Series Americana, the *American Forts Series* presents a wide swath of American history, spanning as it does nearly four centuries and focusing on many separate regions. The various regional histories presented are not noticeably repetitive of those in earlier series.

The thirteen series described above comprise 163 separate titles published from 1940 to 1980. Taken together, they constitute a unique and compelling self-portrait of America that encompasses its people, history, culture, and natural treasures — its mountains, plains, lakes, and trails — over a broad sweep of time measured in centuries.

Every attempt has been made to make this book easy to use. It is first a reference work and as such must be unfailingly dependable in its presentation of factual material. Users of the book will be able — quickly and easily — to identify a first printing of each title. Later printings, to the extent possible, are reported, with the publisher, year of publication, number of printings, and, when available, the number of copies printed. Scholars may discern interesting historical and literary trends from the collateral information I presented, some of it gleaned from the dust jackets of the books themselves, more from correspondence with series authors, illustrators, and their families and descendants, as well as valuable information from the papers and files of publishers, authors, and editors.

This bibliography covers a span of forty-two years — from 1938 to 1980 — the closing years of the Great Depression, World War II, and decades of postwar national development and economic and social change. Some of the books published during the war years include advertisements for war bonds, notices that encourage the donation of books to the armed forces, or identify books published under the paper restrictions of the War Production Board. Such books are not abridged, but are on thinner paper, with jackets that sometimes are too large for the book. A Doubleday, Doran notice read, "This book is standard length, complete and unabridged. Manufactured under wartime conditions in conformity with all government regulations controlling the use of paper and other materials." *Tropic Landfall: The Port of Honolulu*, a volume in the *Seaport Series*, was ready for publication when Pearl Harbor was attacked in 1941. The prologue, "The Port at War," was rewritten just before the book's publication to take into account the attack and its immediate results.

Within this bibliography, I present the thirteen series in chronological order, based on the year the first volume in each series was published. Each section begins with an introduction and publishing history, a biography of the general editor, if any, and a publishing chronology and alphabetical listings of the authors and titles. Within each section, the series titles are presented in alphabetical order. A detailed description of the first edition, first printing of each book is followed by a note providing the number of reprints of the first printing, if any, issued by the original publisher. Some titles were issued in special and limited edition printings. My collection includes most of such printings, but there are a few that I have been unable to acquire or examine. These are listed and noted as "not seen." This is followed by a listing, "Reprints and Reproductions," identifying later printings, sometimes enlarged or revised printings by the original publisher, or printings by other publishers.

Biographies of the book's author and its illustrator, if the book is illustrated, follow. In turn, these are followed by a "Notes on . . ." section, which may contain an account of how the book's author was chosen or some other aspect of the book. This section is followed by a tabulation of book reviews; a listing of selected writings of the author's other published works; and a listing of sources used.

Many of the authors, illustrators, and editors were established figures in the world of books and letters. For them, adequate biographical information was readily available. For others, whose talents were perhaps no less, such information is often limited or unavailable. I have done my best to tell their stories, hoping to preserve some record of their work. I encourage those with additional material or information to contact me.

～

The following notes explain the specifics of each volume's entry:

EDITION, YEAR OF PUBLICATION, AND VOLUME NUMBER: The edition described and its year of publication are followed by a number within brackets reflecting the book's position in the chronological order of publication of the titles in the series, based on copyright dates and publishers' advertising.

TITLE PAGE: A facsimile description of the title page of each volume is provided.

COLLATION: Leaf size measured in inches, the vertical dimension first, then the horizontal, is followed by the number of leaves. Page numbers not actually printed on the page are enclosed within brackets.

CONTENTS: The contents of first editions, first printings, are listed in full and described to a useful but not cumbersome degree. Occasionally a book contains preliminary pages that do not fit into the usual collation. To these I have assigned lower-case letters in brackets. Unless otherwise noted, all type is roman and printing is in black. When italics are used in the description, they reflect italics in the material being described. When a color is used in the description, it persists until another color or black is noted.

ILLUSTRATIONS: Illustrations are identified as double-page, full-page, or small, and are described in that order, followed by a listing of the book's maps, if any. If an illustration or a map has a title, the title is included in the description.

BINDING: The binding is transcribed in quasi–facsimile, with the color of the binding and the Pantone number that most closely identifies it stated. (The publishers' series devices displayed on various bindings are depicted in an appendix.) Spines are read horizontally, i.e., as one reads the titles of most books when they are shelved, from left to right, starting at the top of the spine. Spines that would be read from left to right if the book were lying on its back are described as "read vertically."

DUST JACKET: The color of the jacket paper is noted, usually as white or light cream. Jacket colors and the Pantone numbers that most closely identify them are stated. Descriptions of the spines of the jackets employ the same terms, "read horizontally" and "read vertically," as are used for the bindings.

BIOGRAPHIES: Biographical sketches of editors, authors, and illustrators are provided.

NOTES ON . . .: This section provides details, when available, on how the authors and illustrators of the book were chosen and may include narrative information of a kind not generally found in standard bibliographies. For some volumes, a wealth of such information was available; for others there was little or none.

REVIEWS: *Book Review Digest* is the source of most of the reviews cited, but other reviews are noted when available.

SELECTED WRITINGS BY . . .: This section lists, in the chronological order of their publication, other published works of the authors, the publishers of such works, and the dates of their publication. This information is intended to give the reader an indication of the nature and extent of the published works of the authors, while placing their work in the immediate series, which is printed in bold, at the proper point among their published writings.

SOURCES: This section lists the sources used, including library and museum holdings of the papers of the authors, illustrators, and editors; files and records of various publishers; standard reference works; newspaper files; and correspondence and interviews with authors, illustrators, and editors of the series, their families, and their descendants. Sources are listed in the chronological order of their publication or occurrence.

SERIES AMERICANA

The Publishers

This compilation of brief histories of the publishers of the thirteen Series Americana presented in this work is based almost entirely on the four-volume series, *A History of Book Publishing in the United States* by John Tebbel, published by the R. R. Bowker Company in the years 1972–1981, especially Volume III, "The Golden Age Between Two Wars 1920-1940" and Volume IV, "The Great Change 1940-1980."

BOBBS-MERRILL

The Bobbs-Merrill Company traced its origins to 1838, with the opening of a bookstore in Indianapolis by Samuel Merrill. Operating as Merrill, Meigs, and Company after the Civil War, the firm merged with Bowen, Stewart and Company in 1885 and was renamed Bowen-Merrill Company. W.C. Bobbs, who had joined the original firm in 1879, became a partner in the new company. When Silas Bowen retired in 1895, Bobbs was elected company president. In 1903, after Bowen died, the firm adopted the Bobbs-Merrill name.

In the late 1890s the firm began to publish novels, making publishing history with spectacular sales promotions and numerous best-sellers. Over the decades that followed, the firm published fiction, children's books, textbooks, law books, and periodicals. For many years, the firm had a profitable contract with the state of Indiana for printing state documents. After some drastic cost-cutting, the firm survived the Depression and the war years.

In 1958, Howard W. Sams of Indianapolis announced the purchase of Bobbs-Merrill, which became a subsidiary of Howard W. Sams and Company, Inc., a publisher of educational and technical books. The Bobbs-Merrill firm entered the field of educational testing, and, in 1966, the Sams corporation became a subsidiary of ITT Publishing. Bobbs-Merrill continued as an operating firm under the Sams corporation, concentrating increasingly on the work of its educational and technical division through the 1960s and 1970s, eventually abandoning fiction in favor of reference works.

DOUBLEDAY, DORAN (later DOUBLEDAY)

Doubleday was founded in 1897 as a partnership between Nelson Doubleday and Samuel McClure, a magazine publisher. The new firm, Doubleday & McClure Company, became Doubleday, Page & Company in 1900 when Walter Hines joined the firm as a partner. The founder's son, Nelson Doubleday, joined the firm in 1922 and took control of the company in 1934, after his father's death. In 1927, the firm merged with the George H. Doran Company, becoming the largest publishing entity in the English-speaking world. The firm became Doubleday & Company in 1946 and was sold to Bertelsmann, AG in 1986. In 1988, it became part of the Bantam Doubleday Dell Publishing Group, which in turn became a division of Random House, Inc. in 1998.

Anchor Books, which the firm created in 1953, was the publishing industry's first line of distinguished trade paperback books. Dell Publishing, which included a major paperback house and two hardcover firms, Dial Press and Delacorte Press, was acquired in 1976. By 1980, about 35 percent of Doubleday's sales and pretax profits came from its fifteen or more book clubs; about 25 percent from Laidlaw Brothers, its elementary and high school textbook division; 25 percent from the company's manufacturing operations; and 15 percent from Dell. Additional profits were generated by various operations of the Doubleday Company itself.

DUELL, SLOAN & PEARCE

Duell, Sloan & Pearce was founded on December 1, 1939, by C. Halliwell Duell, Samuel Sloan, and Charles A. Pearce, all relatively young men, each with about ten years' publishing experience. Duell had begun his career with Doubleday, continuing it with Morrow; Sloan. Pearce came from Harcourt, Brace. The entrance of the United States into World War II in 1941 was followed by various restrictions on publishing, but the new firm published two hundred and ninety-five books in its first five years (1939–1944) — fifty-five works of fiction, forty-six Bloodhound Mysteries, the remainder non-fiction. Pearce served in the Army during the war, returning to the firm when the war ended, and Sloan died in an accident in April 1945.

After the war, the firm underwent a rapid expansion which continued into the 1950s, concentrating on non-fiction and publishing about fifty titles a year and maintaining an active backlist of more than five hundred titles. But, with continuing financial difficulties, the firm was acquired by the Meredith Publishing Co. in 1961. In 1969, thirty years after the firm's founding, Hawthorn Books bought Meredith's trade book department, including the inventory and rights to all titles published under the Duell, Sloan & Pearce imprint.

E.P. DUTTON & COMPANY

E.P. Dutton was founded in 1864 when Edward Payson Dutton purchased the Old Corner Bookstore in Boston from Ticknor & Fields and Dutton brought their chief salesman, Charles Augustus Clapp, into the firm. The store prospered through increased retail trade, allowing Dutton to expand the bookstore's small publishing concern, and building a business producing church books. The firm moved to New York City in 1869 and by 1874 had a list of seven hundred religious and children's books.

As the decades passed, the firm developed a flourishing retail business in New York. The firm's turning point is generally thought to have occurred about 1919–1920, with its abandonment of religious book publishing. It became a general trade house, and the retail operation was sold. E. P. Dutton died in 1923 at age ninety-three. In his long career, he published at least ten thousand titles. His last catalog listed four thousand.

The firm prospered in the 1920s under the direction of Dutton's partner, John Macrae. In the 1930s control of the firm gradually passed to Macrae's two sons, John, Jr. and Elliott, and later to John Macrae III. In 1975, the company was sold to Elsevier, a Dutch company, and Dutton continued in business under their management. In 1986, Penguin Group (USA) acquired Dutton Books.

HARPER BROTHERS (later HARPER & ROW and HARPERCOLLINS)

Harper Brothers was founded in 1817 by James and John Harper when they formed their printing firm, J. & J. Harper in New York. In 1824, they advertised their first list of books: — five titles — and the next year their younger brothers, Wesley and Fletcher, became partners. In 1833, the firm's imprint was changed to Harper & Bros. By 1849, the firm had nineteen power presses and a staff of nearly three hundred and fifty and was producing two million volumes a year. In the 1850s, the firm founded its two periodicals, *Harper's New Monthly Magazine* and *Harper's Weekly*.

By 1865, five sons of the four brothers were involved in the family business. In 1877, they inherited management of the firm. In 1896, to continue operations, Harper borrowed heavily from J. P. Morgan & Co. but, by 1899, was unable to meet the interest payments. After some turbulent months with the S. S. McLure Company in control of Harpers, George B. Harvey took over, but he resigned in 1915. C. T. Brainerd became president of the firm and operated it through the war years and until 1922, when the firm was recapitalized. Through the 1920s and the Depression and war years of the 1930s and 1940s, the firm thrived under a series of capable leaders, including Cass Canfield and Eugene Saxton.

In the postwar era, Canfield led the firm as it continued to dominate the nation's book business. In the late 1950s, the firm developed its own paperback imprints. In 1962, seeking to develop a line of elementary and high school textbooks, Harper merged with Row, Peterson & Company of Evanston, Illinois, adopting the corporate name Harper & Row. Harper & Row was acquired by the News Corporation in 1987 and combined with the British publisher William Collins & Sons in 1990 to form HarperCollins Publishers, a firm with publishing groups in the United States, Canada, the United Kingdom, Australia, New Zealand, and India, and, by 2006, annual revenues of more than a billion dollars.

HASTINGS HOUSE

Hastings House Publishing Company was founded in 1936 by Walter and Margaret Frese. The firm's first publication was *A Small House in the Sun,* a collection of photographs of houses in New England by Samuel Chamberlain. For years the company specialized in picture books, guide books, and works of similar character, including many other volumes of Chamberlain's photographic works.

While competing with a number of established publishing houses, including Viking, Random House, and Houghton Mifflin, Hastings House published the largest number of titles in the American Guide Series, produced in the late 1930s under the Federal Writers' Project. The firm's success has been attributed to its ability to make quick decisions and its pioneering use of sheet-fed gravure for illustrations.[1] By 1941, the firm had published fifteen titles in the American Guide Series, eventually adding ten more.

In 1982, Hastings House and Earl Steinbicker, an editor and writer, created the *Daytrips* series. Each book in the series provides a guide to a one-day, self-guided tour from a variety of starting places. The books contain descriptions of popular sites, suggested walking tours, photographs, and maps. In the 21st century, Hastings House publishes travel, history, and children's books, cookbooks, and works of Americana.

McGRAW-HILL

McGraw-Hill began as the McGraw-Hill Book Company in 1909 with the merger of the McGraw Publishing Company, founded by James H. Mc-

1. Penkower, Monty Noam. *The Federal Writers' Project* (University of Illinois Press) p. 129.

Graw in 1899, and the Hill Publishing Company, founded by John A. Hill in 1902. Hill became the new company's president and McGraw the vice president. Hill died unexpectedly in 1916, and McGraw became president. In 1917, the firm was renamed McGraw-Hill Publishing Company, Inc.

By the 1930s, the prosperous firm had developed specialities in business, management, and social science textbooks, and, after World War II, elementary and high school textbooks. In the 1960s, renamed McGraw Hill, Inc., the firm acquired Standard & Poor's, a major provider of financial information and analysis. Company revenues exceeded a billion dollars for the first time in 1980. In 1995, the firm reorganized as the McGraw-Hill Companies, developing three segments, education, financial services, and information and media. In 1999, with its Standard & Poors, BusinessWeek, and McGraw-Hill Education segments flourishing, revenues reached a record four billion dollars. The company also expanded into television, the Internet, research, and consulting.

PRENTICE-HALL

Prentice-Hall, Inc. was founded in 1913 by Richard P. Ettinger and Charles W. Gerstenberg, professors of economics at New York University. The two men had written a case textbook, *Materials in Corporate Finance,* which they decided to publish themselves. (The firm name was formed from the maiden names of their mothers.) The book was such a success that they abandoned teaching and took up publishing. After their third book, a volume on taxation, quickly became obsolete owing to changes in the tax code, they began supplying businesses with timely tax information in looseleaf format, then using portions of the looseleaf material in textbooks that were sold to businesses and colleges. The company did not start selling through bookstores until 1937 and did not publish fiction until 1945.

While the firm continued its steady expansion in literary fiction and nonfiction, the publication of novels quickly became a success. By 1962, the firm had become the largest publisher of college textbooks in the United States. Its book-writing division was an outstanding success, producing such titles as the *Federal Tax Course,* which by 1964 was in its forty-fourth edition and had sold more than a million and a half copies. By 1976, the company had twenty-seven divisions and subsidiaries and annual sales of more than two hundred million dollars.

VANGUARD PRESS

Vanguard Press was organized in 1926 with a grant from the Garland Foundation's American Fund for Public Service. Under the terms of the grant, the firm was to produce inexpensive books for sale to the working class. At least two hundred thousand copies of nearly a hundred titles, clothbound and selling for fifty cents, were published in the firm's first two years. When the firm became independent in 1928, James Henle, a former reporter for New York newspapers and later the managing editor of McCall's magazine, became the company's president. Henle ran the company until 1952, publishing a general list of books, a number of them mildly iconoclastic.

Because Communist or left-wing authors had written some of its books in the 1920s, Vanguard was briefly investigated by the House Committee on Un-American Activities (HUAC). The firm came under fire in 1947 for publishing *Our Fair City*, edited by Robert Allen, and *End as a Man*, by Calder Willingham. Unlike many other publishing houses, Vanguard fought vigorously against every attempt to suppress its titles. In 1957, with an apology, HUAC dropped Vanguard from its list of subversive organizations.

Evelyn Shrifte, who had worked at Vanguard since the early 1930s, became president of the firm in 1952, serving in that position until the company was sold to Random House in 1988.

American Landmarks
1938–1942

Samuel Chamberlain
Photographer

Hastings House
Publisher

1938
Gloucester and Cape Ann: A Camera Impression
Historic Salem in Four Seasons: A Camera Impression
Longfellow's Wayside Inn: A Camera Impression
Historic Boston in Four Seasons: A Camera Impression

1939
Nantucket: A Camera Impression
Lexington and Concord: A Camera Impression

1940
Old Marblehead: A Camera Impression
Portsmouth, N.H.: A Camera Impression

1941
Martha's Vineyard: A Camera Impression

1942
Historic Cambridge in Four Seasons: A Camera Impression

AMERICAN LANDMARKS

Introduction and Publishing History

Samuel Chamberlain, Photographer

THE *American Landmarks* series, ten volumes of "Camera Impressions" of New England, the work of the distinguished printmaker and photographer Samuel Chamberlain, was published by Hastings House Publishers between 1938 and 1942. The books in the series are small, six by seven and one-half inches, and seventy-three pages in length. First printings of the books were priced at $1.25. Each volume contains a foreword; photographic images depicting the architectural landmarks, historical monuments, building interiors, and, at times, the nearby countryside of the volume's subject site; which may be a town or city, an island, or, in one instance, a famous inn. Each title also includes descriptive background information on the area or subject and brief but informative captions for the photographs. Each volume's title page carries the subtitle, or, in some instances, the sub-subtitle, *"A Camera Impression."*

The front of each dust jacket carries the book's title across the top above a photograph of a scene characteristic of the book's subject area, "A Camera Impression by Samuel Chamberlain" below the photograph, and the book's title on the spine. The blurb on the back flap of the jacket of each volume begins, *"'American Landmarks' A Series of Camera Impressions by Samuel Chamberlain"* and continues:

> Much that is significant in the American scene has yet to be recorded by a discriminating lens. Strong is the need of documents which do justice to the beauties of our landscape, our historic shrines.

> Without pretense of being either guides or histories, these little volumes aspire, by means of the photographic image, to catch the essence of some of America's unique landmarks.

> The eloquence of these sunlit pictures, carefully edited and captioned, qualifies them for the pleasant task of sketching the American countryside.

> Presented in sympathetic and inexpensive form, this series should appeal to native and traveler alike.

Samuel Chamberlain and his wife, Narcissa, settled in Marblehead, Massachusetts, in 1934 after an extended stay in Europe, where Chamberlain studied etching and printmaking under well-known, distinguished teachers. Over time, his focus turned from printmaking to photography. His early books on New England villages, farms, architectural landmarks, building interiors, and seaside venues were well received. Walter Frese founded Hastings House specifically to publish Chamberlain's work.

Gloucester and Cape Ann, published in June 1938, is the first title in the *American Landmarks* series. Its publication was noted in the August 7, 1938, edition of *The New York Times*, which observed, "This pictorial presentation of one of the most individual and delightful corners of the American scene should find its way to many an American bookshelf." The front flap of the book's jacket reads, "The many moods of Cape Ann, that colorful finger tip of granite pointing far out into the Atlantic, have been caught by the sparkling photographs which fill these pages. The pageant of Gloucester's fishing fleet, the picturesqueness of Rockport, the placidity of the verdant countryside have delighted artists and travelers for decades."

Three series titles were published later in 1938, *Historic Salem in Four Seasons, Longfellow's Wayside Inn,* and *Historic Boston in Four Seasons.* Like *Gloucester and Cape Ann,* the dust jackets of these three titles all carry a paragraph beginning, "This little volume" or "This little book." Each jacket also carries a brief reference to the book's contents.

The dust jacket of *Historic Salem* notes, "The Salem of today conserves much of the drama and beauty of its romantic past. Eloquent reminders of the earliest settlers, and of the days of witchcraft, still remain. The Salem of Revolutionary days, of the prosperous era of merchant princes and clipper ships, is reflected in its dignified old streets."

The dust jacket of *Longfellow's Wayside Inn* notes, "American antiquity has no more eloquent spokesman than the gracious old Wayside Inn which for two and a half centuries has welcomed travelers along the highway. The atmosphere of age and tranquility which delighted Henry Wadsworth Longfellow has only been enhanced by the passing years."

The dust jacket of *Historic Boston* notes, "The Boston of today has kept intact innumerable reminders of its historic past. Bunker Hill, 'Old Ironsides,' the Old North Church, Faneuil Hall and the site of the Boston Tea Party comprise but a fragment of the rich heritage which has come down from the city's three centuries of existence."

Two series titles were published in 1939: *Nantucket* and *Lexington and Concord.* References on the dust jackets of earlier series titles to "this little volume" or "this little book" have been dropped; the front flaps of the jackets carry a single long paragraph describing in greater detail the book's contents.

The dust jacket of *Nantucket,* notes, "The photographic image has caught the romance of this sandy island, set far out in the immensity of the Atlantic. It has captured a glimpse of these (*sic*) prosperous and adventurous days in the last century when Nantucket was the world's greatest whaling port. These eloquent photographs will be treasured by all those who have had the good fortune to know Nantucket."

The dust jacket of *Lexington and Concord* notes, "Mention of these lovely old towns evokes an immediate picture of the stirring days of 1775. It is fortunate that the historical importance of this subject is matched by its physical beauty. An impressive group of noble old buildings has survived from Revolutionary days." Many of those old buildings are then named.

Two series titles were published in 1940: *Old Marblehead* and *Portsmouth N.H.* Of the former, the dust jacket notes, "Marblehead is one of the few towns which still provide a picturesque, concentrated cross section of early New England, vividly recalling its blazing patriotism, its maritime greatness, its graceful way of living. The opulent mansions of the 18th century merchant princes and the sturdy homes of the fishermen still stand, to serve as reminders of Marblehead's vanished splendor as a seaport."

The dust jacket of *Portsmouth, N.H.* notes, "Few places are as rich in Colonial atmosphere as Portsmouth, one of the rare American cities which retains its character as a proud, patrician, pre-Revolutionary seaport. . . . but Portsmouth's eloquent story is best told by its magnificent old houses. They are its greatest treasure, the most vivid reminder of its richly varied history."

One series title was published in 1941: *Martha's Vineyard.* The book's dust jacket notes, "Martha's Vineyard, the largest, and in many ways the most picturesque island in New England, is a jewel of many facets, each providing rich material for an impressionable lens. Its great open spaces, rolling fields and ponds and salt marshes reflect the overwhelming immensity of the Atlantic. Yet its villages are intimate, sheltered and secure."

Historic Cambridge in Four Seasons, the final title in the series, was published in fall 1942. The book's dust jacket notes, "One of the most significant of America's landmarks, Cambridge's intellectual and historical associations go back to the dawn of American history. It still possesses its rich heritage of old houses, celebrated churches, literary shrines, in addition to the background of Harvard University."

While all ten series titles were reprinted, edition and printings are not stated in the books or on the dust jackets. The presence of the Hastings House device, centered on the back of the dust jacket, with no other image or text presented, seems to identify a first printing. The books carrying the publisher's device in that manner are bound in paper boards of various colors, with cream or white wraparound spines, the book's title printed in cream on the front paper boards and repeated on the spine in a color that is coordinated with the cover, and the front flap of the dust jacket displaying a price of $1.25. Seven series titles fit the foregoing description: *Boston, Cambridge, Gloucester and Cape Ann, Lexington and Concord, Longfellow's Way-*

side Inn, Nantucket, and *Salem.* Printings of three series titles, *Old Marble-head, Martha's Vineyard,* and *Portsmouth, N.H.,* fitting the foregoing description have not been found. It is possible that the backs of the dust jackets of the first printings of these three titles carried advertisements that displaced the Hastings House device.

Eight titles in the series were reprinted by "Stanley F. Baker *Publisher*." The title pages of these volumes have a wide decoration obliterating the "Hastings House Publishers New York" line at the bottom of the page. Some but not all of these reprints have "Stanley F. Baker *Publisher*" printed at the bottom of the title page. The Baker printings also carry the Baker publisher's imprint on the front endflap of the dust jacket. The Hastings House files are no longer available, and no information has been found regarding the Stanley F. Baker publishing firm. No evidence has been found that the Baker firm reprinted *Lexington and Concord* or *Old Marblehead.*

In all, the *American Landmarks* series provides an engaging photographic tour of the New England of the late 1930s and early 1940s. The books are a tribute to American heritage, their photographs the work of a master who clearly loved New England.

Samuel V. Chamberlain
Photographer, *American Landmarks*

Samuel V. Chamberlain was born in Cresco, Iowa, on October 28, 1895, the son of George Ellsworth, a surgeon, and Cora Lee (Summers) Chamberlain. His childhood years were spent in the state of Washington. During World War I, while a student in the architectural program at the Massachusetts Institute of Technology, he joined the American Field Service, a volunteer ambulance corps, and was attached to the French Army Air Forces. He received the Croix de Guerre.

When the war ended, Chamberlain returned to the United States, working at architectural firms and as a commercial artist.

On April 23, 1923, Chamberlain married Narcissa Gellatly, a writer. The couple had two daughters, Narcisse and Stephanie.

In 1925 and 1926, he was assistant professor of architecture at the University of Michigan. In 1927, he received a Guggenheim grant and moved for a short time to London, where he attended the Royal College of Art. In 1934, the couple settled in Marblehead, Massachusetts. While working as a printmaker, Chamberlain began to produce photographs of New England, focusing on the landscape and architecture of popular tourist destinations. Hastings House was founded by Walter Frese specifically to serve as Chamberlain's publisher. Working together, the two produced four dozen books. Including the ten titles in the *American Landmarks Series,* Chamberlain wrote, edited, or was co-author of forty-nine books, five of them with his wife, Narcissa, and illustrated at least fifteen others.

In World War II, Chamberlain served in the U.S. Army Air Forces from 1943 to 1945, rising to major and receiving the Legion of Merit and the Bronze Star Medal.

Chamberlain's work is held by museums in the United States and by the Victoria and Albert Museum in England. He received awards of the Society of American Etchers; the Kate W. Arms prize (1933); the John Taylor Arms prize (1936); a special award from the National Trust for Historic Preservation; and an honorable mention, Paris Salon (1925). He was a Chevalier de la Légion d'Honneur. He was a member of the National Academy of Design, the Society of American Graphic Artists, a fellow of the American Academy of Arts and Sciences, an associate member of the Photographic Society of America, and a member of the Société de la Gravure Originale en Noir.

Samuel V. Chamberlain died in Marblehead, Massachusetts, on January 10, 1975, at age 79.

SOURCES

Contemporary Authors Online. The Gale Group, 2001. Reproduced in *Bibliography Resource Center,* Farmington Hills, Mich.: The Gale Group, 2001. Accessed February 21, 2002.

"2007 Escapes North." "Samuel Chamberlain." 2006 North of Boston Convention & Visitors Bureau Web site, accessed April 7, 2007.

Whittier House Museum of Art Web site (biography of Samuel Chamberlain), accessed August 2007.

HISTORIC BOSTON IN FOUR SEASONS
A CAMERA IMPRESSION

Samuel Chamberlain
October 28, 1895 – January 10, 1975

AL1   First edition, first printing (1938) [4]

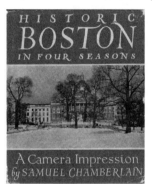

HISTORIC | BOSTON | IN FOUR SEASONS |
[photograph, "Faneuil Hall"] | A CAMERA IM-
PRESSION *by* | *SAMUEL CHAMBERLAIN* |
HASTINGS HOUSE *Publishers* NEW YORK

COLLATION: 6" x 7¼"; 36 leaves. [1–2] 3–7 [8]
9–11 [12] 13–30 [31] 32 34 [35] 36–50 [51] 52–55
[56] 57–59 [60] 61–63 [64] 65–66 [67] 68–72.
Numbers in roman at the inner margin at the
foot of the page.

Note: The verso of the front free endpaper car-
ries a full-page photograph, "The Bowsprits of the Frigate 'Constitution' and
the 'Nantucket' - Charlestown Navy Yard"; the verso of the rear free endpaper carries a full-page photograph, "Arlington Street Church", and a page
number, 73.

CONTENTS: p. [1], title; p. [2], copyright page: "[half-page photograph
"Boston Harbor"| *Copyright, 1938, by Samuel Chamberlain. Printed in the
United States of America* | SET BY HAND IN GARAMOND TYPE BY
ELAINE RUSHMORE | AT THE GOLDEN HIND PRESS, MADISON, NEW
JERSEY"; pp. [3–4], Foreword; pp. 5–72, photographs and text.

BINDING: Crimson paper boards (close to Pantone 201), quarter-bound in
white. Front: [white] *"HISTORIC | BOSTON | IN FOUR SEASONS"*. Spine:
[white background, in crimson] "[read vertically] HISTORIC BOSTON IN
FOUR SEASONS – CHAMBERLAIN". Front endpaper carries a double-page
photograph of the Charles River; rear endpapers carry an untitled double-
page photograph of houses and trees on Beacon Street in winter. A portion
of this photograph, entitled "Essence of Beacon Street," appears on p. 13.

DUST JACKET: Cream paper. Front: "[within a wide crimson band (close to

Pantone 201, in white) *HISTORIC* | *BOSTON* | *IN FOUR SEASONS* | [photograph of the State House] | [within a wide crimson band, in white] A Camera Impression | *by SAMUEL CHAMBERLAIN*". Spine: "[cream background; printing in black] [read vertically] HISTORIC BOSTON IN FOUR SEASONS – CHAMBERLAIN". Back: "[cream background] [Hastings House centered, in crimson]. Front flap: "[upper right] $1.25 | *'AMERICAN LANDMARKS'* | HISTORIC | BOSTON | IN FOUR SEASONS | [short decorative rule] | *A Camera Impression* | *by* SAMUEL CHAMBERLAIN | [blurb] | [publisher's imprint]". Back flap: "'*AMERICAN* | *LANDMARKS*' | [short decorative rule] | A SERIES OF | CAMERA IMPRESSIONS | [short decorative rule] | *by Samuel Chamberlain* | [blurb] | *In the series:* | [list of four series titles, beginning with *Gloucester and Cape Ann* and ending with *Historic Boston*] | *In Preparation:* | 'NANTUCKET', *and others.*".

Published at $1.25 on September 23, 1938; number of copies printed unknown. Copyrighted October 19, 1938; deposited October 20, 1938.

The book is listed in "The Weekly Record," October 8, 1938, p. 1375.

COPIES: CF

REPRINTS AND REPRODUCTIONS

[n.p.]: Stanley F. Baker, Publisher, n.d.

NOTES ON *HISTORIC BOSTON*

Historic Boston is the fourth title in the *American Landmarks* series, and the second of three Chamberlain Camera Impressions to include "In Four Seasons" in the title. In the Foreword of the book, Chamberlain wrote, in part, ". . . these photographic studies seek to preserve some of the atmosphere of old Boston which is personified in Beacon Hill, in the Old North Church, Faneuil Hall and T Wharf, and to record some of the noteworthy landmarks in Back Bay. . . . These photographic impressions are presented with a minimum of text. . . . Let pictures and few words, then, tell the mellow and dramatic story of Boston of today."

REVIEWS

Booklist, October 15, 1938 (p. 66); *Springfield Republican,* December 18, 1938 (p. 7e); *Wisconsin Library Bulletin,* November 1938 (p. 180).

SOURCES

Book Review Digest 1938. New York: The H.W. Wilson Company, 1939, p. 168.

Publisher's Weekly (Fall Index), October 8, 1938, p. 1375.

HISTORIC CAMBRIDGE IN FOUR SEASONS
A CAMERA IMPRESSION

by Samuel Chamberlain
October 28, 1895 – January 10, 1975

AL2   First edition, first printing (1942) [10]

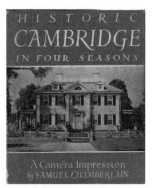

HISTORIC | CAMBRIDGE | IN FOUR SEA-
SONS | [photograph, "Cooper-Frost-Austin
House (1657)"] | A CAMERA IMPRESSION | *by*
SAMUEL   CHAMBERLAIN | HASTINGS
HOUSE · *Publishers* · NEW YORK

COLLATION: 6" x 7¼"; 36 leaves. [1–4] 5–72.
Numbers printed in roman at the inner margin
at the foot of the page.

Note: The verso of the front free endpaper carries a full-page photograph, "Old Town Burying
Ground (Dating from 1636)"; the rear free endpaper carries two photographs
of the Massachusetts Institute of Technology, and a page number, 73.

CONTENTS: p. [1], title; p. [2], copyright page: "[photograph, "Autumn in
the Harvard Yard"] | *Copyright, 1942, by Samuel Chamberlain. Printed in the
United States of America*"; pp. [3–4], Foreword; pp. 5–72, text and photographs.

BINDING: Orange paper boards (close to Pantone 159), quarter-bound in
cream. Front: (cream) *"HISTORIC* | *CAMBRIDGE* | *IN FOUR SEASONS"*.
Spine: [on a cream background, in orange] "[read vertically] HISTORIC
CAMBRIDGE IN FOUR SEASONS – CHAMBERLAIN". Front endpapers
carry a double-page photograph, "The Charles"; the rear endpapers carry a
double-page photograph, "Old Burying Ground."

DUST JACKET: Cream paper. Front: "[within a wide orange band (close to
Pantone 159, in cream) *HISTORIC* | *CAMBRIDGE* | *IN FOUR SEASONS* |
[untitled photograph of the Vassall-Craigie Longfellow House (winter pho-
tograph of the house pictured on p. 54)] | [within a wide orange band, in
cream] A Camera Impression | *by SAMUEL CHAMBERLAIN"*. Spine:

"[cream background; printing in black] [read vertically] HISTORIC CAM-BRIDGE IN FOUR SEASONS – CHAMBERLAIN". Back: "[cream background] [Hastings House device centered, in orange]". Front flap: "[upper right corner] [orange] $1.25 | '*AMERICAN LANDMARKS*' | [black] HISTORIC | CAMBRIDGE | IN FOUR SEASONS | [short decorative rule] | [orange] *A Camera Impression* | *by* SAMUEL CHAMBERLAIN | [blurb] | [publisher's imprint, in orange]". Back flap: "'*AMERICAN* | *LANDMARKS*' | [short decorative rule] | [orange] A SERIES OF | CAMERA IMPRESSIONS | [black] [short decorative rule] | *by Samuel Chamberlain* | [blurb] | [orange] *In the series:* | [list of seven series titles, beginning with *Gloucester and Cape Ann,* and ending with *Historic Cambridge*] | [orange] *Others in Preparation*".

Published at $1.25 on November 9, 1942; number of copies printed unknown. Copyrighted December 14, 1942; deposited December 3, 1942.

The book is not listed in the "Weekly Record."

COPIES: CF

REPRINTS AND REPRODUCTIONS

[n.p.]: Stanley F. Baker, Publisher, n.d.

NOTES ON *HISTORIC CAMBRIDGE*

Historic Cambridge is the tenth and final title in the *American Landmarks* series. As reported in the Hastings House 1939 Spring List, Hastings House had planned to publish *Historic Cambridge* in May 1939, along with *Nantucket* and *Lexington & Concord.* The book was later listed in the *Publishers' Weekly* "1940 Summer Title Index," with a projected publication date of July 1, 1940. There was no further mention of this title until notice of its publication appeared in the 1942 Hastings House Fall List, advising the book would be available in October 1942. Why there were such delays in publication is not known. Dust jackets of earlier books in the series carry *Historic Cambridge* as the seventh title in the series, and only seven series titles, including *Historic Cambridge,* are listed on the book's dust jacket as titles in the series, suggesting that the dust jackets of those books may have been prepared when Hastings House first expected publication of this title. Still, *Historic Cambridge* is the final title in the series.

In the Foreword of the book, Chamberlain wrote, in part, "The story of Cambridge has been told many times, for it has far more than its share of historians. . . . The limited objective of these few pages is to create an *impression* of historic Cambridge by means of the photographic image. By selecting the most significant buildings, the more pictorial compositions, and taking them in good sunlight in all seasons of the year, the camera has tried to capture the essence of this eminent center of American culture."

REVIEWS

Christian Science Monitor, February 27, 1943 (p. 10); *New York Herald Tribune Book Review,* January 17, 1943 (p. 18).

SOURCES

Book Review Digest 1943. New York: The H.W. Wilson Company, 1944, p. 139.

Publishers' Weekly, January 28, 1939 (Spring List), p. 285 and (Spring Book Index), n.p.; May 27, 1939 (Summer Book Index), n.p.; September 26, 1942 (Fall List), n.p.

GLOUCESTER AND CAPE ANN
A CAMERA IMPRESSION

Samuel Chamberlain
October 28, 1895 – January 10, 1975

AL3   First edition, first printing (1938) [1]

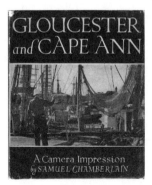

GLOUCESTER | *and* CAPE ANN | A CAMERA IMPRESSION | [untitled photograph of the Eastern Point Light] | By *SAMUEL CHAMBER-LAIN* | HASTINGS HOUSE *Publishers* NEW YORK

COLLATION: 6" x 7¼"; 36 leaves. [1–2] 3–5 [6] 7–45 [46–47] 48–72. Numbers printed in roman at the inner margin at the foot of the page.

Note: The verso of the front free endpaper carries a full-page photograph, "They That Go Down to the Sea in Ships;" the rear free endpaper carries two half-page photographs: "The Fog Horn, Annisquam" and "The Lighthouse, Annisquam," and a page number, 73.

CONTENTS: p. [1], title; p. [2], copyright page: "[photograph, "Forest of Masts"] I *Copyright, 1938, by Samuel Chamberlain. Printed in the United States of America* I SET BY HAND IN GARAMOND TYPE BY ELAINE RUSHMORE AT THE GOLDEN HIND PRESS, MADISON, NEW JERSEY"; pp. [3-4], Foreword; pp. 5-72, photographs and text.

BINDING: Dark-blue paper boards (close to Pantone 288), quarter-bound in cream. Front: [cream] "GLOUCESTER I *and* CAPE ANN". Spine: [cream background, in dark blue] "[read vertically] GLOUCESTER AND CAPE ANN – CHAMBERLAIN". Front endpapers carry a double-page photograph of dories tied at a dock; rear endpapers carry a double-page photograph of a beach scene.

DUST JACKET: Cream paper. Front: "[within a wide dark-blue band (close to Pantone 288, in white) GLOUCESTER I *and* CAPE ANN I [untitled photograph; "Artist Alone"; (An identical photograph appears on p. 31)] I [within a wide dark-blue band, in white] *A* Camera Impression I *by SAMUEL CHAMBERLAIN*". Spine: "[dark-blue background; printing in white] [read vertically] GLOUCESTER AND CAPE ANN – CHAMBERLAIN". Back: "[cream background] [Hastings House device centered, in dark blue]" Front flap: "[upper right corner] [dark blue] $1.25 I '*AMERICAN LANDMARKS*' I [black] GLOUCESTER I *and* CAPE ANN I [short decorative rule] I [dark blue] A CAMERA IMPRESSION I *by Samuel Chamberlain* I [blurb] I [publisher's imprint, in dark blue]". Back flap: "'*AMERICAN* I *LANDMARKS*' I [short decorative rule] I [dark blue] A SERIES OF I CAMERA IMPRESSIONS I [black] [short decorative rule] I *by Samuel Chamberlain* I [blurb] I [dark blue] *In the series:* I [list of seven series titles, beginning with *Gloucester and Cape Ann* and ending with *Historic Cambridge*]" I *Others in Preparation*".

Published at $1.25 on June 27, 1938; number of copies printed unknown. Copyrighted July 19, 1938; deposited July 15, 1938.

The book is listed in "The Weekly Record," July 2, 1938.

Note: Hastings House published at least two printings of *Gloucester and Cape Ann.*

COPIES: CF

REPRINTS AND REPRODUCTIONS

[n.p.]: Stanley F. Baker, Publisher, n.d.

NOTES ON *GLOUCESTER AND CAPE ANN*

Hastings House reported in the July 2, 1938, issue of *Publishers' Weekly* that the first of the "American Landmarks" books were off the press. *Gloucester and Cape Ann* was the first title available. A short review in the August 7, 1938, *New York Times* concluded, "This pictorial presentation of one of the most individual and delightful corners of the American scene should find its way to many an American bookshelf."

In the Foreword of the book, Chamberlain wrote, in part, "This little volume aspires to record an artist's impression of Cape Ann, not upon canvas, but on photographic plates. One hundred pictures cannot hope to tell the story of Gloucester and Cape Ann, but they may perhaps blow a spray of fixatif (*sic*) over the indelible mental picture which every impressionable visitor carries away."

REVIEWS

New York Time Book Review, August 7, 1938 (p. 20); *New Yorker,* July 2, 1938 (p. 52); *Springfield Republican,* June 26, 1938 (p. 7e); *Wisconsin Library Bulletin,* November 1938 (p. 180).

SOURCES

Book Review Digest 1938. New York: The H.W. Wilson Company, 1939, p. 168.

Publishers' Weekly, July 2, 1938, n.p.

The New York Times, August 7, 1938, p. 20.

LEXINGTON AND CONCORD
A CAMERA IMPRESSION

Samuel Chamberlain
October 28, 1895 – January 10, 1975

AL4   First edition, first printing (1939) [6]

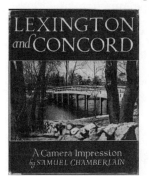

LEXINGTON | *and* CONCORD | [photograph, 'Concord Winter'] | A CAMERA IMPRESSION | *by SAMUEL CHAMBERLAIN* | HASTINGS HOUSE *Publishers* NEW YORK

COLLATION: 6" x 7¼"; 36 leaves. [1–4] 5–72. Numbers in roman at the inner margin at the foot of the page.

Note: The verso of the front free endpaper carries a full-page photograph, "Statue of Captain John Parker, Lexington Common | Henry H. Kitson, Sculptor"; the rear free endpaper carries a full-page photograph, "The 'Minuteman' in a Springtime Setting," and a page number, 73.

CONTENTS: p. [1], title; p. [2], copyright page: "[photograph, *Revolutionary Roadside] Copyright, 1939, by Samuel Chamberlain. Printed in the United States of America* | SET BY HAND IN GARAMOND TYPE BY ELAINE RUSHMORE AT THE GOLDEN HIND PRESS, MADISON, N.J."; pp. [3–4], Foreword; pp. 5–72, text and photographs.

BINDING: Purple paper boards (close to Pantone 526), quarter-bound in white. Front: [white] "LEXINGTON | *and* CONCORD". Spine: [white background, in purple] "[read vertically] LEXINGTON AND CONCORD – CHAMBERLAIN". Front endpapers carry a double-page photograph, "The Tap Room, Buckman Tavern"; rear endpapers carry a double-page photograph, "North Bridge, Concord."

DUST JACKET: White paper. Front: "[within a wide purple band (close to Pantone 526, in white) LEXINGTON | *and* CONCORD | [untitled photograph of North Bridge (the bridge is named in a photograph on the rear endpapers)] | [within a wide purple band, in white] A Camera Impression | *by SAMUEL CHAMBERLAIN*". Spine: "[white background; printing in

black] [read vertically] LEXINGTON AND CONCORD – CHAMBER-
LAIN". Back: "[white background] [Hastings House device centered, in pur-
ple]". Front flap· "[upper right corner] [purple] $1.25 | '*AMERICAN LAND-
MARKS*' | [black] LEXINGTON | and CONCORD | [purple] *A Camera
Impression* | by SAMUEL CHAMBERLAIN | [blurb] | [publisher's imprint,
in purple]". Back flap: "'*AMERICAN | LANDMARKS*' | [short decorative
rule] | [purple] A SERIES OF | CAMERA IMPRESSIONS | [black] [short
decorative rule] | *by Samuel Chamberlain* | [blurb] | *In the series:* | [list of
seven series titles, beginning with *Gloucester and Cape Ann* and ending with
Historic Cambridge]" | *Others in preparation*".

Published at $1.25 on August 30, 1939; number of copies printed unknown.
Copyrighted and deposited September 22, 1939.

The book is not listed in "The Weekly Record."

Note: Hastings House published at least three printings of *Lexington and
Concord.*

COPIES: CF

REPRINTS AND REPRODUCTIONS

None.

NOTES ON *LEXINGTON AND CONCORD*

In the January 28, 1939, Spring List issue of *Publishers' Weekly,* Hastings
House noted that three new titles would be published in May: *Nantucket;
Cambridge;* and *Lexington and Concord. Lexington and Concord* was not published until August 30, 1939, and was available in bookstores on September
14, 1939.

In the Foreword of the book, Chamberlain wrote, in part, "Every American, since his early school days, has been definitely conscious of the two
tranquil New England towns which share the distinction of being the birthplace of the American Revolution. . . . Historical importance here is matched
by physical beauty, a fact which strikes every visitor forcibly, and which this
little book strives to prove by a series of photographic impressions. These
have been taken in all seasons of the year, to portray the varied moods of the
countryside."

REVIEWS

None found.

SOURCES

Publisher's Weekly, January 28, 1939, p. 285.

The New York Times, "Books Published Today," September 14, 1939, n.p.

LONGFELLOW'S WAYSIDE INN
A CAMERA IMPRESSION

Samuel Chamberlain
October 28, 1895 – January 10, 1975

AL5   First edition, first printing (1938) [3]

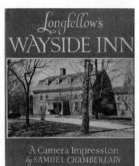

LONGFELLOW'S I WAYSIDE INN I A CAMERA IMPRESSION I [photograph of the Inn] I *by SAMUEL CHAMBERLAIN* I HASTINGS HOUSE *Publishers* NEW YORK

COLLATION: 6" x 7¼"; 36 leaves. [1–2] 3–5 [6–8] 9–25 [26–27] 28–52 [53] 54–55 [56–57] 58–64 [65] 66–67 [68] 69–72. Numbers in roman at the inner margin at the foot of the page.

Note: The verso of the front free endpaper carries a full-page photograph, "The Bar Room"; the rear free end paper carries a full-page photograph, "The Southwest School."

CONTENTS: p. [1], title; p. [2], copyright page: "[photograph of budding trees] I *Copyright, 1938, by Samuel Chamberlain. Printed in the United States of America* I SET BY HAND IN GARAMOND TYPE BY ELAINE RUSH-MORE AT THE GOLDEN HIND PRESS, MADISON, NEW JERSEY"; pp. [3–4], Foreword; pp. 5–72, photographs and text.

BINDING: Green paper boards (close to Pantone 341), quarter-bound in white. Front: "*Longfellow's* I WAYSIDE INN". Spine: [white background, in green] "[read vertically] *Longfellow's* WAYSIDE INN – CHAMBERLAIN". Front endpapers carry a double-page photograph of the Wayside Inn; rear endpapers carry a double-page photograph of a fenced field.

DUST JACKET: Cream paper. Front: "[within a wide green band (close to Pantone 341, in white) *Longfellow's* I WAYSIDE INN I [photograph of the

Wayside Inn] | [within a wide green band, in white] *A Camera Impression* | *by SAMUEL CHAMBERLAIN*". Spine: "[cream background, in green] [read vertically] *Longfellow's* WAYSIDE INN – CHAMBERLAIN" Back· "[cream background] [Hastings House device centered in green]. Front flap: "[upper right corner] $1.25 | *'AMERICAN LANDMARKS'* | *Longfellow's* | WAYSIDE INN | *A Camera Impression* | *by* SAMUEL CHAMBERLAIN | [blurb] | [publisher's imprint]". Back flap: "*'AMERICAN* | *LANDMARKS'* | [short decorative rule] | A SERIES OF | CAMERA IMPRESSIONS | [short decorative rule] | *by Samuel Chamberlain* | [blurb] | *In the series:* | [list of four series titles, beginning with *Gloucester and Cape Ann* and ending with *Historic Boston*] | *In Preparation:* | 'NANTUCKET', *and others.*".

Published at $1.25 on August 29, 1938; number of copies printed unknown. Copyrighted and deposited September 9, 1938.

The book is listed in "The Weekly Record," September 10, 1938, p. 865.

Note: Hastings House published at least two printings of *Longfellow's Wayside Inn.*

COPIES: CF

REPRINTS AND REPRODUCTIONS

[n.p.]: Stanley F. Baker, Publisher, n.d.

Whitefish, Montana: Kessinger Publishing, 2007. Paperback. Published at $17.00.

NOTES ON *LONGFELLOW'S WAYSIDE INN*

This book, the third title in the series, treats a single subject, rather than a New England city, region, or area. In the Foreword of the book, Chamberlain wrote, in part, "This little book exhibits a certain temerity in aspiring to capture, by means of photographs taken in all seasons of the year, some part of the hospitable charm, the tranquillity, the beauty of countryside which the Wayside Inn has reflected since it was

> *'Built in the old Colonial day,*
> *When men lived in a grander way*
> *With ampler hospitality.'"*

REVIEWS

Booklist, October 15, 1938 (p. 66); *Springfield Republican*, October 19, 1938 (p. 8); *Wisconsin Library Bulletin*, November 1938 (p. 180).

SOURCES

Book Review Digest 1938. New York: The H.W. Wilson Company, 1939, p. 168.

Publishers' Weekly, September 10, 1938, p. 865; September 17, 1938 (Fall Index), n.p.

OLD MARBLEHEAD
A CAMERA IMPRESSION

Samuel Chamberlain
October 28, 1895 – January 10, 1975

AL6   First edition, first printing (1940) [7]

OLD |MARBLEHEAD | A CAMERA IMPRESSION | [photograph, 'Fisherman's House'] | *by SAMUEL CHAMBERLAIN* | HASTINGS HOUSE *Publishers* NEW YORK

COLLATION: 6" x 7¼"; 36 leaves. [1–4] 5–72. Numbers in roman at the inner margin at the foot of the page.

Note: The verso of the front free endpaper carries a full-page photograph, "Marblehead Harbor"; the rear free endpaper carries a full-page photograph, "Sunset over Marblehead Fields."

CONTENTS: p. [1], title; p. [2], copyright page: "[photograph, "The Jeremiah Lee Mansion in Midwinter" | *Copyright, 1940, by Samuel Chamberlain. Printed in the United States of America*"; pp. [3–4], Foreword; pp. 5–72, photographs and text.

BINDING: Blue paper boards (close to Pantone 633), quarter-bound in cream. Front: [cream] "OLD | Marblehead". Spine: [on a cream background, in blue] "[read vertically] OLD MARBLEHEAD A CAMERA IMPRESSION – CHAMBERLAIN". Front endpapers carry an untitled double-page photograph of the harbor; rear endpapers carry an untitled double-page photograph of a portion of the town in winter; Abbot Hall in the background. "Abbot Hall in Winter and Summer (A similar photograph appears on p. 13.)"

DUST JACKET: Cream paper. Front: "[within a wide blue band (close to Pantone 632, in white) OLD | *Marblehead* | [photograph of the harbor] | [within a wide blue band, in white] | A Camera Impression | *by SAMUEL CHAMBERLAIN*". Spine: "[white background; printing in blue] [read vertically] OLD MARBLEHEAD A CAMERA IMPRESSION – CHAMBERLAIN". Back: Not seen. Front flap: "[upper right corner] [blue] $1.25 | '*AMERICAN LANDMARKS*' | [black] OLD | MARBLEHEAD | [short decorative rule] | [blue] *A Camera Impression* | *by* SAMUEL CHAMBERLAIN | [black] [blurb] | [publisher's imprint, in blue]". Back flap: "'*AMERICAN* | *LANDMARKS*' | [short decorative rule] | [blue] A SERIES OF | CAMERA IMPRESSIONS | [black] [short decorative rule] | *by Samuel Chamberlain* | [blurb] | *In the series:* | [list of series titles] | *Others in preparation*".

Published at $1.25 on July 8, 1940; number of copies printed unknown. Copyrighted and deposited July 10, 1940.

Note: There is a second notice of copyright for *Old Marblehead* which carries a publication date of July 19, 1940, and a copyright and deposit date of August 9, 1940. The first copyright notice states the book was "completed" June 24, 1940; the second copyright states a "completion" date of July 11, 1940, and appears on the same Copyright Office Record page as *Portsmouth, N.H.* Hastings House released *Old Marblehead* and *Portsmouth, N.H.* for general sale on August 1, 1940.

The book is not listed in "The Weekly Record."

Note: Hastings House published at least two printings of *Old Marblehead*.

COPIES: CF

REPRINTS AND REPRODUCTIONS

New York: Hastings House, 1975. Revised and Enlarged edition by Narcissa G. Chamberlain.[1]

NOTES ON *OLD MARBLEHEAD*

Both *Old Marblehead* and *Portsmouth, N.H.* were published on August 1, 1940. The July 29, 1940, *New York Times* noted that with the publication of these two titles, "[Chamberlain] brings the total number of volumes in his American Landmark Series to nine and the editors of Hastings House say other books are in preparation." This count is incorrect. With the publication of these two titles, the number of titles in the series was actually eight. *Historic Cambridge*, originally scheduled for publication in 1939, was not

1. Samuel Chamberlain's widow.

published until 1942, but the back flaps of the dust jackets of earlier books in the series include *Historic Cambridge* in the list of series titles although it had not yet been published. This could have caused a reviewer to miscount the number of published series titles.

Samuel Chamberlain and his wife, Narcissa, settled in Marblehead in 1934, and the town was always of special interest to him. In the Foreword of the book, Chamberlain wrote, in part, "Few towns are as superbly equipped as Marblehead, Massachusetts, to provide a graphic and concentrated cross section of early New England, its privations, its blazing patriotism, its enterprise and robust individualism, its graceful way of living. . . . But this little book does aspire, by means of the photographic image, to give an *impression* of the beauties of this unforgettable old New England town."

REVIEWS

Booklist, September 1940 (p. 15); *Boston Transcript,* August 17, 1940 (p. 1); *Springfield Republican,* August 4, 1940 (p. 7e).

SOURCES

Book Review Digest 1940. New York: The H.W. Wilson Company, 1941, p. 160.

The New York Times, "Notes on Books and Authors," July 29, 1940, n.p.; "Books Published Today," August 1, 1940, n. p.

MARTHA'S VINEYARD
A CAMERA IMPRESSION

Samuel Chamberlain
October 28, 1895 – January 10, 1975

AL7   First edition, first printing (1941) [9]

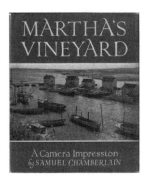

MARTHA'S | VINEYARD | [photograph, "Gay Head Light" | A CAMERA IMPRESSION | *by SAMUEL CHAMBERLAIN* | HASTINGS HOUSE · *Publishers* · NEW YORK

COLLATION: 6" x 7¼"; 36 leaves. [1–2] 3–9 [10–11] 12–31 [32–33] 34–43 [44–45] 46–59 [60–61] 62–72. Numbers in roman at the inner margin at the foot of the page.

Note: The verso of the front free endpaper carries a full-page photograph, "Link with the Mainland – Vineyard Haven"; the rear free endpaper carries a full-page photograph, "Late Afternoon – Gay Head," and a page number, 73.

CONTENTS: p. [1], title; p. [2], copyright page: "[full-page photograph, "Drying Canvas – Menemsha" | *Copyright, 1941, by Samuel Chamberlain. Printed in the United States of America*"; pp. 3–6, Foreword; pp. 7–72, photographs and text.

BINDING: Blue paper boards (close to Pantone 285), quarter-bound in white. Front: [white] "MARTHA'S | VINEYARD". Spine: [white background, in blue] "[read vertically] MARTHA'S VINEYARD – CHAMBERLAIN". Front endpapers carry a double-page photograph of the shore; rear endpapers carry a double-page photograph, "Menemsha Harbor."

DUST JACKET: Cream paper. Front: "[within a wide blue band (close to Pantone 284, in white) MARTHA'S | VINEYARD | [photograph of a harbor scene. | [within a wide blue band, in white] | A Camera Impression | *by SAMUEL CHAMBERLAIN*". Spine: "[blue background; printing in white] [read vertically] MARTHA'S VINEYARD – CHAMBERLAIN". Back: Not seen. Front flap: "[upper right corner] [blue] $1.25 | '*AMERICAN LAND-MARKS*' | [black] MARTHA'S | VINEYARD | [blue] *A Camera Impression* |

by SAMUEL CHAMBERLAIN | [black] [blurb] | [publisher's imprint, in blue]". Back flap: "'*AMERICAN* | *LANDMARKS*' | [short decorative rule] | [blue] A SERIES OF | CAMERA IMPRESSIONS | [black] [short decorative rule] | *by Samuel Chamberlain* | [blurb] | *In the series:* | [list of series titles]".

Published at $1.25 on May 16, 1941; number of copies printed unknown. Copyrighted June 6, 1941; deposited May 17, 1941.

The book is not listed in "The Weekly Record."

Note: Hastings House published at least two printings of *Martha's Vineyard.*

COPIES: CF

REPRINTS AND REPRODUCTIONS

[n.p.]: Stanley F. Baker, Publisher, n.d.

NOTES ON *MARTHA'S VINEYARD*

Martha's Vineyard is the ninth title in the *American Landmarks* series. The book did not receive advance publicity in *Publishers' Weekly.*

In the Foreword of the book, Chamberlain wrote, in part, "Martha's Vineyard, the largest island in New England, and in many ways the most beguiling, has been the subject of books galore. Its historical background, enriched by a romantic pattern of explorers, Indians, whalers and sea captains, has tempted many an author. Artists have painted its airy landscape, its quiet village streets and atmospheric fish wharves for years. But somehow good photographs of the island are rare. This little book attempts to catch some of the indefinable atmosphere of Martha's Vineyard by means of the photographic image. . . . This collection of 'camera impressions' does not aspire to be a history or a guide book, and the brief notes which follow can only provide a thumbnail sketch of the Vineyard's historic past."

REVIEWS

None found.

SOURCES

None.

NANTUCKET
A CAMERA IMPRESSION

Samuel Chamberlain
October 28, 1895 – January 10, 1975

AL8   First edition, first printing (1939) [5]

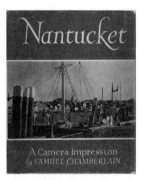

NANTUCKET ‖ A CAMERA IMPRESSION |
[photograph, "The Old Mill (1746)] | *by SAMUEL
CHAMBERLAIN* | HASTINGS HOUSE *Publishers*
NEW YORK

COLLATION: 6" x 7¼"; 36 leaves. [1–4] 5–21
[22–23] 24–72. Numbers in roman at the inner
margin at the foot of the page.

Note: The verso of the front free endpaper caries a
full-page photograph, "Stone Alley"; the rear free
endpaper carries a half-page photograph, "And So
– It's 'Homeward Bound,'" and a page number, 73.

CONTENTS: p. [1], title; p. [2], copyright page: "[photograph, "Old South
Wharf" | *Copyright, 1939, by Samuel Chamberlain. Printed in the United
States of America* | SET BY HAND IN GARAMOND TYPE BY ELAINE
RUSHMORE AT THE GOLDEN HIND PRESS, MADISON, N.J."; pp. [3–4],
Foreword; pp. 5–72, photographs and text.

BINDING: Green paper boards (close to Pantone 328) quarter-bound in
white. Front: {white} "*Nantucket*". Spine: [on a white background, in green]
"[read vertically] NANTUCKET A CAMERA IMPRESSION – CHAMBER-
LAIN". Front endpapers carry a double-page photograph, "Main Street
Square". Rear endpapers carry a double-page photograph, "Old South
Wharf".

DUST JACKET: Cream paper. Front: "[within a wide green band (close to
Pantone328, in white) *Nantucket* | [photograph of a harbor scene] | [within
a wide green band, in white] A Camera Impression | *by SAMUEL CHAM-
BERLAIN*". Spine: "[green background; printing in white] [read vertically]
NANTUCKET A CAMERA IMPRESSION – CHAMBERLAIN". Back:

[cream background] [Hastings House device centered, in green]. Front flap: "[green] [upper right corner] $1.25 I *'AMERICAN LANDMARKS'* I [black] NANTUCKET I [green] A CAMERA IMPRESSION I *by Samuel Chamberlain* I [blurb] I [publisher's imprint, in green]". Back flap: "'*AMERICAN* I *LANDMARKS'* I [short decorative rule] I [green] A SERIES OF I CAMERA IMPRESSIONS I [black] [short decorative rule] I *by Samuel Chamberlain* I [blurb] I [green] *In the series:* I [black] [list of seven series titles, beginning with *Gloucester and Cape Ann,* and ending with *Historic Cambridge*] I *Others in preparation*".

Published at $1.25 on August 30, 1939; the number of copies printed is unknown. Copyrighted and deposited September 22, 1939.

The book is not listed in "The Weekly Record."

Note: Hastings House published at least two printings of *Nantucket.*

COPIES: CF

REPRINTS AND REPRODUCTIONS

[n.p.]: Stanley F. Baker, Publisher, n.d.

NOTES ON *NANTUCKET*

In the January 28, 1939, Spring List issue of *Publishers' Weekly,* Hastings House noted that three new series titles would be published in May: *Nantucket; Cambridge;* and *Lexington and Concord.* The *PW* Summer List moved *Nantucket* to a June 5 publication date. The book was not published until September 14, 1939.

In the Foreword of the book, Chamberlain wrote, in part, "Nantucket, that romantic outpost in the Atlantic, at one time the world's greatest whaling port, has been the subject of many a book. . . . But good photographs of Nantucket seem surprisingly rare. This little book aspires to capture, by means of the photographic image, some of that indefinable native atmosphere which is one of Nantucket's charms. It seeks to emphasize the island's architectural significance, to catch a fleeting glimpse of its great days in the Golden Age of whaling."

REVIEWS

Boston Transcript, September 23, 1939 (p. 2); *New York Herald Tribune Book Review,* July 7, 1940 (*sic*) (p. 12).

SOURCES

Book Review Digest 1940. New York: The H.W. Wilson Company, 1941, p. 160.

Publisher's Weekly, January 28, 1939, p. 285 (Spring List), May 27, 1939 (Summer Index), n.p.

The New York Times, "Books Published Today," September 14, 1939, n.p.

PORTSMOUTH, N.H.
A CAMERA IMPRESSION

Samuel Chamberlain
October 28, 1895 – January 10, 1975

AL9   First edition, first printing (1940) [8]

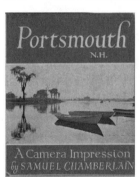

PORTSMOUTH | NEW HAMPSHIRE | [photograph, 'Richard Jackson House (1664)' | A CAMERA IMPRESSION | *by SAMUEL CHAMBERLAIN* | HASTINGS HOUSE · *Publishers* · NEW YORK

COLLATION: 6" x 7¼"; 36 leaves. [1–4] 5–72. Numbers in roman at the inner margin at the foot of the page.

Note: The verso of the front free endpaper carries a full-page photograph, "Chapel Street"; the rear free endpaper carries a full-page photograph, "One of Newcastle's Sleepy Streets," and a page number, 73.

CONTENTS: p. [1], title; p. [2], copyright page: "[full-page photograph, "The Peirce Mansion" (A photograph of the Peirce Mansion also appears on p.13.)| *Copyright, 1940, by Samuel Chamberlain. Printed in the United States of America*"; pp. [3–4], Foreword; pp. 5–72, photographs and text.

BINDING: Red paper boards (close to Pantone 186), quarter-bound in white. Front: [white] "Portsmouth | N.H.". Spine: [on a white background, in red] "[read vertically] PORTSMOUTH, N.H. – CHAMBERLAIN". Front endpapers carry a double-page photograph, "Middle Street"; rear endpapers carry a double-page photograph of a harbor scene.

DUST JACKET: White paper. Front: "[within a wide red band (close to Pantone 185, in white) *Portsmouth* | N.H. | [photograph of three small boats on the Piscataqua. (The photograph also appears on p.32.)] | [within a wide red band, in white] | A Camera Impression | *by SAMUEL CHAMBERLAIN*". Spine: "[white background; printing in black] [read vertically] PORTSMOUTH, N.H. A CAMERA IMPRESSION – CHAMBERLAIN". Back: Not seen. Front flap: "[upper right corner] [red] $1.25 | *'AMERICAN LANDMARKS'* | [black] PORTSMOUTH | N.H. | [red] A CAMERA IMPRESSION | *by Samuel Chamberlain* | [black] [blurb] | [publisher's imprint, in red]". Back flap: "*'AMERICAN | LANDMARKS'* | [short decorative rule] | [red] A SERIES OF | CAMERA IMPRESSIONS | [black] [short decorative rule] | *by Samuel Chamberlain* | [blurb] | *In the series:* | [list of series titles]".

Published at $1.25 on July 19, 1940; number of copies printed unknown. Copyrighted and deposited August 9, 1940.

The book is not listed in "The Weekly Record."

Note: Hastings House published at least two printings of *Portsmouth, N.H.*

COPIES: CF

REPRINTS AND REPRODUCTIONS

[n.p.]: Stanley F. Baker, Publishers, n.d.

NOTES ON *PORTSMOUTH, N.H.*

Both *Old Marblehead* and *Portsmouth, N.H.* were released on August 1, 1940. The July 29, 1940, *New York Times* noted that with the publication of these two titles, "[Chamberlain] brings the total number of volumes in his American Landmark Series to nine and the editors of Hastings House say other books are in preparation." This count is incorrect. With the publication of these two titles, the number of titles in the series was actually eight. *Historic Cambridge*, originally scheduled for publication in 1939, was not published until 1942, but the back flaps of the dust jackets of earlier books in the series include *Historic Cambridge* in the list of series titles although it had not yet been published. This could have caused a reviewer to miscount the number of published series titles.

In the Foreword of the book, Chamberlain wrote, in part, "Few places are as rich in Colonial atmosphere as Portsmouth, New Hampshire which, with Charleston and Annapolis, is one of the rare American cities to retain its character as a proud, patrician, pre-Revolutionary seaport. As such it is superb material for the 'camera impression' which this little book hopes to provide. . . . By means of captioned photographs of Portsmouth's houses, taken in all seasons of the year, this small volume aspires to give an impression of a noble old seaport, where a fine tradition is still maintained."

REVIEWS

Booklist, September 1940 (p. 15); *Boston Transcript,* August 17, 1940 (p. 1); *Springfield Republican,* August 4, 1940 (p. 7e).

SOURCES

Book Review Digest 1940. New York: The H.W. Wilson Company, 1941, p. 160.

The New York Times, "Notes on Books and Authors," July 29, 1940, n.p.; "Books Published Today," August 1, 1940, n. p.

HISTORIC SALEM IN FOUR SEASONS A CAMERA IMPRESSION

Samuel Chamberlain
October 28, 1895 – January 10, 1975

AL10   First edition, first printing (1938) [2]

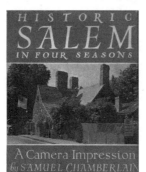

HISTORIC | SALEM | IN FOUR SEASONS | [photograph, "The Custom House (1819) | A CAMERA IMPRESSION BY | *SAMUEL CHAM-BERLAIN* | HASTINGS HOUSE *Publishers* NEW YORK

COLLATION: 6" x 7¼"; 36 leaves. [1–4] 5–11 [12] 13–60 [61–62] 63–68 [69] 70 [71] 72. Numbers in roman at the inner margin at the foot of the page.

Note: The verso of the front free endpaper carries a full-page photograph, "Summer Shadows on Chestnut Street"; the rear free endpaper carries a photograph, "Hamilton Hall (1805) – Samuel McIntyre, Architect", and a page number, 73.

CONTENTS: p. [1], title; p. [2], copyright page: "[full-page photograph, "The Market House (1816)"| *Copyright, 1938, by Samuel Chamberlain. Printed in the United States of America* I SET BY HAND IN GARAMOND TYPE BY ELAINE RUSHMORE AT THE GOLDEN HIND PRESS, MADISON, NEW JERSEY"; pp. [3–4], Foreword; pp. 5–72, photographs and text.

BINDING: Orange paper boards (close to Pantone 145), quarter-bound in cream. Front: [cream] *"HISTORIC I SALEM I IN FOUR SEASONS"*. Spine: [cream background, printing in orange] "[read vertically] HISTORIC SALEM IN FOUR SEASONS – CHAMBERLAIN". Front endpaper carries a double-page photograph of a winter scene with a house in the foreground, a ship's masts in the background; rear endpapers carry a photograph of a Salem street in springtime.

DUST JACKET: Cream paper. Front: "[within a wide orange band (close to Pantone 145, in white) *HISTORIC I SALEM I IN FOUR SEASONS* I [photograph of the House of Seven Gables] I [within a wide orange band, in cream] *A Camera Impression I by SAMUEL CHAMBERLAIN"*. Spine: "[cream background; printing in black] [read vertically] HISTORIC SALEM IN FOUR SEASONS – CHAMBERLAIN". Back: "[cream background] [Hastings House device in orange]". Front flap: "[upper right] $1.25 I *'AMERICAN LANDMARKS'* I HISTORIC I SALEM I IN FOUR SEASONS I [short decorative rule] I *A Camera Impression I by* SAMUEL CHAMBERLAIN I [blurb] I [publishers imprint]". Back flap: "*'AMERICAN I LANDMARKS'* I [short decorative rule] I A SERIES OF I CAMERA IMPRESSIONS I [short decorative rule] I *by Samuel Chamberlain* I [blurb] I *In the series:* I [list of four series titles, beginning with *Gloucester and Cape Ann* and ending with *Historic Boston*] I *In Preparation:* I 'NANTUCKET', *and others*.".

Published at $1.25 on July 25, 1938; number of copies printed unknown. Copyrighted and deposited July 30, 1938.

The Book is listed in "The Weekly Record," July 30, 1938, p. 305.

COPIES: CF

REPRINTS AND REPRODUCTIONS

[n.p.]: Stanley F. Baker, Publisher, n.d.

NOTES ON *HISTORIC SALEM*

Historic Salem is the second title in the *American Landmarks* series, and the first of three Chamberlain Camera Impressions to include photographs taken during the four seasons of the year, the other two being *Historic Boston* and *Historic Cambridge*. In the Foreword of the book, Chamberlain wrote, in part, "Some of Salem's most beautiful moments are in winter, when few visitors see it. To present a more revealing picture of the city's many moods, these photographs have been taken in all seasons of the year. . . . But the realistic Salem of today, still rich with dramatic reminders of the past, is a subject to which the camera may aspire. If a little of Salem's beauty has been caught by this roving lens, its ambition is fulfilled."

REVIEWS

Boston Transcript, September 17, 1938 (p. 1); *New Yorker*, July 30, 1938 (p. 48); *Springfield Republican*, July 24, 1938 (p. 7e); *Wisconsin Library Bulletin*, November 1938 (p. 180).

SOURCES

Book Review Digest 1938. New York: The H.W. Wilson Company, 1939, p. 168.

Publisher's Weekly, July 30, 1938, p. 305.

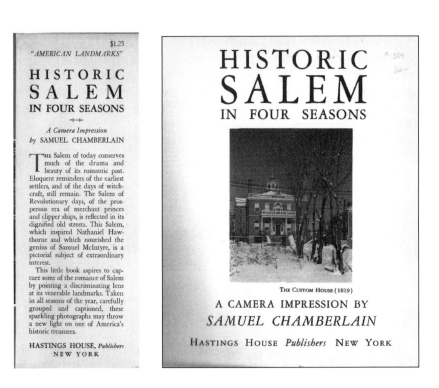

The Seaport Series
1940-1947

Doubleday, Doran
Doubleday & Co.
Publishers

1940
The Port of Gloucester
Harbor of the Sun: The Story of the Port of San Diego

1941
Northwest Gateway: The Story of the Port of Seattle
Baltimore on the Chesapeake

1942
Tropic Landfall: The Port of Honolulu
The Port of New Orleans
Montreal: Seaport and City

1943
The Ports of British Columbia

1944
Quebec: Historic Seaport

1945
Philadelphia: Holy Experiment

1947
Boston: Cradle of Liberty 1630-1776
San Francisco: Port of Gold

THE SEAPORT SERIES

Introduction and Publishing History

DOUBLEDAY, Doran conceived *The Seaport Series* and decided on some of its titles and authors early in 1940. At the time, both the *American Guide Series* and *The Rivers of America* series were firmly established and selling well, and a series on American and Canadian seaports certainly made publishing sense. To promote the series, the publishers capitalized on the regional aspects of each book, preparing special posters and newspaper advertising for each seaport city and its surrounding area. With a few exceptions, the series authors had strong ties to and extensive knowledge of their subjects.

Unlike many other series underway at the time, *The Seaport Series* had no general editor or editor in chief. But it is obvious from the literary design and manufacturing quality of each title that the publisher was deeply involved in the series from start to finish. And, to Doubleday, Doran's credit, the series survived the pervasive wartime personnel shortages and governmental restrictions on paper and publishing.

The *Seaport Series* was launched with the publication of *The Port of Gloucester* by James. B. Connolly on September 20, 1940. The book received favorable comment as did the concept of the series itself. Percy Hutchison's review in the October 6, 1940, *New York Times Book Review* mentioned three additional books in the series "in press or being written" and gave the names of the subject ports and authors. Three other seaports planned for the series were also named, the review noting, "American history is closely bound up with the sea . . . so these books should prove of cultural value as well as intensely interesting for the tales unfolded." *The Port of Gloucester* was followed by publication of *Harbor of the Sun: The Story of the Port of San Diego* by Max Miller on October 26, 1940.

Two series titles were published in 1941: *Northwest Gateway: The Story of the Port of Seattle* by Archie Binns on June 20 and *Baltimore on the Chesapeake* by Hamilton Owens on September 5. Each of these authors had deep roots in his subject port and city.

Tropic Landfall: The Port of Honolulu by Clifford Gessler was published on January 23, 1942, just weeks after the Japanese attack on Pearl Harbor on December 7, 1941. The book carried a five-page prologue, "The Port at War," that included material on the attack and its immediate aftermath. (The prologue is not included in the book's contents listings.) Gessler had worked at the Honolulu *Star-Bulletin* from 1924 to 1934 and was well versed in Hawaiian history and literature.

Two other series titles were published in 1942: *The Port of New Orleans* by Harold Sinclair on July 24 and *Montreal: Seaport and City* by Stephen Leacock on November 13. The United States was at war, and the dust jacket of Leacock's book carried the exhortation, "For Victory Buy United States War Savings Bonds [and] Stamps" and a suggestion that the reader, when finished, "send it to some man in the service who needs good reading" or leave the book with a USO (United Services Organization) library. Leacock had strong ties to his subject city and port, having served on the faculty of McGill University in Montreal for more than thirty years. Judging by available records, however, Sinclair had no obvious ties to New Orleans, although he was clearly an able and respected author.

One title in the series was published in 1943: *The Ports of British Columbia* by Agnes Rothery on June 18. The book included a notice that it was "complete and unabridged, manufactured under wartime conditions in conformity with all government regulations controlling the use of paper and other materials." The back of the dust jacket was devoted almost entirely to a plea presented in large type, reading, in part, "This book, like all books, is a symbol of the liberty and the freedom for which we fight. You, as a reader of books, can do your share in the desperate battle to protect those liberties – Buy War Bonds."

One series title was published in 1944: *Quebec: Historic Seaport* by Mazo de la Roche on July 21. Like *The Ports of British Columbia,* the book's dust jacket carried a plea to buy war bonds and stamps and noted that the book was manufactured in conformity with government regulations.

One series title was published in 1945: *Philadelphia: Holy Experiment* by Struthers Burt on March 22. The dust jacket of the book carried the explicit statement, "The publishers, in accordance with government regulations, have reduced bulk by the use of lightweight paper throughout, and have used smaller margins to allow for more words on each page. You, the reader, are thus provided with a complete, unabridged text, and better assured of a continuing supply of books."

The final two of the twelve titles in *The Seaport Series* were published in 1947: *Boston: Cradle of Liberty: 1630-1776* by John Jennings on March 6 and *San Francisco: Port of Gold* by William Martin Camp on November 13. In 1943, Doubleday, Doran had advertised *The Port of Boston* as due out in 1944. But because Jennings was on active duty in the Navy from 1942 to 1945, the book's publication was delayed.

BALTIMORE ON THE CHESAPEAKE

Hamilton Owens
August 8, 1888 – April 21, 1967

SS1   First edition, first printing (1941) [4]

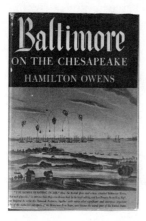

[double serpentine rules] | Baltimore | ON THE CHESAPEAKE | By | HAMILTON OWENS | [single rule] | ILLUSTRATED | [single rule] | [*Seaport* device] | [single rule] | Doubleday, Doran & Company, Inc. | GARDEN CITY, N.Y. 1941 | [double serpentine rules]

COLLATION: 8½" x 6". 176 leaves. [i–iv] v-ix [x] 1-329 [330] 331-342. Numbers printed in roman within brackets in the center at the foot of the page.

Note: Black-and-white illustrations are inserted following pp. 30, 46, 182, 198, 246, 262, 286, and 318.

CONTENTS: p. [i], half-title: "Baltimore on the Chesapeake"; p. [ii], blank; p. [iii], title; p. [iv], copyright page: "PRINTED AT THE *Country Life Press,* GARDEN CITY, N.Y., U.S.A. | [at bottom] CL | COPYRIGHT, 1941 | BY HAMILTON OWENS | ALL RIGHTS RESERVED | FIRST EDITION"; pp. v-vi, "Acknowledgments"; pp. vii–viii, "Contents"; p. ix, "Halftone Illustrations | [list of eight illustrations] | LINECUT ILLUSTRATIONS | [list of five illustrations]; p. [x], blank; pp. 1-329, text; p. [330], blank; pp. 331-342, "Index".

BINDING: Dark teal cloth (close to Pantone 560). Front: *Seaport* device blind-stamped in the center. Spine stamped in gold: "[decorative rule] | [crossed telescopes resting upon a double-scrolled document] | [decorative rule] | BALTIMORE | ON THE | *Chesapeake* | HAMILTON OWENS | [single rule] | DOUBLEDAY DORAN | [decorative rule] | [foul anchor] | [decorative rule] | [sextant] | [decorative rule] | [ship's wheel] | [decorative rule]". Endpapers carry a map in cream and light blue (close to Pantone 549) depicting the Baltimore-Patapsco River-Chesapeake Bay area.

DUST JACKET (white paper): Front: "[within a wide navy blue band (close to Pantone 539), which wraps to the spine, in white] *Baltimore* I ON THE CHESAPEAKE I [yellow (close to Pantone 127)] HAMILTON OWENS I [full-color unsigned illustration, "The Bombs Bursting In Air," which wraps to the spine (the same illustration, in black and white, faces p. 198 of the text)] I [within a light-blue band (close to Pantone 277), which wraps to the spine, in navy blue] [title of the illustration and brief mention of various events and actions resulting from the British attack on "Baltimore Town"]". Spine: "[within the top wide, navy blue band, in white] *Baltimore* I ON THE I CHESAPEAKE I [yellow] HAMILTON I OWENS I [illustration] I [within the bottom light-blue band, in navy blue] DOUBLEDAY I DORAN". Back: "[black] *The Seaport Series* I [blurb] I [list of four titles and their authors, notes on illustrations, and prices (titles in dark pink, close to Pantone 184)] I [lower right] 835–41". Front flap: "[upper right] B.O.C. I Price, $3.50 I BAL-TIMORE ON THE I CHESAPEAKE I HAMILTON OWENS I [blurb] I [lower right] 3923–41". Back flap: "NORTHWEST GATEWAY I *The Story of the Port of Seattle* I ARCHIE BINNS I [blurb promoting *Northwest Gateway*] I Price, $3.00 I [lower right] 3805–41".

Published at $3.50 on September 5, 1941; number of copies printed unknown. Copyrighted October 15, 1941; deposited September 3, 1941, and October 15, 1941.

The book is listed in "The Weekly Record," September 13, 1941, p. 936.

Note: No evidence found that Doubleday, Doran reprinted *Baltimore on the Chesapeake*.

COPIES: CF

SS1a   First edition, first printing, signed edition (1941)

Baltimore on the Chesapeake was issued in a signed edition by Doubleday, Doran & Company in 1941. This book has a special binding, navy blue cloth with a quarter-panel in ivory. A tipped-in leaf preceding the first half-title page bears the signature of Hamilton Owens.

COPIES: CF

REPRINTS AND REPRODUCTIONS

Reproduced on microfilm. New Haven, Conn.: Yale University Library, 1993. 1 reel, 35 mm.

BIOGRAPHY

(James) Hamilton Owens was born in Baltimore, Maryland, on August 8, 1888, the son of Gwinn Fardon and Arabella Pierpoint (Smith) Owens. After early studies at Baltimore City College, he earned a bachelor of arts degree from Johns Hopkins University in 1909.

On March 6, 1913, Owens married Olga von Hartz. The couple had five children: three sons, James Hamilton, Jr., Gwinn, and Lloyd, and two daughters, Olga and Lydia.

Owens worked as a reporter for the *Baltimore News* from 1909 to 1913, when he began working as a drama critic, rewrite man, and editor for the *New York Press*. In 1916, he became assistant to S.S. McClure, founder of *McClure's Magazine,* at the *New York Evening Mail.* The following year, during World War I, Owens served as Secretary of the New York Committee on National Defense. In 1918, he became managing editor of the Foreign Press Bureau of the Commission on Public Information.

In 1922, after a brief career with Guaranty Trust of New York, Owens became editor of the (Baltimore) *Evening Sun* in 1922. He was editor of the *Sun* (a different newspaper) from 1938 until his promotion to editor in chief of both papers in 1943, a post he held until his retirement in 1956. He is credited with coining Maryland's second nickname, "Free State" in 1923. (Maryland is also known as the Old Line State.) In 1937, Owens collaborated with Gerald W. Johnson, Frank R. Kent, and H.L. Mencken to write *The Sunpapers of Baltimore* (Knopf, 1937), a book celebrating the 100th anniversary of the *Baltimore Sun.*

In 1950, Owens received a doctorate of letters from the University of Miami and a doctorate of laws from Johns Hopkins University.

Hamilton Owens died in Baltimore, Maryland, on April 21, 1967, at age 78.

NOTES ON *BALTIMORE ON THE CHESAPEAKE*

Baltimore on the Chesapeake was featured in a full-page Doubleday, Doran advertisement in the August 16, 1941, issue of *Publishers' Weekly* promoting the *Seaport Series* and the addition of the book to the series. Owens was identified as editor of the Baltimore *Sun* in the ad and in the "The Weekly Record."

REVIEWS

Booklist, October 15, 1941 (p. 50); *Nation,* December 20, 1941 (p. 649); *New Republic,* October 6, 1941 (p. 446); *New York Herald Tribune Book Review,* September 21, 1941 (p. 4); *New York Times Book Review,* September 21, 1941

(p. 4); *New Yorker,* September 20, 1941 (p. 111); *Springfield Republican,* September 23, 1941 (p. 8); *Wisconsin Library Bulletin,* November 1941 (p. 176).

SELECTED WRITINGS BY HAMILTON OWENS

(With Gerald W. Johnson, et al) *The Sunpapers of Baltimore* (New York: Knopf, 1937); **Baltimore on the Chesapeake** (New York: Doubleday, Doran, 1941).

SOURCES

Book Review Digest 1941. New York: The H.W. Wilson Company, 1942, p. 687.

Publishers' Weekly, August 16, 1941, p. 433; and September 13, 1941, p. 936

The New York Times Book Review, September 21, 1941, p. 4.

"Owens Retires as Editor of Sunpapers," *Editor & Publisher,* March 31, 1956, p. 70.

The New York Times obituary, April 22, 1967, p. 31.

Who Was Who in America, Volume IV, 1961–1968. Chicago: Marquis-Who's Who, Inc., 1968, p. 726.

Maryland Manual Online, "State Nicknames — MDSOS Kids' Page." Accessed February 19, 2002.

Lears, Lee, Librarian, Maryland Department, Enoch Pratt Free Library, Baltimore, Maryland. Letter to CF, with enclosures, April 30, 2002.

Stimpert, James. Archivist (Arts and Sciences), Milton S. Eisenhower Library, Johns Hopkins University, e-mail message to CF, August 4, 2003.

BOSTON: CRADLE OF LIBERTY
1630-1776

John Jennings
December 30, 1906 – December 4, 1973

SS2   First edition, first printing (1947) [11]

[double serpentine rules] | Boston | CRADLE OF LIBERTY | 1630-1776 | By | JOHN JENNINGS | [single rule] | [*Seaport* device] | [single rule] Doubleday & Company, Inc. | GARDEN CITY 1947 NEW YORK | [double serpentine rules]

COLLATION: 8½" x 6". 176 leaves. [i–vi] vii–x [xi–xvi] 1–315 [316] 317–335 [336]..Numbers printed in roman within brackets in the center at the foot of the page.

Note: Double-sided black-and-white illustrations are inserted following pp. 80, 168, 208, and 264.

Note: On some copies a tipped-in page bearing the author's signature is inserted preceding p. [i].

CONTENTS: p. [i], half-title: "Boston"; p. [ii], "BOOKS BY JOHN JENNINGS | [list of seven titles]"; p. [iii], title; [iv], copyright page: "COPYRIGHT, 1947, BY JOHN JENNINGS | ALL RIGHTS RESERVED | PRINTED IN THE UNITED STATES | AT | THE COUNTRY LIFE PRESS, GARDEN CITY, N.Y. | FIRST EDITION"; p. [v], dedication: "TO THE SEAMEN OF BOSTON WHO, | MORE THAN THE SHIPS THEY SAILED, | MORE THAN THE OWNERS WHO SENT THEM, | MADE THIS THE FOREMOST | PORT OF ALL."; p. [vi], blank; pp. vii–x, "Foreword" [signed "The Author, Washington, D.C. December 1945"].; p. [xi], "Contents"; p. [xii], blank; p. [xiii], "Illustrations"; p. [xiv], blank; p. [xv], half-title: "Boston"; p. [xvi], blank; pp. 1–315, text; p. [316], blank; pp. 317–335, "Index"; p. [336], blank.

BINDING: Medium-blue cloth (close to Pantone 308). Front: *Seaport* device blind-stamped in the center. Spine stamped in gold: "[decorative rule] | [crossed telescopes resting on a double-scrolled document] | [decorative rule] *Boston* | CRADLE OF | LIBERTY | *John* | *Jennings* | [single rule] | DOU-

BLEDAY | [decorative rule] | [foul anchor] | [decorative rule] | [sextant] | [decorative rule] | [ship's wheel] | [decorative rule]". Endpapers carry a double-page map of "The Town of Boston in New England by Capt John Bonner 1722".

DUST JACKET (white paper): Full-color illustration (unsigned) of Boston Harbor wraps to the spine. Front: "[medium cream] Boston | *Cradle of Liberty* | [at bottom, within a medium-cream band, which wraps to the spine, in black] By JOHN JENNINGS | [red, close to Pantone 205] Author of SALEM FRIGATE". Spine: "[medium-cream] Boston | *Cradle of* | *Liberty* | [black] JOHN | JENNINGS | [at bottom, within the medium-cream band, in black] DOUBLEDAY". Back: "[black-and-white photograph of John Jennings] | [brief biography] | *Printed in the U.S.A.*". Front flap: "[upper right] B:C.O.L. | Price, $3.50 | [drawing of Old Faneuil Hall, which also follows p. 208] | Boston | Cradle of Liberty | 1630-1776 | *by John Jennings* | [blurb] | *(Continued on back flap)*". Back flap: "*(Continued from front flap)* | [blurb] | [at lower left corner, printed on the diagonal] BOSTON: CRADLE OF LIBERTY | JENNINGS-DOUBLEDAY".

Published at $3.50 on March 6, 1947; number of copies printed unknown. Copyrighted and deposited March 6, 1947.

Note: No evidence found that the book was listed in "The Weekly Record."

Note: No evidence found that Doubleday reprinted *Boston: Cradle of Liberty*.

COPIES: CF

SS2a   First edition, first printing, Autographed Edition (1947)

Boston: Cradle of Liberty was issued in an "Autographed Edition" by Doubleday, Doran & Company in 1947. The book is signed by John Jennings on a tipped-in leaf following the front free endpaper.

COPIES: CF

REPRINTS AND REPRODUCTIONS

New York: Editions for the Armed Services Number 1306. 1947.

Reproduced on microfilm. New Haven, Conn.: Yale University Library, 1992. 1 reel, 35 mm.

BIOGRAPHY

John Edward Jennings, Jr. was born on December 30, 1906, in Brooklyn, New York, the son of John E. and Florence Thistle Jennings. His father was a surgeon.

Jennings studied at the Colorado School of Mines (1924–1925), at New York University (1925–1926), and at Columbia University (1927–1928). In 1935, he graduated from the Washington Diplomatic and Consular Institute.

In 1931, Jennings married Virginia Lee Storey. The couple had a son, John E. Jennings III. The marriage ended in divorce in 1959. In 1960, he married Elise Durrin Dunlap, an artist.

His first book, *Our American Tropics*, (Crowell, 1938), a travelogue on Southern Florida, Puerto Rico, and the Virgin Islands, was followed by twenty-four books, including a novel written under the pseudonym "Joel Williams" and two novels written under the pseudonym "Bates Baldwin." His last book, *Tattered Ensign* (Crowell) was published in 1966. He contributed short stories to the *Saturday Evening Post, Cosmopolitan, Doc Savage Magazine*, and other periodicals. Thirteen of his novels were best-sellers.

During World War II, Jennings served in the Navy from 1942 to 1945 as officer in charge of the Naval Aviation History Unit.

John Edward Jennings died on December 4, 1973, in Long Island, New York, at age 66.

NOTES ON *BOSTON: CRADLE OF LIBERTY 1630-1776*

In the book's foreword, Jennings wrote, "This does not pretend to be the definitive history of Boston, even for the period which it covers. Such an undertaking would require more years of research than I can give it, and would fill many volumes. . . . But this is not even the ultimate word on the Port. Here you will find no tables of statistics, no tabulated lists of imports and exports, no registers of vessels, no columns of customs receipts. Rather, what I have tried to do here is to tell the story of Boston Port in human terms. I have left out or tried to condense the drier details and have endeavored, as far as possible, to cling to the movement and the high action which when lumped together made the city what it was."

The August 7, 1943, issue of *Publishers' Weekly* carried a two-page Doubleday, Doran advertisement, the first page headed "We're Worried To Death" and continuing "about shipping books to our regular customers this Christmas," urging booksellers to place their orders early, noting, "The printing problem is serious because in these days of paper rationing we can't stock up ahead in sufficient quantities."

The facing page of the ad was headed "But We're Not Worrying Yet" and continued "about eight titles in our Fall Catalogue which have just been postponed to 1944." The list of postponed titles included *The Port of Boston* by John Jennings. As it turned out, the book was not published until 1947, and then under a revised title, *Boston: Cradle of Liberty 1630-1776*.

REVIEWS

Booklist, April 1, 1947 (p. 239); *Bookmark,* May 1947 (p. 10); *Chicago Sun Book Week,* July 13, 1947 (p. 6); *Christian Science Monitor,* March 17, 1947 (p. 16); *Kirkus,* January 1, 1947 (p. 26); *Library Journal,* March 1, 1947 (p. 385); *New York Times Book Review,* March 23, 1947 (p. 6); *New Yorker,* March 8, 1947 (p. 102); *San Francisco Chronicle,* May 25, 1947 (p. 22); *Wisconsin Library Bulletin,* April 1947 (p. 66).

SELECTED WRITINGS BY JOHN JENNINGS

Our American Tropics (New York: Crowell, 1938); *Next to Valour* (New York: Macmillan, 1939); *Call the New World* (New York: Macmillan, 1941); *Gentleman Ranker* (New York: Reynal & Hitchcock, 1942); (Joel Williams, pseud. *The Coasts of Folly* (New York: Reynal & Hitchcock, 1942); *The Shadow and the Glory* (New York: Reynal & Hitchcock, 1943); **Boston: Cradle of Liberty, 1630-1776** (Garden City, N.Y.: Doubleday, 1947); *The Salem Frigate* (New York: Doubleday, 1946); *River to the West: A novel of the Astor Adventure* (Garden City, N.Y.: Doubleday, 1948); *The Sea Eagles: A Story of the American Navy during the Revolution* (Garden City, N.Y.: Doubleday, 1950); *The Pepper Tree: A Story of New England and the Spice Islands* (Boston: Little, Brown, 1950); (Bates Baldwin, pseud.) *The Sultan's Warrior* (New York: Holt, 1951); (Bates Baldwin, pseud.) *Tide of Empire* (New York: Holt, 1952); *The Strange Brigade: A Story of the Red River and the Opening of the Canadian West* (Boston: Little, Brown, 1952); *Clipper Ship Days* (New York: Random House, 1952); *Rogue's Yarn* (Boston: Little, Brown, 1953); *Banners Against the Wind* (Boston: Little, Brown, 1954); *Shadows in the Dusk* (Boston: Little, Brown, 1955); *Chronicle of the Calypso, Clipper* (Boston: Little, Brown, 1955); *The Wind in His Fists* (New York: Holt, 1955); *The Tall Ships* (New York: McGraw-Hill, 1958); *The Golden Eagle* (New York: Putnam, 1959); *Tattered Ensign* (New York: Crowell, 1966).

SOURCES

Publishers' Weekly, August 7, 1943, pp. 384–385; and February 8, 1947 (Doubleday Spring List).

Book Review Digest 1947. New York: The H.W. Wilson Company, 1948, p. 465.

The New York Times Book Review, March 23, 1947, p. 6.

The New York Times obituary, December 6, 1973, p. 50.

Contemporary Authors Online. The Gale Group, 1999. Reproduced in *Biography Resource Center.* Farmington Hills, Mich: The Gale Group, 2001. Accessed February 19, 2002.

THE PORTS OF BRITISH COLUMBIA

Agnes Rothery
January 31, 1888 – August 11, 1954

SS3   First edition, first printing (1943) [8]

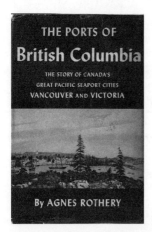

[double serpentine rules] | THE PORTS OF | British Columbia | By | AGNES ROTHERY | [single rule] | ILLUSTRATED WITH PHOTOGRAPHS | [single rule] | [*Seaport* device] | [single rule] Doubleday, Doran & Company, Inc. | GARDEN CITY 1943 NEW YORK | [double serpentine rules]

COLLATION: 8½" x 6". 144 leaves. [i–iv] v-vii [viii] [1–2] 3–279 [280]. Numbers printed in roman within brackets in the center at the foot of the page.

Note: A black-and-white photograph is inserted facing p. [iii]; double sided black and white illustrations are inserted following pp. 48, 96, and 160.

CONTENTS: p. [i], half-title: "THE PORTS OF | British Columbia"; p. [ii], "BOOKS BY AGNES ROTHERY [list of one biography, two juveniles, sixteen essays and travel books, three novels, and one play]"; p. [iii], title; [iv], copyright page: "PRINTED AT THE *Country Life Press*, GARDEN CITY, N.Y., U.S.A. | [within an open book, below an eagle with shield, arrows, and olive branches] THIS BOOK IS | COMPLETE AND UNABRIDGED, | MANUFACTURED UNDER WARTIME | CONDITIONS IN CONFOR-

MITY WITH I ALL GOVERNMENT REGULATIONS I CONTROLLING THE USE OF PAPER I AND OTHER MATERIALS. I [at bottom] CL I COPYRIGHT, 1943 I BY AGNES ROTHERY PRATT I ALL RIGHTS RE- SERVED I FIRST EDITION"; pp. v-vi, "Contents"; p. vii, "Illustrations"; p. [viii], dedication: "For I *Margery Wade*"; p. [1], "PART I I Vancouver and To- day"; p. [2], blank; pp. 3–267, text; p. 268, "Bibliography"; pp. 269–279, "In- dex"; p. [280], blank.

BINDING: Dark-blue cloth (close to Pantone 302). Front: *Seaport* device blind-stamped in the center. Spine stamped in gold: "[decorative rule] I [crossed telescopes resting on a double-scrolled document] I [decorative rule] I THE PORTS I OF I *British* I *Columbia* I ROTHERY I [single rule] I DOUBLEDAY DORAN I [decorative rule] [foul anchor] I [decorative rule] I [sextant] I [decorative rule] I [ship's wheel] I [decorative rule]". Endpapers carry a double-page map titled "British Columbia" in dark green (close to Pantone 341) and cream.

DUST JACKET (white paper): "[Within a wide navy-blue band (close to Pantone 302), which wraps to the spine, in white] THE PORTS OF I British Columbia I THE STORY OF CANADA'S I GREAT PACIFIC SEAPORT CITIES I VANCOUVER AND VICTORIA I [full-color illustration (un- signed), which wraps to the spine, of tall ships underway in a narrow estu- ary, rocks and pine trees in the foreground] I [at bottom, within a navy blue band, which wraps to the spine, in white] By AGNES ROTHERY". Spine: "[within the top navy-blue band, in white] THE PORTS OF I British I Co- lumbia I AGNES I ROTHERY I [within the bottom navy blue band, in white] DOUBLEDAY I DORAN". Back: White background. *"This book is complete and unabridged; manufactured under wartime conditions in con-* I *formity with all government regulations controlling the use of paper and other materi-* als. I [navy blue] [drawing of a hand holding a lighted torch in front of an open book] I THIS BOOK, [black] LIKE ALL BOOKS, I IS A SYMBOL OF THE LIBERTY AND THE I FREEDOM FOR WHICH WE FIGHT. I [navy blue] YOU, [black] AS A READER OF BOOKS, CAN DO I YOUR SHARE IN THE DESPERATE BATTLE I TO PROTECT THOSE LIBERTIES- I [navy blue] Buy I War Bonds I [navy blue] ([black] *Bonds or stamps may be pro- cured at most book* I *stores, all banks, many other places of business. To* I *buy them is to become a true soldier of Democracy.* [navy blue])". Front flap: "[up- per right] T.P.O.B.C. I Price, $3.00 I THE PORTS I OF BRITISH COLUMBIA I BY AGNES ROTHERY I [blurb] I *This book is complete and unabridged;* I *manufactured under wartime conditions in* I *conformity with all government regulations* I *controlling the use of paper and other mate-* I *rials.* I 4228-42". Back flap: "MONTREAL I Seaport and City I By STEPHEN LEACOCK I [blurb promoting *Montreal: Seaport and City*, noting it is the seventh in the

Doubleday, Doran *Seaport Series*] | [at far right] 3609–42 | Price, $3.50".

Published at $3.00 on June 18, 1943; number of copies printed unknown. Copyrighted July 1, 1943; deposited June 10, 1943, and July 2, 1943.

The book is listed in "The Weekly Record," June 26, 1943, p. 2395.

Note: No evidence found that Doubleday, Doran reprinted *The Ports of British Columbia.*

COPIES: CF

REPRINTS AND REPRODUCTIONS

None.

BIOGRAPHY

Agnes Edwards Rothery (Pratt) was born on January 31, 1888, in Brookline, Massachusetts, the daughter of John Jay Elmendorf and Rosamond Dale (Pentecost) Rothery. When she was young, her family moved to Wellesley, Massachusetts, where she lived for twenty-five years and attended college. *The House by the Windmill* (Doubleday, 1923), her seventh book and her first novel, is based in part on the life "full of fun and hospitality" which her family — there were five brothers and sisters — enjoyed at their summer home on Cape Cod.

In 1909, Rothery earned a bachelor of arts degree from Wellesley College. She moved to Philadelphia that year and worked for the *Ladies Home Journal.* She soon returned to Massachusetts, joining the staff of the *Boston Herald* as editor of the woman's page, later becoming editor of the book page. She took a one-year course in English at Radcliffe College (1912–1913), concentrating on playwriting. In 1913, a hundred of her *Boston Herald* essays were collected and published by Houghton as *Our Common Road,* her first book. From 1912 to 1916 she wrote a weekly column for the *Christian Science Monitor* and was a contributing editor to *Youth's Companion* and *House Beautiful.*

On September 24, 1917, Rothery married Harry Rogers Pratt, a musician, composer, and actor. The couple lived in Hartford, Connecticut, for four years. While there she wrote the play *Miss Coolidge.* The couple then spent a year at the Lake Placid Club in New York, where she wrote her second novel, *The High Altar* (Doubleday, 1924). In 1923, she and her husband moved to Charlottesville, Virginia, where he had accepted a position in the Department of Music at the University of Virginia.

Rothery continued to write, producing *New Roads in Old Virginia,* her first book written in the South. Based on summer travel with her husband, Rothery wrote several travel books. *Sweden: The Land and the People* (Viking,

1934) followed a trip to Sweden in 1932. She later wrote books on Norway, Finland, and Denmark. Her husband's photographs illustrated many of her books. In 1946, on the first anniversary of Denmark's liberation from German occupation, Rothery received the Medal of Liberation from King Christian X.

Rothery wrote at least thirty books, including three novels, three books of essays, two juveniles, and a play, as well as magazine articles, short stories, and essays. Her first four books were published under the pseudonym Agnes Edwards. In 1937, when the Association of American Publishers donated two hundred books to the White House to serve as the nucleus of a permanent library, four of Rothery's books were included in the donation.

Agnes Rothery died on August 11, 1954, at age 67.

NOTES ON *PORTS OF BRITISH COLUMBIA*

The book was published in 1943, when life in Canada was dominated by the country's war effort. The front flap of the book's dust jacket notes, in part, "Agnes Rothery is acknowledged as pre-eminent in her field. That field is not exactly that of the travel book — although her volumes are used as guides the world over. Neither is it exactly the field of the reporter. . . . What Agnes Rothery does is to present and interpret a country in such a way that it becomes a reality in its geography, history, people, cities, natural resources, and institutions."

REVIEWS

Booklist, July 15, 1943 (p. 462); *New York Times Book Review,* July 25, 1943 (p. 24); *Weekly Book Review,* August 15, 1943 (p. 5); *Wisconsin Library Bulletin,* July 1943 (p. 108).

SELECTED WRITINGS BY AGNES ROTHERY

Our Common Road (Boston: Houghton, 1913): [Agnes Edwards, pseud.] *The House of Friendship* (Boston: Houghton, 1915); [Agnes Edwards, pseud.] *The Romantic Shore* (Salem, Mass.: The Salem Press Company, 1915); [Agnes Edwards, pseud.] *A Garden Rosary* (Boston: Houghton, 1917); [Agnes Edwards, pseud.] *Cape Cod, New & Old* (Boston: Houghton, 1918); *The Old Coast Road from Plymouth* (Boston: Houghton, 1920); *The House by the Windmill* (Garden City, N.Y.: Doubleday, Page, 1923); *The High Altar* (Garden City, N.Y.: Doubleday, Page, 1924); *Miss Coolidge, a Comedy in One Act* (Hartford, Conn.: The Printery, Inc., 1927); *New Roads in Old Virginia* (Boston: Houghton, 1929); *Central America and the Spanish Main* (Boston: Houghton, 1929); *South America: The West Coast and the East* (Boston: Houghton, 1930);

Into What Port? (New York: Coward-McCann, 1931); *Images of Earth: Guatemala* (New York: Viking, 1934); *Sweden, the Land and the People* (New York: Viking, 1934); *Finland, the New Nation* (New York: Viking, 1936); *Denmark, Kingdom of Reason* (New York: Viking, 1937); *Norway, Changing and Changeless* (New York: Viking, 1939); *South American Roundabout* (New York: Dodd, Mead, 1940); *Virginia, the New Dominion* (New York: D. Appleton-Century, 1940); *Family Album* (New York: Dodd, Mead, 1942); *Washington Roundabout* (New York: Dodd, Mead, 1942); **The Ports of British Columbia** (Garden City, N.Y.: Doubleday, Doran, 1943); *A Fitting Habitation* (New York: Dodd, Mead, 1944); *Central American Roundabout* (New York: Dodd, Mead, 1944); *Balm of Gilead* (New York, Dodd, Mead, 1946); *Scandinavian Roundabout* (New York: Dodd, Mead, 1946); *Iceland Roundabout* (New York: Dodd, Mead, 1948); *The Joyful Gardener* (New York: Dodd, Mead, 1949); *Rome Today* (New York: Dodd, Mead, 1950); *New York Today* (New York: Prentice-Hall, 1951); *Houses Virginians Have Loved* (New York, Rinehart, 1954).

SOURCES

Burke, W.J. and Will D. Howe. *American Authors and Books, 1640-1940.* New York: Gramercy Publishing Co., 1943, p. 603.

Book Review Digest 1943. New York: The H.W. Wilson Company, 1944, p. 703.

The New York Times Book Review, July 25, 1943, p. 24.

"Travel Globetrotter," *Travel Magazine,* October, 1954, p. 40.

Who's Who in America, 1952-1953, p. 1959.

Southwell, Ann L. S. Albert and Shirley Small Special Collections Library, Alderman Library, University of Virginia. E-mail message to CF, March 4, 2003; by U.S. mail, biographical materials from the Library's Agnes Rothery Pratt files.

Slaight, Wilma R., Archivist, Wellesley College Archives, Margaret Clapp Library, Wellesley College. Letter to CF, May 6, 2003, forwarding college records of Agnes Rothery and various press clippings.

THE PORT OF GLOUCESTER

James B. Connolly
October 28, 1868 – January 20, 1957

SS4   First edition, first printing (1940) [1]

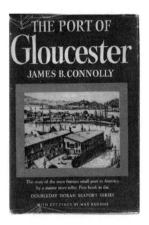

[double serpentine rules] | THE PORT OF | Gloucester | By | James B. Connolly | [single rule] | WITH ETCHINGS BY MAX KUEHNE | [single rule] | [*Seaport* device] | [single rule] Doubleday, Doran & Company, Inc. | NEW YORK 1940 | [double serpentine rules]

COLLATION: 8½" x 6". 176 leaves. [a–b] [i–iv] v [vi] vii–ix [x–xii] 1-333 [334-338]. Numbers printed in roman within brackets in the center at the foot of the page.

Note: An unpaginated tipped-in leaf [a–b] is inserted preceding p. [i].

Note: Unpaginated sepia illustrations are inserted facing pp. 2, 82, 162, 234, and 306.

CONTENTS: pp. [a–b], blank; p. [i], half-title: "THE PORT OF | Gloucester"; p. [ii], "BOOKS BY JAMES B. CONNOLLY | [list of three historical titles, nine short stories, and six novels]; p. [iii], title; [iv], copyright page: "PRINTED AT THE *Country Life Press*, GARDEN CITY, N.Y., U.S.A. | [at bottom] CL | COPYRIGHT, 1940 | BY DOUBLEDAY, DORAN & COMPANY, INC. | ALL RIGHTS RESERVED | FIRST EDITION"; p. v; "Acknowledgment" [signed J.B.C.]; p. vi, blank; pp. vii–viii, "Contents"; p. ix, "Illustrations" | [list of five illustrations]; p. [x], blank; p. [xi], half-title: "THE PORT OF | Gloucester"; p. [xii], blank; pp. 1-326, text; pp. 327-333, "Index"; pp. [334-338], blank.

BINDING: Dark blue cloth (close to Pantone 302). Front: *Seaport* device blind-stamped in the center. Spine stamped in gold: "[decorative rule] | [crossed telescopes resting on a double-scrolled document] | [decorative rule] | THE PORT OF | *Gloucester* | CONNOLLY | [single rule] | DOUBLE-DAY DORAN | [decorative rule] [foul anchor] | [decorative rule] | [sextant]

| [decorative rule] | [ship's wheel] | [decorative rule]". Front endpapers carry a pictorial nautical chart "Le Beau port" in dark cream and navy blue. [Chart is signed, possibly "Loise."]

DUST JACKET (white paper): Front and spine have a navy blue background (close to Pantone 295). Front: "[white] THE PORT OF | Gloucester | JAMES B. CONNOLLY | [portion of black and Kuehne white drawing of the port as seen from Banner Hill, East Gloucester (also found in sepia facing p. 2), within a gold frame] | [at bottom, in white] The story of the most famous small port in America | by a master story-teller. First book in the | DOUBLEDAY DORAN SEAPORT SERIES | WITH ETCHINGS BY MAX KUEHNE". Spine: "[white] THE PORT | OF | Gloucester | JAMES B. | CONNOLLY | [remaining portion of black and white drawing on front of jacket, within a gold frame] | [at bottom, in white] DOUBLEDAY DORAN | SEAPORT SERIES | DOUBLEDAY DORAN". Back: White background. "[dark blue] *Can You Join* | *The Conversation* | [black] WHEN THESE IMPORTANT NON-FICTION | BOOKS ARE DISCUSSED? | [list of six titles and their authors, with prices, published by Doubleday Doran | [to the right of the last two titles, Doubleday, Doran device, an eel coiled around an anchor, within an oval frame] | 760-40". Front flap: "[upper right] P.O.G. | Price, $3.00 | [blurb] | [lower right] 3574-40". Back flap: "*The SEAPORT SERIES* | [blurb promoting the series, advising that additional titles in the series will be published 'from time to time until the stories of all of America's major ports have been told' and concluding 'The next volume will be: | HARBOR OF THE SUN | *The Story of the Port of* | *San Diego* | BY MAX MILLER'] | [lower right] 3575-40".

Published at $3.00 on September 20, 1940; number of copies printed unknown. Copyrighted October 1, 1940; deposited September 4, 1940, and October 1, 1940.

The book is listed in "The Weekly Record," October 5, 1940, p. 1443.

Note: No evidence found that Doubleday, Doran reprinted *The Port of Gloucester.*

COPIES: CF

REPRINTS AND REPRODUCTIONS

Reproduced on microfilm. New Haven, Conn.: Yale University Library, 1992. 1 reel, 35 mm.

Reproduced on microfiche. Ann Arbor, Mich.: University Microfilms International, 1993. 4 microfiche; 11 x 15 cm.

BIOGRAPHIES

James Brendan Connolly was born October 28, 1868, in Boston, Massachusetts, the son of John and Ann (O'Donnell) Connolly. His parents were immigrants from the Aran Islands of Ireland. His father was a fisherman. Connolly entered Harvard University in 1895 but soon departed when the university would not grant him a leave of absence to participate in the first modern Olympic Games in 1896. Connolly traveled to Greece at his own expense and on the opening day of the games won first place in the hop-step-and jump, an event now known as the triple jump. He served with the Ninth Massachusetts Infantry in Cuba during the Spanish-American War before returning to Gloucester, where he lived and wrote more than twenty-five books, many of them about ships, seafarers, or the sea, and more than two hundred short stories.

On September 28, 1904, Connolly married Elizabeth Frances Hurley. The couple had a daughter, Brenda.

During World War I, Connolly worked as a correspondent for Colliers magazine. In 1921, he was Commissioner of American Relief for Ireland during the Black and Tan disturbances.

In 1948, Fordham University awarded Connolly an honorary doctorate in literature. In 1952, Connolly received the same honor from Boston College.

James Brendan Connolly died in Jamaica Plain, Massachusetts, on January 20, 1957, at age 88.

Max Kuehne was born in Halle, Germany on November 7, 1880, and came to the United States as a teenager. He studied with the artists Kenneth Hayes Miller (1876–1952) and Robert Henri (1865–1929), adopting the style of the Ashcan School. In 1913, he married Margaret Gresser. In addition to his paintings, his work included etchings, woodcarvings, and carved picture frames and furniture. From 1917 into the late 1960s he created a variety of furniture and furnishings for individuals and retailers, often entering such work in exhibitions. His art was held by the Metropolitan Museum of Art, the Whitney Museum of American Art, the Victoria and Albert Museum, and the Library of Congress. In 1927, Kuehne received a first honorable mention at the Carnegie Institute's International Exhibition in Pittsburgh, Pennsylvania.

Max Kuehne died in New York City on March 14, 1968, at age 87.

NOTES ON *THE PORT OF GLOUCESTER*

Notice of publication of *The Port of Gloucester* appeared in the August 3, 1940, issue of *Publishers' Weekly*, "P.W. Forecast for Buyers," noting, "First book in the new Seaport Series. Now we have the Rivers of America (F&R), Oceans of the World (Whittlesey), the Seaport Series, and the Sovereign States Series (Dodd). . . ." The notice concluded "Special circulars for New England only."

A September 21, 1940, *Publishers' Weekly* article, "Publishers' Plans for Geographical Series," reported that the publication of "new books in the established and recently announced geographical series of various houses continues apace. . . ." The article included comment on the *Seaport Series*, "which leads off with the publication this week of 'The Port of Gloucester,' by James B. Connolly," and "looks like an extremely exciting project." The article noted that Stewart Alsop had written a forty-eight-page prospectus of the series that was sent to booksellers and reviewers and that Doubleday was making a special circular for each book in the series, two of which were ready, and planned local advertising for *The Port of Gloucester*, with special displays in the Boston area.

REVIEWS

Booklist, November 15, 1940 (p. 114); *New Republic,* January 20, 1941 (p. 94); *New York Herald Tribune Book Review,* October 20, 1940 (p. 6); *New York Times Book Review,* October 6, 1940 (p. 10); *New Yorker,* October 5, 1940 (p. 79); *Springfield Republican,* October 15, 1940 (p. 8).

SELECTED WRITINGS BY JAMES B. CONNOLLY

Jeb Hutton: The Story of A Georgia Boy (New York: Scribners, 1902); *Out of Gloucester* (New York: Scribners, 1904); *The Deep Sea's Toll* (New York: Scribners, 1905); *On Tybee Knoll: A Story of the Georgia Coast* (New York: Barnes, 1905); *The Crested Seas* (New York: Scribners, 1907); *An Olympic Victor: A Story of the Modern Games* (New York: Scribners, 1908); *Open Water* (New York: Scribners, 1910); *Wide Courses* (New York: Scribners, 1912); *Sonnie-Boy's People* (New York: Scribners, 1913); *The Trawler* (New York: Scribners, 1914); *Head Winds* (New York: Scribners, 1916); *Running Free* (New York: Scribners, 1917); *The U-Boat Hunters* (New York: Scribners, 1918); *Hiker Joy* (New York: Scribners, 1920); *Tide Rips* (New York: Scribners, 1922); *Steel Decks* (New York: Scribners, 1925); *Coaster Captain: A Tale of the Boston Waterfront* (New York: Macy-Masius, 1927); *The Book of the Gloucester Fishermen* (New York: John Day, 1927); *Gloucestermen: Stories of the Fishing Fleet*

(New York: Scribners, 1930); *Navy Men* (New York: John Day, 1939); ***The Port of Gloucester*** (Garden City, N.Y.: Doubleday, Doran, 1940); *Canton Captain: The Story of Captain Robert Bennet Forbes* (Garden City, N.Y.: Doubleday, Doran, 1942); *Master Mariner: The Life and Voyages of Amasa Dellano* (Garden City, N.Y.: Doubleday, Doran, 1943); *Sea-Borne: Thirty Years Avoyaging* (Garden City, N.Y.: Doubleday, Doran, 1944).

SOURCES

(Connolly)
Book Review Digest 1940. New York: The H.W. Wilson Company, 1941, p. 194.

The New York Times Book Review, October 6, 1940, p. 10.

Publishers' Weekly, August 3, 1940, p. 323; August 10, 1940, n.p.; September 21, 1940, p. 1101; and October 5, 1940, p. 1443.

The New York Times obituary, January 21, 1957, p. 25.

Boston College Fact Book, 1992‑93. (www.bc.edu) Accessed March 15, 2002.

Contemporary Authors Online. The Gale Group, 2000. Reproduced in *Biography Resource Center.* Farmington Hills, Mich.: The Gale Group, 2001. Accessed February 19, 2002.

Kane, Patrice M. Head, Archives and Special Collections, Fordham University Library. Email message to CF, June 23, 2003; E-mail message to Jean Fitzgerald, June 25, 2003.

(Kuehne)
The New York Times obituary, March 16, 1968, p. 31.

Jackson, Kenneth T., ed. *The Encyclopedia of New York City.* New Haven: Yale University Press; New York: The New-York Historical Society, 1995, ("Henri, Robert," p. 539 and "Miller, Kenneth Hayes," p. 762.)

Hollis Taggart Galleries. *Max Kuehne: Artist and Craftsman.* Web Page http://www.hollistaggart.com/Exhibitions/Kuehne2001/Bio.html. Accessed June 22, 2003.

TROPIC LANDFALL: THE PORT OF HONOLULU

Clifford Gessler
November 9, 1893 – June 9, 1979

SS5   First edition, first printing (1942) [5]

[double serpentine rules] I TROPIC LANDFALL I *The Port of Honolulu* I By I CLIFFORD GESSLER I [single rule] I ILLUSTRATED BY A.S. MacLEOD I I [single rule] I [*Seaport* device] I [single rule] I Doubleday, Doran & Company, Inc. I GARDEN CITY 1942 NEW YORK I [double serpentine rules]

COLLATION: 8½" x 6". 176 leaves. [i–iv] v-vii [viii] ix–xi [xii] xiii–xvii [xviii–xx] 1–321 [322] 323–331 [332]. Numbers printed in roman within brackets in the center at the foot of the page.

Note: Black-and-white A.S. MacLeod illustrations are inserted facing pp. [iii], 4, 44, 80, 104, 188, 252, and 300.

CONTENTS: p. [i], half-title: "Tropic Landfall"; p. [ii], "Books By I CLIFFORD GESSLER I TRAVEL AND HISTORICAL I [list of four titles] I POETRY I [list of two titles]; p. [iii], title; [iv], copyright page: "PRINTED AT THE *Country Life Press*, GARDEN CITY, N.Y., U.S.A. I [at bottom] CL I COPYRIGHT, 1942 I BY CLIFFORD GESSLER I ALL RIGHTS RESERVED I FIRST EDITION"; pp. v-vii, "Of the Sources [signed C.G.]"; p. [viii], blank; pp. ix–x, "Contents"; p. xi, "Illustrations"; p. [xii], blank; pp. xiii–xvii, "Prologue"; p. [xviii], blank; p. [xix], half-title: "Tropic Landfall"; p. [xx], blank; pp. 1–321, text; p. [322], blank; pp. 323–331, "Index"; p. [332], blank.

BINDING: Medium green cloth (close to Pantone 356). Front: *Seaport* device blind-stamped in the center. Spine stamped in gold: "[decorative rule] I [crossed telescopes resting on a double-scrolled document] I [decorative rule] I TROPIC I LANDFALL I THE PORT OF I *Honolulu* I GESSLER I [single rule] I DOUBLEDAY DORAN I [decorative rule] I [foul anchor] I [decorative rule] I [scxtant] I [decorative rule] I [ship's wheel] I [decorative rule]".

Cream endpapers depict a map of Honolulu and the Sandwich Islands in cream and medium blue.

DUST JACKET (white paper). Front and spine carry a full-color illustration of Oahu in yellow, the surrounding ocean in blue] Front: "[black] THE PORT OF HONOLULU | [below the island, in white] TROPIC | LAND-FALL | [yellow, close to Pantone 128] CLIFFORD GESSLER white] Romantic legend and exciting tales | of battle on land and sea mark the story of America's Pacific island port." Spine: "[black] THE PORT | OF | HON-OLULU | [white] TROPIC | LANDFALL | [yellow] CLIFFORD | GESSLER | [white] DOUBLEDAY DORAN". Back: White background. "[blue] *The Seaport Series* | [blurb] | [list of four titles and their authors, notes on illustrations, and prices (titles in dark pink, close to Pantone 185)] | [lower right] 835–41". Front flap: "[blue] [upper right] T.L. | PRICE, *$3.50* | TROPIC LANDFALL: | *The Port of Honolulu* | BY CLIFFORD GESSLER | [blurb] | [lower right] 4115–41". Back flap: "[blue] BALTIMORE ON THE | CHESA-PEAKE | HAMILTON OWENS | [blurb promoting *Baltimore on the Chesapeake*] | 3923–41 | Price, $3.50".

Published at $3.50 on January 23, 1942; number of copies printed unknown. Copyrighted March 11, 1942; deposited January 17, 1942.

The book is listed in "The Weekly Record," January 24, 1942, p. 280.

Note: No evidence found that Doubleday, Doran reprinted *Tropic Landfall: The Port of Honolulu.*

COPIES: CF

REPRINTS AND REPRODUCTIONS

Reproduced on microfilm. New York: New York Public Library, 1990. 1 reel, 33 mm.

BIOGRAPHY

Clifford Franklin Gessler was born on November 9, 1893, in Milton Junction, Wisconsin, the son of Benjamin Franklin and Kathryn (Oviatt) Gessler.

In 1916, Gessler earned a bachelor of arts degree from Milton (Wisconsin) College, where he studied piano, violin, and cello. In 1917, he earned a master of arts degree from the University of Wisconsin. Milton College awarded him an honorary doctorate in literature in 1928.

In 1917, Gessler married Margaret Hull, a prominent music teacher in Hawaii.

Gessler's first book, *Slants* (Honolulu: Honolulu Star Bulletin), a book of poetry, was published in 1924. He wrote ten books, including three books of poetry and four books about Pacific islands. He was a professor of Latin American literature at the University of California.

Beginning in 1917, Gessler worked at eight newspapers. He was an editor of the Honolulu *Star-Bulletin* from 1924 to 1934. In 1937, he joined the staff of the *Oakland Tribune*, where he became the paper's music and dance critic. In 1964, after twenty-six years at the *Tribune*, Gessler retired to his home in Berkeley, California, noting on the music page of the paper that travel and independent writing would "interest" him in his retirement.[1]

Gessler was a member of the Poetry Society of America, the Anthropological Society of Hawaii, the Polynesian Society, the Order of Bookfellows, and the League of American Writers. In 1934, he accompanied the Mangareva Expedition of the Bishop Museum in Honolulu to southeastern Polynesia.

Clifford Gessler died on June 9, 1979, at age 85.

NOTES ON *TROPIC LANDFALL*

In an advertisement in the January 17, 1942, issue of *Publishers' Weekly*, Doubleday, Doran promoted *Tropic Landfall* as "the most timely title in the famous . . . Seaport Series. . . ." The advertisement continued, "The next chapter of our nation's history may well be written in the Port of Honolulu. That's why this latest title in the Doubleday, Doran Seaport Series takes on special significance- *and special saleability*. . . . Brought up-to-the-minute with a special Prologue, written after the attack on Pearl Harbor, this dramatic, readable volume tracks the history of the port, its tales of shipwreck, colorful legends, life under the Hawaiian kings, growth as an American city and as a vast melting pot-and shows how Honolulu has always been a battleground of the Pacific." The five-page Prologue is not listed in the book's table of contents.

REVIEWS

Bookmark, March 1942 (p. 11); *Foreign Affairs*, April 1942 (p. 576); *New York Herald Tribune Book Review*, February 22, 1942 (p. 12); *New York Times Book Review*, February 1, 1942 (p. 3); *New Yorker*, February 7, 1942 (p. 63); *Wisconsin Library Bulletin*, April 1942 (p. 66).

SELECTED WRITINGS BY CLIFFORD GESSLER

Slant (Honolulu: Honolulu Star-Bulletin, 1924); *Kanaka Moon* (New York: Dodd, Mead, 1927); *The Dangerous Islands* (London: M. Joseph, Ltd., 1937); *Hawaii: Isles of Enchantment* (New York: Appleton-Century, 1937); *Road My*

---

1. *Oakland Tribune*, February 2, 1964, n.p.

Body Goes (New York, Reynal & Hitchcock, 1937); *Pattern of Mexico* (New York: Appleton-Century, 1941); ***Tropic Landfall; the Port of Honolulu*** (Garden City, N.Y., Doubleday, Doran, 1942); *The Leaning Wind* (New York: Appleton-Century, 1943); *Tropic Earth* (West Los Angeles, Calif.: Wagon & Star, 1944); *The Reasonable Life; Some Aspects of Polynesian Life: What We May Learn from It in Developing in Our Own Lives the Strength of Quietness* (New York: J. Day, 1950).

SOURCES

The *Oakland Tribune,* February 2, 1964, n.p. (Report of Gessler's retirement from the *Tribune.*)

Book Review Digest 1942. New York: The H.W. Wilson Company, 1943, p. 289.

Publishers' Weekly, January 17, 1942, n.p.; January 24, 1942, p. 280; and January 31, 1942, p. 324 (Doubleday, Doran Spring List).

The New York Times Book Review, February 1, 1942, p. 3.

Oakland Tribune, May 27, 1951, p. C-3. (Music Page article by Gessler.)

Burke, W.J., and Will D. Howe. *American Authors and Books.* New York: Crown Publishers, Revised Edition, 1962, p. 278.

Who Was Who Among North American Authors, 1921–1939, Volume 1, A–J. Detroit, Michigan: Gale Research Company, 1976, p. 581.

Oakland Tribune funeral notice, June 12, 1979.

MONTREAL: SEAPORT AND CITY

Stephen Leacock
December 30, 1869 – March 28, 1944

SS6 First edition, first printing (1942) [7]

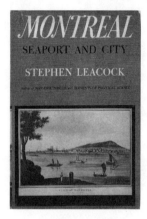

[double serpentine rules] | Montreal | SEAPORT AND CITY | By | STEPHEN LEACOCK | [single rule] | [*Seaport* device] | [single rule] | Doubleday, Doran & Company, Inc. | GARDEN CITY 1942 NEW YORK | [double serpentine rules]

COLLATION: 8½" x 6". 176 leaves. [i–iv] v-vii [viii] ix–xi [xii] [1]-340. Numbers printed in roman in headline at the outer margin of the type page, except for pp. v, ix, xi, 22, 37, 53, 73, 97, 116, 132, 159, 186, 215, 237, 267, 288, 312, 325, 329, and 333, on which the numbers are printed in the center, at the foot of the page.

Note: Black-and-white illustrations are inserted facing pp. [iii], 20, 100, 164, 180, 200, 212, and 312.

CONTENTS: p. [i], half-title: "Montreal"; p. [ii], "SOME BOOKS BY | STEPHEN LEACOCK | [list of twenty-nine titles]; p. [iii], title; [iv], copyright page: "PRINTED AT THE *Country Life Press*, GARDEN CITY, N.Y., U.S.A. | [at bottom] CL | COPYRIGHT, 1942 | BY STEPHEN LEACOCK | ALL RIGHTS RESERVED | FIRST EDITION"; p. v-vii, "Preface [signed Stephen Leacock, McGill University, 1942]"; p. [viii], blank; pp. ix–x, "Contents"; p. xi, "Illustrations"; p. [xii], blank; pp. [1]-328, text; pp. 329-331, Appendix; p. [332], blank; pp. 333-340, "Index".

BINDING: Bright green cloth (close to Pantone 347). Front: *Seaport* device blind-stamped in the center. Spine stamped in gold: "[decorative rule] | [crossed telescopes resting on a double-scrolled document] | [decorative rule] | MONTREAL | *Stephen* | *Leacock* | [single rule] | DOUBLEDAY DORAN | [decorative rule] [foul anchor] | [decorative rule] | [sextant] | [decorative rule] | [ship's wheel] | [decorative rule]". Cream endpapers.

DUST JACKET (white paper): Front and spine have a medium green background (close to Pantone 328). Front: "[white] *MONTREAL* | [black] SEA-

PORT AND CITY | [white] STEPHEN LEACOCK | [black] Author of NON-SENSE NOVELS and ELEMENTS OF POLITICAL SCIENCE | [full-color illustration titled 'View of Montreal' within a black frame]" Spine: "[white] *MONTREAL* | [black] SEAPORT | AND CITY | [white] STEPHEN | LEA-COCK | [black] DOUBLEDAY DORAN | [a portion of the full-color illustration on the front is repeated] | [wide black band]". Back: White background. "*THE SEAPORT SERIES* | [blurb promoting and describing the *Seaport Series*] | [list of six titles and their authors, notes on illustrators, and prices (titles in dark pink, close to Pantone 185)] | [lower right] 835-42". Front flap: "[upper right] M.S.C. | Price, $3.50 | MONTREAL | Seaport and City | By STEPHEN LEACOCK | [blurb] | [lower right] 3609-42". Back flap: "[advertisement including a black-and-white drawing on a dark pink rectangle of a Revolutionary War soldier holding a rifle with text to the right, 'For Victory Buy United States War Savings Bonds Stamps' | [blurb promoting purchase of war bonds and stamps] | [pink rule] | [blurb urging the reader who has finished reading the book to send it to 'some man in the service who needs good reading . . .'] | [dashed pink line] | [mailing label for so sending the book] | LEAVE WITH U S O LIBRARY AFTER READING".

Published at $3.50 on November 13, 1942; number of copies printed unknown. Copyrighted November 27, 1942; deposited October 31, 1942 and November 25, 1942.

The book is listed in "The Weekly Record," November 14, 1942, p. 2066.

Note: No evidence found that Doubleday, Doran reprinted *Montreal: Seaport and City*.

COPIES: CF

REPRINTS AND REPRODUCTIONS

Toronto: McClelland and Stewart, 1963. Revised edition. Edited by John Thomas Culliton.

BIOGRAPHY

Stephen Butler Leacock was born in Swanmoor, Hampshire, England, on December 30, 1869, the son of W. P. and Agnes (Butler) Leacock. When he was six years old, his family emigrated to Canada. Leacock attended Upper Canada College from 1882 to 1887, the Strathroy Collegiate Institute, and the University of Toronto, where he earned a bachelor of arts degree in modern languages in 1891. In 1903, he earned a doctorate in Political Economy from the University of Chicago. From 1889 to 1899, he taught modern languages at Upper Canada College. From 1903 to 1936, he was professor of political economy at McGill University in Montreal, lecturing on economics and political science.

On August 7, 1900, Leacock married Beatrix Hamilton (d. 1925). The couple had a son, Stephen L. Leacock.

Leacock was a prolific writer, a humorist, and a lecturer. His first and most profitable book, *Elements of Political Science* (Houghton), a university textbook, was published in 1906. He wrote at least sixty books, thirty-five of them works of humor. He also wrote plays, pamphlets, literary essays, literary studies, and histories. He wrote two biographies, *Mark Twain* (1932) and *Charles Dickens: His Life and Work* (1933), both published by the English firm Peter Davies. Leacock considered Twain and Dickens the greatest humorists of all time.[1]

The Stephen Leacock Museum occupies the summer house Leacock built in 1928 in Orillia, Ontario.

Leacock was elected to the Royal Society of Canada in 1919. He received the Mark Twain Medal in 1935.

Stephen Leacock died on March 28, 1944, in Toronto, at age 74.

PAPERS: Stephen Leacock's papers are held by the Special Collections Research Center, University of Chicago Library.

NOTES ON *MONTREAL: SEAPORT AND CITY*

In 1941, after Leacock had completed work on a history of Canada, *Canada: The Foundations of Its Future* (Gazette: 1941), Thomas B. Costain, an editor at Doubleday and a former editor of *Maclean's* magazine, a long-time acquaintance of Leacock's, wrote to him suggesting Leacock write his autobiography. When Leacock expressed his reluctance to undertake such a project, Costain suggested a book on Quebec to be part of the *Seaports Series*. Leacock, a Montrealer through and through, convinced Costain that Montreal would be a better choice for such a book and thus *Montreal: Seaport and City* became a title in the series.[2]

REVIEWS

Booklist, January 1, 1943 (p. 182); *Commonweal,* January 29, 1943 (p. 378); *Library Journal,* October 15, 1942 (p. 908); *New York Herald Tribune Book Review,* November 29, 1942 (p. 3); *New York Times Book Review,* December 6, 1942 (p. 10); *Wisconsin Library Bulletin,* December 1942 (p. 185).

1. *The New York Times* obituary, March 9, 1944, p. 21.
2. Legate, David M. *Stephen Leacock: A Biography,* pp. 233–238.

SELECTED WRITINGS BY STEPHEN LEACOCK

Elements of Political Science (Boston: Houghton, 1906); *Baldwin, Lafontaine, Hincks: Responsible Government* (Toronto: Morang, 1907); *Greater Canada: An Appeal: Let Us No Longer Be A Colony* (Montreal: Montreal News Company, 1907); *Literary Lapses: A Book of Sketches.* New York: Lane, 1910; *Nonsense Novels* (New York: Lane, 1911); *Sunshine Sketches of a Little Town* (New York: Lane, 1912); *"Behind the Beyond," and Other Contributions to Human Knowledge* (New York: Lane, 1913); *Adventurers of the Far North: A Chronicle of the Frozen Seas* (Toronto: Brook, 1914); *Arcadian Adventures with the Idle Rich* (New York: Lane, 1914); *The Dawn of Canadian History: A Chronicle of Aboriginal Canada and the Coming of the White Man* (Toronto: Brook, 1914); *The Mariner of St. Malo: A Chronicle of the Voyages of Jacques Cartier* (Toronto: Brook, 1914); *The Methods of Mr. Sellyer: A Book Story Study* (New York: Lane, 1914); *Moonbeams from the Larger Lunacy* (New York: Lane, 1915); *Further Foolishness: Sketches and Satires on the Follies of the Day* (New York: Lane, 1916); *Essays and Literary Studies* (New York: Lane, 1916); *Frenzied Fiction* (New York: Lane, 1918); *The Unsolved Riddle of Social Justice* (New York: Lane, 1920); *Winsome Winnie, and Other New Nonsense Novels* (New York: Lane, 1920); *My Discovery of England* (New York: Dodd, 1922); *College Days* (New York: Dodd, 1923); *Over the Footlights* (New York: Lane, 1923); *The Garden of Folly* (New York: Dodd, 1924); *The Raft* (a play); *Winnowed Wisdom: A New Book of Humour* (New York: Dodd, 1926); *Short Circuits* (New York: Dodd, 1928); *The Iron Man and the Tin Woman, with Other Such Futurities: A Book of Little Sketches of To-day and To-morrow* (New York: Dodd, 1929); *Economic Prosperity in the British Empire* (Boston: Houghton, 1930); *Laugh with Leacock: An Anthology of the Best Works of Stephen Leacock* (New York: Dodd, 1930); *Wet Wit and Dry Humour, Distilled from the Pages of Stephen Leacock* (New York: Dodd, 1931); *Afternoons in Utopia: Tales of the New Times* (New York: Dodd, 1932); *Mark Twain* (London: Peter Davies, 1932); *Charles Dickens; His Life and Work* (London: Peter Davies, 1933); *Lincoln Frees the Slaves* (New York: Putnam, 1934); *Canada: The Foundations of Its Future* (Montreal: Gazette, 1941); **Montreal: Seaport and City** (Garden City, N.Y.: Doubleday, Doran, 1942); *While There is Time: The Case Against Social Catastrophe* (Toronto: McClelland & Stewart, 1945).

SOURCES

Book Review Digest 1942. New York: The H.W. Wilson Company, 1943, p. 457.

Publishers' Weekly, November 14, 1942, p. 2066.

The New York Times Book Review, December 6, 1942, p. 10.

The New York Times obituary, March 29, 1944, p. 21.

Legate, David M. *Stephen Leacock: A Biography.* Toronto: Doubleday Canada Limited, 1970.

Creative Canada: A biographical dictionary of twentieth-century creative and performing artists. Volume Two. Toronto: University of Toronto Press, 1972, pp. 158–160.

Contemporary Authors Online. The Gale Group, 2001. Reproduced in *Biography Resource Center.* Farmington Hills, Mich.: The Gale Group, 2001. Accessed February 19, 2002.

University of Chicago Library, Reference & Business Information Center. E-mail message to CF, June 30, 2003.

THE PORT OF NEW ORLEANS

Harold Sinclair
May 8, 1907 – May 24, 1966

SS7   First edition, first printing (1942) [6]

[double serpentine rules] | THE PORT OF | New Orleans | By | HAROLD SINCLAIR | [single rule] | [*Seaport* device] | [single rule] | Doubleday, Doran & Company, Inc. | GARDEN CITY 1942 NEW YORK | [double serpentine rules]

COLLATION: 8½" x 6". 176 leaves. [i–vi] vii–ix [x] xi–xiii [xiv-xvi] 1–335 [336]. Numbers printed in roman within brackets in the center at the foot of the page.

Note: Black-and-white illustrations are inserted facing pp. [iii], 68, 96, 108, 140, 192, 208, 233, and 248.

CONTENTS: p. [i], half-title: "The Port of New Orleans"; p. [ii], "Books by | HAROLD SINCLAIR | [list of six titles]; p. [iii], title; [iv], copyright page: "PRINTED AT THE *Country Life Press,* GARDEN CITY, N.Y., U.S.A. | [at bottom] CL | COPYRIGHT, 1942 | BY HAROLD SINCLAIR AND ETHEL

MORAN SINCLAIR I ALL RIGHTS RESERVED I FIRST EDITION"; p. [v], dedication: "*For Sidney*";[1] p.[vi], blank; pp. vii–ix, "Author's Note [signed Harold Sinclair I April 1942.]"; p. [x], blank; pp. xi–xii, "Contents"; p. xiii, "Illustrations"; p. [xiv], blank; p. [xv], half title: "The Port of New Orleans"; p. [xvi], blank; pp. 1–326, text; pp. 327–335, "Index"; p. [336], blank.

BINDING: Red cloth (close to Pantone 193). Front: *Seaport* device blind-stamped in the center. Spine stamped in gold: "[decorative rule] I [crossed telescopes resting on a double-scrolled document] I [decorative rule] THE PORT OF I *New Orleans* I SINCLAIR I [single rule] I DOUBLEDAY DO-RAN I [decorative rule] I [foul anchor] I [decorative rule] I [sextant] I [decorative rule] I [ship's wheel] I [decorative rule]". Dark cream endpapers bearing a drawing in gray and dark blue titled, "A View of New Orleans Taken From the Plantation of Marigny".

DUST JACKET (white paper): Front and spine carry a full-color folk-art drawing of the river and the waterfront, farm crops being harvested in the foreground, the city in the background. Lettered on the front: "[medium blue, close to Pantone 285] THE PORT OF I [red, close to Pantone 185] New Orleans I [medium blue] The story of one of America's most enchanting cities — a great seaport I and gateway to the vast Mississippi river valley I [at bottom, within a dark brown band, in white] HAROLD SINCLAIR". Spine: "[medium blue] THE PORT I OF I [red] I New I Orleans I [medium blue] HAROLD I SINCLAIR I [at bottom, within the dark brown band, in white] DOUBLEDAY I DORAN". Back: White background; printing in medium blue. "*The Seaport Series* I [blurb] I [list of six titles and their authors, notes on illustrators, and prices (titles in red)] I [lower right] 385–42". Front flap: "[medium blue] [upper right] P.O.N.O. I Price, $3.50 I THE PORT OF I NEW ORLEANS I By Harold Sinclair I [blurb] I [lower right] 3013–42". Back flap: "[medium blue] [upper right] PRICE, *$3.50* I TROPIC LANDFALL: I *The Port of Honolulu* I By CLIFFORD GESSLER I [blurb promoting *Tropic Land-fall*] I [lower right] 4115–41".

Published at $3.50 on July 24, 1942; number of copies printed unknown. Copyrighted July 28, 1942; deposited July 16, 1942, and July 29, 1942.

The book is listed in "The Weekly Record," July 25, 1942, p. 256.

Note: No evidence found that Doubleday, Doran reprinted *The Port of New Orleans.*

COPIES: CF

1. Sinclair's daughter.

REPRINTS AND REPRODUCTIONS

None.

BIOGRAPHY

Harold (Augustus) Sinclair was born in Chicago, Illinois, on May 8, 1907, the son of Walter Guy, a railroad fireman, and Violet (Wishard) Sinclair.

Sinclair attended public schools in Bloomington, Illinois, but left high school in his junior year to work as a salesman of builders' hardware, working from time to time in Illinois, Texas, and Florida. Self-taught, he began writing in Chicago during the 1920s after becoming acquainted with the bohemian literary set there. During the Depression he returned to Bloomington, where he managed the hardware department of a Sears, Roebuck store for five years.

Sinclair's first book, *Journey Home* (Doubleday), was published in 1936, in the depth of the Depression. His second book, *American Years* (Doubleday, 1938), was a Literary Guild selection. After its publication, he left his job at Sears, Roebuck and became a freelance writer. The next year, 1939, he won a Guggenheim Fellowship in creative writing. During World War II, he worked as a machine operator in a machine shop. In 1948, he began to work as a full-time writer.

In 1933, Sinclair married Ethel Louise Moran. The couple had six children: Ward, Judith, J. Michael, Elizabeth Audrey, Marion Gail, and Sidney Irene. (*The Port of New Orleans* is dedicated "For Sidney.")

Sinclair was a member of the Authors League of America and a contributor of short stories to several popular magazines. He wrote articles for the *Illinois State Historical Journal*, the *St. Louis Post-Dispatch*, and the *Chicago Sun-Times*. His book *The Horse Soldiers* (Harper, 1956) was the basis of the 1959 United Artists movie starring John Wayne and William Holden.

Harold Sinclair died in Bloomington, Illinois, on May 24, 1966, at age 59.

NOTES ON *THE PORT OF NEW ORLEANS*

A full-page advertisement in the June 13, 1942, issue of *Publishers' Weekly* promoting the book featured its dust jacket and an illustration of a busy seaport of an earlier time. The book was announced as "Coming July 24th. Illustrated with eight half-tones. $3.50. Doubleday, Doran." The titles, authors, and prices of the preceding five books in *The Seaport Series* were given at the bottom of the page.

REVIEWS

Booklist, September 1942 (p. 9); *Boston Globe,* July 22, 1942 (p. 19); *Library Journal,* July 1942 (p. 629), *Nation,* November 7, 1942 (p. 489); *New York Herald Tribune Book Review,* July 26, 1942 (p. 4); *New York Times Book Review,* August 2, 1942 (p. 1); *New Yorker,* July 25, 1942 (p. 59); *Saturday Review of Literature,* September 19, 1942 (p. 17); *Wisconsin Library Bulletin,* October 1942 (p. 136).

SELECTED WRITINGS BY HAROLD SINCLAIR

Journey Home (Garden City, N.Y.: Doubleday, Doran, 1936); *American Years* (Garden City, N.Y.: Doubleday, Doran, 1938); *Years of Growth* (Garden City, N.Y.: Doubleday, Doran, 1940); *Westward the Tide* (Garden City, N.Y.: Doubleday, Doran, 1940); *Years of Illusion* (Garden City, N.Y.: Doubleday, Doran, 1941); ***The Port of New Orleans*** (Garden City, N.Y.: Doubleday, Doran, 1942); *Music Out of Dixie* (New York: Rinehart, 1952); *The Horse Soldiers* (New York: Harper, 1956); *The Cavalryman* (New York: Harper, 1958).

SOURCES

Book Review Digest 1942. New York: The H.W. Wilson Company, 1943, p. 708.

Publishers' Weekly, June 13, 1942, p. 2181; and July 25, 1942, p. 256.

The New York Times Book Review, August 2, 1942, p. 1.

The New York Times obituary, May, 25, 1966, p. 47.

Contemporary Authors Online. The Gale Group, 1999. Reproduced in *Biography Resource Center.* Farmington Hills, Mich.: The Gale Group, 2001. Accessed February 19, 2002.

PHILADELPHIA: HOLY EXPERIMENT

Struthers Burt
October 18, 1882 – August 29, 1954

SS8   First edition, first printing (1945) [10]

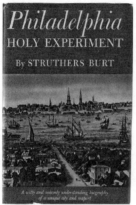

[double serpentine rules] | Philadelphia | HOLY EXPERIMENT | By | STRUTHERS BURT | [single rule] | ILLUSTRATED WITH PHOTOGRAPHS | [single rule] | [*Seaport* device] | [single rule] | Doubleday, Doran & Company, Inc. | GARDEN CITY 1945 NEW YORK | [double serpentine rules]

COLLATION: 8½" x 6". 208 leaves. [i–viii] ix–xiii [xiv-xvi] 1–379 [380] 381–396 [397–400]. Numbers printed in roman within brackets in the center at the foot of the page.

Note: Black-and-white illustrations are inserted facing pp. 48, 49, 80, 81, 104, 105, 112, 113, 144, 145, 176, 177, 208, 209, 328, and 329.

CONTENTS: p. [i], half-title: "Philadelphia"; p. [ii], "BOOKS BY | STRUTHERS BURT | [list of seventeen titles]"; p. [iii], title; p. [iv], copyright page: "[at bottom] COPYRIGHT, 1945 | BY STRUTHERS BURT | ALL RIGHTS RESERVED | PRINTED IN THE UNITED STATES | AT | THE COUNTRY LIFE PRESS, GARDEN CITY, N.Y. | FIRST EDITION"; p. [v], dedication: "TO | JOHN FREDERICK LEWIS, JR. | and his wife, ADA; | two Philadelphians who love their city | and really do something about it. | 'A *great city is that which has the greatest | men and women.*' — WALT WHITMAN."; p. [vi], blank; p. [vii], "AS AN EXAMPLE of how thick the texture of Philadel- | phia is and of how, whenever you touch anything | about it, you touch something interesting, John Fred- | erick Lewis, Jr., distinguished Philadelphian and hard- | working and outstandingly patriotic American, is in | reality Baron Johann Friedrich von Ludwig, and | would still be such if his great-great grandfather had | not the sense to come to this country and settle | on the shores of the Delaware."; p. [viii], blank; pp. ix–x, "Acknowledgments [signed S.B.]"; pp. xi–xii, "Contents"; p. xiii, "Illustrations"; p. [xiv], blank; p. [xv], half-title: "Philadelphia"; p. [xvi], blank; pp. 1–379, text; p. [380], blank; pp. 381–396, "Index"; pp. [397–400], blank.

BINDING: Dark green cloth (close to Pantone 364). Front: *Seaport* device blind-stamped in the center. Spine stamped in gold: "[decorative rule] | [crossed telescopes resting on a double-scrolled document] | [decorative rule] | *Philadelphia* | HOLY | EXPERIMENT | *Struthers* | *Burt* | [single rule] | DOUBLEDAY | DORAN | [decorative rule] | [foul anchor] | [decorative rule] | [sextant] | [decorative rule] | [ship's wheel] | [decorative rule]". Dark cream endpapers, utilized courtesy of the Historical Society of Pennsylvania, depict an illustration in sepia of the waterfront of the Port of Philadelphia, the city in the background, low hills rising in the distance.

DUST JACKET (white paper): "[Within a wide dark olive band (close to Pantone 448), which wraps to the spine, in white] *Philadelphia* | HOLY EX-PERIMENT | By STRUTHERS BURT | [full-color illustration (unsigned), which wraps to the spine, of a harbor scene, houses and trees in the fore-ground, ships and boats in the water, city buildings and churches on the far side of the water] | [at bottom, within a dark olive band, which wraps to the spine, in white] *A witty and warmly understanding biography* | *of a unique city and seaport*". Spine: "[within the top dark olive band, in white] *Philadel-* | *phia* | HOLY | EXPERIMENT | STRUTHERS | BURT | [within the bottom dark olive band, in white] DOUBLEDAY | DORAN". Back: "[red, close to Pantone 185] STRUTHERS BURT | [biographical sketch of Burt, which is continued on the back flap; a black and white photograph of Burt appears on the upper right quadrant of the back of the jacket]". Front flap: "[upper right] P.H.E. | Price, *$3.75* | [single rule] | ✶ IMPORTANT ✶ | This EDI-TION is COMPLETE and UNABRIDGED | THIS IS A FULL-LENGTH BOOK PRINTED IN | A SPECIAL FORMAT DESIGNED TO SAVE | MA-TERIALS AND MANPOWER. | The publishers, in accordance with govern-ment | regulations, have reduced bulk by the use of | lightweight paper throughout, and have used | smaller margins to allow for more words on each | page. You, the reader, are thus provided with a | complete, unabridged text, and better assured of | a continuing supply of books. | [single rule] | Philadelphia | HOLY EXPERIMENT | by Struthers Burt | [blurb]". Back flap: "(*Continued from back of* | *jacket)* | [biographical sketch of Burt continued] | *DOUBLEDAY, DORAN* | *& CO., INC.*"

Published at $3.75 on March 22, 1945; number of copies printed unknown. Copyrighted March 27, 1945 ; deposited March 11, 1945 and March 23, 1945.

The book is listed in "The Weekly Record," March 21, 1945, p. 1309.

No evidence found that Doubleday, Doran reprinted *Philadelphia: Holy Ex-periment.*

CITED: *Bibliography of Pennsylvania History* [7955]

COPIES: CF

REPRODUCTIONS AND REPRINTS

London: Rich and Cowan, 1947.

BIOGRAPHY

Maxwell Struthers Burt was born on October 18, 1882, in Baltimore, Maryland, the son of Horace Brooke, a lawyer, and Hester Ann (Jones) Burt. When he was six months old, the family moved to Philadelphia. Burt always considered himself a Philadelphian. Throughout his life he used "Struthers" as his first name.

Burt was educated in private college-preparatory schools in Philadelphia. When he graduated in 1898, at age sixteen, he went to work as a reporter for the *Philadelphia Times*. In 1900, he entered Princeton University, where he became editor in chief of the *Tiger* and was on the editorial boards of two other student publications. He graduated in 1904, then attended the University of Munich for a year and Merton College at Oxford University for a year and a half. On his return to the United States, he taught English at Princeton for several years. In 1908, he went west, settling in Jackson Hole, Wyoming.

Burt and Katherine Newlin, an American he had met at Oxford, were married on February 2, 1913. The couple had two children, Nathaniel and Julia.

During their early days in Wyoming, Burt and his wife were barely making ends meet. Their first breakthrough came when his short story, "The Water-Hole," was published by *Scribner's* magazine in 1915. Husband and wife would go on to successful writing careers — he as a novelist and writer of short stories and magazine and newspaper articles, she as a novelist, short story writer, and author of serials for women's magazines. In their parallel careers they received more than four hundred acceptances of their written work. Burt's short story, "Each in His Generation," won the 1920 O. Henry Memorial Prize.

Burt was a Chevalier of the Order of the White Rose of Finland, having passionately argued that the United States should supply arms to Finland in 1939 as the country was first threatened and then attacked by the Soviet Union. Near the end of 1941, with war raging in Europe, Burt wrote the *American Authors' Manifesto*, a vigorous and well-reasoned attack on totalitarianism. The manifesto was signed by more than a hundred authors. (Burt had served briefly in the Army Air Service in 1918.)

Burt was a member of the American Institute of Arts and Letters, an

Elector of the Hall of Fame, and a judge for the 1945 O. Henry Award. His reviews appeared in the *Saturday Review of Literature,* the *New York Times,* and the *Philadelphia Record;* his articles and short stories appeared in many leading magazines. In 1942, the Philadelphia Art Alliance named Burt as the person who had done the most for the city's arts.

Burt lived and wrote at his Three Rivers Ranch in Wyoming in the summer for many years, spending the winters at his home, "Hibernia," in Southern Pines, North Carolina.

After attending his fiftieth class reunion at Princeton in June 1954, he returned to Wyoming, became ill, and was hospitalized.

Maxwell Struthers Burt died at Jackson Hole, Wyoming, on August 29, 1954, at age 71.

NOTES ON *PHILADELPHIA: HOLY EXPERIMENT*

In the Acknowledgments section of the book, Burt wrote, "This series wisely, and especially now, considering the paper shortage, does not carry bibliographies; bibliographies for the most part being lists of books one intended to read but didn't. Lists are handed down from historian to historian like the ceremonial beads of Indians. Nevertheless, I think I have read almost everything so far written about Philadelphia, and I have examined numerous documents; at all events, I have done enough of this so that frequently the only relief was aspirin. . . . Philadelphia is a fascinating place and one of the hardest subjects imaginable to write about. The trees are so thick, the little wandering forest byways and paths so numerous and so interesting, that it is almost impossible at times to see the forest."

Burt considered *Philadelphia: Holy Experiment* a biography of the city, not simply an account of the city's history as a seaport. Others, including the *New York Times,* in writing Burt's obituary, and the *Bibliography of Pennsylvania History,* agreed.

REVIEWS

Atlantic, July 1945 (p. 131); *Book Week,* April 1, 1945 (p. 4); *Booklist,* April 15, 1945 (p. 234); *Boston Globe,* March 21, 1945 (p. 21); *Christian Science Monitor,* March 28, 1945 (p. 14); *Cleveland Open Shelf,* November 1945 (p. 21); *Commonweal,* April 27, 1945 (p. 49); *Geography Review,* January 1946 (p. 176); *Kirkus,* January 15, 1945 (p. 29); *Nation,* April 21, 1945 (p. 464); *New York Times Book Review,* April 1, 1945 (p. 3); *New Yorker,* April 14, 1945 (p. 92); *Saturday Review of Literature,* April 14, 1945 (p. 54); *Springfield Republican,* April 15, 1945 (p. 4d); *Time,* March 26, 1945 (p. 99); *Weekly Book Review,* April 1, 1945 (p. 2); *Wisconsin Library Bulletin,* May 1945 (p. 53).

SELECTED WRITINGS BY STRUTHERS BURT

In the High Hills (Boston, New York: Houghton, 1914); *John O'May and Other Stories* (Scribner's, 1918); (editor, with others) *A Book of Princeton Verse, 1916-1919* (Princeton: Princeton University Press, 1916–1919); *Songs and Portraits* (New York: Scribner's, 1920); *Chance Encounters* (New York: Scribner's, 1921); *The Interpreter's House* (New York: Scribner's, 1924); *The Diary of a Dude-Wrangler* (New York: Scribner's, 1924); *When I Grow Up to Middle Age* (New York: Scribner's, 1925); *The Delectable Mountains* (New York: Scribner's, 1927); *They Could Not Sleep* (New York: Scribner's, 1928); *The Other Side* (New York: Scribner's, 1928); *Festival* (New York: Scribner's, 1931); *Entertaining the Islanders* (New York: Scribner's, 1933); *Malice in Blunderland, With Apologies to Lewis Carroll, Whose Name Has So Often Been Taken in Vain* (New York: Scribner's, 1935); *Escape from America* (New York: Scribner's, 1936); *Powder River: Let 'er Buck* (Rivers of America Series) (New York: Farrar & Rinehart, 1938); *Along These Streets* (New York: Scribner's, 1942); *War Songs* (New York: Scribner's, 1943); **Philadelphia: Holy Experiment** (Garden City, N.Y.: Doubleday, Doran, 1945).

SOURCES

Burke, W.J. and Will D. Howe. *American Authors and Books, 1640-1940.* New York: Gramercy Publishing Co., 1943, p. 603.

Publishers' Weekly, September 23, 1944; January 27, 1945, p. 319; February 10, 1945, p. 702; and March 21, 1945, p. 1309.

Book Review Digest 1945. New York: The H.W. Wilson Company, 1946, pp. 102–103.

The New York Times Book Review, April 1, 1945, p. 3.

The New York Times obituary, August 30, 1954, p. 17.

Bibliography of Pennsylvania History. Harrisburg: Pennsylvania Historical and Museum Commission, 1957, p. 612.

Phillips, Jr., Raymond C. *Struthers Burt.* Boise, Idaho: Boise State University (Western Writers Series Number 56), 1983.

Toth, Jr., William P. *Maxwell Struthers Burt,* in Kimbel, Bobby Ellen, ed. *Dictionary of Literary Biography, Volume 86, American Short-Story Writers 1910-1945, First Series.* Detroit: Gale Research Co., 1989, pp. 57–62.

Fitzgerald, Carol. *The Rivers of America: A Descriptive Bibliography.* New Castle, Delaware: Oak Knoll Press in Association with The Center for the

Book in the Library of Congress, 2001, pp. 506–508. (Entry for Struthers Burt.)

Contemporary Authors Online, Gale, 2003. Reproduced in *Biography Resource Center*. Farmington Hills, Mich.: The Gale Group. 2003. Accessed April 13, 2003.

QUEBEC: HISTORIC SEAPORT

Mazo de la Roche
January 15, 1879 – July 12, 1961

SS9   First edition, first printing (1944) [9]

[double serpentine rules] | Quebec | HISTORIC SEAPORT | By | MAZO de la ROCHE | [single rule] | ILLUSTRATED WITH PHOTOGRAPHS | [single rule] | [*Seaport* device] | [single rule] | Doubleday, Doran & Company, Inc. | GARDEN CITY 1944 NEW YORK | [double serpentine rules]

COLLATION: 8½" x 6". 112 leaves. [i–vi] vii–xii 1–203 [204] 205–212. Numbers printed in roman within brackets in the center at the foot of the page.

Note: Black-and-white illustrations are inserted facing pp. 28, 29, 52, 53, 76, 77, 100, 101, 124, 125, 140, 141, 164, 165, 196, and 197.

CONTENTS: p. [i], half-title: "Quebec"; p. [ii], blank; p. [iii], title; p. [iv], copyright page: "[within an open book, below an eagle with shield, arrows, and olive branches] THIS BOOK IS | STANDARD LENGTH, | COMPLETE AND UNABRIDGED, | MANUFACTURED UNDER WARTIME CONDITIONS | IN CONFORMITY WITH ALL GOVERNMENT | REGULATIONS CONTROLLING THE USE | OF PAPER AND OTHER MATERIALS | [at bottom] COPYRIGHT, 1944 | BY MAZO DE LA ROCHE | ALL RIGHTS RESERVED | PRINTED IN THE UNITED STATES | AT | THE COUNTRY LIFE PRESS, GARDEN CITY, N.Y. | FIRST EDITION"; p. [v], dedication:

"FOR I *Katherine Hale* I in friendship and I in appreciation of her vivid sketches I of the Canadian scene."; p. [vi], blank; pp. vii–viii, "Preface", [signed Mazo de la Roche, Windrush Hill, York Mills, 2nd February, 1944.]; pp. ix–x, "Contents"; pp. xi–xii, "Illustrations"; pp. 1–203, text; p. [204], blank; pp. 205–212, "Index".

BINDING: Dark red cloth (close to Pantone 201). Front: *Seaport* device blind-stamped in the center. Spine stamped in gold: "[decorative rule] I [crossed telescopes resting on a double-scrolled document] I [decorative rule] I Quebec I HISTORIC I SEAPORT I MAZO I de la ROCHE I [single rule] I DOUBLEDAY I DORAN I [decorative rule] [foul anchor] I [decorative rule] I [sextant] I [decorative rule] I [ship's wheel] I [decorative rule]". Dark cream endpapers depict a double-page illustration in sepia of the port of Quebec, ships and boats in the water, the city in the background.

DUST JACKET (white paper): Front and spine have a dark red background (close to Pantone 194) with a woven appearance. Front: "[white] Quebec I [black] HISTORIC SEAPORT I [white] MAZO de la ROCHE I [black] *Author of the* JALNA *Novels* I [full-color illustration (unsigned) within a black frame with a thin white interior border, of a harbor; sailboats on the far side; a steamship in the center; and cattle resting in a pasture in the foreground]". Spine: "[white] Quebec I [black] HISTORIC I SEAPORT I [white] MAZO I de la ROCHE I [black] DOUBLEDAY I DORAN I [continuation of the illustration found on the front cover, the black frame with thin white interior border at top and bottom]". Back: White background; printing in black. "*This book is complete and unabridged; manufactured under wartime conditions* I *in conformity with all government regulations controlling the use of paper and* I *other materials.* I *The Seaport Series* I [blurb] I [list of seven titles and their authors, notes on illustrations, and prices, beginning with *Montreal: Seaport and City*, and ending with *The Port of New Orleans*]". Front flap: "[upper right] Q.H.S. I Price, *$3.50* I [within an open book, below an eagle with shield, arrows, and olive branches] THIS BOOK IS I STANDARD LENGTH, I COMPLETE AND UNABRIDGED, I MANUFACTURED UNDER WARTIME CONDITIONS I IN CONFORMITY WITH ALL GOVERNMENT I REGULATIONS CONTROLLING THE USE I OF PAPER AND OTHER MATERIALS I QUEBEC: HISTORIC I SEAPORT I *By Mazo de la Roche* I [blurb] I *This book has not been serialized in any* I *form prior to publication.* I [lower right] 4582–44". Back flap: "[within a blue square (close to Pantone 307), on a white square, in black, to the right of a Revolutionary War soldier holding a rifle] FOR VICTORY I BUY I UNITED I STATES I WAR I SAVINGS I BONDS I STAMPS I [blurb promoting war bonds and stamps] I [blue rule] I [blurb urging the reader who has finished reading the

book to send it to 'some man in the service who needs good reading.' |
[dashed blue line] | [mailing label for so sending the book.] | LEAVE WITH
U S O LIBRARY AFTER READING".

Published at $3.50 on July 21, 1944; number of copies printed unknown.
Copyrighted September 7, 1944; deposited July 26, 1944.

The book is listed in "The Weekly Record," July 20, 1944, p. 338.

Note: No evidence found that Doubleday, Doran reprinted *Quebec: Historic
Seaport.*

COPIES: CF

REPRINTS AND REPRODUCTIONS

London: Macmillan, 1946.

Berlin: Deutsche Buch-Gemeinschaft, 1951. Translation into German with
the title, *Quebec: Roman einer Stadt.* 332 pp.

Boucherville, Québec: Éditions du Ronfleur, 1994. Éd. corr. et rev. / Lorenzo
Proteau. Translation into French with the title *Le Québec, notre province,
notre pays: le Canada, notre histoire.*

BIOGRAPHY

Mazo de la Roche was born on January 15, 1879, in Newmarket, Ontario,
Canada, the daughter of William Richmond, a farmer and salesman, and Alberta (Lundy) Roche. According to her *New York Times* obituary, her father
named her Mazo for a Spanish friend, promising his wife she could name all
subsequent children. (De la Roche was an only child.) She is said to have
adopted "de la Roche" as her surname as a child.

De la Roche attended the University of Toronto and taught school in
Toronto for several years. Never married, she lived with her cousin, Caroline
Clement. In the 1930s she adopted two children, a son, René, and a daughter,
Esme (Mrs. David Rees).

De la Roche's first published work was a book of short stories, *Explorers
in the Dawn* (Knopf, 1922). Her first novel, *Possession,* (Macmillan) was published in 1923. She gained international recognition in 1927, winning the ten-
thousand dollar Atlantic-Little Brown novel contest with *Jalna* (Little,
Brown, 1927). The novel, one of more than a thousand manuscripts entered
in the contest, was in the rejection pile at the *Atlantic Monthly* when an editor, attracted by the manuscript's handsome binding, "picked it out, and
didn't put it down until he had finished reading the book."[1]

1. *Publishers' Weekly* obituary, July 24, 1961, pp. 48–49.

Following the success of *Jalna*, De la Roche moved to London (England), where she lived for twelve years. Throughout her life she worked in longhand, seated in a chair, a pad of paper on her knee, her writing goal at least a thousand words a day. At the time of her death in 1961, her sixteen *Jalna* books, known as the Whiteoak Chronicles, had been translated into sixteen languages and Braille and had sold more than eleven million copies in ninety-two foreign and one hundred and ninety-three English editions. The final book in the series, *Morning at Jalna*, (Little, Brown), was published in 1960. Altogether, her published work includes twenty-two novels, a novella, four works with autobiographical backgrounds, five produced plays, two children's books, anthologies of her published short stories, and *Quebec: Historic Seaport.*

In addition to the Atlantic-Little Brown prize De la Roche won in 1927 for *Jalna,* she won two Daughters of the British Empire prizes for her plays in 1925; the Lorne Pierce Medal of the Royal Society of Canada for distinguished contributions to Canadian literature in 1938; and the University of Alberta National Award in Letters in 1951.

Mazo de la Roche died at her home in Toronto on July 12, 1961, at age 82.

NOTES ON *QUEBEC: HISTORIC SEAPORT*

Quebec: Historic Seaport was promoted by Doubleday with a full-page advertisement in the May 20, 1944, issue of *Publishers' Weekly.* The ad described Mazo de la Roche as "A famous novelist [who] tells the story of the oldest and most picturesque seaport on the American continent, which goes back to the landing of Jacques Cartier in 1535. Miss de la Roche, a Canadian herself, is thoroughly familiar with the history of the citadel city on the St. Lawrence. The naturally romantic style of her writing, so well-known through her *Jalna* novels, is excellently adapted to this historical chronicle of what has always been one of the story-book cities of America."

The book's preface begins, "After having spent the greater part of my life in writing of imaginary characters it has been a novel experience to write an account of historical events, a strange experience to keep my very active imagination in leash. I have found great fascination in these characters of the past, even with their weight of cold dates, treaties, and acts."

REVIEWS

Booklist, September 1944 (p. 15); *Catholic World,* December 1944 (p. 285); *Christian Science Monitor,* August 9, 1944 (p. 16); *Kirkus,* April 1, 1944 (p. 161); *Library Journal,* July 1944 (p. 601); *New York Times Book Review,* July 30, 1944

(p. 10); *New Yorker,* August 5, 1944 (p. 60); *Springfield Republican,* August 13, 1944 (p. 4d); *Weekly Book Review,* December 24, 1944 (p. 6); *Wisconsin Library Bulletin,* November 1944 (p. 145).

SELECTED WRITINGS BY MAZO de la ROCHE

"Whiteoak Chronicles" Series; Novels:
Jalna (Boston: Little, Brown, 1927); *Whiteoaks of Jalna* (Boston: Little, Brown, 1929); *Finch's Fortune* (Boston: Little, Brown, 1931); *The Master of Jalna* (Boston: Little, Brown, 1933); *Young Renny* (Boston: Little, Brown, 1935); *Whiteoak Harvest* (Boston: Little, Brown, 1936); *Whiteoak Heritage* (Boston: Little, Brown, 1940); *Wakefield's Course* (Boston: Little, Brown, 1941); *The Building of Jalna* (Boston: Little, Brown, 1944); *Return to Jalna* (Boston: Little, Brown, 1946); *Mary Wakefield* (Boston: Little, Brown, 1949); *Renny's Daughter* (Boston: Little, Brown, 1951); *Whiteoak Brothers: Jalna 1923* (Boston: Little, Brown, 1953); *Variable Winds at Jalna* (Boston: Little, Brown, 1954); *Centenary at Jalna* (Boston: Little, Brown, 1958); *Morning at Jalna* (Boston: Little, Brown, 1960).

Other Books:
Possession (New York: Macmillan, 1923); *Low Life: A Comedy in One Act* (play; first produced as "Low Life" in Toronto, Ontario, at Trinity Memorial Hall, May 14, 1925) (New York: Macmillan, 1925); *Delight* (New York: Macmillan, 1926); *Come True* (play; first produced in Toronto at Trinity Memorial Hall, May 16, 1927) (New York: Macmillan, 1927); *The Return of the Emigrant* (play, first produced in Toronto at Trinity Memorial Hall, March 12, 1928); *Low Life and Other Plays* (Boston: Little, Brown, 1929); *Portrait of a Dog* (novel) (Boston: Little, Brown, 1930); *Lark Ascending* (Boston: Little, Brown, 1932); *The Thunder of the New Wings* (Boston: Little, Brown, 1932); *Beside a Norman Tower* (Boston: Little, Brown, 1934); *The Very Little House* (Boston: Little, Brown, 1937); *Growth of a Man* (Boston: Little, Brown, 1938); *The Sacred Bullock and Other Stories of Animals* (Boston: Little, Brown, 1939); *The Two Saplings* (New York: Macmillan, 1942); **Quebec: Historic Seaport** (New York: Doubleday, 1944); *Mistress of Jalna* (first produced in Bromley, Kent, England, at New Theatre, November 12, 1951); *A Boy in the House, and Other Stories* (Boston: Little, Brown, 1952); *The Song of Lambert* (New York: Macmillan, 1955); *Ringing the Changes: An Autobiography* (Boston: Little, Brown, 1957); *Bill and Coo* (New York: Macmillan, 1958); *Selected Stories of Mazo de la Roche* (ed. and intro. by Douglas Daymond) (Ottawa: University of Ottawa Press, 1979).

SOURCES

Book Review Digest 1944. New York: The H.W. Wilson Company, 1945, p. 191.

Publishers' Weekly, May 20, 1944, p. 1892; July 20, 1944, p. 338; and July 24, 1961, pp. 48–49 (obituary).

The New York Times Book Review, July 30, 1944, p. 10.

The New York Times obituary, July 13, 1961, p. 29.

Twentieth-Century Romance & Historical Writers, 3rd ed. St. James Press, 1994. Reproduced in *Biography Resource Center.* Farmington Hills, Mich.: The Gale Group, 2001. Accessed February 19, 2002.

Encyclopedia of World Biography, 2nd ed. 17 Vols. Gale Research, 1998. Reproduced in *Biography Resource Center.* Farmington Hills, Mich.: The Gale Group. 2001. Accessed February 19, 2002.

Contemporary Authors Online. The Gale Group, 2000. Reproduced in *Biography Resource Center.* Farmington Hills, Mich.: The Gale Group, 2001. Accessed February 19, 2002.

HARBOR OF THE SUN:
THE STORY OF THE PORT
OF SAN DIEGO

Max Miller
February 9, 1899 – December 27, 1967

SS10   First edition, first printing (1940) [2]

[double serpentine rules] | Harbor of the Sun | THE STORY OF THE PORT OF SAN DIEGO | By | MAX MILLER | [single rule] | ILLUS-TRATED | [single rule] | [*Seaport* device] | [single rule] Doubleday, Doran & Company, Inc. | NEW YORK 1940 | [double serpentine rules]

COLLATION: 8½" x 6". 176 leaves. [a–b] [i–viii] ix–xi [xii] xiii [xiv-xvi] 1–329 [330-334]. Numbers printed in roman within brackets in the center at the foot of the page.

Note: Black-and-white photographs are inserted facing pp. [iii], 34, 46, 62, 130, 158, 194, and 222.

CONTENTS: pp. [a–b], blank; p. [i], half-title: "Harbor of the Sun"; p. [ii], "OTHER BOOKS BY | MAX MILLER | [list of ten titles]; p. [iii], title; p. [iv], copyright page: "PRINTED AT THE *Country Life Press*, GARDEN CITY, N.Y., U.S.A. | [at bottom] CL | COPYRIGHT, 1940 | BY MAX MILLER | ALL RIGHTS RESERVED | FIRST EDITION"; p. [v], dedication: "TO | ROY *and* AIRDRIE PINKERTON | partly because years and years ago when I | first came to San Diego and went into his | newspaper office and asked '*How about* | *it?*' he answered: '*All right. You can go* | *down and see what's been go-ing on along* | *the waterfront.*' Both the new job and the | assignment turned out to be bigger than I | had thought, the waterfront having '*been* | *going on,*' it seems, for some four hun- | dred years. And these years | are this book."; p. [vi], blank; p. [vii], "Acknowledgment"; p. [viii], blank; pp. ix–xi, "Before Starting [signed M.M., La Jolla, California]"; [xii], blank; p. xiii, "Illustrations"; p. [xiv], blank; p. [xv], half-title: "Harbor of the Sun"; p. [xvi], blank; pp. 1–320, text; pp. 321–329, "Index"; pp. [330-334], blank.

BINDING: Red cloth (close to Pantone 186). Front: *Seaport* device blind-stamped in the center. Spine stamped in gold: "[decorative rule] | [crossed telescopes resting on a double-scrolled document] | [decorative rule] HARBOR | OF THE SUN | *Max Miller* | [single rule] | DOUBLEDAY DORAN | [decorative rule] [foul anchor] | [decorative rule] | [sextant] | [decorative rule] | [ship's wheel] | [decorative rule]". Dark cream endpapers.

DUST JACKET (white paper): Front: "[within a wide orange band (close to Pantone 172, which wraps to the spine)] [white] Harbor Of The Sun | [black] THE STORY OF THE PORT OF SAN DIEGO | [black-and-white print, which wraps to the spine, depicting the port, horses and rail cars in the foreground, ships in the bay in the background, a gold band at top and bottom] | [at bottom, within a wide orange band, which wraps to the spine] [black] ILLUSTRATED WITH OLD AND CONTEMPORARY PRINTS AND PHOTOGRAPHS | [white] MAX MILLER | [black] Author of I COVER THE WATERFRONT". Spine: "[within the wide orange band] [white] Harbor | Of | The Sun | [black] MAX | MILLER | [illustration] | [within the bottom orange band, in black] DOUBLEDAY | DORAN". Back: White background. "THE SEAPORT SERIES | [orange] [*Seaport* device] | [blurb promoting the *Seaport Series*, advising that additional titles will be published 'from time to time until the stories of all of America's major ports have been told' and announcing that the next volume in the series will be 'on the Port of Seattle....'] | [lower right] 783–40". Front flap: "[upper right] H.O.T.S. | Price, $3.00 | [blurb] | *Jacket illustration from an old print through | courtesy of* SOCIETY OF THE CALIFORNIA | PIONEERS | [lower right] 3632–40". Back flap: "The Port of Gloucester | *James B. Connolly* | [blurb promoting *The Port of Gloucester*] | *Price, $3.00* | [lower right] 3574–40".

Published at $3.00 on October 18, 1940; number of copies printed unknown. Copyrighted October 25, 1940; deposited October 15, 1940 and October 25, 1940.

The book is listed in "The Weekly Record," October 26, 1940, p. 1708.

Note: No evidence found that Doubleday, Doran reprinted *Harbor of the Sun*.

COPIES: CF

REPRINTS AND REPRODUCTIONS

None.

BIOGRAPHY

Max Carlton Miller was born on February 9, 1899, in Traverse City, Michigan, the son of William Wesley and Bessie (Adams) Miller.

Miller served in the U.S. Navy in World War I in 1917 and 1918, rising to first class petty officer; in World War II, from 1942 to 1945, rising to lieutenant commander; and in the Korean War from 1950 to 1953, leaving the Navy as a commander. Six of his thirty books are based on his experiences at sea in the Navy.

Miller began to write at age eight while living on an isolated homestead in Montana. He attended public schools in Everett, Washington, and was a student at the University of Washington from 1919 to 1923, where he was editor of the student *University of Washington Daily*. After college, Miller worked as a reporter for several newspapers, including the *Seattle Star*, the Melbourne (Australia) *Herald*, and the *San Diego Sun*.

Miller became a full-time writer in 1932, after the success of *I Cover the Waterfront* (Dutton, 1932), a collection of vignettes and essays based on his time with the *Sun*, when his beat was the San Diego port and waterfront. The 1933 movie of the same name starred Claudette Colbert (1903–1996). The book's title was also used as the title of a popular song written by Betty Comden (1918–2006), Adolph Green (1915–2002), and Jule Styne (1905–1994). Over the next thirty years, as Miller produced some twenty-eight books, he became known for the understated simplicity of his writing and his talent for picturing the commonplace. *I Cover the Waterfront*, however, remained his most critically and commercially successful work.

Miller married Margaret Ripley on August 23, 1927. The couple lived in La Jolla, California, the inspiration for Miller's book, *The Town with the Funny Name* (Dutton, 1948), in a part of La Jolla known as the cliff shoreline.

Max Miller died on December 27, 1967, in La Jolla, California, at age 68.

NOTES ON *HARBOR OF THE SUN*

A September 21, 1940, *Publishers' Weekly* article, "Publishers' Plans for Geographical Series," reported that the publication of "new books in the established and recently announced geographical series of various houses continues apace...." The article included comment on Doubleday, Doran's *Seaport Series*, which "leads off with the publication this week of 'The Port of Gloucester,' by James B. Connolly," and "looks like an extremely exciting project." The article reported that the second title in the series, Miller's *Harbor of the Sun*, was to be published on October 18, 1940, also noting that Stewart Alsop has written a forty-eight-page prospectus of the series that was sent to booksellers and reviewers, and that Doubleday planned to make a special circular for each book in the series and was planning autographing parties for Miller when *Harbor of the Sun* reached the bookstores.

REVIEWS

Booklist, November 15, 1940 (p. 114); *Christian Science Monitor,* December 19, 1940 (p. 20); *New Republic,* February 3, 1941 (p. 158); *New York Herald Tribune Book Review,* November 10, 1940 (p. 6); *New York Times Book Review,* December 1, 1940 (p. 12); *New Yorker,* November 2, 1940 (p. 87).

SELECTED WRITINGS BY MAX MILLER

C+:A College Commentary (Seattle: Sunset, 1922); *I Cover the Waterfront* (New York: Dutton, 1932); *He Went Away for Awhile* (New York: Dutton, 1933); *The Beginning of a Mortal* (New York: Dutton, 1933); *The Second House from the Corner* (New York: Dutton, 1934); *The Man on the Barge* (New York: Dutton, 1935); *The Great Trek: The Story of the Five-Year Drive of a Reindeer Herd through the Icy Wastes of Alaska, and Northwestern Canada* (Garden City, N.Y.: Doubleday, 1935); *For the Sake of Shadows* (New York: Dutton, 1936); *Fog and Men on Bering Sea* (New York: Dutton, 1936); *Mexico Around Me* (New York: Reynal, 1937); *A Stranger Came to Port* (New York: Reynal, 1938); **Harbor of the Sun: The Story of the Port of San Diego** (Garden City, N.Y.: Doubleday, 1940); *Reno* (New York: Dodd, 1941); *It Must Be the Climate* (New York: McBride, 1941); *The Land Where Time Stands Still* (New York: Dodd, 1943); *Daybreak for Our Carrier* (New York: Whittlesey, 1944); *The Far Shore* (New York: Whittlesey, 1945); *It's Tomorrow Out Here* (New York: Whittlesey, 1945); *The Lull* (New York: Whittlesey, 1946); *The Town with the Funny Name* (New York: Dutton, 1948); *No Matter What Happens* (New York: Dutton, 1949); *I'm Sure We've Met Before* (New York: Dutton, 1951); *The Cruise of the Cow: Being an Introduction to San Diego, Mexico's Baja California, and a Voyage Into the Gulf of California* (New York: Dutton, 1951); *Always the Mediterranean* (New York: Dutton, 1952); *Speak to the Earth* (New York: Appleton, 1955); *Shinny on Your Own Side, and Other Memories of Growing Up* (Garden City, N.Y.: Doubleday, 1958); *Holladay Street* (New York: New American Library, 1962).

SOURCES

Book Review Digest 1940. New York: The H.W. Wilson Company, 1941, p. 641.

Publishers' Weekly, September 7, 1940, p. 796 (Doubleday, Doran October Books); September 21, 1940, p. 1101; and October 26, 1940, p. 1708.

The New York Times Book Review, December 1, 1940, p. 12.

The New York Times obituary, December 28, 1967, p. 32.

Contemporary Authors Online. The Gale Group, 1999. Reproduced in

Biography Resource Center. Farmington Hills, Mich.: The Gale Group, 2001. Accessed April 28, 2002.

SAN FRANCISCO: PORT OF GOLD

William Martin Camp
July 23, 1911 – May 31,1948

SS11   First edition, first printing (1947) [12]

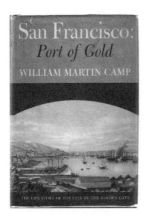

[double serpentine rules] | San Francisco | PORT OF GOLD | By | WILLIAM MARTIN CAMP | [single rule] | [*Seaport* device] | [single rule] | Doubleday & Company, Inc. | GARDEN CITY 1947 NEW YORK | [double serpentine rules]

COLLATION: 8½" x 6". 268 leaves. [a–b] [i–vi] vii–xv [xvi] [1–2] 3–64 [65–66] 67–194 [195–196] 197–336 [337–338] 339–495 [496–498] 499–518. Numbers printed in roman within brackets in the center at the foot of the page.

Note: Black-and-white illustrations are inserted facing pp. 38, 86, 126, 166, 214, 314, 462, and 482.

CONTENTS: pp. [a–b], blank; p. [i], half-title: "San Francisco | PORT OF GOLD"; p. [ii], "Books by | WILLIAM MARTIN CAMP | [list of three titles]"; p. [iii], title; [iv], copyright page: "COPYRIGHT, 1947, BY WILLIAM MARTIN CAMP | ALL RIGHTS RESERVED | PRINTED IN THE UNITED STATES | AT | THE COUNTRY LIFE PRESS, GARDEN CITY, N.Y. | FIRST EDITION"; p. [v], dedication: "*Dedicated to the memory of* | JERRY SCAN-LON | *and a long line of* | *San Francisco newspaper reporters who* | *covered the water front* | *and hoped someday to write a book on it* | *but somehow never did.*"; p. [vi], blank; pp. vii–xii, "Preface" [signed "William Martin Camp, Berkeley, California, 1947"]; pp. xiii–xiv, "Contents"; p. xv, "Illustrations"; p. [xvi], blank; p. [1], division-title: "Part One | THE NEW GOLDEN MOUN-TAIN"; p. [2], blank; pp. 3–64, text; p. [65], division-title: "Part Two | THE BAY"; p. [66], blank; pp. 67–194, text; p. [195], division-title: Part Three | MEN AND SHIPS"; p. [196], blank; pp. 197–336, text; p. [337], division-title: "Part Four | WATER-FRONT WARFARE"; p. [338], blank; pp. 339–495, text; p. [496], blank; p. [497], "Index"; p. [498], blank; pp. 499–518, "Index".

BINDING: Dark green cloth (close to Pantone 350). Spine stamped in gold: "[decorative rule] | [crossed telescopes resting on a double-scrolled document] | [decorative rule] *San Francisco* | PORT | OF GOLD | *William Martin* | *Camp* | [single rule] | DOUBLEDAY | [decorative rule] | [foul anchor] | [decorative rule] | [sextant] | [decorative rule] | [ship's wheel] | [decorative rule]". Front endpapers carry a double-page illustration in sepia described on p. xv as a "Bird's-eye view of San Francisco and the Harbor, 1868, *Photo Courtesy the Bancroft Library;* back endpapers carry an illustration described on p. xv as "San Francisco, after one hundred years as an American seaport. *Photo by Ken McLaughlin, Courtesy the San Francisco Chronicle*".

DUST JACKET (white paper): Front: "[within a medium-green band (close to Pantone 5787), which wraps to the spine, in white] San Francisco: | [black] *Port of Gold* | [white] WILLIAM MARTIN CAMP | [full-color illustration (unsigned), which wraps to the spine, of the Port of San Francisco in the age of sailing ships] | [at bottom, within a black band, which wraps to the spine, in white] THE LIFE STORY OF THE CITY BY THE GOLDEN GATE". Spine: "[within the medium-green band, in white] San | Francisco: | [black] *Port of* Gold | [white] WILLIAM | MARTIN | CAMP | [within the bottom black band, in white] DOUBLEDAY". Back: "[black and white photograph of William Martin Camp, taken by Joe Rosenthal[1]] | [brief biographical sketch of Camp] | *Printed in the U.S.A.*". Front flap: "[upper right] S.F. | *Price,* $5.00 | San Francisco: | PORT OF GOLD | *by* | WILLIAM MARTIN CAMP | [blurb] | *(Continued on back flap)*". Back flap: "*(Continued from front flap)* | [blurb] | [at lower left corner, printed on the diagonal] SAN FRANCISCO: PORT OF GOLD | CAMP-DOUBLEDAY".

Published at $5.00 on November 13, 1947; number of copies printed unknown. Copyrighted and deposited November 4, 1947.

The book is listed in "The Weekly Record," November 30, 1947.

Note: No evidence found that Doubleday reprinted *San Francisco: Port of Gold.*

COPIES: CF

REPRINTS AND REPRODUCTIONS

Reproduced on microfilm. Berkeley, Calif.: University of California, Library Photographic Service, 1989. 1 reel, 35 mm.

---

1. Joe (Joseph J.) Rosenthal, famous for his World War II photograph of five U.S. Marines and a Navy hospital corpsman raising the flag at Iwo Jima, later worked as a photographer at the *San Francisco Chronicle* for thirty-five years.

BIOGRAPHY

William Martin Camp was born on July 23, 1911, in Boonville, Indiana, the son of Noble F. Camp. His mother's maiden name was McNeeley. His father was a foreman in the mining industry. At age 17, Camp ran away from home and joined the Marines. Late in 1929 he was ordered to duty in Shanghai. A voyage to Shanghai in the Navy transport *Henderson* from Norfolk, Virginia, via the Panama Canal and San Francisco gave him his first glimpse of the San Francisco waterfront. In January, 1932, Camp witnessed the Japanese attack on Shanghai and their landing on the Shanghai Bund.

From 1935 to 1938 Camp worked for the *Washington* (D.C.) *Star* and the *Washington Times* while studying law at the Washington College of Law, now part of American University.[2] In 1938, he returned to San Francisco and worked briefly for the *San Francisco Examiner.*

Camp later worked for a year for the *Pan-Pacific Press* in Honolulu. During that time he used the Hawaiian Archives on the grounds of Iolani Palace to study the history of shipping between San Francisco and Hawaii, compiling background information he would later use in writing *San Francisco: Port of Gold.* From 1941 to 1944 he lectured on newspaper writing and reporting at the University of California while covering the waterfront for the *San Francisco Chronicle*, eventually becoming the paper's night city editor.

During World War II Camp again served in the Marine Corps, seeing duty as a combat correspondent in the South Pacific, the Philippines, and China. His first book, *Retreat, Hell!* (Appleton-Century, 1943) was a novel based on Marine Corps action in the Philippines before the fall of Corregidor. The success of his second novel, *Skip to My Lou* (Doubleday, 1945), which dealt with an Ozark family's experiences in California's wartime shipyards, allowed him to take time out from his newspaper job to write *San Francisco: Port of Gold.* At the time of his death in 1948, Camp held the rank of captain in the U.S. Marine Corps Reserve.

Camp and his wife, the former Eleanor Henderson, had three children: William, George, and Daniel. In January, 1948, Camp and his wife purchased a sprawling ranch with vineyards and orchards, "Happy Holler," near Calistoga, California. But a few months later, Camp, despondent over financial problems associated with the ranch, took his life.

William Martin Camp died near Calistoga, California, on May 31, 1948, at age 36.

---

2. The entry on William Camp in *Who Was Who Among English and European Authors, 1931-1949* and two obituaries credit Camp with a bachelor of laws degree, but verification of such a degree has not been found.

NOTES ON *SAN FRANCISCO: PORT OF GOLD*

In his preface to *San Francisco: Port of Gold,* William Martin Camp wrote ". . . this is not a book about the City, but rather one about the Port, the water front of San Francisco. . . . The stories I have included here are in the category of the lesser-known stories. Much has been told, indirectly, in other books about San Francisco, about most of the famous sea captains and shipping lines which have called San Francisco their home Port, and while the water front should be the best-known spot in San Francisco, there is surprisingly little of its past which has been explored."

Near the end of his review of the book in the November 9, 1947 *San Francisco Chronicle,* Joseph Henry Jackson, the paper's book editor, observed, ". . . without setting out to write a straight-line history of a great port Mr. Camp has accomplished something very like it, though in terms of the human-interest tale, the quick bit of action, the colorful incident which his newspaperman's eye unfailingly spots. A lot of people are going to have a good time reading his book and discovering some of the background of a side of the city about which most of them know too little."

San Francisco: Port of Gold was included in Doubleday's Fall List, with a publication date of November 13, 1947. It was advertised as an "anecdote-filled history covering the fabulous waterfront from gold-rush and whaling days to the present."

REVIEWS

Kirkus, October 1, 1947 (p. 568); *New York Herald Tribune Weekly Book Review,* November 30, 1947 (p.2); *San Francisco Chronicle,* November 9, 1947 (p. 12).

SELECTED WRITINGS BY WILLIAM MARTIN CAMP

Retreat, Hell! (New York: Appleton-Century, 1943); *Skip to My Lou* (Garden City, N.Y.: Doubleday, Doran, 1945); *San Francisco: Port of Gold* (Garden City, N.Y.: Doubleday, 1947).

SOURCES

Book Review Digest 1947. New York: The H.W. Wilson Company, 1948, p. 138.

Publishers' Weekly, September 27, 1947, Doubleday Fall List, n.p.; and November 30, 1947, p. 2433;

Preface. *San Francisco: Port of Gold.* Garden City, N.Y.: Doubleday & Company, 1947, pp. vii–xii.

San Francisco Chronicle book review, November 9, 1947, p. 12.

New York Herald Tribune Weekly Book Review, November 30, 1947, p. 2.

San Francisco Chronicle obituary, June 1, 1948, p. 11.

San Francisco Examiner obituary, June 1, 1948, p. 19.

Who Was Who Among English and European Authors, 1931-1949. Omnigraphics, 1978, p. 269.

Contemporary Authors Online, Gale, 2003. Reproduced in *Biography Resource Center.* Farmington Hills, Mich.: The Gale Group, 2003. http://www.galenet.com/servlet/BioRC. Accessed August 6, 2003.

NORTHWEST GATEWAY: THE STORY OF THE PORT OF SEATTLE

Archie Binns
July 30, 1899 – June 28, 1971

SS12   First edition, first printing (1941) [3]

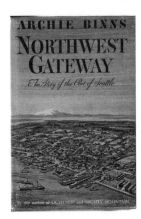

[double serpentine rules] | Northwest Gateway | THE STORY OF THE PORT OF SEATTLE | By | ARCHIE BINNS | [single rule] | ILLUSTRATED | [single rule] | [*Seaport* device] | [single rule] | Doubleday, Doran & Company, Inc. | GARDEN CITY, N.Y. 1941 | [double serpentine rules]

COLLATION: 8¼" x 6". 164 leaves. [a–b] [i–vi] vii–ix [x–xii] 1–313 [314]. Numbers printed in roman within brackets in the center at the foot of the page.

Note: Black-and-white photographs are inserted facing pp. 98, 99, 138, 139, 242, 243, 274, and 275.

CONTENTS: pp. [a–b], blank; p. [i], half-title: "Northwest Gateway"; p. [ii], "BOOKS BY | ARCHIE BINNS | [list of five titles]; p. [iii], title; [iv], copyright page: "PRINTED AT THE *Country Life Press,* GARDEN CITY, N.Y.,

U.S.A. | [at bottom] CL | COPYRIGHT, 1941 | BY ARCHIE BINNS | ALL RIGHTS RESERVED | FIRST EDITION"; p. [v], dedication: "To | FRANK BINNS | who carried a Home Guard rifle | during Seattle's anti–Chinese riots | so that the process of democracy | might be preserved."; p. [vi], blank; pp. vii–viii, "Contents"; p. ix, "Illustrations"; p. [x], blank; p. [xi], half-title: "Northwest Gateway"; p. [xii, blank; pp. 1–304 text; pp. 305–313, "Index"; p. [314], blank.

BINDING: Medium brown cloth (close to Pantone 484). Front: *Seaport* device blind-stamped in the center. Spine stamped in gold: "[decorative rule] | [crossed telescopes resting on a double-scrolled document] | [decorative rule] NORTHWEST | GATEWAY | *Archie Binns* | [single rule] | DOUBLE-DAY DORAN | [decorative rule] | [foul anchor] | [decorative rule] | [sextant] | [decorative rule] | [ship's wheel] | [decorative rule]". Cream endpapers carry a map in cream and light blue (close to Pantone 549) depicting the Olympic Peninsula, Vancouver Island, and the Seattle area.

DUST JACKET (white paper): Front and spine carry an unsigned full-color illustration, the port, waterfront, and city in the foreground, Mt. Rainier in the background. Front: "[black] ARCHIE BINNS | Northwest | Gateway | *The Story of the Port of Seattle* | [at bottom, in white] By the author of LIGHTSHIP and MIGHTY MOUNTAIN". Spine: "[black] ARCHIE | BINNS | NORTHWEST | GATEWAY | *The Story of the* | Port of Seattle | [white] DOUBLEDAY | DORAN | SEAPORT | SERIES". Back: White background. "THE SEAPORT SERIES | [pink, (close to Pantone 239)] [*Seaport* device] | [blurb promoting the Seaport Series, advising that additional titles will be published 'from time to time until the stories of all of America's major ports have been told' and announcing that a forthcoming volume in the series will be *Baltimore on the Chesapeake* by Hamilton Owens] | [lower right] 783–40". Front flap: "[upper right] N.W.G. | Price, $3.00 | NORTHWEST GATEWAY | *The Story of the Port of Seattle* | ARCHIE BINNS | [blurb] | [lower right] 3805–41". Back flap: "HARBOR OF THE SUN | The Story of the Port of San Diego | MAX MILLER | [blurb] | *Price, $3.00* | [lower right] 3632–40".

Published at $3.00 on June 20, 1941; number of copies printed unknown. Copyrighted August 20, 1941; deposited June 11, 1941 and August 16, 1941.

The book is listed in "The Weekly Record," June 21, 1941, p. 2482.

Note: No evidence found that Doubleday, Doran reprinted *Northwest Gateway: The Story of the Port of Seattle*.

COPIES: CF

REPRINTS AND REPRODUCTIONS

Portland, Oregon: Binfords & Mort.

Reproduced on microfilm. New Haven, Conn.: Yale University Library, 1993.
1 reel, 35 mm.

BIOGRAPHY

Archie Fred Binns was born on July 30, 1899, in Port Ludlow, Washington, the son of Frank and Atlanta Sarah (McQuah) Binns.

Binns served in the Field Artillery, U.S. Army, from 1918 to 1923, rising to second lieutenant. In 1922, he earned a bachelor of arts degree from Stanford University.

In 1923, Binns married Mollie Windish. The couple had two children, Jacqueline and Georgia. Mollie Binns died in 1954. At his death in 1971, Binns left six children, Jacqueline and Georgia from his first marriage; Richard and Thomas, both adopted; and Ellen and Margaret, from a second marriage.

During the 1920s, Binns was an editor at the Leonard Scott Publication Co. In 1923, he was Washington correspondent for Scripps-Howard newspapers. His career as a novelist and historian began with his first book, written with Felix Riesenberg, *The Maiden Voyage* (John Day, 1931).

Critics and readers agreed that Binns was at his best when his subject was the Pacific Northwest. One of his earliest jobs was aboard a lightship near Cape Flattery, Washington. His second book was the 1934 work *Lightship* (Reynal & Hitchcock), a fictional account of life aboard such a vessel. The book received favorable, enthusiastic reviews. Over the next thirty-three years, Binns wrote more than a dozen other books, about a third of them non-fiction, but *Lightship* remained his best-known and most popular work.

Archie Binns died in Port Angeles, Washington, on June 28, 1971, at age 71.

NOTES ON *NORTHWEST GATEWAY*

In the January 25, 1941, issue of *Publishers' Weekly*, Doubleday announced that the book would be featured in a promotional booklet on the *Seaport Series*, noting that the book would "probably lead the general institutional ads" in Doubleday's promotion of the series.

REVIEWS

Booklist, September 1941 (p. 7); *Christian Science Monitor*, September 20, 1941 (p. 10); *Commonweal*, September 19, 1941 (p. 522); *Library Journal*, May 15, 1941 (p. 462); *Nation*, July 12, 1941 (p. 40); *New Republic*, September 1, 1941 (p. 286); *New York Herald Tribune Book Review*, July 6, 1941 (p. 3); *New York*

Times, July 6, 1941 (p. 1); *New Yorker,* June 21, 1941 (p. 79); *Wisconsin Library Bulletin,* July 1941 (p. 137).

SELECTED WRITINGS BY ARCHIE BINNS

(with Felix Riesenberg) *The Maiden Voyage* (New York: John Day, 1931); *Lightship* (New York: Reynal & Hitchcock, 1934); *The Laurels Are Cut Down* (New York: Reynal & Hitchcock, 1937); *The Land Is Bright* (New York: Scribner, 1939); *Mighty Mountain* (New York: Scribner, 1940); **Northwest Gateway: The Story of the Port of Seattle** (Seaport Series) (Garden City, N.Y.: Doubleday, 1941); *The Roaring Land* (*New York:* R. M. McBride, 1942); *The Timber Beast* (New York: Scribner, 1944); (contributor) **The Pacific Coast Ranges** (American Mountain Series) (New York: Vanguard, 1946); *You Rolling River* (New York: Scribner, 1947); *The Radio Imp* (Philadelphia: Winston, 1950); *Secret of the Sleeping River* (Philadelphia: Winston, 1952); *Sea in the Forest* (Garden City, N.Y. Doubleday, 1953); *Sea Pup* (New York: Duell, Sloan & Pearce, 1954); (with Olive Kooken) *Mrs. Fiske and the American Theatre* (New York: Crown, 1955); *The Enchanted Islands* (New York: Duell, Sloan & Pearce, 1956); *The Headwaters: A Novel* (New York: Duell, Sloan & Pearce, 1957); *Sea Pup Again* (New York: Duell, Sloan & Pearce, 1965); *Peter Skene Ogden: Fur Trader* (Portland, Oregon: Binford & Mort, 1967).

SOURCES

Book Review Digest 1941. New York: The H.W. Wilson Company, 1942, p. 83.

Publishers' Weekly, January 25, 1941, p. 398; May 3, 1941, pp. 1799 and 1854; May 31, 1941, p. 2149; May 31, 1941, n.p.; and June 21, 1941, p. 2482.

Seattle Post-Intelligencer obituary, July 4, 1971, n.p.

The New York Times Book Review, July 6, 1941, p. 1.

Almanac of Famous People, 6th Edition, Gale Research, 1998. Biography Resource Center, Gale Research, 2001. Accessed February 19, 2002.

Contemporary Authors Online. The Gale Group, 2000. Reproduced in *Biography Resource Center.* Farmington Hills, Mich.: The Gale Group, 2001. Accessed February 19, 2002.

American Folkways
1941–1958

Erskine Caldwell
Editor

Duell, Sloan & Pearce
Publisher

1941
Desert Country
Piñon Country
Short Grass Country
Ozark Country

1942
Blue Ridge Country
High Border Country
Mormon Country
Palmetto Country

1944
Far North Country
Deep Delta Country

1945
Town Meeting Country
North Star Country
Golden Gate Country

1946
Southern California Country: An Island on the Land
Lower Piedmont Country

1947
Corn Country
Big Country: Texas

1949
Redwood Country
Niagara Country

1950
Rocky Mountain Country
Wheat Country

1951
Pittsylvania Country
Gulf Coast Country

1952
Smoky Mountain Country

1954
Adirondack Country

1955
High Sierra Country

1957
Old Kentucky Country
The Other Illinois

AMERICAN FOLKWAYS

Introduction and Publishing History

ERSKINE Caldwell proposed the publication of what would become the *American Folkways* series to Viking Press in 1939. Viking had published five of Caldwell's books in the preceding six years, but rejected his proposal. In his autobiography, *With All My Might* (Peachtree, 1987), Caldwell wrote, "I had become completely absorbed in my interest in editing a series of books describing regional life in the United States and was determined to get the books written and published. By chance, I happened to accept an invitation to one of New York's literary cocktail parties on an opportune occasion. And it was there that I met Charlie Duell, who with Cap Pearce and Sam Sloan, had established the new publishing house of Duell, Sloan, and Pearce, Inc. The three partners promptly offered me a contract to publish the twenty-five volume series of *American Folkways* under my editorship in addition to publishing any books of fiction and nonfiction I would write."[1] Caldwell "jumped at the opportunity," noting, "I was only writing one or two novels a year and maybe twenty-five short stories and maybe going around the world, and I had plenty of time left. So I got the idea for the series, and when a publisher took it on I scurried around the country finding writers I thought were suitable to their regions."[2]

By the fall of 1939, Caldwell began meeting with potential authors, later describing this as "a moonlighting job that let me travel around America. Between writing my own books I'd have a month or two off and would be traveling somewhere, so this was suited to my way of life. . . . These were people I had known or who had been recognized. I'd go to see the person and talk with him on the kind of writing he would produce; then I would select him and the publisher would give him a contract. The book would be sent to me and I'd look at it and pass it on to the editor." Caldwell recalled his original intention as to "present segments of the country, individual regions, which were more distinct in those days." Noting that his motive "was to promote the regionalism of the country," he said, "I've always been a regional writer, and I think the best writing is regional. To write about the Cajuns of Louisiana, the Mexicans along the Rio Grande, the Indians of New Mexico, to me that is regionalism and what I wanted to do was to bring out

1. Caldwell, Erskine. *With All My Might*. Atlanta: Peachtree Publishers, Ltd., 1987, pp. 165–166.
2. Arnold, Edwin T., ed. *Conversations with Erskine Caldwell*. Jackson: University Press of Mississippi, 1998, p. 48.

these various sections of life in America, because every part of the country is different–at least, until we got radio and everybody tried to lose their accent. So we're losing our Southern accents, and our New England accents, because everybody tried to talk like Walter Cronkite."[3]

As for his approach to editing the series, Caldwell noted that he tried to find the "ideal person for a region of the country, someone who had the ability to write, and the knowledge and the inclination to write about this particular field. If it was an agricultural region or manufacturing region or urban region, whatever this particular thing was, this was the person to be selected to write about that. Not only did he have to have the ability to express himself, he also had to have the knowledge, the background to write about it. And so that was my only contribution, because once we got a manuscript, then I would give it to somebody else to do so-called editing. In other words I didn't correct spelling or anything like that."[4]

At a meeting with Stanley Vestal at the University of Oklahoma, Caldwell suggested that Vestal write the first book in the series. In a November 20, 1939, letter to Caldwell, Vestal offered to write on the "region that includes parts of Oklahoma, Kansas, Texas, Colorado, and New Mexico, originally known as The Short Grass, and now better known as the Dust Bowl." In a November 22 letter to Caldwell, Charles A. Pearce wrote that Vestal sounded "interested but expensive." Vestal had asked for an advance of $800 and royalties of 10 percent on the first five hundred copies sold, 12.5 percent on the next two-thousand five-hundred, and 15 percent on all further sales. The publisher's November 28 letter to Vestal explained that Caldwell, as series editor, "playing an important, creative, and cohesive part in the development" of the series, was to share in the margin allowable for royalties. The letter further noted that series authors were to receive 10 percent on the first three thousand copies sold, 11 percent on the next three thousand, and 12 percent for sales above six thousand copies, adding, "We find it therefore impossible to offer a higher royalty which, combined with the editor's royalty, would make the books unprofitable." Pearce further noted, "As to advances against royalties, we have set a standard advance of $250 for the books in this series." But, "in consideration of [Vestal's] position and past record," he was offered a $500 advance, twice that offered to other authors. He agreed to the publisher's terms and was to deliver his manuscript by December 31, 1940.

In a conversation with Charles Pearce, Edgar Lee Masters had expressed interest in writing a book in the series but ultimately decided against the idea. Joseph Mitchell of *The New Yorker* turned down Caldwell's request to write a book on the coastal and Piedmont Carolinas, citing work and family

3. Ibid., pp. 230 and 250.
4. Ibid., 229–230.

obligations. Although Caldwell received unsolicited letters from others offering to write for the series, nothing seems to have come of such offers.

Duell, Sloan and Pearce announced publication of the *American Folkways* series in their Spring List in the January 25, 1941, issue of *Publishers' Weekly*, noting it would be edited by Erskine Caldwell and "Inaugurated in May with Edwin Corle's *Desert Country*." Although the publisher had planned to lead off with Stanley Vestal's *Short Grass Country*, Vestal had suffered a lengthy illness that forced him to ask for an additional six months to complete his book. The *Publishers' Weekly* announcement promoted both *Desert Country* and *Piñon Country*, the first two titles in the series.

Four series titles were published in 1941: *Desert Country* by Edwin Corle on May 22, *Piñon Country* by Haniel Long on June 12, *Short Grass Country* by Stanley Vestal on October 30, and *Ozark Country* by Otto Ernest Rayburn on December 1.

In a March 3, 1941, letter to Caldwell, Stetson Kennedy, author of *Palmetto Country* in the *Folkways* series, addressed the lack of guidance he had received, observing, "I wish I had known of your preference for folk tales and anecdotes before I went so far with the Cuban material. . . . I want to again assure you that I can write a satisfactory volume on this region, and in a surprisingly short time, once I am sure what you want."

To give Caldwell and potential series authors a firmer footing in producing future titles, on June 5, 1941, Kennedy sent Caldwell a draft prospectus of the series, which he believed would help "promote that degree of uniformity and common perspective which is desired for books of the American Folkways Series." The draft continued, "Each author, however, is urged to give his book a maximum of individuality, a distinctive flavor typical of his region's folkways." Later in the prospectus, Kennedy defined folkways as "including all the ways of people; the aim is to translate the daily life of the people into prose." Further on, Kennedy observed, "The region's ecology and natural resources . . . are relevant insofar as they influence regional life and culture. . . . One of the aims of the Series is to provide, on a regional basis a cultural history of America of a new and peculiarly honest kind. It is in viewpoint that folk history primarily differs from the standard text-book variety. . . . In general, the idea is to portray the people who have done the working, fighting, and living that have made history, and to record the unwritten history which has been preserved on their lips."[5]

Caldwell's June 12 response to Kennedy noted, "Your ideas are well stated and quite concrete. Such a folder that would state the aims of the Folk Way Series has never occurred to me in quite so absolute a form. Your interest is very much appreciated, and I will let you know as soon as possible the reac-

5. Stetson Kennedy, letters to Erskine Caldwell, March 3, 1941, and June 5, 1941.

tion of the publishers." In his excellent article, *The American Folkways Series* in the May, 1998 edition of *Firsts,* John D. Townsend reported, "Caldwell liked Kennedy's outline, had it approved by DS&P, and then sent it out as a 'prospectus' or guideline to prospective writers for the series, very often sending along copies of previous titles."[6]

In keeping with Caldwell's intention to publish four *Folkways* titles each year, four series titles were published in 1942: *Blue Ridge Country* by Jean Thomas on March 19, *High Border Country* by Eric Thane on May 21, *Mormon Country* by Wallace Stegner on September 24, and *Palmetto Country* by Stetson Kennedy on November 20.

No series titles were published in 1943.

Two series titles were published in 1944: *Far North Country* by Thames Williamson on March 30 and *Deep Delta Country* by Harnett T. Kane on November 3.

Three series titles were published in 1945: *Golden Gate Country* by Gertrude Atherton on February 28, *Town Meeting Country* by Clarence M. Webster on March 14, and *North Star Country* by Meridel Le Sueur on November 28.

Two series titles were published in 1946: *Southern California Country: An Island on the Land* by Carey McWilliams on March 22 and *Lower Piedmont Country* by H.C. Nixon on November 8.

Caldwell wrote to a number of the *Folkways* authors on January 15, 1947, outlining his plans for further promotion of the series. At the time, fifteen series titles had been published. In his January 20 reply, Stanley Vestal wrote, "if we can get these books recommended as textbooks or supplementary readers it would be grand," also suggesting that the series books be made available to airline and railroad passengers traveling through areas "covered by" the various titles. Jean Thomas, in her January 23 reply to Caldwell, suggested that the annual American Folk Song Festival in Ashland, Kentucky, drawing as many as twenty thousand patrons – admission was free – could be used as a "spring board to launch an unusual, a different campaign to promote the American Folkways Series," proposing that the series authors be invited to attend. Thomas was the founder of the American Folk Song Society, which sponsored the festival. Other series authors may have responded to Caldwell's "form letter," as Thomas called it, but no other responses have been found.

Two series titles were published in 1947: *Corn Country* by Homer Croy on May 9 and *Big Country: Texas* by Donald Day on June 11.

No series titles were published in 1948.

Two series titles were published in 1949: *Niagra Country* by Lloyd Gra-

6. "The American Folkways Series." *Firsts,* Vol. 8, No. 5, May, 1998, p. 55. *Arnold,* op. cit., pp. 47; 285–286.

ham on June 30 and *Redwood Country: The Lava Region and the Redwoods* by Alfred Powers on July 20.

Two series titles were published in 1950: *Rocky Mountain Country* by Albert N. Williams on February 17 and *Wheat Country* by William B. Bracke on April 20.

Two series titles were published in 1951: *Pittsylvania Country* by George Swetnam on January 15 and *Gulf Coast Country* by Hodding Carter and Anthony Ragusin on March 16.

Gulf Coast Country was the twenty-third series title. In several interviews, Caldwell reported that he had edited a total of twenty-three series titles. Even so, the next two series titles, *Smoky Mountain Country* by North Callahan, published on May 9, 1952, and *Adirondack Country* by William Chapman White, published on May 6, 1954, carry Caldwell's name as series editor. Both titles also name Little, Brown and Company as series co-publisher with Duell, Sloan and Pearce.

One series title was published in 1955: *High Sierra Country* by Oscar Lewis on June 30. With this title, the twenty-sixth in the series, Caldwell was no longer named as editor. He had given up the position, saying it was time-consuming and that he had completed what he had set out to do. Little, Brown and Company was again named as series co-publisher.

One series title was published in 1957: *Old Kentucky Country* by Clark McMeekin, the pen name of the writing team Dorothy Park Clark and Isabel McLennan McMeekin, on May 16. Little, Brown and Company was no longer named as series co-publisher.

The twenty-eighth and final title in the series, *The Other Illinois* by Baker Brownell was published on February 18, 1958.

The endpapers of the first eight series titles carry maps of the United States with the focus area of the book highlighted. The endpapers of the next five titles carry maps of the focus area or region only. The endpapers of *Southern California Country*, the fourteenth series title, carry the full map of the U.S., with the focus area highlighted. *Lower Piedmont Country*, the fifteenth series title, has blank endpapers. With the publication of *Corn Country*, the sixteenth series title, the endpaper design returns to the presentation of the U.S. map with the focus area highlighted, a practice maintained through the publication of *Smoky Mountain Country*, the twenty-fourth series title. The final four series titles carry endpaper maps that depict only the focus area or region of the book.

With the publication of *Southern California Country*, the fourteenth title in the series, the design of the front panel of the dust jacket was changed. Until then, the front panel had been illustrated, with a map highlighting the focus area of the book. For succeeding series titles, the front panel of the dust jacket carries a photograph rather than an illustration. For eight series titles, beginning with *Southern California,* these photographs were framed; for the six titles that followed, the photographs were presented without a frame. With the publication of *High Sierra Country* and *Old Kentucky Country,* the twenty-sixth and twenty-seventh series titles, the photograph was moved to a position above the title and the author's name. The dust jacket of *The Other Illinois,* the twenty-eighth and final series title, was radically redesigned, wrapping to the spine and the back of the jacket.

In his evaluation of the series, Caldwell said, "Well, of course it didn't get very much circulation. We did too many books too rapidly, I think. I jumped at the opportunity for Duell, Sloan and Pearce to start this series, and they agreed to do four a year. I had been turned down by Viking Press, and I was so elated with the idea that it ran away with me, and I did it too rapidly, I suppose, with too many people involved. I couldn't pay too much attention to the preparation and reading of manuscripts and revising. All that had to be left to Cap Pearce. I think it would have been a much better series if we had cut it down in half and maybe spread it out over a longer period of time."[7]

Each of the entries that follow includes a biographical sketch of the book's author or authors. Taken as a whole, these thirty sketches portray an impressive group of experienced, qualified, and respected professional writers – novelists, historians, journalists, and educators, all of them familiar with the "Country" they wrote about. The *Folkways* series ranges across America, from Clarence Webster's *Town Meeting Country,* which could not be more New England Yankee in spirit, to Carey McWilliams's *Southern California Country,* the "island on the land," bounded on the west by the Pacific Ocean and on the south by Mexico.

Many series titles were still in print well into the 21st century, and some, such as Stetson Kennedy's *Palmetto Country,* are considered classics. Published from 1941 to 1958, *The American Folkways* series captured much of American life, from the depths of the Great Depression, through the challenging years of World War II, to the bustling postwar decades.

7. *Arnold,* op.cit., pp. 47; 285–286.

ERSKINE CALDWELL

Editor, *American Folkways*

Erskine Preston Caldwell was born on December 17, 1903, in the White Oak community near the village of Moreland, Georgia, the son of Ira Sylvester and Caroline Bell Caldwell. His father was a Presbyterian minister. His mother had been a teacher of English and Latin in women's seminaries and colleges.

Caldwell attended Erskine College in South Carolina in 1920 and 1921; the University of Pennsylvania in 1924, and the University of Virginia from 1922 to 1926. Over the years he worked as a mill laborer, cotton picker, cook, waiter, taxicab driver, farmhand, stonemason's helper, and stagehand in a burlesque theater. He was a reporter for the *Atlanta Journal* in 1925 and a scriptwriter in Hollywood (1933–1934 and 1942–1943). He was a newspaper correspondent in Mexico, Europe, and China (1938–1940) and a war correspondent for *Life*, the newspaper *PM*, and the Columbia Broadcasting System in 1941.

Caldwell wrote twenty-six novels, sixteen collections of stories, fifteen books of nonfiction, two children's books, and a collection of his poetry. His books sold more than eighty million copies and have been translated into more than forty languages. His work appeared in national magazines and various newspapers, including *The Atlantic, Nation, The New Republic, The New Yorker, Punch, The Saturday Review, Time, The Chicago Tribune,* and *The New York Times.* His books included many best-sellers. The novels *Tobacco Road* (1932) and *God's Little Acre* (1933) are among the best-known works of twentieth-century American literature and with *Claudelle Inglish*, (1958, under the title *Claudelle*) were adapted for motion pictures. *Tobacco Road* was also adapted for the stage, running on Broadway for more than seven years while earning Caldwell $2,000 a week in royalties.[1]

Caldwell's early work, which focused principally on poverty, depravity, bigotry, and suffering among poor, small-town, white Southerners, was frequently banned or censored. At the time, the pungent language his characters used was, by some at least, deemed obscene, although by the time of Caldwell's death in 1987 much of that language might generally have been considered acceptable.

Caldwell's first three marriages ended in divorce. With the photographer Margaret Bourke-White, who in 1939 became his second wife, Caldwell wrote four books, including *You Have Seen Their Faces* (1937), a well-known

---

1. *New York Times* obituary, April 13, 1987. p. 1.

non-fiction work about the South. His fourth marriage, in 1957, was to Virginia Moffett Fletcher, who survived him.

Caldwell was admitted to the American Academy of Arts and Letters in 1984. He was also a Georgia Writers Hall of Fame honoree.

Erskine Caldwell died in Paradise Valley, Arizona, on April 11, 1987, at age 83.

SOURCES

Caldwell, Erskine. *With All My Might: An Autobiography.* Atlanta: Peachtree Publishers, Ltd., 1987.

The New York Times obituary, April 13, 1987, p. 1.

Yardley, Jonathan. "Dixie Redux: Two Writers Reassessed" (review of *Erskine Caldwell: The Journey From Tobacco Road,* by Dan B. Miller) (Knopf, 1995). *The* (Miami) *Herald,* January 29, 1995, p. 3I.

Contemporary Authors Online. The Gale Group, 2000. Reproduced in *Biography Resource Center,* Farmington Hills, Mich.: The Gale Group. Accessed February 11, 2002.

Hall of Fame Honorees. Georgia Writers Hall of Fame, A Program of the University of Georgia Libraries. UGA Libraries Home Page, accessed May 15, 2003.

ADIRONDACK COUNTRY

William Chapman White
February 20, 1903 – November 28, 1955

AF1   First edition, first printing (1954) [25]

[*Folkways* device] | [within a gray (close to Pantone 402) rectangle with rounded corners, in cream] EDITED BY ERSKINE CALDWELL | [black] ADIRONDACK | COUNTRY | BY WILLIAM CHAPMAN WHITE | [cream] DUELL, SLOAN & PEARCE · NEW YORK | LITTLE, BROWN & COMPANY · BOSTON

COLLATION: 8½" x 6". 162 leaves. [i–vii] viii [1–3] 4–41 [42] 43–64 [65] 66–178 [179] 180-211 [212] 213–228 [229] 230-246 [247] 248–307 [308–309] 310-315 [316]. Numbers printed in roman in headline at the outer margin of the type page, except for p. 311, on which the number is printed in the center at the foot of the page.

CONTENTS: p. [i], half-title: "*Adirondack Country*"; p. [ii], "AMERICAN FOLKWAYS | EDITED BY ERSKINE CALDWELL | [list of twenty-five titles and their authors, beginning with *Golden Gate Country* and ending with *Far North Country*]"; p. [iii], title; p. [iv], copyright page: "COPYRIGHT 1954, | BY WILLIAM CHAPMAN WHITE | ALL RIGHTS RESERVED. NO PART OF THIS BOOK IN EXCESS OF FIVE | HUNDRED WORDS MAY BE RE-PRODUCED IN ANY FORM WITHOUT | PERMISSION IN WRITING FROM THE PUBLISHER | LIBRARY OF CONGRESS CATALOG CARD NO. 52–12652 | FIRST EDITION | [within a rectangular frame] DUELL, SLOAN AND PEARCE-LITTLE, BROWN | BOOKS ARE PUBLISHED BY | LITTLE, BROWN AND COMPANY | IN ASSOCIATION WITH | DUELL, SLOAN & PEARCE, INC. | *Published simultaneously in Canada | by Little, Brown & Company (Canada) Limited* | PRINTED IN THE UNITED STATES OF AMERICA"; p. [v], dedication: "A DEDICATION | *William Morris was a New York theatrical agent | who came to the Adirondacks for his health. He re- | gained it and lived for another thirty years. | In his gratitude he did much for the region, par- | ticularly for the village of Saranac Lake. Although he | died* twenty years ago, he is still beloved in memory. | It is an Adirondack tradition that if a man needs | help, whether when lost in the woods or for any other | purpose, he need only shout. People of good will drop | their work and come running. | William Morris lived by that tradition in many a | civic and regional project. He was not alone. His story | of finding new strength in the hills, then sharing it, is | the story of many another man who has come at one | time or other to the Adirondacks and remained. The | Adirondack country is the better for them. | To William Morris, and to the many like him, this | book is dedicated."[1]; p. [vi], blank; pp. [vii]-viii, "Contents"; p. [1], half-title: "Adirondack Country"; p. [2], blank; pp. [3]-307, text; p.[308], blank; pp. [309]-310, "Sources and Acknowledgments"; pp. 311-315, "Index"; p. [316], blank.

BINDING: Light green cloth (close to Pantone 624). Front: Folkways device stamped in black, at lower right corner. Spine stamped in black, except where noted: "[thick rule] | [four thin rules] | [within a black panel, in gold] AD-IRON- | DACK | COUNTRY | · | WILLIAM | CHAPMAN | WHITE | [four thin rules] | [thick rule] | [four thin rules] | [at bottom] [four thin rules | [within a black panel, in gold] DUELL, SLOAN | AND PEARCE | [thin rule] | LITTLE, BROWN | [four thin rules] | [thick rule]". Cream endpapers carry a map in dark green (close to Pantone 341) and cream by Stephen J. Voorhies, inset in the upper left corner a map of the region with Adirondack State Park cross-hatched, and, inset in the lower left corner the title "The Adirondack Country showing boundaries of the Adirondack State Park" and a scale of miles.

DUST JACKET (white paper): Front: Medium green (close to Pantone 341); printing in white. "Adirondack | Country | [black] [thin rule] | AMERICAN FOLKWAYS | [thin rule] | [black-and-white photograph of a lake; with mountains in the background] | WILLIAM CHAPMAN WHITE". Spine: Gray background (close to Pantone 407); printing in medium green. "Adirondack | Country | WILLIAM | CHAPMAN | WHITE | [Folkways device in black and white] | DUELL, SLOAN | AND PEARCE | [thin rule] | LITTLE, BROWN". Back: White background; printing in black. "American Folkways | Edited by ERSKINE CALDWELL | [blurb praising the series] | [list of 25 authors and the corresponding title for each] | [publisher's imprint[2]]". Front flap: White background; printing in black. "[upper right] $4.00 | Adirondack | Country | WILLIAM CHAPMAN WHITE | [brief biographical sketch of White, followed by blurb] | (Continued on second flap)". Back flap: White background; printing in black. "(Continued from first flap) | [blurb] | [within a rectangular frame] DUELL, SLOAN AND

1. William Morris was the father of William Chapman White's wife, Ruth.
2. The imprint reads: "Duell, Sloan and Pearce — Little, Brown and Company."

PEARCE-LITTLE, BROWN | BOOKS ARE PUBLISHED BY | LITTLE, BROWN AND COMPANY | IN ASSOCIATION WITH | DUELL, SLOAN & PEARCE, INC."

Published at $4.00, on May 6, 1954;[3] number of copies printed unknown. Copyrighted and deposited May 12, 1954.

The book is listed in "The Weekly Record," May 22, 1954, p. 2204.

Note: Duell, Sloan & Pearce published at least four printings of *Adirondack Country.*

COPIES: CF

REPRINTS AND REPRODUCTIONS

New York: Knopf, 1967 (Borzoi Book). Introduction by Fred Ayvazian. Afterword by Ruth M. White. Drawings by Walter Richards. Reprinted: 1968, 1970, 197?, 1974, 1976, 1980, 1987.

Syracuse, N.Y.: Syracuse University Press, 1985. Paperback. (Reprint of 1967 Knopf edition.) Published at $14.95, 2,052 copies; reprinted in 1990, 2,043 copies; 1998, 1,094 copies; and 2001, 1082 copies. The price was changed to $16.95 in 2002.

BIOGRAPHY

William Chapman White was born in Reading, Pennsylvania, on February 20, 1903, the son of William and Margaret (Dye) White.

In 1923, White earned a bachelor of arts degree from Princeton University and, in 1926, a master of arts degree from the University of Pennsylvania, where he was an instructor in European history, also teaching at various private schools. Awarded a Penfield Scholarship by the University of Pennsylvania, he studied at Moscow University from 1927 to 1929.

In 1936, White married Ruth Morris, the daughter of the New York theatrical agent William Morris. The couple had an adopted son, William M.

During World War II, White worked in London for the United States Office of War Information, creating miniature newspapers in French, German, Norwegian, and Dutch. These newspapers were smuggled into German-occupied countries or air-dropped there by American and British forces. One of them, *L'Amerique en Guerre* (America at War) eventually had a weekly circulation of seven million copies.[4]

After the war, White worked from 1946 to 1950 in the United States as a

---

3. The copyright certificate notes a May 6, 1954, publication date; the May 1, 1954, issue of *PW* reports a publication date of May 19, 1954.
4. *The New York Times* (obituary), November 29, 1955, p. 29.

correspondent for the British "News Review." From 1952 until his death in 1955, he was a columnist for the *New York Herald Tribune*. His article, *Saranac Lake, N.Y.*, was published in the Cities of America series in the August 25, 1951, issue of the *Saturday Evening Post*.

In 1948, for reasons of his health, White and his family moved from New York to the William Morris family home at Saranac Lake. White's affection for the Adirondacks area is reflected in his civic involvement there. He was a board member of the Saranac Lake Rehabilitation Guild, a trustee of the Saranac Lake Free Library, and a board member of the Saranac Lake General Hospital. Shortly before his death, he began the task of reopening the Trudeau Sanatorium as a medical or research center.

White wrote *Adirondack Country* while living in Saranac, thus acquiring special stature as a preeminent recorder of the history and folklore of northern New York and the Adirondack region. He died in 1955 while in Washington, D.C., conducting research on the Ironclad *Monitor* and the Civil War battle between the *Monitor* and the *Merrimac*. White and his wife, Ruth, wrote *Tin Can on a Shingle*, a book about that battle published by E.P. Dutton on May 2, 1957.

William Chapman White died on November 28, 1955, at age 52.

Note: The William Chapman White Memorial Room at the Adirondack Research Center of the Saranac Lake Free Library was funded in part by The William Chapman White Memorial Fund.

NOTES ON *ADIRONDACK COUNTRY*

Adirondack Country was included in the Duell, Sloan and Pearce — Little Brown Winter-Spring List, which also listed books published by Atlantic Monthly Press. The book was featured in the May 1, 1954, issue of *Publishers' Weekly* in the "*PW buyers' forecast for May 17-25*," which noted that the book was scheduled for publication on May 19, 1954.

A mailer from E.L. Gray & Company, a Saranac Lake bookseller, announced, "Here, at long last, is the complete and definitive book on the ADIRONDACK COUNTRY." In a glowing review of *Adirondack Country* in the *New York Times Book Review* that was republished in the (Saranac) *Enterprise*, Carl Carmer, describing the book's last chapter, wrote, in part, "This chapter deserves to be ranked with the very best of American writing about nature — with Thoreau and Burrows, with Joseph Wood Krutch and Edwin Way Teale."

White and Carl Carmer and his wife, Betty, met for the first time in August, 1954. The lengthy caption of a photo of the three taken by Mary Ann Clancy for the *Enterprise*, noting that the Carmers and White admired one another's work, said of the event "Their get-together could therefore be termed the first meeting of the Adirondack Mutual Admiration Society."

The endpapers of *Adirondack Country,* the twenty-fifth title in *The American Folkways Series,* are markedly different from those of previous series titles, providing a more detailed conventional map of the subject area.

REVIEWS

Booklist, July 1, 1954 (p. 416); *Bookmark,* June 1954 (p. 218); *Christian Science Monitor, June 17, 1954 (p. 7); Kirkus,* March 15, 1954 (p. 225); *New York Herald Tribune Book Review,* July 11, 1954 (p. 4); *New York Times Book Review,* July 4, 1954, (p. 9); *Springfield Republican,* July 4, 1954 (p. 5–C); *Wisconsin Library Bulletin,* July 1954 (p. 179).

SELECTED WRITINGS BY WILLIAM CHAPMAN WHITE

These Russians (New York: Scribner's, 1931); *Made in Russia* (New York: Knopf, 1932); *B.E.F.: The Whole Story of the Bonus Army* (by W. W. Waters as told to William C. White) (New York: John Day, 1933); *Lenin* (New York: H. Smith and R. Haas, 1936); *Mouseknees* (New York: Random House, 1939); *Made in the USSR* (New York: Knopf, 1944); *The Pale Blonde of Sands Street* (New York: Viking, 1946); **Adirondack Country** (New York: Duell, Sloan & Pearce, 1954); (with Ruth White) *Tin Can on a Shingle* (New York: Dutton, 1957).

SOURCES

Book Review Digest 1954. New York: The H.W. Wilson Company, 1955, p. 948.

Publishers' Weekly, January 30, 1954, p. 425; May 1, 1954, p. 1918; and May 22, 1954, p. 2204.

The New York Times Book Review, July 4, 1954, p. 9.

The New York Times obituary, November 29, 1955, p. 29.

Who Was Who in America, Volume III, 1951-1960. Chicago: Marquis Who's Who, 1960, p. 911.

Tucker, Michele D. (Curator, Adirondack Collection, Saranac Lake Free Library). Letter to CF, with enclosed biographical information on William Chapman White, July 19, 2002.

White, William M. (Spruce, Michigan), son of William Chapman White. Telephone interview with CF, March 6, 2003.

Syracuse University Press. E-mail messages to CF, September 11, 2007.

BIG COUNTRY: TEXAS

Donald Day
May 11, 1899 – July 22, 1991

AF2   First edition, first printing (1947) [17]

[*Folkways* device] | [within a medium blue (close to Pantone 549) rectangle with rounded corners, in cream] EDITED BY ERSKINE CALDWELL | [black] BIG | COUNTRY: | TEXAS | BY DONALD DAY | [cream] DUELL, SLOAN & PEARCE · NEW YORK

COLLATION: 8½" x 6". 168 leaves. [i–viii] ix–x [1–2] 3–6 [7–8] 9–69 [70–72] 73–144 [145–146] 147–162 [163–164] 165–222 [223–224] 225–280 [281–282] 283–326. Numbers printed in roman in headline at the outer margin of the type page, except for pp. ix, 3, 9, 17, 22, 41, 53, 73, 93, 109, 127, 147, 151, 157, 165, 182, 189, 198, 209, 225, 234, 246, 258, 276, 283, 293, 298, 307, 314, and 316, on which the numbers are printed in the center at the foot of the page.

CONTENTS: p. [i], half-title: "*Big Country: Texas*"; p. [ii], "AMERICAN FOLKWAYS | EDITED BY ERSKINE CALDWELL | [list of seventeen titles and their authors, beginning with *Golden Gate Country* and ending with *Far North Country*] | In Preparation | [list of 11 titles[1]]"; p. [iii], title; p. [iv], copyright page: "COPYRIGHT, 1947, BY | DONALD DAY | *All rights reserved, including the right | to reproduce this book or portions | thereof in any form.* | 1 | PRINTED IN THE UNITED STATES OF AMERICA | AMERICAN BOOK-STRATFORD PRESS, INC., NEW YORK"; pp. [v], dedication: "*To My Mother and Father*"; p. [vi], blank; p. [vii], "Acknowledgments [signed D.D., Amarillo, Texas]"; p. [viii], blank; pp. ix–x, "Contents"[2]; p. [1],

1. The list includes *Pecos Country* by Allan Bosworth, *Buckeye Country* by Louis Bromfield, *Rip Van Winkle Country* by Howard Fast, *Piney Woods Country* by John Faulkner, *Great Lakes Country* by Iola Fuller, *Pacific Northwest Country* by Richard Neuberger, *Hill Country* by Cameron Shipp, *Tidewater Country* by Elswyth Thane, *Gold Rush Country* by Charis Weston, *Pennsylvania Dutch Country* by Harry Emerson Wildes, and *Mile High Country* by Helen Worden, none of which were published in the *Folkways* series.
2. Page x lists "Epilogue" as at p. 315; it begins on p. 314. "Index" is listed as at p. 317; it begins on p. 316.

second half-title: "*Big Country: Texas*"; p. [2], blank; pp. 3–6, "Prologue"; p. [7], "*Part One: | So It Was in the Beginning*"; p. [8], blank; pp. 9–69, text; p. [70], blank; p. [71], "*Part Two: | Built of Hide and Horn*"; p. [72], blank; pp. 73–144, text; p. [145], "*Part Three: | In the Land of Cotton*"; p. [146], blank; pp. 147–162, text; p. [163], "*Part Four: | Waterholes*"; p. [164], blank; pp. 165–222, text; p. [223], "*Part Five: | Black Gold*"; p. [224], blank; pp. 225–280, text; p. [281], "*Part Six: | Men and Intangibles*"; p. [282], blank; pp. 283–313, text; pp. 314–315, "*Epilogue*"; pp. 316–326, "*Index*".

BINDING: Medium blue cloth (close to Pantone 660). Spine stamped in black, except where noted: "[thick rule] | [four thin rules] | [within a black panel, in gold] BIG | COUNTRY | TEXAS | · | DONALD | DAY | [four thin rules] | [thick rule] | [four thin rules] | [at bottom] [four thin rules | [within a black panel, in gold] DUELL SLOAN | AND PEARCE | [four thin rules] | [thick rule]". Cream endpapers carry a map of the United States in medium blue (close to Pantone 660) and cream, with the Big Country area highlighted in cream and "Big Country" on a medium-blue ribbon in the lower right corner

DUST JACKET (white paper): Front: Medium blue background (close to Pantone 285). "[white] Big Country | Texas | [black] [thin rule] | AMERICAN FOLKWAYS | [thin rule] | [black-and-white photograph of a herd of cattle being driven by a cowboy on horseback up a steep incline in rough country, within an irregular horizontal rectangular yellow and black frame] | [yellow, close to Pantone 108] DONALD DAY". Spine: Yellow background. "[medium blue] Big | Country | Texas | [black] | DONALD DAY | [*Folkways* device in black and yellow] | [medium blue] DUELL, SLOAN | AND PEARCE". Back: White background; printing in black. "SOUTHERN CALIFORNIA COUNTRY | *An Island on the Land* | by Carey McWilliams | [quotes from five reviews] | $3.75 | *An American Folkways book* | [publisher's imprint]". Front flap: White background, printing in black. "[upper right] $3.50 | BIG COUNTRY | TEXAS | by | Donald Day | [blurb] | [publisher's imprint]". Back flap: White background; printing in black. "[upper left] $3.50 | CORN COUNTRY | by | Homer Croy | [blurb] | [lower left, printed diagonally, below a dotted line] BIG COUNTRY | Duell | $3.50".

Published at $3.50 on June 11, 1947; number of copies printed unknown. Copyrighted July 8, 1947; deposited June 21, 1947.

The book is listed in "The Weekly Record," July, 5, 1947, p. 95.

Note: No evidence found that Duell, Sloan & Pearce reprinted *Big Country: Texas*.

CITED: *Guns* 292; *Guns* (Revised Edition) 572; *Herd*, 663

COPIES: CF

Note: Beginning with *Corn Country* and this volume, there may have been a price change for *Folkways* titles from $3.00 to $3.50. *Corn Country,* published in May 1947, was advertised at $3.00 in April, but was published at $3.50; the back flap of the book's jacket notes a price of $3.50. The back flap also uses *Big Country,* the title used in earlier advertising, rather than *Big Country: Texas,* as the book's title.

REPRINTS AND REPRODUCTIONS

None.

BIOGRAPHY

Donald Day was born Horace Henry Day, in Millseat, Hays County, Texas, on May 11, 1899, the son of Edward Manning and Lillie (Saunders) Day. His parents were school teachers. In an autobiographical sketch published in the Dallas *Daily Times Herald* in 1947, Day refers to Millseat as "now a defunct place . . . about 30 miles up in the hill country at Wimberley and San Marcos, Tex." (He attended high school in San Marcos.) The sketch does not explain Day's change of given names.[3]

For a short time during World War I, Day served in the U.S. Army. In 1918, he earned a bachelor of arts degree from Southwest Texas Teachers College at San Marcos (now Texas State University). Later, after enrolling at the University of Texas at Austin to study law, he changed his major field of study, earning a master's degree in political science in 1924. In 1940, he earned a doctorate in English from the University of Chicago.

On September 18, 1923, Day married Nina Mae Starnes. The couple had a daughter, Dorothy.

Day taught economics at the University of South Dakota from 1925 to 1927. He worked for a number of years in the insurance industry, principally in personnel and general management. Drawn to the literary life, Day worked as editor of the *Southwest Review* at Southern Methodist University in Dallas from 1943 to 1945. He worked as a staff writer for *Reader's Digest* from 1947 to 1952, and in the mid-1940s was regional editor for *West* magazine. From the late 1940s until the early 1960s, he was West Coast editor for *Reader's Digest.*[4]

Day's best-known books were biographies, including those of Will Rogers, Theodore Roosevelt, Franklin Roosevelt, Woodrow Wilson, and the humorist Josh Billings. Rogers was the subject of three of Day's books. Day

3. [Dallas] *Daily Times Herald,* November 9, 1947, n.p.
4. *The New York Times* (obituary), August 3, 1991, p. 26.

also collaborated with his son-in-law, Harry H. Ullom, on *The Autobiography of Sam Houston* (Norman: University of Oklahoma Press, 1954), which was favorably reviewed.

According to several sources, Day had six marriages. He lived for many years in New York City and Chautauqua, New York, but, in failing health, moved to a nursing home in Connecticut.

Donald Day died on July 22, 1991, in Westport, Connecticut, at age 92.

NOTES ON *BIG COUNTRY: TEXAS*

No background information on the publication of the book or on the selection of Donald Day as its author has been found.

On the whole, the book received favorable reviews.

REVIEWS

Booklist , September 1, 1947 (p. 13); *Chicago Sun Book Week*, July 27, 1947 (p. 2); *Christian Science Monitor*, July 31, 1947 (p. 14); *Commonweal*, July 11, 1947 (p. 315); *Kirkus*, May 15, 1947 (p. 267); *Library Journal*, June 1, 1947 (p. 885); *New York Herald Tribune Weekly Book Review*, November 23, 1947 (p. 36); *New York Times*, July 27, 1947 (p. 10); *San Francisco Chronicle*, July 8, 1947 (p. 14); *Saturday Review of Literature*, January 3, 1948 (p. 27); *Wisconsin Library Bulletin*, October 1947 (p. 139).

SELECTED WRITINGS BY DONALD DAY

The Life and Works of George Washington Harris (Chicago: [n.p.], 1942); (ed., with Mody C. Boatright) *Backwoods to Border* (Austin, Tex.: Texas Folk-Lore Society, 1943); *The Humorous Works of George W. Harris* ([n.p.], 1943); (ed., with Mody C. Boatright) *From Hell to Breakfast* (Austin, Tex.: Texas Folk-Lore Society, 1944); *Big Country: Texas.* (New York: Duell, Sloan & Pearce, 1947); (with Beth Day) *Will Rogers: The Boy Roper* (Boston: Houghton, 1950); (selections by Donald Day) *Franklin D. Roosevelt's Own Story: Told in His Own Words From His Private and Public Papers* (Boston: Little, Brown, 1951); (selected and edited) *Will Rogers on How We Elect Our Presidents* (Boston: Little, Brown, 1952); (selected and edited) *Woodrow Wilson's Own Story* (Boston: Little, Brown, 1952); *Uncle Sam's Uncle Josh* (Boston: Little, Brown, 1953); (ed., with Harry Herbert Ullom) *The Autobiography of Sam Houston* (Norman: University of Oklahoma Press 1954); *The Evolution of Love* (New York: Dial Press, 1954); *Will Rogers: A Biography* (New York: McKay, 1962).

SOURCES

Book Review Digest 1947. New York: The H.W. Wilson Company, 1948, p. 227.

Publishers' Weekly, March 8, 1947, p. 1420; and July 5, 1947, p. 95.

The New York Times Book Review, July 27, 1947, p. 10.

The New York Times obituary, August 3, 1991, p. 26.

[Dallas, Texas] *Daily Times Herald*, November 9, 1947. Brief autobiographical sketch of Donald Day, n.p..

Barnes, Lorraine. "Ike Stand Draws Fire by Author." Undated article, probably mid-1950's, furnished by the University of Texas at Austin.

Westport (Connecticut) *News* obituary, July 26, 1991, n.p.

"Day, Donald." The Handbook of Texas Online. A Project of the General Libraries at the University of Texas at Austin, 2002. Accessed May 21, 2002.

Celia, Deborah A., Reference Librarian, Westport Public Library, Westport, Connecticut. E-mail message to CF, April 3, 2003. (*Westport News* obituary.)

BLUE RIDGE COUNTRY

Jean Thomas
November 14, 1881 – December 7, 1982

AF3   First edition, first printing (1942) [5]

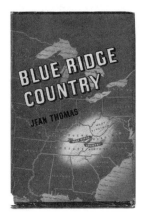

[*Folkways* device] | [within a medium blue (close to Pantone 645) rectangle with rounded corners, in cream] EDITED BY ERSKINE CALDWELL | [black] BLUE RIDGE | COUNTRY | *by* | JEAN THOMAS | [cream] DUELL, SLOAN & PEARCE · NEW YORK

COLLATION: 8½" x 6". 176 leaves. [i–viii] ix–x [1–2] 3–329 [330] 331–338 [339–342]. Numbers printed in roman in headline at the outer margin of the type page, except for pp. ix, 3, 46, 112, 122, 155, 168, 180, 210, 248, and 331, on which the numbers are printed in the center at the foot of the page.

CONTENTS: p. [i], half-title: "BLUE RIDGE COUNTRY"; p. [ii], "AMERI-CAN FOLKWAYS I Edited by ERSKINE CALDWELL I [thin rule] I [list of five titles and their authors, beginning with *Desert Country* and ending with *Blue Ridge Country*] I *In Preparation* I [list of three titles and their authors[1]] I Books by JEAN THOMAS I [thin rule] [list of seven titles]"; p. [iii], title; p. [iv], copyright page: "COPYRIGHT, 1942, BY I JEAN THOMAS I *All rights reserved, including* I *the right to reproduce this book* I *or portions thereof in any form.* I *first edition* I PRINTED IN THE UNITED STATES OF AMERICA"; p. [v], dedication: "*To My Brother* I DOCTOR GEORGE G. BELL I *A once itinerant 'Tooth Dentist'* I *who became the first Republican county judge* I *in more than a quarter of a century* I *at the mouth of Big Sandy* I *and whose unique sentences have become legendary* I *throughout the Blue Ridge*"; pp. [vi–vii], "Appalachian Ritual [nine-stanza poem by Rachel Mack Wilson]"; p. [viii], blank; pp. ix–x, "*Contents*"; p. [1], half-title: "BLUE RIDGE COUN-TRY"; p. [2], blank; pp. 3–329, text; p. [330], blank; pp. 331–338, "Index"; pp. [339–342], blank.

BINDING: Bright blue cloth (close to Pantone 286). Front: *Folkways* device stamped in black at lower right corner. Spine stamped in black, except where noted: "[thick rule] I [four thin rules] I [within a black panel, in gold] BLUE I RIDGE I COUNTRY I · I JEAN I THOMAS I [four thin rules] I [thick rule] I [four thin rules] I [at bottom] [four thin rules I [within a black panel, in gold] DUELL, SLOAN I AND PEARCE I [four thin rules] I [thick rule]". Cream endpapers carry map of the United States in medium blue and cream; "Blue Ridge Country" region is shaded in cream and further identified on a ribbon-like banner, with a similar ribbon in lower right corner.

DUST JACKET (white paper): Front carries a map of the eastern portion of the United States, which is also found on the endpapers, in medium blue, with the 'Blue Ridge Country' region highlighted in cream. "[thick brown rule (close to Pantone 477)] I [white, outlined in brown] BLUE RIDGE I COUNTRY I [brown] JEAN THOMAS I [printed on a medium blue ribbon, in white] BLUE RIDGE COUNTRY [thick brown rule]". Spine: "[thick brown rule] [four thin brown rules on a white band] I [brown, on medium blue] BLUE I RIDGE I COUNTRY I [white] · I JEAN I THOMAS I [brown] [four thin rules, thick rule, four thin rules, with the series device overlaid in the center] I [drawing of a craggy mountain cliff; tall pine tree in back-ground] I [four thin brown rules] I [within a brown panel, in medium blue] DUELL, SLOAN I AND PEARCE I [four thin black rules] I [thick brown rule]". Back: "[white background] [within an arced ribbon, in medium blue] AMERICAN FOLKWAYS I [brown] *Edited by* I Erskine Caldwell I [blurb] I

1. *Florida Country*, the title given in the first four books in the series for a book by Stetson Kennedy, has been retitled *Palmetto Country*.

[medium blue] READY | [brown] [list of five titles and their authors; two are further described on the back flap] | [medium blue] IN PREPARATION | [brown] [list of three titles and their authors, with a brief description of each: *Palmetto Country, Mormon Country,* and *High Border Country*] | [medium blue] *Each Volume, $3.00* | [brown] [publisher's imprint]". Front flap: "[brown] [upper right] $3.00 | [medium blue] BLUE RIDGE COUNTRY | [brown] *by* JEAN THOMAS | [blurb][2] | [publisher's imprint]". Back flap: "[brown] [upper left] $3.00 | ["It is well to have a book like *OZARK COUNTRY to fix the image of this people as it now is, before it is irrevocably changed.* . . . "] | [medium blue] OZARK COUNTRY | [brown] *by* OTTO ERNEST RAYBURN | [blurb] | [publisher's imprint]".

Published at $3.00 on March 19, 1942; number of copies printed unknown. Copyrighted March 31, 1942 ; deposited April 1, 1942.

The book is listed in "The Weekly Record," March 21, 1942, p. 1198.

Note: Duell, Sloan & Pearce published at least four printings of *Blue Ridge Country.*

COPIES: CF

REPRINTS AND REPRODUCTIONS

Reproduced on microfilm. New Haven, Conn.: Yale University Library, 1993. 1 reel. 35 mm.

Reproduced on microfilm. Atlanta, Ga.: SOLINET, 1995. 1 reel. 35 mm.

BIOGRAPHY

Jean Thomas was born on November 14, 1881, in Ashland, Kentucky, the daughter of W. William George and Kate (Smith) Bell. Her given name was Jeanette Mary Francis de Assisi Aloysius Marcissum Garfield (Bell). One of five children, she attended Holy Family School in Ashland, graduating on June 3, 1899.

As a young girl, she became interested in the mountain music she heard in the Ashland area. Later, while working as a court stenographer and traveling on the eastern Kentucky judicial circuit, she began to collect traditional mountain ballads and the stories told by local people, an interest which would dominate her life. It was during this time that she acquired the name "The Traipsin' Woman."

After living in New York City for 13 years, she married Albert Hart Thomas. The young couple moved to Logan, West Virginia, where Albert

2. In reference to Jean Thomas, the blurb refers to her as "he" rather than "she" as founder and director of the American Folk Song Festival.

worked in his family's coal business. The marriage ended in divorce after only a year.

Thomas then traveled from coast to coast, working in a number of jobs. In 1926, on a trip to Kentucky, she heard James William Day, a blind fiddler, playing and singing in front of the Rowan County courthouse. Impressed by his performance, she signed him to a management contract, gave him the stage name Jilson Settle and arranged a concert tour that began in Kentucky and moved on to Lowe's Theater in New York and then to the Royal Albert Hall in London. These events became the subject of Thomas's book *The Singin' Fiddler of Lost Hope Hollow.*

While working as a consultant for NBC in 1930, Thomas staged a folk festival in the backyard of her Ashland home. The next year, she introduced the idea of an annual folk music event. She founded and incorporated the American Folk Song Society and, in 1932, staged the first American Folk Song Festival. By 1938, the Ashland festival had grown to forty-two acts and annually attracted audiences of twenty thousand or more.

Thomas's participation in the Folk Song Society and the annual festival continued until 1972, when ill health forced her to retire. She made arrangements for her extensive collection of folklore to be preserved in her home in Ashland, which was opened to the public as the Jean Thomas Museum in 1979. In 2005, Thomas was named by the Kentucky Commission on Women as one of "Kentucky Women Remembered" whose portraits are on permanent display in the rotunda hall of the state capitol in Frankfort.

Before she wrote *Blue Ridge Country,* Thomas had written six books and was the co-author of a seventh. All were set in whole or in part in Kentucky, and all, including her autobiography, *The Sun Shines Bright* (1940), placed strong emphasis on the folk music and musicians of Kentucky and the Blue Ridge, which includes parts of eight southern states.

Jean Thomas died in Ashland, Kentucky, on December 7, 1982, at age 101.

PAPERS: Much of Jean Thomas's folklore collection was donated by her heirs to the Dwight Anderson Memorial Music Library at the University of Louisville.[3]

NOTES ON *BLUE RIDGE COUNTRY*

Except for a listing in Duell, Sloan & Pearce's Spring List in *Publishers' Weekly,* there was no promotion of the book. The listing in "The Weekly Record" names Jean Thomas as "Thomas, Mrs. Jeannette Bell [The Traipsin' Woman, pseud.]"

3. "Memories of the Traipsin' Woman: Memorabilia of Jean Thomas." Exhibit text by Shirley J. Boyd. Mansbach Memorial Gallery, Ashland Community College, Ashland, Kentucky. October 4–31, 1999.

In a March 19, 1940, letter to Erskine Caldwell, Thomas referred to a letter Caldwell had written to her in care of Henry Holt & Co., the publishers of her book *Big Sandy* that year, noting, "I am pleased to learn of your opinion of my work and I should be proud to undertake a volume covering the mountain region you suggest."

Caldwell replied to her in his letter of March 22, using her Ashland, Kentucky, address. He outlined his plans for the American Folkways series and for a book he called at the time "the Southern Mountain Region." Caldwell wrote, ". . . you, I am convinced, are the one person to write the history of mountain life from Virginia and Kentucky southward."

Thomas's reply, dated three days later, states, "I think your plan for the Series on American Folkways is excellent. I shall be proud to do the volume of the Series on the southern mountain region and consider a year's time quite ample for completion of such a book inasmuch as I have been in the field for some time."

In his April 15 letter to Thomas, Caldwell wrote, ". . . the authors of the books in the Series have complete freedom of selection when it comes to writing the book. In other words, there are no limitations whatsoever . . . selection of material, and its treatment, is entirely in your hands. As I see the books, they will be lively in style, authentic in material, and popular in appeal."

REVIEWS

Booklist, May 1, 1942 (p. 329); *New York Herald Tribune Book Review*, April 5, 1942 (p. 5); *Library Journal*, February 1, 1942 (p. 130); *New Republic*, May 4, 1942 (p. 614); *New York Times*, March 29, 1942 (p. 5); *New Yorker*, March 28, 1942 (p. 79); *Scientific Book Club Review*, April 1942 (p. 4); *Wisconsin Library Bulletin*, May 1942 (p. 86).

SELECTED WRITINGS BY JEAN THOMAS

Devil's Ditties :Being Stories of the Kentucky Mountain People (Chicago: W. W. Hatfield, 1931); *The Traipsin' Woman* (New York: Dutton, 1933); *The Singin' Fiddler of Lost Hope Hollow* (New York: Dutton, 1938); [in collaboration with Joseph A. Leeder, Professor of Music, Ohio State University] *The Singin' Gatherin':Tunes from the Southern Appalachians* (New York: Silver Burdett Company, 1939); *Big Sandy* (New York: Holt, 1940); *The Sun Shines Bright* (New York: Prentice-Hall, 1940); **Blue Ridge Country** (New York: Duell, Sloan & Pearce, 1942); (with music arranged. by Walter Kob) *Ballad Makin' in the Mountains of Kentucky* (New York: Oak Publications, 1964).

SOURCES

Book Review Digest 1942. New York: The H.W. Wilson Company, 1943, p. 770.

Publishers' Weekly, January 31, 1942, p. 326; and March 21, 1942, p. 1198.

The New York Times Book Review, March 29, 1942, p. 5.

Daily Independent (Ashland, Kentucky) obituary, December 8, 1982.

"Memories of the Traipsin' Woman: Memorabilia of Jean Thomas." Exhibit text by Shirley J. Boyd. Mansbach Memorial Gallery, Ashland Community College, Ashland, Kentucky. October 4 – 31, 1999.

Boyd, Shirley. Ashland Community College Library. E-mail messages and letters to CF, May 2002.

From the Jean Thomas Collection, Dwight Anderson Music Library, University of Louisville: Thomas, Jean. Letters to Erskine Caldwell, March 19, 1940; March 25, 1940. Caldwell, Erskine. Letters to Jean Thomas, March 22, 1940; April 15, 1940.

"Alison Lyne Portraits of 2005 Kentucky Women Remembered Honorees for Kentucky Commission on Women." www.lyneart.com/kywomen5.htm. Accessed February 2, 2006.

CORN COUNTRY

Homer Croy
March 11, 1883 – May 24, 1965

AF4   First edition, first printing (1947) [16]

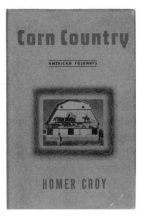

[*Folkways* device] | [within a medium green (close to Pantone 346) rectangle with rounded corners, in cream] EDITED BY ERSKINE CALDWELL | [black] CORN | COUNTRY | *by* | HOMER CROY | [cream] DUELL, SLOAN & PEARCE · NEW YORK

COLLATION: 8½" x 6". 168 leaves. [i–v] vi [vii–viii] [1–2] 3–325 [326–328]. Numbers printed in roman in headline at the outer margin of the type page, except for pp. vi, 3, 8, 15, 21, 26, 32, 39, 46, 55, 66, 75, 90, 98, 111, 122, 129, 144, 153, 158, 164, 181, 201, 212, 222, 232, 238, 246, 255, 260, 268, 273, 278, 284, 288, 304, 310, 314, 316, 318, and 319, on which the numbers are printed in the center at the foot of the page.

CONTENTS: p. [i], half-title: "CORN COUNTRY"; p. [ii], "AMERICAN FOLKWAYS | *Edited by* ERSKINE CALDWELL | [list of sixteen titles and their authors, beginning with *Golden Gate Country* and ending with *Far North Country*] | *In Preparation* | [list of nine titles and their authors[1]]"; p. [iii], title; p. [iv], copyright page: "COPYRIGHT, 1947, BY | HOMER CROY | All rights reserved, including | the right to reproduce this book | or portions thereof in any form | *First Edition* | ['union bug'] | PRINTED IN THE UNITED STATES OF AMERICA"; pp. [v]-vi, "Contents"; p. [vii], "*Foreword* | [thick/thin rule] | *THE PLAN OF THE BOOK*"; p. [viii], blank; p. [1], second half-title: "CORN COUNTRY"; p. [2], blank; pp. 3–317, text; p. 318, "*GRATEFUL THANKS*"; pp. 319–325, "INDEX"; pp. [326–328], blank.

BINDING: Medium tan cloth (close to Pantone 730). Front: *Folkways* device

---

1. The list includes *Buckeye Country* by Louis Bromfield, *Rip Van Winkle Country* by Howard Fast, *Piney Woods Country* by John Faulkner, *Great Lakes Country* by Iola Fuller, *Pacific Northwest Country* by Richard Neuberger, *Tidewater Country* by Elswyth Thane, *Gold Rush Country* by Charis Weston, and *Mile High Country* by Helen Worden, none of which were published in the series, and *Big Country* by Donald Day, published in 1947 as *Big Country: Texas*, as part of the series.

stamped in dark green (close to Pantone 627) at lower right corner. Spine stamped in dark green, except where noted: "[thick rule] | [four thin rules] | [within a black panel, in gold] CORN | COUNTRY | · | HOMER | CROY | [four thin rules] | [thick rule] | [four thin rules] | [at bottom] [four thin rules | [within a black panel, in gold] DUELL, SLOAN | AND PEARCE | [four thin rules] | [thick rule]". Light cream endpapers carry map of the United States in medium green (close to Pantone 347) and light cream, with the Corn Country area shaded in light cream and "Corn Country" on a medium-green ribbon in the lower right corner.

DUST JACKET (white paper): Front: Bright yellow background (close to Pantone 129). "[dark green, close to Pantone 341] CORN COUNTRY | [thin black rule] | AMERICAN FOLKWAYS | [thin black rule] | [black-and-white photograph of a woman viewing a mural painted on a barn; the mural depicts a team of oxen pulling a covered wagon, a man on horseback riding along behind the wagon. At the bottom of the mural is printed 'The Arrival at the Croy Farm in 1867' | [dark green] HOMER CROY". Spine: Dark green background. "[bright yellow] CORN | COUNTRY | [black] HOMER | CROY | [*Folkways* device] | [bright yellow] DUELL, SLOAN | AND PEARCE". Back: "[white background; printing in black] SOUTHERN CALIFORNIA COUN-TRY | *An Island on the Land* | by Carey McWilliams | [quotes from five reviews] | $3.75 | *An American Folkways book* | [publisher's imprint]". Front flap: "[white background; printing in black] [upper right] $3.50 | CORN COUNTRY | by | Homer Croy | [blurb] | [publisher's imprint]". Back flap: "[white background; printing in black] [upper left] $3.00 | BIG COUNTRY | by | Donald Day | [blurb] | [lower left, printed diagonally, below a dotted line] CORN COUNTRY | $3.00[2] | Duell, Sloan & Pearce".

Published at $3.50 on May 9, 1947;[3] number of copies printed unknown. Copyrighted May 14, 1947; deposited May 11, 1947.

The book is listed in "The Weekly Record," June 14, 1947, p. 2968.

Note: No evidence found that Duell, Sloan & Pearce reprinted *Corn Country*.

CITED: *Guns* 268; *Guns* (Revised Edition) 521

COPIES: CF

2. The book was published at $3.50. This may have been the pre-publication price.
3. The Duell, Sloan & Pearce advertisement for the book in the March 8, 1947, issue of *Publishers' Weekly* notes a publication date of April 16, 1947. The copyright certificate, however, notes that the book was published on May 9, 1947. Most of the book's reviews did not appear until June or July 1947.

REPRINTS AND REPRODUCTIONS

None.

BIOGRAPHY

Homer Croy was born on March 11, 1883, a few miles from Maryville, Missouri, the son of Amos J., a farmer, and Susan (Sewell) Croy.

Croy attended rural schools and was one of the first in his area to attend high school. He began to write while in high school and sold his first article to *Puck* magazine when he was fourteen. In 1901, he entered the University of Missouri, working his way through school by writing and editing. He was editor of the university newspaper; editor of *The Asterisk,* a booklet published by the university literary society; and editor in chief of the yearbook. Ironically, because he failed a senior English course, he did not graduate. Still, Croy was a pioneer in the field of journalism at the university and would sometimes claim to be "the first student in the first school of journalism in the world." (The University of Missouri School of Journalism, however, was not established until April 1908 and classes there did not begin until September, after Croy had departed.)[4] In 1956, the university awarded him an honorary doctorate in literature.

After he left the university, Croy worked as a reporter for the *St. Joseph Gazette* and the *St. Louis Post Dispatch* before moving to New York, where he worked as an assistant to Theodore Dreiser[5] at Butterick Publications. Croy left Butterick in 1910, remaining in New York and working essentially as a freelance writer. Sometime later, when he returned to Missouri, he founded a magazine, *The Magazine Maker,* which he sold after a year. In 1912, he was back in New York, working as managing editor of *Leslie's Weekly* and *Judge,* two very popular humor magazines.

On February 7, 1915, Croy married Mae Belle Savel. The couple had three children, two boys who died in childhood, and a daughter, Carol.

In August 1918, Croy went to Paris to work for the YMCA as director of the "Overseas Weekly," which is believed to have been a series of movies as entertainment for the American Expeditionary Forces in France. He held the position for nine months, returning to the United States in the late spring of 1919.[6]

Croy's first novel, *When to Lock the Stable* (Bobbs-Merrill), was published in 1914. His 1923 novel, *West of the Water Tower* (Harper), brought him national recognition. He became a regular contributor to the *Saturday*

4. O'Dell, Charles A. *Homer Croy, Maryville Writer: The First Forty Years, 1883 to 1923.* The Northwest Missouri State University Studies, August, 1972, pp. 16–17.
5. Theodore Dreiser (1871–1945) American novelist and prominent member of the Chicago Group of American writers.
6. O'Dell, op. cit.,p. 38.

Evening Post while producing virtually a book every year for the next twenty years. Between 1914 and 1962, Croy wrote thirty works of fiction, non-fiction, and biography; an autobiography; a collection of reminiscences; eight screenplays; numerous scripts for the radio program "Show Boat;" and numerous magazine articles and short stories.

Homer Croy died in New York City on May 24, 1965, at age 82.

PAPERS: Homer Croy's Papers, 1905–1965 (C2534) are held by the University of Missouri, Columbia.

NOTES ON *CORN COUNTRY*

Duell, Sloan and Pearce introduced the book in a double-page advertisement in the March 8, 1947, issue of *Publishers' Weekly,* quoting a price of $3.00 and an April 16 publication date. The advertisement carried a full-page promotion of the book while the facing page named the Folkways titles already published and their authors and prices. Actual publication was delayed, probably until early May, and the price was raised to $3.50.

On page 83 of the text, paragraph four, line three, "railroad" is misspelled as "railorad."

The book's free-style, semi–alphabetical index is humorously unconventional and worth reviewing. For example, the entry for "Croy Farm" (p. 319) reads, "Croy Farm, 18, and goodness knows how many other times, 18; coyotes on, 272." The entry for "Canton" on the same page reads, "Canton, not the one in China but the one in S. Dakota, 21."

REVIEWS

Booklist, July 15, 1947 (p. 357); *Chicago Sun Book Week,* June 22, 1947 (p. 6); *Christian Science Monitor,* June 7, 1947 (p. 16); *Churchman,* August, 1947 (p. 16); *Kirkus,* March 15, 1947 (p. 180); *Library Journal,* May 1, 1947 (p. 730); *New York Herald Tribune Weekly Book Review,* May 18, 1947 (p. 5); *New York Times Book Review,* June 1, 1947 (p. 16); *San Francisco Chronicle,* June 27, 1947 (p. 14); *Wisconsin Library Bulletin,* June 1947 (p. 95).

SELECTED WRITINGS BY HOMER CROY

When to Lock the Stable (Indianapolis: Bobbs-Merrill, 1914); *How Motion Pictures are Made* (New York: Harper, 1918); *West of the Water Tower* (New

York: Harper, 1923); *They Had to See Paris* (New York: Grosset, 1926); *Fancy Lady* (New York: Harper, 1927); *Caught* (New York: Harper, 1928); *Coney Island* (New York: Harper, 1929); *River Girl* (New York: Harper, 1931); *Headed for Hollywood* (New York: Harper, 1932); *Sixteen Hands* (New York: Harper, 1938); *Mr. Meek Marches On* (New York: Harper, 1941); *Family Honeymoon* (New York: Harper, 1942); (autobiography) *Country Cured* (New York: Harper, 1943); *Wonderful Neighbor* (New York: Harper, 1945); **Corn Country** (New York: Duell, Sloan & Pearce, 1947); *What Grandpa Laughed At* (New York: Duell, Sloan & Pearce, 1948); *Jessie James Was My Neighbor* (New York: Duell, Sloan & Pearce, 1949); *He Hanged Them High: An Authentic Account of the Fanatical Judge Who Hanged Eighty-eight Men* (New York: Duell, Sloan & Pearce, 1952); *Our Will Rogers* (New York: Duell, Sloan & Pearce, 1953); *Wheels West* (New York: Hastings House, 1955); *Last of the Great Outlaws* (New York: Duell, Sloan & Pearce, 1956); *The Lady From Colorado* (New York: Duell Sloan & Pearce, 1957); *Trigger Marshal: The Story of Chris Madsen* (New York: Duell, Sloan & Pearce, 1958); *Star maker: The Story of D. W. Griffith* (New York: Duell, Sloan & Pearce, 1959); *The Trial of Mrs. Abraham Lincoln* (New York: Duell, Sloan & Pearce, 1962).

SOURCES

Book Review Digest 1947. New York: The H.W. Wilson Company, 1948, p. 207.

Publishers' Weekly, March 8, 1947, pp. 1420-1421; and June 14, 1947, p. 2968.

The New York Times Book Review, June 1, 1947, p. 16.

The New York Times obituary, May 25, 1965, p. 41.

O'Dell, Charles A. *Homer Croy, Maryville Writer: The First Forty Years: 1883-1923.* Maryville, Mo.: The Northwest Missouri State University Studies, 1972.

Murphy, Bruce, ed. *Benét's Reader's Encyclopedia,* Fourth Edition. New York: HarperCollins, 1996. (Entry on Theodore Dreiser)

Contemporary Authors Online. The Gale Group, 1999. Reproduced in *Biography Resource Center.* Farmington Hills, Mich.: The Gale Group, 2001. Accessed February 11, 2002.

Dictionary of American Biography, Supplement 7: 1961-1965. American Council of Learned Societies, 1981. Reproduced in *Biography Resource Center.* Farmington Hills, Mich.: The Gale Group, 2001. Accessed June 26, 2002.

DEEP DELTA COUNTRY

Harnett T. Kane
November 8, 1910 – September 4, 1984

AF5 First edition, first printing (1944) [10]

[*Folkways* device] | [within a medium green (close to Pantone 356) rectangle with rounded corners, in cream] EDITED BY ERSKINE CALDWELL | [black] DEEP DELTA | COUNTRY | *by* | HARNETT T. KANE[1] | [cream] DUELL, SLOAN & PEARCE · NEW YORK

COLLATION: 8½" x 6". 152 leaves. [i–iv] v–xx [1–2] 3–74 [75–76] 77–143 [144–146] 147–269 [270] 271–283 [284]. Numbers printed in roman in headline at the outer margin of the type page, except for pp. v, vii, 3, 18, 28, 42, 52, 63, 77, 92, 105, 119, 132, 147, 160, 172, 188, 199, 214, 228, 239, 254, 271, and 273, on which the numbers are printed in the center at the foot of the page.

Note: The "Louisiana Edition" is so identified on the title page and includes an unpaginated leaf signed by the author and inserted following p. [ii].

Note: Between pages [2] and 3 and facing page 3, is a full-page black-and-white photograph attributed to Eugene Delcroix, below which is printed, within quotation marks, "The great Delta is a favored spot and a tormented one, of alternate felicity and frowning hazard and mystery . . . ."

CONTENTS: p. [i], half-title: "DEEP DELTA COUNTRY"; p. [ii], "AMERICAN FOLKWAYS | EDITED BY ERSKINE CALDWELL | [thin rule] | [list of ten titles and their authors, beginning with *Desert Country* and ending with *Far North Country*] | In Preparation | [list of nine titles and their authors[2]] | Other Books by HARNETT T. KANE | [list of two titles]"; p. [iii],

1. The Louisiana Edition is identified on the title page, beneath the author's name, as "LOUISIANA EDITION".
2. The list includes *Buckeye Country* by Louis Bromfield, *Piney Woods Country* by John Faulkner, *Cutover Country* by John T. Frederick, and *Tidewater Country* by Elswyth Thane, none of which were titles in the series, and *Mission Country* by Carey McWilliams, published as *Southern California Country*, as part of the series.

title; p. [iv], copyright page: "COPYRIGHT, 1944, BY | HARNETT T. KANE | *All rights reserved, including* | *the right to reproduce this book* | *or portions thereof in any form.* | *first edition* | WAR EDITION. THIS BOOK IS PRO- DUCED | IN ACCORDANCE WITH CONSERVATION | ORDERS OF THE WAR PRODUCTION BOARD | PRINTED IN THE UNITED STATES OF AMERICA"; pp. v-vi, "Contents"; pp vii–xx, "Introduction"; p. [1], "PART I | *THE 'GLORY DAYS'*"; p. [2], blank; pp. 3–74, text; p. [75], "PART II | *MELT- ING POT*"; p. [76], blank; pp. 77–143, text; p. [144], blank; p. [145], "PART III | *SHADOWS AND TURBULENCE*"; p. [146], blank; pp. 147–269, text; p. [270], blank; pp. 271–272, "*Acknowledgments*; pp. 273–280, "*Selected Bibliog- raphy*"; pp. 281–283, "Index"; p. [284], blank.

BINDING: Medium green cloth (close to Pantone 359). Front: *Folkways* de- vice stamped in black at lower right corner. Spine stamped in black, except where noted: "[thick rule] | [four thin rules] | [within a black panel, in gold] DEEP | DELTA | COUNTRY | · | HARNETT T. | KANE | [four thin rules] | [thick rule] | [four thin rules] | [at bottom] [four thin rules | [within a black panel, in gold] DUELL, SLOAN | AND PEARCE | [four thin rules] | [thick rule]". Light cream endpapers carry map of the Delta area of the Mississippi River to the south and east of New Orleans and Lake Pontchartrain in medium green (close to Pantone 362); and "DEEP DELTA | COUNTRY" is printed in medium green on a light green ribbon.

DUST JACKET (white paper): Front carries the map of the Delta region of the Mississippi River found on the endpapers, in dark green (close to Pan- tone 342). "[thick dark orange rule (close to Pantone 179)] [white, outlined in dark orange] DEEP DELTA | COUNTRY | [solid dark orange] HARNETT T. KANE". Spine: "[four thin dark orange rules on a white band] | [dark or- ange on dark green] DEEP | DELTA | COUNTRY | [white] · | KANE | [dark orange] [four thin rules, thick rule, four thin rules, with the series device overlaid in the center] | [drawing of cypress trees with moss hanging from branches; birds in flight; and an alligator at the foot of a tree] | [four thin dark orange rules] | [within a dark orange panel, in white] DUELL, SLOAN | AND PEARCE | [four thin dark orange rules] | [thick dark orange rule]". Back: "[white background] [within an arced ribbon, in dark orange] AMER- ICAN FOLKWAYS | [dark green] [to the left of the *Folkways* device, which is in dark orange and white] *Edited* | — *by* — [to the right of the *Folkways* de- vice, in dark green] ERSKINE | CALDWELL | [quote from Harold Rugg] | PUBLISHED | [list of ten titles and their authors] | [quote from Lewis Gan- nett] | EACH VOLUME $3.00 | IN PREPARATION | [list of the nine titles and their authors found on p. [ii] of the text] | [dark orange] [publisher's

imprint]". Front flap[3]: "[dark green] [upper right] $3.00 | DEEP DELTA
COUNTRY | by Harnett T. Kane | [blurb] | [publisher's imprint]". Back flap:
"[dark green] $3.00 | FAR NORTH COUNTRY | by Thames Williamson |
[blurb] | [publisher's imprint]".

Published at $3.00 on November 3, 1944; number of copies printed un-
known. Copyrighted December 8, 1944; deposited December 2, 1944.

The book is listed in "The Weekly Record," November 11, 1944, p. 1945.

Note: Duell, Sloan & Pearce published at least six printings of *Deep Delta
Country.*

COPIES: CF

AF5a   First edition, first printing, Louisiana Edition (1945)

As noted, *Deep Delta Country* was issued in a Louisiana Edition that is identified on the title page, beneath the author's name, as "LOUISIANA EDI-
TION." "LOUISIANA EDITION" is also printed at the top of the front flap
of the dust jacket of this edition.

REPRINTS AND REPRODUCTIONS

None.

BIOGRAPHY

Harnett Thomas Kane was born in New Orleans, Louisiana, on November 8, 1910, the son of William J. and Anna (Hiri) Kane. In 1931, he earned a
bachelor of arts degree from Tulane University, where he was editor of both
the college newspaper and the college handbook. In 1932 and 1933, he undertook graduate studies in sociology at Tulane. He never married.

Kane began his writing career while he was a sophomore at Tulane,
working as a reporter for the *New Orleans Item-Tribune.*[4] He worked for the
paper from 1928 to 1943, with assignments covering welfare, business, labor,
and politics, most notably the politics of Huey Long (1893–1935) and the
Long administration. Known as "the Kingfish," Long was a populist but dic-
tatorial governor of Louisiana (1928–1931) and later a U.S. senator
(1931–1935). Long was assassinated in 1935.

Kane is best remembered for his first book, *Louisiana Hayride: The
American Rehearsal for Dictatorship* (Morrow,1941), which exposed extensive

3. "LOUISIANA EDITION" is printed at the top of the front flap of the dust jacket of
that edition.
4. Publication of the morning *Tribune* ceased in 1941.

political corruption in Louisiana and was based on his years covering the Long administration. The book was immensely popular in Louisiana, going into a third printing within a week of its publication, with bookstores unable to keep it in stock. Newspapers in all sections of the country provided generous publicity. The Basement Book Shop and Library in New Orleans reported the largest advance sale in its history for an author's first book.

In 1943 and 1944, while he taught journalism at Loyola University, Kane received successive Guggenheim Fellowships supporting his work on issues of government and civics in the American South.

A lifelong resident of New Orleans, Kane wrote twenty-five books, fiction and non-fiction, about the city and the region. He was a frequent contributor of travel articles and book reviews to the *New York Times* and also wrote for *Colliers, Reader's Digest, Saturday Review, American Mercury, National Geographic,* and other national magazines.

Harnett T. Kane died in New Orleans, Louisiana, on September 4, 1984, at age 73.

PAPERS: A portion of Harnett Kane's papers, 1948–1958, is held by Louisiana State University.

NOTES ON *DEEP DELTA COUNTRY*

Duell, Sloan & Pearce included the book in the "Preview of Bestsellers" in the June 10, 1944, issue of *Publishers' Weekly,* noting, "The author of *The Bayous of Louisiana* knows this region." Two earlier books in the series, *Mormon Country* and *Palmetto Country,* both published in 1942, listed "Delta Country" as a title "in preparation," and named E.P. O'Donnell as the author.

REVIEWS

Book Week, November 26, 1944, (p. 5); *Booklist,* December 15, 1944 (p. 122); *Christian Science Monitor,* January 20, 1945 (p. 12); *Kirkus,* September 15, 1944 (p. 418); *Library Journal,* October 15, 1944 (p. 882); *New York Times Book Review,* December 24, 1944 (p. 9); *New Yorker,* November 18, 1944 (p. 93); *Springfield Republican,* January 14, 1945 (p. 4-d); *Weekly Book Review,* November 5, 1944 (p. 4).

SELECTED WRITINGS BY HARNETT T. KANE

Louisiana Hayride: The American Rehearsal for Dictatorship (New York: Morrow, 1941); *Bayous of Louisiana* (New York: Bonanza, 1943); **Deep Delta Country** (New York: Duell, Sloan & Pearce, 1944); *Plantation Parade—the*

Grand Manner in Louisiana (New York: Morrow, 1945); *New Orleans Woman* (New York: Doubleday, 1946); *Natchez on the Mississippi* (New York: Morrow, 1947); *Bride of Fortune* (New York: Doubleday, 1948); *Queen New Orleans: City by the River* (New York: Morrow, 1949); *Pathway to the Stars* (Garden City, N.Y.: Doubleday, 1950); *Gentlemen, Swords and Pistols* (New York: Bonanza, 1951); *The Scandalous Mrs. Blackford* (New York: Messner, 1951); *Dear Dorothy Dix: The Story of a Compassionate Woman* (Garden City, N.Y.: Doubleday, 1952); *The Lady of Arlington: A Novel Based on the Life of Mrs. Robert E. Lee* (Garden City, N.Y.: Doubleday; 1953); *Spies for the Blue and Gray* (New York: Hanover House, 1954); *The Smiling Rebel: A Novel Based on the Life of Belle Boyd* (Garden City, N.Y. Doubleday, 1955); *Miracle in the Mountains* (Garden City, N.Y.: Doubleday, 1956); *The Gallant Mrs. Stonewall: A Novel Based on the Lives of General and Mrs. Stonewall Jackson* (Garden City, N.Y.: Doubleday, 1957); *The Southern Christmas Book: The Full Story from Earliest Times to Present* (New York: Bonanza, 1958); *The Ursulines: Nuns for Adventure: The Story of the New Orleans Community* (New York: Vision Books, 1959); *The Golden Coast* (Garden City, N.Y.: Doubleday, 1959); *Have Pen, Will Autograph: An Author Meets His Public* (Garden City, N.Y.: Doubleday, 1959); *Gone Are the Days: An Illustrated History of the Old South* (New York: Dutton, 1960); *The Romantic South* (New York: Coward-McCann, 1961); *Place du Tivoli: A History of Lee Circle* (Boston: John Hancock Mutual Life Insurance Co., 1961); *The Amazing Mrs. Bonaparte: A Novel Based on the Life of Betsy Patterson* (New York: Curtis, 1963); *A Picture Story of the Confederacy* (New York: Lothrop, Lee & Shepard, 1965); *Young Mark Twain and the Mississippi* (New York: Random House, 1966).

SOURCES

Book Review Digest 1944. New York: The H.W. Wilson Company, 1945, p. 405.

Publishers' Weekly, May 24, 1941, pp. 2072–2073 ("New Writers: Harnett T. Kane"); June 10, 1944, p. 2148; and November 11, 1944, p. 1945.

The New York Times Book Review. December 24, 1944, p. 9.

Benét, William Rose. *The Reader's Encyclopedia.* New York: Thomas Y. Crowell Co., 1948, p. 648 (Entry on Huey Long).

Emery, Edwin and Henry Ladd Smith. *The Press and America.* New York: Prentice-Hall, 1954, p. 669 (Information on *New Orleans Item-Tribune*).

The New York Times obituary, September 14, 1984, p. B-5.

Who Was Who in America. Volume 8, 1982–1985. Chicago: Marquis Who's Who, 1985, p. 216.

Contemporary Authors Online. The Gale Group, 2000. Reproduced in *Biography Resource Center.* Farmington Hills, Mich.: The Gale Group, 2001. Accessed February 11, 2002.

DESERT COUNTRY

Edwin Corle
May 7, 1906 – June 11, 1956

AF6   First edition, first printing (1941) [1]

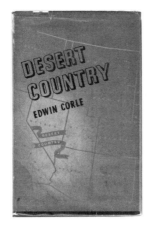

[*Folkways* device] | [within a medium tan (close to Pantone 471) rectangle with rounded corners, in cream] EDITED BY ERSKINE CALDWELL | [black] DESERT | COUNTRY | *by* | EDWIN CORLE | [cream] DUELL, SLOAN & PEARCE · NEW YORK

COLLATION: 8½" x 6". 184 leaves. [i–vi] vii–viii [1–2] 3–65 [66] 67–265 [266] 267–357 [358–360]. Numbers printed in roman in headline at the outer margin of the type page, except for pp. vii, 3, 67, 109, 147, 177, 225, 267, 317, and 349, on which the numbers are printed in the center at the foot of the page.

CONTENTS: p. [i], half-title: "DESERT COUNTRY"; p. [ii], "AMERICAN FOLKWAYS | Edited by ERSKINE CALDWELL | [thin rule] | [list of two titles and their authors, beginning with *Desert Country* and ending with *Piñon Country*] | *In Preparation* | [list of four titles and their authors] | Books by EDWIN CORLE | [thin rule] | [list of six titles]"; p. [iii], title; p. [iv], copyright page: "COPYRIGHT, 1941, BY | EDWIN CORLE | *All rights reserved, including* | *the right to reproduce this book* | *or portions thereof in any form.* | *first edition* | Small portions of this book have appeared | in the following magazines: *The American* | *Mercury, Esquire, Prairie Schooner, Prom-* | *enade,* and *The Yale Review.* | PRINTED IN THE UNITED STATES OF AMERICA | BY QUINN & BODEN COMPANY, INC., RAHWAY, N. J."; p. [v], dedication: "*To* | GWEN BEHR | and | RANCHO YUCCA LOMA"[1]; p. [vi], blank;

1. The actress Gwen Behr was a principal owner of Rancho Yucca Loma, a celebrity resort in the High Mojave Desert near Victorville, California. An adobe house on the ranch was the home of the film star David Manners (1900-1998).

pp. vii–viii, "Contents"; p. [1], half-title: "DESERT COUNTRY"; p. [2], blank; pp. 3–65, text; p. [66], blank; pp. 67–265, text; p. [266], blank; pp. 267–348, text; pp. 349–357, "Index"; pp. [358–360], blank.

BINDING: Dark rust cloth (close to Pantone 484). Front: *Folkways* device stamped in black at lower right corner. Spine, stamped in black except where noted: "[thick rule] I [four thin rules] I [within a black panel, in gold] DESERT I COUNTRY I · I EDWIN I CORLE I [four thin rules] I [thick rule] I [four thin rules] I [at bottom] [four thin rules I [within a black panel, in gold] DUELL, SLOAN I AND PEARCE I [four thin rules] I [thick rule]". Cream endpapers carry map of the United States in rose (close to Pantone 487) and cream; "Desert Country" area is shaded in cream and further identified on two light rust ribbons, with a similar ribbon in lower right corner.

DUST JACKET (gold paper): Front carries the western portion of the United States map found on the endpapers in rose, with the 'Desert Country' region highlighted in cream. "[rose, outlined in black] DESERT I COUNTRY I [solid black] EDWIN CORLE I [printed on a rose ribbon, in cream] DESERT I COUNTRY I [thick black rule]". Spine: "[thick black rule] [four thin black rules on a cream band] I [black] [in outline, on a rose panel] DESERT I COUNTRY I · I [cream] EDWIN I CORLE I [all of the following is printed on a cream panel] [black] [four thin rules, thick rule, four thin rules] I [drawing of a cactus in rose and black; desert in the background] I [four thin black rules] I [within a black panel, in rose] DUELL, SLOAN I AND PEARCE I [four thin black rules] I [thick black rule]". Back: "[gold background] [within an arced ribbon, in medium tan] AMERICAN FOLKWAYS I [black] *Edited by* I Erskine Caldwell I [blurb] I [rose] READY I [black] [list of two titles and their authors: *Desert Country* and *Piñon Country*] I [rose] IN PREPARATION I [black] [list of four titles and their authors, with a brief description of each title: *Ozark Country, High Border Country, Short Grass Country,* and *Blue Ridge Country*] I [rose] *Each Volume, $3.00* I [black] [publisher's imprint]". Front flap: "[upper right] $3.00 I [quote from *Desert Country*] I [rose] Desert Country I [black] *by* EDWIN CORLE I [blurb] I [publisher's imprint]". Back flap: "[upper left] $3.00 I [rose] Pinon Country I [black] *by* HANIEL LONG I [blurb] I [publisher's imprint]".

Published at $3.00 on May 22, 1941; number of copies printed unknown. Copyrighted June 4, 1941; deposited May 22, 1941.

The book is listed in "The Weekly Record," May 24, 1941, p. 2090.

Note: Duell, Sloan & Pearce published at least six printings of *Desert Country.*

CITED: *Herd,* 582; *Guns,* 251; *Guns* 494 (Revised ed.); Paher 382

COPIES: CF

REPRINTS AND REPRODUCTIONS

Reproduced on microfilm. Cambridge, Mass.: Harvard College Library Imaging Services, 2000. 1 reel; 35 mm.

BIOGRAPHY

Edwin Corle was born on May 7, 1906, in Wildwood, New Jersey, the son of Samuel Edwin and Marie Gertrude (Dever) Corle. He attended schools in Wildwood and Philadelphia, completing the first three years of high school in Wildwood. When he was seventeen, the Corle family moved to California and he finished high school in Hollywood. In 1928, he earned a bachelor of arts degree in English from the University of California at Los Angeles.

In 1930, Corle worked as a writer for radio, with occasional work at the studios of RKO and Metro-Goldwyn-Mayer. In 1933 his first published story, "Amethyst," appeared in the *Atlantic Monthly.* The story was included in Edward J. O'Brien's *The Best Short Stories: 1934.* In the next few years, Corle's short fiction and non-fiction pieces were published in the *New Yorker, Scribner's, Liberty, Harper's, Esquire,* and other periodicals. His first book, *Mojave: A Book of Stories* (Liveright), was published in 1934. His first novel, the acclaimed *Fig Tree John* (Liveright), was published in 1935.

Corle continued to write fiction, concentrating on the people of the American Southwest. His work drew good reviews, although he was sometimes criticized for excessive sentimentality and melodrama. *Desert Country* was his first book-length non-fiction work. In 1941, Corle received a Guggenheim Fellowship in creative writing.

Corle's marriage to Helen Freeman in 1932 ended in divorce. In 1944, he married Jean Armstrong. Their daughter, Jeanne, was born in 1945. Corle lived at his home on Hope Ranch, near Santa Barbara, California, until his death in 1956. His library there housed more than six thousand titles and, after his death, his widow, Jean, donated his books and papers to the library of the University of California at Los Angeles. In 1963, she established a book-collection contest that is now called the Edwin and Jean Corle Memorial Book Collection Contests and is an annual event on the Santa Barbara campus of the University of California.

Edwin Corle died in Santa Barbara, California, on June 11, 1956, at age 50.

PAPERS: The Corle mss., 1942–1965 are held by the Lilly Library, Indiana University, Bloomington, Indiana.

NOTES ON *DESERT COUNTRY*

Duell, Sloan & Pearce announced publication of *The American Folkways Series* in their Spring List in the January 25, 1941, issue of *Publishers' Weekly*, noting that the series would be edited by Erskine Caldwell and "inaugurated" in May with Edwin Corle's Desert Country. The April 12, 1941, issue of *PW* carried a two-page Duell, Sloan & Pearce advertisement in which *Desert Country*, the first title in the series, and *Piñon Country*, the second, were promoted, noting that *Desert Country* would be published May 22 and stating, "Erskine Caldwell, the editor, has traveled widely throughout this country; he has sought out, in every locality, the creative writers whom he felt best fitted to speak for their regions."

REVIEWS

Booklist, June 15, 1941 (p. 489); *New York Herald Tribune Book Review*, June 1, 1941 (p. 1); *Catholic World*, November, 1941 (p. 253); *Library Journal*, May 15, 1941 (p. 462); *The New York Times Book Review*, June 1, 1941, (p. 5); *New Yorker*, May 31, 1941 (p. 71); *Saturday Review of Literature*, June 21, 1941 (p. 11); *Scientific Book Club Review*, July 1941 (p. 3); *Wisconsin Library Bulletin*, July 1941 (p. 137).

SELECTED WRITINGS BY EDWIN CORLE

Mojave: A Book of Stories (New York: Liveright., 1934); *Fig Tree John* (New York: Liveright, 1935); *People on the Earth* (New York: Random House, 1937); (contributor, with others, of articles) *Books and Typography designed by Merle Armitage* (New York: Duell, Sloan & Pearce, 1938); *Burro Alley* (New York: Random House, 1938); *Solitaire* (New York: Dutton, 1940); *Desert Country* (New York: Duell, Sloan & Pearce, 1941); *Coarse Gold* (New York: Dutton 1942); *Listen Bright Angel* (New York: Duell, Sloan & Pearce, 1946); *See Your West* (California: Standard Oil Company of California, 1947); *Three Ways to Mecca* (New York: Duell, Sloan & Pearce, 1947); (ed.) *Operations Santa Fe: Atchison, Topeka & Santa Fe Railway System*, by Merle Armitage (New York: Duell, Sloan & Pearce, 1948); *John Studebaker: An American Dream* (New York: Dutton, 1948); *In Winter Light* (New York: Duell, Sloan & Pearce, 1949); (ed.) *Igor Stravinsky* (New York: Duell, Sloan & Pearce, 1949); *The Royal Highway (El Camino Real)* (Indianapolis: Bobbs-Merrill, 1949); *The Widow* (New Haven: Yale University Press, 1950); *People on the Earth*

(Santa Barbara: W. Hebberd, 1950); *The Gila: River of the Southwest* (Rivers of America Series) (New York: Rinehart, 1951); *The Story of the Grand Canyon* (New York: Duell, Sloan & Pearce, 1951); *Apache Devil* (New York: Pyramid Books, 1952); *Billy the Kid* (New York: Duell, Sloan & Pearce, 1953); (intro.) *Glances into California*, by Walter Colton (Early California Travels series) (Los Angeles: G. Dawson, 1955); *Death Valley and the Creek Called Furnace* (with photographs by Ansel Adams) (Los Angeles: Ward Ritchie Press, 1962).

SOURCES

Book Review Digest 1941. New York: The H.W. Wilson Company, 1942, p. 194.

Publishers' Weekly, January 25, 1941, p. 308 (Duell, Sloan & Pearce Spring List), and p. 399; April 12, 1941, p. 1524; April 26, 1941, p. 1750; and May 24, 1941, p. 2090.

The New York Times Book Review, June 1, 1941, p. 5.

The New York Times obituary, June 12, 1956, n.p.

Who Was Who in America, Vol. III, 1951-1960. Chicago: Marquis Who's Who, n.p.

Shirley, Carl R. "Edwin Corle." *Dictionary of Literary Biography Yearbook*: *1985*. Detroit: Gale Research Company, pp. 344-350.

FAR NORTH COUNTRY

Thames Williamson
February 7, 1894 – May 5, 1961

AF7   First edition, first printing (1944) [9]

[*Folkways* device] | [within a medium cream (close to Pantone 4545) rectangle with rounded corners, in cream] EDITED BY ERSKINE CALD-WELL | [black] FAR NORTH | COUNTRY | *by* | THAMES WILLIAMSON | [cream] DUELL, SLOAN & PEARCE · NEW YORK

COLLATION: 8½" x 6". 124 leaves. [i–x] xi [xii] [1–2] 3–77 [78–80] 81–153 [154-156] 157–231 [232] 233–236. Numbers printed in roman in headline at the outer margin of the type page, except for pp. xi, 3, 17, 31, 45, 61, 81, 93, 109, 124, 138, 157, 173, 188, 203, 217, and 233, on which the numbers are printed in the center at the foot of the page.

CONTENTS: p. [i], half-title: "FAR NORTH COUNTRY"; p. [ii], "AMERI-CAN FOLKWAYS | Edited by ERSKINE CALDWELL | [thin rule] | [list of nine titles and their authors, beginning with *Desert Country* and ending with *Far North Country*] | Other Alaska Books by THAMES WILLIAMSON | [list of two titles]"; p. [iii], title; p. [iv], copyright page: "COPYRIGHT, 1944, BY | THAMES WILLIAMSON | *All rights reserved, including* | *the right to repro-duce this book* | *or portions thereof in any form* | 1 | [stylized eagle carrying book in its talons and a ribbon in its beak on which is printed 'Books are weapons in the war of ideas'] | A WARTIME BOOK | THIS COMPLETE EDITION IS PRODUCED | IN FULL COMPLIANCE WITH THE GOV-ERN- | MENT'S REGULATIONS FOR CONSERVING | PAPER AND OTHER ESSENTIAL MATERIALS | PRINTED IN THE UNITED STATES OF AMERICA | BY THE VAIL-BALLOU PRESS, INC., BINGHAMTON, N.Y."; p. [v], dedication: "FOR MY WIFE | She liked Alaska and Alaska liked her"; p. [vi], blank; p. [vii], "'One learns that the world, | though made, is yet being made.'" | "-JOHN MUIR."; p. [viii], blank; p. [ix], "A CALENDAR FOR A GIANT" [introduction to the book]; p. [x], blank; p. xi, "WHAT'S IN THE BOOK?" [Contents]; p. [xii], blank; p. [1], "*Yesterday*"; p. [2], blank; pp. 3-77, text; p. [78], blank; p. [79], "*Today*"; p. [80], blank; pp. 81–153, text; p. [154], blank; p. [155], "*Tomorrow*"; p. [156], blank; pp. 157–231, text; p. [232], blank; pp. 233–236, "Index".

BINDING: Medium blue cloth (close to Pantone 301). Front: *Folkways* device stamped in black at lower right corner. Spine, stamped in black, except where noted: "[thick rule] | [four thin rules] | [within a black panel, in gold] FAR | NORTH | COUNTRY | · | THAMES | WILLIAMSON | [four thin rules] | [thick rule] | [four thin rules] | [at bottom] [four thin rules | [within a black panel, in gold] DUELL, SLOAN | AND PEARCE | [four thin rules] | [thick rule]". Light cream endpapers carry map of Alaska and portions of the Arctic Ocean, the Bering Sea, and the Pacific Ocean; a part of Siberia to the west; and a part of Canada to the east, in sea-foam green (close to Pantone 557) and cream; and "Alaska" printed in sea-foam green on a light cream ribbon at the lower right.

DUST JACKET (white paper): Front carries a portion of the map of Alaska found on the endpapers, in sea-foam green and cream. "[white, outlined in dark orange (close to Pantone 166)] FAR NORTH | COUNTRY | [solid dark orange] THAMES WILLIAMSON". Spine: "[four thin dark orange rules on a white band] | [dark orange on sea-foam green] FAR | NORTH | COUNTRY | [white] · | WILLIAMSON | [dark orange] [four thin rules, thick rule, four thin rules, with the *Folkways* device overlaid in the center] | [drawing of a totem pole] | [four thin dark orange rules] | [within a dark orange panel, in white] DUELL, SLOAN | AND PEARCE | [four thin dark orange rules]". Back: "[white background] [within an arced ribbon, in dark orange] AMERICAN FOLKWAYS | [sea-foam green] *Edited by* | Erskine Caldwell | [blurb] | [dark orange] ALREADY PUBLISHED | [sea-foam green] [list of nine titles and their authors; four are further described on the back flap] | [dark orange] IN PREPARATION | [sea-foam green] [list of four titles and their authors[1] | [dark orange] *Each Volume, $3.00* | [sea-foam green] [publisher's imprint]". Front flap: "[sea-foam green] [upper right] $3.00 | [dark orange] FAR NORTH COUNTRY | [sea-foam green] *by* Thames Williamson | [blurb] | [dark orange] [publisher's imprint]". Back flap: "[dark orange] Desert Country | [sea-foam green] *by* EDWIN CORLE [quotes from two reviews] | [dark orange] High Border Country | [sea-foam green] *by* ERIC THANE | [quote from a review] | [dark orange] Piñon Country | [sea-foam green] *by* HANIEL LONG | [quote from a review] | [dark orange] Short Grass Country | [sea-foam green] *by* STANLEY VESTAL | [quote from a review] | [dark orange] *Each Volume, $3.00* | [sea-foam green] [publisher's imprint]".

1. One title listed, *Black Jack Country* by George Milburn, was never published; another, listed as *Paul Bunyan Country*, was published as *North Star Country* by Meridel Le Sueur.

Published at $3.00 on March 30, 1944; number of copies printed unknown. Copyrighted April 15, 1944; deposited April 15, 1944.

The book is listed in "The Weekly Record," April 1, 1944, p. 1396.

Note: Duell, Sloan & Pearce published at least two printings of *Far North Country*.

CITED: *Guns* 1100

COPIES: CF

REPRINTS AND REPRODUCTIONS

None

BIOGRAPHY

Thames Ross Williamson was born on February 7, 1894, on the Nez Percé Indian reservation near Genesee, Idaho, the son of Benjamin Franklin and Eugenia May (Ross) Williamson. His father, a former scout, was a trader. Williamson's first name, Thames, was pronounced not like that of the English river, but "with a lisp at the start and the rest to rhyme with James."[2]

Williamson ran away from home at age fourteen and for two years traveled and worked his way around the western United States and Alaska, somehow graduating from high school in Spokane, Washington, on June 10, 1910, when he was sixteen. By age twenty he was private secretary to the warden of the Iowa State Prison and editor of the prison magazine. Proficient in many languages, he moved to Chicago, where he worked as an interpreter of Italian, Spanish, and modern Greek at Hull House, the famous Chicago settlement house.

After he returned to Iowa, he attended the University of Iowa, where, in June, 1917, he earned a bachelor of arts degree (cum laude) in modern languages and economics and was admitted to Phi Beta Kappa. Also in 1917, he was awarded a scholarship by Harvard University, earning a master of arts degree in economics and anthropology there in 1918. While at Harvard, Williamson taught night classes at Northeastern College.

In 1917, Williamson married Florence Louise von Zurawski. The couple had a daughter. They were later divorced. In 1927, Williams married Sarah Storer Smith. The couple had two children. She occasionally collaborated with him in his writings, and one of his pseudonyms, S.S. Smith, was derived from her surname and initials.

Williamson taught economics at Simmons College (1920-1921), and economics and sociology at Smith College (1921-1922). From 1925 to 1928 he

2. *Twentieth Century Authors*, 1942, New York: The H. W. Wilson Company, p. 1528.

wrote three textbooks in sociology and civics, earning sufficient income from their sales to leave teaching to devote his time to writing. His later fiction was set in many locales, including the Alaskan tundra, the Ozarks, Pennsylvania Dutch farm country, the Far East, Germany, and Rome in the time of Nero. In 1941, the family moved to California, where he worked as a screenwriter in Hollywood. In 1957, when he retired, he and his wife moved to Carmel.

Williamson wrote forty books, including novels, juveniles, textbooks, and travel books. His 1929 novel, *Hunky,* was a Book-of-the-Month Club selection. His various pseudonyms included Gregory Trent; Edward Dragonet; De Wolfe Morgan; Waldo Fleming, and, as noted, S.S. Smith.

Thames Ross Williamson died in Carmel, California, on May 5, 1961, at age 67.

NOTES ON *FAR NORTH COUNTRY*

The book, like many of the earlier *Folkways* titles, was not heavily promoted by its publisher, Duell, Sloan & Pearce.

The book was widely and favorably reviewed.

REVIEWS

Book Week, April 16, 1944 (p. 3); *Booklist,* May 15, 1944 (p. 316); *Kirkus,* April 1, 1944 (p. 164); *Library Journal,* March 1, 1944 (p. 203); *Nation,* June 3, 1944 (p. 660); *New Republic,* July 3, 1944 (p. 20); *New York Times Book Review,* April 9, 1944 (p. 6); *New Yorker,* April 15, 1944 (p. 84); *Saturday Review of Literature,* July 22, 1944 (p. 39); *Weekly Book Review,* April 9, 1944 (p. 6).

SELECTED WRITINGS BY THAMES WILLIAMSON

Problems in American Democracy (Boston: D.C. Heath & Co., 1922); *Readings in American Democracy* (Boston: D.C. Heath & Co., 1922); *Introduction to Economics* (Boston: D.C. Heath & Co., 1923); *Run, Sheep, Run* (Boston: Small, Maynard & Company, 1925); *Gypsy Down the Lane* (Boston: Small, Maynard & Company, 1926); *The Man Who Cannot Die* (Boston: Small, Maynard & Company, 1926); *Stride of Man* (New York: Coward-McCann, 1928); *Civics at Work: A Textbook in Social and Vocational Citizenship* (Boston: D.C. Heath and Company, 1928); *Hunky* (New York: Coward McCann, 1929); *Opening Davy Jones's Locker* (Boston: Houghton, 1930); *The Flood-fighters: A Boy's Adventures with the Raging Mississippi* (Boston: Houghton, 1931); *In Krusack's House* (New York: Harcourt, 1931); *Sad Indian: A Novel about Mexico* (New York: Harcourt, 1932); *On the Reindeer Trail* (Boston: Houghton, 1932);

(with Sarah Storer Smith) *Glacier Mystery: A Boy's Story of the Tyrolese Alps* (New York: Harcourt Brace,1932); *Against the Jungle* (Boston: Houghton, 1933); *North After Seals* (Boston: Houghton, 1934); *D is for Dutch: A Last Regional Novel* (New York: Harcourt, 1934); The *Lobster War* (Boston: Lothrop, Lee & Shephard, 1935); *Beginning at Dusk: An Interlude* (New York: Doubleday, Doran, 1935); *Under the Linden Tree: An Interlude* (New York: Doubleday, Doran, 1935); *The Cave Mystery* (New York: Harcourt, 1935); *The Falcon Mystery* (New York: Harcourt, 1936); *In the Stone Age: A Boys' Story of Early Paleolithic Times* (New York: Harcourt, 1936); *Spy Mystery: A Boys' Story of Soviet Russia* (New York: Harcourt, 1937); *The Last of the Gauchos: A Boys' Tale of Argentine Adventure* (Indianapolis: Bobbs-Merrill, 1937); *Flint Chipper* (Boston: Lothrop, Lee & Shepard, 1940); **Far North Country** (New York: Duell, Sloan & Pearce, 1944); *Christine Roux* (New York: Current Books, 1945); *Gladiator* (New York: Coward-McCann, 1948).

SOURCES

Book Review Digest 1944. New York: The H.W. Wilson Company, 1945, p. 817.

Burke, W.J. and Will D. Howe. *American Authors and Books: 1640-1940.* New York: Gramercy Publishing Co., 1943, pp. 831–832.

Kunitz, Stanley J. and Howard Haycraft, eds. *Twentieth Century Authors.* New York: The H.W. Wilson Company, 1942, pp. 1528–1529.

Publishers' Weekly, January 29, 1944 (Duell, Sloan & Pearce Spring List); and April 1, 1944, p. 1396.

The New York Times Book Review, April 9, 1944, p. 6.

Carmel Pine Cone-Cymbal (California) obituary, May 11, 1961, p. 6. (Courtesy of Denise Sallee, Local History Librarian, Hamilton Memorial Library, Carmel-by-the-Sea, California).

Seymour-Smith, Martin, and Andrew C. Kimmens, eds. *World Authors 1900-1950. Volume Four.* New York: The H.W. Wilson Company, 1996, pp. 2901–2902 (entry on Thames Ross Williamson).

Carey, Kyle, Reference Assistant, Pusey Library, Harvard University, Cambridge, Massachusetts. Letter to CF, with material from the biographical folder of Thames Ross Williamson. October 9, 2002.

GOLDEN GATE COUNTRY

Gertrude Atherton
October 30, 1857 – June 14, 1948

AF8   First edition, first printing (1945) [11]

[*Folkways* device] | [within a gold (close to Pantone 141) rectangle with rounded corners, in cream] EDITED BY ERSKINE CALDWELL | [black] GOLDEN | GATE | COUNTRY | *by* | GERTRUDE ATHERTON | [cream] DUELL, SLOAN & PEARCE · NEW YORK

COLLATION: 8½" x 6". 136 leaves. [i–viii] ix–xi [xii] [1–2] 3–76 [77–78] 79–169 [170-172] 173–220 [221–222] 223–256 [257–260]. Numbers printed in roman in headline at the outer margin of the type page, except for pp. ix, xi, 3, 15, 26, 44, 79, 101, 130, 140, 173, 196, 223, and 251, on which the numbers are printed in the center at the foot of the page.

CONTENTS: p. [i], half-title: "GOLDEN GATE COUNTRY"; p. [ii], blank; p. [iii], "BOOKS BY GERTRUDE ATHERTON | *Historical Novels* [list of six titles] | *The San Francisco Series* | [list of 10 titles] | *In Other Parts of the World* | [list of fifteen titles] | *Short Stories* | [list of three titles] | *Autobiography* | [one title] | *History* | [list of two titles] | *Miscellaneous* | [list of three titles]"; p. [iv], "AMERICAN FOLKWAYS | EDITED BY ERSKINE CALDWELL | [thin rule] | [list of eleven titles and their authors, beginning with *Golden Gate Country* and ending with *Far North Country*] | In Preparation | [list of eight titles and their authors[1]]"; p. [v], title; p. [vi], copyright page: "COPYRIGHT, 1945, BY | GERTRUDE ATHERTON | *All rights reserved, including | the right to reproduce this book | or portions thereof in any form.* | *first edition* | WAR EDITION. THIS BOOK IS PRODUCED | IN ACCORDANCE WITH CONSERVATION | ORDERS OF THE WAR PRODUCTION BOARD | PRINTED IN THE

---

1. The list includes *Buckeye Country* by Louis Bromfield, *Piney Woods Country* by John Faulkner, *Cutover Country* by John T. Frederick, *Black Jack Country* by George Milburn, and *Tidewater Country* by Elswyth Thane, none of which were published in the series, and *North Star Country* by Meridel Le Sueur, *Mission Country* (issued as *Southern California Country*) by Carey McWilliams, and *Town Meeting Country* by Clarence M. Webster, all of which were published in the series.

UNITED STATES OF AMERICA"; p. [vii], dedication: "To | *George Sheldon Russell*"; p. [viii], blank; pp. ix–x, "Acknowledgments"; p. xi, "Contents"; p. [xii], blank; p. [1], "PART ONE"; p. [2], blank; pp. 3–76, text; p. [77], "PART TWO"; p. [78], blank; pp. 79–169, text; p. [170], blank; p. [171], "PART THREE"; p. [172], blank; pp. 173–220, text; p. [221], "PART FOUR"; p. [222], blank; pp. 223–250, text; pp. 251–256, "Index"; pp. [257–260], blank.

BINDING: Tan cloth (close to Pantone 728). Front: *Folkways* device stamped in dark brown (close to Pantone 407) at lower right corner. Spine stamped in dark brown, except where noted: "[thick rule] | [four thin rules] | [within a dark brown panel, in gold] GOLDEN | GATE | COUNTRY | GERTRUDE | ATHERTON | [four thin rules] | [thick rule] | [four thin rules] | [at bottom] [four thin rules | [within a dark brown panel, in gold] DUELL, SLOAN | AND PEARCE | [four thin rules] | [thick rule]". Cream endpapers carry map of the San Francisco Bay area in dark brown (close to Pantone 469) and cream; "GOLDEN GATE COUNTRY" is printed in dark brown on a cream ribbon.

DUST JACKET (white paper): Front carries the map of the San Francisco Bay area in burgundy (close to Pantone 187) and cream, which is also found on the endpapers. "[navy blue rule (close to Pantone 280)] | [cream outlined in navy blue] GOLDEN GATE | COUNTRY | [solid navy blue] GERTRUDE ATHERTON" Spine: "[four thin navy blue rules on a cream band] | [navy blue] GOLDEN | GATE | COUNTRY | [cream] · | ATHERTON | [navy blue] [four thin rules, thick rule, four thin rules, with the *Folkways* device overlaid in the center] | [drawing of a mission-style church] | [four thin navy blue rules on a cream band] | [within a navy blue panel, in dark brown] DUELL, SLOAN | AND PEARCE | [four thin navy blue rules on a cream band] | [navy blue rule]". Back: "[white background] [within an arced ribbon, in burgundy] AMERICAN FOLKWAYS | [navy blue] [to the left of the *Folkways* device, which is in burgundy and white] *Edited* | — *by* — [to the right of the *Folkways* device, in navy blue] ERSKINE | CALDWELL | [quote from Harold Rugg] | PUBLISHED | [list of twelve titles and their authors] | [quote from Lewis Gannett] | EACH VOLUME $3.00 | IN PREPARATION | [list of seven of the eight titles found on p. [iv] of the text; *Town Meeting Country* has been moved to the list of titles published] | [burgundy] [publisher's imprint]". Front flap: White background; printing in navy blue. "[upper right] $3.00 | GOLDEN GATE | COUNTRY | by | Gertrude Atherton | [blurb] | [publisher's imprint]". Back flap: White background; printing in navy blue. "[upper left] $3.00 | *From the reviews of* | DEEP DELTA | COUNTRY | [quotes from five reviews] | [publisher's imprint]".

Published at $3.00 on February 28, 1945; number of copies printed unknown. Copyrighted March 8, 1945; deposited March 12, 1945.

The book is listed in "The Weekly Record," June 23, 1945, p. 2456.

Note: Duell, Sloan & Pearce published at least four printings of *Golden Gate Country.*

COPIES: CF

REPRINTS AND REPRODUCTIONS

None.

BIOGRAPHY

Gertrude Horn Atherton was born in San Francisco, California, on October 30, 1857, the only child of Thomas Ludovich[2] and Gertrude (Franklin) Horn. Horn was a New England businessman whose family had been in the shipping business there for some two hundred years. His wife, Gertrude, a descendent of Benjamin Franklin, had grown up on a Louisiana plantation.

Atherton's parents were divorced when she was a young girl. She attended public and private schools in California, lived from time to time on her maternal grandfather's San Jose ranch, and at age seventeen went to Lexington, Kentucky, to study at the Sayre Institute. After a year, she returned to California. In 1876, shortly after her return, young Gertrude eloped with George H. Bowen Atherton, then twenty-four. He was the son of a trader with business interests in California and Chile and a Chilean mother, Dominga de Goñi. The couple had two children, George Goñi, who died at age six, and Muriel Florence.

In her mid-twenties, bored with her marriage and domestic life, Atherton began to write, employing various pen names. Around 1883, her first novel, *The Randolphs of Redwoods*, was serialized in the *San Francisco Argonaut*. The novel was based on a contemporary scandal involving a privileged young woman who succumbed to alcoholism. When it became known that Atherton was the author, she was ostracized by San Francisco society. The book was revised and published in England by John Lane, The Bodley Head, in 1899 as *A Daughter of the Vine.*

Atherton's husband died in 1887, while he was on a business trip to Chile. She soon began a full-time literary career, and, in 1888, moved to New York. Her books, presenting liberated women and romantic melodrama, and her sexual candor, drew critical scorn for her work.[3] She left New York in 1895,

2. One source states "Lodowick".
3. Fowler, Dean. *Dictionary of American Biography.* New York: Scribners, 1974, p. 31.

moving to England, where she was well received. She never remarried.

In the 1930s, Atherton returned to California and soon became active in San Francisco society and civic organizations. In 1935, she was awarded an honorary doctorate in literature by Mills College. In 1937, she was awarded an honorary doctorate in law by the University of California, Berkeley.

During more than sixty years as a writer, Atherton moved between the United States and Europe and between California and New York and New England, writing fifty-six books, thirty-four of them novels. In 1943, she became the first living author to donate manuscripts, correspondence, notes, and related papers to the Library of Congress.

Gertrude Atherton died in San Francisco, California, on June 14, 1948, at age 90.

PAPERS: Gertrude Atherton's papers are held by the Library of Congress; the Bancroft Library at the University of California, Berkeley; the New York Public Library; the California Historical Society Library; and the Yale University Library. Her papers relating to the writing of *Golden Gate Country* and *Dido, Queen of Hearts* are held by the Dartmouth College Library.

NOTES ON *GOLDEN GATE COUNTRY*

In a June 14, 1943, letter to Gertrude Atherton, C. Halliwell ("Charles") Duell expressed his pleasure that she would be writing a book for *The American Folkways Series,* noting, "your contribution calls for the highest advance we have ever paid on one of these books." Atherton signed an agreement with Duell, Sloan & Pearce on August 9 to write the book, then entitled "Northern California Country," to be approximately seventy-five thousand words in length. The manuscript was due on or before January 1, 1944, but in a handwritten margin note on the agreement Atherton advised "earlier date possible." She received an advance of $750 and was to receive a royalty of 14 percent on all copies of regular trade editions sold by the publisher in the United States at discounts of less than 48 percent from the catalog price.

Shortly after the contract was signed, at her request the book's title was changed to *Golden Gate Country*. She was well along with the manuscript by December 1943, and the publisher hoped to include the book in the Spring 1944 catalogue. Owing to a problem with her typewriter, she was unable to provide a carbon copy of the manuscript, leading Charles Duell to write in a February 28, 1944, letter, "When your manuscript comes we shall throw a cordon of police around it, as your warning of no carbon copy is quite a caution."

The publisher received the manuscript in mid-April, but thought it needed considerable editing and should include additional material which

would carry the book into the twentieth century. The manuscript was sent
to Erskine Caldwell for his review. By mid-July 1944 the manuscript had
been so heavily edited that it was necessary that it be retyped before it was
sent to the printer. Atherton and Caldwell were to work out the final editing
details, but in the retyping of the manuscript the final chapter and the final
paragraphs of the preceding chapter were not retyped, being deemed by the
publisher, and presumably by Caldwell, as an unsuitable climax. Charles
Duell's letter of October 19 explains, "We have two major points of criticism
to make. The first is that the matters discussed in these sections will be too
soon dated. . . . The second point of criticism is that as a conclusion to your
book the Redwoods, the Save-the-Redwoods League, and so on, receive attention out of all proportion to the interests of the general reader. It simply
unbalances the book at a point where the over-all perspective is at its most
important." He suggested the deletion of the final chapter and the last paragraphs of the preceding chapter, ending the book with a separate paragraph,
"San Francisco was thoroughly alive." This was done, and those words end
the text.

By March 20, sales had passed three thousand and by April 26 had
reached five thousand three hundred. In a May 24 letter responding to Atherton's concerns about the promotion of the book, Duell stated that the firm
had made a special poster on *Golden Gate Country* which was sent "to all of
the California stores at the time of publication," but owing to wartime space
rationing the *San Francisco Chronicle* was unable to accept an ad for the
book until sometime in June.

The fourth printing of *Golden Gate Country*, in November 1945, was to
contain several corrections requested by Atherton, but despite the best ef-
forts of the publisher, the printer, American Book Stratford Press, failed to
include them. By January 1946, the book had sold more than seven thousand
copies.

Gertrude Atherton was eighty-seven when *Golden Gate Country* was
published. In his review in *The New York World-Telegram*, Harry Hansen
wrote, "How Erskine Caldwell came to ask her to do a book for his series of
American Folkways I do not know, but obviously she was the logical candidate when he thought of San Francisco."

REVIEWS

Book Week, March 18, 1945 (p. 6.); *Booklist*, May 1, 1945 (p. 251); *Christian Science Monitor*, March 24, 1945 (p. 12); *Churchman*, June 15, 1945 (p. 18); *Commonweal*, March 30, 1945 (p. 594); *Kirkus*, February 1, 1945 (p. 50); the *New
York Times Book Review*, April 1, 1945 (p. 3); *New Yorker*, March 17, 1945 (p.
95); *Weekly Book Review*, March 18, 1945 (p.12).

SELECTED WRITINGS BY GERTRUDE ATHERTON

Los Cerritos: A Romance of the Modern Time (New York: John W. Lovell, 1890); *The Doomswoman* (New York: Tait and Sons, 1893); *A Whirl Asunder* (New York: Frederick A. Stokes, 1895); *Patience Sparhawk and Her Times, A Novel* (London: John Lane, The Bodley Head, 1897); *American Wives and English Husbands, A Novel* (London: Service and Paton, 1898); *The Valiant Runaways, A Story for Boys* (New York: Dodd, Mead, 1898); *A Daughter of the Vine* (London: John Lane, The Bodley Head, 1899); *The Splendid Idle Forties, Stories of Old California* (New York: Macmillan, 1902); *The Bell in the Fog and Other Stories* (New York: Harper, 1905); *The Traveling Thirds* (New York: Harper, 1905); *Rezanov* (New York: Authors and Newspapers Association, 1906); *Ancestors, A Novel* (New York: Harper, 1907); *Perch of the Devil* (New York: Frederick A. Stokes, 1914); *California: An Intimate History* (New York: Harper, 1914); *Before the Gringo Came; Rezanov; and The Doomswoman* (New York: Frederick A. Stokes, 1915); *The Avalanche, A Mystery Story* (New York: Frederick A. Stokes, 1919); *The Sisters-in-Law, A Novel of Our Time* (New York: Frederick A. Stokes, 1921); *Sleeping Fires, A Novel* (New York: Frederick A. Stokes, 1922); *Adventures of a Novelist* (New York: Liveright, 1932); *The House of Lee* (New York: Appleton-Century, 1940); *The Horn of Life* (New York: Appleton-Century, 1942); **Golden Gate Country** (New York: Duell, Sloan & Pearce, 1945); *My San Francisco: A Wayward Biography* (Indianapolis: Bobbs-Merrill, 1946).

SOURCES

Jackson, Joseph Henry. "'Watch The Parade; Write It All Down'". *San Francisco Chronicle*, November 1, 1942. (Profile of Gertrude Atherton on the celebration of her 85th birthday.)

Book Review Digest 1945. New York: The H.W. Wilson Company, 1946, p. 24.

Publishers' Weekly, January 27, 1945, p. 320; and June 23, 1945, p. 2456.

The New York Times Book Review, April 1, 1945, p. 3.

The New York Times obituary, June 15, 1948, p. 27.

Fowler, Dean. *Dictionary of American Biography.* New York: Charles Scribner & Sons, 1974, pp. 30-31. (Entry on Gertrude Franklin (Horn) Atherton.)

McClure, Charlotte. *Gertrude Atherton.* Western Writers Series No. 23. Boise, Idaho: Boise State University, 1976.

"Women in American History" Encyclopedia Britannica Online, 1999. Accessed May 19, 2002. (Entry for Gertrude Franklin Horn Atherton.)

Gertrude Atherton Papers. Bancroft Library, University of California, Berkeley. (Atherton contract with Duell, Sloan & Pearce; her obituary and an editorial regarding her death; Harry Hanson review of *Golden Gate Country*; Atherton-Duell, Sloan and Pearce correspondence, 1943–1946.) Accessed August 2003.

GULF COAST COUNTRY

Hodding Carter
February 3, 1907 – April 4, 1972
and
Anthony Ragusin
April 22, 1902– March 3,1997

AF9   First edition, first printing (1951) [23]

[*Folkways* device] | [within a green (close to Pantone 376) rectangle with rounded corners, in cream] EDITED BY ERSKINE CALDWELL | [black] GULF | COAST | COUNTRY | BY HODDING CARTER | AND | ANTHONY RAGUSIN | [cream] DUELL, SLOAN & PEARCE · NEW YORK

COLLATION: 8½" x 6". 128 leaves. [i–vi] vii–viii 1–247 [248]. Numbers printed in roman in headline at the outer margin of the type page, except for pp. vii, 1, 7, 14, 22, 32, 42, 49, 55, 60, 72, 79, 93, 98, 104, 110, 117, 125, 134, 143, 149, 155, 168, 176, 181, 190, 199, 208, 215, 228, 235, and 241, on which the numbers are printed in the center at the foot of the page.

CONTENTS: p. [i], half-title: "*Gulf Coast Country* | [thick rule]"; p. [ii], "AMERICAN FOLKWAYS | EDITED BY ERSKINE CALDWELL | [list of twenty-three titles and their authors, beginning with *Golden Gate Country* and ending with *Gulf Coast Country*] | In Preparation | [list of eight titles[1]]";

1. The list includes *Great Lakes Country* by Iola Fuller, *Tidewater Country* by Elswyth Thane, *Pacific Northwest Country* by Richard Neuberger, *Gold Rush Country* by Charis Weston, *Pennsylvania Dutch Country* by Harry Emerson Wildes, *Homesteader Country* by Edward Stanley, and *Ohio Country* by Elrick B. Davis (which would have replaced *Buckeye Country* by Louis Bromfield), none of which were published in the *Folkways* series, and *Adirondack Country* by William C. White, which was published in the series.

p. [iii], title; p. [iv], copyright page: "COPYRIGHT, 1951, I By Hodding Carter and Anthony Ragusin I *All rights reserved, including the right to I reproduce this book or portions I thereof in any form.* I I I PRINTED IN THE UNITED STATES OF AMERICA"; p. [v], dedication: "*To Edith and Betty*";[2] p. [vi], blank; pp. vii–viii, "Contents"; pp. 1–240, text; pp. 241–247, "Index"; p. [248], blank.

BINDING: Light olive cloth (close to Pantone 384). Front: *Folkways* device stamped in black at lower right corner. Spine stamped in black, except where noted: "[four thin rules] I [thick rule] I [four thin rules] I [within a black panel, in gold] GULF I COAST I COUNTRY I · I CARTER I and I RAGUSIN I [four thin rules] I [thick rule] I [four thin rules] I [at bottom] [four thin rules I [within a black panel, in gold] DUELL, SLOAN I AND PEARCE I [four thin rules] I [thick rule]". Cream endpapers carry map of the United States in green (close to Pantone 341) and cream, with the "Gulf Coast Country" area highlighted in cream and further identified on a green ribbon in the lower right corner.

DUST JACKET (white paper): Front: Green/yellow background (close to Pantone 397); printing in black. "Gulf Coast I Country I [thin rule] I AMERICAN FOLKWAYS I [thin rule] I [black and white photograph of several commercial fishing boats along the shore; trees in the foreground with Spanish moss hanging from some of the branches] I HODDING CARTER and ANTHONY RAGUSIN". Spine: Orange background (close to Pantone 157); printing in black. "Gulf Coast I Country I CARTER I and I RAGUSIN I [*Folkways* device in black and orange] I DUELL, SLOAN I AND PEARCE". Back: White background; printing in black. "American Folkways I Edited I by [*Folkways* device] ERSKINE I CALDWELL I [blurb praising the series] I [list of twenty-three titles and their authors and prices] I [publisher's imprint]". Front flap: White background; printing in black. "[upper right] $3.50 I GULF COAST I COUNTRY I by I Hodding Carter and I Anthony Ragusin I [blurb] I *An American Folkways Book* I [publisher's imprint]". Back flap: White background; printing in black. "[upper left] $3.50 I DEEP DELTA COUNTRY I by Harnett T. Kane I [blurb] I [publishers imprint].

Published at $3.50 on March 16, 1951; number of copies printed unknown. Copyrighted April 9, 1951; deposited March 27, 1951.

The book is listed in "The Weekly Record, "March 16, 1951, p. 1371.

Note: No evidence found that *Gulf Coast Country* was reprinted by Duell, Sloan & Pearce.

COPIES: CF

2. "Edith" was the wife of Anthony Ragusin; "Betty" was the wife of Hodding Carter.

REPRINTS AND REPRODUCTIONS

None.

BIOGRAPHIES

(William) Hodding Carter, Jr. was born on February 3, 1907, in Hammond, Louisiana, the son of William Hodding, a farmer, and Irma (Dutart) Carter.

Carter graduated from Bowdoin College in 1927 and attended the Graduate School of Journalism at Columbia University in 1928. In 1939, he attended Harvard University as a Nieman Fellow.

On October 14, 1931, Carter married Betty Werlein, a writer. The couple had three sons: Hodding III, a journalist and government official; Philip D., a journalist; and Thomas, who died at age nineteen.

After his years at Bowdoin and Columbia, Carter returned to the South, teaching freshman English at Tulane University and, in 1929, working as a reporter for the *New Orleans Item-Tribune*. He became night bureau manager for the United Press in New Orleans in 1930 and bureau manager for the Associated Press in Jackson, Mississippi, in 1931 but, after a few months, was fired in a dispute over his release of a story about a controversial sales-tax issue in the Mississippi legislature.

With their combined capital of three hundred and sixty-seven dollars, the Carters went to Hammond, Louisiana, Hodding's birthplace, where they founded and from 1932 to 1936 edited and published a newspaper, *The Daily Courier*. In 1936, they sold the paper and moved to Greenville, Mississippi, where they founded *The Delta Star*. In 1938, they purchased a competing newspaper and merged the two under the name *Delta Democrat-Times*. With several interruptions, including his time at Harvard and his military service, Carter was the paper's publisher and editor until the mid-1960s.

Carter served in the Army from 1940 to 1945, rising to the rank of major and, in Egypt during World War II, establishing the Middle Eastern editions of the Army publications *Stars and Stripes* and *Yank*. Although his first love was always journalism, over his lifetime he wrote short-stories; essays; and poetry; contributed to popular periodicals; and wrote biographies of Lafayette and Robert E. Lee, both written for juvenile readers, and two novels, *The Winds of Fear* (Farrar & Rinehart, 1944) and *Flood Crest* (Rinehart, 1947).

During his wartime service in the Army, Carter lost the use of his right eye. In 1963, after the failure of several operations, he lost the useful vision of his left eye as well, but continued to write, dictating much of his work. That year, 1963, he became writer-in-residence at Tulane University, writing books, magazine articles, and book reviews until the end of the decade.

Carter received a Guggenheim Fellowship in 1945. He won the University of Southern Illinois Elijah Lovejoy Award in 1952, the National Citation of Journalistic Merit of the William Allen White Foundation in 1961, the Bowdoin Prize in 1963, and the Columbia University Journalism Alumni Award in 1971. He received six honorary academic degrees and, in 1946, won a Pulitzer Prize for editorial writing. As noted, he had received a Nieman Fellowship in 1939.

Although Carter's forceful and courageous opposition to racial intolerance was recognized and applauded by newspapers and ordinary citizens across the country, he was also subjected to years of criticism for his liberal views and opposition to racial segregation. He bore all such criticism with patience and good humor, living and working in his beloved South until his death.

Hodding Carter died in Greenville, Mississippi, on April 4, 1972, at age 65.

∿

Anthony Ragusin was born in Biloxi, Mississippi, on April 22, 1902 , the son of Anthony and Mary (Milinovich) Ragusin. His father was a carpenter and a commercial fisherman.

After his father died when Ragusin was eight years old, he worked at a variety of odd jobs, including shoe-shining, shrimp-picking, oyster-shucking, and delivering newspapers. Although he never finished grammar school, he briefly attended Northwestern University on a scholarship. He was a self-trained photographer, whose vivid photographs of Gulf Coast birds and boats were considered classics.

In 1926, Ragusin built a bungalow in Biloxi for his bride, Edith Bill. The couple had no children. Edith died in 1979, and Ragusin lived in the house until his death in 1997.

In 1922, at age twenty, Ragusin became general manager of the Biloxi Chamber of Commerce, a position he held, except for his military service during World War II and the Korean War, until his retirement in 1967. Known locally as "Mr. Biloxi," he was for decades a tireless, dynamic promoter of the town, at first little more than a small fishing village but later a leading city on the so-called American Riviera. Magazines carrying his work included the *Saturday Evening Post, Life,* and *National Geographic.*

During World War II, Ragusin, who had risen to the rank of major in the Army Air Forces, served as a press censor on the staff of the commander in chief of the Pacific Fleet, Admiral Chester Nimitz. He later served on active duty during the Korean War.

Ragusin was a popular and admired figure along the Mississippi Gulf

Coast. In an editorial tribute in the Biloxi *Sun Herald* after his death he was described as "the most single-minded civic worker any city has ever encountered."

Anthony V. Ragusin died on March 3, 1997, in Biloxi, Mississippi, at age 94.

NOTES ON *GULF COAST COUNTRY*

In 1947, Erskine Caldwell asked Hodding Carter to write a book on the Gulf Coast Piney Woods country. In a letter to his agent, Bernice Baumgarten, Carter wrote that he would be happy to do the book, "as we already have enough stuff in our files to write it." In a later letter to her, he wrote that it would be good for his reputation in Mississippi to "turn out Mississippiana," noting, "The only way you can get by with conking people there is to alternate with a little patting." In the summer of 1950, Carter and his wife, Betty, spent a month on the Gulf Coast working on research for the book, which he finished with the participation of his collaborator, Anthony Ragusin.[3]

REVIEWS

Booklist, April 1, 1951 (p. 271); *Bookmark*, April 1951 (p. 153); *Chicago Sunday Tribune*, April 1, 1951 (p. 10); *Christian Science Monitor*, April 7, 1951 (p. 9); *Kirkus*, January 15, 1951 (p. 43); *New York Herald Tribune Book Review*, May 6, 1951 (p. 3); *New York Times Book Review*, June 3, 1951 (p. 6).

SELECTED WRITINGS BY HODDING CARTER

(with Ernest R. Dupuy) *Civilian Defense for the United States* (New York: Farrar & Rinehart, 1942); *Lower Mississippi.* (Rivers of America Series) (New York: Farrar & Rinehart, 1942); *The Winds of Fear* (New York: Farrar & Rinehart, 1944); *Flood Crest* (New York: Rinehart, 1947); (contributor) *The Aspirin Age 1919-1941* (New York: Simon & Schuster, 1949); *Southern Legacy* (Baton Rouge: Louisiana State University Press, 1950); (with Anthony Ragusin) *Gulf Coast Country* (American Folkways Series) (New York: Duell, Sloan & Pearce, 1951); *John Law Wasn't So Wrong: The Story of Louisiana's Horn of Plenty* (Baton Rouge, La.: Esso Standard Oil Co., 1952); *Where Main Street Meets the River* (New York: Rinehart, 1953); *Robert E. Lee and the Road of Honor* (New York: Random House, 1955); (With Betty W. Carter) *So Great a Good: A History of the Episcopal Church in Louisiana and of Christ Church Cathedral, 1805-1955* (Sewanee, Tenn.: University Press of Sewanee, 1955);

---

3. *Hodding Carter: The Reconstruction of a Racist*, by Ann Waldron. Chapel Hill, N.C.: Algonquin Books of Chapel Hill, 1993, p. 198.

Marquis de Lafayette: Bright Sword for Freedom (New York: Random House, 1958); *The South Strikes Back* (Garden City, N.Y.: Doubleday, 1959); **The Angry Scar: The Story of Reconstruction** (Mainstream of America Series) (Garden City, N.Y.: Doubleday, 1959); (contributor) *This is the South* (Chicago: Rand McNally, 1960); *First Person Rural* (Garden City, N.Y.: Doubleday, 1963); (with Betty W. Carter) **Doomed Road of the Empire: The Spanish Trail of Conquest.** (American Trails Series) (New York: McGraw-Hill, 1963); *The Ballad of Catfoot Grimes and Other Verses* (Garden City, N.Y.: Doubleday, 1964); (contributor) *A Vanishing America* (New York: Holt, Rinehart and Winston, 1964); *So the Heffners Left McComb* (Garden City, N.Y.: Doubleday, 1965); *The Commandos of World War II* (New York: Random House, 1966); (ed., with others) *The Past as Prelude: New Orleans, 1718-1968* (New Orleans: Tulane University, 1968); *Their Words Were Bullets: The Southern Press in War, Reconstruction, and Peace* (Athens: University of Georgia Press, 1969); *Man and the River: The Mississippi* (Chicago: Rand McNally, 1970).

Hodding Carter contributed to national magazines including *Reader's Digest, New Republic, Saturday Evening Post, Saturday Review, The New York Times Magazine,* and *Nation.*

SOURCES

Book Review Digest 1951. New York: The H.W. Wilson Company, 1952, pp. 155–156.

Publishers' Weekly, January 27, 1951, p. 340 (Duell, Sloan and Pierce Spring List); and March 17, 1951, p. 1371.

The New York Times Book Review, June 3, 1951, p. 6.

Waldron, Ann. *Hodding Carter: The Reconstruction of a Racist.* Chapel Hill, N.C.: Algonquin Books of Chapel Hill, 1993, p. 198.

[Ragusin] (Biloxi) *Sun Herald* obituary, March 5, 1997, p. A-2

[Ragusin] (Biloxi) *Sun Herald* editorial, March 7, 1997, p. A-8

Fitzgerald, Carol. *The Rivers of America: A Descriptive Bibliography.* New Castle, Del.: Oak Knoll Press, in Association with the Center for the Book in the Library Congress, 2001, pp. 384–386 (entry on Hodding Carter).

Powell, Murella H., Local History & Genealogy Librarian, Biloxi Public Library/Harrison County Library System. E-mail message to CF, March 18, 2003, providing valuable biographical information on Anthony Ragusin.

HIGH BORDER COUNTRY

Eric Thane
February 20, 1907 – July 7, 1998

AF10   First edition, first printing (1942) [6]

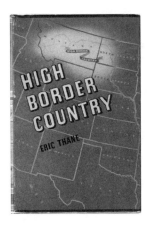

[*Folkways* series device] | [within a blue-gray (close to Pantone 5425) rectangle with rounded corners, in cream] EDITED BY ERSKINE CALD-WELL | [black] HIGH BORDER | COUNTRY | *by* | ERIC THANE | [cream] DUELL, SLOAN & PEARCE · NEW YORK

COLLATION: 8½" x 6". 176 leaves. [i–vi] vii–ix [x] [1–2] 3–331 [332] 333–335 [336–342]. Numbers printed in roman in headline at the outer margin of the type page, except for pp. vii, 3, 60, 70, 111, 145, 161, 224, 256, 267, 288, and 333, on which the numbers are printed in the center at the foot of the page.

CONTENTS: p. [i], half-title: "HIGH BORDER COUNTRY"; p. [ii], "AMERICAN FOLKWAYS | Edited by ERSKINE CALDWELL | [thin rule] | [list of six titles and their authors, beginning with *Desert Country* and ending with *High Border Country*] | *In Preparation* | [list of two titles and their authors[1]]"; p. [iii], title; p. [iv], copyright page: "COPYRIGHT, 1942, BY | ERIC THANE | *All rights reserved, including* | *the right to reproduce this book* | *or portions thereof in any form.* | *first edition* | Small portions of this book, in a slightly different form, | have appeared in *The American Mercury* and in *Direction.* | PRINTED IN THE UNITED STATES OF AMERICA"; p. [v], dedication: "TO THE PIONEERS- | *Saints and Sinners-too few saints and too* | *many sinners, but for better or worse the race* | *that tamed the High Border. To* | *the living of* | *them, honor; to the dead of them, the promise* | *that what they* | *did will never be forgotten. To* | *all of them this book is dedicated.*"; p. [vi], blank; pp. vii–ix, "Contents"; p. [x], blank; p. [1], half-title: "HIGH BORDER COUNTRY"; p. [2], blank; pp. 3–331, text; p. [332], blank; pp. 333–335, "Index"; pp. [336–342], blank.

1. *Florida Country* by Stetson Kennedy was the title used in the first four books in the series. This was changed to *Palmetto Country* in the fifth book, but *Florida Country* has reappeared as "in preparation" in this, the sixth book in the series.

BINDING: Navy blue cloth (close to Pantone 289). Front: *Folkways* device stamped in red (close to Pantone 187) at lower right corner. Spine stamped in red (close to Pantone 187), except where noted: "[thick rule] | [four thin rules] | [within a red panel, in gold] HIGH | BORDER | COUNTRY | · | ERIC | THANE | [four thin rules] | [thick rule] | [four thin rules] | [at bottom] [four thin rules | [within a black panel, in gold] DUELL, SLOAN | AND PEARCE | [four thin rules] | [thick rule]". Cream endpapers carry map of the United States in medium blue (close to Pantone 647) and light blue (close to Pantone 643); within a white border; "High Border Country" region is shaded in cream and further identified on a ribbon-like banner, with a similar ribbon in lower right corner.

DUST JACKET (white paper): Front and spine have an orange-red background (close to Pantone 179). Front carries a map of the central and central-west portion of the United States map found on the endpapers, in orange-red, with the 'High Border Country' region highlighted in cream. "[thick black rule] | [printed on an orange-red ribbon, in cream] HIGH BORDER COUNTRY | [cream, outlined in black] HIGH | BORDER | COUNTRY | [solid black] ERIC THANE | [thick black rule]". Spine: "[thick black rule] [four thin black rules on a cream band] | [black, on orange-red background] HIGH | BORDER | COUNTRY | · | [cream] ERIC | THANE | [black] [four thin rules, thick rule, four thin rules, with the *Folkways* device overlaid in the center] | [drawing of a long gun, powder horn, and a liquor jug hanging from a peg in a log wall] | [four thin black rules] | [within a black panel, in dark cream] DUELL, SLOAN | AND PEARCE | [four thin black rules] | [thick black rule]". Back: "[white background; printing in dark blue (close to Pantone 294), except where noted] [within an arced ribbon, in orange-red] AMERICAN FOLKWAYS | [dark blue] *Edited by* | Erskine Caldwell | [blurb] | [orange-red] READY | [dark blue] [list of five titles and their authors, three of which are described on the back flap, with *Ozark Country* and *Blue Ridge Country* described here] | [orange-red] IN PREPARATION | [dark blue] [list of two titles and their authors, with a brief description of each: *Florida Country*[2] and *Mormon Country*] | [orange-red] *Each Volume, $3.00* | [dark blue] [publisher's imprint]". Front flap: "[dark blue] [upper right] $3.00 | [passage from *High Border Country*] | [orange-red] HIGH BORDER COUNTRY | [dark blue] *by* ERIC THANE | [blurb] | [publisher's imprint]". Back flap: "[dark blue] | LEWIS GANNETT *foresees that the* AMERICAN | FOLKWAYS *series may be* 'a landmark in Amer- | ican regional literature.' | [orange-red] Desert Country | [dark blue] *by* EDWIN CORLE | [blurb] | [orange-red] Piñon Country | [dark blue] *by* HANIEL LONG | [blurb] | [orange-red] Short Grass Country | [dark blue] *by* STAN-

2. Later titled *Palmetto Country*.

LEY VESTAL | [blurb] | [orange-red] *Each Volume, $3.00* | [dark blue] [publisher's imprint]".

Published at $3.00 on May 21, 1942; number of copies printed unknown. Copyrighted and deposited May 23, 1942.

The book is listed in "The Weekly Record," May 23, 1942, p. 1922.

Note: Duell, Sloan & Pearce published at least two printings of *Far North Country.*

CITED: *Guns* 984 and *Guns* 2195 (Revised ed.)

COPIES: CF

REPRINTS AND REPRODUCTIONS

None.

BIOGRAPHY

Ralph Chester Henry was born on February 20, 1907, in Seattle, Washington, the son of H.C. and Lydia Spieth Henry. "Eric Thane" was a pseudonym Henry used in the writing of *High Border Country* and other works. "Eric Thane" and "Thane" are used throughout this biography.

Thane's parents moved to Stevens County, Washington, while Thane was an infant, and he spent the early years of his life there.

Thane attended schools in Washington, Ohio, Idaho, and Montana, graduating from the Eastern Washington College of Education (now Eastern Washington University) in Cheney, Washington. He undertook graduate studies at the University of Montana and received a fellowship in regional writing from the University of Minnesota.

In the late 1930s, Thane moved to Helena, Montana, where he was publicity director for Montana, Inc., now the Montana Chamber of Commerce. During World War II, he served in the Army, first as an enlisted man and later as an officer. After the war, he served in the Army Reserve and, while resuming his work for the Montana Chamber of Commerce and working with the Montana Educational Association, in the Montana National Guard.

Thane taught Montana history at the Helena High School from 1954 until his retirement in 1974. He wrote at least two hundred published articles and short stories. Writing under his given name, Ralph Chester Henry, he wrote three textbooks which were widely used in elementary and secondary schools in Montana. During the 1950s, he wrote book reviews for the *Montana Magazine of History.*

Ralph Chester Henry died in Helena, Montana, on July 7, 1998, at age 91.

NOTES ON *HIGH BORDER COUNTRY*

On September 6, 1943, while serving in the Army and stationed at Fort Hayes, in Ohio, Thane wrote, as Ralph C. Henry, to Stetson Kennedy, the author of *Palmetto Country*. He had read a book review in the *New York Times* written by Kennedy, noting that he was working on a book about Florida.

After identifying himself as the author, Eric Thane, of *High Border Country* and lamenting the book's poor sales, Thane wrote, "I am interested also in this new book of yours. Is Duell, Sloan & Pearce going to publish it? . . . I found Charles A. Pearce a honey of a fellow to deal with, and the company good. But I notice they have put no advertising to speak of behind the Folkway series. Evidently they expect it to pay off; and I sincerely hope it does. I figure so far on my High Border Country I've made about one-third of what I'd have made if I had put in my time writing stuff for the pulp westerns, which was my racket in civilian life, with a too-occasional foray into Redbook, Liberty and The American Mercury. And I mean, damned occasional."

Note: No reply to Thane's letter to Stetson Kennedy has been found.

REVIEWS

Booklist, June 15, 1942 (p. 383); *Books,* May 31, 1942 (p. 4); *Library Journal,* May 15, 1942 (p. 476); *New York Times Book Review,* May 31, 1942 (p. 9).

SELECTED WRITINGS BY ERIC THANE

High Border Country (New York: Duell, Sloan & Pearce, 1942); *The Majestic Land: Peaks, Parks & Prevaricators of the Rockies & Highlands of the Northwest* (Indianapolis: Bobbs-Merrill, 1950).

As Ralph Chester Henry: *Treasure State: The Story of Montanans* (Helena: State Publishing Company, 1954); *The People of Montana: A Study of Montana Government for Students in Montana Schools* (Helena: State Publishing Company, 1958); *Our Land Montana: The Story of Our Treasure State* (Helena: State Publishing Company, 1962).

SOURCES

Book Review Digest 1942. New York: The H.W. Wilson Company, 1943, pp. 352.

Publishers' Weekly, May 23, 1942, p. 1922.

The New York Times Book Review, May 31, 1942, p. 9

Henry, Ralph C. Letter to Stetson Kennedy, September 6, 1943.

Independent Record (Helena, Montana) obituary, July 22, 1998, p. 2C.

Heckerd, Melissa, Assistant Librarian, University of Montana Western, Dillon, Montana. E-mail messages to CF, May 22, 2002 and May 28, 2002. With grateful thanks to Ms. Heckerd, who provided photocopies of material from the University of Montana files relating to Ralph C. Henry/Eric Thane.

HIGH SIERRA COUNTRY

Oscar Lewis
May 5, 1893 – July 11, 1992

AF11   First edition, first printing (1955) [26]

"[within a rectangle with a thin black border, in black] [thin rule] I OSCAR LEWIS I [thin rule] I *HIGH SIERRA* I *COUNTRY* I [*Folkways* device in black and cream] I DUELL, SLOAN & PEARCE I *New York* I LITTLE, BROWN AND COMPANY I *Boston Toronto*"

COLLATION: 8 ½" x 6". 152 leaves. [i–vii] viii–ix [x] [1–3] 4–9 [10] 11–53 [54] 55–78 [79] 80–133 [134] 135–165 [166] 167–208 [209] 210–246 [247] 248–277 [278–281] 282–291 [292–294]. Numbers printed in roman in headline at the outer margin of the type page.

CONTENTS: p. [i], blank; p. [ii], "AMERICAN FOLKWAYS I EDITED BY ERSKINE CALDWELL I [list of twenty-six titles and their authors, beginning with *Golden Gate Country* and ending with *Far North Country*]"; p. [iii], half-title: "*High Sierra Country* I [thick rule]"; p. [iv], blank; p. [v], title; p. [vi], copyright page: "COPYRIGHT, 1955, BY OSCAR LEWIS I ALL RIGHTS RESERVED. NO PART OF THIS BOOK IN EXCESS OF FIVE I HUNDRED WORDS MAY BE REPRODUCED IN ANY FORM WITHOUT I PERMISSION IN WRITING FROM THE PUBLISHER I LIBRARY OF CONGRESS CATALOG CARD NO. 55-9834 I FIRST EDITION I [within a rectangular frame] DUELL, SLOAN AND PEARCE-LITTLE, BROWN I

BOOKS ARE PUBLISHED BY | LITTLE, BROWN AND COMPANY | IN
ASSOCIATION WITH | DUELL, SLOAN & PEARCE, INC. | *Published si-
multaneously in Canada | by Little, Brown & Company (Canada) Limited |*
PRINTED IN THE UNITED STATES OF AMERICA"; pp. [vi]-ix, "Con-
tents"; p. [x], blank; p. [1], half-title: "*High Sierra Country* | [thick rule]"; p.
[2], blank; pp. [3]-277, text; p. [278], blank; p. [279], "*Index* | [thick rule]"; p.
[280], blank; pp. [281]-291, "Index"; pp. [292-294], blank.

BINDING: Dark teal cloth (close to Pantone 322). Spine stamped in gold,
except where noted: "[four thin rules] | [within a dark turquoise panel, in
gold] High | Sierra | Country | · | *Oscar Lewis* | [four thin rules] | [at bottom]
Duell, Sloan, | and Pearce | [thin rule] | *Little, Brown*". Cream endpapers carry
map in green and cream by John Morris, inset in the upper right corner a
map of the region with Sierra Nevada framed and, in the lower left corner
the title, "The Sierra Nevada Country," and a scale of miles, on a scroll.

DUST JACKET (white paper): Front: "[black-and-white photograph of
mountains fills the top half of the cover and wraps to the spine] [thick yellow band (close to Pantone 128), which wraps to the spine; *Folkways* device
in black and dark green (close to Pantone 335) on the right side of the band]
| [on a wide dark green band, which wraps to the spine, in yellow, shaded in
black] HIGH SIERRA | COUNTRY | [white] BY OSCAR LEWIS". Spine:
"[black-and-white photograph wraps from the front to the spine] | [thick
yellow band] | [green background] [yellow, shaded in black] HIGH |
SIERRA | COUNTRY | [white] OSCAR | LEWIS | [black] DUELL, SLOAN |
AND PEARCE | [thin rule] | LITTLE, BROWN". Back: White background;
printing in black. "AMERICAN FOLKWAYS | [blurb praising the series] |
[list of twenty-one authors and the corresponding title for each, beginning
with Gertrude Atherton and ending with Thames Williamson[1]] | [pub-
lisher's imprint[2]]". Front flap: White background; printing in black. "[upper
right] HSC | $4.50 | High Sierra | Country | OSCAR LEWIS | [blurb] | (*Con-
tinued on second flap*)". Back flap: White background; printing in black.
"(*Continued from first flap*) | [blurb] | [within a rectangular frame] DUELL,
SLOAN AND PEARCE-LITTLE, BROWN | BOOKS ARE PUBLISHED BY |
LITTLE, BROWN AND COMPANY | IN ASSOCIATION WITH | DUELL,
SLOAN & PEARCE, INC. | *Jacket design by Samuel H. Bryant*".

Published at $4.50 on June 30, 1955;[3] number of copies printed unknown.
Copyrighted July 5, 1955; deposited July 1, 1955.

1. The list includes Anthony Ragusin, co-author with Hodding Carter of *Gulf Coast Country*. Not all the previously published titles in the series or their authors are included in
the list.
2. The imprint reads: "Duell, Sloan and Pearce — Little, Brown and Company."
3. Publication may have been delayed as the book is not listed in "The Weekly Record"
until July 30, 1955.

The book is listed in "The Weekly Record," July 30, 1955, p. 485.

Note: Duell, Sloan & Pearce published at least three printings of *High Sierra Country.*

CITED: Paher 1133

COPIES: CF

REPRINTS AND REPRODUCTIONS

Westport, Conn: Greenwood Press, 1977.

Reno: University of Nevada Press, 1988. (Paperback). Vintage West Series.

BIOGRAPHY

Oscar Lewis was born on May 5, 1893, in San Francisco, California, the son of William Francis and Anna Amanda (Walter) Lewis. His first published stories were written while he was in high school in Berkeley. After his graduation from high school, Lewis entered the University of California at Berkeley, where he was soon advised by one of his professors to leave the university and become a writer.[4]

In 1917 and 1918, Lewis served in Europe with an ambulance squad sponsored by the University of California. After the Armistice in 1918, he remained in Europe for a year, supporting himself by writing for American periodicals. Over the years, his work appeared in *Harper's, Scribner's, Atlantic Monthly, Saturday Review, New Republic,* and other popular periodicals.

In June 1925, Lewis married Betty Mooney. His stepson, Addison, retained the surname Mooney.

Lewis's stature as a historian developed in the 1920s and 1930s as he worked as a freelance writer, contributing stories and articles to young people's magazines, including *Youth's Companion, St. Nicholas,* the *American Boy,* and *Boys' Life.* In the mid-1930s, he abandoned magazine work and devoted himself exclusively to writing books.[5] He wrote twenty-five books, many of them works of Western history and biography, and was co-author or editor of others. Among his books are *The Big Four: The Story of Huntington, Stanford, Hopkins, and Crocker* (Knopf, 1938); *Silver Kings* (Knopf, 1947); and *Here Lived the Californians* (Rinehart, 1957). He contributed articles to *Colophon* and wrote the introductions to various books of Western history and literature. He considered *High Sierra Country* one of the three more important of his books, the other two being *The Big Four* and *Silver Kings.*[6]

From 1948 to 1960, Lewis was a member of the San Francisco Art Com-

4. *The New York Times* (obituary), July 15, 1992, p. D19.
5. *Sutter's Fort: Gateway to the Gold Fields* (Prentice-Hall, Inc., 1966), "About The Author," following p. 222.
6. *Contemporary Authors New Revision Series, Volume 46* (1995), p. 223.

mission. He was a member of the Book Club of California for decades, serving as its secretary and editing its *Quarterly News Letter* at various times. He wrote *The First 75 Years: The Story of the Book Club of California, 1912-1987,* which was published by the Club in 1987. The Club's annual Oscar Lewis Awards recognize achievements in western history and the book arts.

Oscar Lewis died at his home in San Francisco on July 11, 1992, at age 99.

NOTES ON *HIGH SIERRA COUNTRY*

With the publication of *High Sierra Country,* Erskine Caldwell is no longer named as series editor on the title pages or the dust jackets of series titles, nor is a series editor named.

The endpaper maps in *High Sierra Country,* like those in *Adirondack Country,* are more detailed and conventional than those in the preceding twenty-four series titles.

REVIEWS

Booklist, November 1, 1955 (p. 100); *Christian Science Monitor,* August 25, 1955 (p. 11); *Kirkus,* May 15, 1955 (p. 340); *Library Journal,* August 1955 (1701); *New York Herald Tribune Book Review,* July 31, 1955 (p. 4); *New York Times Book Review,* October 2, 1955 (p. 12); *New Yorker,* October 1, 1955 (p. 145); *San Francisco Chronicle,* July 29, 1955 (p. 15).

SELECTED WRITINGS BY OSCAR LEWIS

Hearn and His Biographers (San Francisco: Westgate Press, 1930); *Lola Montez: The Mid-Victorian Bad Girl in California* (San Francisco: Colt Press, 1938); *The Big Four: The Story of Huntington, Stanford, Hopkins, and Crocker* (New York: Knopf, 1938); (with Carroll D. Hall) *Bonanza Inn* (New York: Knopf, 1939); *I Remember Christine* (New York: Knopf, 1942); *The Uncertain Journey* (New York: Knopf, 1945); *Silver Kings* (New York: Knopf, 1947); *Sea Routes to the Gold Fields* (New York: Knopf, 1949); *California Heritage* (New York: Crowell, 1949); *The Lost Years: A Biographical Fantasy* (New York: Knopf, 1951); *Sagebrush Casinos* (Garden City, N.Y.: Doubleday, 1953); *Hawaii, Gem of the Pacific* (New York: Random House, 1954); *George Davidson, Pioneer West Coast Scientist* (Berkeley: University of California Press, 1954); *The Town That Died Laughing* (Boston: Little, Brown, 1955); *The Story of California* (Garden City, N.Y.: Garden City Books, 1955); **High Sierra Country** (American Folkways Series) (New York: Duell, Sloan & Pearce, 1955); *Bay Window Bohemia: An Account of the Brilliant Artistic World of Gaslit San Francisco* (Garden City, N.Y.: Doubleday, 1956); *The Story of Ore-*

gon (Garden City, N.Y.: Garden City Books, 1957); *Here Lived the Californi-ans* (New York: Rinehart, 1957); *The War in the Far West: 1861-1865* (Garden City, N.Y.: Doubleday, 1961); *Sutter's Fort: Gateway to the Gold Fields* (American Forts Series) (Englewood Cliffs, N.J.: Prentice-Hall, 1966); *San Francisco: From Mission to Metropolis* (Berkeley, Calif.: Howell-North Books, 1966); *The Sacramento River* (New York: Holt, Rinehart & Winston, 1970); *To Remember Albert M. (Mickey) Bender: Notes for a Biography, with an appreciation by Elise S. Haas, R. Grabhorn & A. Hoyem* (Oakland, Calif., 1973); *The United States Conquest of California* (New York: Arno Press, 1976).; *The First 75 Years: The Story of the Book Club of California, 1912-1987* (San Francisco: Book Club of California, 1987); (ed., with Albert Sperisen) *California's Wayside Inns: Relics of Stagecoach Days* (San Francisco: Book Club of California, 1988).

SOURCES

Book Review Digest 1955. New York: The H.W. Wilson Company, 1956, p. 549.

The New York Times Book Review, October 2, 1955, p. 12.

The New York Times obituary, July 15, 1992, p. D19.

Publishers' Weekly, July 30, 1955, p. 485.

The Book Club of California Web page. www.bccbooks.org

"About the Author," following p. 222 of *Sutter's Fort: Gateway to the Gold Fields,* by Oscar Lewis (Englewood Cliffs, N.J.: Prentice-Hall, Inc., 1966).

Contemporary Authors New Revision Series, Vol. 46, Dean, Pamela S., Ed. Detroit, Gale Research Inc., 1995, p. 222.

Contemporary Authors Online, Gale, 2003. Reproduced in *Biography Resource Center.* Farmington Hills, Mich.: The Gale Group, 2003. Accessed March 16, 2003.

THE OTHER ILLINOIS

Baker Brownell
December 12, 1887 – April 5, 1965

AF12   First edition, first printing (1958) [28]

[within a rectangle with a thin black border, in black] [thin rule] | BAKER BROWNELL | [thin rule] | *THE OTHER* | *ILLINOIS* | [thin rule] [*Folkways* device] | DUELL, SLOAN & PEARCE | *New York* | [thin rule]

COLLATION: 8½" x 6". 144 leaves. [i–vi] vii [viii] [1–2] 3–261 [262] 263–276 [277–280]. Numbers printed in roman in headline at the outer margin of the type page, except for pp. vii, 3, 23, 34, 54, 76, 93, 116, 132, 152, 163, 179, 193, 216, 234, 254, 263, and 269, on which the numbers are printed in the center at the foot of the page.

CONTENTS: p. [i], blank; p. [ii], "AMERICAN FOLKWAYS | [list of 22 titles and their authors, beginning with *Golden Gate Country* and ending with *Far North Country*]"; p. [iii], half-title: "*The Other Illinois* | [thin rule]"; p. [iv], "*By the SAME AUTHOR* | [list of ten titles]; p. [v], title; p. [vi], copyright page: "COPYRIGHT © 1958 BY BAKER BROWNELL | All rights reserved. No part of this book in excess of | five hundred words may be reproduced in any form | without permission in writing from the publisher. | Library of Congress Catalog Card No. 58–6766 | *First Edition* | MANUFACTURED IN THE UNITED STATES OF AMERICA | VAN REES PRESS · NEW YORK"; p. vii, "Contents"; p. [viii], blank; p. [1], half-title: "*The Other Illinois* | [thin rule]"; p. [2], blank; pp. 3–261, text; p. [262], blank; pp. 263–268, "Notes"; pp. 269–276, "Index"; pp. [277–280], blank..

BINDING: Yellow cloth (close to Pantone 108). Spine: "[thick orange rule (close to Pantone 485)] | [four thin orange rules] | [within an orange panel, in gold] THE | OTHER | ILLINOIS | · | BAKER | BROWNELL | [four thin orange rules] | [thick orange rule] | [at bottom, in orange] DUELL, SLOAN | AND PEARCE. Light cream endpapers carry two maps in turquoise (close to Pantone 322) and light cream of Southern Illinois. On the left page is a map showing major highways and railroads; an inset of states contiguous to Illinois identifies the Southern Illinois region. The right page carries a map of Southern Illinois showing the Wilderness Trail route and the limit of physiographic regions.

DUST JACKET (white paper): A wide yellow band (close to Pantone 127) covers the top half of the jacket front, spine, and back; a wide orange band (close to Pantone 142) covers the bottom half of the jacket front, spine, and back. Front: "[on the left half of the wide yellow band is an orange-and-black photograph, which wraps to the spine and the right half of the wide yellow band on the jacket back, of children swimming in a mountain stream; high rocks in the background] [to the right of the photograph, on the wide yellow band, in black] *Baker | Brownell* | THE | OTHER | [printed half on the yellow band and half on the orange band, in black] ILLINOIS | [in the center of the wide orange band in black and yellow, is the *Folkways* device] | [three thin black rules wrap to the spine and the back] | [at lower right, a black-and-yellow photograph of three young people looking up at a stone wall through which a stream is flowing]". Spine: "[beneath the top photograph, within the wide yellow band, in black] *Brownell* | [within the wide orange band, in black] THE | OTHER | ILLINOIS | [at bottom, in black] Duell, Sloan | and Pearce". Back: "[upper right] [photograph wraps from front and spine] | [lower left] [black and yellow photograph of a lake or river; a bare tree in the foreground]". Front flap: White background; printing in black. "[upper right] $4.50 | *An American Folkways book* | THE OTHER ILLINOIS | *by* BAKER BROWNELL | [blurb, with brief biographical sketch of the author] | *Jacket by H. Lawrence Hoffman* | [publisher's imprint[1]]". Back flap: White background; printing in black. "*An American Folkways book* [upper right] $4.00 | OLD KENTUCKY COUNTRY | *by* CLARK McMEEKIN | [blurb] | [publisher's imprint]".

Published at $4.50 on February 18, 1958; number of copies printed unknown. Copyrighted and deposited on June 18, 1958.

The book is not listed in "The Weekly Record."

Note: No evidence found that Duell, Sloan & Pearce reprinted *The Other Illinois*.

COPIES: CF

REPRINTS AND REPRODUCTIONS

None.

1. Little, Brown has been dropped from the publisher's imprint for this title. Only Duell, Sloan and Pearce is noted.

BIOGRAPHY

Baker Brownell was born in St. Charles, Illinois, on December 12, 1887, the son of Eugene A. and Esther Burr Baker Brownell.

Brownell attended public schools in St. Charles. In 1910, he earned a bachelor's degree from Northwestern University, having completed his last undergraduate year at Harvard, where he earned a master's degree in philosophy in 1911. In 1912, at Harvard, he was named a James Walker Traveling Fellow in Philosophy. He traveled to Europe and attended Tuebingen University in Germany (1912–1913) and Cambridge University in England in 1913.

Later in 1913, he worked as an editorial writer for the *Chicago Tribune.* From 1914 until 1917 he lived in Emporia, Kansas, where he taught English at the Kansas State Normal College and edited the journal *Teaching.*

In 1916, he married Helena Maxwell. The marriage ended in divorce. In 1933, he married Adelaide Howard. The couple had a son, Eugene Howard.

In 1916, President Wilson called out the U.S. Army and mobilized the National Guard after the attack on an American border town by Mexican marauders. At the time, Brownell served in the Army as a sergeant. In World War I, he served in the Army as a lieutenant and later in the Navy as an ensign.

Brownell was an assistant professor of English at the University of Idaho (1919–1920), after which he returned to Chicago and worked as an editorial writer for the *Chicago Daily News.* In 1921, he joined the Northwestern University faculty. He was professor of contemporary thought in the School of Journalism (1925–1934) and in the College of Liberal Arts (1934–1947). From 1947 until 1953, he was professor of philosophy, becoming professor emeritus in 1953. He later made his home in Fairhope, Alabama, where he lived until his death.

Brownell's course in Contemporary Thought at Northwestern, one of the first of its kind, included weekly lectures by experts in a wide variety of fields of research and scholarship. He was the editor of a twelve-volume work, *Man and His World* (Van Nostrand, 1929), sixty lectures delivered in his Contemporary Thought course. He wrote or was co-author of ten books. His book *Architecture and Modern Life* (Harper, 1937) was written with Frank Lloyd Wright.

Baker Brownell died in Fairhope, Alabama, on April 5, 1965, at age 77.

PAPERS: Baker Brownell's papers are held at the University Library, Northwestern University, University Archives, Evanston, Illinois.

NOTES ON *THE OTHER ILLINOIS*

The book is the final volume in the *American Folkways* series and differs in design from earlier books in the series. It is a compilation of fifteen essays written by Baker Brownell, each presented as a separate chapter. (Chapter 15 concludes with a number of acknowledgments.) As in *High Sierra Country* and *Old Kentucky Country*, the two preceding volumes in the series, no series editor is named. And, as in those two volumes and *Adirondack Country*, the endpaper maps are more detailed and conventional than those in the preceding twenty-four volumes.

REVIEWS

Chicago Sunday Tribune, February 23, 1958 (p. 3); *Kirkus*, January 1, 1958 (p. 27); *New York Times Book Review*, April 6, 1958 (p. 3).

SELECTED WRITINGS BY BAKER BROWNELL

The New Universe: An Outline of the Worlds in which We Live (New York: D. Van Nostrand, 1926); *Earth Is Enough: An Essay on Religious Realism* (New York: Harper, 1933); (with Frank Lloyd Wright) *Architecture and Modern Life* (New York: Harper, 1937); *Art is Action: A Discussion of Nine Arts in A Modern World* (New York: Harper, 1939); *The Philosopher in Chaos: An Attempt to Make Head and Tail of the Modern World* (New York: D. Van Nostrand, 1941); *The Human Community: Its Philosophy and Practice in a Time of Crisis* (New York: Harper, 1950); *The College and the Community: A Critical Study of Higher Education* (New York: Harper, 1952); **The Other Illinois** (New York: Duell, Sloan & Pearce, 1958).

SOURCES

Book Review Digest 1958. New York: The H.W. Wilson Company, 1959, p. 158.

The New York Times Book Review, April 6, 1958, p. 3.

Publishers' Weekly, January 27, 1958 (Duell, Sloan and Pearce Spring List), p. 38.

Lentz, E. G., Southern Illinois University. Review of *The Other Illinois*. *Journal of the Illinois State Historical Society*, Volume LI, Number 2, Summer 1958, n.p.

Fairhope (Alabama) *Courier* obituary, April 8, 1965, n.p.

Chicago Sun-Times obituary, April 8, 1965, n.p.

US Border Patrol Beginning, www.usborderpatrol.com, accessed July 1, 2006.

Baker Brownell Papers, Series 12/13, Northwestern University Archives, Evanston, Il.

Olson, Janet C., Assistant University Archivist, University Library, Northwestern University, Letter to CF, April 10, 2003, and research materials on Baker Brownell.

OLD KENTUCKY COUNTRY

Clark McMeekin

Dorothy Park Clark
September 14, 1899 – June 23, 1983
and
Isabel McLennan McMeekin
November 19, 1895 – September 4, 1973

AF13   First edition, first printing (1957) [27]

[within a rectangle with a thin black border, in black] [thin rule] I CLARK McMEEKIN I [thin rule] I *OLD KENTUCKY I COUNTRY* I [thin rule] [*Folkways* device] I DUELL, SLOAN & PEARCE I *New York* I [thin rule].

COLLATION: 8½" x 6". 112 leaves. [i–vi] vii–ix [x] [1–2] 3–214. Numbers printed in roman in headline at the outer margin of the type page, except for pp. vii, 3, 16, 29, 43, 57, 71, 79, 92, 103, 112, 124, 134, 147, 164, 175, 188, 198, and 209, on which the numbers are printed in the center at the foot of the page.

CONTENTS: p. [i], blank; p. [ii], "AMERICAN FOLKWAYS I [list of 21 titles and their authors, beginning with *Golden Gate Country* and ending with *Far North Country*]"; p. [iii], half-title: "*Old Kentucky Country* I [thin rule]"; p. [iv], "*By* CLARK McMEEKIN I [list of 11 titles]; p. [v], title; p. [vi], copyright page: "COPYRIGHT © 1957 *by* DUELL, SLOAN & PEARCE, INC. I All rights reserved. No part of this book in excess of I five hundred words may be reproduced in any form I without permission in writing from the publisher. I

Library of Congress Catalog Card No. 57-7574 | *First Edition* | MANUFAC-
TURED IN THE UNITED STATES OF AMERICA | VAN REES PRESS ·
NEW YORK"; pp. vii–ix, "Contents"; p. [x], dedication: "TO ALL OTHER
KENTUCKIANS, OUR KITH AND KIN. | TO THE MEN, WOMEN, AND
CHILDREN WHOM WE HAVE NOT | MENTIONED IN THIS BOOK. |
TO THE DREAMERS AND THE DOERS, THE PLODDERS AND THE |
PROFLIGATES, WHO ADDED THEIR WHOLESOME SALT AND THEIR
| PUNGENT SPICE TO THE FEAST OF HISTORY."; p. [1], half-title: "*Old
Kentucky Country* | [thin rule]"; p. [2], blank; pp. 3–208, text; pp. 209–214,"In-
dex".

BINDING: Medium green cloth (close to Pantone 363). Spine: "[thick dark
green rule (close to Pantone 343)] | [four thin dark green rules] | [within a
dark green panel, in gold] OLD | KENTUCKY | COUNTRY | · | CLARK |
McMEEKIN | [four thin dark green rules] | [thick dark green rule] | [at bot-
tom, in gold] DUELL, SLOAN | AND PEARCE. Light cream endpapers carry
a double-page map of Kentucky in blue-green (close to Pantone 340) and
light cream by D.T. Pitcher titled "Old Kentucky Country"; the upper left
quadrant carries a map of the Northeast and Midwest states, with Kentucky
shaded; the right page carries a drawing of a cardinal, the state bird, and
drawing of a log house with smoke rising from a chimney. Below the map is
a drawing of a long gun and below that a "Scale of Miles."

DUST JACKET (white paper): Front: "[black-and white photograph wraps
to the spine; a scene of grazing horses; tall trees in the background] | [thin
white rule, which wraps to the back cover] | [medium green band (close to
Pantone 359), which wraps to the back cover; on the far right side of the
green band the *Folkways* device is overlaid in the center] | [within a dark
green band in white, shaded in black] OLD KENTUCKY | COUNTRY |
[medium green] BY CLARK McMEEKIN". Spine: "[within the bottom dark
green band in white, shaded in black] OLD | KENTUCKY | COUNTRY |
[black] CLARK | McMEEKIN | DUELL, SLOAN | AND PEARCE". Back:
"[black-and-white photograph of a river cascading over rocks to form a wa-
terfall; trees in the background and foreground] | [thin white rule] | [printed
on the medium green band, which wraps from the front, in black] Pho-
tographs courtesy of Caufield and Shook, Louisville, Kentucky | [within a
white band, in black] AMERICAN FOLKWAYS | [two-column list of 21 ti-
tles and their authors, beginning with *Golden Gate Country* and ending with
Far North Country]". Front flap: White background; printing in black. "[up-
per left] *An American Folkways book* [upper right] $4.00 | OLD KENTUCKY
COUNTRY | *by* CLARK McMEEKIN | [blurb] | [publisher's imprint[1]]". Back

1. "Little, Brown and Company" has been dropped from the publisher's imprint for this
title. Only Duell, Sloan and Pearce is named.

flap: White background; printing in black. "[black-and-white photograph of Clark McMeekin, identified as Dorothy Park Clark and Isabel McLennan McMeekin] | [brief biographical sketches of the authors]".

Published at $4.00 on May 16, 1957; number of copies printed unknown. Copyrighted and deposited November 12, 1957.

The book is listed in "The Weekly Record," June 3, 1957, p. 112.

Note: No evidence found that Duell, Sloan & Pearce reprinted *Old Kentucky Country*.

COPIES: CF

REPRINTS AND REPRODUCTIONS

None.

BIOGRAPHIES

Clark McMeekin was the pen name of the writing team of Dorothy Park Clark and Isabel McLennan McMeekin, who lived and wrote in Louisville, Kentucky. Working individually, the two had published mysteries, short stories, and children's books under their own names, but they did not become widely recognized and successful until they began to write together as Clark McMeekin.

In the mid-1930s, in their first collaboration, Clark and McMeekin produced a novel but were unable to find a willing publisher. Undaunted, in 1938 they began research for *Show Me a Land*, finishing it a year later. The book was immediately accepted for publication by Appleton-Century in 1940, received good reviews, and became a best-seller. From 1940 to 1961, the Clark McMeekin team produced twelve successful historical novels, two plays, and several local histories. During World War II, two of their books, *Red Raskall* (1943) and *Black Moon* (1945), both published by Appleton-Century, were issued in Armed Services Editions.

≈

Dorothy Dowden Park Clark was born on September 14, 1899, in Osceola, Iowa, the daughter of William Herbert Park, a lawyer, and Eugenia Christy (Dowden) Park.

After her father's death when she was four, Park lived with her mother and sister, Pauline, in the Kentucky Bluegrass country, not far from Lexington, and later lived in Frankfort, where Park graduated from high school. She attended Randolph-Macon Woman's College in Lynchburg, Virginia, for two years, and, from 1919 to 1922, the College of Music in Cincinnati, Ohio, preparing for a career as a music teacher in the Louisville public schools. She later took several courses at Columbia University.

On September 1, 1923, she married Edward Reep Clark, an accountant. The couple had two daughters, Christy and Martha.

Clark began to write when she was nine. She wrote twenty mystery and romantic pulp-fiction stories in the late 1920s and early 1930s as well as puppet plays and two operettas. Her stories appeared in *Liberty, Coronet, Maclean's,* and other periodicals. She wrote three mystery novels published in the late 1940s and 1950.[2] She was best known, however, as the "Clark" in "Clark McMeekin."

Dorothy Park Clark died on June 23, 1983, In Louisville, Kentucky, at age 82.

∾

Isabel Stewart McLennan McMeekin was born on November 19, 1895, in Louisville, Kentucky, the daughter of Alexander McLennan, a Scottish-Canadian, and Margaret Rosannah (Harbison) McLennan. Her father died when she was two.

McMeekin's maternal ancestors were among the founders and earliest settlers of Louisville. She grew up in Louisville and attended Westover, a boarding school in Middlebury, Connecticut, graduating in 1914. She later attended the University of Chicago for a year. McMeekin spent a summer teaching at a branch of the Pine Mountain School, and would later write that her experience there led her to the writing of poems, children's plays, juvenile books, and, in time, historical novels and collaborative works.[3]

On April 11, 1921, she married Samuel Head McMeekin, an executive at Churchill Downs, the site of the Kentucky Derby. The couple had three children, a son and two daughters.

Beginning in 1929, McMeekin wrote books dealing with cooking, horticulture, and histories of pioneer days. *Journey Cake* (J. Messner, 1942), her first book for children, won the Julia Ellsworth Ford Award for children's books. She wrote *Louisville: the Gateway City* (J. Messner, 1946), a title in the *Cities of America Biographies* series.

Isabel McMeekin died in Louisville, Kentucky, on September 4, 1973, at age 77.

PAPERS: Some of the papers of Isabel McLennan McMeekin, 1960-1972, are held by the Filson Historical Society. A\M167.

2. *Current Biography Yearbook,* 1957 (H. W. Wilson Company), pp. 348–349.
3. Ibid., p. 347.

NOTES ON *OLD KENTUCKY COUNTRY*

Unlike *Smoky Mountain Country, Adirondack Country,* and *High Sierra Country,* the preceding three titles in the Folkways series, the book does not name Little, Brown and Company as publisher or co-publisher. Further, as in *High Sierra Country,* no series editor is named.

The endpaper maps in the book, like those in *Adirondack Country* and *High Sierra Country,* are more detailed and conventional than those in the twenty-four earlier series volumes.

The book was included in the 1957 Duell, Sloan & Pearce Spring List, with a planned April publication.

REVIEWS

Booklist, September 1, 1957 (p. 17); *Kirkus,* April 15, 1957 (p. 319); *Library Journal,* June 1, 1957 (p. 1532); *New York Herald Tribune Book Review,* July 14, 1957 (p. 3).

SELECTED WRITINGS BY CLARK McMEEKIN

Show Me A Land (New York: Appleton-Century, 1940); *Reckon with the River* (New York: Appleton-Century, 1941); *Welcome Soldier* (New York: Appleton-Century, 1942); *Red Raskall* (New York: Appleton-Century, 1943); *Black Moon* (New York: Appleton Century, 1945); *Gaudy's Ladies* (New York: Appleton-Century-Crofts, 1948); *City of the Flags* (New York: Appleton-Century-Crofts, 1950); *Room at the Inn* (New York: Putnam, 1953); *Tyrone of Kentucky* (New York: Appleton-Century-Crofts, 1954); *The October Fox* (New York: Putnam, 1956); **Old Kentucky Country** (New York: Duell, Sloan & Pearce, 1957); *The Fairbrothers* (New York: Putnam, 1961).

SOURCES

Book Review Digest 1957. New York: The H.W. Wilson Company, 1958, p. 591.

New York Herald Tribune Book Review, July 14, 1957, p. 3.

Publishers' Weekly, June 20, 1942, p. 2285 (Julia Ellsworth Ford Foundation Award to McMeekin); January 28, 1957 (Duell, Sloan and Pearce Spring List), p. 35; and June 3, 1957, p. 112.

Candee, Marjorie Dent. *Current Biography Yearbook.* New York: The H.W. Wilson Company, 1957, 1958, pp. 347–349.

Kreke, Jean, Telereference Department, Louisville Free Public Library. E-mail message to CF regarding Clark McMeekin entry in the *Encyclopedia of Louisville,* March 25, 2003.

Kleber, John E., ed. (with others). *Encyclopedia of Louisville*. Entry for Clark McMeekin. Lexington, Ky.: University Press of Kentucky, 2000, pp. 601–602.

LOWER PIEDMONT COUNTRY

H.C. Nixon
December 29, 1886 – August, 10, 1967

AF14   First edition, first printing (1946) [15]

[*Folkways* device] | [within a rust (close to Pantone 207) rectangle with rounded corners, in cream] EDITED BY ERSKINE CALDWELL | [black] LOWER | PIEDMONT | COUNTRY | *by* | H.C. NIXON | [cream] DUELL, SLOAN & PEARCE · NEW YORK

COLLATION: 8½" x 6". 135 leaves. [i–viii] ix–xi [xii] xiii–xxiii [xxiv] [1–2] 3–244 | [245–246]. Numbers printed in roman in the center at the foot of the page.

CONTENTS: p. [i], half-title: "LOWER PIED-MONT COUNTRY"; p. [ii], "AMERICAN FOLK-WAYS | *Edited by* ERSKINE CALDWELL | [list of fifteen titles and their authors, beginning with *Golden Gate Country* and ending with *Far North Country*] | *In Preparation* | [list of ten titles and their authors[1]]"; p. [iii], title; p. [iv], copyright page: "COPYRIGHT, 1946, BY | H.C. NIXON | All rights reserved, including | the right to reproduce this book | or portions thereof in any form. | *First Printing* | PRINTED IN THE UNITED STATES OF AMER-ICA | BY J.J. LITTLE & IVES COMPANY, NEW YORK; p. [v], dedication: "*To* | *the Memory of* | MY PARENTS | *of* | *Piedmont, Alabama* | *R.F.D.*"; p. [vi], blank; p. [vii], "Contents"; p. [viii], blank; pp. ix–xi, "Acknowledg-ments"; p. [xii], blank; pp. xiii–xxiii, "Foreword"; p. [xxiv], blank; p. [1], sec-

---

1. The list includes *Buckeye Country* by Louis Bromfield, *Rip Van Winkle Country* by Howard Fast, *Piney Woods Country* by John Faulkner, *Great Lakes Country* by Iola Fuller, *Pacific Northwest Country* by Richard Neuberger, *Tidewater Country* by Elswyth Thane, *Gold Rush Country* by Charis Weston, and *Mile-High Country* by Helen Worden, none of which were published in the series, and *Corn Country* by Homer Croy and *Big Country* by Donald Day, both of which were published in the series.

ond half-title: "LOWER PIEDMONT COUNTRY"; p. [2], blank; pp. 3–233, text; pp. 234–238, "Book Notes"; pp. 239–244, "Index"; pp. [245–246], blank.

BINDING: Taupe cloth (close to Pantone 452). Front: *Folkways* device stamped in rust (close to Pantone 484) at lower right corner. Spine stamped in rust, except where noted: "[thick rule] | [four thin rules] | [within a rust panel, in gold] LOWER | PIEDMONT | COUNTRY | [thin rule] | NIXON | [four thin rules] | [thick rule] | [four thin rules] | [at bottom] [four thin rules | [within a rust panel, in gold] DUELL, SLOAN | AND PEARCE | [four thin rules] | [thick rule]". Cream endpapers.

DUST JACKET (white paper): Front: "[rust background (close to Pantone 704) [white] Lower Piedmont | Country | [black-and-white photograph of a house in the "hills" within an irregular black and light green (close to Pantone 441) rectangular frame] | [black] AMERICAN FOLKWAYS | [grey] H.C. NIXON". Spine: "[light green background] [rust] LOWER | PIEDMONT | COUNTRY | [black] NIXON | [*Folkways* device in black and light green] | [rust] DUELL, SLOAN | AND PEARCE". Back: "[white background; printing in black] SOUTHERN CALIFORNIA COUNTRY | *An Island on the Land* | by Carey McWilliams | [quotes from five reviews] | $3.75 | *An American Folkways book* | [publisher's imprint]". Front flap: White background; printing in black. "[upper right] $3.00 | quote from the text | LOWER PIEDMONT | COUNTRY | by H.C. Nixon | [blurb] | *An American Folkways book* | [publisher's imprint]". Back flap: White background; printing in black. "$3.00 | [quote from *Short Grass Country*] | Short Grass Country | *by* STANLEY VESTAL | [blurb] | [publisher's imprint]".

Published at $3.00 on November 8, 1946; number of copies printed unknown. Copyrighted November 22, 1946; deposited November 15, 1946.

The book is listed in "The Weekly Record," November 30, 1946, p. 3032.

Note: No evidence found that Duell, Sloan & Pearce reprinted *Lower Piedmont Country.*

COPIES: CF

REPRINTS AND REPRODUCTIONS

Freeport, N.Y.: Books for Libraries Press, 1971. Essay Index Reprint Series. Published at $10.50.

Reprinted as *Lower Piedmont Country: The Uplands of the Deep South*, with a new Introduction and bibliography by Sarah N. Shouse. University, Ala.: The University of Alabama Press, April 27, 1984. Published at $21.75; paperback, $9.95.

Electronic reproduction. Boulder, Colo.: NetLibrary, Inc., 2000. (An electronic book accessible through the World Wide Web) http://www.netLi-brary.com/urlapi.ask?action=summary&v=1&bookid=20243

BIOGRAPHY

Herman Clarence Nixon was born in Merrellton, Alabama, on December 29, 1886, the son of William Dawson Nixon, a teacher and farmer who operated a successful country store, and Nancy (Green) Nixon.

President Arthur had appointed William Nixon the Merrellton postmaster in 1885. The Nixon country store, at the "Junction," where the Southern and Seaboard railroads crossed, became a center of community life, serving as country store, post office, and railroad station. Nixon's mother, who encouraged him to read and write, shared family and community history with him, but the store was the foundation of his education and it was there that he absorbed the folkways and lifestyles of "Possum Trot," the name he chose for his boyhood community in his book, *Possum Trot: Rural Community, South* (University of Oklahoma Press, 1941).

In 1903 Nixon enrolled at the State Normal School in Jacksonville, Alabama, graduating in 1907. He then attended Alabama Polytechnic Institute in Auburn (now Auburn University), earning a bachelor's degree in 1909 and a master's degree in history in 1910.

Back in Merrellton, Nixon joined the faculty of Jacksonville State Normal School as assistant professor of English, also teaching French, German, and Latin. While there he was the school correspondent for an Anniston, Alabama newspaper. In 1913, he received a scholarship from the University of Chicago, which he attended intermittently over the next twelve years, earning a doctorate (magna cum laude) in 1925.

In World War I, Nixon joined the Army in 1917, serving in an ordnance unit that sailed for France in July 1918. After the Armistice, he was accepted into the American Peace Commission in Paris. He returned to the U.S. in December 1919.

In 1925, Nixon joined the Vanderbilt University faculty as assistant professor of history. In 1928, he became an associate professor of history at Tulane University; and, within five years, full professor and department chairman. He resigned from Tulane in 1938. From 1938 to 1940, he was a visiting professor at the University of Missouri, returning to Vanderbilt in 1940. He was promoted to full professor in 1953 and retired in 1955.

Nixon married Anne Richardson Trice on June 16, 1927. The couple had three children.

Nixon was one of twelve contributors to *I'll Take My Stand: The South and the Agrarian Tradition* (Harper & Brothers, 1930). In the book, Nixon joined other Southern intellectuals to present a critique of the modern world, "a rebuke to materialism, a corrective to the worship of Progress, and a reaffirmation of man's aesthetic and spiritual needs."[2]

Nixon played key roles in support of President Roosevelt's assistance to the South during the Great Depression. He supported the creation of the Tennessee Valley Authority and the Subsistence Homesteads program and was one of the organizers of the Southern Conference for Human Welfare. During these years, he was a strong and active supporter of many liberal, progressive initiatives designed to relieve poverty and promote social justice, often in the face of hostile opposition.[3]

Herman Clarence Nixon died in Nashville, Tennessee, on August 10, 1967, at age 80.

PAPERS: A portion of Herman Clarence Nixon's papers is held by Vanderbilt University.

NOTES ON *LOWER PIEDMONT COUNTRY*

In her biography of Clarence Nixon, *Hillbilly Realist,* Sarah Newman Shouse reported that Erskine Caldwell had read Nixon's *Possum Trot . . .* and asked Nixon, a native Alabamian, to write on the region enclosed in the triangle formed by Atlanta, Birmingham, and Chattanooga. Nixon worked on the manuscript through 1945. When the publisher Charles Pearce read Nixon's first draft, he wrote, "It's good stuff certainly, up to the best that has so far appeared in the Folkways Series. I guess I have only one criticism and that is that there isn't more of it."[4]

REVIEWS

Book Week, December 8, 1946 (p. 20); *Booklist,* January 15, 1947 (p. 150); *Christian Science Monitor,* December 21, 1946 (p. 14); *Kirkus,* September 15, 1946 (p. 479); *Library Journal,* November 1, 1946 (p. 1540); *Weekly Book Review,* January 5, 1947 (p. 5).

SELECTED WRITINGS BY H.C. NIXON

Alexander Beaufort Meek (Auburn: Alabama Polytechnic Institute Historical Studies, 1910); *Social Security for Southern Farmers* (Southern Policy Paper No. 2) (Chapel Hill: University of North Carolina Press, 1936); *Forty Acres and Steel Mules* (Chapel Hill: University of North Carolina Press, 1938);

2. Rubin, Louis D., Jr. Introduction to the Torchbook Edition (Harper & Row,1962) of *I'll Take My Stand: The South and the Agrarian Tradition,* p. xiv.
3. Harwell, Sara. "Herman Clarence Nixon, 1886–1967." *The Tennessee Encyclopedia of History and Culture.* Nashville: Tennessee Historical Society, 1998.
4. Shouse, Sarah Newman. "Hillbilly Realist: Herman Clarence Nixon of Possum Trot." University of Alabama Press, 1986, p.159.

Possum Trot: Rural Community, South (Norman: University of Oklahoma Press, 1941); *The Tennessee Valley: A Recreation Domain* (Nashville: Vanderbilt University Press, 1945); **Lower Piedmont Country** (New York: Duell, Sloan & Pearce, 1946); *American Federal Government: A General View* (New York: Scribner, 1952).

Nixon's work was widely published in historical reviews, quarterlies, and journals, including the *Virginia Quarterly Review, Journal of Politics,* and *Journal of Southern History.* As noted, Nixon was a contributor to *I'll Take My Stand: The South and the Agrarian Tradition by Twelve Southerners* (Harper & Brothers, 1930).

SOURCES

Book Review Digest 1946 New York: The H.W. Wilson Company, 1947, p. 614.

Publishers' Weekly, October 5, 1946, p. 1719; and November 30, 1946, p. 3032.

New York Herald Tribune Weekly Book Review, January 5, 1947, p. 5.

I'll Take My Stand: The South and the Agrarian Tradition by Twelve Southerners. New York: Harper Torchbooks. The Academy Library. Harper & Row, 1962.

Shouse, Sarah Newman. *Hillbilly Realist: Herman Clarence Nixon of Possum Trot.* University, Ala.: The University of Alabama Press, 1984.

Harwell, Sara. "Herman Clarence Nixon, 1886–1967." *The Tennessee Encyclopedia of History and Culture.* Nashville: Tennessee Historical Society, 1998.

MORMON COUNTRY

Wallace Stegner
February 18, 1909 – April 13, 1993

AF15   First edition, first printing (1942) [7]

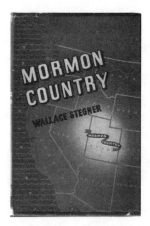

[*Folkways* device] | [within a dark turquoise (close to Pantone 323) rectangle with rounded corners, in cream] EDITED BY ERSKINE CALDWELL | [black] MORMON | COUNTRY | *by* | WALLACE STEGNER | [cream] DUELL, SLOAN & PEARCE · NEW YORK

COLLATION: 8½" x 6". 186 leaves. [i–viii] ix–x [1–2] 3–235 [236–238] 239–349 [350] 351–362. Numbers printed in roman in headline at the outer margin of the type page, except for pp. ix, 3, 21, 25, 33, 52, 57, 72, 84, 100, 108, 128, 136, 142, 171, 182, 187, 209, 227, 239, 251, 259, 269, 281, 293, 302, 319, 331, 344, and 351, on which the numbers are printed in the center, at the foot of the page.

CONTENTS: p. [i], half-title: "MORMON COUNTRY"; p. [ii], "AMERICAN FOLKWAYS | Edited by ERSKINE CALDWELL | [thin rule] | [list of eight titles and their authors, beginning with *Desert Country* and ending with *Palmetto Country*] | In Preparation | [list of two titles and their authors[1]]"; p. [iii], title; p. [iv], copyright page: "COPYRIGHT, 1942, BY | WALLACE STEGNER | *All rights reserved, including | the right to reproduce this book | or portions thereof in any form.* | *first edition* | PRINTED IN THE UNITED STATES OF AMERICA"; p. [v], dedication: "*For Mary, as all of them are.*"; p. [vi], blank; p. [vii], "Acknowledgments"; p. [viii], blank; pp. ix–x, "Contents"; p. [1], "PART I | THE ROCK OUR FATHERS PLANTED"; p. [2], blank; pp. 3–235, text; p. [236], blank; p. [237], "PART II | THE MIGHT OF THE GENTILE"; p. [238], blank; pp. 239–349, text; p. [350], blank; pp. 351–362, "Index".

1. The two titles listed are: *Black Jack Country*, by George Milburn, and *Delta Country*, by E. P. O'Donnell. *Black Jack Country* is not a title in the series, nor did George Milburn write a book in the series. *Delta Country* was published as *Deep Delta Country* and written by Harnett Kane. E. P. O'Donnell did not write a book in the series.

BINDING: Burgundy cloth (close to Pantone 194). Front: *Folkways* device stamped in black at lower right corner. Spine stamped in black, except where noted: "[thick rule] | [four thin rules] | [within a black panel, in gold] MOR-MON | COUNTRY | · | WALLACE | STEGNER | [four thin rules] | [thick rule] | [four thin rules] | [at bottom] [four thin rules | [within a black panel, in gold] DUELL, SLOAN | AND PEARCE | [four thin rules] | [thick rule]". Light cream endpapers carry map of the United States in dark turquoise and cream; "Mormon Country" region is shaded in cream and further identified on a ribbon-like banner.

DUST JACKET (cream paper): Front carries the map of the western portion of the United States found on the endpapers, in dark turquoise, with the 'Mormon Country' region highlighted in cream. "[thick burgundy rule (close to Pantone 195)] | [white, outlined in burgundy] MORMON | COUN-TRY | [solid burgundy] WALLACE STEGNER | [printed on a turquoise ribbon, in cream] MORMON COUNTRY [thick burgundy rule]". Spine: "[thick burgundy rule] [four thin burgundy rules on a cream band] | [burgundy, on dark turquoise] MORMON | COUNTRY | [cream] · | WALLACE | STEGNER | [burgundy] [four thin rules, thick rule, four thin rules, with the *Folkways* device overlaid in the center] | [drawing of three tall trees (Lombardy poplars) in dark turquoise on a cream background] | [four thin burgundy rules] | [within a burgundy panel, in cream] DUELL, SLOAN | AND PEARCE | [four thin burgundy rules] | [thick burgundy rule]". Back: "[cream background] [within an arced ribbon, in burgundy] AMERICAN FOLKWAYS | [dark turquoise] *Edited by* | Erskine Caldwell | [blurb] | [burgundy] READY | [turquoise] [list of eight titles and their authors; the first four of these titles are further described on the back flap] | [burgundy] IN PREPARATION | [dark turquoise] [list of two titles and their authors, with a brief description of each[2] | [burgundy] *Each Volume, $3.00* | [turquoise] [publisher's imprint]". Front flap: "[dark turquoise] [upper right] $3.00 | [burgundy] Mormon Country | [turquoise] *by* WALLACE STEGNER | [blurb] | [publisher's imprint]". Back flap: "[burgundy] Desert Country | [dark turquoise] *by* EDWIN CORLE [quotes from two reviews] | [burgundy] High Border Country | [turquoise] *by* ERIC THANE | [quote from a review] | [burgundy] Piñon Country | [dark turquoise] *by* HANIEL LONG | [quote from a review] | [burgundy] Short Grass Country | [dark turquoise] *by* STANLEY VESTAL | [quote from a review] | [burgundy] *Each Volume, $3.00* | [dark turquoise] [publisher's imprint]".

Published at $3.00 on September 24, 1942; number of copies printed unknown. Copyrighted September 28, 1942; deposited September 25, 1942.

2. See Note 1, above.

The book is listed in "The Weekly Record," October 10, 1942, p. 1608.

Note: Duell, Sloan & Pearce published at least four printings of *Mormon Country.*

CITED: Paher 1863; Colberg A6.1.a

COPIES: CF

REPRINTS AND REPRODUCTIONS

New York: Bonanza Books, 1968. At least two printings.

New York: Hawthorn Books, 1975. Paperback. Published at $3.95.

Lincoln: University of Nebraska Press, 1981. A Bison Book. Paperback. Published at $6.95; at least eight printings.

Lincoln: University of Nebraska Press, September 1, 2003. Paperback Published at $15.00. With a new introduction by Richard W. Etulain.

Reproduced on microfilm. New Haven, Conn.: Yale University Library, 1993. 1 reel. 35 mm.

BIOGRAPHY

Wallace Earle Stegner was born on February 18, 1909, in Lake Mills, Iowa, the son of George H. and Hilda (Paulson) Stegner, who were Scandinavian immigrants. During the first twelve years of Stegner's life, his father moved the family to North Dakota, Washington, Saskatchewan, Montana, and Wyoming before settling in Salt Lake City in 1921. Stegner attended public school in Salt Lake City and later worked his way through the University of Utah, earning a bachelor of arts degree in 1930. He undertook graduate study at the University of Iowa, earning a master of arts degree in 1932 and a doctorate in 1935.

On September 1, 1934, Stegner married Mary Stuart Page. The couple had a son, Stuart Page.

At various times from 1930 to 1937, Stegner served as an instructor at Augustana College in Illinois and at the University of Utah at Salt Lake City. In 1937, he taught at the University of Wisconsin. From 1939 to 1945 he was the Briggs-Copeland Instructor of Composition at Harvard University. In 1945 he began teaching English, creative writing, and literature at Stanford University, founding the university's prestigious Creative Writing Center and serving as its director until 1971, when he left and began to devote his time to writing.

Stegner's first novel, *Remembering Laughter*, was published in 1937. The book, which recounts an adulterous triangle on an Iowa farm, won the first prize, $2,500, in a contest sponsored by Little, Brown and Company. He later wrote other books, including *Mormon Country*, his first non-fiction work. He achieved national recognition in 1943 with the publication of *The Big Rock Candy Mountain* (Duell, Sloan & Pearce), a semi–autobiographical novel in which two brothers come to grips with their lives after finally understanding their father's failings.

Many years after the publication of *The Big Rock Candy Mountain*, Stegner published a collection of his short stories and essays, *Where the Bluebird Sings to the Lemonade Springs* (subtitled *Living and Writing in the West*) (Viking, 1992). Both titles are taken from the well-known hobo's song about the imaginary land of the good life, "the land of milk and honey ... and you don't need any money."

After Stegner left Stanford in 1971, he wrote *Angle of Repose* (Doubleday, 1971). In 1972, the book won the Pulitzer Prize for fiction. It was adapted as an opera by Andrew Imbrie and Oakley Hall and produced by the San Francisco Opera Company in 1976.

The American West was a player in Stegner's work for more than fifty years. He was a fervent environmentalist, with a complex view of the West. "The West does not need to explore its myths much further; it has relied on them too long," he told a reporter in 1981. "The West is politically reactionary and exploitative: admit it. The West as a whole is guilty of inexplicable crimes against the land: admit that, too. The West is rootless, culturally half-baked. So be it." But despite all this, he continued, the West remains "the New World's last chance to be something better, the only American society still malleable enough to be formed."[3]

Stegner's awards and recognition include O. Henry Awards in 1942, 1950, and 1954; and, in 1945, the Houghton-Mifflin Life-in-America Award. He won the Ainsfield Wolfe Award for his work on *One Nation*, a photographic study of racial and religious prejudice among ethnic groups in the United States, which was initiated by the editors of *Look* and for which Stegner wrote the text. In 1977, he won the National Book Award for *The Spectator Bird*. He received Guggenheim Fellowships in 1950 and 1959 and a Rockefeller Fellowship in 1950-1951. In 1967, he received a Gold Medal from the Commonwealth Club of California for *All the Little Live Things* and, in 1976, a second Gold Medal, for *The Spectator Bird*. He received at least seven honorary doctorates.

Stegner was deeply involved in the conservation movement and in environmental causes. In 1961, he accepted an invitation to be an assistant to Stewart Udall, the U.S. Secretary of the Interior. While he held the post for

3. *The New York Times*, April 15, 1993, Page A1 (obituary).

only three months, his research there resulted in Udall's writing of *The Quiet Crisis* (1963), an overview of the conservation movement and the condition of the nation's forests, prairies, swamps, and deserts. Udall later appointed Stegner to the National Parks Advisory Board; he was a board member from 1962 to 1966 and chairman during his last year there. Still later, he served a three-year term on the Board of Directors of the Sierra Club, with which he maintained an affiliation for nearly forty years.

In a speech Stegner delivered in 1960, he said, in part, "I want to speak for the wilderness idea as something that has helped form our character and that has certainly shaped our history as a people. Something will have gone out of us as a people if we ever let the remaining wilderness be destroyed." These few words became a mission statement for conservationists and were used to introduce the bill that established the National Wilderness Preservation System in 1964.

Stegner wrote thirty books, including thirteen novels, and was editor or co-editor of twenty books, a contributor to a dozen other works, and a contributor of short stores, essays, and articles to *Esquire, Vogue, Atlantic, New Yorker, Harper's,* and other popular periodicals. For more than twenty years, he co-edited the annual Stanford University Press *Stanford Short Stories.* He was West Coast editor for Houghton-Mifflin for nearly ten years.

At the San Francisco Main Library, a public-private partnership which opened on April 18, 1996, the Wallace E. Stegner Environmental Center, which houses the Wallace Stegner Environmental Collection, is one of the library's "affinity centers." The Center's stated goal is "to inspire understanding and appreciation of the interconnectedness of life on earth by providing environmental literature and innovative public programs."

In March, 1993, Stegner was in Santa Fe, New Mexico, where he had gone to accept an award from the Montana & Plains Booksellers Association. On the evening of March 28, he was severely injured in an auto accident. He was taken by ambulance to St. Vincent Hospital in Santa Fe, where, on April 13, 1993, he died. He was 84.

NOTES ON *MORMON COUNTRY*

The book is one of two non-fiction works Stegner wrote about the Mormons. The second, *The Gathering of Zion: The Story of the Mormon Trail* (McGraw-Hill, 1964), is a volume in the *American Trails Series.* As noted, Stegner had lived in Salt Lake City and attended the University of Utah, and *Mormon Country,* while it presents a short history of the Mormons who settled in the area, focuses on the sense of community and the stability of Mormon society. Stegner was not a Mormon and, in fact, in his introduction to

The Gathering of Zion he makes his view of the Mormons clear, stating:

> Suffering, endurance, discipline, faith, brotherly and sisterly
> charity, the qualities so thoroughly celebrated by Mormon writers,
> were surely well distributed among them, but theirs also was a nor-
> mal amount of human cussedness, vengefulness, masochism, back-
> biting, violence, ignorance, selfishness, and gullibility. So far as it is
> possible, I shall take them from their own journals and reminis-
> cences and letters, and I shall try to follow George Bancroft's rule
> for historians: I shall try to present them in their terms and judge
> them in mine. That I do not accept the faith that possessed them
> does not mean I doubt their frequent devotion and heroism in its
> service. Especially their women. Their women were incredible.[4]

In his 1996 biography, *Wallace Stegner: His Life and Work* (Viking), Jackson J. Benson wrote, "Stegner has said that he wrote *Mormon Country* in
Cambridge out of 'nostalgia' for the West, passing it off rather lightly. But
the book really stands at a crossroads in the author's career." Benson notes
that Stegner "had traveled many times throughout the territory and camped
out in so many places and knew them so well that he thought of Mormon
country as his own."[5]

REVIEWS

Booklist, November 15, 1942 (p. 100); *Books*, October 11, 1942 (p. 3); *Boston
Globe*, November 11, 1942 (p. 21); *Library Journal*, September 15, 1942 (p. 794);
New Republic, December 28, 1942 (p. 866); *New York Times Book Review*, Oc-
tober 25, 1942 (p. 20); *Saturday Review of Literature*, January 2, 1943 (p. 21);
Wisconsin Library Bulletin, November 1942 (p. 162).

SELECTED WRITINGS BY WALLACE STEGNER

Remembering Laughter (Boston: Little, Brown, 1937); *The Potter's House*
(Muscatine, Iowa: Prairie Press, 1938); *On a Darkling Plain* (New York: Harcourt, 1940); *Fire and Ice* (New York: Duell, Sloan & Pearce, 1941); **Mormon
Country** (American Folkways Series) (New York: Duell, Sloan & Pearce,
1942); *The Big Rock Candy Mountain* (New York: Duell, Sloan & Pearce,
1943); *Second Growth* (Boston: Houghton, 1947); *The Women on the Wall*
(Boston: Houghton, 1948); *The Preacher and the Slave* (Boston: Houghton,
1950); *The City of the Living and Other Stories* (Boston: Houghton, 1956); *A

4. Stegner, Wallace. *The Gathering of Zion.* New York: McGraw-Hill, p. 12.
5. Benson, Jackson J. *Wallace Stegner: His Life and Work.* New York: Viking, 1996, p. 122.

Shooting Star (New York: Viking, 1961); ***The Gathering of Zion: The Story of the Mormon Trail*** (American Trails Series) (New York: Mc-Graw-Hill, 1964); *All the Little Live Things* (New York: Viking, 1967); *Angle of Repose* (Garden City, N.Y.: Doubleday, 1971); *The Spectator Bird* (Garden City, N.Y.: Doubleday, 1976); *Recapitulation* (Garden City, N.Y.: Doubleday, 1979); *Crossing to Safety* (New York: Random House, 1987); *Where the Bluebird Sings to the Lemonade Springs: Living and Writing in the West* (New York: Viking, 1992); *Collected Stories of Wallace Stegner* (New York: Random House, 1994).

SOURCES

Book Review Digest 1942. New York: The H.W. Wilson Company, 1943, p. 733.

Publishers' Weekly, August 22, 1942, p. 526; September 26, 1942, p. 1099; and October 10, 1942, p. 1608.

The New York Times Book Review, October 25, 1942, p. 20.

Lewis, Merrill and Lorene. "Wallace Stegner." Boise State College Western Writers Series, Number 4. Boise State College, Boise, Idaho, 1972.

The New York Times obituary, April 15, 1993, p. A1.

Benson, Jackson J. *Wallace Stegner: His Life and Work*. New York: Viking, 1996.

Contemporary Authors Online. The Gale Group, 2000. Reproduced in *Biography Resource Center*. Farmington Hills, Mich.: The Gale Group, 2002.

Owens, Wendy, Librarian, Wallace Stegner Environmental Center, San Francisco Public Library. E-mail message to CF, February 9, 2006.

NIAGARA COUNTRY

Lloyd Graham
November 14, 1893 – October 10, 1991

AF16   First edition, first printing (1949) [19]

[*Folkways* device] | [within a green (close to Pantone 341) rectangle with rounded corners, in cream] EDITED BY ERSKINE CALDWELL | [black] NIAGARA | COUNTRY | BY LLOYD GRAHAM | [cream] DUELL, SLOAN & PEARCE · NEW YORK

COLLATION: 8½" x 6". 168 leaves. [i–x] xi–xiii [xiv] [1–2] 3–301 [302–304] 305–321 [322]. Numbers printed in roman in headline at the outer margin of the type page, except for pp. xi, 3, 30, 54, 74, 125, 152, 196, 248, 262, and 305, on which the numbers are printed in the center at the foot of the page.

CONTENTS: p. [i], half-title: "*Niagara Country* | [thin rule]"; p. [ii], "AMERICAN FOLKWAYS | EDITED BY ERSKINE CALDWELL | [list of eighteen titles and their authors, beginning with *Golden Gate Country* and ending with *Niagara Country*] | In Preparation | [list of nine titles[1]]"; p. [iii], title; p. [iv], copyright page: "COPYRIGHT, 1949, BY | Lloyd Graham | *All rights reserved, including the right to | reproduce this book or portions | thereof in any form* | First Printing | PRINTED IN THE UNITED STATES OF AMERICA"; p. [v], dedication: "*To Joan*"; p. [vi], blank; p. [vii], "*Preface* [signed L.G.]"; p. [viii], blank p. [ix], "*Acknowledgments*"; p. [x], blank; pp. xi–xiii, "Contents"; p. [xiv], blank; p. [1], second half-title: "*Niagara Country* | [thin rule]"; p. [2], blank; pp. 3-301, text; p. [302], blank; p. [303], "*Index*" | [thin rule]"; p. [304], blank; pp. 305-321, "Index"; p. [322], blank.

---

1. The list includes *Great Lakes Country* by Iola Fuller, *Tidewater Country* by Elswyth Thane, *Pacific Northwest Country* by Richard Neuberger, *Gold Rush Country* by Charis Weston, *Pennsylvania Dutch Country* by Harry Emerson Wildes, and *Buckeye Country* by Louis Bromfield, none of which were published in the *Folkways* series, and *Wheat Country* by William Bracke, *Rocky Mountain Country* by Albert N. Williams, and *Redwood Country* by Alfred Powers, all of which were published in the series.

BINDING: Green cloth (close to Pantone 341). Spine stamped in black, except where noted: "[four thin rules] [thick rule] | [four thin rules] | [within a black panel, in gold] NIAGARA | COUNTRY | · | LLOYD | GRAHAM | [four thin rules] | [thick rule] | [at bottom] [four thin rules] | [within a black panel, in gold] DUELL, SLOAN | AND PEARCE | [four thin rules] | [thick rule]". Cream endpapers carry map of the United States in green and cream, with "Niagara Country" identified on a curved arrow in green and in cream on a green ribbon.

DUST JACKET (white paper): Front: Green background (close to Pantone 342). "[yellow (close to Pantone 127)] Niagara | Country | [black] [thin rule] | AMERICAN FOLKWAYS | [thin rule] | [black-and-white photograph of Niagara Falls enclosed in an irregular horizontal rectangular yellow and black frame] | [yellow] LLOYD GRAHAM". Spine: Yellow background. "[green] Niagara | Country | [black] THE NIAGARA FRONTIER | OF THE UNITED STATES | AND CANADA | LLOYD | GRAHAM | [*Folkways* device in black and yellow] | [green] DUELL, SLOAN | AND PEARCE". Back: "[white background; printing in black] SOUTHERN CALIFORNIA COUNTRY | *An Island on the Land* | by Carey McWilliams | [quotes from five reviews] | $3.75 | *An American Folkways book* | [publisher's imprint]". Front flap: "[white background; printing in black] [upper right] $3.50 | NIAGARA | COUNTRY | by | Lloyd Graham | [blurb] | *An American Folkways Book* | [publisher's imprint]". Back flap: "[white background; printing in black] [upper left] $3.50 | REDWOOD | COUNTRY | *The Lava Region and the* | *Redwoods* | by | Alfred Powers | [blurb] | *An American Folkways Book* | [publisher's imprint]".

Published at $3.50 on June 30, 1949; number of copies printed unknown. Copyrighted July 8, 1949; deposited July 8, 1949.

The book is listed in "The Weekly Record," August 20, 1949, p. 766.

Note: Duell, Sloan & Pearce published at least two printings of *Niagara Country.*

COPIES: CF

REPRINTS AND REPRODUCTIONS

None.

BIOGRAPHY

Lloyd Saxon Graham was born in Theresa, New York, on November 14, 1893.

While still in high school, Graham was a correspondent for the *Standard*, a Watertown, New York, newspaper. His first professional newspaper job was as a reporter for the *Rochester Herald*. He was twenty at the time and was attending the Rochester Business Institute while working at the *Herald*. He later worked for the *Watertown Times*, and then the East Liverpool, Ohio, *Tribune*. In 1915, he moved to Buffalo. His first job in Buffalo was as a reporter for the *Buffalo Courier*, where he worked for two years before leaving to become director of public relations for the Buffalo YMCA.

Graham soon began to write short stories and magazine articles. He left his job at the YMCA and from 1922 to 1934 supported his family as a full-time freelance writer. By his own estimate, during those years he wrote articles for at least three hundred and fifty magazines at an annual rate of nearly a million words, the equivalent of nearly ten books.[2]

In 1934, as the effects of the Great Depression intensified, the American magazine market shrank. Graham resumed his public relations position at the YMCA, working there until 1940, when he joined the staff of the Buffalo Chamber of Commerce. He became editor of the Chamber's publication, *Buffalo Business*, a post he held from 1940 until his retirement in 1961. Under Graham's direction, *Buffalo Business* was developed from a four-page weekly bulletin into a wide-ranging monthly magazine, described at the time of his retirement as "the voice of commerce and industry on the Niagara Frontier."[3]

During those years, Graham continued to write, producing numerous newspaper and magazine articles, writing three books, and collaborating on two others. For twenty years during this time he taught a course in creative writing at the evening school of the University of Buffalo.

Graham's 1945 book, *The Desperate People* (Foster & Stewart), which recounts the creation of the U.S. Constitution, was translated into Japanese and, in 1948, approved by the Occupation authorities for publication in Japan, with a preface by Graham.[4]

At the time of his death, Graham was survived by his second wife, Betty Jean McClary Graham, and three sons. Graham's first wife, Kathryn, had predeceased him.

Lloyd Graham died in Buffalo, New York, on October 10, 1991, at age 97.

NOTES ON *NIAGARA COUNTRY*

The book was promoted by Duell, Sloan & Pearce in the March 19, 1949,

2. Froehlich, Walter. "Tips for Eisenhower Found in Lloyd Graham's Books." *Buffalo Courier-Express*, December 5, 1952, p. 19.
3. Joseph, Bill. "'30' for L.G.", *Buffalo Business*, January 1962, p. 24.
4. *Buffalo Courier-Express*, January 18, 1948, [n.p.].

issue of *Publishers' Weekly* in an advertisement styled "Nature — Travel — Folkways." The advertisement described the Niagara region as ". . . once the pawn of nations and the scene of bitter Indian strife-now a land of beauty and the heart of an industrial empire."

Prior to the book's publication, the *Buffalo Courier-Express* promoted it as containing "a wealth of information on the history and folklore of the Niagara region, including Buffalo, much of which never previously appeared in book form."

The Buffalo Chamber of Commerce hosted a luncheon on June 30, 1949, the book's publication date, honoring Graham and celebrating the publication of his book. More than a hundred business and civic leaders from the Niagara Frontier area attended the luncheon.

REVIEWS

Booklist, July 15, 1949 (p. 390); *Buffalo Courier Express*, July 3, 1949 (Section 7, p. 8); *Buffalo Evening News* (Magazine), July 2, 1949 (p. 5); *Commonweal*, August 12, 1949 (p. 446); *Kirkus*, April 15, 1949 (p. 224); *Library Journal*, June 1, 1949 (p. 891); *New York Herald Tribune Weekly Book Review*, July 17, 1949 (p. 5); *New York Times Book Review*, August 7, 1949 (p. 19); *New Yorker*, September 17, 1949 (p. 114); *Saturday Review of Literature*, January 21, 1950 (p. 11).

SELECTED WRITINGS BY LLOYD GRAHAM

Rip Cord: Thrills with Parachutes (Buffalo, N.Y.: Foster & Stewart Publishing Corp., 1936); (with Samuel R. Guard) *Francis Parnell Murphy, Governor of New Hampshire: Biography of an American* (East Aurora, N.Y.; Roycroft Shops, 1940); (with Frank H. Severance) *The First Hundred Years of the Buffalo Chamber of Commerce* (Buffalo, N.Y.: Foster & Stewart Publishing Corp., 1945); *The Desperate People* (Buffalo, N.Y.: Foster & Stewart Publishing Corp., 1945); *Niagara Country* (New York: Duell, Sloan & Pearce, 1949).

SOURCES

Book Review Digest 1949. New York: The H.W. Wilson Company, 1950, p. 364.

"Buffalo Literary Seed Soon to Bloom in Japan." *Buffalo Courier-Express*, January 18, 1948, [n.p.].

"Lloyd Graham Writes Book on Niagara Region." *Buffalo Courier-Express*, January 30, 1949, p. 5-B.

Buffalo Courier-Express, June 19, 1949, Section 7, p. 5; June 26, 1949, Section 7, p. 6; July 1, 1949, p. 10; July 3, 1949, Section 7, p. 8.

Buffalo Evening News (Magazine), July 2, 1949, p. 5.

The New York Times Book Review, August 7, 1949, p. 19.

Publishers' Weekly, January 29, 1949 (DSP Spring List), p. 366; March 19, 1949, p. 1282; and August 20, 1949, p. 752 and p. 766.

Froehlich, Walter. "Tips for Eisenhower Found in Lloyd Graham's Books." *Buffalo Courier-Express,* December 5, 1952, p. 19.

Joseph, Bill. "'30' for L.G." *Buffalo Business.* January 1962, pp. 24–26.

Buffalo News obituary, October 11, 1991, p. B-6.

Buffalo and Erie County Historical Society Research Library. Photocopies of materials from their files.

Buffalo and Erie County Public Library Special Collections. Photocopies of materials from their files.

NORTH STAR COUNTRY

Meridel Le Sueur
February 22, 1900 – November 14, 1996

AF17   First edition, first printing (1945) [13]

[*Folkways* device] | [within a medium blue (close to Pantone 549) rectangle with rounded corners, in cream] EDITED BY ERSKINE CALDWELL | [black] NORTH | STAR | COUNTRY | *by* | MERIDEL LE SUEUR | [cream] DUELL, SLOAN & PEARCE · NEW YORK

COLLATION: 8½" x 6". 168 leaves. [i–vi] vii–viii [1–2] 3–29 [30-32] 33–80 [81–82] 83–111 [112–114] 115–196 [197–198] 199–249 [250–252] 253–297 [298–300] 301–321 [322] 323–327 [328]. Numbers printed in roman in headline at the outer margin of the type page, except for pp. vii, 3, 12, 17, 24, 33, 42, 57, 73, 83, 91, 96, 102, 115, 125, 136, 153, 167, 177, 187, 199, 208, 217, 226, 237, 243, 253, 261, 271, 275, 281, 289, 301, 308, 316, and 323, on which the numbers are printed in the center at the foot of the page.

The "Paul Bunyan Edition" of the book contains an unpaginated leaf signed by the author, inserted following p. [ii].

CONTENTS: p. [i], half-title: "NORTH STAR COUNTRY"; p. [ii], "AMER-ICAN FOLKWAYS | Edited BY ERSKINE CALDWELL | [thin rule] | [list of 13 titles and their authors, beginning with *Desert Country* and ending with *North Star Country*] | In Preparation | [list of six titles and their authors[1]]"; p. [iii], title; p. [iv], copyright page: "COPYRIGHT, 1945, BY | MERIDEL LE SUEUR | *All rights reserved, including | the right to reproduce this book | or portions thereof in any form.* | *First Printing* | PRINTED IN THE UNITED STATES OF AMERICA"; p. [v], dedication: "*For my Mother and Arthur*"; p. [vi], blank; pp. vii–viii, "Contents"; p. [1], "They Shall Come Rejoicing"; p. [2], blank; pp. 3–29, text; p. [30], blank; p. [31], "The Light Is Sweet"; p. [32], blank; pp. 33–80, text; p. [81], "Woe to My People!"; p. [82], blank; pp. 83–111, text; p. [112], blank;; p. [113], "Thunder On, Democracy"; p. [114], blank; pp. 115–196, text; p. [197], "Rise, O Days"; p. [198], blank; pp. 199–249, text; p. [250], blank; p. [251], "Struggle"; p. [252], blank; pp. 253–297, text; p. [298], blank; p. [299], "Stride On, Democracy"; p. [300], blank; pp. 301–321, text; p. [322], blank; pp. 323–327, "Index"; p. [328], blank.

BINDING: Navy blue cloth (close to Pantone 289). Front: *Folkways* device stamped in red (close to Pantone 202) at lower right corner. Spine stamped in red, except where noted: "[thick rule] | [four thin rules] | [within a red panel, in gold] NORTH | STAR | COUNTRY | MERIDEL | LE SUEUR | [four thin rules] | [thick rule] | [four thin rules] | [at bottom] [four thin rules | [within a red panel, in gold] DUELL, SLOAN | AND PEARCE | [four thin rules] | [thick rule]". Light cream endpapers carry map of the Minnesota and Wisconsin area, Lake Michigan, and Lake Superior in medium blue (close to Pantone 645) and light cream; at upper left, "NORTH STAR COUNTRY" is printed in medium blue on a light cream ribbon.

DUST JACKET (white paper): Front carries the map of the Minnesota and Wisconsin area, Lake Michigan, and Lake Superior in light blue (close to Pantone 657) and cream, which is also found on the endpapers. "[thick rust rule (close to Pantone 470)] [white outlined in rust] NORTH STAR | COUNTRY | [solid rust] MERIDEL LE SUEUR". Spine: "[four thin rust rules on a light cream band] | [rust] NORTH | STAR | COUNTRY | [cream] LE SUEUR | [rust] [four thin rules, thick rule, four thin rules, with the *Folkways* device overlaid in the center] | [drawing of a canoe carrying seven persons:

1. The list includes *Buckeye Country* by Louis Bromfield, *Piney Woods Country* by John Faulkner, *Cutover Country* by John T. Frederick, *Black Jack Country* by George Milburn, and *Tidewater Country* by Elswyth Thane, none of which were published in the series, and *Mission Country* by Carey McWilliams, which was published in the series as *Southern California Country*.

five Indians, one frontiersman, and a clergyman] | [four thin rust rules] | [within a rust band, in light cream] DUELL, SLOAN | AND PEARCE | [four thin rust rules] | [thick rust rule]". Back: "[white background] [within an aiced ribbon, in light blue] AMERICAN FOLKWAYS | [rust] [to the left of the *Folkways* device, which is in light blue and white] *Edited* | — *by* — [to the right of the AFS device, in rust] ERSKINE | CALDWELL | [quote from Harold Rugg[2]] | PUBLISHED | [list of 13 titles and their authors | [quote from Lewis Gannett] | EACH VOLUME $3.00 | IN PREPARATION | [list of the same six titles found on p. [ii] of the text] | [light blue] [publisher's imprint]". Front flap : White background; printing in rust. "[upper right] $3.00 | NORTH STAR | COUNTRY | by Meridel Le Sueur | [blurb] | [publisher's imprint]". Back flap: White background; printing in rust. "$3.00 | [quote from *Town Meeting Country*[3]] | TOWN MEETING COUNTRY | by | Clarence Webster | [blurb] | [publisher's imprint]".

Published at $3.00, probably on November 28, 1945; number of copies printed unknown. Copyrighted December 13, 1945; deposited December 14, 1945.

The book is not listed in "The Weekly Record."

Note: No evidence found that Duell, Sloan and Pearce reprinted *North Star Country*.

COPIES: CF

AF17a First edition, PAUL BUNYAN EDITION, signed (1945)

Duell Sloan & Pearce published "The Paul Bunyan Edition" of *North Star Country*, which was issued with a tipped-in leaf following p. [ii], which reads:

> "*Paul Bunyan* | *Edition* | of | North Star Country | by | Meridel Le Sueur | [signature of Le Sueur] | [thick/thin rule]"

REPRINTS AND REPRODUCTIONS

New York: Book Find Club, 1945.

Lincoln: University of Nebraska Press, 1984. A Bison Book. Published January 17, 1985. New Foreword by Blanche H. Gelfant.

---

2. Harold Ordway Rugg (1886–1960), author, educator, civil engineer. Pioneer in curriculum design unifying the social sciences and content based on research and experimentation.
3. The quote reprints in full the last paragraph of Chapter 1 of *Town Meeting Country*.

Reproduced on microfilm. Cambridge, Mass.: Harvard University Library Micro reproduction Service, 198-. 1 reel; 35 mm.

Minneapolis: University of Minnesota Press, September 1998. The Fesler-Lampert Minnesota Heritage Book Series. Paperback. Published at $15.95.

BIOGRAPHY

Meridel Le Sueur was born in Murray, Iowa, on February 22, 1900, the daughter of William Winston, an itinerant Church of Christ minister, and Marian Lucy Wharton.

In 1910, Le Sueur's mother, Marian, left her husband, taking Meridel and her two younger brothers with her. Meridel spent the next years in Perry, Oklahoma, at her grandmother's home, while her mother, a feminist social-ist, earned a living lecturing on women's issues. In 1914, the family moved to Fort Scott, Kansas, where Marian headed the English department at People's College, a socialist institution. In 1917, she married Alfred Le Sueur, a lawyer and a committed socialist, who adopted the three children.[4]

Meridel attended high school in Fort Scott, Kansas. She studied dance and physical fitness at the American College of Physical Education in Chicago (1916–1917), and later studied acting at the American Academy of Dramatic Art in New York City. She appeared in two silent films, *The Perils of Pauline* (1914) and *The Last of the Mohicans* (1920). After joining the Com-munist Party in 1924, she began to write for various left-wing publications.

In 1927, Le Sueur married Harry Rice, born Yasha Rabanoff in Russia, a Marxist labor-organizer. The couple had two daughters, Rachel and Debo-rah, and were divorced in the early 1930s.

Le Sueur's short story, "Persephone," was published In 1927 in the *Dial*, a New York journal of the arts. She soon became known for her focus on the working class, especially women, and for her lyrical style. Her work was reg-ularly published until the onset of the Cold War following World War II. In 1947, she was blacklisted by the House Un-American Activities Committee (HUAC). While the Alfred Knopf house continued to publish her highly praised children's books, the income from them was meager, and she began to teach writing. For a time, she was an instructor in writing courses at the University of Minnesota, but the radicalism of the 1960s and the rise of fem-inism brought her attention from a new class of readers and she continued to write and to publish into her nineties.[5]

Le Sueur was inducted into the Iowa Women's Hall of Fame in 1996. She

4. *Meridel Le Sueur: An Inventory of Her Papers.* Minnesota Historical Society, Manu-script Collections.
5. Biographical Note, Meridel Le Sueur Papers, Special Collections Department, Univer-sity of Delaware Library.

received a *California Quarterly* annual award; grants from the Bush Foundation, a private grant-making foundation serving Minnesota and the Dako-
tas; from the University of Minnesota; and an American Book Award from
the Before Columbus Foundation in 1991 for her *Harvest Song: Collected Stories and Essays* (Oklahoma University Press, 1990).

Meridel Le Sueur died in Hudson, Wisconsin, on November 14, 1996, at
age 96.

PAPERS: Meridel Le Sueur's Papers are held by the University of Delaware
Library; the Minnesota Historical Society; and the Augsburg (Minneapolis)
College Library.

NOTES ON *NORTH STAR COUNTRY*

The first notice of the publication of the book appeared in the Duell,
Sloan & Pearce Spring List in the January 27, 1945, issue of *Publishers' Weekly.*
The book was scheduled for publication in May. Later that year, it was included in the publisher's Fall List in *Publishers' Weekly*, with an October
publication date. It was published on November 28, 1945.

REVIEWS

Book Week, December 23, 1945 (p. 4); *Booklist*, January 15, 1946 (p. 162);
Kirkus, October 1, 1945 (p. 447); *Library Journal*, October 15, 1945 (p. 978);
Saturday Review of Literature, January 5, 1946 (p. 11); *Weekly Book Review*,
December 16, 1945, (p. 3).

SELECTED WRITINGS BY MERIDEL LE SUEUR

Annunciation (Los Angeles: Platen Press, 1935); *Salute to Spring and Other
Stories* (New York: International Publishers, 1940); **North Star Country** (New
York: Duell, Sloan & Pearce, 1945); *Little Brother of the Wilderness: The Story
of Johnny Appleseed* (New York: Knopf, 1947); *Nancy Hanks of Wilderness
Road: A Story of Abraham Lincoln's Mother* (New York: Knopf, 1949); *Spar-
row Hawk* (New York: Knopf, 1950); *Chanticleer of Wilderness Road: A Story
of Davy Crockett* (New York: Knopf, 1951); *The River Road: A Story of Abraham Lincoln* (New York: Knopf, 1954); *Crusaders: The Radical Legacy of Marian and Arthur Le Sueur* (New York: Blue Heron, 1955); *Conquistadores* (New
York: F. Watts, 1973); *The Mound Builders* (New York: F. Watts, 1974); (poems) *Rites of Ancient Ripening* (Minneapolis: Vanilla Press, 1975); *Harvest:
Collected Stories* (Cambridge, Mass.: West End, 1977); *Song for My Time: Stories of the Period of Repression* (Cambridge, Mass.: West End, 1977); *Women
on the Breadlines* (Cambridge, Mass.: West End, 1977); *The Girl* (Cambridge,

Mass.: West End, 1979); *Ripening: Selected Work, 1927-1980* (Old Westbury, N.Y.: Feminist Press, 1982); (with John Crawford) *Worker Writers* (Cambridge, Mass.: West End, 1982); *I Hear Men Talking and Other Stories* (Cambridge, Mass.: West End, 1984); *Winter Prairie Woman* (Minneapolis: Midwest Villages and Voices, 1990); *Harvest Song: Collected Stories and Essays* (Norman: Oklahoma University Press, 1990); *The River Road: A Story of Abraham Lincoln* (Duluth, Minn.: Holy Cow!, 1991).

SOURCES

Book Review Digest 1945. New York: The H.W. Wilson Company, 1946, p. 425.

Publishers' Weekly, January 27, 1945, p. 320 (Spring List); and September 22, 1945, p. 1184 (Fall List).

Richards, Carmen Nelson and Genevieve Rose Breen, eds. *Minnesota Writes: A Collection of Autobiographical Stories by Minnesota Prose Writers*. Minneapolis: The Lund Press, Inc., 1945, pp. 39–41.

Saturday Review of Literature, January 5, 1946, p. 11.

Richards, Carmen Nelson, ed. *Minnesota Writers: A Collection of Autobiographical Stories by Minnesota Prose Writers*. Minneapolis: T.S. Denison & Company, Inc., 1961, pp. 192–196.

Goddard, Connie. "Le Sueur's Wilderness Series Now Complete." *Publishers' Weekly*, October 4, 1991, vol. 238, No. 44, p. 60.

The New York Times obituary, November 24, 1996, p. 46.

South Florida Sun-Sentinel obituary, November 25, 1996. p. 7B.

Contemporary Authors Online. The Gale Group, 2000. Reproduced in *Biography Resource Center*, Farmington Hills, Mich.: The Gale Group, 2002.

"Harold Ordway Rugg" *Dictionary of American Biography, Supplement 6: 1956-1960*. American Council of Learned Societies, 1980. Reproduced in *Biography Resource Center*, Farmington Hills, Mich.: The Gale Group, 2003.

Minnesota Historical Society Manuscript Collections.

University of Delaware Library, Special Collections Department.

OZARK COUNTRY

Otto Ernest Rayburn
May 6, 1891 – October 30, 1960

AF18   First edition, first printing (1941) [4]

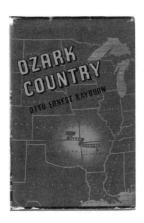

[*Folkways* device] | [within a red (close to Pantone 193) rectangle with rounded corners, in cream] EDITED BY ERSKINE CALDWELL | [black] OZARK | COUNTRY | *by* | OTTO ERNEST RAYBURN | [cream] DUELL, SLOAN & PEARCE · NEW YORK

COLLATION: 8½" x 6". 184 leaves. [i–vi] vii–ix [x–xii] [1–2] 3–345 [346] 347–352 [353–356]. Numbers printed in roman in headline at the outer margin of the type page, except for pp. vii, 3, 35, 55, 77, 101, 127, 174, 197, 215, 239, 247, 261, 276, 292, 317, 337, and 347, on which the numbers are printed in the center at the foot of the page.

CONTENTS: p. [i], half-title: "OZARK COUNTRY"; p. [ii], "AMERICAN FOLKWAYS | Edited by ERSKINE CALDWELL | [thin rule] | [list of four titles and their authors, beginning with *Desert Country* and ending with *Ozark Country*] | *In Preparation* | [list of four titles and their authors[1]] | Books by OTTO ERNEST RAYBURN | [thin rule] | [list of four titles]"; p. [iii], title; p. [iv], copyright page: "COPYRIGHT, 1941, BY | OTTO ERNEST RAYBURN | *All rights reserved, including | the right to reproduce this book | or portions thereof in any form. | first edition* | PRINTED IN THE UNITED STATES OF AMERICA"; p. [v], dedication: "TO | *Lutie Beatrice, Glovon, and Billy*"; p. [vi], blank; pp. vii–ix, "Contents"; p. [x], blank; p. [xi], "Foreword" [signed Otto Ernest Rayburn, Caddo Gap, Arkansas]; p. [xii], blank; p. [1], half-title: "OZARK COUNTRY"; p. [2], blank; pp. 3–345, text; p. 346, blank; pp. 347–352, "Index"; pp. [353–356], blank.

BINDING: Red cloth (close to Pantone 187). Front: *Folkways* device stamped in black at lower right corner. Spine, stamped in black, except where noted: "[thick rule] | [four thin rules] | [within a black panel, in gold] OZARK |

1. The list includes *Florida Country* by Stetson Kennedy; the title was changed to *Palmetto Country*.

COUNTRY I · I OTTO ERNEST I RAYBURN I [four thin rules] I [thick rule] I [four thin rules] I [at bottom] [four thin rules I [within a black panel, in gold] DUELL, SLOAN I AND PEARCE I [four thin rules] I [thick rule]". Cream endpapers carry map of the United States in red (close to Pantone 186) and cream; "Ozark Country" region is shaded in cream and further identified on two ribbon-like banners.

DUST JACKET (dark-cream paper): Front carries the central portion of the United States map found on the endpapers in red (close to Pantone 186), with the "Ozark Country" region highlighted in cream. "[thick black rule] I [dark cream outlined in black] OZARK I COUNTRY I [solid black] OTTO ERNEST RAYBURN I [printed on a red ribbon, in cream] OZARK COUN-TRY I [thick black rule]". Spine: "[thick black rule] I [four thin black rules on a cream band] I [black] [on red] OZARK I COUNTRY I · I [cream] OTTO ERNEST I RAYBURN I [black] [four thin rules, thick rule, four thin rules, with the *Folkways* device overlaid in the center] I [drawing of a grist mill at the edge of a creek] I [four thin black rules] I [within a black panel, in dark cream] DUELL, SLOAN I AND PEARCE I [four thin black rules] I [thick black rule]". Back: "[gold background] [within an arced ribbon, in red] AMERICAN FOLKWAYS I [black] *Edited by* I Erskine Caldwell I [blurb] I [red] READY I [black] [list of four titles and their authors: *Desert Country, Piñon Country, Short Grass Country,* and *Ozark Country*] I [red] IN PREPA-RATION I [black] [list of four titles and their authors, with a brief descrip-tion of each: *Florida Country², Mormon Country, High Border Country,* and *Blue Ridge Country*] I [red] *Each Volume, $3.00* I [black] [publisher's im-print]". Front flap: "[black] [upper right] $3.00 I [passage from *Ozark Coun-try*] I [red] OZARK COUNTRY I [black] *by* OTTO ERNEST RAYBURN I [blurb] I [publisher's imprint]". Back flap: "[black] I LEWIS GANNETT *fore-sees that the* AMERICAN I FOLKWAYS *series may be* 'a landmark in Amer- I ican regional literature.' I [red] Desert Country I [black] *by* EDWIN CORLE I [blurb] I [red] Piñon Country I [black] *by* HANIEL LONG I [blurb] I [red] Short Grass Country I *by* STANLEY VESTAL I [blurb] I [red] *Each Volume, $3.00* I [black] [publisher's imprint]".

Published at $3.00 on December 1, 1941; number of copies printed unknown. Copyrighted February 10, 1942 ; deposited December 4, 1942.

The book is listed in "The Weekly Record," December 6, 1941, p. 2132.

Note: Duell, Sloan & Pearce published at least five printings of *Ozark Coun-try.*

---

2. Later titled *Palmetto Country.*

CITED: *Guns* 1824 (Revised Ed.)

COPIES: CF

REPRINTS AND REPRODUCTIONS

None.

BIOGRAPHY

Otto Ernest Rayburn was born on May 6, 1891, in Bloomfield, Davis County, Iowa, the son of William Grant and Sarah Jane (Turpin) Rayburn. While Rayburn was a youngster, his family moved to Woodson County, Kansas.

In 1909 and 1910, Rayburn attended Marionville College in Marionville, Missouri. In 1917, during World War I, Rayburn enlisted in the army, serving in France and taking part in several campaigns, including the Argonne.

During a life that included the publication of four magazines, work as a newspaper columnist and as a book editor, and the writing of six books, Rayburn worked as a school teacher or school superintendent for thirty years. He began teaching in Kansas at Rose Hill in Butler County and at Buffalo in Wilson County. Beginning in 1924, Rayburn spent six years as the school superintendent at the Kingston Community Project, a joint school-church educational venture in the hills in Kingston, Arkansas. On September 26, 1925, while at Kingston, he married Lutie Beatrice Day of Hopkins County, Texas. The couple had two children, Glovon and Billy.

From 1932 until 1936, the family lived in Commerce, Texas. In 1936, they moved to Caddo Gap, Arkansas, a village in the Ozarks. In 1943, Rayburn became a part-time teacher at the Caddo Gap Consolidated School and, after his first year there, superintendent of the school, a position he held for three years. He lived out his life in various towns and villages in the Ozarks.

Rayburn published *Ozark Life* (1925–1930); *Arcadian Magazine* (1931–1932); *Arcadian Life* (1933–1942); and *Ozark Guide* (1943–1960), magazines described by Ethel C. Simpson as "rich in the treasure so dear to Rayburn's heart: Ozark folklore and customs, sketches of local characters and events, historical or linguistic notes on the region."[3]

From 1952 to 1956, Rayburn was director of the Ozark Folk Festival. In 1955, he began to compile the *Ozark Folk Encyclopedia*. His passion for the Ozarks, along with his lifelong accumulation of information about the region, resulted in a unique, invaluable resource for scholars of the Ozarks. At the time of his death, the encyclopedia comprised two hundred and twenty-nine volumes, each a loose-leaf notebook. Never intended for publication,

3. Simpson, Ethel. "Arkansas Lives — The Ozark Quest of Otto Rayburn." *Arkansas Libraries*, Vol. 39/No. 1, pp. 12–19.

the encyclopedia is held in the Special Collections Department of the University of Arkansas Library in Fayetteville.[4]

Otto Ernest Rayburn died on October 30, 1960, in Fayetteville, Arkansas, at age 69.

PAPERS: Otto Ernest Rayburn's papers are held in the Special Collections Division of the University of Arkansas Library.

NOTES ON *OZARK COUNTRY*

In his autobiography, *Forty Years in the Ozarks,* Rayburn recounts how he came to write the book:

> My big moment came in 1940 when Fate patted me on the back in a friendly way. I had spent years in preparation for big-time writing and now opportunity came like a flash of lightning. I was selected to do the book on the Ozarks for the American Folkway [*sic*] Series.
>
> When I heard of this proposed series, I wrote the publishers, Duell, Sloan and Pearce, New York, sending them some samples of my work. In a few days I received a letter from Erskine Caldwell, of Tobacco Road fame, who had been selected to edit the series.

In his May 1, 1940, reply to Rayburn's letter, Caldwell wrote, "I am very happy to hear that you want to do the book on the Ozarks for the American Folkways Series. I believe you are the ideal person to write this book, and I have great hopes of it being one of the outstanding volumes of the series. . . . I have been carried away by the extracts from your writing that you have sent us. . . . I like your fresh use of words, and I hope you will feel free to employ this style in the book. . . . I would suggest that you plan your book with the idea of presenting the Ozarks not as a tourist area, but as though you were seeing it as a historian of contemporary America."[5]

Rayburn resigned from his position as superintendent of the Caddo Gap Consolidated School, returned to part-time teaching there, and began to write the book.

The book was featured on the cover of *The New York Times Book Review* of January 18, 1942. There were no special promotions in *Publishers' Weekly.*

---

4. Shipley, Ellen. "The Literary Enterprises of Otto Ernest Rayburn." *Arkansas Libraries,* Vol. 39/No. 1, p. 22.
5. Rayburn, Otto Ernest. *Forty Years in the Ozarks: An Autobiography.* Eureka Springs, Arkansas: Ozark Guide Press, pp. 77–78.

REVIEWS

Arkansas Gazette, December 28, 1941 (p. 4); *Booklist,* January 15, 1942 (p. 176); *Chicago Sun,* March 8, 1942 (n.p.); *Christian Science Monitor,* April 18, 1942 (n.p.); *Daily Oklahoman,* March 22, 1942 (p. D7); *Library Journal,* November 15, 1941 (p. 999); *New York Herald Tribune Book Review,* December 21, 1941 (p. 2); *New York Times Book Review,* January 18, 1942 (p. 1); *Scientific Book Club Review,* December 1941 (p. 4); *Spectator,* n.d.; Springfield *(Missouri) News,* n.d.

SELECTED WRITINGS BY OTTO ERNEST RAYBURN

An Ozarker Looks at Life, Volume 1: Through the Inward Real (Kingston, Ark.: Kingscraft Press, 1927); (ed.) *An Arcadian Anthology of Verse* (6 volumes) (Olney, Ill.: Taylor Press, 1931–1936); *Dream Dust* (Olney, Ill.: Taylor Press, 1934); **Ozark** **Country** (New York: Duell, Sloan & Pearce, 1941); *The Eureka Springs Story* (Eureka Springs, Ark.: Times-Echo Press, 1954); (autobiography) *Forty Years in the Ozarks* (Eureka Springs, Ark.: Ozark Guide Press, 1957); (publisher) *Ozark Guide* (magazine); *Rayburn's Roadside Chats.*

SOURCES

Book Review Digest 1941. New York: The H.W. Wilson Company, 1942, pp. 742.

Publishers' Weekly, December 6, 1941, p. 2132.

The New York Times Book Review, January 18, 1942, p. 1.

Rayburn, Otto Ernest. *Forty Years in the Ozarks: An Autobiography.* Eureka Springs, Ark.: Ozark Guide Press, pp. 77–78.

Deane, Ernie. "Lover of Ozarks Finds Prize Nuggets." "Ernie Deane: The Arkansas Traveler," *Arkansas Gazette,* October 22, 1958, n.p.

Arkansas Gazette obituary, November 1, 1960, p. 10-B.

"Champion of the Ozarks." *Arkansas Gazette,* November 2, 1960, p. A-4.

Simpson, Ethel C. "Arkansas Lives: The Ozark Quest of Otto Rayburn." *Arkansas Libraries,* Vol. 39/No. 1, pp. 12–19.

Shipley, Ellen. "The Literary Enterprises of Otto Ernest Rayburn." *Arkansas Libraries,* Vol. 39/No.1, pp. 20-23.

Who Was Who Among North American Authors, 1921-1939. Volume 2, K-Z. Detroit, Mich.: Gale Research Company, 1976, p. 1196.

Prichard, Anne, Special Collections Division, University Libraries, University of Arkansas. Letters to CF, with enclosures, June 5, 2002 and June 11, 2002.

PALMETTO COUNTRY

Stetson Kennedy
October 5, 1916 -

AF19   First edition, first printing (1942) [8]

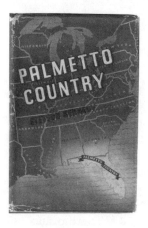

[*Folkways* device] | [within a green (close to Pantone 364) rectangle with rounded corners, in cream] EDITED BY ERSKINE CALDWELL | [black] PALMETTO | COUNTRY | *by* | STETSON KENNEDY | [cream] DUELL, SLOAN & PEARCE · NEW YORK

COLLATION: 8½" x 6". 176 leaves. [i–viii] ix–xii [1–2] 3–107 [108] 109–145 [146] 147–191 [192] 193–211 [212] 213–255 [256] 257–267 [268] 269–333 [334] 335–340. Numbers printed in roman in headline at the outer margin of the type page, except for pp. ix, 3, 43, 59, 67, 89, 109, 121, 147, 163, 183, 193, 201, 213, 239, 257, 269, 297, and 335, on which the numbers are printed in the center at the foot of the page.

CONTENTS: p. [i], half-title: "PALMETTO COUNTRY"; p. [ii], "AMERICAN FOLKWAYS | Edited by ERSKINE CALDWELL | [thin rule] | [list of eight titles and their authors, beginning with *Desert Country* and ending with *Palmetto Country*] | *In Preparation* | [list of two titles and their authors[1]]"; p. [iii], title; p. [iv], copyright page: "COPYRIGHT, 1942, BY | STETSON KENNEDY | *All rights reserved, including* | *the right to reproduce this book* | *or portions thereof in any form.* | *first edition* | PRINTED IN THE UNITED STATES OF AMERICA"; p. [v], dedication: "*To* | FOLK IN GENERAL | *and* | EDITH IN PARTICULAR"; p. [vi], blank; p. [vii], [paragraph

1. The two titles listed are: *Black Jack Country*, by George Milburn, and *Delta Country*, by E. P. O'Donnell. *Black Jack Country* is not a title in the series, nor did George Milburn write a book in the series. *Delta Country* was published as *Deep Delta Country* and written by Harnett Kane. E. P. O'Donnell did not write a book in the series.

expressing appreciation for the assistance of several people, including B.A. Botkin, Fellow in Folklore at the Library of Congress; *Direction, The Crisis,* and *Opportunity* magazines; and the Florida Writers' Project for access to its archives, "particularly material collected by" six persons, including Zora Neale Hurston]; p. [viii], blank; pp. ix–xii, "Contents"; p. [1], half-title: "PAL-METTO COUNTRY"; p. [2], blank; pp. 3–107, text; p. [108], blank; pp. 109–145, text; p. [146], blank; pp. 147–191, text; p. [192], blank; pp. 193–211, text; p. [212], blank; pp. 213–255, text; p. [256], blank; pp. 257–267, text; p. [268], blank; pp. 269–333, text; p. [334], blank; pp. 335–340, "Index".

BINDING: Medium green cloth (close to Pantone 575). Front: *Folkways* device stamped in black at lower right corner. Spine stamped in black, except where noted: "[thick rule] | [four thin rules] | [within a black panel, in gold] PALMETTO | COUNTRY | · | STETSON | KENNEDY | [four thin rules] | [thick rule] | [four thin rules] | [at bottom] [four thin rules | [within a black panel, in gold] DUELL, SLOAN | AND PEARCE | [four thin rules] | [thick rule]". Light cream endpapers carry map of the United States in medium green and cream; "Palmetto Country" region is shaded in cream and further identified on a ribbon-like banner.

DUST JACKET (white paper): Front carries the map of the southeastern portion of the United States found on the endpapers, in medium green (close to Pantone 363), with the 'Palmetto Country' region highlighted in cream. "[dark orange rule (close to Pantone 179)] | [white outlined in dark orange] PALMETTO | COUNTRY | [solid dark orange] STETSON KENNEDY | [printed on a medium green ribbon, in light green] PAL-METTO COUNTRY [thick dark orange rule]". Spine: "[thick dark orange rule] [four thin dark orange rules on a white band] | [dark orange on medium green] PALMETTO | COUNTRY | [white] · | STETSON | KENNEDY | [dark orange] [four thin rules, thick rule, four thin rules, with the *Folkways* device overlaid in the center] | [drawing of a single tall pal-metto tree, planted on a small island in a bay] | [four thin dark orange rules] | [within a dark orange panel, in white] DUELL, SLOAN | AND PEARCE | [four thin dark orange rules] | [thick dark orange rule]". Back: "[white background] [within an arced ribbon, in dark orange] AMERICAN FOLKWAYS | [medium green] *Edited by* | Erskine Caldwell | [blurb] | [dark orange] READY | [medium green] [list of eight titles and their authors; the first four of these titles are further described on the back flap] | [dark orange] IN PREPARATION | [medium green] [list of two titles and their authors, with a brief description of each[2] | [dark orange] *Each Volume, $3.00* | [medium green] [publisher's imprint]". Front flap: "[medium green] [upper right]

2. See Note 1, above.

$3.00 | [dark orange] Palmetto Country | [medium green] *By* STETSON KENNEDY | [blurb] | [publisher's imprint]". Back flap: "[dark orange] Desert Country | [medium green] *by* EDWIN CORLE [quote from two reviews] | [dark orange] High Border Country | [medium green] *by* ERIC THANE | [quote from a review] | [dark orange] Piñon Country | [medium green] *by* HANIEL LONG | [quote from a review] | [dark orange] Short Grass Country | [medium green] *by* STANLEY VESTAL | [quote from a review] | [dark orange] *Each Volume, $3.00* | [medium green] [publisher's imprint]".

Published at $3.00 on November 20, 1942; number of copies printed unknown. Copyrighted December 16, 1942; deposited December 15, 1942.

The book is listed in "The Weekly Record," December 12, 1942, p. 2385.

Note: Duell, Sloan & Pearce published at least three printings of *Palmetto Country.*

COPIES: CF

REPRINTS AND REPRODUCTIONS

Tallahassee, Fla.: Florida A&M University Press, August 29,1989. New Afterword. Published at $14.95. Reprinted in 1991 with "An Appreciation from Woody Guthrie" following the copyright page.

New Haven, Conn.: Yale University Library, 1993. 1 reel. 35 mm.

Ann Arbor, Mich.: UMI, 1994. 4 microfiches; 11 x 15 cm.

BIOGRAPHY

Stetson Kennedy was born in Jacksonville, Florida, on October 5, 1916, the son of George Wallace and Willye (Stetson) Kennedy. He studied at the University of Florida, the New School for Social Research, and the University of Paris. He left the University of Florida in 1937 to join the Florida Writers' Project of the Works Progress Administration, where he was head of the unit on folklore, oral history, and social-ethnic studies. Often accompanied by Zora Neale Hurston, he traveled within Florida with a bulky sound recorder he has described as the size of a coffee table, recording folk songs, stories, and anecdotes from the common people of the state, black and white, Latin and Greek, sponge fisherman, turpentiners, farmhands, and backwoodsmen. At a young age — he was in his early twenties — he was already becoming a recognized and respected folklorist.

Even before his affiliation with the Florida Writers' Project, Kennedy

displayed a powerful concern for human rights, this in the then highly seg-
regated Deep South, with much of his life spent in fighting for such rights,
while affiliated at various times with the CIO Political Action Committee;
the Anti–Defamation League of B'nai B'rith; the Non-Sectarian Anti–Nazi
League; the Congress of Peoples for Peace, in Austria; and with other organizations. Kennedy was a correspondent for newspapers in New York City
and Baltimore and was the editor of the Florida edition of the *Pittsburgh
Courier,* one of the nation's leading black newspapers.

Kennedy had many distinguished friends and associates, including Zora
Neal Hurston, Richard Wright, W.E.B. Dubois, and Jean Paul Sartre, in a
multiracial world, his literary work reflecting that and his enduring passion
for human rights. Consider his literary works: the present volume, *Palmetto
Country* (Duell, 1942); *Southern Exposure* (Doubleday, 1946); *I Rode With the
Ku Klux Klan* (Arco,1954); *The Klan Unmasked* (Editions Morgan, 1957); *Jim
Crow Guide to the U.S.A.* (Lawrence & Wishart, 1959); and *After Appomattox:
How the South Won the War* (University Press of Florida, 1994). All have a
Southern flavor, and all are addressed in some degree to race. His *Jim Crow
Guide* was first published in Paris by Juilliard and edited by Jean Paul Sartre,
after Kennedy was unable to find a publisher in the U.S. for the highly con-
troversial work.

Kennedy's honors and awards reflect his passion for human rights. In
2003, his home in Fruit Cove, Florida, was designated a Literary Landmark.
In 2005, he was admitted to the Florida Artists Hall of Fame. Also in 2005,
the Florida Communities Trust approved the creation of Beluthahatchee
Park. The park was to measure about five acres and include Kennedy's home,
which was to be maintained as a museum on an as-is basis, as if Kennedy,
who was to remain there until his death, has just gone out for a walk. The
park museum was to be complemented by three adjoining rustic homesteads housing studio-workshop retreats, an artist-in-residence, and a park
custodian.[3]

In 1947, Kennedy received the Peoples Award, Negro Freedom Rally,
Madison Square Garden. In 1991 he received the Cavallo Prize of $10,000,
awarded for civic courage in exposing wrongdoing. He received the NAACP
Freedom Award in 1992 and, in 1998, the Florida Folk Heritage Award from
the Division of Cultural Affairs of the State of Florida. In 2003, he became a
Fellow of the Society of Professional Journalists, recognized for his com-
pelling work over decades of reporting and writing about the American
South.

Kennedy's writings were published in the *New York Times, Nation, New
Republic, Saturday Review of Literature, New York Post, Pittsburgh Courier,* St.

3. *Florida Times-Union,* September 19, 2005, p. B-2.

Petersburg Times, Baltimore Afro-American, Amsterdam News, Associated Ne-gro Press, Southern Folklore Quarterly, Southern Changes, Southern Patriot, Common Ground, and the *Journal of Country Music.*

In 1992, Kennedy received the Jules Verne Medal, Monnaie de Paris, Prix de l'Édit de Nantes, which is awarded by an international congress spon-sored by Juridica on Human Rights and the Force of Law, Nantes, France.

In August 2008, Kennedy received the first Literary Legends Award from the organizers of the Florida Heritage Book Festival.

Kennedy lives and workes at his home, Beluthahatchee, in Fruit Cove, Florida, just south of Jacksonville.

PAPERS: Stetson Kennedy's papers are held by the University of Georgia and the University of South Florida.

NOTES ON *PALMETTO COUNTRY*

On August 19, 1940, Erskine Caldwell wrote to Stetson Kennedy, express-ing his interest in Kennedy's contribution of "Here Hung Isleno, For Living With A Brown," in a contest held by the journal *Direction.* "I should like to know if you have ever thought of writing a book dealing with that region," Caldwell wrote, continuing, "My reason for asking is that I am editing a se-ries to be called 'American Folkways', the first volume of which will be pub-lished shortly, and it seemed to me that perhaps you might be interested in writing about that region of America. I should like very much to hear from you."

In his August 21 reply, Kennedy wrote, "I appreciate to the utmost the opportunity you offer me, and I am confident that I could make a contribu-tion to your series on 'American Folkways' that would be satisfactory in every respect." After summarizing his experience as "folklore editor with the Florida Writers' and Music Projects," describing his extensive holdings of material on life in the South, noting that his writings on the Southern scene had been "substantially influenced" by Caldwell's work, and mentioning his age, which was twenty-three, Kennedy wrote, "Probably I should reassure you that my approach to folklore is functional and social, with the purpose of discovering and pointing out the relationship of the lore to the past and contemporary life of the people who keep it alive; I am not at all inclined to regard folklore with a purely academic preoccupation with its intrinsic qual-ities, to the neglect of its social significance." He concluded, "I should like nothing better than to work with you, and trust you will send me more in-formation about your plans for a volume on this region."

In his August 25 reply, Caldwell wrote, "I was very glad to receive your letter. And I think you should by all means consider doing one of the volumes for <u>American Folkways</u>. I will be glad to take up the matter with you if you think it will be possible to complete such a book during the next twelve months. It is my hope that you will be able to include some of the surrounding territory in your volume. The plan of the Series is such that we do not wish to devote a volume to a single state. If you could include the whole of Florida and a portion of South Georgia and southern Alabama, the thing would be ideal for us. Do you think it will be possible for you to do this?" Further along in the letter, Caldwell wrote, "I think we are already off on the right foot, because it is evident that you understand our desire to throw the word 'folklore' out the window, for our purposes, and to create the usage of the term 'folkways!.' To me, the term 'folkways' means the study of contemporary life in terms of its social and economic implications. . . . Your knowledge of local customs and habits of thought is the ideal basis for such a study." Caldwell continued, "We should like to have a volume running to about 250 pages—something like 75,000 words—and the rest is up to you. There is no working plan to impose upon an author."

In his August 28 reply, Kennedy wrote in part, "I believe that Florida and the southern parts of Georgia and Alabama do comprise something of a distinct cultural region. . . . A volume on the folk culture of this region, with emphasis on the contemporary and with an eye to the future, would for the most part have to deal with the native whites, Negroes, and the tourists. The tourists, bless them, complicate matters considerably, as they represent every state and racial group in America."[4]

In a May 14, 1991, letter to CF, Stetson Kennedy, referring to his "some thirty" letters from Erskine Caldwell, wrote, "This is apparently the only collection of his 'guidance' to the authors of the Folkways books. I was astounded to discover that he had no guidelines whatever at the outset, and so wrote several pages, which the publisher sent [to Kennedy] with his [Caldwell's] approval and signature." This exchange of views between Kennedy and Caldwell is described in more detail in the Introduction to the American Folkways Series.

Duell, Sloan & Pearce promoted the book, along with Wallace Stegner's *Mormon Country,* in a large advertisement in the August 22, 1942, issue of *Publishers' Weekly,* with a publication date of November 20. The title was included in the publisher's Fall List, which also noted the November publication date. But publication was delayed and the book was not released until the second week of December.

---

4. Caldwell-Kennedy correspondence from Erskine Caldwell Papers, Syracuse University Library, Special Collection Research Center.

REVIEWS

Booklist, January 15, 1943 (p. 199); *Library Journal,* November 15, 1942 (p. 1013); *New York Herald Tribune Book Review,* January 17, 1943 (p. 2); *New York Times Book Review,* December 27, 1942 (p. 4).

SELECTED WRITINGS BY STETSON KENNEDY

Palmetto Country (New York: Duell, Sloan & Pearce, 1942); *Southern Exposure* (Garden City, N.Y.: Doubleday, 1946); *I Rode with the Ku Klux Klan* (London: Arco Publishers, 1954); *The Klan Unmasked* (Editions Morgan, 1957); *Jim Crow Guide to the U.S.A.* (London: Lawrence & Wishart, 1959); *After Appomattox: How the South Won the War* (Gainesville: University Press of Florida, 1994); *Grits & Grunts: Folkloric Key West* (Sarasota: Pineapple Press, 2008).

SOURCES

Book Review Digest 1942. New York: The H.W. Wilson Company, 1943, p. 421.

Publishers' Weekly. August 22, 1942, p. 527; September 26, 1942 (Duell, Sloan & Pearce Fall List), p. 1099; and December 12, 1942, p. 2385.

The New York Times Book Review, December 27, 1942, p. 4.

Kennedy, Stetson. Letters to CF, May 14, 1991 and July 17, 1993.

Cooter, Diane L. Syracuse University Library, Special Collection Research Center. Erskine Caldwell Papers. (Caldwell-Kennedy correspondence quoted in "Notes on Palmetto Country," above.)

University of Georgia. Erskine Caldwell Papers. Caldwell-Kennedy correspondence.

Florida Literary Landmarks, a publication of Florida Center for the Book, Fort Lauderdale: 2005.

PIÑON COUNTRY

Haniel Long
March 9, 1888 – October 17, 1956

AF20   First edition, first printing (1941) [2]

[*Folkways* device] | [within a dark turquoise (close to Pantone 327) rectangle with rounded corners, in cream] EDITED BY ERSKINE CALD-WELL | [black] PIÑON | COUNTRY | *by* | HANIEL LONG | [cream] DUELL, SLOAN & PEARCE · NEW YORK

COLLATION: 8½" x 6". 172 leaves. [i–viii] ix–xi [xii] [1–2] 3–327 [328–332]. Numbers printed in roman in headline at the outer margin of the type page, except for pp. ix, 3, 11, 22, 31, 39, 45, 58, 70, 79, 86, 101, 116, 122, 130, 138, 146, 157, 162, 171, 184, 191, 198, 206, 218, 227, 240, 254, 262, 271, 303, and 319, on which the numbers are printed in the center at the foot of the page.

CONTENTS: p. [i], half-title: "PIÑON COUNTRY"; p. [ii], "AMERICAN FOLKWAYS | Edited by ERSKINE CALDWELL | [thin rule] | [list of two titles and their authors, beginning with *Desert Country* and ending with *Piñon Country*] | *In Preparation* | [list of four titles and their authors] | Books by HANIEL LONG | [thin rule] | [list of five titles]"; p. [iii], title; p. [iv], copyright page: "COPYRIGHT, 1941, BY | HANIEL LONG | *All rights reserved, including | the right to reproduce this book | or portions thereof in any form.* | *first edition* | PRINTED IN THE UNITED STATES OF AMER-ICA | BY QUINN & BODEN COMPANY, INC., RAHWAY, N.J."; p. [v], dedication: "*To friends in or out of my book who have | shared what they know of life in the piñon | country and so given me more of it than I | could ever gain by myself - and to the | friend, too, who told me to write the book*[1]"; p. [vi], blank; p. [vii], "ACKNOWLEDGMENTS"; p. [viii], blank; pp. ix–xi, "Contents"; p. [xii], blank; p. [1], half-title: "PIÑON COUNTRY"; p. [2], blank; pp. 3–318, text; pp. 319–327, "Index"; pp. [328–332], blank.

1. The "friend, too, who told me to write the book" may have been Santa Fe poet Witter Bynner. See "Notes on *Piñon Country*," below.

BINDING: Turquoise cloth (close to Pantone 327). Front: *Folkways* device stamped in burgundy (close to Pantone 216) at lower right corner. Spine, stamped in burgundy, except where noted: "[thick rule] | [four thin rules] | [within a burgundy panel, in gold] PIÑON | COUNTRY | · | HANIEL | LONG | [four thin rules] | [thick rule] | [four thin rules] | [at bottom] [four thin rules | [within a burgundy panel, in gold] DUELL, SLOAN | AND PEARCE | [four thin rules] | [thick rule]". Cream endpapers carry map of the United States in turquoise (close to Pantone 326) and cream; "Piñon Country" region is shaded in cream and further identified on two ribbon-like banners.

DUST JACKET (dark cream paper): Front carries the western portion of the United States map found on the endpapers in turquoise (close to Pantone 326), with the "Piñon Country" region highlighted in cream. "[burgundy, close to Pantone 216] [in outline] PIÑON | COUNTRY | [solid] HANIEL LONG | [printed on a turquoise ribbon, in cream] PIÑON | COUNTRY | [thick burgundy rule]". Spine: "[thick burgundy rule] | [four thin burgundy rules on a cream band] | [within a turquoise panel] [burgundy] PIÑON | COUNTRY | · | [cream] HANIEL | LONG | [below turquoise panel, on cream background] [burgundy] [four thin rules, thick rule, four thin rules] | [drawing of a piñon tree in burgundy and turquoise; hills in the background] | [on cream background] [four thin burgundy rules] | [within a burgundy panel, in turquoise] DUELL, SLOAN | AND PEARCE | [four thin burgundy rules] | [thick burgundy rule]". Back: "[dark cream background] [within an arced ribbon, in turquoise] AMERICAN FOLKWAYS | [burgundy] *Edited by* | Erskine Caldwell | [blurb] | [turquoise] READY | [burgundy] [list of two titles and their authors: *Piñon Country* and *Desert Country*] | [turquoise] IN PREPARATION | [burgundy] [list of four titles and their authors, with a brief description of each: *Ozark Country, High Border Country, Short Grass* Country, and *Blue Ridge Country*] | [turquoise] *Each Volume, $3.00* | [burgundy] [publisher's imprint]". Front flap: "[burgundy] [upper right] $3.00 | [turquoise] Pinon Country | [burgundy] *by* HANIEL LONG | [blurb] | [publisher's imprint]". Back flap: "[upper left, in burgundy] $3.00 | [four line quote from *Desert Country*] | [turquoise] Desert Country | [burgundy] *by* EDWIN CORLE | [blurb and brief note on Corle] | [publisher's imprint]".

Published at $3.00 on June 12, 1941; number of copies printed unknown. Copyrighted June 14, 1941; deposited June 13, 1941.

The book is listed in "The Weekly Record," June 14, 1941, p. 2394.

Note: Duell, Sloan & Pearce published at least three printings of *Piñon Country*.

CITED: *Guns* 631; *Guns* 1358 (Revised Ed.); *Legacy from Haniel Long,* 12a[2]

COPIES: CF

REPRINTS AND REPRODUCTIONS

Santa Fe, New Mexico: The Sunstone Press, 1975. "Living History Series." Introduction by Fray Angelico Chavez.[3] Paperback. Published at $6.95.

Lincoln: University of Nebraska Press, December 11, 1986. A Bison Book. Foreword by Tony Hillerman. Paperback. Published at $8.95.

Reproduced on microfilm. Ann Arbor, Mich.: University Microfilms International. 1 reel; 35 mm.

BIOGRAPHY

Haniel Clark Long was born on March 9, 1888, in Rangoon, Burma, the son of Samuel Parker and May Clark Long. His parents were Methodist missionaries. In 1891, when he was three, the family returned to the United States, settling in Pittsburgh, Pennsylvania. When he was ten, the family moved to Duluth, and later to Minneapolis.

Long entered Harvard University in 1907, earning a bachelor of arts degree in 1910. He returned to Pittsburgh, joining the faculty of the English Department at the newly founded Carnegie Technology School (later the Carnegie Institute of Technology, now Carnegie Mellon University). In 1920, as associate professor, he was named head of the English Department.

On August 12, 1913, Long married Alice Lavinia Knoblauch, a painter and poet. The couple had a son, Anton.

Long's first published work was *Poems* (Moffatt, 1920). In ill health, Long served on the Carnegie faculty as a part-time professor from 1926 until 1929, when he resigned and moved his family to Santa Fe, joining the Santa Fe writers' colony that included Witter Bynner, Oliver La Farge, Paul Horgan, Mary Austin, Roark Bradford, Angelico Chavez, and others. In 1933, in the depths of the Depression, the group founded Writers' Editions, a cooperative publishing house. Writers' Editions published seventeen books, including the first thousand copies of Long's *Pittsburgh Memoranda* (1935), which was written in Pittsburgh; his best-known work, *Interlinear to Cabeza de Vaca: His Relation to the Journey from Florida to the Pacific, 1528-1536;* and two other of Long's books. During World War II, severe government restrictions on paper forced the group to cease publishing.

In July 1937, Long joined the staff of the New Mexico *Sentinel* as editor of "New Mexico Writers," a weekly section of poetry and prose. Although

2. Long, Anton V., comp. Naples, NY: The Brookside Press, 1977.
3. Chavez was associated with Haniel Long in Writers' Editions, a cooperative regional publishing venture that concentrated on works by New Mexican poets and authors.

the section was a literary success, publishing the work of many New Mexican writers and poets, known and unknown, it was discontinued by the *Sentinel* in 1939.

During the 1940s, Long contributed poetry and prose to New Mexican journals, newspapers, and periodicals, and wrote several books, including *Piñon Country*. Shortly before his death, he finished the novel *Spring Returns* (Pantheon, 1958), which was published posthumously, as were other works still in manuscript.

Haniel Long died on October 17, 1956, at the Mayo Clinic in Minnesota, where he had gone for heart surgery. He was 68. His death occurred three days after the death of his wife, Alice, at a hospital in Santa Fe.

PAPERS: Haniel Long Papers, 1932–1968, MSS 156 SC, are held by the Center for Southwest Research, General Library, University of New Mexico; the Haniel Long Papers, 1900-1956. Collection Number 672, is held by the UCLA Library, Department of Special Collections.

NOTES ON *PIÑON COUNTRY*

A two-page Duell, Sloan & Pearce advertisement in the April 12, 1941, issue of *Publishers' Weekly* (p. 1524), promoted the first two titles in the *Folkways* series, *Desert Country* and *Piñon Country*, noting that *Piñon Country* would be published June 12. The advertisement stated,"Erskine Caldwell, the editor, has traveled widely throughout this country; he has sought out, in every locality, the creative writers whom he felt best fitted to speak for their regions. Today, two books are ready and four more are in manuscript."

In a September 14, 1991, letter to CF, written in response to a query asking how Haniel Long, who was a relative newcomer among the region's numerous writers, was chosen to write the book, Long's daughter-in-law, Helen Long, wrote:

Tony [Anton, the son of Haniel and Alice Long] said that he himself questioned whether he should be the one to do it and I believe that Erskine Caldwell went to Santa Fe to sell him. I would imagine that the success of *Pittsburgh Memoranda* had something to do with the selection. Sections of that book had been published in various versions in newspapers and magazines during the 20's and early 30's and finally it came out in 1935 from Writers' Editions with a second edition in 1939."

Long's dedication in *Piñon Country* makes reference to "the friend, too, who told me to write the book[.]" But it is not certain who that friend was. Long enjoyed a close relationship with Witter Bynner, a friend from his Harvard days and later in Pittsburgh during the years 1913 to 1920, and later still in Santa Fe, from 1923 on. The two men were key participants in the organization and operation of Writers' Editions, the cooperative regional publishing venture which ultimately published four of Long's books. It may well have been Witter Bynner who "told" Long "to write the book."

REVIEWS

Booklist, June 15, 1941 (p. 489); *Christian Science Monitor*, June 26, 1941 (p. 20); *Commonweal*, November 14, 1941 (p. 98); *Library Journal*, June 1, 1941 (p. 519); *New York Herald Tribune Book Review*, June 15, 1941 (p. 4); *New York Times*, June 22, 1941 (p. 4); *New Yorker*, June 14, 1941 (p. 78); *Saturday Review of Literature*, June 21, 1941 (p. 22); *Scientific Book Club Review*, July 1941 (p. 3); *Wisconsin Library Bulletin*, July 1941 (p. 138).

SELECTED WRITINGS BY HANIEL LONG

Poems (New York: Moffatt, Yard, 1920); *Notes for a New Mythology* (Chicago: Bookfellows, 1926); *Atlantides* (Santa Fe: Writers' Editions, 1933); *Pittsburgh Memoranda* (Santa Fe: Writers' Editions, 1935); *Interlinear to Cabeza de Vaca: His Relation of the Journey from Florida to the Pacific, 1528-1536* (Santa Fe: Writers' Editions, 1936); *Walt Whitman and the Springs of Courage* (Santa Fe: Writers' Editions, 1938); *Malinche (Doña Marina)* (Santa Fe: Rydal Press, 1939); *Piñon Country* (New York: Duell, Sloan & Pearce, 1941); *French Soldier* (Santa Fe: Santa Fe Press, 1942); *Children, Students, and a Few Adults* (Santa Fe: Santa Fe Press, 1942); *The Grist Mill* (Santa Fe: Rydal Press, 1945); *A Letter to St. Augustine after Re-reading His Confessions* (New York: Duell, Sloan & Pearce, 1950); *Spring Returns* (New York: Pantheon, 1958); (James H., Maguire, ed) (poems) *My Seasons* (Boise, Idaho: Ahsahta Press, 1977).

Many of Long's poems were published in *Poetry: A Magazine of Verse, Southwest Review, Nation, New Mexico Quarterly,* and the *New Republic.*

Long's non-fiction appeared regularly in the *New Mexico Sentinel* and *Southwest Review.*

SOURCES

Book Review Digest 1941. New York: The H.W. Wilson Company, 1942, pp. 558-559.

Publishers' Weekly, January 25, 1941, p. 308 (Duell, Sloan and Pearce Spring List); April 12, 1941, p. 1524; May 24, 1941, p. 2078; and June 14, 1941, p. 2394.

The New York Times Book Review, June 22, 1941, p. 4.

Sarton, May. "The Leopard Land: Haniel and Alice Long's Santa Fe". *Southwest Review*, Winter 1972.

Long, Anton V. (son of Haniel Long), comp. *Legacy from Haniel Long.* Naples, NY: The Brookside Press, 1977.

Long, Helen (daughter-in-law of Haniel Long). Letter to CF, with enclosures, September 14, 1991. Enclosures Include a letter from Anton V. Long and Helen Long dated December 1, 1987, addressed to "Family, friends, and correspondents both known to us and unknown who have an interest in the work of Haniel Long," stating that on April 21, 1987, he (Anton Long) had signed over to UCLA all his rights and responsibilities as literary executor for his father, Haniel Long.

Quartermain, Peter, ed. *Dictionary of Literary Biography, Volume 45: American Poets, 1880-1945, First Series.* The Gale Group, 1986, pp. 229–237.

"Haniel Long Centenary Celebration" printed program, Tuesday, March 8, 1988, [at] The First United Methodist Church of Pittsburgh. Twelve pages, unnumbered, printed by Geyer Printing Company.

Haniel Long Papers, Center for Southwestern Research, General Library, University of New Mexico. Accessed January 14, 2006.

Contemporary Authors Online, Gale, 2006. Reproduced in *Biography Resource Center.* Farmington Hills, Mich.: Thomson Gale. 2006. Accessed January 14, 2006.

PITTSYLVANIA COUNTRY

George Swetnam
March 11, 1904 – April 3, 1999

AF21   First edition, first printing (1951) [22]

[*Folkways* device] | [within a gray (close to Pan-
tone 404) rectangle with rounded corners, in
cream] EDITED BY ERSKINE CALDWELL |
[black] PITTSYLVANIA | COUNTRY | BY
GEORGE SWETNAM | [cream] DUELL, SLOAN
& PEARCE · NEW YORK

COLLATION: 8½" x 6". 167 leaves. [a–b] [i–vi]
vii–xiii [xiv] [1–2] 3–311 [312] 313–315 [316–320].
Numbers printed in roman in headline at the
outer margin of the type page, except for pp. vii,
ix, 3, 9, 36, 59, 69, 87, 117, 137, 155, 178, 191, 207, 214,
227, 233, 249, 256, 267, 277, 287, 298, 304, 309, and
313, on which the numbers are printed in the center at the foot of the page.

CONTENTS: pp. [a–b], blank; p. [i], half-title: "*Pittsylvania Country* | [thin
rule]"; p. [ii], "AMERICAN FOLKWAYS | EDITED BY ERSKINE CALD-
WELL | [list of 22 titles and their authors, beginning with *Golden Gate Coun-
try* and ending with *Pittsylvania Country*] | In Preparation | [list of nine ti-
tles[1]]"; p. [iii], title; p. [iv], copyright page: "COPYRIGHT, 1951, BY |
GEORGE SWETNAM | *All rights reserved, including the right to | reproduce
this book or portions | thereof in any form.* | I | PRINTED IN THE UNITED
STATES OF AMERICA"; p. [v], dedication: "*To Ruth*"; p. [vi], blank; pp.
vii–viii, "Author's Note"; pp. ix–xiii, "Contents"; p. [xiv], blank; p. [1], half-
title: "*Pittsylvania Country* | [thin rule]"; p. [2], [map of western Pennsylva-

---

1. The list includes *Great Lakes Country* by Iola Fuller, *Tidewater Country* by Elswyth
Thane, *Pacific Northwest Country* by Richard Neuberger, *Gold Rush Country* by Charis
Weston, *Pennsylvania Dutch Country* by Harry Emerson Wildes, *Homesteader Country* by
Edward Stanley, and *Ohio Country* by Elrick B. Davis (which would have replaced *Buckeye Country* by Louis Bromfield), none of which were published in the Folkways series,
and *Gulf Coast Country* by Hodding Carter and Anthony Ragusin and *Adirondack Country* by William C. White, both of which were published in the series.

nia titled "Pittsylvania Country"]; pp. 3–311, text; p. [312], blank; pp. 313–315, "Index"; pp. [316–320], blank.

BINDING: Medium brown cloth (close to Pantone 463). Front: *Folkways* device stamped in black at lower right corner. Spine stamped in black, except where noted: "[thick rule] I [four thin rules] I [within a black panel, in gold] PITT- I SYLVANIA I COUNTRY I · I GEORGE I SWETNAM I [four thin rules] I [thick rule] I [four thin rules] I [at bottom] [four thin rules I [within a black panel, in gold] DUELL, SLOAN I AND PEARCE I [four thin rules] I [thick rule]". Cream endpapers carry map of the United States in rust (close to Pantone 484) and cream, with "Pittsylvania Country" area highlighted in cream and further identified on a rust ribbon in the lower right corner.

DUST JACKET (white paper): Front: Red background (close to Pantone 200). "[grey, close to Pantone 404)] Pittsylvania I Country I [black] [thin rule] I AMERICAN FOLKWAYS I [thin rule] I [black-and-white photograph of a pusher tug and barge on the Ohio River approaching the junction of the Allegheny and the Monongahela Rivers] I [grey] GEORGE SWETNAM". Spine: Grey background. "[red] Pittsylvania I Country I SWETNAM I [black] [*Folkways* device] I [red] DUELL, SLOAN I AND PEARCE". Back: White background; printing in black. "Edited I by [*Folkways* device] ERSKINE I CALDWELL I [blurb praising the series] I [list of 21 titles and their authors and prices] I [publisher's imprint]". Front flap: White background; printing in black. "[upper right] $3.50 I PITTSYLVANIA I COUNTRY I by I George Swetnam I [blurb] I *Photograph courtesy Standard Oil of New* Jersey I *An American Folkways Book* I [publisher's imprint]". Back flap: White background; printing in black. "[upper left] $3.50 I NIAGARA I COUNTRY I by I Lloyd Graham I [blurb] I *An American Folkways Book* I [publisher's imprint].

Published at $3.50 on January 15, 1951; number of copies printed unknown.[2] Copyrighted February 26, 1951; deposited January 24, 1951.

Note: Duell, Sloan & Pearce published at least two printings of *Pittsylvania Country.*

The book is listed in "The Weekly Record," January 20, 1951, p. 257.

CITED: *Bibliography of Pennsylvania History* [7081]

COPIES: CF

2. In an interview in the *Pittsburgh Post-Gazette* in 1997, George Swetnam reported "about 12,000" copies were printed.

REPRINTS AND REPRODUCTIONS

Greensburg, Pa.: McDonald/Sward Publishing Company, 1992. Paperback.

BIOGRAPHY

George F. Swetnam was born in Hicks Station, Ohio, on March 11, 1904, the son of William Wylie, an itinerant school teacher and school principal, and Flora May (Stafford) Swetnam, who was a well-known author at the turn of the century. As a child, he lived with his family in Kentucky, North Carolina, Tennessee, Georgia, South Carolina, and Mississippi.

Swetnam attended the University of South Carolina and the University of Alabama, and graduated from the University of Mississippi in 1928 having earned a bachelor of arts degree in English. He then earned a bachelor of arts degree in divinity from Columbia Theological Seminary in Columbia, South Carolina, where he studied archeology and Semitic languages. He later earned a master of arts degree in theology from Auburn Theological Seminary. In 1930, he earned a doctorate in Assyriology at the Hartford (Connecticut) Seminary Association. Soon thereafter, he joined the faculty of the University of Alabama as a teacher of English, but, as the Great Depression deepened and the university became unable to meet its payroll, Swetnam and other faculty members were let go.

After a brief time running a photo studio he had founded and is said simply to have handed over to someone else, he went on the road, living three years as a hobo, later claiming to have ridden in more railroad boxcars than any other person possessing a doctoral degree.

In 1936, Swetnam married Ruth Kulamer. The couple had three children, a daughter, Anne, and two sons, George and John.

After his time as a hobo, Swetnam managed and edited a weekly newspaper in Tennessee before moving to Uniontown, Pennsylvania, where he was a staff writer and managing editor of the *Uniontown Evening Standard.* He was an ordained Presbyterian minister, serving as such for seven years in Uniontown. After a falling out with the owner of the *Evening Standard,* he moved to Pittsburgh, where he joined the staff of the *Pittsburgh Press* in 1943, beginning as a reporter and becoming a copy editor, a features writer, and a columnist. For decades Swetnam wrote a column in the paper's Sunday Family Magazine, sometimes using the pen name "Acker Petit" (an old small typeface) for a second article in an issue carrying his column. After his retirement in 1973, he wrote a semi–monthly column, "Looking Backward," for the *North Hills News Record,* writing the column into his ninety-fourth year.[3]

3. *Pittsburgh Post-Gazette* (obituary), April 7, 1999, p. A-19.

During his time at the *Press,* Swetnam wrote five books, including a three-volume history of Pittsburgh published in 1955 and a history of transportation in Pennsylvania, published in 1964. After his retirement in 1973, he wrote another three books and co-authored an additional four.

Swetnam was editor of the *Keystone Folklore Quarterly* from 1959 to 1965, and was the founder of the Institute of Pennsylvania Rural Life and Culture. In 1954, he received the Lawrence S. Mayers National Peace Award; the award was presented to him by Vice President Richard Nixon at the White House.

As his health began to fail, Swetnam moved from his home in Glenshaw to a health-care facility in Wexford. (Both towns are in the Pittsburgh area.) Shortly thereafter, he moved to a care facility in Morrisville, New York, in order to be near his daughter, Anne M. Perry, in nearby Hamilton.

George F. Swetnam died on April 3, 1999, in Morrisville, New York, at age 95.

PAPERS: The George Swetnam Papers, 1781–1981 are held by Indiana University of Pennsylvania, University Archives and Special Collections (MG#5), Indiana, Pennsylvania.

NOTES ON *PITTSYLVANIA COUNTRY*

In an interview in the January 12, 1997, *Pittsburgh Post-Gazette,* George Swetnam was said to have felt "a need to write books, but about what?" Swetnam then describes how he came to write the book:

> I was determined to turn over every stone until I found one with a *bug* under it. I found a book about Niagara Falls published by Duell, Sloane [*sic*] & Pearce. I noticed Erskine Caldwell, the famous Southern novelist, was editor of Duell's American Folkways Series. I wrote to him and said I didn't see anything [in the series] about this area, and I sent along some of my pieces. As I had hoped, he wrote back, saying why not try something? I wrote a synopsis and a chapter and finished the book, "Pittsylvania Country," in a year while at the [Pittsburgh] Press. The book was printed in an edition of about 12,000. It was a best-seller, especially here.

In a December 17, 1949, letter to Swetnam, Caldwell noted, "we all agree that there is a fine book in the material," referring to the synopsis and first chapter that Swetnam had sent to him. Later in his letter, Caldwell referred to "the important matter of a suitable title," observing, "So far we seem to have made little progress, and I confess that I am of little help. I have thought of 'Western Pennsylvania Country' and 'Steel and Coal Country'. Neither is very good. Perhaps you have had some more ideas since writing last. I think

it is always helpful to both the author and the publisher to have a title decided upon in advance for a book of this nature." Swetnam's obituary in the
Pittsburgh Post-Gazette (April 7, 1999), reports, "He used the name 'Pittsyl
vania Country' for Western Pennsylvania, tracing the term to the 18th century."

REVIEWS

Booklist, March 1, 1951 (p. 234); *Bookmark*, February, 1951 (p. 108); *Kirkus*,
December 1, 1950 (p. 716); *Library Journal*, February 1, 1951 (p. 182); *New York
Herald Tribune Book Review*, February 4, 1951 (p. 14); *San Francisco Chroni-
cle*, March 11, 1951 (p. 19); *Saturday Review of Literature*, May 5, 1951 (p. 16);
U.S. Quarterly Book Review, June 1951 (p. 184); *Wisconsin Library Bulletin*,
September 1951 (p. 213).

SELECTED WRITINGS BY GEORGE SWETNAM

Pittsylvania Country (New York: Duell, Sloan & Pearce, 1951); *The Bicentennial History of Pittsburgh and Allegheny County* (Hopkinsville, Ky.: Historical
Record Association, 1955); (with Jacob A. Evanson) *Early Western Pennsyl-
vanian Hymns and Hymn-Tunes: 1816-1846* (Coraopolis, Pa.: Yahres Publications, 1958); *Where Else but Pittsburgh!* (Pittsburgh: Davis & Wade, Inc.,
1958); (with John Lofton, et al) Pittsburgh's First Unitarian Church (Pittsburgh: The Boxwood Press, 1961); *The McKees Rocks Story* (Pittsburgh: Pittsburgh National Bank, 1964); *Pennsylvania Transportation* (Gettysburg: The
Pennsylvania Historical Association, 1964); *Andrew Carnegie* (Boston:
Twayne Publishers, 1980); *Devils, Ghosts, and Witches: Occult Folklore of the
Upper Ohio Valley* (Greensburg, Pa.: McDonald/Sward Publishing Co., 1988);
(with Helene Smith) *The Carnegie Nobody Knows* (Greensburg, Pa.: Mc-
Donald/Sward Publishing Co., 1989); *The Governors of Pennsylvania 1790-
1990* (Greensburg, Pa.: McDonald/Sward Publishing Co., 1990); (with He-
lene Smith) *A Guidebook to Historic Western Pennsylvania* (Pittsburgh:
University of Pittsburgh Press, 1991).

SOURCES

Caldwell, Erskine. Letter to George Swetnam, December 17, 1949.

Book Review Digest 1951. New York: The H.W. Wilson Company, 1952, p. 862.

Publishers' Weekly, January 20,1951, p. 287, and January 27, 1951, p. 340 (Duell,
Sloan and Pearce Spring List).

Library Journal, February 1, 1951, p. 182.

Saturday Review of Literature, May 5, 1951, p. 16.

"George Swetnam's 'Pittsylvania,'" *Pittsburgh Post-Gazette,* January 12, 1997, p. E-10.

Pittsburgh Post-Gazette obituary, April 7, 1999, p. A-19.

Zorich, Phillip, Special Collections Librarian, University Library, Indiana University of Pennsylvania. George Swetnam Papers, 1781–1981, including Caldwell-Swetnam correspondence.

Chad, Barry, Senior Librarian, Pennsylvania Department, Carnegie Library of Pittsburgh. "George Swetnam: Chronicler of All Things Pittsylvanian." (www.clpgh.org/clp/Pennsylvania/swetnam.html) Accessed July 8, 2002.

REDWOOD COUNTRY: THE LAVA REGION AND THE REDWOODS

Alfred Powers
June 3, 1887 – July 24, 1983

AF22   First edition, first printing (1949) [18]

[*Folkways* device] | [within a dark red (close to Pantone 201) rectangle with rounded corners, in cream] EDITED BY ERSKINE CALDWELL | [black] REDWOOD | COUNTRY: | The Lava Region and The Redwoods | BY ALFRED POWERS | [cream] DUELL, SLOAN & PEARCE · NEW YORK

COLLATION: 8½" x 6". 160 leaves. [a–b] [i–iv] v–xv [xvi] xvii–xviii [xix–xxii] 1–153 [154–156] 157–284 [285–286] 287–292 [293–296]. Numbers printed in roman in headline at the outer margin of the type page, except for pp. v, ix, xvii, 3, 12, 20, 26, 36, 51, 58, 62, 70, 75, 81, 93, 102, 110, 115, 126, 134,

145, 157, 168, 189, 212, 220, 228, 238, 252, 259, 262, 272, 283, and 287, on which the numbers are printed in the center at the foot of the page.

CONTENTS: pp. [a–b], blank; p. [i], half-title: "*REDWOOD COUNTRY* | *The Lava Region* | *and The Redwoods*"; p. [ii], "AMERICAN FOLKWAYS | EDITED BY ERSKINE CALDWELL | [list of 19 titles and their authors, beginning with *Golden Gate Country* and ending with *Redwood Country*] | In Preparation | [list of eight titles[1]]"; p. [iii], title; p. [iv], copyright page: "COPYRIGHT, 1949, BY | ALFRED POWERS | *All rights reserved, including the right to repro-* | *duce this book or portions thereof in any form.* | *First Edition* | PRINTED IN THE UNITED STATES OF AMERICA"; pp. v–viii, Contents; pp. ix–xv, "Foreword"; p. [xvi], blank; pp. xvii–xviii, "A Note on Sources"; p. [xix], half-title: "*REDWOOD COUNTRY* | *The Lava Region* | *and The Redwoods*"; p. [xx], blank; p. [xxi], "*REDWOODS*"; p. [xxii], blank; pp. 1–2, "*Song of the Redwood Tree*" | by | Walt Whitman]; pp. 3–153, text; p. [154], blank; p. [155], "*LAVA REGION*"; p. [156], "*Lava Desert*" | By Joaquin Miller" pp. 157–284, text; p. [285], "*INDEX*"; p. [286], blank; pp. 287–292, "Index"; pp. [293–296], blank.

BINDING: Red cloth (close to Pantone 207). Front: *Folkways* device stamped in black at lower right corner. Spine stamped in black, except where noted: "[thick rule] | [four thin rules] | [within a black panel, in gold] REDWOOD | COUNTRY | The Lava Region | and the Redwoods | · | ALFRED | POWERS | [four thin rules] | [thick rule] | [four thin rules] | [at bottom] [four thin rules | [within a black panel, in gold] DUELL, SLOAN | AND PEARCE | [four thin rules] | [thick rule]". Cream endpapers carry map of the United States in brown (close to Pantone 201) and cream, with the Redwood Country area highlighted in cream and "Redwood Country" on a red ribbon in the lower right corner.

DUST JACKET (white paper): Front:Dark red background (close to Pantone 201). "[yellow (close to Pantone 614)] Redwood | Country | [black] The Lava Region and the Redwoods | [black] [thin rule] | AMERICAN FOLKWAYS | [thin rule] | [black-and-white photograph by Ansel Adams within an irregular horizontal rectangular yellow-and-black frame] | [yellow] ALFRED POWERS". Spine: Yellow background. "[brown] Redwood | Country | [black] The Lava Region | and the Redwoods | ALFRED | POWERS | [*Folkways* device in black and yellow] | [brown] DUELL, SLOAN, | AND

1. The list Includes *Great Lakes Country* by Iola Fuller, *Tidewater Country* by Elswyth Thane, *Pacific Northwest Country* by Richard Neuberger, *Gold Rush Country* by Charles Weston, *Pennsylvania Dutch Country* by Harry Emerson Wildes, and *Buckeye Country* by Louis Bromfield, none of which were published in the Folkways series, and *Wheat Country* by William Bracke and *Rocky Mountain Country* by Albert N. Williams, both of which were published in the series.

PEARCE". Back: "[white background; printing in black] SOUTHERN CAL-
IFORNIA COUNTRY | *An Island on the Land* | by Carey McWilliams |
[quotes from five reviews] | $3.75 | *An American Folkways book* | [publisher's
imprint]". Front flap: "[white background; printing in black] [upper right]
$3.50 | REDWOOD | COUNTRY | *The Lava Region and the* | *Redwoods* | by |
Alfred Powers | [blurb] | *Jacket Photograph by Ansel Adams* | *An American
Folkways Book* | [publisher's imprint]". Back flap: "[white background; print-
ing in black] [upper left] $3.50 | NIAGARA | COUNTRY | by | Lloyd Gra-
ham | [blurb] | *An American Folkways Book* | [publisher's imprint].

Published at $3.50 on July 20, 1949; number of copies printed unknown.
Copyrighted August 12, 1949; deposited July 22, 1949.

The book is listed in "The Weekly Record," August 20, 1949, p. 769.

Note: No evidence found that Duell, Sloan and Pearce reprinted *Redwood
Country*.

CITED: *Mount Shasta* MS712

COPIES: CF

REPRINTS AND REPRODUCTIONS

None.

BIOGRAPHY

Alfred Powers was born on a cattle ranch near Delana, Arkansas, on
June 3, 1887, the son of Andrew C. and Elizabeth (Prescott) Powers. His father was a rancher. Powers spent his early years in Oklahoma and Texas before moving west. He often said that building trails in the Cascades, his first
real job, had a lasting influence on his life and his unending interest in the
Northwest.

Powers attended the University of Oklahoma before enrolling in the
University of Oregon in 1907. He earned a bachelor's degree in rhetoric from
Oregon in 1910 and was admitted to Phi Beta Kappa.

During World War I, Powers served in France as a member of the famed
Rainbow Division, the 42nd Division of the U.S. Army, which was made up
of National Guard troops from all over the United States and was the first
American unit to see combat in the war.

After his return from France, Powers was an assistant director of the
Northwestern Division of the American Red Cross, in Seattle, with manage-
ment responsibilities for Oregon and Washington and the Territory of
Alaska. From 1920 until 1922, he was University Editor for the School of
Journalism of the University of Oregon. In 1922, he joined the university fac-

ulty as assistant director of the extension division, becoming dean of the division in 1926. When he retired from the University of Oregon in 1961, he was dean of creative writing and publishing.[2] For many years, Powers taught an evening writing class at the Lincoln High School in Portland (now Lincoln Hall at Portland State University). Scores of Northwest journalists and writers are said to have been his students.

In 1919, Powers married Harriet Elizabeth Morsman. The couple had two children, John and Elizabeth. Powers and his second wife, the former Molly Douglas Averill, were married in 1961.

Powers wrote a dozen books, collaborated on or contributed to others, and wrote many magazine articles. From 1935 to 1937, he was associated with the Oregon division of the Federal Writers' Project, where he was a contributing writer to the Oregon state guide, *Oregon: End of the Trail.*

Alfred Powers died in Portland, Oregon, on July 24, 1983, at age 96.

NOTES ON *REDWOOD COUNTRY*

Duell, Sloan & Pearce promoted the book in an advertisement in the March 19, 1949, issue of *Publishers' Weekly* which read, below the book's title, "The land of the giant Redwoods, of Crater Lake, and the hauntingly beautiful Mount Shasta, along with the whole great lava region, comprise the scene of this American Folkways Book."

REVIEWS

Booklist, September 15, 1949 (p. 31); *Commonweal,* August 19, 1949 (p. 470); *Kirkus,* May 15, 1949 (p. 264); *Library Journal,* July 1949 (p. 1023); *New York Herald Tribune Weekly Book Review,* October 9, 1949 (p. 18); *San Francisco Chronicle,* July 18, 1949 (p. 12); *Saturday Review of Literature,* September 10, 1949 (p. 22); *Wisconsin Library Bulletin,* December 1949 (p. 9).

SELECTED WRITINGS BY ALFRED POWERS

(contributor) *Marooned in Crater Lake: Stories of the Skyline Trail, the Umpqua Trail, and the Old Oregon Trail* (Portland: Metropolitan Press, 1930); *Early Printing in the Oregon Country* (Portland: The Portland (Oregon) Club of Printing House Craftsmen, 1933); *History of Oregon Literature* (Portland: Metropolitan Press, 1935); *Hannibal's Elephants* (New York: Longmans, 1944); *Legends of the Four High Mountains* (Portland: Junior Historical Journal, 1944); *Poems of the Covered Wagons* (Portland: Pacific Publishing House, 1947); *Chains for Columbus* (Philadelphia: Westminster, 1948); *Prisoners of*

2. *The Oregonian,* (obituary) July 27, 1983, p. B8.

the Redwoods: An Adventure Story of San Francisco and the Northern California Coast in the Fifties (New York: Coward-McCann, 1948); **Redwood Country** (New York: Duell, Sloan & Pearce, 1949); *A Long Way to Frisco: A Folk Adventure Novel of California and Oregon in 1852* (Boston: Little Brown, 1951); (with Emil R. Peterson) *A Century of Coos and Curry: History of Southwest Oregon* (Portland: Binfords & Mort [for] Coos-Curry Pioneer and Historical Association, 1952); *True Adventures on Westward Trails* (Boston: Little Brown, 1954); *Alexander's Horses* (New York: Longmans, 1959); (with Leland Huot) *Homer Davenport of Silverton: Life of A Great Cartoonist* (Bingen, Wash.: West Shore Press, 1973).

SOURCES

Benét, William Rose, Ed. *The Reader's Encyclopedia.* New York: Thomas Y. Crowell Company, 1948, p. 904 (listing on Rainbow Division).

Book Review Digest 1949. New York: The H.W. Wilson Company, 1950, p. 744.

Publishers' Weekly, January 29, 1949, p. 550; March 19, 1949, p. 1282; August 20, 1949, p. 769; and September 3, 1949 (Duell, Sloan & Pearce Fall List), p. 906.

Saturday Review of Literature, September 10, 1949, p. 22.

New York Herald Tribune Weekly Book Review, October 9, 1949, p. 18.

(Portland) *Oregonian* obituary, July 27, 1983, p. B-8.

Barash, Elizabeth (daughter of Alfred Powers). Telephone interview with CF, March 26, 2003; letter to CF, April 17, 2003.

ROCKY MOUNTAIN COUNTRY

Albert N. Williams
December 26, 1914 – September 18, 1962

AF23   First edition, first printing (1950) [20]

[*Folkways* device] I [within a blue (close to Pantone 641) rectangle with rounded corners, in cream] EDITED BY ERSKINE CALDWELL I [black] ROCKY I MOUNTAIN I COUNTRY I BY ALBERT N. WILLIAMS I [cream] DUELL, SLOAN & PEARCE · NEW YORK

COLLATION: 8½" x 6". 160 leaves. [i–vi] vii–xxv [xxvi–xxx] [1–2] 3–289 [290]. Numbers printed in the center at the foot of the page.

CONTENTS: p. [i], half-title: "*Rocky Mountain Country* I [thin rule] I *Also by Albert N. Williams* I *LISTENING* I *(Critical Essays)*"; p. [ii], "AMERICAN FOLKWAYS I EDITED BY ERSKINE CALDWELL I [list of 20 titles and their authors, beginning with *Golden Gate Country* and ending with *Rocky Mountain Country*] I In Preparation I [list of eight titles[1]]"; p. [iii], title; p. [iv], copyright page: "COPYRIGHT, 1950 BY I Albert N. Williams I *All rights reserved, including the right* I *to reproduce this book or portions* I *thereof in any form.* I First Printing I PRINTED IN THE UNITED STATES OF AMERICA"; p. [v], dedication: "*For My Father* I This is his country"; p. [vi], blank; pp. vii–x, "Contents"; pp. xi–xxv, "Introduction"; pp. [xxvi–xxx], five maps entitled "Rocky Mountain Country[2]; p. [1], half-title: "*Rocky Mountain Country* I [thin rule] I *Also by Albert N. Williams* I *LISTENING* I *(Critical Essays)*"; p. [2], blank; pp. 3–277, text; p. 278, "Ac-

---

1. The list Includes *Great Lakes Country* by Iola Fuller, *Tidewater Country* by Elswyth Thane, *Pacific Northwest Country* by Richard Neuberger, *Gold Rush Country* by Charis Weston, *Pennsylvania Dutch Country* by Harry Emerson Wildes, *Buckeye Country* by Louis Bromfield, and *Homesteader Country* by Edward Stanley, none of which were published in the *Folkways* series, and *Wheat Country* by William Bracke, which was published in the series.
2. The five maps are subtitled "Early Exploration;" "Frémont's Rocky Mountain Crossings and the Battle of Glorieta Pass, 1862;" "Early Trails;" "Major Mineral Fields;" and "The Three Circle Tours."

knowledgments"; pp. 279–282, "Bibliographical Note"; pp. 283–289, "Index"; p. [290], blank.

BINDING: Blue cloth (close to Pantone 302). Front: *Folkways* device stamped in black at lower right corner. Spine stamped in black, except where noted: "[four thin rules | [thick rule] | [four thin rules] | [within a black panel, in gold] ROCKY | MOUNTAIN | COUNTRY | · | ALBERT N. | WILLIAMS | [four thin rules] | [thick rule] | [at bottom] [four thin rules | [within a black panel, in gold] DUELL, SLOAN | AND PEARCE | [four thin rules] | [thick rule]". Cream endpapers carry map of the United States in blue (close to Pantone 641) and cream; "Rocky Mountain Country" area is shaded in cream and further identified on a blue ribbon in lower right corner.

DUST JACKET (white paper): Front: Blue background (close to Pantone 298). "[rust (close to Pantone 470)] Rocky Mountain | Country | [black] [thin rule] | AMERICAN FOLKWAYS | [thin rule] | [black-and-white photograph of snow-capped mountains; a lake in the foreground, framed with an irregular horizontal rectangular rust and black frame] | [rust] ALBERT N. WILLIAMS". Spine: Rust background. "[blue] Rocky | Mountain | Country | [black] The High Rockies | between Santa Fe | and Cheyenne | WILLIAMS | [*Folkways* device] | [blue] DUELL, SLOAN | AND PEARCE". Back: "[white background; printing in black] SOUTHERN CALIFORNIA COUNTRY | *An Island on the Land* | by Carey McWilliams | [quotes from five reviews] | $3.75 | *An American Folkways book* | [publisher's imprint]". Front flap: White background; printing in black. "[upper right] $3.50 | Rocky Mountain | Country | by | Albert N. Williams | [blurb] | *An American Folkways Book* | [publisher's imprint]". Back flap: "[white background; printing in black] [upper left] $3.50 | [quote from *The Saturday Review of Literature* review of *Redwood Country*] | REDWOOD | COUNTRY | *The Lava Region and the* | *Redwoods* | by | Alfred Powers | [blurb] | *An American Folkways Book* | [publisher's imprint].

Published at $3.50 on February 17, 1950; number of copies printed unknown. Copyrighted March 17, 1950; deposited February 27, 1950.

The book is listed in "The Weekly Record," April 8, 1950, p. 1719.

Note: No evidence found that Duell, Sloan and Pearce reprinted *Rocky Mountain Country*.

COPIES: CF

REPRINTS AND REPRODUCTIONS

Reproduced on microfilm. New Haven, Conn.: Yale University Library, 1993. 1 reel, 35 mm.

BIOGRAPHY

Albert Nathaniel Williams, Jr. was born in Dennison, Texas, on January 26, 1914, the son of Albert Nathaniel and Clara Lillian (Skeel) Williams. The senior Williams was a prominent business executive, serving as president of Western Union Telegraph Co. during the war years 1941–1945 and later as president of other national corporations.

Williams prepared for college at the Blake School in Minnesota. After attending Macalester College and Northwestern University in the early 1930s, he entered Yale University as a freshman, graduating in 1936.

After a short time as an advertising copywriter, Williams joined the National Broadcasting Company in 1937 as a program director, creating many of the network's dramatic public service programs. After leaving NBC in 1941, he worked for a year as a freelance radio and advertising copywriter. In 1942, with the United States at war, he joined the State Department, working in the Office of the Coordinator of Inter-American Affairs as chief of the Script Services Division of the Latin-American radio service. In 1943, he joined the Navy, serving as a communications officer. When the war ended in 1945, he returned to government service as editor in chief of the English Features Section of the Voice of America.

In the summer of 1947, Williams moved to his family's ranch in Littleton, Colorado, and joined the faculty of the University of Denver, teaching English. In 1949, he became assistant to the chancellor and director of development. In 1954, he moved to Chicago, where he worked as executive director of the Associated Colleges of Illinois until 1960, when he and a partner founded a fund-raising enterprise, the Fund Fulfillment Corporation of Chicago.

Williams was married three times, first to Jeahnne de Mare, with whom he had two children, Christopher Healy and Holliday (a girl); second; to Martha Rountree; and third to Ann West, with whom he had a son, Albert. (Martha Rountree was the co-creator and long-time moderator of the NBC news program "Meet the Press.")

Williams wrote ten books, three with Western themes, two biblical histories, four books written with his wife, the former Ann West, relating to biblical figures and the Scriptures, and a collection of critical articles.

In 1958, Williams received an honorary doctorate in letters from Lincoln College in Lincoln, Illinois.

Albert N. Williams died in St. Louis, Missouri, on September 18, 1962, at age 47.

NOTES ON *ROCKY MOUNTAIN COUNTRY*

The book is the first volume in the Folkways series to contain maps — five maps altogether. Williams wrote the book while a member of the faculty of the University of Denver.

REVIEWS

Booklist, March 1, 1950 (p. 217); *Commonweal,* March 10, 1950 (p. 586); *Kirkus,* December 15, 1949 (p. 684); *Library Journal,* February 15, 1950 (p. 321); *New York Herald Tribune Book Review,* February 26, 1950 (p. 4); *New York Times,* February 26, 1950 (p. 36); *San Francisco Chronicle,* February 23, 1950 (p. 22); *Saturday Review of Literature,* April 8, 1950 (p. 11).

SELECTED WRITINGS BY ALBERT N. WILLIAMS

Listening: A Collection of Critical Articles on Radio (Denver: University of Denver Press, 1948); **Rocky Mountain Country** (New York: Duell, Sloan & Pearce, 1950); *The Water and the Power: Development of the Five Great Rivers of the West* (New York: Duell, Sloan & Pearce, 1951); The *Black Hills: Mid-Continent Resort* (Dallas: Southern Methodist University Press, 1952); *The Holy City* (New York: Duell, Sloan & Pearce, 1954); *Paul, the World's First Missionary: A Biography of the Apostle Paul* (New York: Association Press, 1954); *Simon Peter, Fisher of Men: A Fictionalized Autobiography of the Apostle Peter* (New York: Association Press, 1954); *John Mark, First Gospel Writer* (New York: Association Press, 1956); *Key Words of the Bible: A New Guide to Better Understanding of the Scriptures* (New York: Duell, Sloan & Pearce, 1956); *What Archeology Says about the Bible* (New York, Association Press, 1957).

SOURCES

Book Review Digest 1950. New York: The H.W. Wilson Company, 1951, pp. 974–975.

Publishers' Weekly, January 25, 1950 (Duell, Sloan & Pearce Spring List) [n.p.]; and April 8, 1950, p. 1719.

The New York Times Book Review, February 26, 1950, p. 36.

Who Was Who in America, Vol. IV, 1961–1968. Chicago: Marquis - Who's Who, Inc. (Entry on Williams, Albert Nathaniel, father of Albert N. Williams, Jr.)

Williams III, Albert N. (son of Albert N. Williams, Jr.). E-mail messages to CF, August 5, 2002.

Williams, Christopher (son of Albert N. Williams, Jr.). E-mail message to CF, August 6, 2002.

Moon, Danelle. Manuscripts and Archives, Sterling Memorial Library, Yale University. E-mail message to CF, March 27, 2003, and various documents from the library archives pertaining to Albert Williams.

SHORT GRASS COUNTRY

Stanley Vestal
August 15, 1887 – December 25, 1957

AF24   First edition, first printing (1941) [3]

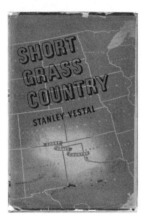

[*Folkways* device | [within a green rectangle (close to Pantone 335) with rounded corners, in cream] EDITED BY ERSKINE CALDWELL | [black] SHORT GRASS | COUNTRY | *by* | STANLEY VESTAL | [cream] DUELL, SLOAN & PEARCE · NEW YORK

COLLATION: 8½" x 6". 160 leaves. [i–viii] ix–x [1–2] 3–297 [298] 299–304 [305–310]. Numbers printed in roman in headline at the outer margin of the type page, except for pp. ix, 3, 10, 25, 44, 72, 96, 108, 121, 140, 172, 188, 209 , 217, 232, 255, 279, and 299, on which the numbers are printed in the center at the foot of the page.

CONTENTS: p. [i], half-title: "SHORT GRASS COUNTRY"; p. [ii], "AMER-ICAN FOLKWAYS | Edited by ERSKINE CALDWELL | [thin rule] | [list of three titles and their authors, beginning with *Desert Country* and ending with *Short Grass Country*] | *In Preparation* | [list of five titles and their authors[1]] | Books by STANLEY VESTAL | [thin rule] | [list of fifteen titles]"; p. [iii], title; p. [iv], copyright page: "COPYRIGHT, 1941, BY | STANLEY VESTAL | *All rights reserved, including* | *the right to reproduce this book* | *or*

1. The list includes *Florida Country* by Stetson Kennedy; the title was changed to *Palmetto Country*.

portions thereof in any form. | *first edition* | PRINTED IN THE UNITED STATES OF AMERICA"; p. [v], dedication: "*To* | AUNT ANNE"; p. [vi], blank; p. [vii], "ACKNOWLEDGMENTS"; p. [viii], blank; pp. ix–x, "Contents"; p. [1], half-title: "SHORT GRASS COUNTRY"; p. [2], blank; pp. 3–297, text; p. [298], blank; pp. 299–304, "Index"; pp. [305–310], blank.

BINDING: Tan cloth (close to Pantone 727). Front: *Folkways* device stamped in brown (close to Pantone 483) at lower right corner. Spine, stamped in brown, except where noted: "[thick rule] | [four thin rules] | [within a burgundy panel, in gold] SHORT | GRASS | COUNTRY | · | STANLEY | VESTAL | [four thin rules] | [thick rule] | [four thin rules] | [at bottom] [four thin rules | [within a brown panel, in gold] DUELL, SLOAN | AND PEARCE | [four thin rules] | [thick rule]". Cream endpapers carry map of the United States in medium green (close to Pantone 347) and cream; "Short Grass Country" region is shaded in cream and further identified on two ribbon-like banners.

DUST JACKET (gold paper): Front carries the western portion of the United States map found on the endpapers in medium green (close to Pantone 347), with the 'Short Grass Country' region highlighted in cream. "[thick brown rule, close to Pantone 497] | [brown] [in outline] SHORT | GRASS | COUNTRY | [solid] STANLEY VESTAL | [printed on a medium green ribbon, in cream] SHORT GRASS COUNTRY | [thick brown rule]". Spine: "[thick brown rule] | [four thin brown rules on a cream band] | [brown] [on medium green background] SHORT | GRASS | COUNTRY | · | [cream] STANLEY | VESTAL | [brown] [four thin rules, thick rule, four thin rules, with the *Folkways* device overlaid in the center] | [drawing of saddle, spurs, boots, and a lasso] | [four thin brown rules] | [within a brown panel, in medium green] DUELL, SLOAN | AND PEARCE | [four thin brown rules] | [thick brown rule]". Back: "[gold background] [within an arced ribbon, in medium green] AMERICAN FOLKWAYS | [brown] *Edited by* | Erskine Caldwell | [blurb, signed by Erskine Caldwell] | [medium green] READY | [brown] [list of three titles and their authors: *Desert Country, Piñon Country,* and *Short Grass Country*] | [medium green] IN PREPARATION | [burgundy] [list of five titles and their authors, with a brief description of each: *Florida Country,*[2] *Ozark Country, Mormon Country, High Border Country,* and *Blue Ridge Country*] | [medium green] *Each Volume, $3.00* | [brown] [publisher's imprint]". Front flap: "[brown] [upper right] *$3.00* | [passage from *Short Grass Country*] | [medium green] Short Grass Country | [brown] *by* STANLEY VESTAL | [blurb] | [publisher's imprint]". Back flap: "[brown] | LEWIS GANNETT *foresees that the* AMERICAN | FOLKWAYS *series may*

2. Later titled *Palmetto Country*.

be 'a landmark in Amer- I ican regional literature.' I [medium green] Desert Country I [brown] *by* EDWIN CORLE I [quotes from three reviews] I [medium green] Piñon Country I [brown] *by* HANIEL LONG I [quotes from two reviews] I [medium green] *Each Volume, $3.00* I [brown] [publisher's imprint]".

Published at $3.00 on October 30, 1941; number of copies printed unknown. Copyrighted November 6, 1941; deposited November 1, 1941.

The book is listed in "The Weekly Record," November 1, 1941, p. 1792.

Note: Duell, Sloan & Pearce published at least three printings of *Short Grass Country*.

CITED: *Guns* 1028; *Guns* 2270 (Revised Ed.); *Herd* 2407

COPIES: CF

REPRINTS AND REPRODUCTIONS

Greenwood Press. Westport, Conn: Greenwood Press, 1970. Published at $11.25.

BIOGRAPHY

(Walter) Stanley Vestal was born on August 15, 1887, on a homestead on the Kansas frontier, the son of Walter Malory and Isabella Louise (Wood) Vestal. Vestal's father, a lawyer, died a few months after the child's birth and mother and child returned to her mother's home in Fredonia, in southeast Kansas.

When Vestal was nine, his mother married James Robert Campbell, the superintendent of Fredonia schools. In 1898, Campbell was named superintendent of schools in Guthrie, capital of the Oklahoma Territory. During these years, Walter began to use the name Walter Stanley Campbell. In 1915, when he joined the Oklahoma University faculty and began to work as a writer, he adopted "Stanley Vestal" as a pen name.

Vestal was educated in public schools in Kansas and Oklahoma. He attended Southwestern State College in Weatherford, Oklahoma Territory, majoring in Latin and Greek. In 1908, he and nine classmates composed the first Southwestern State College graduating class. Owing to a political dispute between the Republicans who had controlled the Territory, and the Democrats who took control when Oklahoma became a state in November, 1907, Vestal and his classmates were not awarded academic degrees.

In 1908, Vestal became the first Rhodes Scholar from the new state, winning a three-year scholarship.. (There had been earlier Rhodes Scholars from the Oklahoma Territory.) In 1911, he earned a bachelor's degree from Merton

College at Oxford. In 1916, after maintaining his Oxford University status, he was named master of arts, in effect an honorary degree.

During World War I, Vestal served in France as captain and battery commander, 335th Field Artillery, 87th Division. He spent six months in France with the Allied Expeditionary Forces, but saw no action.

On December 26, 1917, Vestal married Isabel Jones. The couple had two children, Dorothy and Malory. They were divorced in 1939.

Vestal was successful in the two lives he lived under the two names he used professionally. As Stanley Vestal he was known and respected as a distinguished historian of the American West and the American Indian. As Walter S. Campbell he was known and respected as a professor of English and literature and an ingenious and effective teacher of writing. In 1938, he established a school of writing at the University of Oklahoma that became nationally known and commercially successful. He served on the faculty of the University of Oklahoma for forty-three years, from 1915 until his death.

Vestal wrote more than twenty-four books and edited others. His four books on the craft of writing were widely used as classroom and correspondence course texts. He wrote more than two hundred articles, book reviews, and forewords or introductions to other books, his work appearing in popular magazines and dozens of regional and specialized periodicals. A member of the Authors' League, he wrote more than a dozen biographical sketches in the *World Book Encyclopedia*.

Stanley Vestal died in Oklahoma City on December 25, 1957, at age 70.

NOTES ON *SHORT GRASS COUNTRY*

A Duell, Sloan & Pearce ad in the September 13, 1941, *Publishers' Weekly* gave a publication date of October 3 for the book. It was published on October 30, 1941.

Ray Tassin's 1973 biography, *Stanley Vestal: Champion of the Old West*, included the following account:

Erskine Caldwell, who had just been hired to edit a series of books on American folkways to be published by Duell, Sloan and Pearce of New York ... asked Vestal to lead off the series with a book on the short grass country. Vestal was committed to too many other projects at the time, but agreed to write the book for later in the series. Houghton Mifflin was Vestal's regular publisher, having printed nine of his fourteen books. They were reluctant for him to write for a rival firm, but agreed to permit it. [p. 223]

REVIEWS

Booklist, December 1, 1941 (p. 111); *Library Journal*, October 15, 1941 (p. 903); *New York Herald Tribune Book Review*, November 30, 1941 (p. 2); *New York*

Times Book Review, November 30, 1941 (p. 4); *Saturday Review of Literature,* December 13, 1941 (p. 11); *Scientific Book Club Review,* December 1941 (p. 4).

SELECTED WRITINGS BY STANLEY VESTAL

Fandango: Ballads of the Old West (Boston: Houghton, 1927); (ed.) *The Oregon Trail* (by Francis Parkman) (Oklahoma City: Harlow Publishing Co., 1927); *Kit Carson: The Happy Warrior of the Old West: A Biography* (Boston: Houghton, 1928); *Happy Hunting Grounds* (Chicago: Lyons and Carnahan, 1928); *'Dobe Walls: A Story of Kit Carson's Southwest* (Boston: Houghton, 1929); *Sitting Bull: Champion of the Sioux: A Biography* (Boston: Houghton, 1932); *Warpath: The True Story of the Fighting Sioux Told in a Biography of Chief White Bull* (Boston: Houghton, 1934); *New Sources of Indian History, 1850-1891: The Ghost Dance — The Prairie Sioux* (Norman: University of Oklahoma Press, 1934); *The Wine Room Murder* (Boston: Little, Brown, 1935); *Mountain Men* (Boston: Houghton, 1937); (Walter D. Merton, pseud.); *Sallow Moon* (privately printed, ca. 1937); *Revolt on the Border* (Boston: Houghton, 1938); *The Old Santa Fe Trail* (Boston: Houghton, 1939); *King of the Fur Traders: Pierre Esprit Radisson* (Boston: Houghton, 1940); **Short Grass Country** (New York: Duell, Sloan & Pearce, 1941); *Big-Foot Wallace* (Boston: Houghton, 1942); *The Missouri* (Rivers of America Series) (New York: Farrar & Rinehart, 1945); *Jim Bridger: Mountain Man* (New York: Morrow, 1946); *Wagons Southwest: Story of Old Trail to Santa Fe* (New York: American Pioneer Trails Association, 1946); *Warpath and Council Fire: The Plains Indians' Struggle for Survival in War and in Diplomacy, 1851-1891* (New York: Random House, 1948); *Queen of the Cow Towns: Dodge City: "The Wickedist Little City in America": 1872-1886* (New York: Harper, 1952); *Joe Meek: The Merry Mountain Man: A Biography* (Caldwell, Idaho: Caxton Printers, 1952); *The Book Lover's Southwest* (Norman: University of Oklahoma Press, 1955); *The Indian Tipi: Its History, Construction, and Use. With a History of the Tipi by Stanley Vestal* (by Reginald Laubin) (Norman: University of Oklahoma Press, 1957).

SOURCES

Book Review Digest 1941. New York: The H.W. Wilson Company, 1942, pp. 143.

Publishers' Weekly, September 13, 1941, p. 869; and November 1, 1941, p. 1792.

The New York Times Book Review, November 30, 1941, p. 4.

Tassin, Ray. *Stanley Vestal: Champion of the Old West.* Glendale, Calif.: The Arthur H. Clark Company, 1973, pp. 40-41, 223, 227-228.

Fitzgerald, Carol. *The Rivers of America: A Descriptive Bibliography.* New Castle, Delaware: Oak Knoll Press in association with The Center for the Book in the Library of Congress, 2001. (Entry on Stanley Vestal for *The Missouri.*)

SMOKY MOUNTAIN COUNTRY

North Callahan
August 7, 1908 – December 20, 2004

AF25 First edition, first printing (1952) [24]

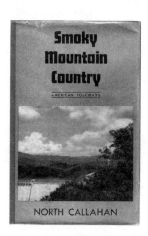

[*Folkways* device] | [within a taupe (close to Pantone 451) rectangle with rounded corners, in cream] EDITED BY ERSKINE CALDWELL | [black] SMOKY | MOUNTAIN | COUNTRY | BY NORTH CALLAHAN | [cream] DUELL, SLOAN & PEARCE · NEW YORK | LITTLE, BROWN & COMPANY · BOSTON

COLLATION: 8½" x 6". 136 leaves. [i–vii] viii–xii [xiii–xiv] [1–3] 4–14 [15] 16–36 [37] 38–54 [55] 56–73 [74] 75–102 [103] 104–116 [117] 118–140 [141] 142–167 [168] 169–194 [195] 196–213 [214] 215–231 [232] 233–250 [251] 252–257 [258]. Numbers printed in roman in headline at the outer margin of the type page.

CONTENTS: p. [i], half-title: "*Smoky Mountain Country*"; p. [ii], "AMERICAN FOLKWAYS | EDITED BY ERSKINE CALDWELL | [list of 24 titles and their authors, beginning with *Golden Gate Country* and ending with *Far North Country*] | In Preparation | [list of eight titles[1]]"; p. [iii], title; p. [iv], copyright page: "COPYRIGHT 1952, | BY NORTH CALLAHAN | ALL

---

1. The list includes *Ohio Country* by Elrick B. Davis (which would have replaced *Buckeye Country* by Louis Bromfield), *Great Lakes Country* by Iola Fuller, *Pacific Northwest Country* by Richard Neuberger, *Homesteader Country* by Edward Stanley, *Tidewater Country* by Elswyth Thane, *Pennsylvania Dutch Country* by Harry Emerson Wildes, and *Gold Rush Country* by Charis Weston, none of which were published in the *Folkways* series, and *Adirondack Country* by William C. White, which was published in the series.

RIGHTS RESERVED. NO PART OF THIS BOOK IN EXCESS OF FIVE | HUNDRED WORDS MAY BE REPRODUCED IN ANY FORM WITHOUT | PERMISSION IN WRITING FROM THE PUBLISHER | LIBRARY OF CONGRESS CATALOG CARD NO. 52–6783 | FIRST EDITION | [within a rectangular frame] DUELL, SLOAN AND PEARCE-LITTLE, BROWN | BOOKS ARE PUBLISHED BY | LITTLE, BROWN AND COMPANY | IN ASSOCIATION WITH | DUELL, SLOAN & PEARCE, INC. | *Published simultaneously* | *in Canada by McClelland and Stewart Limited* | PRINTED IN THE UNITED STATES OF AMERICA"; p. [v], dedication: *To* | *My Father and Mother* | *True Offspring of the Smokies*"; p. [vi], blank; pp. [vii–xii], "Foreword" [includes acknowledgments]"; pp. [xiii–xiv], "Contents"; p. [1], half-title: "*Smoky Mountain Country*"; p. [2], blank; pp. [3]-250, text; pp. [251]-257, "Index"; p. [258], blank.

BINDING: Light blue cloth (close to Pantone 659). Front: *Folkways* device stamped in black at lower right corner. Spine stamped in black, except where noted: "[thick rule] | [four thin rules] | [within a black panel, in gold] SMOKY | MOUNTAIN | COUNTRY | · | NORTH | CALLAHAN | [four thin rules] | [thick rule] | [four thin rules] | [at bottom] [four thin rules | [within a black panel, in gold] DUELL, SLOAN | AND PEARCE | thin rule | LITTLE, BROWN | [four thin rules] | [thick rule]". Cream endpapers carry map of the United States in blue (close to Pantone 659) and cream, with the "Smoky Mountain Country" region highlighted in cream and further identified on a blue ribbon in the lower right corner.

DUST JACKET (white paper): Front: Light blue (close to Pantone 643); printing in black. "Smoky | Mountain | Country | [thin rule] | AMERICAN FOLKWAYS | [thin rule] | [black-and-white photograph of low mountains in the background; a dam in the foreground] | NORTH CALLAHAN". Spine: Orange background (close to Pantone 145); printing in white. "Smoky | Mountain | Country | The land of | ballads | and frontier | memories, | of Oak Ridge | and TVA | CALLAHAN | [*Folkways* device in black and white] | DUELL, SLOAN | AND PEARCE | [thin rule] | LITTLE, BROWN". Back: White background; printing in black. "American Folkways | Edited by ERSKINE CALDWELL | [blurb praising the series] | [list of 24 authors and the corresponding series title for each] | [publisher's imprint[2]]". Front flap: White background; printing in black. "[upper right] $4.00 | Smoky | Mountain | Country | by NORTH CALLAHAN | [blurb] | (continued on back flap)". Back flap: White background; printing in black. "(continued from first flap) | [blurb] | Photograph courtesy of the Tennessee | Valley Authority | [within a rectangular frame] DUELL, SLOAN AND

2. The imprint reads: "Duell, Sloan and Pearce — Little, Brown and Company."

PEARCE-LITTLE, BROWN I BOOKS ARE PUBLISHED BY I LITTLE, BROWN AND COMPANY I IN ASSOCIATION WITH I DUELL, SLOAN & PEARCE, INC.".

Published at $4.00 on May 9, 1952;[3] number of copies printed unknown. Copyrighted May 14, 1952; deposited May 13, 1952.

The book is listed in "The Weekly Record, "June 14, 1952, p. 2487.

Note: Duell, Sloan & Pearce published at least two printings of *Smoky Mountain Country.*

COPIES: CF

REPRINTS AND REPRODUCTIONS

Sevierville, TN: Smoky Mountain Historical Society, 1988. Edition limited to 1,000 copies. Published at $19.95.

Reproduced on microfilm. Atlanta, Ga.: SOLINET, 1994. 1 reel; 35 mm.

BIOGRAPHY

North Callahan was born on August 7, 1908, on a farm in Fork Creek, near Sweetwater, Tennessee, the son of R.B. and Naomi (North) Callahan. In 1930, he earned a bachelor of arts degree from the University of Chattanooga (now the University of Tennessee at Chattanooga). He later attended Columbia University, earning a master of arts degree in American history in 1950. He earned a doctorate in American civilization from New York University in 1955, where he was a Penfield Fellow.

From 1930 to 1935, Callahan was a teacher and principal in various Tennessee public schools. From 1935 to 1937, he was an advisor on education for the Tennessee Valley Authority (TVA) and the Civilian Conservation Corps (CCC). From 1937 to 1939, he worked as a reporter, editor, and columnist for various newspapers in Tennessee and Texas. He was the New York correspondent for the *Dallas News* from 1939 to 1944, a period that included four years of the U.S. involvement in World War II. During these years he became a syndicated columnist and also served in the Army from 1940 to 1945.

During his Army service, Callahan was based at Governor's Island in the New York City harbor, rising to the rank of lieutenant colonel. He wrote recruiting publicity for the Army; edited *Army Life* magazine, which was distributed nationwide to schools, libraries, and government officials; and

3. According to the copyright certificate, the book was published May 9, 1952; the book was not available until June 5, 1952.

supervised a nationwide radio series, "The Voice of the Army."

In 1944, Callahan married Jennie Waugh. The couple had two children, North Callahan, Jr. and Mary Alice. They were divorced. Callahan later married Helen Pemberton, who died in 2004.

Callahan worked as a public relations consultant in New York City from 1945 to 1950. He began his university teaching career in the mid-1950s as professor of history at Finch College (1956–1957), then at New York University, where he served as associate professor of history (1956–1962) and professor of history from 1962 to 1973, when he retired and was named professor emeritus.

After his retirement, he lectured at several universities in Great Britain, served as head of the Civil War Round Table of New York and as a member of the New York City Bicentennial Commission, and founded the American Revolution Round Table. He contributed to newspapers and magazines and was a consultant on American history to American Express, Twentieth-Century Fox, and the National Cash Register Company.

In 1964, Callahan received an honorary doctorate in humane letters from the University of Chattanooga (now, as noted, the University of Tennessee at Chattanooga). In 1983, he received the Distinguished Alumnus Award of the University of Tennessee, at the time making him the only person in the university's history to have received both these honors.

Callahan wrote two novels, six biographies, four works of history, two books about the U.S. Army, and an account of the creation and work of the Tennessee Valley Authority.

North Callahan died in Chattanooga, Tennessee, on December 20, 2004, at age 96.

PAPERS: North Callahan's papers are held by the Lupton Library, University of Tennessee at Chattanooga (North Callahan Collection — 6.5 linear feet; MSS 070). The collection of more than two thousand volumes contains original manuscripts of his books, including materials relating to *Smoky Mountain Country;* unpublished notes; a collection of personal photographs; and Callahan's personal research library.

NOTES ON *SMOKY MOUNTAIN COUNTRY*

In an April 10, 2003, typewritten letter to CF, Callahan wrote:

My Smoky Mountain book originated at Columbia University in a seminar under the Pulitzer Prize-winning Richard Hofstadter and was about the recent Senatorial campaign of Estes Kefauver. You can imagine the hilarious reception of its discussion. Later I revised the manuscript and offered it to Duell-Sloan and Pearce. They were going to turn it down when my friend Estes rescued it. (You will note it was published by Little Brown.)[4]

I did not work closely with Erskine Caldwell whose main contribution was asking me to include as much humor as possible, so I dug up all the old jokes which are included. I was not familiar with the American Folkways series. The publisher did not make any serious demands. I was satisfied with the promotion of the book, the little Jewish girl at DS&P placing me on numerous TV and radio shows. I even appeared on the Grand Old Opera, though this came about through a whiz of a former Wac I knew in the army. (See the exact quotes on the jacket).

1952 was a good time for a book to be published. Newspapers carried pages and did reviews and the other media gave more time to books.... SMC has been reprinted three times by the publisher and now has been reprinted by the Smoky Mountain Historical Society. I think I am still in Who's Who in America.... All the best, [signed] North Callahan. P.S. [handwritten] I did get to know Charlie Duell well — a nice guy.

This is the first title in the series to be identified as published by Little, Brown and Company in association with Duell, Sloan & Pearce, Inc. The new publisher's imprint appears on the back of the dust jacket, a brief statement of the new publishing relationship is on the copyright page and the back flap of the dust jacket, and the co-publishers are named on the title page and the book's spine.

REVIEWS

Booklist, July 1, 1952 (p. 357); *Bookmark,* July 1952 (p. 238); *Chicago Sunday Tribune,* September 14, 1952 (p. 11); *Christian Century,* September 10, 1952 (p. 1032); *Christian Science Monitor,* August 7, 1952 (p. 7); *Kirkus,* April 1, 1952 (p. 252); *Library Journal,* July 1952 (p. 1194); *New York Herald Tribune Book Review,* June 15, 1952 (p. 7); *New York Times Book Review,* July 6, 1952 (p. 4); *San*

4. Richard Hofstadter, 1917–1970. American historian and professor at Columbia University for many years. Winner of Pulitzer Prizes for *The Age of Reform* (1955) and *Anti–Intellectualism in American Life* (1963). Estes Kefauver, 1903–1963. U.S. Congressman (1939–1948) and U.S. Senator (1948–1963) from Tennessee. He was an unsuccessful candidate for the Democratic presidential nomination in 1952 and 1956.

Francisco Chronicle, August 10, 1952 (p. 10); *Saturday Review of Literature,* July 12, 1952 (p. 33); *Springfield Republican,* August 3, 1952 (p. 6–D).

SELECTED WRITINGS BY NORTH CALLAHAN

The Armed Forces As a Career (New York: McGraw-Hill, 1947); **Smoky Mountain Country** (New York: Duell, Sloan & Pearce - Little, Brown, 1952); *Henry Knox: General Washington's General* (New York: Rinehart, 1958); *Daniel Morgan: Ranger of the Revolution* (New York: Holt, Rinehart & Winston, 1961); *Royal Raiders: The Tories of the American Revolution* (Indianapolis: Bobbs-Merrill, 1963); *Carl Sandburg: Lincoln of Our Literature: A Biography* (New York: New York University Press, 1970); *George Washington: Soldier and Man* (New York: Morrow, 1972); *TVA: Bridge Over Troubled Waters* (South Brunswick, N.J.: A.S. Barnes, 1980); *Peggy* (New York: Cornwall Books, 1983); *Daybreak* (New York: Cornwall Books, 1985); *Carl Sandburg: His Life and Works* (University Park: Pennsylvania State University Press, 1987); *Thanks Mr. President: The Trail-Blazing Second Term of George Washington* (New York: Cornwall Books, 1991).

SOURCES

Book Review Digest 1952. New York: The H.W. Wilson Company, 1953, pp. 144–145.

Duell, Sloan & Pearce *Book News* Press Release for *Smoky Mountain Country.* May 19, 1952.

Publishers' Weekly, June 14, 1952, p. 2487.

The New York Times Book Review, July 6, 1952, p. 4.

HarperCollins Dictionary of Biography. New York: HarperCollins, 1993.

Benét's Reader's Encyclopedia, Fourth Edition. New York: HarperCollins Publishers, Inc., 1996. (Entries on Richard Hofstadter and Estes Kefauver.)

The New York Times death notice, Dr. Jennie Waugh Callahan, October 2, 1998, Late Edition, p. C-19.

Contemporary Authors Online. The Gale Group, 2001. Reproduced in *Biography Resource Center.* Farmington Hills, Mich.: The Gale Group, 2001.

"North Callahan Essay Contest," The University of Tennessee at Chattanooga (contest announcement and rules), April 15, 2002.

Townsend, Gavin, Director of University Honors Program, University of Tennessee at Chattanooga. E-mail message to CF, with attachments, April 1, 2003.

Callahan, Dr. North. Letter to CF, April 10, 2003.

Chattanoogan obituary, December 28, 2004.

The New York Times, New York Regional Edition obituary, January 6, 2004.

SOUTHERN CALIFORNIA COUNTRY: AN ISLAND ON THE LAND

Carey McWilliams
December 13, 1905 – June 27, 1980

AF26   First edition, first printing (1946) [14]

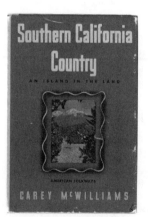

[*Folkways* device] | [within a bright green (close to Pantone 369) rectangle with rounded corners, in cream] EDITED BY ERSKINE CALDWELL | [black] SOUTHERN | CALIFORNIA | COUNTRY | An Island on the Land | BY CAREY McWILLIAMS | [cream] DUELL, SLOAN & PEARCE · NEW YORK

COLLATION: 8½" x 6". 200 leaves. [i–vi] vii–xii [1–2] 3–387 [388]. Numbers printed in roman in headline at the outer margin of the type page, except for pp. vii, ix, 3, 21, 49, 70, 84, 96, 113, 138, 165, 183, 205, 227, 249, 273, 314, 330, 350, 371, and 379, on which the numbers are printed in the center at the foot of the page.

CONTENTS: p. [i], half-title: "SOUTHERN | CALIFORNIA | COUNTRY"; p. [ii], "AMERICAN FOLKWAYS | Edited by ERSKINE CALDWELL | [thin rule] | [list of 14 titles and their authors, beginning with *Desert Country* and ending with *Southern California Country*] | In Preparation | [list of nine titles and their authors[1]”; p. [iii], title; p. [iv], copyright page: “COPYRIGHT, 1946, BY | CAREY McWILLIAMS | *All rights reserved, including | the right to reproduce this book | or portions thereof in any form.* | *First Printing* | PRINTED IN THE UNITED STATES OF AMERICA | AMERICAN BOOK-STRATFORD PRESS, INC., NEW YORK; p. [v], dedication: “Dedicated | to | ROBERT WALKER KENNY, | -Native Son-”; p. [vi], blank; pp. vii–viii, “Foreword”; pp. ix–xii, “Contents”; p. [1], second half-title: “SOUTHERN | CALIFORNIA | COUNTRY”; p. [2], blank; pp. 3-378, text; p. 379-387, “Index”; p. [388], blank.

BINDING: Green cloth (close to Pantone 370). Front: *Folkways* device stamped in dark green (close to Pantone 343) at lower right corner. Spine stamped in dark green, except where noted: “[thick rule] | [four thin rules] | [within a dark green panel, in gold] Southern | California | Country | Carey | McWilliams | [four thin rules] | [thick rule] | [four thin rules] | [at bottom] [four thin rules | [within a dark green panel, in gold] DUELL, SLOAN | AND PEARCE | [four thin rules] | [thick rule]”. Cream front endpapers carry a map of the United States in green (close to Pantone 376) and cream, with “Southern California Country” highlighted in cream. “SOUTHERN CALIFORNIA COUNTRY” is printed in cream on a green ribbon. Rear endpapers are blank.

DUST JACKET (white paper): Front: “[medium blue background (close to Pantone 5483)] [yellow (close to Pantone 127)] Southern California | Country | [black] AN ISLAND IN THE LAND[2] | [black-and-white photograph of a lake scene, with snow-capped mountains in the background, bordered with an irregular yellow rectangular frame] | [black] AMERICAN FOLK-WAYS | [yellow] CAREY McWILLIAMS”. Spine: “[yellow background] [medium blue] SOUTHERN | CALIFORNIA | COUNTRY | [black] McWILLIAMS | [*Folkways* device in black and yellow] | DUELL, SLOAN | AND PEARCE”. Back: “[yellow background] [within an arced ribbon, in medium blue] AMERICAN FOLKWAYS | [black] [to the left of the *Folkways* device, which is in medium blue and yellow] *Edited* | - *by* - [to the right of the *Folkways* device, in black] ERSKINE | CALDWELL | [quote from Harold

1. The list includes *Buckeye Country* by Louis Bromfield, *Piney Woods Country* by John Faulkner, *Great Lakes Country* by Iola Fuller Goodspeed, *Pacific Northwest Country* by Richard Neuberger, *Tidewater Country* by Elswyth Thane, *Gold Rush Country* by Charis Weston, and *Mile-High Country* by Helen Worden, none of which were published in the series, and *Big Country* by Donald Day and *Lower Piedmont Country* by Henry C. Nixon, both of which were published in the series.
2. The tag line here is incorrect. It should read, “An Island on the Land,” not in the Land. The error was corrected on the dust jacket of the second printing.

Rugg³] | PUBLISHED | [list of 13 titles and their authors] | [quote from Lewis Gannett] | EACH VOLUME $3.00 | IN PREPARATION | [list of six titles⁴] | [medium blue] [publisher's imprint]". Front flap: White background; printing in black. "[upper right] $3.75 | SOUTHERN CALIFORNIA | COUNTRY | By Carey McWilliams | [blurb] | [publisher's imprint]". Back flap: White background; printing in black. "$3.00 | NORTH STAR | COUNTRY | by Meridel Le Sueur | [blurb] | [publisher's imprint]".

Published at $3.75 on March 22, 1946; number of copies printed unknown. Copyrighted March 22, 1946; deposited March 26, 1946

The book is listed in "The Weekly Record," March 23, 1946, p. 1770.

Note: Duell, Sloan & Pearce published at least two printings of *Southern California Country*.

CITED: *Libros Californios*, p. 78

COPIES: CF

REPRINTS AND REPRODUCTIONS

Freeport, N.Y.: Books for Libraries Press, 1970.

Santa Barbara, Calif.: Peregrine Smith, 1973. (Published as *Southern California: An Island on the Land*). Published at $3.95.

Reproduced on microfilm. Berkeley, Calif.: University of California, Library Photographic Service, 1989. 1 reel; 35 mm.

BIOGRAPHY

Carey McWilliams was born in Steamboat Springs, Colorado, on December 13, 1905, the son of Jeremiah (Jerry) Newby, a cattle rancher, land dealer, and state senator, and Harriet (Hattie) (Casley) McWilliams.

In 1922, McWilliams enrolled at the University of Southern California, where he earned a bachelor's degree and, in 1927, a law degree. He practiced law for a decade. His first book, *Ambrose Bierce: A Biography* (Boni & Liveright), was published in 1929.

3. Harold Ordway Rugg (1986–1960), author, educator, civil engineer. Pioneer in curriculum design unifying the social sciences and content based on research and experimentation.
4. Included in the list are *Buckeye Country* by Louis Bromfield, *Piney Woods Country* by John Faulkner, *Cutover Country* by John T. Frederick, *Black Jack Country* by George Milburn, and *Tidewater Country* by Elswyth Thane, none of which were published in the series. Also included in the list is *Mission Country*, the former title of this volume, *Southern California Country*, by Carey McWilliams.

On July 12, 1930, McWilliams married Dorothy Hedrick. The couple had a son, Wilson Carey. The marriage ended in divorce. On September 10, 1941, McWilliams married Iris Dornfield, a novelist. The couple had a son, Jerry Ross.

During the Great Depression, while conducting research for a second book, McWilliams studied farm labor and various labor strikes of agricultural workers. His book, *Factories in the Field* (Little, Brown), was published in 1939 (as was John Steinbeck's *The Grapes of Wrath*). Earlier in 1939, McWilliams had left the practice of law and accepted an appointment as California Commissioner of Immigration and Housing, a position he held for four years. His involvement in disputes over migrant workers and immigrants in that position aroused intense enmity among the state's agricultural business interests. After Earl Warren, a Republican, was elected governor in 1942, he fired McWilliams, who then began a full-time writing career.

Over the next seven years, McWilliams wrote seven books, including two wide-ranging analyses of California culture and five books analyzing the problems of migrant labor, various minorities and their social problems, and anti–Semitism in America. His book *North from Mexico* (Lippincott, 1949), examined the social status of Mexican-Americans and foresaw the Latino coloration of present-day California.[5] *Factories in the Field,* his second book, is generally considered the most influential of his books.

In 1945, McWilliams became West Coast contributing editor of the *Nation,* an influential magazine with roots deep in nineteenth-century liberalism. In 1951, he moved to New York City and became associate editor of the magazine, and, in 1955, editor. During his thirty years there, the *Nation* addressed McCarthyism, civil liberties, the Central Intelligence Agency, the Federal Bureau of Investigation, inhumane prison conditions, the death penalty, the military-industrial complex, American involvement in the Vietnam War, and other subjects and issues.

In *Contemporary Authors Online,* in a neat summation of Carey McWilliams's life, Lloyd J. Graybar wrote, "In 1975, McWilliams retired, having spent four decades identifying many of the questions that engaged American liberalism. On many occasions, McWilliams was called a socialist, a Communist, and a soft-headed liberal. He was not any of these, he insisted in his memoirs, but rather a Western radical, a radical who was concerned with issues rather than with the theoretical precision of his own arguments."[6]

Carey McWilliams died in Manhattan on June 27, 1980, at age 74.

5. Cannon, Lou. Profile of Carey McWilliams for State Net. www.statenet.com 1998–2000.
6. Graybar, Lloyd J. *Carey McWilliams: 1905-1980. Contemporary Authors Online.*

PAPERS: Carey McWilliams's papers are held by the University of California, Los Angeles; and the Bancroft Library, University of California, Berkeley.

NOTES ON *SOUTHERN CALIFORNIA COUNTRY*

In reference to the book, the May 11, 1946, issue of *Publishers' Weekly* reported, "Recently DS&P held a cocktail party for the author [McWilliams] at the Beverly Hills Hotel, in Beverly Hills, with authors, book trade people, reviewers, story editors, and various leaders of public opinion — university professors, editors, columnists, radio commentators, union officials and community group leaders — among the guests. . . . DS&P is also having considerable advertising for the book in Southern California papers."

REVIEWS

Book Week, March 31, 1946 (p. 3); *Booklist,* April 1, 1946 (p. 245); *Bookmark,* November 1946 (p. 11); *Catholic World,* September 1946 (p. 570); *Christian Science Monitor,* April 10, 1946 (p. 16); *Current History,* September 1946 (p. 230); *Kirkus,* February 15, 1946 (p. 84); *Library Journal,* April 1, 1946 (p. 483); *Nation,* June 8, 1946 (p. 697); *New Republic,* May 20, 1946 (p. 739); *New York Times Book Review,* April 7, 1946 (p. 6); *Saturday Review of Literature,* May 4, 1946 (p. 22); *Survey G,* September 1946 (p. 333); Weekly Book Review, April 14, 1946, (p.1).

SELECTED WRITINGS BY CAREY McWILLIAMS

Ambrose Bierce: A Biography (Boni & Liveright, 1929); *The New Regionalism in American Literature* (Seattle: University of Washington Bookstore, 1930); *Louis Adamic and Shadow-America* (Los Angeles: A. Whipple, 1935); *Factories in the Field: The Story of Migratory Farm Labor in California* (Boston: Little, Brown, 1939); *Ill Fares the Land: Migrants and Migratory Labor in the United States* (Boston: Little, Brown, 1942); *Brothers Under the Skin* (Boston: Little, Brown, 1943); *Prejudice: Japanese-Americans: Symbol of Racial Intolerance* (Boston: Little, Brown, 1944); **Southern California Country: An Island on the Land** (New York: Duell, Sloane & Pearce, 1946); *A Mask for Privilege: Anti–Semitism in America* (Boston: Little, Brown, 1948); *California: The Great Exception* (New York: Current Books, 1949); *North from Mexico: The Spanish-Speaking People of the United States* (Philadelphia: Lippincott, 1949); *Witch Hunt: The Revival of Heresy* (Boston: Little, Brown, 1950); *The Mexicans in America: A Student's Guide to Localized History* (New York: Teachers College Press, 1968); *The Education of Carey McWilliams* (New York: Simon & Schuster, 1979).

SOURCES

Book Review Digest 1946. New York: The H.W. Wilson Company, 1947, p. 534.

Publishers' Weekly, January 26, 1946, p. 412; March 23, 1946, p. 1770; and May 11, 1946, p. 2560.

The New York Times obituary, June 28, 1980, p.18.

Tebbel, John and Mary Ellen Zuckerman. *The Magazine in America 1741-1990*. New York: Oxford University Press,1991. (Various entries on the *Nation* and on Carey McWilliams.)

Cannon, Lou. Profile of Carey McWilliams for State Net. www.statenet.com. 1998-2000.

Contemporary Authors Online. The Gale Group, 1999. Reproduced in *Biography Resource Center*. Farmington Hills, Mich.: The Gale Group, 2002. Accessed July 1, 2002.

TOWN MEETING COUNTRY

Clarence M. Webster
September 16, 1892 – January 24, 1959

AF27   First edition, first printing (1945) [12]

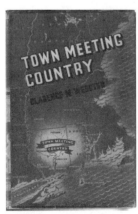

[*Folkways* device] I [within a taupe (close to Pantone 452) rectangle with rounded corners, in cream] EDITED BY ERSKINE CALDWELL I [black] TOWN I MEETING I COUNTRY I *by* I CLARENCE M. WEBSTER I [cream] DUELL, SLOAN & PEARCE · NEW YORK

COLLATION: 8½" x 6". 128 leaves. [i–vi] vii–ix [x] [1–2] 3–241 [242] 243–246. Numbers printed in roman in headline at the outer margin of the type page, except for pp. vii, 3, 10, 19, 46, 98, 107, 138, 175, 236, and 243, on which the numbers are printed in the center at the foot of the page.

CONTENTS: p. [i], half-title: "TOWN MEETING COUNTRY"; p. [ii],

"AMERICAN FOLKWAYS | Edited BY ERSKINE CALDWELL | [thin rule] | [list of 12 titles and their authors, beginning with *Golden Gate Country* and ending with *Town Meeting Country*] | In Preparation | [list of seven titles and their authors[1]]"; p. [iii], title; p. [iv], copyright page: "COPYRIGHT, 1945, BY | CLARENCE M. WEBSTER | *All rights reserved, including | the right to reproduce this book | or portions thereof in any form* | I | [eagle carrying book in its talons and a ribbon in its beak on which is printed 'Books are weapons in the war of ideas'] | A WARTIME BOOK | THIS COMPLETE EDITION IS PRODUCED | IN FULL COMPLIANCE WITH THE GOV- ERN- | MENT'S REGULATIONS FOR CONSERVING | PAPER AND OTHER ESSENTIAL MATERIALS | MANUFACTURED IN THE UNITED STATES OF AMERICA | BY THE VAIL-BALLOU PRESS, INC., BINGHAM- TON, N.Y."; p. [v], dedication: "To the memory of my mother | whose ancestors helped settle | the Town Meeting Country"; p. [vi], blank; pp. vii–ix, "Contents"; p. [x], blank; p. [1], half-title: "TOWN MEETING COUNTRY"; p. [2], blank; pp. 3–235, text; pp. 236–241, "Epilogue"; p. [242], blank; pp. 243–246, "Index".

BINDING: Taupe cloth (close to Pantone 451). Front: *Folkways* device stamped in black at lower right corner. Spine stamped in black, except where noted: "[thick rule] | [four thin rules] | [within a black panel, in gold] TOWN | MEETING | COUNTRY | · | CLARENCE M. | WEBSTER | [four thin rules] | [thick rule] | [four thin rules] | [at bottom] [four thin rules | [within a red panel, in gold] DUELL SLOAN | AND PEARCE | [four thin rules] | [thick rule]". Light cream endpapers carry map of the Connecticut-Rhode Island area in taupe (close to Pantone 452) and light cream; with the Town Meeting Country region highlighted in cream and further identified on a taupe ribbon-like banner on which "TOWN MEETING COUNTRY" is printed in light cream.

DUST JACKET (white paper): Front carries the map of the Connecticut-Rhode Island area in taupe (close to Pantone 452) and light cream, which is also found on the endpapers. "[thick red rule (close to Pantone 199)] | [white outlined in red] TOWN | MEETING | COUNTRY | [solid red] CLARENCE M. WEBSTER | [thick red rule]". Spine: "[thick red rule] | [four thin red rules on a light cream band] | [red] TOWN | MEETING | COUNTRY | [light cream] · | WEBSTER | [red] [four thin rules, thick rule, four thin rules, with the *Folkways* device overlaid in the center] | [drawing of a tree, a church in

1. The list includes *Buckeye Country* by Louis Bromfield, *Piney Woods Country* by John Faulkner, *Cutover Country* by John T. Frederick, *Black Jack Country* by George Milburn, and *Tidewater Country* by Elswyth Thane, none of which were published in the series, and *North Star Country* by Meridel Le Sueur and *Mission Country* (issued as *Southern California Country*) by Carey McWilliams, both of which were published in the series.

the background] | [four thin red] | [within a red panel, in light cream] DU-
ELL, SLOAN | AND PEARCE | [four thin rust rules] | [thick red rule]". Back:
"[white background] [within an arced ribbon, in red] AMERICAN FOLK-
WAYS | [taupe] |to the left of the *Folkways* device, which is in red and white]
Edited | - *by* - [to the right of the *Folkways* device, in taupe] ERSKINE |
CALDWELL | [quote from Harold Rugg] | PUBLISHED | [list of 12 titles
and their authors | [quote from Lewis Gannett] | EACH VOLUME $3.00 |
IN PREPARATION | [list of the same seven titles found on p. [ii] of the text]
| [red] [publisher's imprint]". Front flap: White background; printing in
taupe. "[upper right] $3.00 | [quote from Chapter 1 of the book] | TOWN
MEETING COUNTRY | by | Clarence Webster | [blurb] | [publisher's im-
print]". Back flap: White background; printing in taupe. "[upper right] $3.00
| *From the reviews of* | DEEP DELTA | COUNTRY | [quotes from five re-
views] | [publisher's imprint]".

Published at $3.00 on March 14, 1945; number of copies printed unknown.
Copyrighted March 15, 1945; deposited March 19, 1945.

The book is listed in "The Weekly Record," March 24, 1945, p. 1314.

Note: Duell, Sloan & Pearce published at least two printings of *Town Meeting Country.*

COPIES: CF

REPRINTS AND REPRODUCTIONS

"Country Fair," an excerpt from pp. 159–161, and words from a New England
folk rhyme from p. 145 of *Town Meeting Country* appear in *A Treasury of
New England Folklore: The Stories, Legends, Tall Tales, Traditions, Ballads and
Songs of the Yankee People.* Revised Edition. Edited by B.A. Botkin. New York:
Bonanza, 1965, pp. 432–434.

Westport, Conn.: Greenwood Press, 1970. Published at $11.00.

Reproduced on microfilm. New Haven, Conn.: Yale University Library, 1992.

BIOGRAPHY

Clarence Mertoun Webster was born in Hampton, Connecticut, on September 16, 1892.[2]
Webster earned a bachelor of arts degree from Clark University in 1915.

2. The 1900 U.S. Census, Hampton Town, Windham County, Connecticut, lists a Clarence
M. Webster, identified as the stepson of Henry and Mary Clapp, with a date of birth of
September, 1892. Thus it is probable that Webster's father had died and his mother, Mary,
had remarried. The entry reports her age as 41; years married 2; and one child, age 7.

He then undertook graduate studies at the University of Michigan, earning a master of arts degree in 1916. In 1933, he enrolled at Brown University, earning a doctorate in English in 1935.

During his World War I service in the U.S. Army in Europe, Webster was severely wounded in a gas attack. The disability he suffered persisted throughout his life and was a significant factor in his death more than forty years later.

On June 8, 1922, Webster married Elsiena Bottema, a native of the Netherlands. The couple had no children.

From 1919 through the early 1930s, Webster held teaching positions at the University of Michigan, Albion College, the University of Denver, Battle Creek College, and the University of Tennessee. In 1933, he returned to New England to continue his education at Brown University. Between 1931 and 1936 he wrote nineteen articles for various newspaper and periodicals and the book *Puritans at Home* (Harcourt Brace, 1936). In 1935, following the completion of his graduate studies at Brown, Webster left academia, becoming a freelance writer and, from 1936 to 1942, writing thirty-four short stories and sketches and serving as a contributing editor at *Yankee* magazine.

From October 1942 until his death in 1959, Webster taught English at Brown University. He began as an instructor, became assistant professor in 1946 and associate professor in 1949, and was named to a full professorship a week before his death in 1959. During these years, he wrote dozens of book reviews as well as *Town Meeting Country*. A respected scholar in the field of 18th-century English literature, Webster was a devoted teacher and spent most of his working hours in the classrooms at Brown. His seminar on Jonathan Swift (1667–1745) was considered one of the finest graduate courses the university had offered in the generation preceding his death.

George K. Anderson, in his report to the Brown faculty on Webster's death, observed, "Nothing delighted him more than to speak for the Yankee way of life, because he believed in it, and his two best books-*Puritans at Home* (1936) and *Town Meeting Country* (1945)-were at once the statement, the defence, and the justification of his thesis."[3]

Clarence M. Webster died in Providence, Rhode Island, on January 24, 1959, at age 67.

NOTES ON *TOWN MEETING COUNTRY*

Publication of the book was first announced in the June 10, 1944, issue of *Publishers' Weekly* in a "DS&P Preview of Bestsellers." In the January 27,

3. Anderson, George K. "The Yankee at His Best." Minute on the death of Clarence M. Webster. *Brown Alumni Monthly*. Volume 59, No. 7, April 1959, p. 19.

1945, issue of *Publishers' Weekly,* the book was included in the Duell, Sloan & Pearce Spring List. It was published on March 14, 1945.

On September 24, 1945, Webster was one of ten Rhode Island authors introduced at the Providence Public Library's Book Fair, where the book was featured.

REVIEWS

American History Review, October 1945 (p. 135); *Book Week,* April 1, 1945 (p.7); *Booklist,* April 15, 1945 (p. 235); *Bookmark,* November 1945 (p. 13); *Christian Science Monitor,* April 21, 1945 (p. 14); *Churchman,* August 1945 (p. 15); *Cleveland Open Shelf,* May 1945 (p. 10); *Commonweal,* April 6, 1945 (p. 628); *Kirkus,* December 15, 1944 (p. 560); *Library Journal,* March 15, 1945 (p. 265); *New York Times Book Review,* March 25, 1945 (p. 3); *Providence Journal,* March 18, 1945 (n.p.); *Springfield Republican,* May 20, 1945 (p. 4–D); *U.S. Quarterly Booklist,* June 1945 (p. 33); *Weekly Book Review,* April 1, 1945 (p. 4).

SELECTED WRITINGS BY CLARENCE WEBSTER

Puritans at Home (New York: Harcourt, Brace, 1936); ***Town Meeting Country*** (New York: Duell, Sloan & Pearce, 1945).

SOURCES

Book Review Digest 1945. New York: The H.W. Wilson Company, 1946, p. 749.

Publishers' Weekly, June 10, 1944, p. 2148; January 27, 1945, p. 320; and March 24, 1945, p. 1314.

The New York Times Book Review, March 25, 1945, p. 3.

"Biographical Notes - Clarence M. Webster, associate professor of English at Brown University." April 1955 press release by the Public Relations Office of Brown University.

Providence Journal obituary, January 25, 1959, p. C-28.

Anderson, George K. "The Yankee at His Best". (April 1959) *Brown Alumni Monthly,* Volume 59, Number 7, p. 19.

Lynch, Gayle D., Archives Assistant, Brown University Library. Letter to CF, with enclosures, June 10, 2002.

Brown University Archives.

WHEAT COUNTRY

William B. Bracke
October 31, 1912 – May 14, 1968

AF28   First edition, first printing (1950) [21]

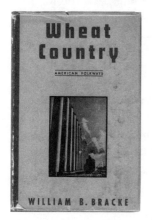

[*Folkways* device] | [within a dark blue (close to Pantone 294) rectangle with rounded corners, in cream] EDITED BY ERSKINE CALDWELL | [black] WHEAT | COUNTRY | BY WILLIAM B. BRACKE | [cream] DUELL, SLOAN & PEARCE · NEW YORK

COLLATION: 8½" x 6". 159 leaves. [i–vi] vii–viii [1–2] 3–309 [310]. Numbers printed in the center at the foot of the page.

CONTENTS: p. [i], half-title: "*Wheat Country* | [thin rule]"; p. [ii], "AMERICAN FOLKWAYS | EDITED BY ERSKINE CALDWELL | [list of 21 titles and their authors, beginning with *Golden Gate Country,* and ending with *Wheat Country*] | In Preparation | [list of six titles[1]]"; p. [iii], title; p. [iv], copyright page: "COPYRIGHT, 1950, BY | William B. Bracke | *All rights reserved, including | the right to reproduce this book | or portions thereof in any form.* | I | PRINTED IN THE UNITED STATES OF AMERICA"; p. [v], dedication: "*for | my Mother*"; p. [vi], blank; pp. vii–viii, "Contents"; p. [1], half-title: "*Wheat Country* | [thin rule]"; p. [2], blank; pp. 3–298, text; pp. 299–309, "Index"; pp. [310], blank.

BINDING: Light blue cloth (close to Pantone 659). Front: *Folkways* device stamped in black at lower right corner. Spine stamped in black, except where noted: "[four thin rules] | [thick rule] | [four thin rules] | [within a black panel, in gold] WHEAT | COUNTRY | · | WILLIAM B. | BRACKE | [four thin rules] | [thick rule] | [at bottom] [four thin rules | [within a black panel,

---

1. The list includes *Great Lakes Country* by Iola Fuller, *Tidewater Country* by Elswyth Thane, *Pacific Northwest Country* by Richard Newberger [sic], *Gold Rush Country* by Charis Weston, *Pennsylvania Dutch Country* by Harry Emerson Wildes, and *Buckeye Country* by Louis Bromfield, none of which were published in the *Folkways* series. In the listing, Richard Neuberger's surname is misspelled.

in gold] DUELL, SLOAN I AND PEARCE I [four thin rules] I [thick rule]".
Cream endpapers carry map of the United States in blue (close to Pantone
645) and cream; "Wheat Country" area is shaded in cream and further identified on a blue ribbon in lower right corner.

DUST JACKET (white paper): Front: Yellow background (close to Pantone
128). "[blue (close to Pantone 646)] Wheat I Country I [black] [thin rule] I
AMERICAN FOLKWAYS I [thin rule] I [black-and-white photograph by
Margaret Bourke-White of wheat elevators and storage bins; a train in the
foreground] I [blue] WILLIAM B. BRACKE". Spine: Blue background. "[yel-
low] Wheat I Country I [black] The Center I of Kansas I and the U.S. I [yel-
low] BRACKE I [*Folkways* device] I [yellow] DUELL, SLOAN I AND
PEARCE". Back: White background; printing in black. "[black-and-white
photograph of William B. Bracke attributed to 'Hixon's'] I [brief biographical sketch of Bracke[2]]". Front flap: White background; printing in black.
"[upper right] $3.50 I WHEAT COUNTRY I by I William B. Bracke I [blurb]
I *Jacket photograph by I Margaret Bourke-White* I [publisher's imprint]". Back
flap: White background; printing in black. "[upper left] $3.50 I CORN
COUNTRY I by I Homer Croy I [blurb] I [publishers imprint]".

Published at $3.50 on April 20, 1950; number of copies printed unknown.
Copyrighted May 10, 1950; deposited May 5, 1950.

The book is listed in "The Weekly Record," April 22, 1950, p. 1849.

Note: No evidence found that Duell, Sloan and Pearce reprinted *Wheat
Country*.

COPIES: CF

REPRINTS AND REPRODUCTIONS

Reproduced on microfilm. New Haven, Conn.: Yale University Library, 1993.
1 reel 35 mm.

BIOGRAPHY

William Bollman Bracke was born on October 31, 1912, on a farm in
Atchison, Kansas, the son of F. F. Bracke. A third-generation Kansan, he attended local schools and graduated from Atchison High School in 1930.

Bracke entered the University of Kansas that year, 1930. Majoring in
English, he earned a bachelor's degree in 1934 and a master of arts degree in
1935. From 1935 until the U.S. entered World War II in December, 1941, he

2. The biographical sketch makes reference to the "Kansas *Star-Times*" as a newspaper for
which Bracke wrote book reviews. Those reviews were written for the *Kansas City Star*.

worked as a high-school teacher. In 1942, he joined the Army Air Forces, serving more than four years as a public relations officer.

After his service in the war, Bracke joined the faculty of the University of Kansas as an Instructor of English from 1946 to 1949. For a time, he held a position as a visiting professor at the Wisconsin State Teachers College in Whitewater, Wisconsin. He was a frequent reviewer of books for the *St. Louis Star-Times* and the *Kansas City Star,* covering a wide range of literature.

In the early fall of 1948, while he was on the University of Kansas faculty, Bracke visited various communities in Kansas to obtain material for *Wheat Country*. By October, he had completed three chapters of the book. In April 1949, in the middle of the university term, Bracke unexpectedly resigned, citing pressure from his publishers to complete the book, noting, "My publishers want the book completed by the first of May. I didn't think I could finish it by then, and I was not returning to K.U. next fall."[3] His resignation was the subject of several speculative news articles, none of which provided any further information.

Later in 1949, Bracke joined the faculty of Washington State College (now Washington State University) in Pullman, where he was an assistant professor of journalism and literature when *Wheat Country* was published in April, 1950.[4] He was at Washington State College only a single year, leaving in 1950.[5]

The biographical sketch of Bracke on the back of the *Wheat Country* dust jacket states, "Currently he is teaching at Washington State College in Pullman, Washington, where he holds a full professorship in the Department of English." As noted, Bracke was at Washington State College for only a year and was an assistant professor there. The sketch also states, "He received his early education in the local schools, took his bachelor's degree at the University of Kansas, and his Ph.D. from Cornell." Cornell University, however, has no record of Bracke's receiving a doctorate there or of his having attended Cornell at any level at any time.[6] At some point, Bracke returned to the city of his birth, Atchison, Kansas.

William B. Bracke died on May 14, 1968, in Atchison, Kansas, at age 55.

---

3. "Two Instructors Leave Suddenly," *University Daily Kansan*, University of Kansas, April 27, 1949, [n.p.].

4. "Faculty," *Graduate Magazine*, University of Kansas Alumni Association, June, 1950, p. 32.

5. Stark, Lawrence R. Assistant Archivist, Washington State University. Letter to CF, May 29, 2002.

6. Muratori, Fred. Reference Librarian, Olin & Uris Libraries, Cornell University. E-mail to CF, May 30, 2006.

NOTES ON *WHEAT COUNTRY*

During the Kansas Writers conference sponsored by the University of Kansas Department of English in 1948, Erskine Caldwell interviewed William Bracke, then an instructor of English at the university, and chose him to write *Wheat Country*. Caldwell had become interested in Bracke after reading his book reviews in the *Kansas City Star* and the *St. Louis Star-Times*, as well as one of Bracke's short stories in *Sewanee Review*.[7]

The book received mixed reviews. Milton Tabor's April 21, 1950, review in the *Topeka Capital* began, "Kansas gets a rather thoro (sic) working over in 'Wheat Country. . . . [Bracke] is inclined toward the cynical, but his story is well told and only the more conservative Jayhawkers will suffer from the reading." In sharp contrast, Hal Borland's April 23, 1950, review in *The New York Times Book Review* said of the book, in part, "It speculates, not too profoundly, on Kansas journalism, Kansas prohibition, and Kansas politics." Later in his review, Borland noted, "William Bracke shovels his material in, often with skimped punctuation and occasionally with sentences of which he, as an English teacher, should be ashamed."

REVIEWS

Booklist, July 1, 1950 (p. 332); Chicago Sunday Tribune, July 23, 1950 (p.4); *Kirkus*, February 15, 1950 (p. 126); *New York Herald Tribune Book Review*, April 30, 1950 (p. 5); *New York Times Book Review*, April 23, 1950 (p. 21); *Saturday Review of Literature*, May 13, 1950 (p. 49); *Topeka Capital*, April 21, 1950 (n.p.); *Wisconsin Library Bulletin*, June 1950 (p. 25).

SELECTED WRITING BY WILLIAM B. BRACKE

Wheat Country (New York: Duell, Sloan & Pearce, 1950).

SOURCES

"English Instructor is Author of Book on Wheat Country for Caldwell Series," *University Daily Kansan*, University of Kansas, October 4, 1948, [n.p.].

"Two Instructors Leave Suddenly," *University Daily Kansan*, University of Kansas, April 27, 1949, [n.p.].

Book Review Digest 1950. New York: The H.W. Wilson Company, 1951, p. 103.

Bracke, William B. *Wheat Country* dust jacket; biographical material on the back. (1950)

7. "English Instructor Is Author Of Book On Wheat Country For Caldwell Series," *University Daily Kansan*, University of Kansas, October 4, 1948. [n.p.].

Publishers' Weekly, January 25, 1950 (Duell, Sloan & Pearce Spring List) [n.p.]; and April 22, 1950, p. 1849.

Tabor, Milton. "Kansas Author Pens Picture of State in 'Wheat Country.'" *Topeka Capital,* April 21, 1950, n.p.

Borland, Hal. "Kansas Ways." *The New York Times Book Review,* April 23, 1950, p. 21.

"Faculty," *Graduate Magazine,* Lawrence, Kansas, University of Kansas Alumni Association, June 1950, Vol. 48, No. 9, p. 32.

"Author To Be Speaker," *Kansas City Star,* September 4, 1951.

Kansas Alumni. Vol. 67, No. 5. February 1969. "A Last Salute," p. 39

Grace, William. Reference Section. Kansas State Historical Society (Topeka). Letter to CF, June 3, 2002, with enclosure.

Stark, Lawrence R., Assistant Archivist, Washington State University. Letter to CF, May 29, 2002.

Hawkins, Mary, Librarian. Reader Services, Kenneth Spencer Research Library, Kansas Collection, Special Collections, University Archives, The University of Kansas. Letter to CF, July 15, 2002, with enclosures; E-mail message to CF, July 12, 2002.

Muratori, Fred. Reference Librarian, Olin & Uris Libraries, Cornell University. E-mail message to CF, May 30, 2006.

AMERICAN MOUNTAIN SERIES
1942–1952

Roderick Peattie
Editor

The Vanguard Press, Inc.
Publisher

1942
The Friendly Mountains: Green, White, and Adirondacks

1943
The Great Smokies and the Blue Ridge: The Story of the Southern Appalachians

1945
The Rocky Mountains

1946
The Pacific Coast Ranges

1947
The Sierra Nevada: The Range of Light

1948
The Berkshires: The Purple Hills
The Inverted Mountains: Canyons of the West

1949
The Cascades: Mountains of the Pacific Northwest

1952
The Black Hills

AMERICAN MOUNTAIN SERIES

Introduction and Publishing History

Roderick Peattie, Editor

THE *American Mountain Series* was announced in an article in the April 11, 1942, *Publishers' Weekly*. The article noted that Vanguard Press would launch the series with the book "The Friendly Mountains: White, Green, Taconic and Adirondacks" and named Roderick Peattie, who was identified as a professor of geography at Ohio State University, as the series editor. The purpose of the series, as stated by Peattie and unnamed Vanguard editors, was described as follows:

> The books are not to be mountaineering books in any restricted sense; they are for the general reader, the climber, the hiker, winter sports enthusiast, armchair traveler, travel reader and the layman interested in the human and social aspects as well as the natural history of our mountain regions. As it goes on, the series will comprise a systematic coverage of the American mountains in popular terms. Following "The Friendly Mountains," there will be books on the Rockies, the Sierra Nevada, the Pacific Coast Range, the Cascades and the Southern Appalachians including the Great Smokies. "The Friendly Mountains" will be liberally illustrated with photographs of mountains and mountain scenes. The text will be made up of chapters by many experts on the Northeastern region.

Except for *The Rocky Mountains* by Wallace Atwood, each title in the series had multiple authors. The nine titles in the series and their authors are listed in a publishing chronology in the Appendix.

The Friendly Mountains: Green, White, and Adirondacks was published on October 10, 1942. The book's subtitle omitted "Taconic."

One series title was published in 1943: *The Great Smokies and the Blue Ridge: The Story of the Southern Appalachians* on December 10, 1943. The back of the book's dust jacket further described the purpose of the series: "There have been volumes on American rivers and seaports, but none on this country's proudest heritage–its beautiful, sweeping mountain ranges. The American Mountain Series will survey for American readers the ranges east and west, north and south, from the lofty and snowcapped to the gentle and congenial."

No series titles were published in 1944.

One series title was published in 1945: *The Rocky Mountains* on October 15.

One series title was published in 1946: *The Pacific Coast Ranges* on June 17.

One series title was published in 1947: *The Sierra Nevada: The Range of Light* on November 1.

Two series titles were published in 1948: *The Berkshires: The Purple Hills* on May 10 and *The Inverted Mountains: Canyons of the West* on December 16.

One series title was published in 1949: *The Cascades: Mountains of the Pacific Northwest* on November 28.

No series titles were published in 1950 or 1951.

The series ended in 1952 with the publication of *The Black Hills* on May 22.

The Great Smokies and the Blue Ridge (1943) was reprinted by Vanguard in 1972. Apparently, no other title in the series was reprinted, other than by reproduction on microfilm.

Fifty-seven authors contributed to the *American Mountain Series*. Edited by an academic, Roderick Peattie, and written in large measure by specialists in various fields, the series provided accurate, useful, practical information likely to appeal to readers with specific interests. But it was rather narrow, restricted as it was to American mountains, and it ran its course in a decade.

⟿

RODERICK PEATTIE
Editor, *American Mountain Series*

Roderick Peattie was born on August 1, 1891, in Omaha, Nebraska. He attended the University of Chicago, receiving a bachelor of science degree in 1914. In 1920, he earned a doctoral degree from Harvard University. He was a specialist in physiography and served as a summertime assistant in that field at the University of Chicago at various times during the summers of the years from 1916 to 1919.

On June 11, 1917, Peattie married Margaret Rhodes. The couple had three children, Roderick, Anne, and Michael. Margaret died in 1945 and, in October 1947, Peattie married Ruth Cavett.

Peattie was an Austin Teaching Fellow at Harvard (1916–1917), while also participating in field topographic surveys for the U.S. Geological Survey. In 1918, during World War I, Peattie served in the Allied Expeditionary Forces as an instructor at the Army Engineers School.

In 1919 and 1920, Peattie worked as a field geologist for the Cosden Oil and Gas Company, at the same time serving as an assistant professor of geology at Williams College. In 1920, he joined the faculty of Ohio State University as associate professor of geography, rising to the rank of professor in 1925, a position he held until his death in 1955.

From 1921 to 1938, Peattie was a summer lecturer at various times at the University of California, Clark University, Northwestern University, and the University of Wisconsin. The nine titles in *The American Mountain Series* were published under his editorship from 1942 to 1952. During World War II, he served as chief of the War Information Office of the Union of South Africa in 1944 and 1945.

Peattie was a member of the Association of American Geographers and a Fellow of the Ohio Academy of Science. He wrote two textbooks, *College Geography* (Ginn, 1926) and *Mountain Geography: A Critique and Field Study* (Harvard University Press, 1936). His other books include *Exploring Geography* (Harcourt, 1937), *Geography in Human Destiny* (G. W. Stewart, 1940), *The Incurable Romantic* (Macmillan, 1941), *How To Read Military Maps* (G. W. Stewart, 1942), and *Struggle on the Veld* (Vanguard, 1947).

Roderick Peattie died in June 1955, at age 63.

THE BERKSHIRES: THE PURPLE HILLS

Edited by Roderick Peattie

AM1   First edition, first printing (1948) [6]

THE I BERKSHIRES: I *The Purple Hills* I EDITED BY I RODERICK PEATTIE I CONTRIBUTORS: I *Walter Prichard Eaton* I *A. Kenneth Simpson* I *George J. Wallace* I *Bartlett Hendricks* I *Theodore Giddings, Haydn Mason* I *William S. Annin, Margaret Cresson* I THE VANGUARD PRESS, INC. I NEW YORK

The foregoing is printed within a white vertical rectangle superimposed on a two-page black-and-white photograph of the Sourla Farm in Cheshire, Massachusetts.

COLLATION: 9¼" x 6¼". 210 leaves. [a–f] [1–6] 7–11 [12–16] 17–30 [31–32] 33–74 [75–76] 77–112 [113–114]115–143 [144–146]

147–186 [187–188] 189–219 [220-222] 223–256 [257-260] 261–274 [275–276] 277–313 [314-316] 317–353 [354-356] 357–377 [378-380] 381–398 [399–400] 401–414. Numbers printed in roman in the outer margin at the foot of the page.

Note: Single unpaginated leaves bearing black-and-white photographs on glossy paper are inserted facing pp. 62, 63, 94, 95, 126, 127, 158, 159, 190, 191, [222], 223, 286, 287, 318, and 319.

CONTENTS: p. [a], half-title: "THE BERKSHIRES"; pp. [b-c], title; p. [d], copyright page: "COPYRIGHT 1948, BY VANGUARD PRESS, INC. | No portion of this book may be reprinted in any form without the written | permission of the publisher, except by a reviewer who wishes to quote | brief passages for inclusion in a review for a newspaper or magazine. | Published simultaneously in Canada by the Copp Clark Co., Ltd. | Manufactured in the United States of America by | H. Wolff, New York, N.Y. | TITLE PAGE PHOTOGRAPH: The Sourla Farm in Cheshire, Mass. | (Courtesy of Howard E. Foote.)"; pp. [e-f]-[1], "Contents"; p. [2], blank; pp. [3–5], "Illustrations"; p. [5], ACKNOWLEDGMENT: Photographs number 1, 23, and 24 are printed by | courtesy of Bartlett Hendricks; numbers 2, 3, 12, 13, 17, 18, and 28 | courtesy of S. Waldo Bailey; numbers 4, 6, 7, 8, and 9, courtesy of | Alvah W. Sanborn; number 5, courtesy of Alvah W. Sanborn and Hustace | H. Poor; numbers 10, 15, and 27, courtesy of Arthur Palme; numbers | 11, 14, 25, and 26, courtesy of Howard E. Foote; number 16, courtesy | of Clement R. Gardner; numbers 19, 29, 30, and 34, courtesy of Haydn | Mason; number 20, courtesy of Berkshire Garden Center; numbers | 21, 22, and 32, courtesy of H.S. Babbit, Jr.; number 31, courtesy of | Vera V. Fielding; number 33, courtesy of Mrs. Byron H. Porter; num- | ber 35, courtesy of Will Plouffe."; p. [6], blank; pp. pp. 7–11, "Introduction [signed Roderick Peattie]; p. [12], blank; p. [13], "Part One | THE BERKSHIRE SCENE"; p. [14], blank; p. [15], "WHAT ARE THE | BERKSHIRE HILLS? | by Walter Prichard Eaton"; p. [16], blank; pp. 17–30, text; p. [31], "WITH WHAT THE HILLS | ARE CLOTHED | by A. Kenneth Simpson"; p. [32], blank; pp. 33–74, text; p. [75], "FOUR SEASONS OF BERKSHIRE | BIRD LORE | by George J. Wallace"; p. [76], blank; pp. 77–112, text; p. [113], "BYWAYS TO PLEASURE | by Bartlett Hendricks"; p. [114], blank; pp. 115–130, text; p. [131], map titled 'Berkshire County'; p. 132, blank; pp. 133–143, text; p. [144], blank; p. [145], "STREAMS AND CASTING | by Theodore Giddings"; p. [146], blank; pp. 147–186, text; p. [187], "MAN CHANGES THE LANDSCAPE | THROUGH GARDENING | by A. Kenneth Simpson"; p. [188], blank; p. 189–219, text; p. [220], blank; p. [221], "WINTER SPORTS AMONG | THE HILLS | by Bartlett Hendricks"; p. [222], blank; pp. 223–256, text; p. [257], "Part Two | THE BERKSHIRE | PEOPLE-PAST AND

| PRESENT"; p. [258], blank; p. [259], "INDIAN LEGENDS | *by Haydn Mason*"; p. [260], blank; pp. 261–274, text; p. [275], "TWO HUNDRED AND FIFTY | YEARS OF HISTORY | *by Walter Prichard Eaton*"; p. [276], blank; pp. 277–313, text; p. [314], blank; p. [315], "BERKSHIRE FOLK AND | FOLK-WAYS | *by William S. Annin*"; p. [316], blank; pp. 317–353, text; p. [354], blank; p. [355], "THE INVADERS AND WHAT | THEY HAVE MEANT | *by Margaret Cresson*"; p. [356], blank; pp. 357–377, text; p. [378], blank; p. [379], "THE BERKSHIRE FESTIVAL | *by Margaret Cresson*"; p. [380], blank; pp. 381–398, text; p. [399], "INDEX"; p. [400], blank; pp. 401–414, "Index".

BINDING: Tan cloth (close to Pantone 453). Front: "[medium brown] THE BERKSHIRES | [*Mountain* device, in red and blue] | [dark blue] RODER-ICK PEATTIE". Spine: "[medium brown] THE | BERKSHIRES | [*Mountain* device, in red and blue] | [dark blue] RODERICK | PEATTIE | [medium brown] VANGUARD". Cream endpapers carry a double-page map by Graphic Associates in cream and dark brown (close to Pantone 505) titled "Berkshire County". Top edges plain.

DUST JACKET (white paper): Front and spine carry a black-and-white photograph, "Autumn Road, Middlefield, Near Glendale Falls," which is also found facing p. [222] of the text. Front: "[within a dark rose rectangle (close to Pantone 701), in black] THE | Berkshires | THE PURPLE HILLS | *Edited by Roderick Peattie*". Spine "[within a dark rose rectangle, in black] THE | BERKSHIRES | *Edited by* | Roderick | Peattie | VANGUARD". Back: "Other Titles in the | AMERICAN MOUNTAIN SERIES | edited by RODERICK PEATTIE | [list of five titles with quotes from reviews] | *Each volume - illustrated with mountain photographs and maps* — $5.00 | [publishers imprint]". Front flap: "[blurb] | [list of the table of contents with the author noted for each contribution] | *With numerous illustrations* | [lower right] $5.00". Back flap: Blank.

Published at $5.00 on May 10, 1948; number of copies printed unknown. Copyrighted and deposited May 5, 1948.

The book is listed in "The Weekly Record," May 15, 1948, p. 2125.

Note: No evidence found that Vanguard reprinted *The Berkshires: The Purple Hills*.

COPIES: CF

REPRINTS AND REPRODUCTIONS

Reproduced on microfilm. New Haven, Conn.: Yale University Library, 1988. 1 reel. 35 mm.

Reproduced on microfilm. Amherst, Mass.: University Library, University of Massachusetts Amherst, 2000. Filmed by Northeast Document Conservation Center. Western Massachusetts local history monographs Reel 10. 1 reel, with other items, 35 mm.

BIOGRAPHIES

William S. Annin was born in 1894. He was a regular contributor to the "Our Berkshires" column in the *Berkshire Eagle* of Pittsfield, Massachusetts. Annin began his work as columnist there in October 1941. He later joined the paper's staff, first as a copy editor and later as an editorial writer. He was a farmer, a teacher, and a town official as well as a newspaperman. Annin's wife, Katharine (1893–1990), succeeded him as an "Our Berkshires" columnist, becoming the first woman to serve as one of the column's regulars. William Annin died in April 1957.

Margaret (French) Cresson was born in 1889. She was the daughter of Daniel Chester French (1850-1931), the sculptor of the seated figure of Abraham Lincoln at the Lincoln Memorial in Washington, D.C., the Minute Man at Concord, Massachusetts, and other noted works. A sculptor herself, her work was exhibited in Paris, at the Corcoran Gallery of Art in Washington, and in other museums and private collections. She wrote *Journey Into Fame: The Life of Daniel Chester French* (Harvard University Press, 1947) and *Daniel Chester French* (Norton, 1947). She was instrumental in the preservation of Chesterwood, her family's estate in Stockbridge, Massachusetts, which is administered as a museum by the National Trust for Historic Preservation. She died on October 1, 1973, at age 84.

Walter Prichard Eaton was born in Malden, Massachusetts, on August 24, 1878. He attended Harvard University and later worked at several newspapers as a reporter and drama critic. In 1933 he became associate professor of playwriting at Yale University, later serving as chairman of the university Drama Department. He was one of the original columnists in the "Our Berkshires" column of the *Berkshire Eagle* when the column began in 1940. Eaton, a well-known drama critic and lecturer, wrote books and articles on theater, gardening, and the outdoors. He died on February 26, 1957.

Theodore Giddings was born in Pittsfield, Massachusetts, on May 31, 1906, the son of Charles and Edith M. Giddings. He graduated from Brown University in 1929. He was hired by the *Berkshire Eagle* in 1928, while still at Brown, and worked as a reporter until 1937 and as city editor from 1938 to 1971. He wrote the field and stream column in the "Our Berkshires" feature of the *Eagle* from 1948 until 2003, the seventy-fifth anniversary of his joining

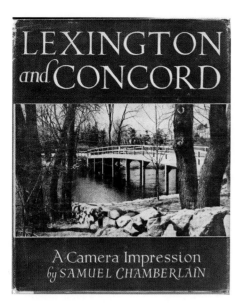

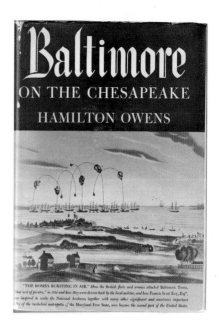

Lexington and Concord: A Camera Impression by Samuel F. Chamberlain, the sixth title in the *American Landmarks Series,* was published by Hastings House in 1939.

Baltimore on the Chesapeake by Hamilton Owens, the fourth title in *The Seaport Series,* was published by Doubleday, Doran in 1941. The unsigned cover illustration is titled "The Bombs Bursting in Air."

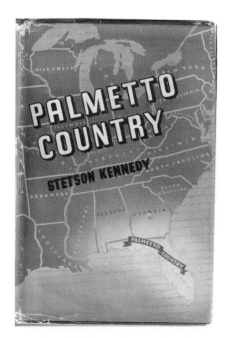

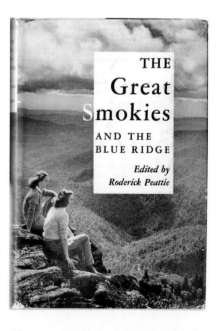

Palmetto Country by Stetson Kennedy, the eighth title in the *American Folkways Series,* was published by Duell, Sloan & Pearce in 1942.

The Great Smokies and the Blue Ridge, the second title in the *American Mountain Series,* was published by Vanguard Press, Inc. in 1943. The series was edited by Roderick Peattie.

Several titles from Bobbs-Merrill's *American Lakes Series* are showcased in this undated photo of a Scribner's window display. Photo courtesy The Lilly Library, Indiana University, Bloomington, Indiana.

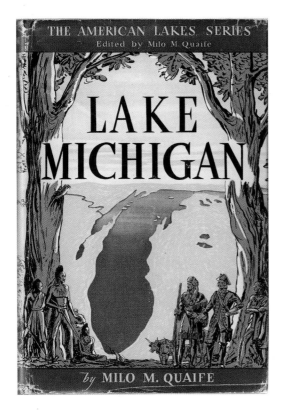

Lake Michigan by Milo M. Quaife, the third title in *The American Lakes Series,* was published by Bobbs-Merrill in 1944. The series was edited by Quaife.

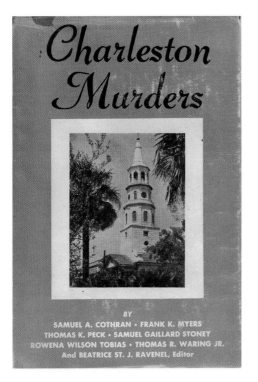

Charleston Murders, the seventh title in the *Regional Murder Series*, was published by Duell, Sloan & Pearce in 1947. The series was edited by Marie Rodell.

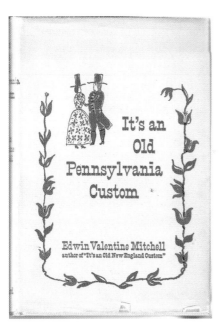

It's an Old Pennsylvania Custom by Edwin Valentine Mitchell, the second title in the *American Customs Series*, was published by Vanguard Press in 1947. Mitchell wrote four of the seven titles in the *American Customs* series.

The Proper Bostonians by Cleveland Amory, the first title in the *Society in America* series, was published by E.P. Dutton in 1947.

Bookshop display of *The National Road* by Philip D. Jordan, the third title in the Bobbs-Merrill *American Trails Series,* was published in 1948. Photo courtesy The Lilly Library, Indiana University, Bloomington, Indiana.

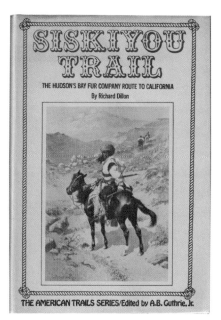

Siskiyou Trail: The Hudson's Bay Fur Company Route to California by Richard Dillon, the twelfth title in *The American Trails Series,* was published by McGraw-Hill in 1975.

Richard Dillon, author of *Siskiyou Trail,* at his home in Mill Valley, California (August 14, 2003).

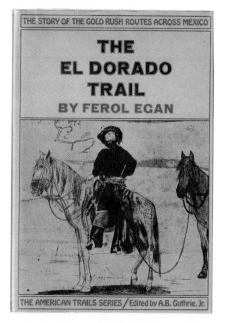

The El Dorado Trail: The Story of the Gold Rush Routes Across Mexico by Ferol Egan, the ninth title in *The American Trails Series,* was published by McGraw-Hill in 1970.

Ferol Egan, author of *The El Dorado Trail: The Story of the Gold Rush Routes Across Mexico,* at his home in Berkeley, California (August 16, 2003).

Carol Fitzgerald interviewing David Lavender at his home in Ojai, California (August 30, 2002). In three of the thirteen series described in this book, Lavender wrote a total of six books.

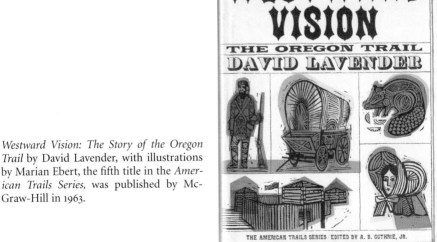

Westward Vision: The Story of the Oregon Trail by David Lavender, with illustrations by Marian Ebert, the fifth title in the *American Trails Series,* was published by Mc-Graw-Hill in 1963.

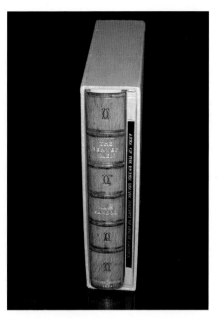

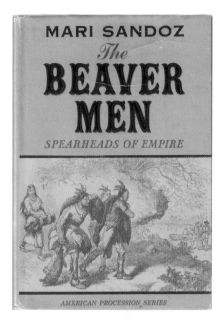

Special signed limited edition of 185 copies of *The Beaver Men: Spearheads of Empire* by Mari Sandoz, published by Hastings House in 1964. This edition was produced and distributed by James F. Carr.

Trade edition of *The Beaver Men: Spearheads of Empire* by Mari Sandoz, the ninth title in the *American Procession Series*. The book was published by Hastings House in 1964.

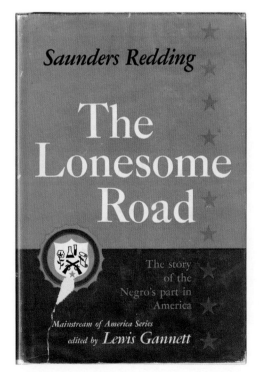

The Lonesome Road: The Story of the Negro's Part in America by Saunders Redding, the eleventh title in *The Mainstream of America Series,* was published by Doubleday in 1958.

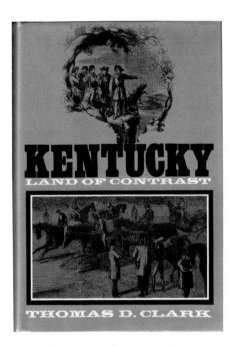

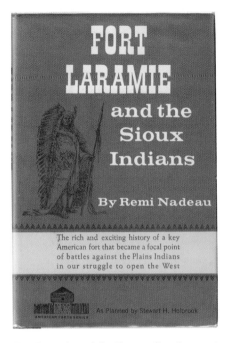

Kentucky: Land of Contrast by Thomas D. Clark, the eleventh title in the *Regions of America Series,* was published by Harper & Row in 1968.

Fort Laramie and the Sioux Indians by Remi Nadeau, the fifth title in *The American Forts Series,* was published by Prentice-Hall, Inc. in 1967.

Remi Nadeau, author of *Fort Laramie and the Sioux Indians,* at his home in Santa Barbara, California (August 12, 2003).

the paper. In 2002, he received the Francis W. Sargent Conservation Award of the Massachusetts Department of Fisheries and Wildlife. He died on June 6, 2005, at age 99.

Bartlett Hendricks was born in Pittsfield, Massachusetts, on January 22, 1910. He was curator of natural science at the Berkshire Museum in Pittsfield from 1931 to 1989. An accomplished photographer, he founded the Berkshire Museum Camera Club in 1937. The museum presented an exhibition of his work in 2004. His "Field List of the Birds of Berkshire County" was published by the museum in 1941. Hendricks was a founder of the Mt. Greylock Ski Club and was instrumental in the creation of the Jiminy Peak ski area. He died on September 19, 2002, at age 92.

Haydn Mason was born in Connecticut on May 27, 1891. His parents were English. The Mason family moved to Massachusetts when Haydn was a child, settling in Berkshire County. As a young man, Mason traveled to the American West, where he developed a scholarly interest in American Indians and their legends. Upon his return to Berkshire County, he began to study the Indians who had once lived among the hills of the Berkshires. The five legends Mason recounts in *The Berkshires* are almost poetically presented, reflecting the depth of his studies and his respect for Indian beliefs and practices. He died in February 1982, at age 90.

A. Kenneth Simpson was born in 1902. A graduate of Massachusetts State College, he worked for a time with the Bureau of Entomology of the U.S. Department of Agriculture. He was deeply interested in the forest covering and flowers of the Berkshire hills and became director of the Berkshire Garden Center in Stockbridge, Massachusetts. When *The Berkshires* was published in 1948, Simpson had studied Berkshire gardens for twenty years and was a popular judge at flower and vegetable shows. He was one of the original "Our Berkshires" columnists in the *Berkshire Eagle*, and had previously written "Garden Center Notes" for the paper. His "Our Berkshires" columns also focused on flowers and gardening. He died in 1972.

George J. Wallace was born in 1907 in Waterbury, Vermont. He grew up on a farm, becoming interested in birds while still a schoolboy. In 1928, he began studies at the University of Michigan, earning bachelor's and master's degrees and, in 1936, a doctorate in ornithology. After working as a biologist with the Vermont Fish and Game Service for less than a year, he worked for five years as warden of the Pleasant Valley Bird and Wildlife Sanctuary in Lenox, Massachusetts. He later joined the faculty of Michigan State College (later University), where he taught for thirty-one years, until his retirement in 1972. His textbook, *An Introduction to Ornithology* (Macmillan, 1955), went through three editions. His autobiography, *My World of Birds: Memoirs of an Ornithologist* (Dorrance) was published in 1979. He died on March 8, 1986, at age 79.

NOTES ON *THE BERKSHIRES: THE PURPLE HILLS*

Notice of publication of the book was included in the Vanguard Press 1948 Spring List in the January 31, 1948, issue of *Publishers' Weekly*. The April 24, 1948, "P.W. Forecast for Buyers" included a May 10 publication date, a note that the book has "special interest for skiing enthusiasts and those interested in [Berkshire] music festivals" and would receive local advertising and imprinted postcards for Berkshire [book] shops. The note concluded that the book would be a good "summer vacation item for all New England stores."

REVIEWS .

Booklist, July 1, 1948 (p. 366); *Commonweal*, July 9, 1948 (p. 312); *Kirkus*, April 15, 1948 (p. 204); *Library Journal*, May 15, 1948 (p. 812); *New York Herald Tribune Book Review*, May 23, 1948 (p. 5); *New York Times Book Review*, May 23, 1948 (p. 31); *New Yorker*, September 4, 1948 (p. 82); *Saturday Review of Literature*, July 3, 1948 (p. 29); *Wisconsin Library Bulletin*, November 1948 (p. 184).

SOURCES

Book Review Digest 1948. New York: The H.W. Wilson Company, 1949, p. 653.

Peattie, Roderick. Introduction to *The Berkshires* (Vanguard, 1948), pp. 7–11.

Publishers' Weekly, January 31, 1948, p. 513; April 24, 1948, p. 1832; May 15, 1948, p. 2125.

The New York Times Book Review, May 23, 1948, p. 31.

"Six Decades of 'Our Berkshires'" the *Berkshire Eagle*, December 29, 2000, n.p. NewsBank, Inc. infoweb.newsbank.com Accessed January 29, 2007.

(Cresson) "Margaret Cresson, Sculptor, 84, Dead" *The New York Times*, October 3, 1973, n.p.

(Cresson) Jackson, Linda W., Manager of Collections and Interpretation, Chesterwood. E-mail message to CF, May 8, 2007. (Advice regarding sources.)

(Eaton) Answers.com, "Walter Prichard Eaton," n.p., n.d. Accessed May 8, 2007.

(Eaton) "Literary Connections to the Berkshire Taconic Landscape." "Human History," lastgreatplaces.org Accessed May 9, 2001.

(Giddings) Giddings, Anna W., letter to CF, June 6, 2005, enclosing valuable correspondence and press clippings relating to her husband, Theodore Giddings.

(Hendricks) Beck, Lesley Ann. "Remembering Bartlett Hendricks," *Berkshires Week,* September 30, 2004, n.p.

Wallace) Hardy, John William. "In Memoriam: George J. Wallace," in *The Auk 104* (Quarterly Journal of Ornithology), April 1987, pp. 316–317.

THE BLACK HILLS

Edited by Roderick Peattie

AM2   First edition, first printing (1952) [9]

The Black Hills | EDITED BY RODERICK PEAT-TIE | THE CONTRIBUTORS: *Leland D. Case, Badger Clark,* | *Paul Friggens, R.V. Hunkins, Clarence S. Paine,* | *Elmo Scott Watson* | THE VAN-GUARD PRESS, INC. NEW YORK

The foregoing is printed within a white vertical rectangle superimposed on a two-page black-and-white photograph titled "Needles Highway Scene."

COLLATION: 91/4" x 61/4". 161 leaves. [a–b] [1–10] 11–15 [16] 17–320. Numbers printed in roman in headline at the outer margin of the page, except for pp. 11, 17, 30, 75, 125, 151, 177, 194, 221, 244, 280, and 311, on which the numbers are printed in the outer margin at the foot of the page.

Note: Single unpaginated leaves bearing black-and-white photographs on glossy paper are inserted facing pp. 34, 35, 66, 67, 128, 129, 160, 161, 192, 193, 224, 225, 256, 257, 288, and 289.

CONTENTS: p. [a], half-title: "THE BLACK HILLS"; p. [b], blank; p. [1], blank; pp. [2–3], title; p. [4], copyright page: "COPYRIGHT, 1952, by The Vanguard Press, Inc. | Published Simultaneously in Canada by the Copp Clark Company, | Ltd., Toronto | No portion of this book may be reprinted in any form without the | written permission of the publisher, except by a reviewer who wishes | to quote brief passages for inclusion in a review for a newspaper or | magazine. | Manufactured in the United States of America by H. Wolff, | New York, N.Y. | TITLE PAGE PHOTOGRAPH: Needles Highway Scene. | (Photo courtesy of the Miller Studio.)"; pp. [5–6], "Contents"; pp. [7–8], "Illustrations"; p. [8], ACKNOWLEDGMENTS: Photographs number 1, 3, and 4 are | printed by courtesy of L.D. Case and the Miller Studio; number 6, | courtesy of L.D. Case and the Yale University Press; numbers 2, 5, | and 16, courtesy of the Miller Studio; numbers 7, 10, 26, 31, 32, | courtesy of the Bell Studio; numbers 9 and 14, courtesy of the Adams | Memorial Hall Museum; numbers 11 and 19, courtesy of the South | Dakota State Highway Commission; numbers 8, 24, 27, 28, and 29, | courtesy of the South Dakota State Highway Commission and the | Miller Studio; number 20, courtesy of the Harms Studio; number 23, | courtesy of the South Dakota State Publicity Department and H. | Ervind Larsen; number 25, courtesy of the Publishers' Photo Service; | numbers 33 and 34, courtesy of the Black Hills Studio, Inc.; numbers | 22 and 30, courtesy of the South Dakota Chamber of Commerce; num- | ber 35, courtesy of the *Engineering and Mining Journal*; numbers 13, | 15, 17, and 18, courtesy of the Bettmann Archive."; p. [9], half-title: "THE BLACK HILLS"; p. [10], blank; pp. 11–15, "INTRODUCTION | *by Roderick Peattie*"; p. [16], blank; pp. 17–29, "CHAPTER ONE | THE BLACK HILLS | *by Badger Clark*"; pp. 30–74, "CHAPTER TWO | WHERE B.C. MEANS BEFORE CUSTER | by *Leland D. Case*"; pp. 75–124, "CHAPTER THREE | HISTORY CATCHES UP | *by Leland D. Case*"; pp. 125–150, "CHAPTER FOUR | CRAZY HORSE- | THE GREATEST AMONG THEM | *by Elmo Scott Watson*"; pp. 151–176, "CHAPTER FIVE | WILD BILL HICKOK AND | CALAMITY JANE | *by Clarence S. Paine*"; pp. 177–193, "CHAPTER SIX | 'DON'T FENCE ME IN!' | *by Paul Friggens*"; pp. 194–220, "CHAPTER SEVEN | THE TOURISTS COME | *by Badger Clark*"; pp. 221–243, "CHAPTER EIGHT | THE MOUNTAIN THAT HAD ITS | FACE LIFTED | *by Badger Clark*"; pp. 244–279, "CHAPTER NINE | THE BLACK HILLS- | A STOREHOUSE OF MINERAL TREASURE | *by R.V. Hunkins*"; pp. 280–310, "CHAPTER TEN | AMERICA'S GREATEST GOLD MINE- | THE HOMESTAKE | *by R.V. Hunkins*"; pp. 311–320, "Index".

BINDING: Tan cloth (close to Pantone 453). Front: "[black] THE BLACK HILLS | [*Mountain* device in red and blue] | [dark red] RODERICK PEATTIE". Spine: "[black] THE | BLACK | HILLS | [*Mountain* device in red and blue] I [dark red] RODERICK I PEATTIE I [black] VANGUARD". Cream endpapers. Top edges plain.

DUST JACKET (white paper): Front and spine carry a black-and-white photograph titled "Needles Highway Scene," which is also found on the title page of the book. Front: "[within a white horizontal rectangle, in black] THE I BLACK HILLS I *Edited by Roderick Peattie*". Spine "[within a white rectangle, in black] THE I BLACK I IILLS I *Edited by* I Roderick I Peattie I Vanguard". Back: "[black] Other Volumes in the I AMERICAN MOUNTAIN SERIES I edited by RODERICK PEATTIE I [list of eight titles with quotes from reviews] I *Each volume illustrated with magnificent photographs and maps*". Front flap: "[blurb] I *With magnificent photographs* I [lower right] $5.00". Back flap: "[blurb, which is identical to that found on the front flap] I *All volumes of the* I AMERICAN MOUNTAIN SERIES I *are available at your book seller or:* I THE VANGUARD PRESS, INC. I 424 Madison Avenue, New York 17, N.Y.".

Published at $5.00 on May 22, 1952; number of copies printed unknown. Copyrighted June 3, 1952; deposited May 26, 1952.

The book is listed in "The Weekly Record," June 14, 1952, p. 2495.

Note: No evidence found that Vanguard reprinted *The Black Hills*.

CITED: *Guns* 758; *Guns* (Revised Ed.) 1699; *Herd* 1774

COPIES: CF

REPRINTS AND REPRODUCTIONS

Reproduced on microfilm. New Haven, Conn.: Yale University Library, 1989. 1 reel. 35 mm.

BIOGRAPHIES

Leland D. Case was born in Iowa on May 8, 1900. He attended Dakota Wesleyan University (1918–1920) and Macalester College, earning a bachelor's degree in 1922. In 1926, he earned a master's degree from Northwestern University, later undertaking studies at the universities of Minnesota and Chicago. He worked as a newspaperman in South Dakota (1923–1925) and with the Paris edition of the *New York Herald Tribune* (1926–1927) and was co-publisher of the *Evening Star* in Hot Springs, South Dakota, from 1928 until 1934. He was editor of *Rotarian Magazine* in Chicago (1930-1950) and its field editor from 1950 to 1952; editorial director of the *Christian Advocate* and founder and editorial director of *Together* from 1955 until 1963; and director of the Pacific Center for Western Historical Studies at the University of the Pacific from 1965 to 1967. He died in December, 1986, at age 86.

(Charles) Badger Clark was born in Iowa on January 1, 1883, and moved to the Dakota Territory with his family that year. After graduating from Deadwood High School, Clark attended Wesleyan University in Mitchell, South Dakota, but left after a year, traveling to Arizona and Cuba before returning. In 1925, he built a small cabin he called "Badger Hole" in Custer State Park, where he lived until his death in 1957. The cabin is now part of Custer State Park. Clark's first book of poetry was published in 1915. Known as the "cowboy poet," Clark wrote six books; at least two hundred poems, including "A Cowboy's Prayer," his best-known poem; and thirty short stories. In 1938, South Dakota Governor Leslie Jensen appointed Clark South Dakota Poet Laureate, a position he held for twenty years. He died on September 26, 1957, at age 74.

Paul Friggens was born in South Dakota on October 4, 1909. In 1931, he graduated from the University of South Dakota, earning a bachelor's degree. With the Great Depression raging, he organized a state capital news bureau in Pierre, South Dakota, thereby creating a job for himself. He later worked for United Press International (UPI); then worked as a feature writer and Sunday magazine editor and book critic for the Newspaper Enterprise Association (NEA); and then worked as an executive representative for the Associated Press in New York City. In 1946, he became an editor of *Farm Journal*. He became a staff writer for the *Reader's Digest* in 1960, later becoming the magazine's roving editor. The Paul Friggens Memorial Scholarship Fund at the University of South Dakota was established by his daughter, Myriam. Paul Friggens died on November 9, 1987, at age 78.

Ralph Valentine Hunkins was born on February 14, 1890. When Hunkins wrote "The Black Hills — A Storehouse of Mineral Treasure," his chapter for the book, he was superintendent of schools in Lead, South Dakota. He wrote many education-related articles and a children's book, *Tepee Days: Tales of the Prairies* (American Book Company, 1941). Hunkins was well-versed in local history, especially the history and workings of the famous Homestake gold mine. He died in May 1975, at age 85.

Clarence S. Paine was born on June 9, 1908, in Lincoln, Nebraska. He attended the University of Illinois, earning a bachelor's degree, and the University of Nebraska, earning a master's degree in library science. In 1938, he became head librarian and professor of library science at Beloit College, becoming director of libraries at Beloit in 1945. In January 1948, he became head of city libraries in Oklahoma City. In 1958, he moved to Lansing, Michigan, where he served as director of public libraries and school libraries. Paine was an expert on the history of the American West and a frequent contributor to professional journals. He died on September 30, 1978, at age 70. [The Clarence S. Paine Papers, 1871–1948 are held by the Center for Western Studies, Augustana College, Sioux Falls, South Dakota.]

Elmo Scott Watson was born in Illinois in 1892. He attended Colorado College, later earning a master's degree at Northwestern University and a doctorate from Illinois Wesleyan University. In 1918, he became an instructor in journalism at the University of Illinois. In 1924, he joined the faculty of the Medill School of Journalism at Northwestern University, serving there until 1950. From 1932 until 1945, he edited *Publishers' Auxiliary,* a national monthly publication serving community newspapers, and wrote a regular column, "Dear Ed.," in the publication. A historian and a lifelong student of the American Indian, he wrote seven books, including *The Illinois Wesleyan Story, 1850-1950* (Illinois Wesleyan Press, 1950). He became chairman of the Department of Journalism at the University of Denver in 1950, a post he held until his death the next year. He died in 1951. [The Elmo Scott Watson Papers, 1816–1951 (bulk 1920-1951) are held by the Newberry Library, Roger and Julie Baskes Department of Special Collections, Midwest Manuscript Collection, Chicago, Illinois.]

NOTES ON *THE BLACK HILLS*

The book was included in the Vanguard Press 1952 Spring List in the January 26, 1952, issue of *Publishers' Weekly*, projecting a June publication. Although the copyright records reflect a copyright and publication date of May 22, 1952, the book may not have been available until early June.

REVIEWS

Booklist, July 1, 1952 (p. 358); *Christian Science Monitor,* August 14, 1952 (p. 7); *Kirkus,* April 1, 1952 (p. 249); *Library Journal,* May 15, 1952 (p. 891); *New York Herald Tribune Book Review,* June 15, 1952 (p. 6); *New York Times Book Review,* May 25, 1952 (p. 12); *San Francisco Chronicle,* June 29, 1952 (p. 11).

SOURCES

Book Review Digest 1952. New York: The H.W. Wilson Company, 1953, pp. 701–702.

Publishers' Weekly, January 26, 1952 (Vanguard Fall List), p. 406; June 14, 1952, p. 2495.

The New York Times Book Review, May 25, 1952, p. 12.

(Case) *Contemporary Authors Online.* The Gale Group, 2001. Reproduced in *Biography Resource Center.* Farmington Hills, Mich.: The Gale Group, 2001. Accessed February 20, 2002.

(Clark) South Dakota State Historical Society. "Charles Badger Clark, Jr." Profile from www.history.org. Accessed January 24, 2003.

(Clark) University of South Dakota, Special Collections, "Badger Clark, Papers 1928–1940." Accessed January 24, 2003.

(Clark) Block, Bradley, Chief of Interpretation, Interpretive and Educational Services Program, Custer State Park. E-mail message to CF, February 2, 2007.

(Friggens) University of South Dakota, "Paul Friggen [*sic*] Memorial Scholarship Fund Award Description," printed May 9, 2003.

(Hunkins) "Homestake Mining Company," www.homestaketour.com Accessed May 15, 2007.

(Paine) Center for Western Studies. http://inst.augie.edu/CWS/findingaids3.html Accessed January 24, 2003.

(Paine) Burwell, Fred, Librarian, Beloit College Library, Beloit, Wisconsin. Biographical material from Beloit College files and Beloit College Faculty files, May 2007.

(Watson) Inventory of the Elmo Scott Watson Papers, 1816–1951, Elmo Scott Watson Papers, Edward E. Ayer Manuscript Collection, The Newberry Library, Chicago. Accessed January 24, 2003.

(Watson) "Publishers' Auxiliary," National Newspaper Association. www.nna.org Accessed May 15, 2007.

THE CASCADES: MOUNTAINS OF THE PACIFIC NORTHWEST

Edited by Roderick Peattie

AM3   First edition, first printing (1949) [8]

THE CASCADES | *Mountains of the Pacific North-west* | EDITED BY RODERICK PEATTIE | THE CONTRIBUTORS: *Margaret Bundy Callahan, Harry | W. Hagen, Weldon F. Heald, Charles D. Hessey, Jr., | Ellsworth D. Lumley, Herbert Lundy, Grant McConnell, | Walter F. McCulloch, James Stevens* | THE VANGUARD PRESS NEW YORK

The foregoing is printed within a white vertical rectangle superimposed on a two-page black-and-white photograph titled "Skiing at Mount Baker, on Artists' Point."

COLLATION: 9¼" x 6¼". 209 leaves. [1–10] 11–18 [19–20] 21–64 [65–66] 67–96 [97–98] 99–138 [139–140] 141–167 [168–170] 171–213 [214–216] 217–270 [271–272] 273–299 [300–302] 303–333 [334–336] 337–363 [364–366] 367–395 [396–398] 399–401 [402] 403–417 [418]. Numbers printed in roman in headline at the outer margin of the page, except for pp. 11, 21, 67, 99, 141, 171, 217, 273, 303, 337, 367, 399, and 403, on which the numbers are printed in the center at the foot of the page.

Note: Single unpaginated leaves bearing black-and-white photographs on glossy paper are inserted facing pp. 36, 37, 68, 69, 132, 133, 164, 165, 260, 261, 292, 293, 324, 325, 356, and 357.

CONTENTS: p. [1], half-title: "THE CASCADES"; pp. [2–3], title; p. [4], copyright page: "COPYRIGHT, 1949, BY THE VANGUARD PRESS, INC. | Published simultaneously in Canada by the Copp Clark Co., Ltd. | No portion of this book may be reprinted in any form without the written | permission of the publisher, except by a reviewer who wishes to quote brief | passages for inclusion in a review for a newspaper or magazine. | Manufactured in the United States of America by H. Wolff, New York, N.Y. | TITLE PAGE PHOTOGRAPH: Skiing at Mount Baker, on Artists' Point. | (Photo by

Bob & Ira Spring)"; pp. [5–6], "Contents"; pp. [7–8], "Illustrations"; p. [8], ACKNOWLEDGMENTS: Photographs number 1, 4, 6, 10, 13, 16, 17, 25, 27, 28, 29, 30, I and 31 are printed by courtesy of Ira & Bob Spring; numbers 2, 14, and 15, by I courtesy of Al Monner; numbers 3, 5, 12, 24, and 26, courtesy of Ray Atkeson; I numbers 8 and 9, courtesy of K.S. Brown; numbers 11 and 21, courtesy of I William L. Dawson from the National Audubon Society; number 23, courtesy I Edward F. Dana from the National Audubon Society; number 18, courtesy I Alfred M. Bailey from the National Audubon Society; number 22, courtesy I W.E. Shore from the National Audubon Society; number 20, courtesy Gayle I Pickwell from the National Audubon Society; number 19, courtesy Ruth and I H.D. Wheeler from the National Audubon Society; number 7, courtesy of the I Art Commercial Studios."; p. [9], "INTRODUCTION I by Roderick Peattie"; p. [10], blank; pp. 11–18, "Introduction [signed R.P.]"; p. [19], "THE LAST FRONTIER I by Margaret Bundy Callahan"; p. [20], blank; pp. 21–64, text; p. [65], "THE CASCADE RANGE I by Grant McConnell"; p. [66], blank; pp. 67–96, text; p. [97], "CASCADE HOLIDAY I by Weldon F. Heald"; p. [98], blank; pp. 99–138, text; p. [139], "LOGGING AND MINING I by James Stevens"; p. [140], blank; pp. 141–167. text'; p. [168], blank; p. [169], "THE CASCADE FOREST I by Walter F. Mc-Culloch"; p. [170], blank; pp. 171–213, text; p. [214], blank; p. [215], "THE FLOWERS IN OUR I BIT OF PARADISE I by Harry W. Hagen"; p. [216], blank; pp. 217–270, text; p. [271], "THE BIRDS OF THE CASCADES I by Ellsworth D. Lumley"; p. [272], blank; pp. 273–299, text; p. [300], blank; p. [301], "WHERE THE DRY FLY IS QUEEN I by Herbert Lundy"; p. [302], blank; pp. 303–333, text; p. [334], blank; p. [335], "MOUNTAINEERING I by Grant McConnell"; p. [336], blank; pp. 337–363, text; p. [364], blank; p. [365], "SKIS ON THE CASCADES I by Charles D. Hessey, Jr."; p. [366], blank; pp. 367–395, text; p. [396], blank; p. [397], "APPENDIX I by Weldon F. Heald"; p. [398], blank; pp. 399–401, "Appendix"; p. [402], blank; pp. 403–417, "Index"; p. [418], blank.

BINDING: Tan cloth (close to Pantone 453). Front: "[medium brown, close to Pantone 724] THE CASCADES I [Mountain device in red and blue] I [dark blue] RODERICK PEATTIE". Spine: "[medium brown] THE I CAS-CADES IMountain device in red and blue] I [dark blue] RODERICK I PEAT-TIE I [medium brown] VANGUARD". Cream endpapers. Top edges plain.

DUST JACKET (white paper): Front and spine carry a navy blue-and-white photograph, a skier in the foreground, snow-covered mountains in the background. Front: "[within a white rectangle, in navy blue] THE I CASCADES I Mountains of the I Pacific Northwest I Edited by Roderick Peattie". Spine "[within a white rectangle, in navy blue] THE I CASCADES I Mountains I of the | Pacific | Northwest | *Edited by* | *Roderick* | *Peattie* | Vanguard". Back: "[navy blue] Other Volumes in the | AMERICAN MOUNTAIN SERIES | edited by RODERICK PEATTIE | [list of seven titles with quotes from reviews] | *Each volume — illustrated with mountain photographs and maps* — $5.00 | [publishers imprint]". Front flap: "[blurb] | *With magnificent and unusual photographs* | [lower right] $5.00". Back flap: "BOOKS | *are wonderful* | GIFTS | [blurb promoting American Booksellers Association Give-A-Book Certificates] | [American Booksellers Association emblem] | *Buy* GIVE-A-BOOK CERTIFICATES | *Wherever You See This Emblem* | [publisher's imprint]".

Published at $5.00 on November 28, 1949; number of copies printed unknown.

Copyrighted and deposited November 28, 1949.

The book is listed in "The Weekly Record," December 10, 1949, p. 2397.

Note: No evidence found that Vanguard reprinted *The Cascades: Mountains of the Pacific Northwest.*

COPIES: CF

REPRINTS AND REPRODUCTIONS

Reproduced on microfilm. New Haven, Conn.: Yale University Library, 1988. 1 reel. 35 mm.

BIOGRAPHIES

Margaret Bundy Callahan was the wife of the well-known Pacific Northwest painter, Kenneth Callahan (1905–1956). The couple were married in 1930 and had a son, Brian. She was a writer for Northwest newspapers and magazines and an editor of the *Town Crier* literary magazine, which was published in Seattle in the years 1912–1937. The Callahans lived in Seattle in the 1930s and 1940s, but spent their summers and many weekends in other seasons on the 160-acre tree farm they called "Hemlock Heaven," in the Mount Pilchuck region of the Cascades. She had visited the Cascades in her childhood and, after her marriage, began a serious and extensive exploration and studies of the Cascades, their people, and their peaks and hidden valleys. She was the only woman of the nine contributors to *The Cascades.* She died in 1961.

Harry W. Hagen was born on November 4, 1907. In the introduction to *The Cascades,* Roderick Peattie, the editor, noted, "I take great pride in discovering Harry W. Hagen. He is not by profession a botanist but a mailman. I love him because he is a layman who has discovered the flowers of the mountains and as a layman has studied the flora and has become an authority on the matter." Harry Hagen died on June 9, 2001, at age 93.

Weldon F. Heald was an architect and an expert on the Sierra mountain peaks. From his early childhood, he was fascinated with mountains and their fauna and flora, geology, climate, and history. During World War II, he worked as an Army climatologist. He wrote more than six hundred articles on the history, ecology, conservation and preservation of mountains, wilderness, deserts, forests, and parks in one hundred and twenty-seven publications.[1] From 1961 to 1967, Heald was a consultant on national parks and monuments to the Secretary of the Interior. He was a prominent member of the Sierra Club; a trustee of the National Parks Association; and Western vice president of the American Alpine Club, and served on the Committee on Glaciers of the American Geophysical Union. He died in July 1967, at age 66.

Charles D. Hessey, Jr. was born on February 20, 1908. He was a freelance writer who was fond of mountain climbing, fishing, and especially skiing. His article "Gateways to the North Cascades" was published in the October 1967 *Sierra Club Bulletin*. Hessey had extensive experience as a mountain skier in the Colorado Rockies and especially the Cascades, where he had skied hundreds of miles. He died in January, 1990.

Ellsworth D. Lumley was a teacher at Roosevelt High School in Seattle when he wrote "The Birds of the Cascades" in *The Cascades*. At the time, he was the National Bird Chairman of the National Council of State Garden Clubs and had been president of the Seattle Audubon Society for four years. He had earlier been a ranger-naturalist in the Cascades for seven years. He wrote various articles on birds, including "The 'Phoebe' Call of the Chicadee" in the June 1934 edition of *The Auk* and "Birds of the San Juan Islands, Washington," in the September 1935 issue of *The Murrelet*. The latter article was co-written with Robert C. Miller and F.S. Hall. Ellsworth D. Lumley died in 1951.

Herbert Lundy was born on February 8, 1907. He attended the University of Oregon, earning a degree in journalism in 1928, when he began work at the *Tillamook Herald*. He joined the *Oregonian* in 1936 as a reporter and political writer, becoming associate editor in 1945 and editorial page editor in 1956. Lundy was deeply interested in the natural resources of the Pacific Northwest. Editorials he wrote on conservation issues in 1952 won a national citation for the *Oregonian* from the Izaak Walton League of America. Lundy retired in 1977 after forty-one years at the paper and twenty-one years as editorial page editor. He died on March 1, 1994, at age 87.

1. Sierra Club Hundred Peaks Section, "2M Heald Peak," angeles.sierraclub.org

Grant McConnell was born on June 27, 1915. He attended Reed College, earning a bachelor of arts degree in 1937. He studied at Oxford University from 1938 to 1939 and at Harvard University from 1939 to 1940 and earned a doctorate from the University of California, Berkeley, in 1951. He was an instructor in economics at Mount Holyoke College from 1939 to 1940, and worked at the U.S. Department of Agriculture and the Office of Price Administration from 1940 until 1942. He served in the Navy from 1943 to 1946, seeing action in the Pacific and rising to lieutenant. From 1951 to 1971, he held various academic positions as a political scientist at the University of California, Berkeley, the University of Chicago, and the University of California, Santa Cruz. He contributed to many political science journals and popular magazines. *Private Power and American Democracy* (Knopf, 1966) is considered the most important of his five scholarly books. He died on September 27, 1993, at age 78.

Walter F. McCulloch was born in 1905 in British Columbia and studied at the University of British Columbia, the University of Washington, the State University of New York, the University of Southern California, and Oregon State University. He joined the staff of the Oregon State University College of Forestry in 1937, and was later on the forestry staffs of Syracuse University and Michigan State University. During World War II, he was Assistant State Forester of Oregon, rejoining Oregon State University College of Forestry in 1945 and serving as dean from 1955 to 1966. The introduction to *The Cascades* notes, "For thirty-six years [McCulloch] ranged the forests of British Columbia. He worked in the eastern forests of the Central States, only to return to the West and the Cascades." McCulloch is noted for his book *Woods Words* (Oregon Historical Society, 1958), a comprehensive dictionary of loggers' terms. He died in 1973.

James Stevens was born in Iowa on November 15, 1892. He was a lumberman who popularized tales of Paul Bunyan and Babe the Blue Ox while working in an Oregon logging camp. His first version of the Bunyan legends, *Paul Bunyan* (Knopf, 1925), sold more than two hundred-fifty thousand copies. In 1916, while working in a lumber camp in Idaho, he sold four poems to the *Saturday Evening Post,* later contributing poems to anthologies. He worked for the West Coast Lumbermen's Association as director of public relations from 1937 to 1957, when he retired. He wrote nine books and more than two hundred magazine articles and stories during a writing career spanning more than fifty years.[2] He died on December 31, 1971, at age 79.

---

2. *The New York Times* obituary, January 1, 1972, p. 22.

NOTES ON *THE CASCADES*

Vanguard's Fall List in the September 3, 1949, issue of *Publishers' Weekly* included a November 10, 1949, publication date and reported Vanguard's plans for a special promotion of the book in bookstores in Oregon and Washington, to include posters, a four-page circular, and cooperative advertising. The book's copyright certificate carries a publication date of November 28, 1949.

REVIEWS

Booklist, January 15, 1950 (p. 171); *Kirkus,* September 15, 1949 (p. 533); *Library Journal,* October 1, 1949 (p. 1459); *New York Herald Tribune Book Review,* November 27, 1949 (p. 4); *New York Times Book Review,* January 1, 1950 (p. 6); *Wisconsin Library Bulletin,* December 1949, (p. 9).

SOURCES

Book Review Digest 1949. New York: The H.W. Wilson Company, 1950, p. 724.

Publishers' Weekly, September 3, 1949 (Vanguard Fall List), p. 1010 and p. 1152; September 17, 1949, p. 1421; and December 10, 1949, p. 2397.

Introduction. *The Cascades: Mountains of the Pacific Northwest.*

The New York Times Book Review, January 1, 1949, p. 6.

(Callahan) the *Seattle Times* obituary (Kenneth Callahan), May 11, 1986, n.p.

(Heald) The *Arizona Daily Star,* December 27, 1996, p. 10A. (Obituary of Phyllis Warde Heald)

(Heald) Sierra Club, Hundred Peaks Section, Angeles Chapter, *Summit Signatures,* 2M Heald Peak. Updated February 25, 2003.

(Lumley) (Co-author) "Birds of the San Juan Islands, Washington." *The Murrelet,* September 1935, No. 3.

(Lundy) The *Oregonian* obituary, March 2, 1994, p. B10.

(McConnell) *Writers Directory,* 14th ed., St. James Press, 1999. Reproduced in *Biography Resource Center.* Farmington Hills, Mich.:The Gale Group. 2001. Accessed February 22, 2002.

(McConnell) *Contemporary Authors Online.* The Gale Group, 2001. Reproduced in *Biography Resource Center.* Farmington Hills, Mich.:The Gale Group. 2001. Accessed February 22, 2002.

(McConnell) Meister, Robert. "Grant McConnell" (In Memoriam) in *PS:*

Political Science & Politics, June 1994, vol. 27, no. 2, pp. 285–287. Reproduced in *Biography Resource Center.* Farmington Hills, Mich.:The Gale Group. 2001. Accessed February 22, 2002.

(McCulloch) Oregon State University College of Forestry. "These Deans Guided the School's Progress". www.cof.orst.edu/cof/visitors/history /deans/index.php. Accessed May 9, 2003.

(Stevens) *The New York Times* obituary, January 1, 1972, p. 22.

(Stevens) *Contemporary Authors Online.* The Gale Group, 2000. Reproduced in *Biography Resource Center,* Farmington Hills, Mich.: The Gale Group. 2001.

THE FRIENDLY MOUNTAINS: GREEN, WHITE, AND ADIRONDACKS

Edited by Roderick Peattie

AM4   First edition, first printing (1942) [1]

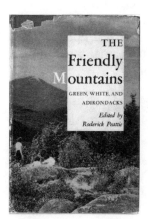

THE FRIENDLY | MOUNTAINS | GREEN, WHITE, AND ADIRONDACKS | *Edited by* | *RODERICK PEATTIE* | Author of "The Incurable Romantic," | "Mountain Geography," etc. | *The contributors:* | ROBERT BALK, VICTOR CONRAD | ZEPHINE HUMPHREY, RODERICK PEATTIE | HENRY POTTER, LOUIS B. PUFFER | HUGH M. RAUP, KATHARINE TOLL | THE VANGUARD PRESS | NEW YORK

The foregoing is printed within a white rectangle superimposed on a two-page black-and-white photograph of a range of low mountains, a large tree on the left, a lake in the foreground.

COLLATION: 9¼" x 6¼". 171 leaves. [i–viii] ix–xii [13–14] 22 [23–24] 25–74 [75–76] 77–84 [85] 86 [87] 88–121 [122–124] 125–141 [142–144] 145–185 [186–188] 189–215 [216–218] 219–271 [272–274] 275–301 [302] 303–328

[329–330] 331–341 [342]. Numbers printed in roman at the foot in the outer margin of the page.

> Note. Two unpaginated leaves (a–d) on glossy paper are inserted following p. [ii]; single unpaginated leaves bearing black-and-white photographs on glossy paper are inserted facing pp. 64, 65, 80, 81, 128, 129, 144, 145, 192, 193, 208, 209, 240, 241, 256, and 257.

CONTENTS: pp. [i–ii], blank; [a], half-title: "THE FRIENDLY MOUN-TAINS"; p. [b-c], title; p. [d], copyright page: "Copyright 1942, by The Van-guard Press, Inc. I *No portion of this book may be reprinted in any I form with-out the written permission of the pub- I lisher, except by a reviewer who wishes to quote I brief passages in connection with a review for a I newspaper or mag-azine* I PRINTED IN THE U.S.A. BY H. WOLFF, NEW YORK"; p. [iii–v], "Contents"; p. [vi], blank; pp. [vii–viii], "Illustrations"; pp. ix–xii, "Preface [signed Roderick Peattie]"; p. [13], "THE FOUR I RANGES I *by Roderick Peattie*"; p. [14], blank; pp. 15–22, text; p. [23], "HISTORY OF I THE MOUN-TAIN SETTLEMENT I *by Zephine Humphrey*"; p. [24], blank; pp. 25–74, text; p. [75], "THE GEOLOGIC STORY I OF THE MOUNTAINS I *by Robert Balk*"; p. [76], blank; pp. 77–141, text; ;p. [142], blank; p. [143], "ADVEN-TURES IN I MOUNTAIN BOTANY I *by Hugh M. Raup*"; p. [144], blank; pp. 145–185, text; p. [186], blank; p. [187], "THE ROUND OF NATURE IN I THE FRIENDLY MOUNTAINS I *by Henry Potter and Roderick Peattie*"; p. [188], blank; pp. 189–215, text; p. [216], blank; p. [217], "HOW TO ENJOY I THE MOUNTAINS IN SUMMER I *by Louis B. Puffer*"; p. [218], blank; pp. 219–271, text; p. [272], blank; p. [273], "WINTER SPORTS IN I THE FOUR RANGES I *by Katharine Toll*"; p. [274], blank; pp. 275–301, text; p. [302], blank; [unpag-inated page], "APPENDICES"; [unpaginated page], blank; pp. 303–311, "Points of Geological Interest"; pp. 312–313, "Guides and Maps"; pp. 314–319, "Some Mountain Elevations"; pp. 320–328, "Principal Ski Areas"; p. [329], "INDEX"; p. [330], blank; pp. 331–341,"INDEX"; p. [342], blank.

BINDING: Medium blue cloth (close to Pantone 285). Front: "[red, close to Pantone 186] THE FRIENDLY MOUNTAINS I [*Mountain* device, in red and green] I [green] RODERICK PEATTIE". Spine: "[red] THE I FRIENDLY I MOUNTAINS I [*Mountain* device, in red and green] I [green] RODERICK I PEATTIE I [red] VANGUARD". Cream endpapers carry a map by L.B.P. in dark green and cream of Maine, New Hampshire, Vermont, and portions of New York and Canada, titled "Here Is Where the Friendly Mountains Are".

DUST JACKET (white paper): Front and spine carry a black-and-white pho-tograph of a mountain scene; a woman standing on the left and two com-panions seated to her right; under a pale blue sky. Front: "[within a white rectangle, in black] THE I Friendly I [white, on blue sky] M [black, within the white rectangle] ountains I GREEN, WHITE, AND I ADIRONDACKS I *Edited by I Roderick Peattie"*. Spine "[within a white rectangle, in black] THE FRIENDLY I MOUNTAINS I *Green, White, and I Adirondacks* I EDITED BY I RODERICK PEATTIE I VANGUARD PRESS". Back: "A MESSAGE TO THE READER I Of its kind there is no greater beauty I to be found than that of the Friendly Mountains. Nor is there greater I experience in freedom, inde-pendence, and peace that soothes the soul. I Are Germans to be allowed to dive-bomb the lovely villages of Ver- I mont? Are the Japanese to infiltrate the peaceful hemlock forests I of the Presidential Range? Are enemy officers to make whoopee at I Lake Placid? I It is possible they may-unless we back our national effort with I bonds. One should not only buy bonds, but more bonds and continue I to buy yet more bonds. It is unthinkable that the en-emy should defile I the peace of The Friendly Mountains. I RODERICK PEATTIE I [within a rectangle with a thin black border is an advertisement for U.S. War Bonds and Stamps, 'Invest in Victory!']". Front flap: "[blurb] I *(Jacket photography courtesy of Pierson Studio)* I [lower right] $3.50". Back flap: "*Also Published by the Vanguard Press* I [thin rule] I Abraham Lincoln I & the Fifth Column I *By* GEORGE FORT MILTON I *Author of* I *'Conflict - The American Civil War,' etc.* I [five quotes from reviewers and historians] I *Illustrated with photographs and contem- I porary cartoons.* I [publisher's im-print] I *at all bookstores"*.

Published at $3.50 on November 30, 1942; number of copies printed un-known. Copyrighted December 11, 1942; deposited December 5, 1942.

The book is not listed in "The Weekly Record."

Note: No evidence found that Vanguard reprinted *The Friendly Mountains*.

COPIES: CF

REPRINTS AND REPRODUCTIONS

Reproduced on microfilm. New Haven, Conn.: Yale University Library, 1989. 1 reel. 35 mm.

BIOGRAPHIES

Robert Balk was born on May 31, 1899, in Reval, Estonia. His family moved to Germany in 1904. He attended the University of Breslau, earning a doc-torate in 1923, and emigrated to the United States in 1924. Over the years, he held academic positions at Columbia University, the New York State Mu-seum, Hunter College, Mount Holyoke College, and the University of

Chicago. In 1952, Balk and his wife, Christina Lochman Balk (d. March 8, 2006), a paleontologist, moved to Socorro, New Mexico, where he was principal geologist for the New Mexico Bureau of Mines. He died in an airplane accident on February 19, 1955, at age 55. The Robert Balk Fellowship at the New Mexico Institute of Mining and Technology, where Christina Balk was a member of the faculty, and a memorial fund at Johns Hopkins University, were established by Balk's widow. [Robert Balk's papers are held in Special Collections, Milton S. Eisenhower Library, The Johns Hopkins University.]

Victor Conrad was born on August 25, 1876, in Vienna, Austria. He studied biology and physics at the University of Vienna, completing his studies in 1900. Following the annexation of Austria into the German Reich in 1938, Conrad emigrated to the United States. In 1939 and 1940 he worked at the Pennsylvania State University Department of Meteorology, later working as a teacher and researcher at Harvard University until the mid-1950s. Conrad wrote at least two hundred and forty papers relating to meteorology, climatology, and seismology. In 2003, the Conrad Observatory at the Geophysical Observatory of the Central Institute for Meteorology and Geodynamics in Austria, one of the most modern, advanced geophysical observatories in the world, was named for him. He died on April 25, 1962, at age 85.

Zephine Humphrey (Fahnestock) was born on December 15, 1874, in Philadelphia, Pennsylvania. She graduated from Smith College in 1896, earning a bachelor's degree. Following her marriage to the artist Wallace Weir Fahnestock (1877–1962), she moved to Dorset, Vermont. She was a popular regional writer and wrote twenty books, including *Over Against Green Peak* (Holt, 1908), *The Story of Dorset* (Tuttle, 1924), *The Beloved Community* (Dutton, 1930), and *Green Mountains to Sierras* (Dutton, 1936). She died on November 14, 1956, at age 81. [Her papers, the Zephine Humphrey Collection, 1918–1959, are held by the University of Vermont Bailey/Howe Library in Vermont.]

Roderick Peattie. See Roderick Peattie, Editor, *The American Mountain Series.*

[**Louis**] **Henry Potter** was born on August 4, 1891. He was a self-trained field botanist and ornithologist and a lifelong farmer. When he wrote "The Round of Nature" for *The Friendly Mountains,* he lived on four hundred acres of valley farm and hill forest in the Taconic Mountains of Vermont. Although Potter did not attend high school, he was associated for decades with many of the leading naturalists in the Northeast. He is said to have observed, "I didn't have much schooling, but I had a lot of education." When he was 89, Potter was awarded an honorary doctorate in science by the University of Vermont. He died on May 27, 1986, at age 94.

Louis Blackmer Puffer was born on July 24, 1886, in Bennington, Vermont, the son of Norman Martin Puffer, a Civil War veteran, and Olive F. Blackmer Puffer. He attended Rensselaer Polytechnic Institute, earning a degree in civil engineering in 1909. In 1921, he joined the faculty of the University of Vermont, becoming full professor and head of the Department of Civil Engineering in 1937. On December 6, 1912, Puffer married Ruth Bascom Resseguie. The couple had three children. Puffer was the fiftieth person to become an Adirondack 46er, after having climbed all forty-six of the four-thousand foot peaks in the Adirondacks. He was president of the Burlington Section of the Green Mountain Club. A member of the Adirondack Mountain Club, for many years he was a trustee of the group's main club. He died on October 11, 1951, at age 65.

Hugh M. Raup, a botanist, ecologist, and geographer, was born on February 4, 1901, in Springfield, Ohio, the son of Gustavus Phillip and Fannie (Mitchell) Raup. He attended Wittenberg College (now Wittenberg University), earning a bachelor's degree in 1923. At Wittenberg, while he continued his studies, he was an instructor in biology. In 1925, he earned a master's degree. In 1928, he earned a doctorate from the University of Pittsburgh. He then returned to Wittenberg as assistant professor. He joined the Harvard faculty in 1932. During his thirty-five years at Harvard, he was associated with the Arnold Arboretum, the Black Rock Forest, the Department of Botany, and the Harvard Forest. Following his retirement in 1967, he was a visiting professor at Johns Hopkins University for three years, after which he and his wife, Lucy, lived in Petersham, Massachusetts, until his death on August 10, 1995, at age 94.

Katharine Toll graduated from Wellesley College a few years before she wrote her contribution to *The Friendly Mountains,* "Winter Sports in the Four Ranges." She was the daughter of a professor at Amherst. According to a brief sketch in the preface of *The Friendly Mountains,* Toll had "skied every run from Maine to Sun Valley." And, the sketch continued, "Her winters are spent ringing country telephones to report snow conditions to the *Boston Post* from every ski tow in New England."

NOTES ON *THE FRIENDLY MOUNTAINS*

Vanguard Press included notice of an October publication of the book, the first title in the *Mountain* series, in its Fall List in the September 26, 1942, issue of *Publishers' Weekly.* The book was well-received by reviewers and was featured in a page-long blurb on the back cover of *The Great Smokies,* the second volume in the series, with quotes from reviews in three major newspapers and the *Literary Guild.*

REVIEWS

Books, December 20, 1942 (p. 2); *Library Journal,* November 1, 1942 (p. 951); *New York Times Book Review,* January 3, 1943 (p. 5); *Scientific Book Club Review,* November 1942 (p. 3).

SOURCES

Book Review Digest 1942. New York: The H.W. Wilson Company, 1943, pp. 596–597.

Publishers' Weekly, April 11, 1942, p. 1413; September 26, 1942, p. 1175.

Preface. *The Friendly Mountains,* pp. ix–xii.

Back of dust jacket of *The Great Smokies and the Blue Ridge.*

The New York Times Book Review, January 3, 1943, p. 5.

(Balk) "Biographical Note." Balk, (Robert), 1899–1955. Papers 1922–1956. Ms. 215. Special Collections, The Milton S. Eisenhower Library, The Johns Hopkins University.

(Balk) Patrick, Kathryn, Archives Assistant, Mount Holyoke College Library. E-mail message to CF, February 2, 2007.

(Conrad) Hammerl, Christa. "Victor Conrad-First Head of the Seismological Service of Austria at ZAMG." Geophysical Research Abstracts, Vol. 7, 11203, 2005.

(Conrad) Bundes Immobilien Gesellschaft, Conrad Observatory. BIG & ZAMG/presseinfo/Conrad Observatorium. 14.05.2002.

(Humphrey) *The New York Times* obituary, November 16, 1956, n.p.

(Humphrey) The Zephine Humphrey Collection, Special Collections, University of Vermont Library, finding aid. Accessed May 8, 2003.

(Potter) Doherty, Prudence. Special Collections, Bailey/Howe Library, University of Vermont. E-mail message to CF, with attachments, January 24 2007.

(Potter) Thorne, Frank and Libby. *Henry Potter's Field Guide to the Hybrid Ferns of the Northeast.* Woodstock, Vt.: Vermont Institute of Natural Science, 1989. Biographical information from "About Henry Potter," pp. ix–x.

(Puffer) "Biographical Note" from the Vermont Historical Society Library VHS Home Page Manuscripts Web Site. www.vermonthistory.org/arccat/findaid/puffer.htm. Accessed January 23, 2007.

(Raup) Harvard University, "Memorial Minute: Hugh M. Raup" www.news.harvard.edu/gazette/1998/02.12/MemorialMinute. Accessed May 8, 2003.

THE GREAT SMOKIES AND THE BLUE RIDGE

Edited by Roderick Peattie

AM5   First edition, first printing (1943) [2]

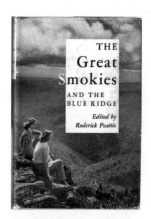

THE | GREAT SMOKIES | AND THE | BLUE RIDGE | THE STORY OF THE | SOUTHERN APPALACHIANS | *Edited by* | *RODERICK PEAT-TIE* | Author of "The Incurable Romantic," | "Mountain Geography," etc. | *The contributors:* | EDWARD S. DRAKE, RALPH ERSKINE, | ALBERTA PIERSON HANNUM, | JOHN JACOB NILES, DONALD CULROSS PEATTIE, | HENRY S. SHARP, ARTHUR STUPKA | THE VANGUARD PRESS | NEW YORK

The foregoing is printed within a white rectangle superimposed on a two-page black-and-white photograph of a range of low mountains in the background, farmland in a valley, and trees in the foreground.

COLLATION: 91/4" x 61/4". 194 leaves. [a–b] [i–iv] v-x [3–4]¹ 5–13 [14] 15–350 [351–352] 353–359 [360] 361–372 [373–378]. Numbers printed in roman in the outer margin at the foot of the page.

1. The book has unusual page numbering. The preliminary pages end with Page x. The text begins with an unnumbered half-title which would correspond to Page [3]. There are no pages [1–2]. Pages [i–iv] are printed on glossy paper.

Note: Single unpaginated leaves bearing black-and-white photographs on glossy paper are inserted facing pp. 90, 91, 122, 123, 154,
155, 186, 187, 218, 219, 250, 251, 282, 283, 314, and 315.

CONTENTS: pp. [a–b], blank; [i], half-title: "THE GREAT SMOKIES"; pp.
[ii–iii], title; p. [iv], copyright page: "Copyright, 1943, by Vanguard Press,
Inc. | No portion of this book may be reprinted in any form | without the
written permission of the publisher, except | by a reviewer who wishes to
quote brief passages for | inclusion in a review for a newspaper or magazine.
| This book has been produced in full compliance with all | government reg-
ulations for the conservation of paper, | metal, and other essential materials.
| Published for Vanguard Press, Inc., by Modern Age Books, Inc. | Manufac-
tured in the United States of America | by H. Wolff, New York, N.Y."; pp. [v-
viii], "Contents"; p. [ix–x], "Illustrations"; p. x, "[below list of illustrations]
Acknowledgment: Photographs number 1, 5, 6, 21, 26, and 28 are printed by
courtesy | of Bayard Wootten, Chapel Hill, N.C.; numbers 2, 3, 8, and 9, cour-
tesy of the U.S. | Forest Service; numbers 4 and 12, courtesy of Elliot Lyman
Fisher, Asheville, N.C.; | numbers 7, 10, and 11, courtesy of the National Park
Service; number 13, courtesy of | the Wildflower Preservation; numbers 15,
16, 23, 24, and 25, courtesy of Carlos C. | Campbell, Knoxville, Tenn.; number
14, courtesy of Wylie Bowmaster, Norris, Tenn.; | numbers 17 and 18, by
Hansel Mieth, courtesy of *Life Magazine,* copyright, Time. | Inc., 1943; num-
bers 20, 22, and 29, courtesy of the North Carolina Department of | Conser-
vation and Development, Raleigh, N.C.; number 19, courtesy of Mrs. Lucy |
Morgan; number 27, courtesy of Shannon Meriweather."; p. [3], half-title,
"THE GREAT SMOKIES"; p. [4], blank; pp. 5–13, "An Introduction and A
Statement of Philosophy | *by Roderick Peattie*"; p. [14], blank; pp. 15–72, "IN-
DIAN DAYS AND THE COMING | OF THE WHITE MAN | *by Donald Cul-
ross Peattie*"; pp. 73–151, "THE MOUNTAIN PEOPLE | *by Alberta Pierson
Hannum*"; pp. 152–171, "MEN, MOUNTAINS, AND TREES | *by Donald Cul-
ross Peattie*"; pp. 172–199, "BLUE RIDGE WILD FLOWERS | *by Donald Cul-
ross Peattie*"; pp. 200-216, "ADVENTURES AMONG THE | MOUNTAIN
CRAFTSMEN | *by Ralph Erskine*"; pp. 217–238, "FOLK BALLAD AND
CAROL*² | *by John Jacob Niles*"; pp. 239–262, "WHAT ABOUT THE CLI-
MATE? | *by Ralph Erskine*"; pp. 263–289, "THROUGH THE YEAR IN THE |
GREAT SMOKY MOUNTAINS | NATIONAL PARK, MONTH | BY
MONTH | *by Arthur Stupka*"; pp. 290-319, "THE GEOLOGIC STORY | *by
Henry S. Sharp*"; pp. 320-350, "HOW SHALL I PLAN MY TRIP? | *by Edward
S. Drake*"; p. [351], "AN APPENDIX | OF FURTHER READING"; p. [352],

2. [footnote] "Mr. Niles insists, and rightly, that the discussion of the ballad cannot be
confined to the area of this book."

blank; pp. 353–359, appendix; p. [360], blank; pp. 361–372, "Index"; pp. [373–378], blank.

BINDING: Medium cream cloth. Front: "[medium brown] THE GREAT SMOKIES | [*Mountain* device, in blue and red] | [blue] AND THE BLUE RIDGE". Spine: "[medium brown] THE GREAT | SMOKIES | AND THE | BLUE RIDGE | [*Mountain* device, in blue and red] | [blue] RODERICK | PEATTIE | [medium brown] VANGUARD". Cream endpapers carry a map by "M.R." in dark blue and cream of the Smoky Mountains, titled "The Great Smokies and the Blue Ridge".

DUST JACKET (white paper): Front and spine carry a black-and-white photograph of a mountain scene; with the mountains in medium green; two young women sitting at the top of a rocky ledge overlooking the mountains. Front: "[within a white rectangle, in black] THE | Great | [outside the rectangle in white] S [black, within the white rectangle] mokies | AND THE | BLUE RIDGE | *Edited by* | *Roderick Peattie*". Spine "[within a white rectangle, in black] THE GREAT | SMOKIES | AND THE | BLUE RIDGE | EDITED BY | RODERICK PEATTIE |VANGUARD PRESS". Back: "*The First Volume in the American Mountain Series* | [thin rule] | The Friendly Mountains | GREEN, WHITE AND ADIRONDACKS | *Edited by Roderick Peattie* | *The Contributors:* ROBERT BALK, VICTOR CONRAD, ZEPHINE HUMPHREY, | RODERICK PEATTIE, HENRY POTTER, LOUIS B. PUFFER, HUGH M. RAUP, and | KATHARINE TOLL. | [three-paragraph blurb] | quotes from three reviews] | *Illustrated with twenty-six beautiful photographs -*". Front flap: "'*Without doubt one of the best books* | *ever written about the Southern moun-* | *tains.*' -GERALD W. JOHNSON in | The N.Y. Herald Tribune | [blurb] | With many illustrations". Back flap: "[blurb, identical to that found on the front flap] | *With many* illustrations | [lower left] $3.75".

Published at $3.75 on December 10, 1943; number of copies printed unknown. Copyrighted December 17, 1943; deposited December 13, 1943.

The book is listed in "The Weekly Record," December 25, 1943, p. 2331.

Note: Vanguard reprinted *The Great Smokies and the Blue Ridge* in 1972.

COPIES: CF

REPRINTS AND REPRODUCTIONS

Reproduced on microfilm. Ann Arbor, Mich.: University Microfilms International, 1987(?). 1 reel, 35 mm.

BIOGRAPHIES

Edward S. Drake is briefly described in Roderick Peattie's introduction to *The Great Smokies:* "Edward S. Drake, the one-time friend of the Grand Old Man of the Mountains, Horace Kephart, is seized with an irrepressible madness about twelve times a year. The cure is once again to return to the Appalachians. I know of no one who has sent more visitors on to the region and sent them with more exact road directions." (Horace Kephart [1895–1948] was a renowned naturalist, woodsman, and author who settled in western North Carolina in 1904 to study the Carolina region. During the last decade of his life he was active in promoting the establishment of the Great Smoky Mountains National Park.)

Ralph Erskine is briefly described in the introduction to *The Great Smokies:* "Ralph Erskine, though of Wisconsin extraction, annually visited his father's home in North Carolina. Gradually those visits have lengthened until now he lives in Pacolet Valley and seldom leaves it. His especial interest in the mountains has extended from the days of horseback to those of the auto. His sense of the artistic has led him to a fine appreciation of the mountain crafts. He has been a sportsman and when he tells of the hunt it is from first hand."

Alberta Pierson Hannum was born in Condit, Ohio, on August 3, 1906, the daughter of James Ellsworth and Caroline Adelle (Evans) Pierson. In 1927, she earned a bachelor's degree from Ohio State University. On January 7, 1929, she married Robert Fulton Hannum, a businessman. She wrote eight books, including the novel *Roseanna McCoy* (Holt, 1947) and *Look Back with Love: A Recollection of the Blue Ridge* (Vanguard, 1969). She contributed to national and foreign magazines. In 1968, she received an honorary doctorate in letters from West Virginia University. In 1971 she received the annual book award of the Columbus, Ohio, branch of the American Association of University Women, and, in 1974, a community service award from the American Association of University Professors. She died in February 1985.

John Jacob Niles was born into a musical family on April 28, 1892, in Louisville, Kentucky, and was taught music theory by his mother. Niles began collecting folk music in his teens and composed his first song, "Go 'Way from My Window," in 1908. During World War I, he served in the U.S. Army Signal Corps as a reconnaissance pilot. He moved to New York in 1925. His first book, *Singing Soldiers* (Scribner's), was published in 1927. He composed the well-known ballads *I Wonder As I Wander* and *Black Is the Color of My True Love's Hair* and was a popular lecturer on American folk music. In his introduction to *The Great Smokies,* Roderick Peattie reported that he was the first "to persuade [Niles] to put pen to paper in other than musical script." Niles died on March 1, 1980, at age 87.

Donald Culross Peattie was born on June 21, 1898, in Chicago, Illinois, the son of Robert Burns and Ella Wilkenson Peattie. His father was a journalist. Peattie attended the University of Chicago from 1916 to 1918, later attending Harvard University and earning a bachelor's degree in 1922. On May 23, 1923, he married Louise Redfield. Peattie worked as a botanist at the U.S. Department of Agriculture from 1922 to 1924, when he became a freelance writer. He wrote twenty works of non-fiction; eight juveniles; four works of fiction; and was co-author or editor of five other books. He was a popular writer, whose many books covered nature, history, and biography. From 1925 to 1934, he wrote a column on nature for the *Washington Star*. In 1935, Peattie received a Gold Medal from the Limited Editions Club for *An Almanac for Moderns* (Putnam). In 1936 he received a Guggenheim Fellowship for creative writing. He died on November 16, 1964, at age 66.

Henry S. Sharp was born on March 26, 1902, in Stuyvesant Falls, New York. He graduated from Cornell University in 1924 and later attended Columbia University, earning a master's degree in 1926 and a doctorate in 1929. He was married to Gertrude Hargrave. He taught at Denison University and later at Columbia University before joining the faculty of Barnard College in 1941 as chairman of the Department of Geology. He retired in 1967. Sharp was a classical geomorphologist. He conducted geological research on Okinawa and the Palau Islands for the military geology branch of the U.S. Geological Survey. In the introduction to *The Great Smokies,* Roderick Peattie described Sharp as "one of a half-dozen men in the country competent to write upon the complicated geologic history of the Great Smokies and the Blue Ridge." Sharp died on October 20, 1969, at age 67.

Arthur Stupka was born on October 25, 1905, in Cleveland, Ohio. After graduating from Ohio State University, he worked for the National Park Service. In 1935, he became the first park naturalist at The Great Smoky Mountains National Park. He served in that capacity for the next twenty-five years and continued as the park biologist for the next four years. He married Margaret McCloud. His second marriage was to Grace Grossman. Stupka wrote *Notes on the Birds of Great Smoky Mountains National Park* (1963) and *Trees, Shrubs, and Woody Vines of Great Smoky Mountains National Park* (1964), both published by the University of Tennessee Press. Stupka died on April 12, 1999, at age 93. In a remembrance in the April 25, 1999, *Knoxville News-Sentinel,* J. B. Owen wrote, "old-timers remember Art Stupka as the soft-spoken, top authority on Great Smoky Mountains birds."

NOTES ON *THE GREAT SMOKIES AND THE BLUE RIDGE*

The book was included in Vanguard's 1943 Fall List in the September 25, 1943, issue of *Publishers' Weekly*. The United States was at war, and a paragraph on the copyright page reads, "This book has been produced in full compliance with all government regulations for the conservation of paper, metal, and other essential materials." A review in the December 19, 1943, *Weekly Book Review* included the observation, "It is far from being a guide book in the ordinary sense. . . . but it is pleasant reading even in these days when gasoline rationing makes vacation touring out of the question."

REVIEWS

Book Week, January 2, 1944 (p. 4); *Booklist*, January 15, 1944 (p. 182); *New York Times Book Review*, December 26, 1943 (p. 7); *New Yorker*, January 1, 1944 (p. 68); *Scientific Book Club Review*, December 1943 (p. 3); *New York Herald Tribune Book Review*, December 19, 1943 (p. 3).

SOURCES

Book Review Digest 1943. New York: The H.W. Wilson Company, 1944, p. 638.

Publishers' Weekly, September 25, 1943, pp. 1132–1133; December 25, 1943, p. 2331.

The New York Times Book Review, December 26, 1943, p. 7.

Peattie, Roderick. Introduction to *The Great Smokies and the Blue Ridge*, pp. 5–13.

(Drake) Hunter Library, "Horace Kephart." Special Collections: Manuscript Collections. Western Carolina University. www.wcu.edu/library/special-coll/manuscripts/kephart.

(Hannum) *Contemporary Authors Online*. The Gale Group, 2000. Reproduced in *Biography Resource Center*. Farmington Hills, Mich.: The Gale Group, 2001. Accessed February 22, 2002.

(Niles) "John Jacob Niles (1892–1980)". *The Hymns and Carols of Christmas*. www.hymnsandcarolsofchristmas.com. Accessed January 22, 2007.

(Peattie, Donald C.) *Contemporary Authors Online, Gale, 2007. Reproduced in Biography Resource Center*. Farmington Hills, Mich.: Thomson Gale. 2007. Accessed April 27, 2007.

(Sharp) Glassman, Donald, Barnard College Archivist, Wollman Library. E-mail messages to CF, February 5 and 15, 2007, and letter to CF postmarked

February 7, 2007, with enclosures: "Minute on the Death of Henry S. Sharp." n.d., and unidentified newspaper obituary, n.p., n.d.

(Stupka) The *Knoxville News-Sentinel* obituary, April 14, 1999, n.p.; and remembrance by J. B. Owen. April 25, 1999, n.p.

THE INVERTED MOUNTAINS: CANYONS OF THE WEST

Edited by Roderick Peattie

AM6   First edition, first printing (1948) [7]

THE | INVERTED | MOUNTAINS: | *Canyons of the West* | EDITED BY | RODERICK PEATTIE | CONTRIBUTORS: *Weldon F. Heald* | *Edwin D. McKee* | *Harold S. Colton* | THE VANGUARD PRESS, INC. | NEW YORK

The foregoing is printed within a white vertical rectangle superimposed on a two-page black-and-white photograph of the North Rim of the Grand Canyon, a view from Cape Royal.

COLLATION: 91/4" x 61/4". 200 leaves. [i–iv] v-x [1–2] 3-7 [8–10] 11–40 [41–42] 43–65 [66–68] 69–82 [83–84] 85–107 [108–110] 111–128 [129–130] 131–149 [150-152] 153–184 [185–186] 187–207 [208–210] 211–252 [253–254] 255–285 [286–288] 289–321 [322–324] 325–376 [377–378] 379–390. Numbers printed in roman in the outer margin at the foot of the page.

Note: Unpaginated single leaves bearing a map on the obverse; blank on the verso are inserted between pp. 14 and 15, and pp. 146 and 147. Single unpaginated leaves bearing black-and-white photographs on glossy paper are inserted facing pp. 24, 25, 56, 57, 88, 89, 120, 121, 182, 183, 214, 215, 278, 279, 310, and 311.

CONTENTS: p. [i], half-title: "THE INVERTED MOUNTAINS"; pp. [ii–iii], title; p. [iv], copyright page: "COPYRIGHT, 1948, BY VANGUARD PRESS,

INC. | No portion of this book may be reprinted in any form without the written | permission of the publisher, except by a reviewer who wishes to quote | brief passages for inclusion in a review for a newspaper or magazine. | Published Simultaneously in Canada by the Copp Clark Co., Ltd. | Manufactured in the United States of America by | H. Wolff, New York, N.Y. | TITLE PAGE PHOTOGRAPH: North rim Grand Canyon, view from Cape Royal. | (Union Pacific Railroad Photo.)"; pp. v-viii, "Contents"; p. ix–x], "Illustrations"; p. x, ACKNOWLEDGMENT: Photographs number 1, 3, 7, 9, 16, 22, and 23 are printed by | courtesy of the National Parks Service; 2, 4, 5, 6, 12, 13, 18, 21, 25, and 27, courtesy | of Weldon F. Heald; numbers 8, 10, 14, 17, 19, 20, 24, 26, courtesy of E.D. McKee; | number 28, courtesy of Orlo Childs; numbers 29, 30, 31, 32 and 33, courtesy of the | American Museum of Natural History, New York; number 11, courtesy of Union Pacific | Railroad; number 15, courtesy of the Santa Fe System Lines."; p. [1], "INTRODUCTION"; p. [2], blank; pp. 3–7, introduction [signed Roderick Peattie]; p. [8], blank; p. [9], "CHAPTER ONE | CANYON PREVIEW | *By Weldon F. Heald*"; p. [10], blank; pp. 11–14, text; [unpaginated leaf; obverse bears an unsigned map of part of Utah and Arizona titled "The Canyon Country; verso blank]; pp. 15–40, text; p. [41], "CHAPTER TWO | FEATURES OF THE CANYON | COUNTRY | *By Edwin D. McKee*"; p. [42], blank; pp. 43–65, text; p. [66], blank; p. [67], "CHAPTER THREE | FOSSIL LIFE OF THE CANYON | COUNTRY | *By Edwin D. McKee*"; p. [68], blank; pp. 69–82, text; p. [83], "CHAPTER FOUR | THREE HUNDRED YEARS OF | SPAIN | *By Weldon F. Heald*"; p. [84], blank; pp. 85–107, text; p. [108], blank; p. [109], "CHAPTER FIVE | INDIAN LIFE-PAST AND PRESENT | *By Harold S. Colton*"; p. [110], blank; pp. 111–128, text; p. [129], "CHAPTER SIX | THE AMERICANS COME | *By Weldon F. Heald*"; p. [130], blank; pp. 131–146, text; [unpaginated leaf; obverse bears a map courtesy of the National Park Service titled 'Grand Canyon National Park'; verso blank]; pp. 147–149, text; p. [150], blank; p. [151], "CHAPTER SEVEN | THE COLORADO RIVER | *By Weldon F. Heald*"; p. [152], blank; pp. 153–184, text; p. [185], "CHAPTER EIGHT | RIDING GRAND CANYON RAPIDS | *By Weldon F. Heald*"; p. [186], blank; pp. 187–207, text; p. [208], blank; p. [209], "CHAPTER NINE | THE CANYON WILDERNESS | *By Weldon F. Heald*"; p. [210], blank; pp. 211–252, text; p. [253], "CHAPTER TEN | ON FOOT AND IN THE SADDLE | *By Edwin D. McKee*"; p. [254], blank; pp. 255–285, text; p. [286], blank; p. [287], "CHAPTER ELEVEN | THE CANYON TRAILS | *By Edwin D. McKee*"; p. [288], blank; pp. 289–321, text; p. [322], blank; p. [323], "CHAPTER TWELVE | ENVIRONMENT CONTROLS LIFE | *By Edwin D. McKee*"; p. [324], blank; pp. 325–376, text; p. [377], "INDEX"; p. [378], blank; pp. 379–390, "Index".

BINDING: Tan cloth (close to Pantone 453). Front: "[medium brown, close to Pantone 724] THE INVERTED MOUNTAINS | [*Mountain* device in red and blue] RODERICK PEATTIE". Spine: "[medium brown] THE | IN-VERTED | MOUNTAINS | [*Mountain* device in red and blue] | [dark green] RODERICK | PEATTIE | [medium brown] VANGUARD". Cream endpapers. Top edges stained medium brown.

DUST JACKET (white paper): Front and spine carry a black-and-white photograph, of the North Rim of the Grand Canyon, a view from Cape Royal, which is also the title page photograph. Front: "[within a white rectangle, in black] THE | INVERTED | MOUNTAINS | CANYONS OF THE WEST | *Edited by* | *Roderick Peattie*". Spine "[within a white rectangle, in black] THE | INVERTED | MOUNTAINS | CANYONS | OF THE WEST | *Edited by* | *Roderick* | *Peattie* | Vanguard". Back: "Other Volumes in the | AMERICAN MOUNTAIN SERIES | edited by RODERICK PEATTIE | [list of six titles with quotes from reviews] | *Each volume — illustrated with mountain photographs and maps* — $5.00 | [publishers imprint]". Front flap: "[blurb] |[lower right] $5.00". Back flap: "BOOKS | *are wonderful* | GIFTS [blurb promoting American Booksellers Association Give-A-Book Certificates] | [American Booksellers Association emblem] | *Buy* GIVE-A-BOOK CERTIFICATES | *Wherever You See This Emblem* | [publisher's imprint]".

Published at $5.00 on December 16, 1948; number of copies printed unknown. Copyrighted December 20, 1948; deposited December 16, 1948.

The book is listed in "The Weekly Record," January 1, 1949, p. 72.

Note: No evidence found that Vanguard reprinted *The Inverted Mountains: Canyons of the West.*

CITED: *Guns* 759; *Guns* (Revised Ed.) 1700; Paher 1539; Farquhar 72

COPIES: CF

REPRINTS AND REPRODUCTIONS

None.

BIOGRAPHIES

Weldon F. Heald. For a biography of Weldon F. Heald, see *The Cascades: Mountains of the Pacific Northwest.*

Edwin Dinwiddie McKee was born on September 24, 1906. A graduate of Cornell University, he studied the geology and natural history of the Grand

Canyon for fifty years. He was the Park Naturalist at Grand Canyon National Park from 1929 until 1940, when he became associate professor of geology at the University of Arizona. He was named chairman of the university's Department of Geology in 1951. In 1953, he joined the U.S. Geological Survey, becoming a research geologist, work he would continue until his death. In 1957 he was awarded an honorary doctorate in science from Arizona State College (now Northern Arizona University). In 1970, he was named Honorary Member of the Society for Sedimentary Science and, in 1975, received the Society's highest medal of recognition, the William H. Twenhofel Medal for Excellence in Sedimentary Geology. McKee Point, a Colorado River overlook on the Hualapai Reservation, was named in his honor. He died in July 1984. [The Edwin and Barbara McKee Collection is held by the Cline Library, Northern Arizona University.]

Harold Sellers Colton was born on August 29, 1881. In 1928, Colton and his wife, the artist Mary Russell-Ferrell Colton (1889–1971), founded the Museum of Northern Arizona at Flagstaff, a private, nonprofit institution dedicated to the preservation of the history and varied cultures of northern Arizona. Colton had taught zoology at the University of Pennsylvania before the couple moved to Arizona. The Harold S. Colton Memorial Research Library, which is housed in the museum's Research Center building, began with the donation of the Coltons' personal library. The library's collection is strongest in the fields of archaeology, ethnology, geology, and paleontology, and the museum itself is a regional center of learning, serving more than one hundred thousand visitors annually. Harold Sellers Colton died on December 29, 1970, at age 89.

NOTES ON *THE INVERTED MOUNTAINS*

Notice of publication of the book was included in the Vanguard Press 1948 Fall List in the September 25, 1948, issue of *Publishers' Weekly*. The book was advertised at $5.00, with a publication date of October 29, 1948. The announced publication date was not met. The book was not received for copyright until December 16, 1948, and it did not appear in "The Weekly Record" until January 1, 1949.

"PW's Guide to the ABA Convention Exhibit of Books" in the May 15, 1948, issue of *PW* had earlier reported that Vanguard would "show dummies of ten books scheduled for publication in September or later" at the convention. *The Inverted Mountains* was one of the books listed.

REVIEWS

Booklist, February 15, 1949 (p. 209); *Kirkus,* September 15, 1948 (p. 497); *Library Journal,* November 1, 1948 (p. 1593); *New York Herald Tribune Book Review,* January 23, 1949 (p. 9); *New York Times Book Review,* January 16, 1949 (p. 33); *Saturday Review of Literature,* January 15, 1949 (p. 37).

SOURCES

Book Review Digest 1949. New York: The H.W. Wilson Company, 1950, p. 724.

Publishers' Weekly, May 15, 1948, pp. 2075 and 2077; September 25, 1948 (Vanguard Fall List), p. 1320; January 1, 1949, p. 72.

The New York Times Book Review, January 16, 1949, p. 33.

(Colton) Evans, Ed, Librarian, Harold S. Colton Memorial Research Library, Flagstaff, Arizona. Telephone conversation with CF, May 11, 2007.

(Colton) Museum of Northern Arizona website. musnaz.org Accessed May 11, 2007.

(McKee) www.findagrave.com Accessed April 24, 2007.

(McKee) Trost, Maxine and Lori Olson, compil. University of Wyoming American Heritage Center Guide to Environmental and Natural Resource Collections at the American Heritage Center, 1995, p. 50.

THE PACIFIC COAST RANGES

Edited by Roderick Peattie

AM7   First edition, first printing (1946) [4]

THE PACIFIC COAST RANGES | *EDITED BY RODERICK PEATTIE* | THE CONTRIBUTORS: *Archie Binns, John Walton Caughey, Lois Crisler,* | *Aubrey Drury, Idwal Jones, Donald Culross Peattie, Thomas Emerson* | *Ripley, Richard Joel Russell, Judy Van der Veer, Daniel E. Willard* | *THE VANGUARD PRESS — NEW YORK*

The foregoing is printed within a white horizontal rectangle superimposed on a two-page black-and-white photograph of the Channel Islands from hills above Santa Barbara, by infra-red photography, taken by Josef Muench.

COLLATION: 9¼" x 6¼". 210 leaves. [i–iv] v–ix [x] xi–xviii [1–2] 3–22 [23–24] 25–43 [44–46] 47–75 [76–78] 79–102 [103–104] 105–134 [135–136] 137–163 [164–166] 167–185 [186–188] 189–218 [219–220] 221–243 [244–246] 247–284 [285–286] 287–317 [318–320] 321–353 [354–356] 357–379 [380-386] 387–402. Numbers printed in roman in headline at the outer margins of the type page, except for pp. v, xi, xiii, 3, 25, 47, 79, 105, 137, 167, 189, 221, 247, 287, 321, 357, and 387, on which the numbers are printed in the center at the foot of the page.

Note: Single unpaginated leaves bearing black-and-white photographs on glossy paper are inserted facing pp. 18, 19, 50, 51, 82, 83, 114, 115, 178, 179, 210, 211, 274, 275, 306, and 307.

CONTENTS: pp. [i], half-title: "THE PACIFIC COAST RANGES"; pp. [ii–iii], title; p. [iv], copyright page: "COPYRIGHT 1946, BY VANGUARD PRESS, INC. | No portion of this book may be reprinted in any form without the written | permission of the publisher, except by a reviewer who wishes to quote | brief passages for inclusion in a review for a newspaper or magazine. | Published Simultaneously in Canada by the Copp Clark Co., Ltd. | Manufactured in the United States of America by H. Wolff, New York,

| N.Y. | TITLE PAGE PHOTOGRAPH: The Channel Islands from hills above | Santa Barbara — by infra-red photography. (Courtesy of Josef | Muench.)";
pp. v-ix, "Contents"; p. [x], blank; pp. xi-xii, "Illustrations"; p. xii, "[below list of illustrations] MAPS BY GUY-HAROLD SMITH[1] | *Acknowledgment:* Photographs number 1, 3, 11, 16, 19, and 29 are printed by | courtesy of Josef Muench; numbers 2, 4, 23, courtesy of the Redwood Em- | pire Association; number 5, courtesy of Gabriel Moulin, and numbers 13, 14 | and 17, courtesy of Gabriel Moulin and the Save-the-Redwoods League; | numbers 6 and 8, courtesy of the Los Angeles County Chamber of Commerce; | number 7, courtesy of Everett F. Chandler; numbers 9, 10, and 12, courtesy | of William and Irene Finley; numbers 15 and 28, courtesy of Edward Weston; | numbers 18, 25, and 26, courtesy of Wilkes and the Santa Barbara Chamber of | Commerce; numbers 20 and 21, courtesy of the National Park Service; number | 22, courtesy of Frank Woodfield and the Astoria Chamber of Commerce; | number 24, courtesy of the Palm Springs Chamber of Commerce; number 27, | courtesy of the Northern Pacific Railway."; pp. xiii-xviii, "Introduction [by Roderick Peattie]; pp. [1], "'FATHER SERRA'S ROSARY' | BY DONALD CULROSS PEATTIE"; p. [2], blank; pp. 3-22, text; p. [23], "THE FIRST IN-HABITANTS | OF THE COAST RANGES | BY JOHN WALTON CAUGHEY"; p. [24] blank; pp. 25-43, text; p. [44], blank; p. [45], "FOOT-STEPS OF SPRING— | A WILD FLOWER TRAIL | BY DONALD CUL-ROSS PEATTIE"; p. [46], blank; pp. 47-75, text; p. [76], blank; p. [77], "GLIMPSES OF WILD LIFE | BY AUBREY DRURY"; p. [78], blank; pp. 79-102, text; p. [103], "FOOTHILLS | BY JUDY VAN DER VEER"; p. [104], blank; pp. 105-134, text; p. [135], "FARM, ROCK, AND | VINE FOLK | BY IDWAL JONES"; p. [136], blank; pp. 137-163, text; p. [164], blank; p. [165], "HEADLANDS IN | CALIFORNIA WRITING | BY JOHN WALTON CAUGHEY"; p. 166], blank; pp. 167-185, text; p. [186], blank; p. [187], "THE WILDERNESS | MOUNTAINS | BY LOIS CRISLER"; p. [188], blank; pp. 189-218, text; p. [219], "TIMBER | BY THOMAS EMERSON RIPLEY"; p. [220], blank; pp. 221-243, text; p. [244], blank; p. [245], "PEOPLE OF THE OREGON | COAST RANGE | BY ARCHIE BINNS"; p. [246], blank; pp. 247-284, text; p. [285], "PEOPLE OF THE | WASHINGTON COAST RANGE | BY ARCHIE BINNS"; p. [286], blank; pp. 287-317, text; p. [318], blank; p. [319], "THE GEOLOGICAL STORY | BY DANIEL E. WILLARD"; p. [320], blank; pp. 321-353, text; p. [354], blank; p. [355], "CLIMATIC TRANSITIONS | AND CONTRASTS | BY RICHARD JOEL RUSSELL"; p. [356], blank; pp. 357-379, text; p. [380], "[editorial note by Roderick Peattie, noting "Here ends the volume, but here is no end to the delights of the Pacific Coast

1. Guy-Harold Smith (1865-1976) was Chair of the Department of Geography at Ohio State University from 1934 to 1963. He was an authority in the field of cartography with special reference to population and physiographic maps.

Ranges. No volume of the 'American Mountain Series' has told or will tell of such variety of human kind and human experience. . . .]"; p. [381], "MAPS | OF THE PACIFIC COAST RANGES"; p. [382], blank; p. [383], [untitled map by Guy-Harold Smith (after Raisz) of the Olympic Mountains]; p. [384], [untitled map by Guy-Harold Smith (after Raisz) of the Coastal Range and Cascade Mountains]; p. [385], [untitled map by Guy-Harold Smith of the Sierra Nevada Mountains]; p. 386], [untitled map by Guy-Harold Smith of the San Rafael Range and the San Bernardino Range]; pp. 387–402, "Index".

Maps by Guy-Harold Smith appear on pp. [383], [384], [385], and [386].

BINDING: Medium cream cloth. Front: "[medium brown] THE PACIFIC COAST RANGES | [*Mountain* device, in red and green] | [black] RODER-ICK PEATTIE". Spine: "[medium brown] THE | PACIFIC | COAST | RANGES | [*Mountain* device in red and green] | [dark green] RODERICK | PEATTIE | [medium brown] VANGUARD". Cream endpapers. Top edges stained red.

DUST JACKET (white paper): Front and spine carry a black-and-white photograph, "Sunshine in the Mill Creek redwoods," which is also found facing p. 178 of the text. Front: "[within a rectangle with a bright yellow border, in yellow] THE | PACIFIC | COAST | RANGES | [below the rectangle] *Edited by Roderick Peattie*". Spine "[yellow] THE | PACIFIC | COAST | RANGES | *Edited by* | *Roderick* | *Peattie* | VANGUARD". Back: "Other Titles in | THE AMERICAN MOUNTAIN SERIES | [list of three titles, their authors, quotes from reviews, number of copies sold, and price]". Front flap: "[blurb] | [publisher's imprint] | [lower right] $3.75". Back flap: Blank.

Published at $3.75 on June 17,1946; number of copies printed unknown. Copyrighted June 17, 1946; deposited June 16, 1946.

The book is listed in "The Weekly Record," June 29, 1946, p. 3356.

Note: No evidence found that Vanguard reprinted *The Pacific Coast Ranges*.

CITED: *Libros Californios*, p. 79

COPIES: CF

REPRINTS AND REPRODUCTIONS

Reproduced on microfilm. New Haven, CT: Yale University Library, 1988. 1 reel, 35 mm.

BIOGRAPHIES

Archie Binns. For a biography of Archie Binns, see *Northwest Gateway: The Story of the Port of Seattle* in the *Seaport Series*.

John Walton Caughey was born in Wichita, Kansas, on July 3, 1902. He attended the University of Texas and later undertook graduate studies, earning a doctorate from the University of California, Berkeley in 1928. In 1930, he joined the faculty of the University of California, Los Angeles, rising to chairman of the Department of History. He was on the boards of the American Historical Association and the Organization of American Historians and was editor of the *Pacific Historical Review* from 1947 to 1968. He wrote books and articles on Los Angeles and the West. He died on December 15, 1995, at age 93. [The John Walton Caughey Papers, 1930-1982, are held in Special Collections, University of California, Los Angeles.]

Lois Crisler was born in Spokane, Washington, on August 9, 1896. She was educated in Washington and taught English and creative writing at the University of Washington. On December 7, 1941, she married Herbert Crisler, who became an Olympic National Park ranger and photographer. The Crislers produced several wildlife movies; including "The Olympic Elk," which was sold to Disney in 1952. For several years, she wrote a column, "Olympic Trail Talk," for the *Port Angeles Evening News.* Her book *Captive Wild* (Harper & Row, 1968) describes the domestication of wolf cubs she and her husband brought back from Alaska to their home at Lake George, Colorado. Following her divorce, she returned to Seattle, where she died on June 3, 1971, at age 74.

Aubrey Drury was born on June 10, 1891, the son of Wells and Ella Lorraine (Bishop) Drury. Drury wrote a tourist guide which was published by Harper's as *California: An Intimate Guide* in 1935. In 1947, Harper's published a revised edition of the book with the subtitle "From the Days of the Mission Fathers to the Celebration Surrounding One Hundred Years of Statehood." Drury was instrumental in expanding the Save-the-Redwoods League, raising funds for the organization and building up its membership. He was administrative secretary of the League from 1940 to 1959. He died on October 23, 1959, at age 68.

Idwal Jones was born on December 8, 1890, in Festiniog in Wales. His father was an engineer and geologist. The family emigrated to Pennsylvania in 1902. Educated at home owing to health concerns, Jones later studied engineering. He wrote book reviews for the *San Francisco Chronicle* in 1915 and later worked as a drama critic for the *San Francisco Daily News.* For a time, he served as a foreign correspondent in Rome and Paris. He returned to the United States in 1930 and worked as an editor and columnist for the *New York American* and as a book critic for *Life* magazine. He was a novelist and a specialist on California folklore and wrote seven books and numerous articles on California geology, folklore, and viticulture. He died on November 14,

1964, at age 73. [The Idwal Jones Papers, 1936–1950, are held by Special Collections, University of California, Los Angeles; the Idwal Jones Collection, 1920-1964 is held by Special Collections, University of California, Santa Barbara.]

Donald Culross Peattie. For a biography of Donald Culross Peattie, see *The Great Smokies and the Blue Ridge.*

Thomas Emerson Ripley was born in Rutland, Vermont, on September 19, 1865, the son of William Y. W. and Cornelia A. (Thomas) Ripley. He attended Yale University, earning a bachelor's degree in 1888. In 1890, he began a career in the lumber industry with the Wheeler-Osgood Company in Tacoma, Washington. In 1893, he became manager of the company's Boston office, working as such until 1902, when a fire destroyed the company's plant and he returned to Tacoma. He retired from the company in 1927 and, in 1929, turned to writing. His first book, *A Vermont Boyhood* (Appleton, 1937), was a best seller. Ripley was married to Charlotte H. Clements in 1891, and later to Dorothy Hellyer. He was an accomplished artist, painting well into his old age, when his eyesight began to fail. He died on December 14, 1956, at age 91.

Richard Joel Russell was born in Hayward, California, on November 16, 1895. He attended the University of California, Berkeley, graduating with a degree in geology and, in 1926, earning a doctorate. After a brief time as an associate professor at Texas Tech University, he joined the faculty of Louisiana State University, where he taught for forty-three years. A distinguished scientist, at age sixty he began to concentrate on coastal research, founding the Coastal Studies Institute in 1954. He was president of the Association of American Geographers in 1948 and president of the Geological Society of America in 1957. In 1959, he became a member of the National Academy of Sciences. He died on September 17, 1971, at age 75.

Judy Van der Veer was born on October 17, 1907, in Oil City, Pennsylvania, the daughter of Tunis Herbert and Alice (Case) Van der Veer. In 1919, the family moved to California. As a child on her father's ranch in Ramona, after she had broken a leg and for a while could not attend school, she began to write poetry. She later dropped out of high school after deciding to live in the country and write. She was a novelist and a poet and wrote children's books. Her stories, articles, and poems appeared in various magazines and anthologies. Her columns about ranch life were published in the *Christian Science Monitor* for twenty years. She died on November 22, 1982, at age 75.

Daniel E. Willard was born in Nile, New York, on August 22, 1862. He attended Alfred College, New York, earning a bachelor's degree in 1888 and a master's degree in 1890. From 1895 to 1910, he was professor of natural resources and geology at North Dakota Normal School and at North Dakota

College. He was a development and agricultural specialist for the Northern Pacific Railway from 1910 to 1920 and for the Great Northern Railway from 1920 to 1924. A scientist who wrote for the popular reader, Willard wrote books on the geology and landscapes of North Dakota, Minnesota, Montana, and California. His book *Adventures in Scenery: A Popular Reader of California Geology* was published by the Jacques Cattell Press in 1942. Willard died in 1947. ["Daniel Everett Willard: An Inventory of His Reminiscences" is held by the Minnesota Historical Society.]

NOTES ON *THE PACIFIC COAST RANGES*

The book was included in the Vanguard Spring List in the January 26, 1946, issue of *Publishers' Weekly*, with publication projected for March.

REVIEWS

Book Week, July 7, 1946 (p. 5); *Booklist*, July 15, 1946 (p. 364); *Kirkus*, April 1, 1946 (p. 166); *Library Journal*, June 1, 1946 (p. 823); *New York Times Book Review*, August 25, 1946 (p. 23); *San Francisco Chronicle*, July 23, 1946 (p. 14); *U.S. Quarterly Booklist*, December 1946 (p. 317); *Weekly Book Review*, June 23, 1946, p. 5; *Wisconsin Library Bulletin*, October 1946 (p. 130).

SOURCES

Book Review Digest 1946. New York: The H.W. Wilson Company, 1947, p. 645.

Publishers' Weekly, January 26, 1946, p. 641; June 29, 1946, p. 3356.

The New York Times Book Review, August 25, 1946, p. 23.

(Caughey) Online Archive of California. www.oac.cdlib.org Accessed January 17, 2003.

(Crisler) Petite, Irving. "In Memoriam: A Tribute to Lois Brown Crisler." The *Seattle Times Magazine*, January 23, 1972, p. 8.

(Crisler) "Author Dies". Brief obituary notice in the book section of the July 4, 1971, edition of a local paper, probably the *Seattle Times*. n.d., n.p.

(Crisler) Special Collections, University of Washington Libraries. (Various press clippings.)

(Drury) "Thurtell and Related Families" entry on Ella Lorraine Bishop Drury, mother of Aubrey Drury. www.geocities.com/thurtellfamily/gp/fam01010.html. Accessed January 17, 2003.

(Jones) Online Archive of California. Accessed April 19, 2007.

(Ripley) Gripp, Jody. Special Collections, Tacoma Public Library. Letter to CF, forwarding biographical material, February 5, 2007.

(Ripley) *Tacoma News Tribune* obituary, December 14, 1956, pg. 1.

(Russell) Walker, H. Jesse (Louisiana State University). "Richard Joel Russell (1895–1971): Coastal Enthusiast."

(Van der Veer) Morgan, Neil, "In Cuyamacas, Color of August Links Ranchers to Weekenders." *San Diego Union-Tribune*, August 26, 2001, p. A-3.

(Van der Veer) *Contemporary Authors Online*, Gale, 2003. Reproduced in *Biography Resource Center*. Farmington Hills, Mich.: The Gale Group. 2003. Accessed May 8, 2003.

(Willard) Minnesota Historical Society Finding Aid for "Daniel Everett Willard: An Inventory of His Reminiscences at the Minnesota Historical Society. www.mnhs.org/library/findaids/P2297.html

THE ROCKY MOUNTAINS

Wallace W. Atwood
October 1, 1872 – July 24, 1949

AM8   First edition, first printing (1945) [3]

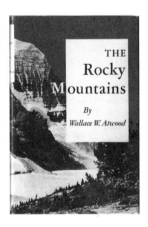

THE ROCKY | MOUNTAINS | *by* | WALLACE W. ATWOOD | *President, Clark University* | THIRD VOLUME IN THE | AMERICAN MOUNTAIN SERIES | EDITED BY RODERICK PEATTIE | THE VANGUARD PRESS | NEW YORK

The foregoing is printed within a white rectangle superimposed on a two-page black-and-white photograph of the Rocky Mountains; snow-capped peaks in the background; a field of flowers in bloom in the foreground.

COLLATION: 9¼" x 6¼". 162 leaves. [1–16] 17–24 [25–28] 29–48 [49–52] 53–70 [71–74] 75–85 [86–88] 89–103 [104–106] 107–128 [129–132] 133–149 [150–

152] 153–159 [160-162] 163–168 [169–172] 173–181 [182–184] 185–193 [194–196] 197–236 [237–240] 241–266 [267–270] 271–273 [274] 275–291 [292] 293–296 [297–307] 308–309 [310] 311–315 [316] 317–324. Numbers printed in roman in the outer margin at the foot of the page.

Note: Single unpaginated leaves bearing black-and-white photographs on glossy paper are inserted facing pp. 36, 37, 68, 69, 100, 101, [132], 133, [196], 197, 228, 229, 260, 261, [292], and 293. An unpaginated map is inserted between p. 296 and p. [297].

CONTENTS: pp. [1], half-title: "THE ROCKY MOUNTAINS"; pp. [2–3], title; p. [4], copyright page: "Copyright, 1945, by Vanguard Press, Inc. | No portion of this book may be reprinted in any | form without the written permission of the pub- | lisher, except by a reviewer who wishes to quote | brief passages for inclusion in a review for a | newspaper or magazine. | MANUFACTURED IN THE UNITED STATES OF AMERICA | BY H. WOLFF, NEW YORK, N.Y."; p. [5], dedication: "TO | HARRIET T.B. ATWOOD, | to the other members of my family, and to more | than one hundred students who have accompanied | me on one or more of my pack-train expeditions | through the Rocky Mountains"; p. [6], blank; pp. [7–8], "Acknowledgments [signed W.W.A., Worcester, Massachusetts]"; pp. [9–11], "Contents"; p. [12], blank; pp. [13–14], "Illustrations"; p. [14], "[below list of illustrations] Acknowledgment: Photographs number 1, 13, 22, 28, 29, and 32 are printed by | courtesy | of W.W. Atwood; numbers 2, 15, 16, 17, 18, and 21, courtesy of the | U.S. Forest Service; number 3, courtesy of the U.S. Department of Mines and | Resources; number 4, courtesy of the National Park Service; numbers 5, 8, 24, | and title page, courtesy of the National Parks Bureau, Ottawa, Canada; num- | bers 6, 7, and 23, courtesy of the Canadian Pacific Railway; numbers 9, 12, 14, | 19, 27, 30, and 31, courtesy of George Grant; number 10, courtesy of Eugene | Kingman; numbers 11 and 25, courtesy of the U.S. Geological Survey; number | 20, courtesy of Barnum Brown; number 26, courtesy of the U.S. Department of | the Interior."; p. [15], "A PREVIEW OF THE ROCKIES | [small illustration by Erwin Raisz[1]]"; p. [16], blank; pp. 17–[25], text [signed Roderick Peattie]"; p. [26], blank; p. [27], "CHAPTER ONE | CLIMBING TO HIGH PLACES"; p. [28], blank; pp. 29–[49], text; p. [50], blank; p. [51], CHAPTER TWO | OPENING A FIELD SEASON"; p. [52], blank; pp. 53–[71], text; p. [72], blank; p. [73], "CHAPTER THREE | THE | MOUNTAIN DRAMA UNFOLDS"; p. [74], blank; pp. 75–[86], text; p. [87], "CHAPTER FOUR | FROM THE AIR | AND FROM THE SADDLE"; p. [88], blank; pp. 89–[104], text; p. [105],

1. Erwin J. Raisz (1893-1968) was an internationally renowned cartographer known for his minutely detailed, hand-drawn, pen-and-ink maps, based on field observations and aerial photography.

"CHAPTER FIVE | UNDERSTANDING | MOUNTAIN SCENERY"; p. [106], blank; pp. 107–[129], text; p. [130], blank; p. [131], "CHAPTER SIX | THE ART OF CAMPING"; p. [132], blank; pp. 133–[150], text; p [151], "CHAPTER SEVEN | MOUNTAINS ARE WORN AWAY"; p. [152], blank; pp. 153–159, text; p. [160], blank; p. [161], "CHAPTER EIGHT | A DAY IN THE WIND RIVER | MOUNTAINS"; p. [162], blank; pp. 163–[169], text; p. [170], blank; p. [171], "CHAPTER NINE | MOUNTAINS RISE AGAIN"; p. [172], blank; pp. 173–[182], text; p. [183], "CHAPTER TEN | THE LAST GREAT ICE AGE"; p. [184], blank; pp. 185–[194], text; p. [195], "CHAPTER ELEVEN | BONANZA IN THE ROCKIES"; p. [196], blank; pp. 197–[237], text; p. [238], blank; p. [239], "CHAPTER TWELVE | INDIANS, RANCH-MEN, | FARMERS, AND TOURISTS"; p. [240], blank; pp. 241–[267]; text; p. [268], blank; p. [269], "THE NATIONAL PARKS IN THE | ROCKY MOUN-TAIN REGION"; p. [270], blank; pp. 271–272, text; p. 273, map; p. [274], blank; pp. 275–290, text; p. 291, map; p. [292], blank; pp. 293–296, text; [un-paginated fold-out map]; p. [297], "CROSS-SECTION DRAWINGS | *Based upon field studies by the author | and prepared for reproduction by* | DR. ER-WIN RAISZ"; pp. [298–305], [drawings with explanatory text]"; p. [306], blank; p. [307], "GEOLOGIC CALENDAR FOR THE | ROCKY MOUNTAIN REGION"; pp. 308–309, calendar; p. [310], blank; pp. 311–315, "Bibliography"; p. [316], blank; pp. 317–324, "Index".

ILLUSTRATIONS: Small illustrations appear on pp. [15], [25], [49], [86], [129], [150], [169], [182], [194], [237], [267], and [307].

Half-page illustrations appear on pp. [27], [51], [73], [87], [104], [105], [131], [151], [161], [171], [183], [195], [239], and [269]. Pages [298–305] bear cross-section illustrations by Dr. Erwin Raisz.

Maps by G.H.B. appear on p. 273, "Park to Park Highways in the Rocky Mountain Region"; p. 291, "Park to Park Highways in the Canadian Rockies". Inserted between pp. 296 and [297], is a map by Erwin Raisz, "Rocky Mountains of the United States and Southern Canada" prepared especially to accompany "The Rocky Mountains".

BINDING: Medium cream cloth. Front: "[red] THE ROCKY MOUNTAINS | [*Mountain* device, in black and red] | [black] WALLACE W. ATWOOD". Spine: "[red] THE ROCKY | MOUNTAINS | [*Mountain* device, in black and red] | [black] WALLACE W. | ATWOOD | [red] VANGUARD". Gold endpapers. Top edges stained red.

DUST JACKET (white paper): Front and spine carry a black and white photograph of the Rockies in winter; rust sky. Front: "[within a white rectangle, in black] THE I Rocky I [outside the rectangle in white] M [black, within the white rectangle] ountains I *By* I *Wallace W. Atwood*". Spine "[within a white rectangle, in black] THE I ROCKY I MOUNTAINS I BY I WALLACE W. I ATWOOD I VANGUARD PRESS". Back: *"Other Volumes in the American Mountain Series* I [thin rule] I Edited by RODERICK PEATTIE I The Great Smokies I and the Blue Ridge I THE STORY OF THE SOUTHERN AP-PALACHIANS I [list of contributors] I [quotes from three reviews] I *6" x 9" Illustrated with mountain photographs $3.75* I The Friendly Mountains I GREEN, WHITE, AND ADIRONDACKS I [quote from one review] I *6" x 9" Illustrated with mountain photographs $3.75* I [thin rule] I [publishers imprint]". Front flap: "[three-paragraph blurb] I [lower right] $3.75". Back flap: "[black and white photograph of Wallace W. Atwood] I [brief biographical sketch] I [publishers imprint]".

Published at $3.75 on October 15, 1945; number of copies printed unknown. Copyrighted October 17, 1945; deposited October 8, 1945.

The book is listed in "The Weekly Record," October 20, 1945, p. 1864.

Note: No evidence found that Vanguard reprinted *The Rocky Mountains.*

CITED: *Herd* 183

COPIES: CF

REPRINTS AND REPRODUCTIONS

Reproduced on microfilm. New Haven, CT: Yale University Library, 1988. 1 reel, 35 mm.

BIOGRAPHY

Wallace W. Atwood was born in Chicago, Illinois, on October 1, 1872, the son of Thomas Green Atwood and Adelaide Adelia (Richards) Atwood. His father owned a planing mill.

Atwood attended the University of Chicago, earning a bachelor of arts degree in 1897 and a doctorate in 1903. On September 22, 1900, he married Harriet Towle Bradley. The couple had four children.

Atwood worked for the New Jersey Geological Survey in 1897 and for the Wisconsin Natural History Survey from 1898 to 1899. He joined the University of Chicago faculty as a fellow in 1899, rising to associate professor of physiography and general geology. In 1913, he joined the Harvard University faculty as professor of physiography.

Atwood became president of Clark University in 1920. While president and also head of a major graduate department, he established the Graduate

School of Geography at Clark. At the time, this was only the second fully-staffed, independent doctoral program in geography in any American university. Clark University remained for more than fifty years the leading producer of doctorates in geography in America. Atwood contributed as well to geographic education at the elementary, junior, and senior high school levels, acting as author or co-author of school geographies that over his lifetime sold more than ten million copies.[2] He was president of Clark University for twenty-six years, retiring in 1946.

From 1929 to 1933, Atwood was president of the National Parks Association. He was president of the Association of American Geographers (1933–1934), and, from 1932 to 1935, president of the Pan-American Institute of Geography and History.

Wallace Atwood died on July 25, 1949, at age 76.

NOTES ON *THE ROCKY MOUNTAINS*

Vanguard Press first announced publication of the book in their 1945 Spring List in the January 27, 1945, issue of *Publishers' Weekly,* with a planned publication date of March 29. Publication was delayed, and the book appeared on Vanguard's Fall List in the September 22, 1945, issue of *PW,* noting a September publication. Written with somewhat of a textbook flavor, the book was acclaimed by the *Scientific Book Club Review* and *Book Week.* Stewart Holbrook, writing in the October 28, 1945, *Weekly Book Review,* noted, "Much of the book is done in an old-fashioned intimate travelogue manner, a method which may be found irritating by some readers, and which, in any case, has its limitations." The book is the only volume in the series to have only one author.

REVIEWS

Book Week, November 18, 1945 (p. 22); *Booklist,* November 15, 1945 (p. 93); *Kirkus,* May 1, 1945 (p. 194); *Library Journal,* June 15, 1945 (p. 585); *New York Herald Tribune Book Review,* October 28, 1945 (p. 14); *Scientific Book Club Review,* November 1945 (p. 2); *Wisconsin Library Bulletin,* December 1945 (p. 126).

SOURCES

Book Review Digest 1945. New York: The H.W. Wilson Company, 1946, pp. 24–25.

2. Koelsch, William A. "Atwood, Wallace Walter," Dictionary of American Biography, Supplement Four, 1946–1950, p. 32.

Publishers' Weekly, January 27, 1945, p. 406; September 22, 1945 (Vanguard Fall List), pp. 1282–1283; October 20, 1945, p. 1864.

Library Journal, June 15, 1945, p. 585.

The New York Times obituary, July 26, 1949, p. 27.

Garraty, John A. and Edward T. James, editors. *Dictionary of American Biography, Supplement Four, 1946-1950.* "Atwood, Wallace Walter," biographical entry by William A. Koelsch. New York: Charles Scribners' Sons, 1974, pp. 31-33.

Robert H. Goddard Library Web Site, Dr. Wallace W. Atwood Biographical Note. Accessed January 18, 2003.

Linn, Mott, Clark University Archives. E-mail messages to CF, January 17, 2003; January 20, 2003.

Raisz Landform Maps, raiszmaps@theworld.com (biography of Erwin Raisz).

THE SIERRA NEVADA:
THE RANGE OF LIGHT

Edited by Roderick Peattie

AM9   First edition, first printing (1947) [5]

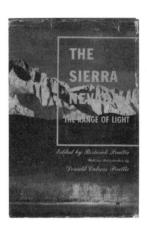

THE SIERRA NEVADA: | *The Range of Light* | EDITED BY RODERICK PEATTIE | WITH AN INTRODUCTION BY DONALD CULROSS PEATTIE | CONTRIBUTORS: David R. Brower, Charles A. Harwell, | Weldon F. Heald, Idwal Jones, Oliver Kehrlein, François E. | Matthes, Lester Rowntree, Richard J. Russell, Mary Tresider | *THE VANGUARD PRESS, INC* · NEW YORK

The foregoing is printed within a white horizontal rectangle superimposed on a two-page black-and-white photograph by Ansel Adams titled "Winter Storm in Yosemite Valley."

COLLATION: 9¼" x 6¼". 202 leaves. [a–f] [1–2] 3–15 [16] 17–387 [388] 389–398. Numbers printed in roman in the outer margin at the foot of the page.

> Note: Single unpaginated leaves bearing black-and-white photographs on glossy paper are inserted facing pp. 30, 31, 62, 63, 94, 95, 126, 127, 158, 159, 190, 191, 286, 287, 318, and 319.

CONTENTS: p. [a], half-title: "THE SIERRA NEVADA"; pp. [b-c], title; p. [d], copyright page: "COPYRIGHT 1947, BY VANGUARD PRESS, INC. | No portion of this book may be reprinted in any form without the written | permission of the publisher, except by a reviewer who wishes to quote brief | passages for inclusion in a review for a newspaper or magazine. | Published simultaneously in Canada by the Copp Clark Co., Ltd. | Manufactured in the United States of America by H. Wolff, New York, N.Y. | TITLE PAGE PHOTOGRAPH: Winter storm in Yosemite Valley. (Courtesy of | Ansel Adams.)"; pp. [e-f], "Contents"; p. [1-2], "Illustrations"; p. [2], *Acknowledgment:* Photographs numbers 1, 4, 10, 12, 14, 16, 22, 23, 24, | and 26 are printed by courtesy of Ansel Adams; number 2, courtesy of | Weldon F. Heald; number 3, courtesy of the Auto Club of Southern Cali– | fornia; number 5, courtesy of Joseph N. Le Conte; numbers 6, 13, 15, 17, | 19, 20, and 25, courtesy of Josef Muench; numbers 7 and 21, courtesy of | Cedric Wright; number 8, courtesy of Rolf Pundt; number 9, courtesy of | David R. Brower; number 11, courtesy of John Lohman and Yosemite Park | and Curry Company; number 18, courtesy of Charles Webber. | MAPS PREPARED BY WELDON F. HEALD".; pp. 3–15, "Introduction [signed Donald Culross Peattie]"; p. [16], blank; p. 17–50, "CHAPTER ONE | SIERRA PANORAMA | *By Weldon F. Heald*"; pp. 51–92, "CHAPTER TWO | EMPIRE IN THE SKY | *By Weldon F. Heald*"; pp. 93–130, "CHAPTER THREE | 'ON A TRAIL OF BEAUTY' | - - - *Navajo chant | By Lester Rowntree*"; pp. 131–165, "CHAPTER FOUR | THE TREES AND FORESTS | *By Mary Tresidder*"; pp. 166–214, "CHAPTER FIVE | A GEOLOGIST'S VIEW | *By François E. Matthes*"; pp. 215–255, "CHAPTER SIX | WINTER SPORTS | *By David R. Brower*"; pp. 256–296, "CHAPTER SEVEN | MOTHER LODE FOLK | *By Idwal Jones*"; pp. 297–322, "CHAPTER EIGHT | SOME BIRDS | OF THE SIERRA NEVADA | *By Charles Albert Harwell*"; pp. 323–340, "CHAPTER NINE | SIERRA CLIMATE | *By Richard Joel Russell*"; pp. 341–387, "CHAPTER TEN | YOSEMITE, A MECCA FOR | MOUNTAINEERS | *By Oliver Kehrlein*"; p. [388], blank; [inserted at this point is an unpaginated triple fold-out map drawn by Joseph F. Hirsch titled 'Topographical Map of A Section of California Showing the Sierra Nevada, Great Central Valley, and Coast Ranges'. 'Map Prepared for The Sierra Nevada — Range of Light by Weldon F. Heald']; pp. 389–398, "Index".

BINDING: Tan cloth (close to Pantone 453). Front: "[medium brown, close to Pantone 470] THE SIERRA NEVADA | [*Mountain* device, in red and green] | [dark green] RODERICK PEATTIE". Spine: "[medium brown] THE | SIERRA | NEVADA | [*Mountain* device, in red and green] | [dark green] RODERICK | PEATTIE | [medium brown] VANGUARD". Cream endpapers. Top edges plain.

DUST JACKET (white paper): Front and spine carry a black-and-white photograph by Ansel Adams, "The Range of Light; Lone Pine Peak (left), Mount Whitney (right)," which is also found facing p. 319 of the text. Front: "[within a rectangle with a bright yellow border (close to Pantone 108, in bright yellow] THE | SIERRA | NEVADA: | THE RANGE OF LIGHT | [below the rectangle, in bright yellow] *Edited by Roderick Peattie | With an Introduction by | Donald Culross Peattie*". Spine "[bright yellow] THE | SIERRA NEVADA | *Edited by | Roderick | Peattie* | VANGUARD". Back: "Other Titles in the | AMERICAN MOUNTAIN SERIES | edited by RODERICK PEATTIE | [list of four titles with quotes from reviews] | *Illustrated with mountain photo-*

graphs and maps | *Each volume $4.50 · at all bookstores* | [publishers imprint]".
Front flap: "[blurb] | table of contents by chapter titles and authors | [lower
right is clipped; it may have carried a higher price for later distribution]".
Back flap: "[blurb, identical to that found on the front flap] | [publisher's
imprint] | [lower left, on the diagonal; a dashed line under which is printed]
THE SIERRA NEVADA | THE VANGUARD PRESS, INC. | $4.50".

Published at $4.50 on November 11, 1947; number of copies printed un-
known. Copyrighted and deposited November 11, 1947.

The book is listed in "The Weekly Record," December 6, 1947, p. 2596.

Note: No evidence found that Vanguard reprinted *The Sierra Nevada*.

COPIES: CF

REPRINTS AND REPRODUCTIONS

Reproduced on microfilm. New Haven, Conn.: Yale University Library, 1988.
1 reel. 35 mm.

BIOGRAPHIES

David R. Brower was born in Berkeley, California, on July 1, 1912, the son of
Ross J. and Mary Grace (Barlow) Brower. He attended the University of California, Berkeley, from 1929 to 1931. In 1933 he joined the Sierra Club. During
World War II, he served in the Army Mountain Troops (1942–1945), rising to
lieutenant and receiving the Combat Infantryman Badge and the Bronze
Star. With time out for wartime service, he was editor of the University of
California Press from 1941 to 1952. On May 1, 1943, he married Anne Hus, a
freelance editor. The couple had four children. From 1952 to 1969, he was executive director of the Sierra Club. In 1972, he was elected its honorary vice-
president. In 1977, he received the John Muir Award, the club's highest honor.
He was a founder, officer, or member of many environmental organizations
and received many environmental awards. He died on November 5, 2000, at
age 88.

Charles A. Harwell was born on October 3, 1910. From 1929 to 1940, he was
Park Naturalist of Yosemite National Park, directing the Yosemite School of
Field Natural History and working with local Indians on programs to record
and maintain their tribal customs. In 1940, he left the Park Service, accept-
ing a position at the National Audubon Society and becoming a popular lecturer for the organization. He was known for his ability to mimic, by
whistling, the songs and calls of scores of birds of the Sierra region. (In
"Some Birds of the Sierra Nevada," a chapter in *The Sierra Nevada*, Harwell

wrote that at least a hundred kinds of birds have settled in the region and at least another hundred, migratory birds, are found there in the summer.) He died in March 1981.

Weldon F. Heald. For a biography of Weldon F. Heald, see *The Cascades: Mountains of the Pacific Northwest.*

Idwal Jones. For a biography of Idwal Jones, see *The Pacific Coast Ranges.*

Oliver Kehrlein was born on April 1, 1882. He was a veteran mountaineer, with years of climbing experience in Europe, Alaska, Canada, and California. Kehrlein lived in San Francisco and was a newspaperman and a radio personality there. He was active in the Sierra Club as a director and as California chairman of the glacier study committee. The Sierra Club's Otto Kehrlein Award honors service to the club's outing programs over an extended period of time at either the local or the national level. Oliver Kehrlein died in April 1967, at age 85.

François E. Matthes was born in Holland in a family of Belgian origin. He emigrated to the United States, graduating from the Massachusetts Institute of Technology with a degree in engineering, after which he entered the U.S. Geological Survey, where he soon distinguished himself by mapping the Bighorn Mountains. He became an expert on the delineation of land forms and later mapped the Grand Canyon of Arizona, Yosemite Valley, Mount Rainier, and what became Glacier National Park. In 1919, acting as a scientific guide for King Albert of Belgium during his visit to Yosemite, Matthes received the cross of Chevalier of the Order of Leopold II. In 1947, he received an honorary doctorate from the University of California for his work on the Sierra Geology.[1] He worked with the Geological Survey for 51 years. He died in June 1948.

Lester Rowntree (Gertrude Lester Rowntree) was born in 1879 in the Lake Country of England. A pioneering botanist, she annually traveled the mountains, deserts, and forests of California collecting seeds and plants. She wrote hundreds of magazine articles. She wrote four children's books and *Hardy Californians: A Woman's Life with Native Plants* (Macmillan, 1936) and *Flowering Shrubs of California and Their Value to the Gardner* (Stanford University Press, 1939), two books that were highly acclaimed. Rowntree was a popular public lecturer who argued passionately for the protection of the state's flora, and a mountain mystic who worshiped on Sierra peaks, bathed in alpine streams, and lived for months on beans and bread.[2] She died in Feb-

1. *The Sierra Nevada*, Introduction, p.13.
2. "Lester Rowntree," *Hardy Californians.* University of California Press book listing. uc-press.edu/books

ruary 1979 at age 100. [The Lester Rowntree papers are held by the Archives, California Academy of Sciences.]

Richard J. Russell. For a biography of Richard J. Russell, see *The Pacific Coast Ranges.*

Mary Tresidder was born Mary Curry in Ogden, Utah, on November 29, 1893. She was a member of a family famous for its early hotel business in Yosemite. (Curry Village, founded in 1899, featured tents, cabins, and motel rooms.) Curry spent her childhood in the Yosemite Valley, riding, fishing, climbing, and skiing, as the seasons dictated. Her book, *The Trees of Yosemite: A Popular Account,* was published by the Stanford University Press in 1948. She was married to Dr. Donald B. Tressider, the fourth president of Stanford University, who died in 1948. Mary Tressider died in October, 1970, at age 76.

NOTES ON *THE SIERRA NEVADA: THE RANGE OF LIGHT*

The book was included in the Vanguard Press 1947 Fall List in the September 27, 1947, issue of *Publishers' Weekly.*

In his introduction to the book, Donald Culross Peattie wrote, "My task in preparing this volume has been to complete as best I could work begun by my brother, Roderick Peattie (a professional geographer and editor of this series as a whole), when he was unable to do so." Later in the introduction, he noted, ". . . the nine contributors [to the book] are, each one of them, experts in their own right, and what they have to tell you is the epitome of their knowledgeable experience in these mountains."

Note: No explanation found of Roderick Peattie's inability to complete the work he had begun on *The Sierra Nevada.*

REVIEWS

Booklist, January 1, 1948 (p. 171); *Kirkus,* November 15, 1947 (p. 645); *New York Herald Tribune Book Review,* December 28, 1947 (p. 5); *New York Times Book Review,* December 28, 1947 (p. 3); *San Francisco Chronicle,* January 4, 1948 (p. 17); *U. S. Quarterly Booklist,* March 1948 (p. 61).

SOURCES

Book Review Digest 1947. New York: The H.W. Wilson Company, 1948, p. 653.

Publishers' Weekly, September 27, 1947, p. 1478; December 6, 1947, p. 2596.

The New York Times Book Review, December 28, 1947, p. 3.

(Brower) "David Brower." *Newsmakers 1990*, Issue 4. Gale Research, 1990. Reproduced in *Biography Resource Center*. Farmington Hills, Mich.: The Gale Group, 2002. Accessed September 16, 2002.

(Brower) *Contemporary Authors Online*, Gale, 2002. Reproduced in *Biography Resource Center*. Farmington Hills, Mich.: The Gale Group, 2002. Accessed September 16, 2002.

(Harwell) Bingaman, John W. *Guardians of the Yosemite: A Story of the First Rangers* (Desert Printers, 1961), Chapter XXIII, Part III, "Park Naturalists of Yosemite National Park."

(Kehrlein) Introduction to *The Sierra Nevada*.

(Matthes) Introduction to *The Sierra Nevada*.

(Matthes) *The Washington Post*, January 26, 1948, p.B2. (Matthes death notice)

(Rowntree) University of California Press, *Hardy Californians*. (Notice of publication of 2006 revised edition) ucpress.edu/books)

(Tresidder) *Oakland Tribune*, September 5, 1962, n.p. (Notice of dedication of new facility at Stanford University)

(Tresidder) Introduction to The Sierra Nevada.

The American Lakes Series
1944–1949

Milo Quaife
Editor

The Bobbs-Merrill Company
Publisher

THE AMERICAN LAKES SERIES

Introduction and Publishing History

Milo Quaife, Editor

*T*he *American Lakes Series* may have been inspired by the success of Farrar & Rinehart's popular *Rivers of America* series, which debuted in June 1937 and continued into 1974. The first title in the *American Lakes* series was published on March 15, 1944. Bobbs-Merrill, the publisher, announced the series earlier in 1944 in *Publishers' Weekly,* noting that the first titles would be devoted to the Great Lakes and would be written for the general reading public by historians of known scholarly standing.[1] In a later advertisement, the publisher stated that the books would "provide an accurate history of the role the individual lake played in the settling of its environs, the development of American commerce, and the noble and thrilling role it may have played in the wars of America," continuing, "Local color, majestic natural scenery, and heroic characters will be presented in rich detail."[2]

The publisher planned an aggressive sales campaign, with promotional posters, a circular, and a brochure about the series. Individual titles were to be marketed regionally, and, in the regional area of a given volume, autographed copies would be supplied to dealers on their original orders.

Milo M. Quaife, a noted historian and expert on the Great Lakes, was named general editor of the series. At the time, Quaife was Secretary of the Burton Historical Collection at the Detroit Public Library. He had written several works of history and was a hands-on editor. In a November 9, 1944, letter to Dale Morgan, himself a noted historian and later the author of *The Great Salt Lake* in the series, Quaife set the tone for the series, noting, "We are intent on bringing out books which shall be as scholarly as possible while at the same time possessing the quality of literary appeal to the ordinary intelligent reader." In a January 6, 1945, letter to Morgan, Quaife wrote, "A body of water, apart from its human associations, has no history, save perhaps in a geological sense. The physical conditions presented supply the stage which conditions the human actions which take place on it. . . . The human story will be the chronological narrative of whatever man has contributed to the area."

In a later letter to Morgan, Quaife wrote, "You impose upon me the necessity of a bit of explanation. In these lake books we are endeavoring with such success as may be possible to achieve, to carry water on both shoulders,

1. *Publishers' Weekly.* "Tips From the Publishers." January 29, 1944, p. 502.
2. *Publishers' Weekly.* February 19, 1944, p. 836. (Bobbs—Merrill advertisement).

so to speak, by making the volumes both scholarly and popular. If they are not popular, they will not sell, and consequently you and I will not eat; if they are not scholarly, I will have sacrificed my lifetime effort to build up a reputation for historical scholarship in the particular field to which I have devoted my labors."[3] In short, the series was to be scholarly and historical, literary and appealing, and focused on the subject lake and its surrounding area.

Quaife wrote an introduction for each of the ten titles in the series, providing information about the author or authors of the book and their knowledge of the subject lake and its region. The first title, *Lake Huron* by Fred Landon, an associate professor of history and librarian at the University of Western Ontario, was published on March 15, 1944. *Lake Superior* by Grace Lee Nute, professor of history at Hamline University, was published on July 31, 1944 and *Lake Michigan* by Milo M. Quaife, the series editor, also on July 31, 1944.

Two series titles were published in 1945: *Lake Ontario* by Arthur Pound on May 15 and *Lake Erie* by Harlan Hatcher on August 14.

As the publisher had planned, the first five titles in the series were on the five Great Lakes, Huron, Superior, Michigan, Ontario, and Erie. These formed the cornerstone of the series, were advertised together, sometimes as a gift package of the five books, and sold well. The five titles to follow were *Lake Pontchartrain, Lake Champlain and Lake George, The Great Salt Lake, Lake Okeechobee,* and *Sierra-Nevada Lakes.*

Two series titles were published in 1946: *Lake Pontchartrain* by W. Adolphe Roberts on October 7 and *Lake Champlain and Lake George* by Frederic F. Van de Water on November 15.

One series title was published in 1947: *The Great Salt Lake* by Dale Morgan on April 4.

One series title was published in 1948: *Lake Okeechobee: Wellspring of the Everglades,* by Alfred Jackson Hanna and Kathryn Abbey Hanna on February 20.

The tenth and last title in the series, *Sierra-Nevada Lakes,* also written by a husband and wife team, George Hinkle and Bliss Hinkle, was published on April 14, 1949.

In six years, two of them with the country at war, the American Lakes series had been written and published, receiving enthusiastic reviews and widespread acclaim. Eleven American lakes and the areas in which they lay had been the subject of scholarly historical examination and reporting. The ten titles in the series stand as authentic American history, well-written, well-edited, and enjoyably readable.

Research on the *The American Lakes Series* was enriched by the Dale Mor-

3. Dale Morgan Papers, Bancroft Library, University of California at Berkeley.

gan Papers at the Bancroft Library, University of California, which include extensive correspondence between Dale Morgan and Milo Quaife; and the Bobbs-Merrill manuscript papers at the Lilly Library, Indiana University.

∾

MILO QUAIFE
Editor, *The American Lakes Series*

Milo M. Quaife was born on October 6, 1880, near Nashua, Iowa, the son of Albert Edward and Barbara S. (Hine) Quaife. After his graduation from Nashua High School, he attended Iowa College (now Grinnell College), where he earned a bachelor's degree in philosophy in 1903. In 1905, he earned a master of arts degree from the University of Missouri. In 1908, after earning a doctorate at the University of Chicago, Quaife joined the faculty of the Lewis Institute of Technology in Chicago, where he taught history from 1908 until 1914, rising to full professor.

In June, 1909, Quaife married Letitia M. Joslin (one source says Goslin). The couple had a son, Donald, and three daughters, Helen, Dorothy, and Mary.

A writer, editor, and historian, from 1914 to 1924 Quaife was superintendent and editor at the Wisconsin State Historical Society in Madison. From 1924 to 1947, he was secretary-editor of the Burton Historical Collection at the Detroit Public Library.

From 1944 to 1949, Quaife organized and edited the ten titles of *The American Lakes Series*. He was later editor of the annual titles of the Lakeside Classics of Western Americana, an advisor on Western history to the Yale University Press, a member of the editorial board of the *Northwest Ohio Quarterly*, and editor of the *Mississippi Valley Historical Review*.

Quaife wrote or edited books and journals of history, especially the history of the American Midwest.

Milo M. Quaife died in an auto accident in Northern Michigan on September 1, 1959, at age 79.

∾

W.R. LOHSE
Illustrator, *The American Lake Series*

Willis Rudolph Lohse was born on January 30, 1890, in Dresden, Germany.

After emigrating to the United States, Lohse maintained a studio in New

York City, working as a painter and designer and producing illustrations for book jackets, endpapers, and children's books.

The 1920 U.S. Census reports that Lohse was married to "Rosanna," and that the couple had a son, Roland.

Lohse illustrated the dust jackets and title pages of the ten titles in *The American Lakes Series* and the jackets and endpapers of the three titles in the Bobbs-Merrill's *The American Trails Series* published in 1947 and 1948.

Willis Lohse died in New York City in February 1969, at age 79.

LAKE CHAMPLAIN AND LAKE GEORGE

Frederic F. Van de Water
September 30, 1890 – September 16, 1968

AL1   First edition, first printing (1946) [7]

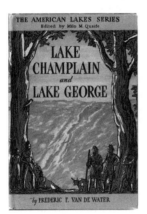

LAKE | CHAMPLAIN AND | LAKE GEORGE | FREDERIC F. VAN DE WATER

The foregoing is printed on a green-and-white illustration, a large tree in the foreground at the right; a young woman on horseback and a hunter in buckskins and a fur cap to the left of the tree; other human figures and an ox-drawn covered wagon behind them and to their right; and a lake and scattered hills in the background.

COLLATION: 8½" x 6". 192 leaves. [a–b] [1–16] 17–354 [355–356] 357–362 [363–364] 365–381 [382]. Numbers printed in roman in headline at the outer margin of the type page, except for pp. 17, 29, 40, 52, 61, 74, 87, 102, 118, 127, 140, 153, 170, 181, 191, 204, 221, 237, 247, 270, 282, 297, 312, 325, 336, 347, 357, and 365, on which the numbers are printed in the center, at the foot of the page.

Note: Black-and-white photographs are inserted facing pp. [16],[1] 17,[2] 30, 31, 62, 63, 94, 95, 126, 127, 158, 159, 190, 191, 222, 223, 254, 255, 286, 287, 318, and 319.

1. "List of Illustrations" on p. [13] incorrectly states p. [14].
2. "List of Illustrations" on p. [13] incorrectly states p. 15.

CONTENTS: p. [a], blank; p. [b], "THE AMERICAN LAKES SERIES | *Published:* | [list of seven titles and their authors, beginning with *Lake Huron* and ending with *Lake Champlain and Lake George*] | *In Preparation:* | [list of two titles and their authors: *The Great Salt Lake* and *Lake Okeechobee*]; p. [1], half title: "LAKE CHAMPLAIN AND LAKE GEORGE"; p. [2], series title: "[set within a green-and-white illustration of an Indian campsite above a lake; a large tree in the foreground at the left; Indian figures beside the tree and down the hill to their left; a lake and scattered hills in the background] The | AMERICAN | LAKES SERIES | Edited by Milo M. Quaife | THE BOBBS-MERRILL COMPANY | Publishers | INDIANAPOLIS · NEW YORK"; p. [3], title; p. [4], copyright page, "COPYRIGHT, 1946, BY THE BOBBS-MERRILL COMPANY | PRINTED IN THE UNITED STATES OF AMERICA | *First Edition*"; p. [5], dedication: "*To* | STERLING AND CAROLYN | *with abiding* affection"; p. [6], blank; pp. [7-10], "EDITORIAL INTRODUCTION [signed M.M. Quaife, Detroit Public Library]"; pp. [11-12], Contents; p. [13-14], "LIST OF ILLUSTRATIONS"; p. [15], half-title: "LAKE CHAMPLAIN AND LAKE GEORGE"; p. [16], blank; pp. 17-354, text; p. [355[, "ACKNOWLEDGMENTS AND | BIBLIOGRAPHICAL NOTE"; p. [356], blank; pp. 357-358, "ACKNOWLEDGMENTS"; pp. 358-362, "BIBLIOGRAPHICAL NOTE"; p. [363], "INDEX"; p. [364], blank; pp. 365-381, Index; p. [382], blank.

BINDING: Forest-green cloth (close to Pantone 343), stamped in gold. Front: "THE AMERICAN LAKE SERIES | [outline of Lake Champlain and Lake George] | LAKE CHAMPLAIN | AND | LAKE GEORGE". Spine: "LAKE | CHAMPLAIN | AND | LAKE | GEORGE | — | FREDERIC | F. | VAN de WATER | [at bottom] BOBBS | MERRILL". Front endpapers carry maps attributed to W. R. Lohse in gold and white: on the left, "Map of the northern portion of Lake Champlain; on the right, "Map of Lake George and the southern portion of Lake Champlain." Rear endpapers carry a double-page map attributed to W.R. Lohse titled "Map of Lake Champlain & Lake George".

DUST JACKET (white paper): Front and spine carry a W.R. Lohse illustration of two large trees in the foreground framing a group of three, a frontiersman, a soldier, and an Indian, to the right, an ox-drawn covered wagon behind them, and other Indians to the left, where a tepee stands in front of a third large tree, a stylized depiction of Lake Champlain in the background. Front: "[at top, within a gold band, which wraps to the spine, in black] THE AMERICAN LAKES SERIES | Edited by Milo M. Quaife | [superimposed on the illustration, in black] | LAKE | CHAMPLAIN | *and* | LAKE GEORGE | [at bottom, within a gold band, which wraps to the spine, in black] *by* FREDERIC F. VAN DE WATER". Spine: "[within the top gold band, in black] LAKE

CHAMPLAIN | LAKE GEORGE | [illustration] | [within the bottom gold band, in black] VAN DE WATER | *Bobbs Merrill*". Back: "[within a rectangular frame with thick/thin rules] THE AMERICAN LAKES SERIES | *under the general editorship of* | MILO M. QUAIFE | [blurb] | *Published* | [list of seven titles and their authors, with brief biographical information, beginning with *Lake Huron*, and ending with *Lake Champlain and Lake George* | *In Preparation* | [list of two titles and their authors, with brief biographical information: *The Great Salt Lake; Lake Okeechobee*]". Front flap: "LAKE CHAMPLAIN | AND LAKE GEORGE | [blurb] | *(Continued on back flap)* | [at bottom right] $3.50". Back flap: "*(Continued from front flap)* | [blurb]".

Published at $3.50 on November 15, 1946; number of copies printed unknown. Copyrighted November 15, 1946; deposited November 9, 1946.

The book is listed in "The Weekly Record," December 7, 1946, p. 3155.

Note: No evidence found that Bobbs-Merrill reprinted *Lake Champlain and Lake George*.

COPIES: CF

AL1a   First edition, Special Autographed Edition (1946)

Lake Champlain and Lake George was issued with a special publisher's autograph page, signed by the author, tipped in following the front free endpaper. The number of such copies issued has not been determined.

REPRINTS AND REPRODUCTIONS

Port Washington, N.Y.: I. J. Friedman, 1969. Empire State Historical Publication Series No. 68.

BIOGRAPHY

Frederic Franklyn Van de Water was born on September 30, 1890, in Pompton, New Jersey, the son of Frederic Franklyn and Virginia Belle (Terhune) Van de Water.

Van de Water studied at New York University from 1910 to 1912 and at Columbia University from 1912 to 1914, earning a bachelor's degree in literature.

On October 4, 1916, Van de Water married Eleanor Gay. The couple had a son, Frederic Franklyn.

After his graduation from Columbia in 1914, Van de Water worked as a reporter for the *New York American*. From 1915 until 1922, he worked as a reporter, feature writer, and night city editor at the *New York Tribune*, then as the paper's book critic from 1922 to 1924. From 1924 to 1928, he worked at the *Ladies Home Journal.* He was a book critic for the *New York Evening Post* from 1928 to 1932, and a member of the corporation of the Vermont Savings Bank from 1936 until his death in 1968.

A historian, journalist, critic, editor, and author, Van de Water wrote at least twenty books, including mysteries, novels, biographies, histories, travel writings, and essays. During the Depression, after spending two years diligently looking for a Colonial house with a view, he and his wife left New York City and moved to Dummerston, a small Vermont community. By adoption, Van de Water became a professional Vermonter, writing *Rudyard Kipling's Vermont Feud* (Reynal & Hitchcock, 1939), *The Reluctant Republic: Vermont 1724-1791* (John Day, 1941), and *In Defense of Worms and Other Angling Heresies* (Duell, 1949). Regarding the theme of this last-named book, he once said, "What I bring back from my Vermont fishing is likely to lie longer in my mind than in my stomach."

Van de Water was a Fellow of the International Institute of Arts and Letters. In 1952, he received an honorary doctorate in humanities from Middlebury College. In 1963, he received an Honors Medallion from Columbia University. He was an honorary life member of the Adventurers Club.

Frederic F. Van de Water died on September 16, 1968, in Brattleboro, Vermont; at age 77.

PAPERS: Frederic Van de Water's papers are held by the Bailey/Howe Library at the University of Vermont.

NOTES ON *LAKE CHAMPLAIN AND LAKE GEORGE*

In a June 12, 1945, letter to Professor Leon Dean of the University of Vermont Library, Van de Water wrote that he was "about to start a book on the Lake Champlain and Lake George Valleys which is to be the sixth of the Lakes of America series that Bobbs Merrill is publishing." . . . His letter continued, "Could you determine for me, therefore, whether the university library has any collection relative to the history, social and economic as well as national, of Burlington's particular area and could you clear the way for me to get at it when I do come up?"

Apparently the library was able to help, for in a September 11 letter to University of Vermont librarian Doris Harvey, Van de Water wrote, "The old man is in trouble again — even more trouble than usual. Sooner or later, he'll be descending on you again but you can postpone the evil day if you can dig from the archives for him one not specially large fact that persistently eludes him and that all the historians in all the libraries he has infested seem to pass lightly over."

The "fact" Van de Water was pursuing was related to the 1776 Battle of Valcour Island, namely, "how many British troops came up as far as Crown Point and what regiments were concerned?" In her September 20, reply, Harvey wrote that after researching the matter and conferring with Professor Dean she believed that the number of such troops "has never been put into print." A few days later, Van de Water responded, "It's nice to have you end up just where I did."

There are many other requests for research assistance in Van de Water's letters to Harvey. Notable as well is a brief note to him in which she reports that she had completed the "correction of references" in a portion of the galley proof of the book. Her assistance is acknowledged in the book, and a coda to the correspondence is found in Harvey's letter of December 18, 1946: "Thank you for the autographed copy of your book, 'Lake Champlain and Lake George' . . . the fact that it is autographed makes it much more interesting and valuable to me."

REVIEWS

Booklist, January 1, 1947 (p. 130); *Kirkus*, November 1, 1946 (p. 573); *New York Times Book Review*, December 8, 1946 (p. 38); *San Francisco Chronicle*, December 8, 1946 (p.13).

SELECTED WRITINGS BY FREDERIC F. VAN DE WATER

Grey Riders: The Story of the New York State Troopers (New York: Putnam, 1922); *Horsemen of the Law* (New York: Appleton, 1926); *Elmer 'n Edwina* (New York: Appleton, 1928); *Hurrying Feet* (New York: Appleton, 1928); *Still Waters* (Garden City, N.Y.: Doubleday, 1929); *Alibi* (Garden City, N.Y.: Doubleday, 1930); *Havoc* (Garden City: Doubleday, 1931); *The Real McCoy* (Garden City: Doubleday, 1931); *Plunder* (Garden City: Doubleday (Crime Club), 1933); *Glory Hunter: A Life of General Custer* (Indianapolis: Bobbs-Merrill, 1934); *Rudyard Kipling's Vermont Feud* (New York: Reynal & Hitchock, 1938); *A Home in the Country* (New York: Reynal & Hitchcock,1937); *We're Still in the Country* (New York: John Day, 1938); *Fathers Are Funny* (New York: John Day, 1939); *The Reluctant Republic: Vermont 1724-1791* (New York: John Day, 1941); *Members of the Family* (New York: John Day, 1942; *Mrs. Applegate's Affair* (New York: Duell, Sloan and Pearce, 1944); *Fool's Errand* (New York: Duell, Sloan & Pearce,1945); **Lake Champlain and Lake George** (Indianapolis: Bobbs-Merrill, 1946); *Reluctant Rebel* (New York: Duell, Sloan & Pearce, 1948); *Catch A Falling Star* (New York: Duell, Sloan & Pearce, 1949); *In Defense of Worms and Other Angling Heresies* (New York: Duell, Sloan & Pearce,

1949); *The Captain Called It Mutiny* (New York: I. Washburn, 1954); *This Day's Madness* (New York: I. Washburn, 1957); *Day of Battle* (New York: I. Washburn, 1958).

SOURCES

Book Review Digest 1946. New York: The H.W. Wilson Company, 1947, p. 840.

Burke, W.J. and Will D. Howe. *American Authors and Books 1640-1940.* New York: Gramercy Publishing Company, 1943, p. 779.

Publishers' Weekly, September 21, 1946, p. 1419; October 5, 1946 (Bobbs-Merrill Fall List), p. 1761; and December 7, 1946, p. 3155.

The New York Times Book Review, December 8, 1946, p. 38.

The New York Times obituary, September 17, 1968, p. 47.

Publishers' Weekly obituary, September 30, 1968, p. 47.

Who Was Who in America, With World Notables, Volume V; 1969–1973. Chicago: Marquis, 1973, p. 740.

Contemporary Authors Online. The Gale Group, 2000. Reproduced in *Biography Resource Center.* Farmington Hills, Mich.: The Gale Group. 2001. Accessed February 14, 2002.

Doherty, Prudence J., Reference Specialist, Special Collections, Bailey/Howe Library, University of Vermont. E-mail message to CF, April 2, 2002, and, by mail, various letters from Frederic Van de Water's papers held by the Bailey/Howe Library.

The Bobbs-Merrill mss., 1885-1957. The Lilly Library, Indiana University, Bloomington, Indiana.

LAKE ERIE

Harlan Henthorne Hatcher
September 9, 1898 – February 25, 1998

AL2   First edition, first printing (1945) [5]

LAKE | ERIE | HARLAN HATCHER

The foregoing is printed on a green-and-white illustration, a large tree in the foreground at the right; a young woman on horseback and a hunter in buckskins and a fur cap to the left of the tree; other human figures and an ox-drawn covered wagon behind them and to their right; and a lake and scattered hills in the background.

COLLATION: 8½" x 6". 210 leaves. [a–b] [1–14] 15–396 [397–398] 399–416 [417–418]. All numbers printed in roman in headline at the outer margin of the type page, except for pp. 15, 20, 25, 35, 47, 65, 71, 85, 91, 104,111, 123, 137, 148, 161, 175, 227, 233, 240, 247, 270, 280, 292, 300, 311, 315, 320, 332, 341, 356, 362, 377, 395, 399, 400, and 405, on which the numbers are printed in the center, at the foot of the page.

Note: Black-and-white photographs are inserted facing pp. 30, 31, 62, 63, 94, 95, 126, 127, 158, 159, 190, 191, 222, 223, 254, 255, 286, 287, 318, 319, 350, and 351.

CONTENTS: p. [a], blank; p. [b], "THE AMERICAN LAKES SERIES | *Published:* | [list of five titles and their authors, beginning with *Lake Huron* and ending with *Lake Erie*] | *In Preparation:* | [list of three titles and their authors: *Lakes Champlain and George; The Great Salt Lake,* and *Lake Pontchartrain*]; p. [1], half title: "LAKE ERIE"; p. [2], series title: "[set within a green and white illustration of an Indian campsite above a lake; a large tree in the foreground at the left; Indian figures beside the tree and down the hill to their left; a lake and scattered hills in the background] The | AMERICAN | LAKES SERIES | Edited by Milo M. Quaife | THE BOBBS-MERRILL COMPANY | Publishers | INDIANAPOLIS · NEW YORK"; p. [3], title; p. [4],

copyright page, "COPYRIGHT, 1945, BY THE BOBBS-MERRILL COM-
PANY | PRINTED IN THE UNITED STATES | *First Edition*"; p. [5], dedica-
tion: "*For* | LINDA LESLIE HATCHER | AND | ANNE HUME VANCE"; p.
[6], blank; pp. [7–8], "EDITORIAL INTRODUCTION [signed M.M. Quaife,
Detroit Public Library]"; pp. [9–10], Contents; p. [11–12], "LIST OF ILLUS-
TRATIONS"; p. [13], "Part I"; p. [14], blank; pp. 15–396, text; p. [397], "AC-
KNOWLEDGMENTS, | BIBLIOGRAPHICAL NOTE | AND INDEX"; p.
[398], blank; pp. 399, "ACKNOWLEDGMENTS"; pp. 400–404, "BIBLIO-
GRAPHICAL NOTE"; pp. 405–416, Index; pp. [417–418], blank.

BINDING: Forest-green cloth (close to Pantone 343), stamped in gold.
Front: "THE AMERICAN LAKE SERIES | [outline of the Great Lakes, with
Lake Erie highlighted] | LAKE ERIE". Spine: "LAKE | ERIE | — | HARLAN |
HATCHER | [at bottom] BOBBS | MERRILL". Front endpapers carry a dou-
ble-page map attributed to W. R. Lohse in gold and white, titled "A Map of
Lake Erie." Back endpapers carry a double-page map attributed to W.R.
Lohse in gold and white, titled "Map of the Great Lakes."

DUST JACKET (white paper): Front and spine carry an illustration attributed to W.R. Lohse of two large trees in the foreground framing a group of
three, a frontiersman, a soldier, and an Indian, to the right, an ox-drawn
covered wagon behind them, and other Indians to the left, where a tepee
stands in front of a third large tree, a stylized depiction of Lake Erie in the
background. Front: "[at top, within a dark-orange band (close to Pantone
032), which wraps to the spine, in black] THE AMERICAN LAKES SERIES |
Edited by Milo M. Quaife | [illustration] | [at bottom, within a dark-red
band, which wraps to the spine, in black] *by* HARLAN HATCHER". Spine:
"[within the top dark-orange band, in black] LAKE | ERIE | [illustration] |
[within the bottom dark-orange band, in black] HATCHER | *Bobbs Merrill*".
Back: "[within a rectangular frame with thick/thin rules] THE AMERICAN
LAKES SERIES | *under the general editorship of* | MILO M. QUAIFE | [blurb]
| *Published* | [list of five titles and their authors, with brief biographical in-
formation, beginning with *Lake Huron,* and ending with *Lake Erie*] | *In
Preparation* | [list of three titles and their authors, with brief biographical
information: *The Great Salt Lake;*[1] *Lakes Champlain and George;* and *Lake
Pontchartrain*]". Front flap: "LAKE ERIE | [blurb] | *(Continued on back flap)*
| [at bottom right] $3.50". Back flap: "*(Continued from front flap)* | [blurb]".

Published at $3.50 on August 14, 1945; number of copies printed unknown.
Copyrighted and deposited August 14, 1945.

1. The description of *The Great Salt Lake* by Dale Morgan notes he is the author of The
Homboldt: Highroad to The West. "Homboldt" should read "Humboldt". This error was
corrected in subsequent printings.

The book is listed in the "Weekly Record," August 18, 1945, p. 618.

Note: No evidence found that Bobbs-Merrill reprinted *Lake Erie*.

CITED: *Bibliography of Pennsylvania History* [8287]

COPIES: CF

AL4a   First edition, Special Autographed Edition (1945)

Lake Erie was issued with a special publisher's autograph page, signed by the author, tipped in following the front free endpaper. The number of such copies issued has not been determined.

REPRINTS AND REPRODUCTIONS

Westport, Conn.: Greenwood Press, 1971.

Reproduced on microform. Ann Arbor, Mich.: UMI, 1994. 5 microfiches and 1 reel, 35 mm.

BIOGRAPHY

Harlan Henthorne Hatcher was born in Ironton, Ohio, on September 9, 1898, the son of Robert Ellison, a school teacher, and Malinda B. (Leslie) Hatcher. His first wife, Frank (Dot) Wilson Colfax, predeceased him. On April 3, 1942, he married Anne Gregory Vance. The couple had two children, Robert Leslie and Anne Linda.

In 1918, during World War I, Hatcher served in the U.S. Army. In World War II, from 1942 to 1944 he was an instructor at the U.S. Navy Pre-Flight School at Chapel Hill, North Carolina, rising to the rank of lieutenant.

Hatcher attended Ohio State University, earning a bachelor's degree in 1922, a master's degree in 1923, and a doctorate in 1927, concentrating in American literature. At Ohio State, he was an instructor (1922–1928), assistant professor (1928–1932), professor of English (1932–1944), dean of the College of Arts and Sciences (1944–1948), and vice president (1948–1951).

In 1951, Hatcher became president of the University of Michigan, a post he held until 1967, when he was named president emeritus. During that time, university enrollment more than doubled, new campuses were opened in Flint and Dearborn, and the university concluded a major private fundraising campaign.

Hatcher's distinguished academic career was not without controversy. In 1954, during the era of Senator Joseph R. McCarthy's notorious anti-Communist activities, Hatcher fired two professors and censured another for their refusal to cooperate in hearings before the House Un-American Activities Committee (HUAC). Decades later, a faculty board agreed to compensate the three. Although Hatcher offered his regrets, he said that the university had done "the very level best" it could at the time.

Hatcher began his writing career in the late 1920s with the publication of *The Versification of Robert Browning* (Ohio State University Press, 1928). He wrote three novels, several academic studies, and books dealing with the history of the Great Lakes region. In 1937 and 1938, he was the Ohio State Director of the Federal Writers' Project, and was editor of the Ohio Guide. During his academic career he lectured widely and served on various boards and national and international committees.

Harlan Hatcher died at his home in Ann Arbor, Michigan, on February 25, 1998, at age 99.

NOTES ON *LAKE ERIE*

The book was listed among the titles in preparation in the Bobbs-Merrill announcement of the series in the February 19, 1944, issue of *Publishers' Weekly*. The author was identified as Lieutenant Harlan Hatcher, U.S.N.R., who was noted as "on war leave from Ohio State University, where he is Professor of English; editor of *The Ohio Guide*; author of *The Buckeye Country* and of three novels."

The book was featured in a Bobbs-Merrill advertisement in the September 9, 1945, issue of the *New York Times Book Review*, beside a review of the book, and was included in the Bobbs-Merrill 1945 Fall List in the September 22, 1945, *Publishers' Weekly*.

REVIEWS

Book Week, August 26, 1945 (p. 9); *Booklist*, September, 1945 (p. 13); *Bookmark*, November, 1945 (p. 10); *Cleveland Open Shelf*, November, 1945 (p. 23); *Current History*, December, 1945 (p. 548); *Kirkus*, June 1, 1945 (p. 238); *New York Times Book Review*, September 9, 1945 (p. 12); *Saturday Review of Literature*, October 13, 1945 (p. 51); *Springfield Republican*, September 16, 1945 (p. 4-D); *U.S. Quarterly Booklist*, December, 1945 (p. 31); *Weekly Book Review*, August 26, 1945 (p. 2).

SELECTED WRITINGS BY HARLAN HATCHER

The Versification of Robert Browning (Columbus, Ohio: Ohio State University Press, 1928); *Tunnel Hill* (Indianapolis: Bobbs-Merrill, 1931); *Patterns of the Wolfpen* (Indianapolis: Bobbs-Merrill, 1934); *Creating the Modern Amer-*

ican Novel (New York: Farrar & Rinehart, 1935); *Central Standard Time* (New York: Farrar & Rinehart, 1937); *The Buckeye Country: A Pageant of Ohio* (New York: Putnam, 1940); (ed.) *The Ohio Guide* (New York: Oxford University Press, 1940); (Editor) *Modern Continental, British and American Dramas* (3 vols.) (New York: Harcourt, 1941); *The Great Lakes* (New York: Oxford University Press, 1944); **Lake Erie** (Indianapolis: Bobbs-Merrill, 1945); *The Western Reserve: The story of New Connecticut in Ohio* (Indianapolis: Bobbs-Merrill, 1949); A *Century of Iron and Men* (Indianapolis: Bobbs-Merrill, 1950); *Giant from the Wilderness* (Cleveland: World Publishing, 1955); (with Erich A. Walter) *A Pictorial History of the Great Lakes* (New York: Crown, 1963); *The Persistent Quest for Values: What are We Seeking?* (Columbia: University of Missouri Press, 1966).

SOURCES

Book Review Digest 1945. New York: The H.W. Wilson & Company, 1946, p. 308.

Publishers' Weekly, February 19, 1944, p. 837; August 18, 1945, p. 617; and September 22, 1945, p. 1151.

The New York Times Book Review, September 9, 1945, p. 12.

Wilkinson, Norman B., comp. *Bibliography of Pennsylvania History.* Second Edition of Writings on Pennsylvania History: A Bibliography. Harrisburg: Pennsylvania Historical and Museum Commission, 1957, p. 635.

Detroit Free Press obituary, February 26, 1998, p. 3B.

The New York Times obituary, March 4, 1998, p. B10.

Contemporary Authors Online. The Gale Group, 2001. Reproduced in *Biography Resource Center.* Farmington Hills, Mich.: The Gale Group, 2001. Accessed February 14, 2002.

Michigan Historical Collections, Bentley Historical Library, University of Michigan, Finding Aid for Harlan Henthorne Hatcher Papers, 1837–1998. Accessed January 30, 2003.

Oglesby, Carl. "Democratic Moral Values?" *The New York Times Magazine,* May 15, 2005, p. 20.

The Bobbs-Merrill mss., 1885–1957. The Lilly Library, Indiana University, Bloomington, Indiana.

THE GREAT SALT LAKE

Dale L. Morgan
December 18, 1914 – March 30, 1971

AL3   First edition, first printing (1947) [8]

THE GREAT | SALT LAKE | DALE L. MORGAN

The foregoing is printed on a green-and-white illustration, a large tree in the foreground at the right; a young woman on horseback and a hunter in buckskins and a fur cap to the left of the tree; other human figures and an ox-drawn covered wagon behind them and to their right; and a lake and scattered hills in the background.

COLLATION: 8½" x 6". 220 leaves. [a–b] [1–16] 17–432 [433–438]. All numbers printed in roman in headline at the outer margin of the type page, except for pp. 17, 32, 44, 60, 62, 80, 95, 113, 130, 148, 176, 203, 224, 250, 261, 283, 304, 323, 348, 367, 387, 409, and 423, on which the numbers are printed in the center, at the foot of the page.

Note: Black-and-white photographs are inserted facing pp. 30, 31, 62, 63, 94, 95, 126, 127, 158, 159, 190, 222, 223, 254, 255, 286, 287, 318, 319, 350, and 351.

CONTENTS: p. [a], blank; p. [b], "THE AMERICAN LAKES SERIES | *Published:* | [list of eight titles and their authors, beginning with *Lake Huron* and ending with *The Great Salt Lake*] | *In Preparation:* | [list of one title and its authors: *Lake Okeechobee*]; p. [1], half title: "THE GREAT SALT LAKE"; p. [2], series title: "[set within a green and white illustration of an Indian campsite above a lake; a large tree in the foreground at the left; Indian figures beside the tree and down the hill to their left; a lake and scattered hills in the background] The | AMERICAN | LAKES SERIES | Edited by Milo M. Quaife | THE BOBBS-MERRILL COMPANY | Publishers | INDIANAPOLIS · NEW YORK"; p. [3], title; p. [4], copyright page, "COPYRIGHT, 1947, BY DALE L. MORGAN | PRINTED IN THE UNITED STATES OF AMERICA | *First Edi-*

tion"; p. [5], dedication: "*To* | MAURICE AND LUCIE HOWE"; p. [6], blank; pp. [7–9], "EDITORIAL INTRODUCTION [signed M.M. Quaife, Detroit Public Library]"; p. [10], blank; p. [11], Contents; p. [12], blank; p. [13], "LIST OF ILLUSTRATIONS"; p. [14], "LIST OF MAPS"; p. [15], half-title: "THE GREAT SALT LAKE"; p. [16], blank; pp. 17–406, text; p. [407[, "ACKNOWL-EDGMENTS, | BIBLIOGRAPHICAL NOTE AND INDEX"; p. [408], blank; pp. 409–411, "ACKNOWLEDGMENTS"; pp. 411–422, "BIBLIOGRAPHICAL NOTE"; pp. 423–432, Index; pp. [433–438], blank.

BINDING: Forest-green cloth (close to Pantone 343), stamped in gold. Front: "THE AMERICAN LAKE SERIES | [outline of Great Salt Lake] | *The* | GREAT SALT LAKE". Spine: "*The* | GREAT | SALT | LAKE | — | DALE L. | MORGAN | [at bottom] BOBBS | MERRILL". Front endpapers carry a map attributed to W. R. Lohse in gold and white titled "Map of the Great Salt Lake". Rear endpapers carry a map attributed to W. R. Lohse in gold and white titled "Western Trails and Explorations 1776–1840".

DUST JACKET (white paper): Front and spine carry an illustration attrib-uted to W.R. Lohse of two large trees in the foreground framing a group of two frontiersmen and an Indian to the right, an ox-drawn covered wagon behind them, and other Indians to the left, where a tepee stands in front of a third large tree, a stylized depiction of Great Salt Lake in the background. Front: "[at top, within an orange band (close to Pantone 143), which wraps to the spine, in black] THE AMERICAN LAKES SERIES | Edited by Milo M. Quaife | [illustration] | [at bottom, within a black band, which wraps to the spine, in orange] *by* DALE L. MORGAN". Spine: "[within the top orange band, in black] THE GREAT | SALT LAKE | [illustration] | [within the bot-tom black band, in orange] MORGAN | *Bobbs Merrill*". Back: "[within a rec-tangular frame with thick/thin rules] THE AMERICAN LAKES SERIES | *under the general editorship of* | MILO M. QUAIFE | [blurb] | *Published* | [list of eight titles and their authors, with brief biographical information, begin-ning with *Lake Huron,* and ending with *The Great Salt Lake* | *In Preparation* | list of one title and its authors, with brief biographical information: *Lake Okeechobee*]". Front flap: "THE GREAT SALT LAKE | [blurb] | *(Continued on back flap)* | [at bottom right] $3.75". Back flap: "*(Continued from front flap)* | [blurb]".

Published at $3.75 on April 4, 1947;[1] number of copies printed unknown. Copyrighted and deposited April 3, 1947.

1.The copyright certificate notes a publication date of April 3, 1947; the March 8, 1947 is-sue of *PW* noted the book would be available on April 4, 1947. An earlier Bobbs-Merrill announcement in *PW* noted the book would be available on April 7, 1947.

The book is listed in "The Weekly Record," April 12, 1947, p. 2056.

Note: No evidence found that Bobbs-Merrill reprinted *The Great Salt Lake.*

CITED: Saunders 19

COPIES: CF

AL2a   First edition, Special Autographed Edition (1947)

The Great Salt Lake was issued with a special publisher's autograph page, signed by the author, tipped in following the front free endpaper. The number of such copies issued has not been determined.

REPRINTS AND REPRODUCTIONS

Albuquerque: University of New Mexico Press, 1973. Introduction by Ray Allen Billington. Paperback.

Lincoln: University of Nebraska Press, 1986. Paperback. Published at $10.95; hardback published at $28.50.

Reproduced on microfilm. New Haven, Conn.: Yale University Library, 1993. 1 reel, 35 mm.

Salt Lake City: University of Utah Press, 1995. (Co-published with the Annie Clark Tanner Trust Fund). Foreword by Harold Schindler.

BIOGRAPHY

Dale Lowell Morgan was born on December 18, 1914, in Salt Lake City, Utah, the son of James Lowell and Emily (Holmes) Morgan. After the death of his father when Dale was five years old, Morgan's mother was left to support four young children on her public school teacher's salary. At age fourteen, Morgan lost his hearing as a result of meningitis. He was a descendant of Orson Pratt, a member of the original Quorum of Twelve Apostles in the Church of Jesus Christ of Latter-day Saints.

Morgan earned a bachelor of arts degree from the University of Utah in 1937. That year, Morgan began work in the Works Progress Administration's Historical Records Survey in Utah, where he wrote seven of the county sections for the collection *Inventories of County Archives of Utah.* From 1940 to 1942, he was the State Supervisor of the Utah Writers' Project, making him, in effect, the editor-in-chief of the Federal Writers' Project state guide, *Utah: A Guide to the State* (Hastings House, 1941). The Utah State Institute of Fine

Arts was the statewide sponsor of the Utah Writers' Project, and the Utah guide is widely admired as one of the finer state guides.

During the war years 1942–1945, Morgan worked in the Office of Price Administration in Washington, D.C. He was the guiding force behind the first National Union Catalogue of works on Mormonism, which others expanded into *A Mormon Bibliography, 1830-1930,* published by the University of Utah Press in 1978. *The Great Salt Lake* is judged his most important work on Mormonism, with its masterly account of the Mormon trek to Utah and the establishment of the Church there.

In 1945, Morgan received a one-year fellowship from the Guggenheim Foundation which included a grant of $2,000. In 1947, having activated the grant, he set out on a year-long journey through New England, Pennsylvania, Ohio, Illinois, Missouri, Kansas, and then across the United States, tracing the route of the early founders of Mormonism and collecting material, especially regional newspaper articles, for the history he planned to write. Although Morgan eventually completed seven chapters and two appendices of the book, he never finished it.

In 1954, Morgan became editor of the Guide Program of Manuscripts at The Bancroft Library of the University of California at Berkeley, where he worked as an editor and author for the next sixteen years, until his retirement in 1970 owing to ill health.

In 1960, Morgan became a Fellow of the Utah State Historical Society. In 1961, he received the Henry R. Wagner Memorial Award of the California Historical Society and, in 1962, its Fellowship Award. In 1964, he was recognized as a Distinguished Alumnus by the University of Utah Alumni Association. In 1965, he received the Award of Merit of the American Association for State and Local History. He wrote at least forty books and many scholarly articles, reviews, introductions, and monographs.

Dale L. Morgan died on March 30, 1971, in Accokeek, Maryland, at age 56.

PAPERS: Dale Morgan's papers were deposited at The Bancroft Library of the University of California at Berkeley. They have been microfilmed and in that form are held by the Manuscript Division of the University of Utah Special Collections.

NOTES ON *THE GREAT SALT LAKE*

The Dale Lowell Morgan Papers at The Bancroft Library at the University of California, Berkeley include correspondence between Morgan and Milo Quaife, the editor of the American Lakes Series. The following account is derived from that correspondence.

In a November 9, 1944, letter to Dale Morgan, Milo Quaife reported that under his editorship the first three titles in the *Lakes* series, *Lake Huron, Lake Superior,* and *Lake Michigan,* had been published and were enjoying excellent sales and uniformly good reviews. Quaife noted that Bobbs-Merrill was "intent on bringing out books which shall be as scholarly as possible while at the same time possessing the quality of literary appeal to the ordinary intelligent reader," continuing, "I think our book on the Great Basin (centered around Great Salt Lake, of course) ought to prove one of the most interesting and valuable in the entire series. If you should care to undertake to write it for us, I will be glad to inform you more at length concerning my editorial conception for the book, and I will wish, of course, to have your own ideas on the subject. If you are disposed to accept my invitation, you will find yourself in excellent company for we are obtaining only the best authors who can be had to write the several volumes in the series."

Morgan's lengthy reply to Quaife, in his letter of November 13, reported that during his work as director of the Utah Writers' Project of the Works Projects Administration from 1940 to 1942 he had "mapped out a popular book on Great Salt Lake which [he] thought would be a worthwhile enterprise for the Project, and one of definite popular appeal." He had "worked out a tentative outline" and had then "turned over the book" to one of his editors "to carry through the research program and write sample chapters and synopsis which the national office could discuss with a publisher."

The entry of the United States into World War II in December 1941 had disrupted plans for the book, but, before Morgan left Utah to work in Washington, D.C., his letter continued, he "made arrangements with the State Historical Society to accept custody of the files of the Writers' Project, in the event WPA should be terminated, and some three months after I departed Utah, this indeed came to pass." Noting that "to write the book you propose would entail less labor for me than any other conceivable book, and I should take a great deal of pleasure in the job," Morgan added, "And yet, despite the fact that a book on Great Salt Lake for your series would not be quite the same thing as the book proposed to be done by the Writers' Project — it would, indeed, be considerably different — the fact of my having been associated with the Writers' Project in the suspended Great Salt Lake book raises somewhat difficult ethical questions in my mind."

In the same letter, Morgan expressed an additional concern, noting that he was under contract with Farrar & Rinehart for the writing of two books, a juvenile biography of John C. Frémont (1813–1890) and a major work "designed as a study of American life from 1800 until the Civil War." In the end, however, after an exchange of letters with Quaife, Morgan resolved both these concerns. He eventually agreed with Quaife that his work on an earlier book on Great Salt Lake did not impose an ethical conflict, principally on the grounds that the Federal Writers' Project was, in Quaife's words, "dead and buried." As for his contract with Farrar & Rinehart, in a December 26 letter to Quaife, Morgan reported that Stanley Rinehart, his publisher, had written that he had no objection to Morgan's writing the Great Salt Lake book for Bobbs-Merrill. With these two impediments behind him, Morgan agreed to write the book and, by January 24, 1945, the contractual details had been worked out. The manuscript was to be delivered by April 1, 1946.

Morgan's work on the book proceeded more slowly than he or his editor and publisher had hoped. By December 1945, Morgan had informed Laurance Chambers, editor in chief at Bobbs-Merrill, that he would not finish the book by the agreed date. Quaife gently chided him, noting that the authors of the previously published *Lakes* books, including Quaife's *Lake Michigan,* had completed their work on time.

By May 1946, Morgan had sent several chapters of the book to Quaife, cautioning that he thought much cutting, sharpening, and condensation was still necessary and adding that although the manuscript might be delivered by July, August 1 was probably a more realistic date. During this time, the question of maps to be included in the book, and the inadequacy of the maps in the earlier *Lakes* volumes, was addressed. The manuscript was completed and delivered to the publisher in late October.

Bobbs-Merrill announced the pending publication of the book in its 1947 Spring List in the February 8, 1947, issue of *Publishers' Weekly,* noting, "Mr. Morgan's fine style and scholarship distinguish the eighth volume of the American Lakes Series." The March 8, 1947, PW carried a full-page advertisement for the book, noting, "The Great Salt Lake clings to its air of mystery as much today as in its myth-shrouded past. . . . Mr. Morgan's vivid style and distinguished scholarship make of this volume a truly notable work of regional literature."

Richard L. Saunders, in his 1990 descriptive bibliography of the works of Dale Morgan, observes that the *Lakes* series was an attempt by Bobbs-Merrill to "recapture a market share from Farrar & Rinehart's widely successful Rivers of America Series. *Great Salt Lake* dealt more with the historical context of the lake than the body of water itself, describing the epochal history of the lake itself, early exploration and mapping, the settlement of Salt Lake City, tourism and recreation, and the advent of railroads beside and across the lake. Besides his incomplete history of the Mormons, this work contains the only published example of Morgan's historical treatment of his religious culture."

REVIEWS

American History Review, October 1947 (p. 127); *Booklist,* May 15, 1947 (p. 288); *Christian Science Monitor,* May 5, 1947 (p. 16); *Kirkus,* February 1, 1947 (p. 92); *New York Herald Tribune Weekly Book Review,* April 20, 1947 (p. 5); *New York Times Book Review,* April 27, 1947 (p. 26); *San Francisco Chronicle,* June 8, 1947 (p. 24); *Springfield Union,* July 21, 1947 (p. 5); *U. S. Quarterly Booklist,* September 1947 (p. 281); *Wisconsin Library Bulletin,* May 1947 (p. 80).

SELECTED WRITINGS BY DALE L. MORGAN

(contributor [Morgan wrote the "sketches" on Tooele, Daggett, Weber, Carbon, Utah, Uintah, and Emery counties during the years 1939 and 1940]) *Inventory of the County Archives of Utah* (Ogden, Utah: The Utah Historical Records Survey Project, 1939–1941); *A History of Ogden* (Ogden, Utah: Ogden City Commission, 1940); (ed., with others) *Utah: A Guide to the State* (American Guide Series) (New York: Hastings House, 1941); (with others) *Provo: Pioneer Mormon City* (American Guide Series) (Portland, Oregon: Binfords and Mort, 1942); (ed.) *Tales of Utah, 1941-42: Collection of News Stories* (Salt Lake City: Utah Writers' Project, Works Progress Administration, 1942); *The Humboldt: High Road to the West* (Rivers of America Series) (New York: Farrar & Rinehart, 1943) **The Great Salt Lake** (Indianapolis: Bobbs-Merrill, 1947); (ed. and author of introduction) *The Exploration of the Colorado River in 1869* (Salt Lake City: Utah State Historical Society, 1947); (ed. and author of introduction) *The Exploration of the Colorado River* and *The High Plateaus of Utah in 1871-72* (2 vols.) (Salt Lake City: Utah State Historical Society, 1948–49); (contributor) "The Mountain States" in *The American Guide, A Source Book and Complete Guide for the United States* (New York: Hastings House, 1949); (contributor) "Salt Lake City, City of the Saints" in *Rocky Mountain Cities,* edited by Ray West (New York: Norton, 1949); (ed.) *Santa Fe and the Far West,* reprinted from *Niles National Register, 1841* (Los Angeles: Printed for Glen Dawson, 1949).

Life in America: The West (Grand Rapids: Fideler, 1952); *Jedediah Smith and the Opening of the West* (Indianapolis: Bobbs-Merrill, 1953); (with Carl I. Wheat) *Jedediah Smith and His Maps of the American West* (San Francisco: California Historical Society, 1954); (ed.) *Rand McNally's Pioneer Atlas of the American West* (Chicago: Rand-McNally, 1956); (contributor) *Mapping the Transmississippi West, 1540-1861* by Carl I. Wheat, (5 vols.) [Morgan wrote the chapter on Mormon maps (Chapter 36) in the fourth volume of this work and the two books comprising Volume 5] (San Francisco: Institute of

Historical Cartography, 1957–1963); (ed.) *The Overland Diary of James A. Pritchard from Kentucky to California in 1949. With a Biography of Captains James A. Pritchard by Hugh Pritchard Williamson* (Denver: Fred A. Rosenstock, 1959); (ed.) *California As I Saw It: Pencillings by the Way of Its Gold and Gold Diggers! and Incidents of Travel by Land and Water by William S. M'Collum, M.D. A returned [sic] Adventurer* (Los Gatos, Calif.: Talisman Press, 1960); *Kansas in Maps* (Topeka: Kansas State Historical Society, 1961);[2] (contributor) "The Significance and Value of the Overland Journal" in *Probing the American West: Papers of the Conference on the History of Western America* (Santa Fe: Museum of New Mexico Press, 1961); (ed., with George P. Hammond) *A Guide to the Manuscript Collections of the Bancroft Library.* Vol. 1 (Berkeley: University of California Press, 1963); (contributor) "Opening of the West: Explorers and Mountain Men" in *Book of the American West* (Jay Monaghan, ed.) (New York: Messner, 1963); (ed.) *Overland in 1846: Diaries and Letters of the California-Oregon Trail* (2 vols.) (Georgetown, Cal.: Talisman Press, 1963); (ed., with Allan Nevins) "The Map of Oregon and Upper California" in *Geographical Memoir Upon Upper California,* by John C. Frémont (Sacramento: Book Club of California, 1964); (ed., with James R. Scobie and author of introduction) *Three Years in California: William Perkins' Journal of Life at Sonora, 1849-52* (Berkeley: University of California Press, 1964); (ed.) *The West of William H. Ashley: The International Struggle for the Fur Trade of the Missouri, the Rocky Mountains, and the Columbia, with Explorations Beyond the Continental Divide, Recorded in the Diaries and Letters of William H. Ashley and his Contemporaries, 1822-1838* (Denver: Fred A. Rosenstock, Old West Publishing Company, 1964).

(ed.) *Dakota War Whoop: Indian Massacres and War in Minnesota* by Harriett E. Bishop McConkey (Chicago: Donnelly, 1965); (Contributor) "GPH." In *GPH: An Informal Record of George P. Hammond and His Era in the Bancroft Library* (Berkeley: Friends of the Bancroft Library, 1965); (with Charles Kelly) *Old Greenwood: The Story of Caleb Greenwood, Trapper, Pathfinder, and Early Pioneer* (Rev. ed.) (Georgetown, Cal.: Talisman Press, 1965); (ed., with George P. Hammond) *Captain Charles M. Weber: Pioneer of the San Joaquin and Founder of Stockton, California* (Berkeley: Friends of the Bancroft Library, 1966); (ed.) *Honolulu: Sketches of Life in the Hawaiian Islands from 1828 to 1861,* by Laura Fish Judd (Chicago: Donnelly, 1966); (ed., with

2. In his invaluable descriptive bibliography of the published writings of Dale L. Morgan, *Eloquence from a Silent World* (Salt Lake City: The Cardamon Press, 1990), Richard L. Saunders lists this book as Number 35 (p. 16), noting that although the work is listed under the authorship of Robert W. Baughman "it is certain that Morgan was responsible for most or all of this work or substantial editing." Saunders adds convincing details to support this statement, concluding that the work is "unquestionably" of Morgan's creation.

Eleanor Towles Harris) *The Rocky Mountain Journals of William Marshall Anderson: The West in 1834* (San Marino: Huntington Library, 1967); (ed.) *Three Years in the Klondike,* by Jeremiah Lynch (Chicago: Donnelly, 1967); (ed.) *In Pursuit of the Golden Dream: Reminiscences of San Francisco and the Northern and Southern Mines, 1849-57,* by Howard Calhoun Gardiner (Stoughton, Mass.: Western Hemisphere, Inc., 1970); (contributor) "Western Travels and Travelers in the Bancroft Library" in *Travelers on the Western Frontier,* edited by John F. McDermott (Urbana: University of Illinois Press, 1970).

Published Posthumously:

(Foreword) *The Beginning of the West: Annals of the Kansas Gateway to the American West, 1540-1854,* by Louise Barry (Topeka: Kansas State Historical Society, 1972); (contributor) *A Mormon Bibliography, 1830-1930: Books, Pamphlets, Periodicals, and Broadsides Relating to the First Century of Mormonism,* edited by Chad J. Flake (Salt Lake City: University of Utah Press, 1978); *Dale Morgan on Early Mormonism: Correspondence & A New History,* edited by John Philip Walker (Salt Lake City: Signature Books, 1986).

SOURCES

Book Review Digest 1947. New York: The H.W. Wilson Company, 1948, p. 647.

Dale Lowell Morgan Papers, BANC MSS 71/161. Bancroft Library, University of California, Berkeley. Reel #6 & Reel #16. Letters to/from Milo Milton Quaife, 1940-1950.

Publishers' Weekly, February 8, 1947 (Bobbs-Merrill Spring List), p. 623; March 8, 1947, p. 1429; and April 12, 1947, p. 2056.

The New York Times Book Review, April 27, 1947, p. 26.

AB Bookman's Weekly obituary, May 24, 1971, p. 1738.

Conway, Martha G., ed., and Marie Evans and David Versical, assoc. eds. *Contemporary Authors, Volume 104* (obituary). Detroit: Gale Research Company, 1982, p. 29.

Walker, John Phillip, editor. *Dale Morgan on Early Mormonism: Correspondence & A New History.* Salt Lake City: Signature Books, 1986, p. 15.

Saunders, Richard L. *Eloquence from a Silent World: A Descriptive Bibliography of the Published Writings of Dale L. Morgan.* Salt Lake City: The Caramon Press, 1990, pp. 8-9.

The Bobbs-Merrill mss., 1885–1957. The Lilly Library, Indiana University, Bloomington, Indiana.

Fitzgerald, Carol. *The Rivers of America. A Descriptive Bibliography.* New Castle, Del.: Oak Knoll Press in Association with The Center for the Book in the Library of Congress, 2001. (Entry on *The Humboldt.*)

LAKE HURON

Fred Landon
November 5, 1880 – August 1, 1969

AL4   First edition, first printing (1944) [1]

LAKE | HURON | FRED LANDON

The foregoing is printed on a green-and-white illustration, a large tree in the fore-ground at the right; a young woman on horseback and a hunter in buckskins and a fur cap to the left of the tree; other hu-man figures and an ox-drawn covered wagon behind them and to their right; and a lake and scattered hills in the back-ground.

COLLATION: 8½" x 6". 200 leaves. [a–b] [1–16] 17–94 [95–96] 97–230 [231–232] 233–282 [283–284] 285–372 [373–374] 375–379] [380–382] 383–398. All numbers printed in roman in headline at the outer margin of the type page, except for pp. 17, 28, 39, 61, 71, 97, 115, 137, 148, 175, 200, 233, 247, 257, 272, 285, 304, 325, 335, 345, 366, 375, and 377, on which the numbers are printed in the center at the foot of the page.

Note: Black-and-white double-sided leaves of photographs are in-serted following pp. 36,[1] 80, 122, 166, 208, 250, 278, 316, and 338; a one-page photograph follows p. 360.

CONTENTS: p. [a–b], blank; p. [1], half-title: "LAKE HURON"; p. [2], series title: "[set within a green and white illustration of an Indian campsite above

1. A reproduction of an early map of Lake Huron faces p. 36.

a lake; a large tree in the foreground at the left; Indian figures beside the tree and down the hill to their left; a lake and scattered hills in the background] The I AMERICAN I LAKES SERIES I Edited by Milo M. Quaife I THE BOBBS-MERRILL COMPANY I Publishers I INDIANAPOLIS · NEW YORK"; p. [3], title; p. [4], copyright page, "COPYRIGHT, 1944, BY THE BOBBS-MERRILL COMPANY I PRINTED IN THE UNITED STATES I *First Edition*"; p. [5], dedication page: "TO MY DAUGHTER I *Mary*"; p. [6], blank; pp. [7–8], "EDITORIAL INTRODUCTION (signed M.M. Quaife, Detroit Public Library)"; pp. [9–10], FOREWORD; pp. [11–12], TABLE OF CONTENTS; p. [13], "LIST OF ILLUSTRATIONS"; p. [14], blank; p. [15], "Part I I EARLY DAYS ON LAKE HURON"; p. [16], blank; pp. 17–94, text; p. [95], "Part II I ISLANDS, SHORES AND RIVERS"; p. [96], blank; pp. 97–230, text; p. [231], "Part III I FOUR LAKE HURON STORIES"; p. [232], blank; pp. 233–282, text; p. [283], "Part IV I THE SHIPS AND THE MEN WHO I SAIL THEM"; p. [284], blank; pp. 285–372, text; p. [373], "ACKNOWLEDG-MENTS I AND I BIBLIOGRAPHICAL NOTE"; p. [374], blank; pp. 375–376, "A WORD OF THANKS (signed F.L.)"; pp. 377–379, "BIBLIOGRAPHICAL NOTE"; p. [380], blank; p. [381], "INDEX"; p. [382], blank; pp. 383–398, Index.

BINDING: Forest-green cloth (close to Pantone 343), stamped in gold. Front: "THE AMERICAN LAKE SERIES I [outline of the Great Lakes, with Lake Huron highlighted] I LAKE HURON". Spine: "LAKE I HURON I — I FRED I LANDON I [at bottom] BOBBS I MERRILL". Front endpapers carry a map attributed to W.R. Lohse, in gold and white, titled "Map of Lake Huron". Rear endpapers carry a map attributed to W.R. Lohse, in gold and white, titled "Map of the Great Lakes".

DUST JACKET (white paper): Front and spine carry an illustration attributed to W.R. Lohse of two large trees in the foreground framing a group of three, a frontiersman, a soldier, and an Indian, to the right, an ox-drawn covered wagon behind them, and other Indians to the left, where a tepee stands in front of a third large tree, a stylized depiction of Lake Huron in the background. Front: "[at top, within a black band, which wraps to the spine, in medium tan] THE AMERICAN LAKES SERIES I Edited by Milo M. Quaife I [illustration] I [at bottom, within a black band, which wraps to the spine, in medium tan] *by* FRED LANDON". Spine: "[within the top black band, in medium tan] LAKE I HURON I [illustration] I [within the bottom black band, in medium tan] LANDON I Bobbs Merrill". Back: "[within a rectangular frame bordered by thin/thick rules] THE AMERICAN LAKES SERIES I *under the general editorship of* I MILO M. QUAIFE I [four-paragraph blurb announcing the series] I *Published* I [*Lake Huron*, with brief biographical information on Landon] | *In Preparation* | [list of four titles and their authors, with brief biographical information: *Lake Superior, Lake Michigan, Lake Ontario,* and *Lake Erie*]". Front flap: "LAKE HURON | [blurb] | (Continued on back flap) | [at bottom right] $3.50". Back flap: "(Continued from front flap) | [blurb]".

Published at $3.50 on March 27, 1944;[2] number of copies printed unknown. Copyrighted March 30, 1944; deposited February 21, 1944.

The book is listed in "The Weekly Record," March 25, 1944, p. 1306.

Note: No evidence found that Bobbs-Merrill reprinted *Lake Huron.*

COPIES: CF

AL3a   First edition, Special Autographed Edition (1944)

Lake Huron was issued with a special publisher's autograph page, signed by the author, tipped in following the front free endpaper. The number of such copies issued has not been determined.

REPRINTS AND REPRODUCTIONS

New York: Russell & Russell, 1972.

Reproduced on microform. Ann Arbor, Mich.: Preservation Office Microfilming Unit, University of Michigan, University Library, 1987. 1 reel, 35 mm./Microfilm (negative).

BIOGRAPHY

Fred Landon was born in London, Ontario, on November 5, 1880, the son of Abraham and Hannah Helena (Smith) Landon. He attended public schools in London and worked briefly for a local dry goods firm there before joining the Northern Navigation Company of Sarnia, Ontario, in 1901. He came to love the Great Lakes and their history while sailing the lakes, mainly on the company's ship the *United Empire.* In 1903, Landon enrolled at Western University, now the University of Western Ontario, where, as one of a class of seven, he earned a bachelor of arts degree in 1906 and a master's degree in 1919.

2. Library of Congress copyright information notes a March 27, 1944, publication date. "Tips from Publishers" in the January 29, 1944, issue of *Publishers' Weekly,* reported that Bobbs-Merrill had set a March 15 publication date. According to an entry in Fred Landon's diary, the book was on sale at the Wendell Holmes Bookshop in Ottawa on March 17, 1944.

In 1914, Landon married Margaret Smith. The couple had three children.

From 1906 to 1916, Landon worked on the editorial staff of the *London* (Ontario) *Free Press*. From 1916 to 1923, he was chief librarian of the London Public Library, where he developed the local history collections which are housed in the library's London Room. In 1923, Landon became the first full-time librarian at the University of Western Ontario, and, over the years, associate professor of history, first vice president, and dean of graduate studies. When he retired in 1950, he was awarded an honorary doctorate in letters from the university and an honorary doctorate in laws from McMaster University.

Landon and Jesse E. Middleton wrote *The Province of Ontario: A History, 1645-1927*, published in five-volumes by Dominion Publishing in 1928. Landon's best known work is *Western Ontario and the American Frontier* (Ryerson Press, 1941), a title in the series "The Relations of Canada and the United States."

Landon's interest in history extended to the American Civil War, the life of Abraham Lincoln, the Underground Railway, Negro refugees in Canada, and the abolition of slavery in the United States. His work was published in the *Journal of Negro History* in 1918. He played a major role in the development of Canada's libraries.[3]

Landon won the J.B. Tyrrell Historical Medal of the Royal Society of Canada in 1945 and the Cruikshank Medal of the Society in 1967. The Fred Landon Prize in Canadian History is awarded to a graduating student in the Department of History at the University of Western Ontario for excellence in Canadian history. The award was endowed by Margaret Landon in memory of her husband.

Fred Landon died in London, Ontario, on August 1, 1969, at age 88.

PAPERS: The Fred Landon Papers are held by the J.J. Talman Regional Collection, University of Western Ontario. The Landon papers include thirty-eight boxes of personal, research, and teaching papers, especially papers dealing with Landon's interest in Negro history, the American Civil War, and Great Lakes shipping.

NOTES ON *LAKE HURON*

In the foreword to the book, Landon wrote, "This book is a history of Lake Huron and of the St. Clair River into which it empties. It is an attempt

3. Armstrong, Frederick H. "Fred Landon, 1880-1969." *Ontario History* (Ontario Historical Society), Vol. LXII, No. 1, March, 1970.

to tell of some of the happenings around and upon these waters in the years since Champlain first saw a portion of Georgian Bay. These happenings relate to men and to ships, for ships have personality too, and much will be said of them in these pages."

Landon received his first copies of the book on February 29, 1944. The book went on sale at the Wendell Holmes Bookshop in Ottawa on March 17. Oscar Cargill's review in *The New York Times Book Review* observed, "Fred Landon has provided his successors with a model which will cost them blood, sweat and tears to equal." But, Cargill also noted, "Evidently it is the plan of the series . . . to exclude a full account of the natural life and of the geological history. The latter exclusion is especially to be lamented, for Huron had a history — before the advent of any man. . . ." Sterling North's review in *Book Week* said the book "will stand comparison with any book in the Rivers of America series, and it taps a veritable mine of new materials."

REVIEWS

Booklist, April 1, 1944 (p. 267); *Bookmark,* May 1944 (p. 13); *Canadian Forum,* August 1944 (p. 118); *Canadian Historical Review,* December 1944 (p. 436); *Kirkus,* January 15, 1944 (p. 35); *Library Journal,* April 15, 1944 (p. 356);*New York Herald Tribune Book Review,* March 26, 1944 (p. 2); *New York Times,* March 26, 1944 (p. 7); *Saturday Review of Literature,* April 15, 1944 (p. 68); *Weekly Book Review,* April 9, 1944 (p. 3); *Wisconsin Library Bulletin,* May 1944 (p. 69).

SELECTED WRITINGS BY FRED LANDON

(co-author with Jesse E. Middleton) *The Province of Ontario: A History, 1645-1927* (Toronto: Dominion Publishing Corp., Ltd., 1928); *Western Ontario and the American Frontier* (Toronto: Ryerson Press, 1941); *Lake Huron* (Indianapolis: Bobbs-Merrill, 1944); *An Exile from Canada to Van Diemen's Land* (Toronto: Longman's Green, 1960); (contributor) *Dictionary of Canadian Biography, London* (Ontario) *Free Press, Inland Seas,* and *Journal of Negro History.*

SOURCES

Book Review Digest 1944. New York: H.W. Wilson Company, 1945, p. 435.

Publishers' Weekly, January 29, 1944 (Bobbs-Merrill Early Spring List), pp. 358–359; January 29, 1944, "Tips From the Publishers," p. 502; February 19, 1944, pp. 836–837; and March 25, 1944, p. 1306.

The New York Times Book Review, March 26, 1944, p. 7.

Book Week, March 26, 1944, p. 2. (Review by Sterling North).

Armstrong, Frederick H. "Fred Landon, 1880-1969." *Ontario History* (Ontario Historical Society) Volume LXII, No. 1, March, 1970, pp. 1-4.

Regnier, Theresa, The J.J. Talman Regional Collection, the D.B. Weldon Library, the University of Western Ontario, London, Ontario. March 20, 2002, letter to CF, with attachments.

Regnier, Theresa. E-mail message to CF, March 20, 2002, quoting three references to *Lake Huron* in Landon's 1944 diary.

The Bobbs-Merrill mss., 1885–1957. The Lilly Library, Indiana University, Bloomington, Indiana.

LAKE MICHIGAN

Milo M. Quaife
October 6, 1880 – September 1, 1959

AL5   First edition, first printing (1944) [3]

LAKE | MICHIGAN | MILO M. QUAIFE

The foregoing is printed on a green-and-white-illustration, a large tree in the foreground at the right; a young woman on horseback and a hunter in buckskins and a fur cap to the left of the tree; other human figures and an ox-drawn covered wagon behind them and to their right; and a lake and scattered hills in the background.

COLLATION: 8½" x 6". 194 leaves. [a–b] [1–14] 15–170 [171–172] 173–278 [279–280] 281–369 [370] 371–384 [385–386]. All numbers printed in roman in headline at the outer margin of the type page, except for pp. 15, 21 28, 37, 49, 61, 69, 77, 87, 100, 111, 122, 135, 147, 158, 173, 186, 198, 208, 221, 231, 248, 262, 281, 291, 303, 312, 329, 344, 361, and 364, on which the numbers are printed in the center, at the foot of the page.

Note: Black-and-white photographs are inserted facing pp. 24, 25, 50, 51, 66, 67, 102, 103, 136, 137, 160, 161, 190, 191, 228, 229, 266, 267, 306, 307, 348, and 349.

CONTENTS: p. [a], blank; p. [b], "THE AMERICAN LAKES SERIES | *Published:* | [list of three titles and their authors, beginning with *Lake Huron* and ending with *Lake Michigan*] | *In Preparation:* | [list of two titles and their authors: *Lake Ontario* and *Lake Erie*]; p. [1], half-title: "LAKE MICHIGAN"; p. [2], series title: "[set within a green and white illustration of an Indian campsite above a lake; a large tree in the foreground at the left; Indian figures beside the tree and down the hill to their left; a lake and scattered hills in the background] The | AMERICAN | LAKES SERIES | Edited by Milo M. Quaife | THE BOBBS-MERRILL COMPANY | Publishers | INDIANAPOLIS · NEW YORK"; p. [3], title; p. [4], copyright page, "COPYRIGHT, 1944, BY THE BOBBS-MERRILL COMPANY | PRINTED IN THE UNITED STATES OF AMERICA | *First Edition*"; p. [5], dedication: "*To* LETITIA[1] | PILOT OF MY MATRIMONIAL BARK"; p. [6], "*I remember the black wharves and the slips,* | *and the sea-tides tossing free;* | . . . . | *And the beauty and mystery of the ships* | *And the magic of the sea.* | — LONGFELLOW, 'My Lost Youth'"; p. [7–8], "PRELUDE [signed M.M. Quaife, Detroit Public Library]"; p. [9–10], Contents; p. [11], "LIST OF ILLUSTRATIONS"; p. [12], blank; p. [13], "Part I | FROM BARK CANOE TO STEEL LEVIATHAN"; p. [14], blank; pp. 15–170, text; p. [171], "Part II | TALK OF MANY THINGS"; p. [172], blank; pp. 173–278, text; p. [279], "Part III | ALL AROUND THE COAST"; p. [280], blank; pp. 281–363, text; pp. 364–369, "ACKNOWLEDGMENTS" and "BIBLIOGRAPHICAL NOTE"; p. [370], blank; pp. 371–384, Index; pp. [385–386], blank.

BINDING: Forest-green cloth (close to Pantone 343), stamped in gold. Front: "THE AMERICAN LAKE SERIES | [outline of the Great Lakes, with Lake Michigan highlighted] | LAKE MICHIGAN". Spine: "LAKE | MICHIGAN | MILO | M. | QUAIFE] [at bottom] BOBBS | MERRILL". Front endpapers carry a map attributed to W. R. Lohse in gold and white, titled "Map of Lake Michigan." Rear endpapers carry a double-page map attributed to W. R. Lohse in gold and white, titled "Map of the Great Lakes".

DUST JACKET (white paper): Front and spine carry an illustration attributed to W.R. Lohse of two large trees in the foreground framing a group of three, a frontiersman, a soldier, and an Indian, to the right, an ox-drawn covered wagon behind them, and other Indians to the left, where a tepee stands in front of a third large tree, a stylized depiction of Lake Michigan in the background. Front: "[at top, within a royal-blue band, which wraps to the spine, in gold] THE AMERICAN LAKES SERIES | Edited by Milo M.

1. Milo Quaife's wife.

Quaife | [illustration] | [at bottom, within a royal-blue band, which wraps to the spine, in gold] *by* MILO M. QUAIFE". Spine: "[within the top royal-blue band, in gold] LAKE | MICHIGAN | [illustration] | [within the bottom royal-blue band, in gold] QUAIFE | *Bobbs Merrill*". Back: "[within a rectangular frame with thick/thin rules] THE AMERICAN LAKES SERIES | *under the general editorship of* | MILO M. QUAIFE | [four-paragraph blurb setting forth the theme of the series and noting that the authors chosen to write a book in the series are 'capable historians whose scholarly standing is well established.'] | *Published* | [list of three titles and their authors, with brief biographical information, beginning with *Lake Huron,* and ending with *Lake Michigan*] | *In Preparation* | [list of two titles and their authors, with brief biographical information: *Lake Ontario,* and *Lake Erie*]". Front flap: "LAKE MICHIGAN | [blurb] | *(Continued on back flap)* | [at bottom right] $3.50". Back flap: "*(Continued from front flap)* | [blurb]".

Published at $3.50 on July 31, 1944; number of copies printed unknown. Copyrighted August 2, 1944; deposited July 10, 1944.

The book is listed in "The Weekly Record," July 29, 1944, p. 341.

Note: No evidence found that Bobbs-Merrill reprinted *Lake Michigan.*

COPIES: CF

AL5a   First edition, Special Autographed Edition (1944)

Lake Michigan was issued with a special publisher's autograph page, signed by the author, tipped in following the front free endpaper.[2] The number of such copies issued has not been determined.

REPRINTS AND REPRODUCTIONS

Reproduced on microfilm. New Haven, Conn.: Yale University Library, 1993. 1 reel, 35 mm.

BIOGRAPHY

For a biography of Milo M. Quaife, see "Milo Quaife, Editor, *The American Lakes Series.*"

NOTES ON *LAKE MICHIGAN*

Milo Quaife, the book's author and general editor of the *Lakes* series, was one of the country's foremost editors and writers. An expert in Northwestern United States history, he was secretary of the Burton Historical Collection in the Detroit Public Library when he wrote *Lake Michigan.*

2. In at least one copy, the page is inserted following p. [4].

REVIEWS

Annals of the American Academy, January 1945 (p. 228); *Booklist,* September 1944 (p. 17); *Library Journal,* September 15, 1944 (p. 765); *New York Herald Tribune Weekly Book Review,* July 30, 1944 (p. 1); *New York Times,* August 27, 1944 (p. 17); *New Yorker,* August 12, 1944 (p. 62); *Saturday Review of Literature,* October 28, 1944 (p. 24); *Springfield Republican,* September 3, 1944 (p. 4-D); *Weekly Book Review,* July 30, 1944 (p. 1); *Wisconsin Library Bulletin,* October 1944 (p. 129).

SELECTED WRITINGS BY MILO M. QUAIFE

Chicago and the Old Northwest, 1673-1835: A Study of the Evolution of the Northwestern Frontier, Together with a History of Fort Dearborn (Chicago: University of Chicago Press, 1913); *Chicago's Highways Old and New: From Indian Trail to Motor Road* (Chicago: D..G. Keller, 1923); *The Kingdom of St. James: A Narrative of the Mormons* (New Haven: Yale University Press, 1930); *Checagou: From Indian Wigwam to Modern City, 1673-1835* (Chicago: University of Chicago Press, 1933); *Condensed Historical Sketches for Each of Michigan's Counties* (Detroit: J. L. Hudson, 1940); (with Sidney Glazer) *Michigan: From Primitive Wilderness to Industrial Commonwealth* (New York: Prentice-Hall, 1948); **Lake Michigan** (Indianapolis: Bobbs-Merrill, 1944).

SOURCES

Book Review Digest 1944. New York: The H.W. Wilson Company, 1945, pp. 619–620.

Publishers' Weekly, February 19, 1944, pp. 836–837; and July 29, 1944, p. 341.

New York Herald Tribune Weekly Book Review, July 30, 1944 (p. 1).

The New York Times Book Review, August 27, 1944, p. 17.

Detroit News obituary, September 2, 1959, p. 12–A.

The New York Times obituary, September 4, 1959, p. 6.

Bates, Roy M., County and City Historian, Allen County-Fort Wayne (Indiana) Historical Society, *The Old Fort Bulletin,* 1959–1960. "Dr. Milo M. Quaife." Three-page remembrance.

Contemporary Authors Online. The Gale Group, 2001. Reproduced in *Biography Resource Center.* Farmington Hills, Mich.: The Gale Group, 2001 . Accessed February 11, 2002.

Connole, Kerry, Graduate Student Assistant, Bentley Historical Library, The

University of Michigan. Letter to CF, May 8, 2002, with biographical material on Milo Quaife.

The Bobbs-Merrill mss., 1885–1957. The Lilly Library, Indiana University, Bloomington, Indiana.

LAKE OKEECHOBEE: WELLSPRING OF THE EVERGLADES

Alfred Jackson Hanna
May 5, 1893 – March 13, 1978
and
Kathryn Abbey Hanna
November 5, 1895 – April 16, 1967

AL6 First edition, first printing (1948) [9]

LAKE | OKEECHOBEE | WELLSPRING OF THE EVERGLADES | ALFRED JACKSON HANNA | AND | KATHRYN ABBEY HANNA

The foregoing is printed on a green-and-white illustration, a large tree in the foreground at the right; a young woman on horseback and a hunter in buckskins and a fur cap to the left of the tree; other human figures and an ox-drawn covered wagon behind them and to their right; and a lake and scattered hills in the background.

COLLATION: 8½" x 6". 192 leaves. [a–b] [1–14] 15–356 [357–358] 359–365 [366] 367–379 [380-382]. All numbers are printed in roman in headline at the outer margin of the type page, except for pp. 15, 25, 35, 53, 72, 82, 91, 105, 118, 134, 152, 164, 173, 185, 196, 204, 217, 222, 235, 244, 254, 270, 278, 287, 291, 302, 317, 327, 338, 348, 359, and 367, on which the numbers are printed in the center at the foot of the page.

Note: Black-and-white two-sided photographs are inserted following pp. 30, 62, 126, 158, 190, 222, 286, and 318.

CONTENTS: p. [a], blank; p. [b], THE AMERICAN LAKES SERIES | *Published:* | [list of nine titles and their authors, beginning with *Lake Huron* and ending with *Lake Okeechobee*] | *In preparation:* | [one title, with authors, *The Sierra Lakes*]"; p. [1], half-title: "LAKE OKEECHOBEE"; p. [2], series title: "[set within a green and white illustration of an Indian campsite above a lake; a large tree in the foreground at the left; Indian figures beside the tree and down the hill to their left; a lake and scattered hills in the background] The | AMERICAN | LAKES SERIES | Edited by Milo M. Quaife | THE BOBBS-MERRILL COMPANY | Publishers | INDIANAPOLIS • NEW YORK"; p. [3], title; p. [4], copyright page, "COPYRIGHT, 1948, BY THE BOBBS-MERRILL COMPANY | PRINTED IN THE UNITED STATES OF AMERICA | *First Edition*"; p. [5], dedication page: "TO PIONEERS | OF THE PAST AND THE PRESENT | WHOSE FAITH AND WORKS HAVE FASHIONED | OKEECHOBEELAND"; p. [6], blank; pp. [7-8], "EDITORIAL INTRODUCTION (signed M. M. Quaife, Detroit, Michigan)"; pp. [9-10], Contents; pp. [11-12], "LIST OF ILLUSTRATIONS"; p. [13], blank; p. [14], half title: "LAKE OKEECHOBEE"; pp. 15-356, text; p. [357], "BIBLIOGRAPHICAL NOTES | AND INDEX"; p. [358], blank; pp. 359-365, "BIBLIOGRAPHICAL NOTES"; p. [366], blank; pp. 367-379, "INDEX"; p. [380-382], blank.

BINDING: Forest-green cloth (close to Pantone 343), stamped in gold. Front: "THE AMERICAN LAKE SERIES | [outline of Lake Okeechobee] | LAKE | OKEECHOBEE". Spine: "LAKE | OKEECHOBEE | — | HANNA | [at bottom] BOBBS | MERRILL". Front and rear endpapers carry maps attributed to W.R. Lohse in gold, and white; on the left, "Map of Lake Okeechobee"; on the right, "Map of Florida".

DUST JACKET (white paper): Front and spine carry an illustration attributed to W.R. Lohse of two soldiers and an Indian standing in front of palm trees to the right, two other Indians to the left standing in front of a gnarled tree tangled in vines, the two groups framing a stylized depiction of Lake Okeechobee in the background. Front: "[at top, within a black band, which wraps to the spine, in white] THE AMERICAN LAKES SERIES | Edited by Milo M. Quaife | [illustration] | [at bottom, within a black band, which wraps to the spine, in white] *by* ALFRED JACKSON HANNA | *and* KATHRYN ABBEY HANNA". Spine: "[within the top black band, in white] LAKE | OKEECHOBEE | [illustration] | [within the bottom black band, in white] HANNA | *Bobbs Merrill*". Back: "[within a rectangular frame with a thin/thick rule] THE AMERICAN LAKES SERIES | *under the general editorship of* | MILO M. QUAIFE | [blurb] | *Published* | [list of nine titles and their authors, with brief biographical information, beginning with Lake Huron and ending with Lake Okeechobee". Front flap: "LAKE OKEECHOBEE | Wellspring of the Everglades | [blurb] | (Continued on back flap) | [at bottom right] $4.00". Back flap: "(Continued from front flap) | [blurb]".

Published at $4.00 on February 20, 1948; number of copies printed unknown. Copyrighted February 24, 1948; deposited February 18, 1948.

The book is listed in "The Weekly Record," March 6, 1948, p. 1283.

Note: No evidence found that Bobbs-Merrill reprinted *Lake Okeechobee*.

CITED: H243, *Catalog of the P. K.. Yonge Library of Florida History* at the University of Florida, Gainesville

COPIES: CF

AL6a   First edition, Special Autographed Edition (1948)

Lake Okeechobee: Wellspring to the Everglades was issued with a special publisher's autograph page, signed by both authors, tipped in following the front free endpaper. The number of such copies issued has not been determined.

REPRINTS AND REPRODUCTIONS

Dunwoody, Ga: N.S. Berg, 1973.

Reproduced on microform. New Haven, Conn.: Yale University Library, 1993. 1 reel, 35 mm.

BIOGRAPHIES

In 1952, the Hannas received grants in history from the Social Science Research Council and the American Philosophical Society for research in France. They were later honored by the award of the Cross of Chevalier, Order of Palmes Academiques, from the Republic of France. They wrote five books together. Their biographies follow.

∼

Alfred Jackson Hanna was born on May 5, 1893, in Tampa, Florida, the son of Josiah Calvin and Sarah Emily (Jackson) Hanna. In 1917, he graduated from Rollins College in Winter Park, Florida, earning a bachelor of arts degree. He undertook graduate studies at the University of Madrid in 1931 and at the National University of Mexico in 1934.

Hanna's career of more than sixty years at Rollins College began as an undergraduate when he was secretary to the faculty and later secretary to the college president. After his graduation, he served as registrar and as as-

sistant to the president, assistant treasurer, and vice president. In 1938, he became professor of history and, later, chairman of the history department
and director of Inter-American studies. From 1946 to 1970, he was Alexan
der Weddell Professor of History, and, from 1951 to 1970, vice president. In
1970, he retired and was named vice president emeritus.

On July 5, 1941, Hanna married Kathryn Abbey.

Hanna was the founder of the Union Catalog of Floridiana and a contributor to the Dictionary of American Biography, the Dictionary of American History, and journals of history. His book reviews appeared in the *New
York Times* and the *New York Herald Tribune*. In 1977, he received the Award
of Merit of the American Association for State and Local History.

Alfred Jackson Hanna died on March 13, 1978, in Winter Park, Florida,
at age 84.

～

Kathryn Trimmer Abbey Hanna was born on November 5, 1895, in
Chicago, Illinois, the daughter of Charles Peters and Julia (Trimmer) Abby.

In 1918 and 1919, she was an instructor at Lenox Hall, in St. Louis, Missouri. At Northwestern University, she earned a bachelor of arts degree in
1917, a master of arts degree in 1922, and a doctorate in 1926. In 1919, she
joined the faculty of Hood College in Frederick, Maryland, as instructor until 1921, associate professor (1922–1923), and head of the department of history (1923–1924). She taught at the Florida State College for Women (now
Florida State University) as associate professor (1926–1927), then as professor (1927–1930). From 1930 until her retirement in 1941, she was head of the
department of history, geography, and political science. She married Alfred
J. Hanna on July 5, 1941.

Kathryn Hanna wrote academic papers, articles, and reviews and contributed to dictionaries, encyclopedias, and historical publications. In 1936
and 1937, she worked in the Survey of Federal Archives, a nationwide survey
of the records of the Federal Government outside Washington, D.C., serving
as regional director for Florida. In 1945, she chaired the Florida State Library
Board, helping plan *Florida Becomes a State,* a volume of selected documents
commemorating the centennial of Florida's admission to the Union. She
was a member of the Southern Historical Association and was its president
in 1953 and 1954. In 1947, she received an honorary doctorate from Rollins
College.

Kathryn Abbey Hanna died on April 16, 1967, in Winter Park, Florida, at
age 71.

NOTES ON *LAKE OKEECHOBEE*

The book was included in Bobbs-Merrill's 1948 Spring List, with a projected publication date of February 20, 1948.

In an article headlined "Storm Puts Dent in Their Book," the October 3, 1947, *Jacksonville Journal* reported that the Hannas were awaiting reports from the Army Corps of Engineers on recent storm damage in the Okeechobee area before completing the chapter "Hell and High Water," which addresses the destructive power of the lake at times of heavy rains and strong winds. "Both assert the forthcoming book will be composed of virtually new material. Months of intensive research and checking have been added to several years' study of the Lake Okeechobee region," the newspaper reported.

REVIEWS

Booklist, March 15, 1948 (p. 246); *Chicago Sunday Tribune,* March 14, 1948 (n.p.); *Miami Daily News,* March 21, 1948 (n.p.); *Miami Herald,* February 29, 1948 (n.p.); *New York Herald Tribune Weekly Book Review,* March 7, 1948 (p. 3); *New York Historical Quarterly,* XXXII, July, 1948. No. 3 (p. 225); *New York Times Book Review,* March 7, 1948 (p. 19); *Orlando Sentinel,* March 19, 1948 (n.p.); (Rollins College) *Flamingo,* Vol. 23, No, 3, Spring, 1948 (p. 51); *San Francisco Chronicle,* May 16, 1948 (p. 16); *U.S. Quarterly Booklist,* June 1948 (p. 177); *St. Petersburg Times,* March 7, 1948 (n.p.); *Tampa Sunday Tribune,* February 29, 1948 (p. 18–A); *Wisconsin Library Bulletin,* October 1948 (p. 64).

SELECTED WRITINGS BY ALFRED JACKSON HANNA

Fort Maitland: Its Origin and History (Maitland, Fla.: The Fort Maitland Committee, 1935); *Founding of Rollins College 1885-1935* (Winter Park, Fla.: Rollins Press, 1936); *Flight into Oblivion* (Richmond, Va.: Johnson Publishing Co, 1938); *A Bibliography of the Writings of Irving Bacheller* (Winter Park, Fla.: Rollins College, 1939); (contributor) Wilgus, A. Curtis, ed. *Hispanic American Essays: A Memorial to James Alexander Robertson* (Chapel Hill: University of North Carolina Press, 1942); (with James Branch Cabell) *The St. Johns: A Parade of Diversities* (Rivers of America Series) (New York: Farrar & Rinehart, 1943); *Recommended Readings on Florida: A Standard Guide to the Best Books on Florida, with Helpful Explanations and Critical Evaluations* (Winter Park, Fla.: Union Catalog of Floridiana, 1945); *A Prince in Their Midst: The Adventurous Life of Achille Murat on the American Frontier* (Norman: University of Oklahoma Press, 1946); (with Kathryn Abbey) **Lake Okeechobee: Wellspring of the Everglades** (Indianapolis: Bobbs-Merrill,

1948); (with Kathryn Abbey Hanna) *Florida's Golden Sands* (Indianapolis: Bobbs Merrill, 1950); (with Kathryn Abbey Hanna) *Confederate Exiles in Venezuela* (Limited ed.) (Tuscaloosa, Ala.: Confederate Publishing Co., 1960); *The Beginnings of Nyasaland and North-eastern Rhodesia, 1859-95* (Oxford: Clarendon Press, 1956); (with Kathryn Abbey Hanna) *Napoleon III and Mexico: American Triumph Over Monarchy* (Chapel Hill: University of North Carolina Press, 1971); (with Kathryn Abbey Hanna) *Napoleon III y Mexico* (Mexico: Fonda de Cultura Economica, 1973).

SELECTED WRITINGS BY KATHRYN ABBEY HANNA

Florida: Land of Change (Chapel Hill: University of North Carolina Press, 1941); (with Cleo Rainwater) *Our Journey Through Florida* (New York: American Book Company, 1957).

SOURCES

Book Review Digest 1948. New York: The H.W. Wilson Company, 1949, p. 356.

Publishers' Weekly, January 31, 1948 (Bobbs-Merrill Spring List), p. 371; and March 6, 1948, p. 1283.

New York Herald Tribune Weekly Book Review, March 7, 1948, p. 3.

The New York Times Book Review, March 7, 1948, p. 19.

Who Was Who, Volume V, 1969-1973. Chicago: Marquis Who's Who, Inc., 1973, p. 304.

Gainesville: University of Florida Libraries, 1977. *Catalog of the P.K. Yonge Library of Florida History, Volume 2, Fis-K,* p. 411.

Fitzgerald, Carol. *The Rivers of America: A Descriptive Bibliography.* New Castle, Del.: Oak Knoll Press in Association with the Center for the Book in the Library of Congress, 2001. (Entry on A.J. Hanna in *The St. Johns: A Parade of Diversities.*)

Rollins College, Department of Archives and Special Collections. Kathryn Hanna and A.J. Hanna Collections.

The Bobbs-Merrill mss., 1885–1957. The Lilly Library, Indiana University, Bloomington, Indiana.

LAKE ONTARIO

Arthur Pound
June 1, 1884 – January 14, 1966

AL7 First edition, first printing (1945) [4]

LAKE | ONTARIO | ARTHUR POUND

The foregoing is printed on a green-and-white illustration, a large tree in the foreground at the right; a young woman on horseback and a hunter in buckskins and a fur cap to the left of the tree; other human figures and an ox-drawn covered wagon behind them and to their right; and a lake and scattered hills in the background.

COLLATION: 8½" x 6". 192 leaves. [1–16] 17–87 [88–90] 91–232 [233–234] 235–352 [353–354] 355–363 [364–366] 367–384. All numbers printed in roman in headline at the outer margin of the type page, except for pp. 17, 25, 30, 39, 54, 66, 91, 109, 119, 129, 138, 147, 171, 185, 201, 211, 235, 255, 266, 279, 300, 312, 326, 334, 345, 355, and 367, on which the numbers are printed in the center, at the foot of the page.

Note: Black-and-white photographs are inserted facing pp. 32, 33, 64, 65, 96, 97, 128, 129, 164, 165, 192, 193, 224, 225, 256, 257, 288, 289, 320, 321, 352, and [353].

CONTENTS: p. [1], blank; p. [2], "THE AMERICAN LAKES SERIES | *Published:* | [list of four titles and their authors, beginning with *Lake Huron* and ending with *Lake Ontario*] | *In Preparation:* | [list of one title and its author, *Lake Erie*]; p. [3], half title: "LAKE ONTARIO"; p. [4], series title: "[set within a green and white illustration of an Indian campsite above a lake; a large tree in the foreground at the left; Indian figures beside the tree and down the hill to their left; a lake and scattered hills in the background] The | AMERICAN | LAKES SERIES | Edited by Milo M. Quaife | THE BOBBS-MERRILL COMPANY | Publishers | INDIANAPOLIS · NEW YORK"; p. [5], title; p. [6], copyright page, "COPYRIGHT, 1945, BY THE BOBBS-MERRILL COMPANY | PRINTED IN THE UNITED STATES | *First Edition*"; p. [7], dedica-

tion: "THIS BOOK IS DEDICATED TO MY FRIENDS IN OSWEGO I AND
ROCHESTER WHO GUARD LOFTY HISTORIC TRADI- I TIONS FOR
THE DELIGHT OF THEIR COMMUNITIES AND I THE JOYFUL EDU-
CATION OF THEIR CHILDREN GEN- I ERATION UNTO GENERATION.
WHO CAN BREATHE I SUCH AIR WITHOUT FEELING HIS VERY SOUL
EXPAND?"; p. [8], blank; pp. [9–10], "EDITORIAL INTRODUCTION
[signed M.M. Quaife, Detroit Public Library]"; pp. [11–12], Contents; p.
[13–14], "LIST OF ILLUSTRATIONS"; p. [15], "Part I I VORTEX OF EM-
PIRE"; p. [16], blank; pp. 17–87, text; pp. [88], blank; p. [89], "Part II I WARS
AND RECONSTRUCTION"; p. [90], blank; pp. 91–232, text; p. [233], "Part
III I SHORE JOURNEY"; p. [234], blank; pp. 235–352, text; p. [353] "AC-
KNOWLEDGMENTS-" I and I "BIBLIOGRAPHICAL NOTE"; p. [354],
blank; pp. 355–356, "ACKNOWLEDGMENTS"; pp. 357–363, "BIBLIO-
GRAPHICAL NOTE"; p. [364], blank; p. [365], "INDEX"; p. [366], blank;
pp. 367–384, Index.

BINDING: Forest-green cloth (close to Pantone 343), stamped in gold.
Front: "THE AMERICAN LAKE SERIES I [outline of the Great Lakes, with
Lake Ontario highlighted] I LAKE ONTARIO". Spine: "LAKE I ONTARIO I
— I ARTHUR I POUND I [at bottom] BOBBS I MERRILL". Front endpapers carry a double-page map attributed to W. R. Lohse in gold and white,
titled "Map of Lake Ontario." Rear endpapers carry a double-page map attributed to W. R. Lohse in gold and white, titled "Map of the Great Lakes".

DUST JACKET (white paper): Front and spine carry an illustration attributed to W.R. Lohse of two large trees in the foreground framing a group of
three, a frontiersman, a soldier, and an Indian, to the right, an ox-drawn
covered wagon behind them, and other Indians to the left, where a tepee
stands in front of a third large tree, a stylized depiction of Lake Ontario in
the background. Front: "[at top, within a gold band, which wraps to the
spine, in black] THE AMERICAN LAKES SERIES I Edited by Milo M.
Quaife I [illustration] I [at bottom, within a black band, which wraps to the
spine, in lavender] *by* ARTHUR POUND". Spine: "[within the top gold band,
in black] LAKE I ONTARIO I [illustration] I [within the bottom black band,
in lavender] POUND I *Bobbs Merrill*". Back: "[within a rectangular frame
with thick/thin rules] THE AMERICAN LAKES SERIES I *under the general
editorship of* I MILO M. QUAIFE I [four-paragraph blurb setting forth the
theme of the series and noting that the authors chosen to write a book in
the series are 'capable historians whose scholarly standing is well established.'] I *Published* I [list of four titles and their authors, with brief biographical information, beginning with *Lake Huron*, and ending with *Lake Ontario*] I *In Preparation* I [list of one title and its author, with brief

biographical information: *Lake Erie*]". Front flap: "LAKE ONTARIO |
[blurb] | *(Continued on back flap)* | [at bottom right] $3.50". Back flap:
"*(Continued from front flap)* | [blurb]".

Published at $3.50 on May 15, 1945; number of copies printed unknown.
Copyrighted May 17, 1944; deposited April 29, 1944.

The book is listed in "The Weekly Record," May 12, 1945, p. 1936.

Note: No evidence found that Bobbs-Merrill reprinted *Lake Ontario*.

COPIES: CF

AL7a   First edition, Special Autographed Edition (1945)

Lake Ontario was issued with a special publisher's autograph page, signed by
the author, tipped in following the front free endpaper. The number of such
copies issued has not been determined.

REPRINTS AND REPRODUCTIONS

Port Washington, N.Y.: Kennikat Press, 1970. Empire State Historical Publication Series No. 87. Published at $12.50.

Reproduced on microfilm. New Haven, CT: Yale University Library, 1993. 1
reel. 35 mm.

Reproduced on microfiche. Ann Arbor, Mich.: UMI, 2004. 5 microfiches.

BIOGRAPHY

Arthur Pound was born on June 1, 1884, in Pontiac, Michigan, the son of
John and Elizabeth Pound. Pound's father was in the dry goods business.
Pound graduated from Pontiac High School in 1903, then joined the
staff of the *Press*, a daily newspaper published in Pontiac. After two years
there, he enrolled at the University of Michigan, earning the bulk of his ex-
penses by working for newspapers in Detroit, Ann Arbor, and Toledo, Ohio.
He was news editor and managing editor of the college newspaper and, for a
year, editor of the college magazine, graduating in 1907. After his graduation, Pound worked as an editor for the Bobbs-Merrill Company of Indianapolis.
On April 22, 1908, Pound married Mary Madelon Patterson of Flint,
Michigan. The couple had four daughters.
A journalist, author, poet, and historian, Pound was an editorial writer
for *The Grand Rapids Press* from 1914 to 1917. After service in the Navy dur-

ing World War I, he gained national recognition with the publication of his "Iron Man" papers in the *Atlantic Monthly*. In 1921, the Iron Man papers were published in book form by Atlantic Monthly Press as *The Iron Man in Industry*.

In the early 1920s, Pound worked in New York, writing editorials for the *New York Evening Post* and the *New York Herald*. In 1924 and 1925, Pound was editor of the Atlantic Monthly Press. From 1925 to 1927, he was associate editor of the *Independent* magazine.

On October 25, 1934, at a dinner and celebration in Pontiac, Stewart Beach, like Pound a native of Pontiac and a magazine editor, presented a biographical sketch, "My Friend Pound." Referring to the Iron Man papers, Beach said, "Probably no more thoughtful and penetrating essays on the sociology and economics of the Machine Age have been written." At the dinner, it was noted that in the preceding eight years Pound had written eleven books, four on American Colonial history and biography, two on the business firms General Motors and American Telephone and Telegraph, two volumes of financial memoirs, two novels, and a book of verse. Beach noted that critics had "expressed their amazement that one man is able to do so much and to do it so well."[1]

From 1940 to 1946, Pound was the New York State Historian. With World War II under way, the organization's publications and historical site-marker programs were suspended. Joseph F. Meany, Jr., in his history of the office of New York State Historian, notes, "Dr. Pound's energies were taken up in organizing arrangements for the protection of the state's historical records in the event that the state capitol came under axis air attack."[2]

Pound founded and was first president of the Society for Colonial History. In 1952, he received an honorary doctorate in literature from the University of Michigan.

Arthur Pound died on January 14, 1966, in Ann Arbor, Michigan, at age 81.

NOTES ON *LAKE ONTARIO*

The book was included on the Bobbs-Merrill 1945 Spring List and was promoted by Bobbs-Merrill with a full-page advertisement in the April 21, 1945, issue of *Publishers' Weekly*.

1. Beach, Stewart. "My Friend Pound." Biographical sketch presented to the guests at the Arthur Pound Homecoming, Pontiac, Michigan, October 25–26, with the compliments of the Atlantic Monthly, pp. 5–6.
2. Meany, Jr., Joseph F. "New York: The State of History." Originally compiled September, 1994. Revised October, 2001.

REVIEWS

Book Week, June 3, 1945 (p. 3); *Booklist,* June 1, 1945 (p. 285); *Canadian Historical Review,* September 1945 (p. 323); *New York Times,* June 17, 1945 (p. 8); *Saturday Review of Literature,* October 13, 1945 (p. 51); *Springfield Republican,* June 6, 1945 (p. 6); *U.S. Quarterly Booklist,* December 1945 (p. 33); *Weekly Book Review,* May 27, 1945 (p. 5).

SELECTED WRITINGS BY ARTHUR POUND

The Iron Man In Industry: An Outline of the Social Significances of Automatic Machinery (Boston: Atlantic Monthly Press, 1922); *The Telephone Idea: Celebrating the Fiftieth Anniversary of the Telephone* (New York: Greenberg, 1926); *They Told Barron; Conversations and Revelations of an American Pepys In Wall Street* (New York, Harper, 1930); *Johnson of the Mohawks: A biography of Sir William Johnson, Irish Immigrant, Mohawk War Chief, American Soldier, Empire Builder* (New York: Macmillan, 1930); *Native Stock: The Rise of the American Spirit Seen In Six Lives* (New York: Macmillan, 1931); *More They Told Barron: The Notes of Clarence W. Barron, Publisher of the Wall Street Journal and The Boston News Bureau* (New York: Harper, 1931); *Mountain Morning and Other Poems* (Albany, N.Y.: Argus Press, 1932); *The Penns of Pennsylvania and England* (New York: Macmillan, 1932); *Washington in Albany* (Albany Institute of History and Art, 1932); *Around the Corner* (New York: Sears Publishing Company, 1933); *The Turning Wheel: The Story of General Motors Through Twenty-Five Years, 1908-1933* (Garden City, N.Y.: Doubleday, Doran, 1934); *Once A Wilderness* (New York: Reynal and Hitchcock, 1934); *The Golden Earth: The Story of Manhattan's Landed Wealth in Process* (New York: Macmillan, 1934); *Second Growth* (New York: Reynal and Hitchcock, 1935); *Industrial America: Its Way of Work and Thought* (Boston: Little, Brown, 1936); *Hawk of Detroit* (New York: Reynal & Hitchcock, 1939); *Salt of the Earth: The Story of Captain J. B. Ford and Michigan Alkali Company, 1890-1940* (Boston: Atlantic Monthly, 1940); **Lake Ontario** (Indianapolis: Bobbs-Merrill, 1945); *The Automobile and an American City* (Detroit: Published for the Detroit Historical Society, by Wayne State University Press, 1962); *The Only Thing Worth Finding: The Life and Legacies of George Gough Booth* (Detroit: Wayne State University Press, 1964).

SOURCES

Beach, Stewart. "My Friend Pound." A remembrance of Arthur Pound. Presented to the guests at the Arthur Pound Homecoming, Pontiac, Michigan, October 25–26, 1934, with the compliments of the Atlantic Monthly.

Publishers' Weekly, February 19, 1944, p. 837; January 27, 1945, (Bobbs-Merrill Spring List), p. 291; April 21, 1945, p. 1625 (?); and May 12, 1945, p. 1936;

Book Review Digest 1945. New York: The H.W. Wilson Company, 1946, p. 569

Burke, W. J., and Will D. Howe. *American Authors and Books 1640-1940.* NY: Gramercy Publishing Co, 1943, p. 601.

Ann Arbor News obituary, January 14, 1966 [n.p.]

The New York Times obituary, January 15, 1966, p. 27

Contemporary Authors Online. The Gale Group, 2000. Reproduced in *Biography Resource Center,* Farmington Hills, Mich.: The Gale Group, 2001. Accessed February 14, 2002.

Connole, Kerry. Graduate Student Assistant, Bentley Historical Library, The University of Michigan. Letter to CF, with enclosures, May 8, 2002.

Meany, Jr., Joseph F. "New York: The State of History." www.nysm.nysed.gov Accessed May 3, 2005.

The Bobbs-Merrill mss., 1885–1957. The Lilly Library, Indiana University, Bloomington, Indiana.

LAKE PONTCHARTRAIN

W. Adolphe Roberts
October 15, 1886 – September, 1962

AL8   First edition, first printing (1946) [6]

LAKE | PONTCHARTRAIN | W. ADOLPHE ROBERTS

The foregoing is printed on a green-and-white illustration, a large tree in the foreground at the right; a young woman on horseback and a hunter in buckskins and a fur cap to the left of the tree; other human figures and an ox-drawn covered wagon behind them and to their right; and a lake and scattered hills in the background.

COLLATION: 8½" x 6". 190 leaves. [a–b] [1–18] 19–125 [126–128] 129–229 [230—232] 233–344 [345–346] 347–357 [358–360] 361–376 [377–378]. All numbers printed in roman in headline at the outer margin of the type page, except for pp. 19, 33, 48, 63, 79, 90, 107, 129, 141, 159, 171, 184, 201, 210, 222, 233, 247, 265, 276, 292, 305, 313, 322, 328, 340, 347, 349, 351,and 361, on which the numbers are printed in the center, at the foot of the page.

Note: Black-and-white photographs are inserted facing pp. 30, 31, 62, 63, 94, 95, [126], [127], 158, 159, 190, 191, 222, 223, 254, 255, 286, 287, 318, and 319.

CONTENTS: p. [a], blank; p. [b], "THE AMERICAN LAKES SERIES | *Published:* | [list of six titles and their authors, beginning with *Lake Huron* and ending with *Lake Pontchartrain*] | *In Preparation.* | [list of three titles and their authors: *Lake Champlain and Lake George; The Great Salt Lake,* and *Lake Okeechobee*]; p. [1], half title: "LAKE PONTCHARTRAIN"; p. [2], series title: "[set within a green and white illustration of an Indian campsite above a lake; a large tree in the foreground at the left; Indian figures beside the tree and down the hill to their left; a lake and scattered hills in the background] The | AMERICAN | LAKES SERIES | Edited by Milo M. Quaife |

THE BOBBS-MERRILL COMPANY | Publishers | INDIANAPOLIS · NEW YORK"; p. [3], title; p. [4], copyright page, "COPYRIGHT, 1946, BY THE BOBBS-MERRILL COMPANY | PRINTED IN THE UNITED STATES OF AMERICA | *First Edition*"; p. [5], dedication: "DEDICATED TO | NELL"; p. [6], blank; pp. [7–8], "EDITORIAL INTRODUCTION [signed M.M. Quaife, Detroit Public Library]"; pp. [9–12], "PRELUDE"; pp. [13–14], Contents; pp. [15–16], "LIST OF ILLUSTRATIONS"; p. [17], "Part I | THE EARLY LAKE"; p. [18], blank; pp. 19–125, text; p. [126], blank; p. [127], "PART II | A CENTURY OF ROMANCE"; p. [128], blank; pp. 129–229, text; p. [230], blank; p. [231], "PART III | THE WAR PERIOD"; p. [232], blank; pp. 233–302, text; p. [303], "PART IV | THE LAKE IN OUR TIMES"; p. [304], blank; pp. 305–344, text; p. [345], "APPENDICES, ACKNOWLEDGMENTS | AND BIBLIOGRAPHICAL NOTE"; p. [346], blank; pp. 347–348, "APPENDIX A"; pp. 349–350, "APPENDIX B"; p. 351, "ACKNOWLEDGMENTS" | pp. 351–357, "BIBLIOGRAPHICAL NOTE"; p. [358], blank; p. [359], "INDEX"; p. [360], blank; pp. 361–376, Index; pp. [377–378], blank.

BINDING: Forest-green cloth (close to Pantone 343), stamped in gold. Front: "THE AMERICAN LAKE SERIES | [outline of the Great Lakes, with Lake Pontchartrain highlighted] | LAKE | PONTCHARTRAIN". Spine: "LAKE | PONTCHAR- | TRAIN | — | W. ADOLPHE | ROBERTS | [at bottom] BOBBS | MERRILL". Front endpapers carry a double-page map attributed to W. R. Lohse in gold and white, titled "Map of Lake Pontchartrain and the Island of Orleans." Rear endpapers carry a double-page map attributed to W. R. Lohse in gold and white, titled "French Louisiana on the Gulf Coast centering about New Orleans and Lake Pontchartrain".

DUST JACKET (white paper): Front and spine carry an illustration attributed to W.R. Lohse of two large trees in the foreground framing a group of three, a frontiersman, a soldier, and an Indian to the right and other Indians to the left, where a tepee stands in front of a third large tree, a stylized depiction of Lake Pontchartrain in the background. Front: "[at top, within a green band, which wraps to the spine, in black] THE AMERICAN LAKES SERIES | Edited by Milo M. Quaife | [superimposed on the illustration, in black] | LAKE | PONTCHARTRAIN | [at bottom, within a black band, which wraps to the spine, in medium tan] *by* W. ADOLPHE ROBERTS". Spine: "[within the top green band, in black] LAKE | PONTCHARTRAIN | [illustration] | [within the bottom black band, in medium tan] ROBERTS | *Bobbs Merrill*". Back: "[within a rectangular frame with thick/thin rules] THE AMERICAN LAKES SERIES | *under the general editorship of* | MILO M. QUAIFE | [blurb] | *Published* | [list of six titles and their authors, with brief biographical information, beginning with *Lake Huron,* and ending with *Lake Pontchartrain*]

"*In Preparation* | [list of three titles and their authors, with brief biographical information: *Lake Champlain and Lake George; The Great Salt Lake; Lake Okeechobee*]". Front flap: "LAKE PONTCHARTRAIN | [blurb] | *(Continued on back flap)* | [at bottom right] $3.50". Back flap: "*(Continued from front flap)* | [blurb]".

Published at $3.50 on October 7, 1946; number of copies printed unknown. Copyrighted October 7, 1946; deposited October 1, 1946.

The book is listed in the "Weekly Record", October 12, 1946, p. 2267.

Note: Bobbs-Merrill published at least two printings of *Lake Pontchartrain*.

COPIES: CF

AL8a   First edition, Special Autographed Edition (1946)

Lake Pontchartrain was issued with a special publisher's autograph page, signed by the author, tipped in following the front free endpaper. The number of such copies issued has not been determined.

REPRINTS AND REPRODUCTIONS

None.

BIOGRAPHY

Walter Adolphe Roberts was born in Jamaica on October 15, 1886, the son of an Anglican chaplain of a British army regiment. He grew up on a coffee plantation that had been in his family for generations. At age eighteen, he moved to New York City. He became a member of the prewar Greenwich Village literary renaissance and a friend of such notables as Edna St. Vincent Millay, Margaret Sanger, and Van Wyck Brooks. After wartime service in the Paris bureau of the *Brooklyn Eagle,* he returned to the United States and began a career that would include editorship of several well-known magazines and the writing of novels, historical works, and verse.[1] At times, he used the pseudonym Stephen Endicott.

In 1938, Roberts moved to New Orleans to finish his biography of the naval hero of the Confederacy, Admiral Raphael Semmes. The book, *Semmes of the Alabama* (Bobbs-Merrill), was published later in the year. Roberts's best-known works are a biography, *Sir Henry Morgan: Buccaneer and Governor* (Covici Friede, 1933), and a narrative history, *The Caribbean: The Story of Our Sea of Destiny* (Bobbs-Merrill, 1940).

1. *New York Times* obituary, September 17, 1962, p. 31.

In *Decoding the History of Black Mysteries,* Paula L. Woods wrote ". . . it was Jamaican writer W. Adolphe Roberts who was the first Black to publish a mystery novel, The Haunting Hand [Macaulay], in 1926. Yet Roberts' effort wasn't recognized for almost three quarters of a century, perhaps because his characters were not Black."[2]

In the 1930s, Roberts worked with the Jamaica Progressive League in Harlem, which sought independence for Jamaica. Jamaica's independence was granted by Great Britain on August 6, 1962.

In 1950, Roberts received the Order of Carlos Manuel de Cespedes Caballero from the government of Cuba. In 1961, he received the Order of the British Empire.

In 1956, Roberts returned to Kingston, Jamaica, where he taught at Kingston University, served as chairman of the board of the Institute of Jamaica, and was general editor of The Pioneer Press.

W. Adolphe Roberts died in London, England, in September, 1962, at age 75.

NOTES ON *LAKE PONTCHARTRAIN*

Bobbs-Merrill announced publication of the book in its Fall List in the August 17, 1946, issue of *Publishers' Weekly,* with a planned publication date of September 25, 1946. A later Bobbs-Merrill advertisement noted the October 7, 1946, publication date.

REVIEWS

Book Week, November 17, 1946 (p. 10); *Booklist,* November 1, 1946 (p. 68); *Christian Science Monitor,* October 28, 1946 (p. 14); *Kirkus,* August 1, 1946 (p. 370); *New York Times Book Review,* November 10, 1946 (p. 26); *San Francisco Chronicle,* December 8, 1946 (p. 13); and *Weekly Book Review,* October 27, 1946 (p. 4).

SELECTED WRITINGS BY W. ADOLPHE ROBERTS

The American Parade (quarterly magazine) (Parade Publishing Co., 1926); *The Haunting Hand* (New York: Macaulay, 1926); *Pan and Peacock* (Boston: Four Seas, 1928); *The Mind Reader* (New York: Macaulay, 1929); [pseud. Stephen Endicott] *Mayor Harding of New York* (New York: Mohawk, 1931); *The Moralist* (New York: Mohawk, 1931); [pseud. Stephen Endicott] *The Strange Career of Bishop Sterling* (New York: Meteor, 1932); *Sir Henry Morgan: Buccaneer and Governor* (New York: Covici Friede, 1933); *The Top-floor Killer* (London, I. Nicholson and Watson, 1935); *Semmes of the Alabama* (In-

2. Woods, Paula L. "Decoding the History of Black Mysteries," Crisis Publishing, 2001.

dianapolis: Bobbs-Merrill, 1938); *The Caribbean: The Story of Our Destiny* (Indianapolis: Bobbs-Merrill, 1940); *The Pomegranate* (Indianapolis: Bobbs-Merrill, 1941); The *U.S. Navy Fights* (Indianapolis: Bobbs-Merrill, 1942); *The French in the West Indies* (Indianapolis: Bobbs-Merrill, 1942); [trilogy] *Royal Street: A Novel of Old New Orleans* (1944) *Brave Mardi Gras: A New Orleans Novel of the '60s* (1946), and *Creole Dusk: A New Orleans Novel of the '80s* (1948) (Indianapolis: Bobbs-Merrill); **Lake Pontchartrain** (Indianapolis: Bobbs-Merrill, 1946); *The Single Star: A Novel of Cuba in the '90s* (Indianapolis: Bobbs-Merrill, 1949); *Lands of the Inner Sea: The West Indies and Bermuda; Havana: The Portrait of a City* (New York: Coward-McCann, 1953); *Jamaica: The Portrait of an Island* (New York: Coward-McCann, 1955); *Six Great Jamaicans: Biographical Sketches* (Kingston, Jamaica: Pioneer Press, 1957).

SOURCES

"Writer Arrives to Gather Data about Semmes," (New Orleans) *Times-Picayune*, April 13, 1938, p. 9.

Book Review Digest 1946. New York: The H.W. Wilson Company, 1947, p. 691.

Publishers' Weekly, August 17, 1946, p. 646; October 5, 1946, (Bobbs-Merrill Fall List) p. 1761; and October 12, 1946, p. 2267.

The New York Times Book Review (advertisement), October 13, 1946, p. 33.

The New York Times Book Review, November 10, 1946, p. 26.

The New York Times obituary, September 17, 1962, p. 31.

Woods, Paula L. "Decoding the History of Black Mysteries." Crisis Publishing Company, Incorporated Sep/Oct 2001.

The Bobbs-Merrill mss., 1885–1957. The Lilly Library, University of Indiana, Bloomington, Indiana.

Contemporary Authors Online. The Gale Group, 2000. Reproduced in *Biography Resource Center,* Farmington Hills, Mich.: The Gale Group, 2001. Accessed February 14, 2002.

SIERRA-NEVADA LAKES

George Henry Hinkle
April 8, 1896 – November 8, 1950
and
Bliss M. Hinkle
June 6, 1896 – September 23, 1949

AL9   First edition, first printing (1949) [10]

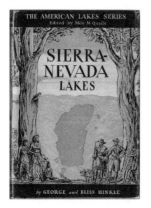

SIERRA- | NEVADA | LAKES | GEORGE and BLISS HINKLE

The foregoing is printed on a green-and-white illustration, a large tree in the foreground at the right; a young woman on horseback and a hunter in buckskins and a fur cap to the left of the tree; other human figures and an ox-drawn covered wagon behind them and to their right; and a lake and scattered hills in the background.

COLLATION: 8½" x 6". 194 leaves. [a–b] [1–18] 19–383 [384–386]. Numbers printed in roman in headline at the outer margin of the type page, except for pp. 19, 31, 38, 43, 52, 71, 73, 89, 91, 110, 111, 128, 153, 170, 173, 189, 213, 233, 251, 255, 276, 298, 327, 351, 359, and 365, on which the numbers are printed in the center at the foot of the page.

Note: Black-and-white two-sided photographic plates are inserted following pp. 30, 62, 126, 158, 190, 222, 286, and 318.

CONTENTS: p. [a], blank; p. [b], "THE AMERICAN LAKES SERIES | *Published:* | [list of ten titles, beginning with Lake Huron, and ending with Sierra-Nevada Lakes]; p. [1], half-title: "SIERRA-NEVADA LAKES"; p. [2], series title: "[set within a green and white illustration of an Indian campsite above a lake; a large tree in the foreground at the left; Indian figures beside the tree and down the hill to their left; a lake and scattered hills in the background] The | AMERICAN | LAKES SERIES | Edited by Milo M. Quaife | THE BOBBS-MERRILL COMPANY, INC. | Publishers | INDIANAPOLIS · NEW YORK"; p. [3], title; p. [4], copyright page, "COPYRIGHT, 1949, BY

THE BOBBS-MERRILL COMPANY, INC. I PRINTED IN THE UNITED STATES OF AMERICA I *First Edition*"; p. [5], dedication page: "*To* Mother I WHOSE LIFE HAS SPANNED MUCH I OF THIS EPOCH"; p. [6], blank; p. [7–10], "EDITORIAL INTRODUCTION [signed M.M. Quaife, Detroit, Michigan]"; p. [11], "AUTHORS' PREFATORY NOTE [signed G. H. B. H]"; p. [12], blank; p. [13[, Contents; p. [14], blank; p. [15–16], "LIST OF ILLUS-TRATIONS"; p. [16] [lower half], "MAPS"; p. [17], half-title: "SIERRA-NEVADA LAKES"; p. [18], blank; pp. 19–355, text; p. [356], blank; p. [357], "ACKNOWLEDGMENTS, I BIBLIOGRAPHICAL NOTES I AND INDEX"; p. [358], blank; pp. 359–360, "ACKNOWLEDGMENTS"; pp. 360-363, "BIBLI-OGRAPHICAL NOTES"; p. [364], blank; pp. 365–383, "INDEX"; pp. [384–386], blank.

BINDING: Forest-green cloth (close to Pantone 343), stamped in gold. Front: "THE AMERICAN LAKE SERIES I [outline of Lake Tahoe and four nearby lakes] I SIERRA-NEVADA I LAKES. Spine: "SIERRA- I NEVADA I LAKES I HINKLE I [at bottom] BOBBS I MERRILL". Endpapers carry a map attributed to W.R. Lohse in gold and white, titled "Map of the Pacific Coast, California and Nevada," and an "Enlarged Section of Map showing Lake Tahoe and its neighborhood".

DUST JACKET (white paper): Front and spine carry an illustration attrib-uted to W.R. Lohse of two large trees in the foreground framing a group of two frontiersmen and an Indian to the right, an ox-drawn covered wagon behind them, and other Indians to the left, where a tepee stands in front of a third large tree, a stylized depiction of Lake Tahoe and four nearby lakes in the background. Front: "[at top, within a black band, which wraps to the spine, in orange (close to Pantone 144)] THE AMERICAN LAKES SERIES I Edited by Milo M. Quaife I [illustration] I [at bottom, within a black band, which wraps to the spine, in orange] *by* GEORGE *and* BLISS HINKLE". Spine: "[within the top black band, in orange] SIERRA- I NEVADA *Lakes* I [illustration] I [within the bottom black band, in orange] HINKLE I *Bobbs Merrill*". Back: "[within a rectangular frame with thick/thin rules] THE AMERICAN LAKES SERIES I *under the general editorship of* I MILO M. QUAIFE I *Published* I [list of ten titles, with their authors and brief biogra-phical information, beginning with LAKE HURON, and ending with SIERRA-NEVADA LAKES]". Front flap: "SIERRA-NEVADA LAKES I [blurb] I (*Continued on back flap*) I [at bottom right] $4.00". Back flap: "(*Continued from front flap*) I [blurb]".

Published at $4.00 on April 14, 1949; number of copies printed unknown. Copyrighted April 18, 1949; deposited February 16, 1949.

The book is listed in "The Weekly Record," April 16, 1949, p. 1692.

Note: No evidence found that Bobbs-Merrill reprinted *Sierra Nevada Lakes.*

CITED: Paher 869

COPIES: CF

A9a   First edition, Special Autographed Edition (1949)

Sierra-Nevada Lakes was issued with a special publisher's autograph page, signed by both authors, tipped in following the front free endpaper. The number of such copies issued has not been determined.

REPRINTS AND REPRODUCTIONS

Reno: University of Nevada Press, 1987. New foreword by Gary F. Kurutz. A Vintage West Reprint.

BIOGRAPHIES

George Henry Hinkle was born on April 8, 1896, in Truckee, California, the son of George Toreson and Emma Hill Hinkle.

At Stanford University, Hinkle earned a bachelor of arts degree (1926); a master of arts degree (1928); and a doctorate (1937). He was professor of English at Stanford in 1937, and later taught English at the University of California, Berkeley and at San Francisco State University.

On June 8, 1918, Hinkle married Bliss McGlashan. The couple had three children, Sue Arden, Marilyn Joan, and Richard Gordon.

George Hinkle was a descendant of a long line of American pioneers, some of them early settlers in New England. For years, one of his grandfathers led a nomadic life, moving from mining camp to mining camp in the West, having left Sutter's Fort in the late 1850s. Hinkle's other grandfather was a circuit rider whose "parish" embraced 2,500 square miles and whose best returns when the collection plate was passed, according to family tradition, were often achieved in honky-tonks and gambling halls. Hinkle's chief scholarly interest was the transmission of folk legends as they affect history.

George Hinkle, who grew up in Truckee, had memories of performances of Shakespearean works and the Dumas play *Camille* in the town's opera house, which was above a saloon.

George Henry Hinkle died in San Francisco, California, on November 8, 1950, at age 54.

Bliss McGlashan Hinkle was born on June 6, 1896, in Truckee, California, the daughter of Charles Fayette McGlashan and Leonora Gertrude Keiser (Waterhouse) McGlashan. Her father was an attorney and editor.

Charles McGlashan is credited with preserving an accurate account of the Donner Party tragedy with his 1879 book, *The History of the Donner Party* (Truckee, Calif.: Crowley and McGlashan). George and Bliss Hinkle wrote the foreword and notes and assembled the bibliography of the 1947 Stanford University Press reissue of the book. *Sierra-Nevada Lakes* deals at length with the Donner Party in Chapters 4 and Chapter 5

At a high school in Elk Grove, California, Bliss Hinkle taught courses in English literature for many years. (She had earned a bachelor of arts degree from the University of California, Berkeley.) At the time she and her husband, George, wrote *Sierra-Nevada Lakes,* she was principal of the Tahoe Branch of Placer Union High School.

Bliss McGlashan Hinkle died in San Francisco, California, on September 23, 1949, at age 53.

PAPERS: George Henry Hinkle and Bliss McGlashan Hinkle papers, circa 1880-1950 are held by the University of California, Berkeley. The collection contains materials used to write *Sierra-Nevada Lakes.*

NOTES ON *SIERRA-NEVADA LAKES*

The book was included in the Bobbs-Merrill 1948 Fall List, with a planned publication date of November 1, 1948, but was not published until 1949. The January 29, 1949, *Publishers' Weekly* reported that the book would "include the history of Lake Tahoe and its neighbors, a long-neglected chapter of California history," and that there would be autographed first editions for pre-publication orders taken by bookstores in the region.

The Bobbs-Merrill 1949 Spring List announced a March 1949 publication date for the book. A full-page advertisement in the March 12, 1949, issue of *PW* reported a publication date of April 15, 1949, promoting the book as an "important new volume in the popular American Lakes Series." The advertisement emphasized the Hinkles' background, noting they "combine a thorough historical training with the intimate, almost instinctive knowledge that comes with having been born and brought up in the region."

REVIEWS

Booklist, May 14, 1949 (p. 310); *Christian Science Monitor,* May 16, 1949 (p. 12); *Commonweal,* August 12, 1949 (p. 445); *Library Journal,* April 1, 1949 (p.

545); *New York Herald Tribune Weekly Book Review,* April 17, 1949 (p. 3); *New York Times,* April 17, 1949 (p. 5); *San Francisco Chronicle,* May 8, 1949 (p. 18); *Saturday Review of Literature,* April 16, 1949 (p. 21); *Wisconsin Library Bulletin,* May 1949 (p. 87).

SELECTED WRITINGS BY GEORGE AND BLISS HINKLE

(Foreword, notes, and bibliography) *History of the Donner Party* (Stanford, Calif.: Stanford University Press, 1947); *Sierra-Nevada Lakes* (Indianapolis: Bobbs-Merrill, 1949).

SOURCES

Book Review Digest 1949. New York:: The H.W. Wilson Company, 1950, p. 421.

Publishers' Weekly, September 25, 1948, p. 1173; January 29, 1949, p. 343; January 29, 1949, p. 535; March 12, 1949, p. 1218; April 16, 1949, p. 1692.

Dust jacket, Editorial Introduction, and Authors' Prefatory Note, *Sierra-Nevada Lakes.*

Reno Gazette Journal obituary of Bliss Hinkle, September 29, 1949, n.p.

McGlashan, M. Nona. *Give Me A Mountain Meadow.* Fresno, Calif: Valley Publishers, 1977.

Earl, Phillip I. "This Was Nevada." [Las Vegas] *Review Journal.* Lifestyles, February 15, 1998, n.p.

McGlashan, Christney. E-mail messages to CF providing biographical information on the Hinkle family, 2002.

Scott, Larry, Department of Special Collections, Stanford University. E-mail message to CF regarding George Hinkle's academic degrees, February 10, 2003.

Maher, Michael, Librarian, Nevada Historical Society. Faxed letter to CF, with attachments, February 21, 2003.

Hinkle, Richard (son of George and Bliss Hinkle). Completed questionnaires providing biographical information on his parents. Received September 2, 2003.

The Bobbs-Merrill mss., 1885–1957. The Lilly Library, Indiana University, Bloomington, Indiana.

LAKE SUPERIOR

Grace Lee Nute
October 13, 1895 – May 10, 1990

AL10   First edition, first printing (1944) [2]

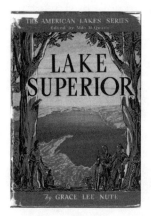

LAKE | SUPERIOR | GRACE LEE NUTE

The foregoing is printed on a green-and-white illustration, a large tree in the foreground at the right; a young woman on horseback and a hunter in buckskins and a fur cap to the left of the tree; other human figures and an ox-drawn covered wagon behind them and to their right; and a lake and scattered hills in the background.

COLLATION: 8½" x 6". 190 leaves. [a–b] [1–18] 19–109 [110-112] 113–212 [213–214] 215–287 [288–290] 291–350 [351–352] 353–359 [360–362] 363–376 [377–378]. All numbers printed in roman in headline at the outer margin of the type page, except for pp. 19, 37, 70, 83, 89, 113, 145, 171, 195, 215, 240, 275, 291, 320, 331, 353, 359, and 363, on which the numbers are printed in the center, at the foot of the page.

Note: Black-and-white double-sided leaves of photographs are inserted following pp. 40,[1] 72, 106, 134, 160, 188, 210, 232, 256, 284, and 316.

CONTENTS: p. [a], blank; p. [b], "THE AMERICAN LAKES SERIES | *Published:* | [list of three titles and their authors, beginning with *Lake Huron* and ending with *Lake Michigan*] | *In Preparation:* | [list of two titles and their authors: *Lake Ontario* and *Lake Erie*]; p. [1], half title: "LAKE SUPERIOR"; p. [2], series title: "[set within a green and white illustration of an Indian campsite above a lake; a large tree in the foreground at the left; Indian figures beside the tree and down the hill to their left; a lake and scattered hills in the background] The | AMERICAN | LAKES SERIES | Edited by Milo M. Quaife | THE BOBBS-MERRILL COMPANY | Publishers | INDIANAPOLIS · NEW YORK"; p. [3], title; p. [4], copyright page, "COPYRIGHT, 1944, BY THE

1. A reproduction of an early map of Lake Superior faces p. 40.

BOBBS-MERRILL COMPANY | PRINTED IN THE UNITED STATES | *First Edition*"; p. [5], dedication: "*To* | THOSE WHO TRY TO KEEP THE FORESTS GREEN, | THE LAKES FULL, AND WILD LIFE | PRESENT ABOUT THE SHORES | OF LAKE SUPERIOR"; p. [6], blank; pp. [7–8], "EDITORIAL INTRODUCTION [signed M.M. Quaife, Detroit Public Library]"; pp. [9–11], "BIG SEA-WATER"; p. [12], blank; pp. [13–14], Contents; p. [15], "LIST OF ILLUSTRATIONS"; p. [16], blank; p. [17], "Part I | FOOTPRINTS ON THE SANDS OF TIME"; p. [18], blank; pp. 19–109, text; p. [110], blank; p. [111], "Part II | VULCAN'S SHOP AND NEPTUNE'S REALM"; p. [112], blank; pp. 113–212, text; p. [213], "Part III | THE CORD OF THE BOW"; p. [214], blank; pp. 215–287, text; p. [288], blank; p. [289], "Part IV | AN ARC OF ROCKS"; p. [290], blank; pp. 291–327, text; p. [328], blank; p. [329], "Part V | RED AND WHITE ART"; p. [330], blank; pp. 331–350, text; p. [351], blank; p. [352], "BIBLIOGRAPHICAL NOTE | AND | ACKNOWLEDGMENTS"; pp. 353–358, "BIBLIOGRAPHICAL NOTE"; p. 359, "ACKNOWLEDGMENTS"; p. [360], blank; p. [361], "INDEX"; p. [362], blank; pp. 363–376, Index; pp. [377–378], blank.

BINDING: Forest-green cloth (close to Pantone 343), stamped in gold. Front: "THE AMERICAN LAKE SERIES | [outline of the Great Lakes, with Lake Superior highlighted]ʻ | LAKE SUPERIOR". Spine: "LAKE | SUPERIOR | — | GRACE | LEE | NUTE | [at bottom] BOBBS | MERRILL". Front endpapers carry a double-page map attributed to W. R. Lohse in gold and white, titled "Map of Lake Superior," with an inset on the upper left page titled "The Cities of Duluth, Minn. and Superior, Wis." Rear endpapers carry a double-page map attributed to W.R Lohse in gold and white, titled "Map of the Great Lakes".

DUST JACKET (white paper): Front and spine carry an illustration attributed to W.R. Lohse of two large trees in the foreground framing a group of three, a frontiersman, a soldier, and an Indian, to the right, an ox-drawn covered wagon behind them, and other Indians to the left, where a tepee stands in front of a third large tree, a stylized depiction of Lake Superior in the background. Front: "[at top, within a red band, which wraps to the spine, in white] THE AMERICAN LAKES SERIES | Edited by Milo M. Quaife | [illustration] | [at bottom, within a red band, which wraps to the spine, in white] *by* GRACE LEE NUTE". Spine: "[within the top red band, in white] LAKE | SUPERIOR | [illustration] | [within the bottom red band, in white] NUTE | *Bobbs Merrill*". Back: "[within a rectangular frame bordered by thin/thick rules] THE AMERICAN LAKES SERIES | *under the general editorship of* | MILO M. QUAIFE | [four-paragraph blurb] | *Published* | [list of three titles and their authors, with brief biographical information, beginning with *Lake Huron,* and ending with *Lake Michigan*] | *In Preparation* | [list of two titles and their authors, with brief biographical information: *Lake Ontario* and *Lake Erie*]". Front flap: "LAKE SUPERIOR | [blurb] | *(Continued on back flap)* | [at bottom right] $3.50". Back flap: "*(Continued from front flap)* | [blurb]".

Published at $3.50 on July 31, 1944; number of copies printed unknown. Copyrighted August 2, 1944; deposited July 1, 1944.[2]

The book is listed in "The Weekly Record," July 29, 1944, p. 341.

Note: No evidence found that Bobbs-Merrill reprinted *Lake Superior.*

COPIES: CF

AL10a First edition, Special Autographed Edition (1944)

Lake Superior was issued with a special publisher's autograph page, signed by the author, tipped in following the front free endpaper. The number of such copies issued has not been determined.

REPRINTS AND REPRODUCTIONS

Reproduced on microfilm. New Haven, CT: Yale University Library, 1993. 1 reel. 35 mm.

Minneapolis: University of Minnesota Press. Paperback. Published at $15.95 in May 2000.

BIOGRAPHY

Grace Lee Nute was born on October 13, 1895, in North Conway, in the White Mountains of New Hampshire. Her family had been associated with New Hampshire for decades, going back to 1631. "According to tradition fortified somewhat by the family coat of arms in England," she wrote, the family was descended from the Danish king, Canute.[3] Canute led the Norse forces invading England and reigned as King of England from 1016 to 1035.

Nute studied at Fryeburg Academy in Maine and the Westfield State Normal School in Massachusetts. She earned a bachelor's degree from Smith

2. An apparent misprint in records at the Library of Congress. *Lake Superior* and *Lake Michigan* have consecutive copyright numbers, 182097 and 182098. But copyright records for *Lake Michigan* carry a date of deposit of July 10, 1944. July 1, 1944, was a Saturday, not a regular workday at the Library of Congress. July 10, 1944, was a Monday, a regular workday. The actual date of deposit of *Lake Superior* was almost certainly July 10.
3. "Grace Lee Nute," in *Minnesota Writers: A Collection of Autobiographical Stories by Minnesota Prose Writers*, Denison,1961, p. 325.

College in 1917, with a major in English. At Radcliffe College of Harvard University, she specialized in American history, earning a master's degree in 1918 and a doctorate in 1921. While at Radcliffe, she studied under the direction of the historian Frederick Jackson Turner for four years. In 1921, with Turner's encouragement, Nute became head of the newly created manuscript division at the Minnesota Historical Society. In 1946, she became a research associate there. She retired in 1957.

From 1927 to 1960, Nute was a history professor at Hamline University in St. Paul and lectured at the University of Minnesota and Macalester College. In 1943, she received an honorary doctorate in letters from Hamline.

Nute studied the science of historical manuscripts and the physics and chemistry of photography. She was a pioneer in the use of microfilm and photocopying to preserve manuscripts, and wrote manuals on the subject.

Her first book, *The Voyageur* (Appleton), was published in 1931. She received a Guggenheim Fellowship in 1934, and spent a year in Europe. Her book *Caesars of the Wilderness: Medard Chouart, Sieur Des Groesilliers, and Pierre Esprit Radisson, 1618-1710* (Appleton), which she described as a joint biography of Minnesota's first known white explorers, Radisson and Des Groesilliers, was published in 1943. A student of history, natural history, biography, and historical manuscripts, Nute wrote books, brochures, and articles in all those fields.

In 1938, she traveled to Sweden to research Charles Lindbergh's ancestry.[4] Her book on the subject, tentatively entitled *From Father to Son*, was never published. She won a Ford Foundation grant in 1945 and an Award of Merit from the Western History Association in 1981. From 1960 until 1966, she was director of the James J. Hill papers project at the James J. Hill Reference Library in St. Paul.[5]

Grace Lee Nute died on May 4, 1990, in Menlo Park, California, at age 94.

PAPERS: Nute's papers, 1924-1945, 1957 are held by the Minnesota Historical Society, St. Paul, Minnesota.

NOTES ON *LAKE SUPERIOR*

In *1945*, in *Minnesota Writes*, Nute wrote, "My most recent book is also my most successful financially — *Lake Superior*. It, like *The Voyageur's Highway*, is a true labor of love. I fell under the spell of the great lake from the moment I first glimpsed it. Oddly, no book had ever been written about it when I engaged myself in 1942 to prepare a volume on it in the *American*

4. Charles A. Lindbergh (1902-1974) American aviator, author, inventor, and explorer.
5. James J. Hill (1838-1916) Minnesota railway magnate.

Lakes series. That summer and the following one I spent largely on the lake or its shore, growing more fascinated with every passing week."[6]

The book did not receive any special promotion, only the notice of its intended publication in the February 19, 1944, issue of *Publishers' Weekly.*

REVIEWS

Annals of the American Academy, January 1945 (p. 228); *Booklist,* September 1944 (p. 17); *Kirkus,* July 15, 1944 (p. 310); *Library Journal,* October 1, 1944 (p. 818); *New York Herald Tribune Weekly Book Review,* July 30, 1944 (p. 1); *New York Times,* August 27, 1944(p. 17); *New Yorker,* August 12, 1944 (p. 62); *Saturday Review of Literature,* October 28, 1944 (p. 24); *Springfield Republican,* July 30, 1944 (p. 4-D); *Weekly Book Review,* July 30, 1944 (p. 1); *Wisconsin Library Bulletin,* October 1944 (p. 129).

SELECTED WRITINGS BY GRACE LEE NUTE

The Voyageur (New York: Appleton, 1931); *The Voyageur's Highway: Minnesota's Border Lake Land* (St. Paul: Minnesota Historical Society, 1941); *Caesars of the Wilderness: Medard Chouart, Sieur Des Groesilliers and Pierre Esprit Radisson, 1618-1710* (New York: Appleton, 1943); **Lake Superior** (Indianapolis: Bobbs-Merrill, 1944); *Calendar of the American Fur Trader's Papers* (Washington, D.C.: U.S. Government Printing Office, 1945); *Rainy River Country: A Brief History of the Region Bordering Minnesota and Ontario* (St. Paul: Minnesota Historical Society, 1950); *A History of Minnesota Books and Authors* (Minneapolis: University of Minnesota Press, 1958).

SOURCES

Book Review Digest 1944. New York: The H.W. Wilson Company, 1945, pp. 565-566.

Publishers' Weekly, February 19, 1944, p. 837; and July 29, 1944, p. 341.

New York Herald Tribune Weekly Book Review, July 30, 1944, (p. 1).

The New York Times Book Review, August 27, 1944, p. 17.

Richards, Carmen Nelson, and Genevieve Rose Breen, eds. *Minnesota Writes: A Collection of Autobiographical Stories by Minnesota Prose Writers.* Minneapolis: The Lund Press, Inc. 1945, pp. 120-127.

Richards, Carmen Nelson, ed. *Minnesota Writers: A Collection of Autobio-*

---

6. *Minnesota Writes,* p. 125.

5

graphical Stories by Minnesota Prose Writers. Minneapolis: T.S. Denison & Company, Inc. 1961, pp. 225–229.

The New York Times obituary, May 16, 1990, p. B8.

Contemporary Authors Online. The Gale Group, 2000. Reproduced in *Biography Resource Center.* Farmington Hills, Mich.: The Gale Group, 2001. Accessed February 14, 2002.

Barrett, Andrea (Minnesota Historical Society, Project Coordinator), Minnesota Author Biographies Project: Grace Lee Nute. Minneapolis Historical Society, 1999. http://people.mnhs.org/authors Accessed March 7, 2002.

The Bobbs-Merrill mss., 1885–1957. The Lilly Library, Indiana University, Bloomington, Indiana.

Regional Murder Series
1944–1948

Marie F. Rodell
General Editor

Duell, Sloan & Pearce
Publisher

1944
New York Murders

1945
Chicago Murders

1946
Denver Murders

1947
San Francisco Murders
Los Angeles Murders
Cleveland Murders
Charleston Murders

1948
Detroit Murders
Boston Murders

REGIONAL MURDER SERIES
Introduction and Publishing History

D
UELL, Sloan & Pearce announced a series of non-fictional books reporting on murders in the February 26, 1944, issue of *Publishers' Weekly*, with publication to begin in the fall of the year. Each title would feature the name of the city where the murders had occurred. Murder cases that had been "examined too often in the past" would be avoided unless new light could be shed on them. Although three titles, San Francisco, Chicago, and New York, were named, neither the series title nor the editor, Marie F. Rodell, was mentioned in the announcement.

Rodell, a literary agent, editor, mystery novelist, and the author of a textbook on mystery fiction writing, was head of the Bloodhound Mysteries department at Duell, Sloan & Pearce at the time. The series eventually included nine titles published from 1944 to 1948, each styled A *Bloodhound Book*.

San Francisco Murders had been announced as the first series title but the schedule was changed. *New York Murders*, edited by Ted Collins, was published on October 27, 1944.

One series title was published in 1945: *Chicago Murders*, edited by Sewell Peaslee Wright, on June 6.

One series title was published in 1946: *Denver Murders*, edited by Lee Casey, on April 24.

Four series titles were published in 1947: *San Francisco Murders*, edited by Joseph Henry Jackson, on May 21; *Los Angeles Murders*, edited by Craig Rice, on June 11; *Cleveland Murders*, edited by Oliver Weld Bayer, on October 9; and *Charleston Murders*, edited by Beatrice St. J. Ravenel, on October 30.

The final titles in the series were published in 1948: *Detroit Murders*, edited by Alvin C. Hammer, on April 21 and *Boston Murders*, edited by John N. Makris, on September 22.

Each series title included the editor's preface summarizing the cases reported in the book or explaining how they were chosen and, occasionally, mentioning cases that were not chosen. Each case is the subject of a chapter in the book, with the chapter's author or authors named. Sixty-six authors contributed to the series. In four titles, the editor wrote a chapter in the book. Many of the authors were journalists who had covered murders or murder trials in their careers. The nine titles contain a total of sixty-nine chapters.

The award of an "Edgar" is reported in a number of the biographical sketches. The Edgar Allan Poe Awards — the Edgars — are made by the Mystery Writers of America (MWA) to authors of distinguished work in various categories of the mystery genre. Other MWA awards that recognize achievements in the mystery field include the Grand Master Award, the Ellery Queen Award, the Raven Award, the Robert L. Fish Memorial Award, and the Mary Higgins Clark Award. In 1949, Marie F. Rodell received an Edgar for her editorship of the *Regional Murder Series*.

∽

MARIE F. RODELL
Editor, *Regional Murder Series*
January 31, 1912 – November 9, 1975

Marie Freid Rodell was born on January 31, 1912. She was a graduate of Vassar College and headed the Bloodhound Mysteries department at Duell, Sloan & Pearce from 1939 to 1948.

As a literary agent, Rodell represented Rachel Carson, Joseph Alsop, Stewart Alsop, Barry Commoner, Christopher and Oliver La Farge, Philip Van Doren Stern, and other writers. She wrote a textbook, *Mystery Fiction: Theory and Technique* (Duell, Sloan & Pearce, 1943). Under the pseudonym Marion Randolph, she wrote three mystery novels: *Breathe No More* (1940), *This'll Kill You* (1940), and *Grim Grow the Lilacs* (1941), all published by Henry Holt & Co.

Rodell was a co-founder of the Mystery Writers of America (MWA) in 1945 and one of its first four officers. She was present at the creation of the organization at a luncheon meeting with Lawrence Treat and Clayton Rawson. After some discussion there of "British crime writers who met irregularly and had a ritual involving a pledge always to play fair with their readers and to make various other promises for the good of their craft," the MWA was conceived.[1]

In 1941, Rodell wrote a long article, "Murder for Rent, Murder for Sale" in *Publishers' Weekly*, arguing that mystery novels could create a broader and more lucrative market, first, by increasing the standard price of the mystery novel, two dollars, by fifty cents, and second, by increasing the sales of such novels to public libraries, raising the numbers of a given mystery novel on library shelves from two to "four or eight or twelve," thereby "renting" the books to more people.[2]

In 1948, Rodell founded a literary agency in Manhattan which later became the Rodell-Frances-Collins agency. In 1949, she won a Special Edgar Award for her editorship of the *Regional Murder Series*.

Marie Rodell died on November 9, 1975, in New York City, at age 63.

1. Zeman, Barry and Angela. "Mystery Writers of America: A Historical Survey." www.mysterywriters.org.
2. *Publishers' Weekly*, January 15, 1941, pp. 828–830.

BOSTON MURDERS

Edited by John N. Makris
1916 – December 12, 1975

RM1   First edition, first printing (1948) [9]

Boston I *MURDERS* I [thin rule] I *by* I MARJORIE CARLETON I LAWRENCE DAME I TIMOTHY FULLER I JAMES A. KELLEY I WILLIAM SCHOFIELD I PAUL WHELTON I *and* I JOHN N. MAKRIS, *editor* I [thin rule] I [Bloodhound device] I NEW YORK I *DUELL, SLOAN AND PEARCE*

COLLATION: 8" x 5½". 112 leaves. [1–6] 7–11 [12–14] 15–39 [40–42] 43–77 [78–80] 81–110 [111–112] 113–129 [130–132] 133–148 [149–150] 151–172 [173–174] 175–207 [208] 209–223 [224]. Numbers printed in roman in the center at the foot of the page.

CONTENTS: p. [1], half–title:"[within a rectangle] Boston Murders"; p. [2], series title: "*Regional* I *MURDER SERIES* I EDITED BY I MARIE F. RODELL I [thin rule] I Vol. I. NEW YORK MURDERS I Vol. II. CHICAGO MURDERS I Vol. III. DENVER MURDERS I Vol. IV. SAN FRANCISCO MURDERS I Vol. V. LOS ANGELES MURDERS I Vol. VI. CLEVELAND MURDERS I Vol. VII. CHARLESTON MURDERS I Vol. VIII. DETROIT MURDERS I Vol. IX. BOSTON MURDERS I [Bloodhound device]"; p. [3], title; p. [4], copyright page: "Copyright, 1948, by I Duell, Sloan & Pearce, Inc. I All rights reserved, including the I right to reproduce this book or I portions thereof in any form. I first printing I Printed in the United States of America"; p. [5], "*CONTENTS*"; p. [6], blank; pp. 7–11, *Preface* [signed John N. Makris]"; p. [12], blank; p. [13], "*1845* I '*Maria Met a Gentleman*' I [within a rectangle] The Bickford Case I [below rectangle] by I Marjorie Carleton I [brief biographical sketch of Carleton]"; p. [14], blank; pp. 15–39, text; p. [40], blank; p. [41], "*1908* I '*Twelve Parts of a Lady*' I [within a rectangle] The Chester S. Jordan Case I [below rectangle] by I Paul Whelton I [brief biographical sketch of Whelton]"; p. [42], blank; pp. 43–77, text; p. [78], blank; p. [79], "*1913* I '*He Fought to Kill*' I [within a rectangle] The Kid Carter Case I [below rectangle] I by I William G. Schofield I [brief biographical sketch of

Schofield]"; p. [80], blank; pp. 81–110, text; p. [111], "*1918* I 'A Man of Too Much Distinction' I [within a rectangle] The Harry Manster Case I [below the rectangle] by I Timothy Fuller I [brief biographical sketch of Fuller]"; p. [112], blank; pp. 113–129, text; p. [130], blank; p. [131], "*1924* I 'The Haunted Man' I [within a rectangle] The Kearney Case I [below rectangle] by I Lawrence Dame I [brief biographical sketch of Dame]"; p. [132], blank; pp. 133–148, text; p. [149], "*1925* I 'The Brown Derby Murder' I [within a rectangle] The Corey-Price Case I [below rectangle] by I James A. Kelley I [brief biographical sketch of Kelley]"; p. [150], blank; pp. 151–172, text; p. [173], "*1927* I 'Who Killed Fantasia?' I [within a rectangle] The Joseph Fantasia Case I [below rectangle] by I John N. Makris I [brief biographical sketch of Makris]"; p. [174], blank; pp. 175–207, text; p. [208], blank; pp. 209–220, "*A Calendar of Boston Murder Trials*"; pp. 221–223, "*Bibliography*"; p. [224], blank.

BINDING: Red paperboards (close to Pantone 201) with black cloth quarter panel on front, spine, and back; stamped in red. Spine: "[read vertically] BOSTON MURDERS I [read horizontally] I [Bloodhound device] I DUELL, SLOAN I AND PEARCE". Cream endpapers.

DUST JACKET (white paper): Front carries a black-and-white photograph of a Boston Street; a church or town hall with a steeple featured in the foreground. Front: "[orange (close to Pantone 152)] BOSTON MURDERS I By I Marjorie Carleton, Lawrence Dame, I Timothy Fuller, James A. Kelley, I William G. Schofield, Paul Whelton I *and* John N. Makris, *Editor*". Spine: "[Bloodhound device] I [read vertically] [orange background; printing in black] BOSTON MURDERS I [read horizontally] I Duell, I Sloan I and I Pearce". Back: White background; printing in black. "[list naming the editor and the six authors, with a brief biographical sketch of each]". Front flap: "[upper right] $3.00 I BOSTON MURDERS I by I Marjorie Carleton, Lawrence Dame, I Timothy Fuller, James A. Kelley, I William G. Schofield, Paul Whelton I and John N. Makris, *Editor* I [blurb] I *A Bloodhound Book* I [publisher's imprint]". Back flap: "REGIONAL MURDER SERIES I [list of the nine titles, their editors, and the price of each book] I [publisher's imprint]".

Published at $3.00 on September 22, 1948; number of copies printed unknown. Copyrighted October 1, 1948; deposited September 21, 1948.

The book is listed in "The Weekly Record," November 4, 1948, p. 985.

Note: No evidence found that Duell, Sloan & Pearce reprinted *Boston Murders*.

COPIES: CF

REPRINTS AND REPRODUCTIONS

None.

BIOGRAPHIES[1]

John N. Makris (1916 –December 12, 1975), editor of *Boston Murders* and the author of a chapter in the book, was born in Watertown, Massachusetts. He sold his first crime story when he was sixteen and later wrote hundreds of such stories. In 1938, he began writing in the true-crime field, later becoming a detective. When *Boston Murders* was published in 1948, Makris had recently served as special investigator for the defense in two murder cases. Makris wrote *The Silent Investigators: The Great Untold Story of the United States Postal Inspection Service* (Dutton, 1959).

Marjorie Carleton (?? – June 4, 1964), a 1917 graduate of Smith College, was a writer, playwright, novelist, pianist, and composer. She wrote nine novels, four plays, and musical compositions. Her best-known novel is *Cry Wolf* (Morrow, 1945). In 1957, she was nominated for an Edgar Award for her novel *The Night of the Good Children* (Morrow, 1957). During World War II, she was a member of the reviewing staff of the *Boston Herald*, writing as many as forty book reviews in a year. Her stories appeared in *Redbook*, *Cosmopolitan*, and other popular magazines. Some of Carleton's musical compositions were broadcast on radio and at least one was performed by the Boston Symphony Orchestra. She was a member of the New England Woman's Press Association, the Professional Women's Club of Boston, and the Boston Authors Club.

Lawrence Dame (July 2, 1898 – May 27, 1981), a journalist, worked for the *Paris Tribune* and the *New York Times*. When *Boston Murders* was published in 1948, he was art editor of the *Boston Herald* and an editorial writer for the *Boston Traveler*. In the early 1950s, he was a staff critic at *Art News* in London and wrote for newspapers in Turkey and Italy. He was briefly associate editor of the *Nantucket Inquirer and Mirror* before moving to Florida, where he was arts and book critic for *Palm Beach Illustrated*, writing as "Baron Pomfret." He was later art editor of the *Palm Beach Post*. Dame wrote three nonfiction books: *New England Comes Back* (Random House, 1940), *Yucatan* (Random House, 1941), and *Maya Mission* (Doubleday, 1968), and was a contributor to newspapers and magazines in the United States and Europe.

---

1. Where birth or death dates are not stated, the information was not found.

Timothy Fuller (November 22, 1914 – May 2, 1971) was born in Newton, Massachusetts. He left Harvard in his junior year to write *Harvard Has A Homicide* (Little, Brown, 1936), the first mystery novel ever serialized in the *Atlantic Monthly*. From 1941 to 1950, he wrote four mystery novels: *Reunion With Murder* (1941), *Three Thirds of a Ghost* (1941), *This is Murder, Mr. Jones* (1943), and *Keep Cool, Mr. Jones* (1950), all published by Little, Brown. His short stories were published in popular magazines.

James A. Kelley (September 4, 1908 – October 13, 1980) was a reporter who worked at the *Boston Herald* and the *Boston Traveler*. During his 43 years with the *Traveler*, he worked on most of the major stories of his time; among them were the Domenick Bonomi murder trial in 1956 and the sinking of the submarine Squalus in 1939. When *Boston Murders* was published in 1948, Kelley had covered crime, including many major New England crimes, for twenty years. He was also a photographer and lecturer. A yachting enthusiast, he wrote articles on yachts and yachting.

William G. Schofield (June 13, 1909 – April 1, 1996) attended Brown University from 1927 to 1930. He began his newspaper career in Providence. Later, after living and writing for a while in New Orleans and Mexico, he returned to Rhode Island. From 1936 to 1940, he was a feature writer for the *Providence Journal*. He was a columnist at the *Boston Traveler* (1940–1942) and (1946–1967). During World War II, he served in the Navy (1942–1946), rising to the rank of lieutenant commander. In the years 1952 to 1967, he was the *Traveler*'s chief editorial writer. He left the *Traveler* in 1967, joining the Raytheon Company as manager of editorial services. He was later associate director of public information and an editorial consultant for Boston University. Schofield founded the Freedom Trail, the historic tour of Boston. He wrote or was co-author of twelve books, including works of non-fiction, among them *Freedom by the Bay: The Boston Freedom Trail* (Rand McNally, 1974).

Paul Whelton (1895? – April 23, 1953) worked in city rooms and was a crime reporter in Boston, New York, and Los Angeles for thirty years. When *Boston Murders* was published in 1948, he was a writer for the *Boston Daily Record and Sunday Advertiser* and had written hundreds of factual accounts of murder for newspapers. From 1944 to 1951, he wrote six mystery novels in the "Garry Dean" series. In World War I, he was an Army aviator.

NOTES ON *BOSTON MURDERS*

The book was included in the Duell, Sloan & Pearce 1948 Fall List, with no publication date noted. There was no statement in the book, the last title in the series, of a title or titles in preparation, as there had been in the earlier titles in the series.

REVIEWS

Chicago Sun Book Week, September 24, 1948 (n.p.); *Kirkus*, September 1, 1948 (p. 461); *New York Herald Tribune Weekly Book Review*, November 28, 1948 (p. 34); *New Yorker*, September 25, 1948 (p. 119); *San Francisco Chronicle*, September 26, 1948 (p. 23); *Springfield Republican*, September 26, 1948 (p. 10–B).

SOURCES

Book Review Digest 1948. New York: The H.W. Wilson Company, 1949, pp. 545–546.

Publishers' Weekly, September 4, 1948, p. 985; and September 25, 1948 (Duell, Sloan and Pearce Fall List) p. 1203.

(Carleton) Class of 1917 Records, 25th Reunion Book, Smith College Archives. Special thanks to Nanci A. Young, College Archivist.

(Carleton) *The New York Times* obituary, June 5, 1964.

(Dame) *Contemporary Authors Online*, Gale, 2006. Reproduced in Biography Resource Center. Farmington Hills, Mich.: Thomson Gale. 2006. Accessed July 21, 2006.

(Kelley) *Boston Globe* obituary, October 15, 1980.

(Makris) *Boston Globe* obituary, December 15, 1975.

(Schofield) *Contemporary Authors Online*, Gale, 2006. Reproduced in Biography Resource Center. Farmington Hills, Mich.: Thomson Gale. 2006. Accessed July 21, 2006.

(Whelton) *The New York Times* obituary, April 24, 1953.

Boston Murders, biographical sketches in the book and on the dust jacket.

CHARLESTON MURDERS

Edited by Beatrice St. Julien Ravenel
October 2, 1904 – December 2, 1990

RM2   First edition, first printing (1947) [7]

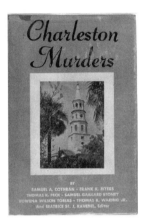

Charleston | *MURDERS* | [thin rule] | *by* | SAMUEL A. COTHRAN | FRANK K. MYERS | THOMAS K. PECK | SAMUEL GAILLARD STONEY | ROWENA WILSON TOBIAS | THOMAS R. WARING JR. | *and* | BEATRICE ST. J. RAVENEL, *editor* | [thin rule] | [Bloodhound device] | NEW YORK | *DUELL, SLOAN AND PEARCE*

COLLATION: 8" x 5½". 112 leaves. [i–viii] 1–8 [9–10] 11–38 [39–40] 41–68 [69–70] 71–107 [108–110] 111–129 [130–132] 133–158 [159–160] 161–188 [189–190] 191–216. Numbers printed in roman in the center at the foot of the page.

CONTENTS: p. [i], half-title:*"Charleston* | *MURDERS"*; p. [ii], series title: *"Regional* | *MURDER SERIES* | EDITED BY | MARIE F. RODELL | [thin rule] | Vol. I NEW YORK MURDERS | Vol. II CHICAGO MURDERS | Vol. III DENVER MURDERS | Vol. IV SAN FRANCISCO MURDERS | Vol. V LOS ANGELES MURDERS | Vol. VI CLEVELAND MURDERS | Vol. VII CHARLESTON MURDERS | [Bloodhound device] | *In Preparation* | DETROIT MURDERS | BOSTON MURDERS"; p. [iii], title; p. [iv], copyright page: "Copyright, 1947, by | Duell, Sloan & Pearce Inc. | All rights reserved, including the | right to reproduce this book or | portions thereof in any form. | first printing | Printed in the United States of America"; p. [v], "*CONTENTS*"; p. [vi], blank; p. [vii], half-title:*"Charleston* | *MURDERS"*; p. [viii], blank; pp. 1–8, *"Preface"*; p. [9], "*1788* | [within a rectangle] The Footpad's Memorial | [below rectangle] by | Samuel Gaillard Stoney | [brief biographical sketch of Stoney]"; p. [10], blank; pp. 11–38, text; p. [39], "*1819* | [within a rectangle] Lovely Lavinia | and the Drunken Hangman | [below rectangle] by | Beatrice St. J. Ravenel | [brief biographical sketch of Ravenel]"; p. [40], blank; pp. 41–68, text; p. [69], "*1889* | [within a rectangle] The Killing | of Captain Dawson | [below rectangle] | by | Thomas K. Peck | [brief biographical sketch of Peck]"; p. [70], blank; pp. 71–107, text; p. [108], blank; p. [109], "*1927* | [within a rectangle] Self Defense from Ambush | [below the rectangle] by | Thomas R. Waring Jr. | [brief biographical sketch of Waring]"; p. [110], blank; pp. 111–129, text; p. [130], blank; p. [131], "*1928* | [within a rectangle] The Annapolis Graduate | and the Country Boy | [below rectangle] by | Frank K. Myers | [brief biographical sketch of Myers]"; p. [132], blank; pp. 133–158, text; p. [159], "*1935* | [within a rectangle] God's Avenging Angel | [below rectangle] by | Rowena Wilson Tobias | [brief biographical sketch of Tobias]"; p. [160], blank; pp. 161–188, text; p. [189], "*1936* | [within a rectangle] First Come, First Serve | [below rectangle] by | Samuel A. Cothran | [brief biographical sketch of Cothran]"; p. [190], blank; pp. 191–216, text.

BINDING: Blue-gray cloth (close to Pantone 444); navy blue quarter cloth (close to Pantone 444) on front, spine, and back, stamped in yellow. Spine: "[read vertically] *Charleston Murders* | [read horizontally] | [Bloodhound device] | DUELL, SLOAN | AND PEARCE". Cream endpapers.

DUST JACKET (cream paper): Front and spine have a dark rose background (close to Pantone 197). Front: "[black] *Charleston* | *Murders* | [black-and-white photograph of St. Michael's Church, in Charleston, taken by Thomas K. Peck, set on a white rectangle] | [below photograph, in white] BY | SAMUEL A. COTHRAN · FRANK K. MYERS | THOMAS K. PECK · SAMUEL GAILLARD STONEY | ROWENA WILSON TOBIAS · THOMAS R. WARING JR. | And BEATRICE ST. J. RAVENEL, Editor". Spine: "[black] [Bloodhound device] | [read vertically] *Charleston Murders* | [read horizontally, in white] Duell, Sloan | and | Pearce". Back: White background; printing in black. "[list naming the editor and the six authors, with a brief biographical sketch of each]". Front flap: "[upper right] $3.00 | CHARLESTON MURDERS | *by* | Samuel A. Cothran, Frank K. Myers, | Thomas K. Peck, Samuel Gaillard | Stoney, Rowena Wilson Tobias, | Thomas R. Waring, Jr., and | Beatrice St. J. Ravenel, *editor* | [blurb] | *A Bloodhound Book* | [publisher's imprint]". Back flap: "REGIONAL MURDER SERIES | NEW YORK MURDERS | [list of authors and price] | CHICAGO MURDERS | [list of authors and price] | DENVER MURDERS | [list of authors and price] | SAN FRANCISCO MURDERS | [list of authors and price] | LOS ANGELES MURDERS | [list of authors and price] | CLEVELAND MURDERS | [list of authors and price] | *In Preparation* | DETROIT MURDERS | BOSTON MURDERS | [publisher's imprint] | [lower left, on the diagonal] CHARLESTON MURDERS | Duell | $3.00".

Published at $3.00 on October 30, 1947; number of copies printed unknown. Copyrighted and deposited October 30, 1947.

The book is listed in "The Weekly Record," November 1, 1947, p. 2225.

Note: No evidence found that Duell, Sloan &Pearce reprinted *Charleston Murders*.

COPIES: CF

REPRINTS AND REPRODUCTIONS

None.

BIOGRAPHIES[1]

Beatrice St. J. (Julien) Ravenel (October 2, 1904 – December 2, 1990), editor of *Charleston Murders* and the author of a chapter in the book, was born in Charleston, South Carolina, and graduated from the College of Charleston. When *Charleston Murders* was published in 1947, she was book editor and a reporter for the *Charleston News and Courier*. Ravenel wrote *Architects of Charleston* (Charleston: Carolina Art Association, 1946) and articles for *Antiques* magazine.

Samuel A. Cothran (December 13, 1915 –), as a student at Davidson College, worked as a correspondent for the *Charlotte Observer* and the *Greenwood Index Journal*. He completed a postgraduate course in journalism at the University of South Carolina, and started as a police reporter at the *Charleston News and Courier* in 1939. In World War II, he joined the Army in 1941, serving in the infantry and rising to lieutenant colonel. After his Army service, he rejoined the paper. He became managing editor in 1960. In 1968, Cothran became editor and publisher of the *Aiken* (South Carolina) *Standard and Review*, a morning paper with a circulation of 4,000 and a minuscule staff. In 1989, when Cothran retired at age seventy-three, the paper, renamed the *Aiken Standard*, had a staff of ninety-three and circulation of sixteen thousand.

Frank K. Myers (May 24, 1907–June 17, 1977) was born in Charleston, South Carolina, the son of a Charleston attorney and federal judge of the same name. He was a graduate of the University of North Carolina. A former state news editor for the *Augusta* (Georgia) *Chronicle*, he covered dozens of sensational murder trials. Myers served in the Marine Corps during World War II, joining the *Charleston News and Courier* after his return to civilian life. When *Charleston Murders* was published in 1947, Myers was assistant state news editor of the paper.

Thomas K. Peck (February 20, 1913 – October 31, 1971) was born in Utica,

1. Where birth or death dates are not stated, the information was not found.

New York. He moved to New York City at an early age and in 1931 was a police reporter on the staff of the *New York Herald Tribune*. He later worked for two years as a reporter and photographer for the *Buffalo Times*. In 1935, he became a photographer for the Washington, D.C. studio Harris and Ewing, covering government events. In 1936, after moving to Charleston, Peck joined the *Charleston News and Courier* as a photographer. In 1943, he became telegraph editor and, in 1955, Sunday editor. In 1957, he moved to the *Charleston Evening Post* as assistant state editor and later became assistant telegraph editor. His photograph of St. Michael's Church is featured on the dust jacket of *Charleston Murders*.

Samuel Gaillard Stoney (August 29, 1891 – July 1968) an architect and novelist, was a student of South Carolina's low country architecture. He was born in Charleston and graduated from the College of Charleston. After studying architecture in Georgia and working as an architect in Atlanta and New York, he returned to Charleston, where he wrote *Charleston, Azaleas and Old Bricks* (Houghton, Mifflin, 1937); *Plantations of the Carolina Low Country* (Carolina Art Association, 1939); and *This is Charleston* (Carolina Art Association, 1944). With Gertrude Shelby , he wrote *Black Genesis* (Macmillan, 1930) and a novel, *Po' Buckra* (Macmillan, 1930).

Rowena Wilson Tobias (Tarshish) (November 6, 1912 – December 1975) was born in Waycross, Georgia, and graduated from the University of Georgia. She wrote feature articles for the *New York Times* and worked for the *Savannah Morning News* and the *Charleston Evening Post*. She was the drama critic and literary editor of the *Charleston News and Courier*.

Thomas R. Waring Jr. (May 30, 1907 – March 8, 1993) had a fifty-year career as a journalist. In 1927, after graduating from the University of the South, in Sewanee, Tennessee, he worked for the *Charleston News and Courier*. In 1929, he moved to New York and worked on the city staff of the *New York Herald Tribune*. In 1931, he returned to Charleston and became city editor of the *Charleston News and Courier*, and, in 1942, managing editor. In 1974, he became editor of the (Charleston) *Evening Post*; a position his father, Thomas R. Waring, had held from 1897 to 1935. He retired in 1977.

NOTES ON *CHARLESTON MURDERS*

The book was included in Duell, Sloan & Pearce's 1947 Fall List with no publication date noted.

The *Saturday Review of Literature* included the book in a section titled "The Criminal Record," the magazine's guide to detective fiction. The book was given a "verdict" of "Informative," noting that it was liberally "splashed with Ca'lina color, enlivened with such monikers as Rumpty Rattles, amply incarnadined and frequently overwritten."

Samuel Stoney was the only one of the seven author-contributors to the book who had never worked at the *Charleston News and Courier.*

The book is difficult to find, in any condition.

REVIEWS

Chicago Sun Book Week, October 31, 1947 (n.p.); *Kirkus,* October 15, 1947 (p. 590); *New York Herald Tribune Weekly Book Review,* November 2, 1947 (p. 24); *San Francisco Chronicle,* November 9, 1947 (p. 27); *Saturday Review of Literature,* November 1, 1947 (p. 45).

SOURCES

Book Review Digest 1947. New York: The H.W. Wilson Company, 1948, p. 740.

Publishers' Weekly, September 27, 1947, p. 1358; and November 1, 1947, p. 2225.

Saturday Review of Literature, November 1, 1947, p. 45.

(Myers) (Charleston, S.C.) *The Post and Courier* obituary, June 19, 1977. n.p.

(Tobias) *American Jewish Archives* website, information on Rowena Wilson Tobias (Tarshish). Accessed August 6, 2006.

(Waring) *Editor and Publisher* website. Accessed August 8, 2006.

Charleston Murders, biographical sketches in the book and on the dust jacket.

CHICAGO MURDERS

Edited by Sewell Peaslee Wright
August 7, 1897 – March 1970

RM3 First edition, first printing (1945) [2]

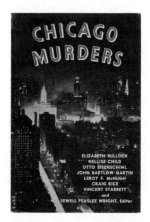

Chicago | *MURDERS* | [thin rule] | *by* | ELIZA-BETH BULLOCK | NELLISE CHILD | OTTO EISENSCHIML | JOHN BARTLOW MARTIN | LEROY F. McHUGH | CRAIG RICE | VINCENT STARRETT | *and edited by* | *SEWELL PEASLEE WRIGHT* | [thin rule] | [Bloodhound device] | NEW YORK | *DUELL, SLOAN AND PEARCE*

COLLATION: 8" x 5½". 112 leaves. [i–x] 1–213 [214]. Numbers printed in roman in the center, at the foot of the page.

CONTENTS: p. [i], half-title: "*Chicago* | *MUR-DERS*"; p. [ii], series title: "*Regional* | *MURDER SERIES* | EDITED BY | MARIE F. RODELL | [thin rule] | Vol. I NEW YORK MURDERS | Vol. II CHICAGO MURDERS | [Bloodhound device] | *In Preparation* | Vol. III SAN FRANCISCO MURDERS"; p. [iii], title; p. [iv], copyright page: "Copyright, 1945, by | Duell, Sloan & Pearce, Inc. | All rights reserved, including the | right to reproduce this book or | portions thereof in any form. | first edition | WAR EDITION | Produced in accordance with | paper conservation orders of | the War Production Board. | Printed in the United States of America"; p. [v], "*ACKNOWLEDGMENTS*"; p. [vi], blank; p. [vii], "*TABLE OF CONTENTS*"; p. [viii], blank; p. [ix], half-title: "*Chicago* | *MURDERS*"; p. [x], blank; pp. 1–13, "PREFACE [unsigned, but identified in the Table of Contents as 'by Sewell Peaslee Wright']"; pp. 14–44, "THE CHICAGO CAREER OF DR. CREAM-1880 | *by Vincent Starrett*"; pp. 45–69, "THE ROCK ISLAND EXPRESS MURDER-1886 | *by Elizabeth Bullock*"; pp. 70–84, "THE CASE OF H.H. HOLMES-1894 | *by John Bartlow Martin*"; pp. 85–118, "THE ORPET-LAMBERT CASE-1916 | *by Otto Eisenschiml*"; pp. 119–142, "THE WYNEKOOP CASE-1933 | *by Craig Rice*"; pp. 143–185, "JOSEPH BOLTON, THE ALMOST INDESTRUCTIBLE HUSBAND | *by Nellise Child*"; pp. 186–213, "THE PEACOCK CASE-1936 | *by LeRoy F. McHugh*"; p. [214], blank.

BINDING: Dark rust cloth (close to Pantone 484), stamped in black. Spine: "[read vertically] CHICAGO MURDERS | [read horizontally] [Bloodhound device] | DUELL SLOAN | AND PEARCE". Cream endpapers.

DUST JACKET (cream paper): Front and spine carry a black-and-white photograph of a night view of the City of Chicago. Front: "[blue, close to Pantone 632, shaded with white] CHICAGO | MURDERS | [at lower right, in white] ELIZABETH BULLOCK | NELLISE CHILD | OTTO EISENSCHIML | JOHN BARTLOW MARTIN | LEROY F. McHUGH | CRAIG RICE | VINCENT STARRETT | and | SEWELL PEASLEE WRIGHT, Editor". Spine: "[read vertically] [blue, shaded with white] CHICAGO MURDERS | [read horizontally] [Bloodhound device] | [white] DUELL, | SLOAN | AND |PEARCE". Back: White background; printing in black. "REGIONAL MURDER SERIES | Edited by Marie F. Rodell | NEW YORK MURDERS edited by Ted Collins $2.75 | [list of the seven chapters and their authors] | CHICAGO MURDERS | edited by Sewell Peaslee Wright $2.75 | [list of the seven chapters and their authors] | SAN FRANCISCO MURDERS | edited by Joseph Henry Jackson $2.75 | [list of the nine chapters and their authors] | [publisher's imprint]". Front flap: "[upper right] $2.75 | CHICAGO | MURDERS | by Elizabeth Bullock, Nellise Child, Otto | Eisenschiml, John Bartlow Martin, Leroy | F. McHugh, Craig Rice, Vincent Starrett | and Sewell Peaslee Wright, Editor | [blurb] | A Bloodhound Book | [publisher's imprint]". Back flap: "About the Editor and the Authors | of CHICAGO MURDERS | [list of the editor and authors with a brief biographical sketch of each] | [publisher's imprint]".

Published at $2.75 on June 6. 1945; number of copies printed unknown. Copyrighted June 8, 1945; deposited June 9, 1945.

The book is listed in "The Weekly Record," June 9, 1945, p. 2313.

Note: No evidence found that Duell, Sloan & Pearce reprinted *Chicago Murders*.

COPIES: CF

REPRINTS AND REPRODUCTIONS

New York: Bantam Books, 1947.

New York: Editions for the Armed Services, No. 992

BIOGRAPHIES[1]

Sewell Peaslee Wright (August 7, 1897 – March 1970), the editor of *Chicago Murders*, wrote mysteries for popular magazines for many years. His interest

1. Where birth or death dates are not stated, the information was not found.

in true crime — the incidents themselves, stories about such incidents, and novels based on them — was said to be a practical one, since he owned and operated a criminological laboratory.

Elizabeth Bullock was mystery editor for Farrar & Rinehart and reviewed mysteries for the *Chicago Sun*.

Nellise Child (Rosenfeld) (September 16, 1901 – June 11, 1981), a novelist and playwright, wrote eight books, including the mysteries *Wolf in the Fold* (Doubleday, 1941) and *If I Come Home* (AMS Press, 1977). She wrote several plays, including *Sister Oakes, The Happy Ending, After the Gleaners*, and *Weep for the Virgin*.

Otto Eisenschiml (June 16, 1880 – December 1963), an expert on the Civil War and Abraham Lincoln, wrote a dozen works on those subjects, including histories, speeches, and a play presented in the Coolidge Auditorium of the Library of Congress in 1950. His *Story of Shiloh*, published in 1946 under the auspices of the Civil War Round Table and decorated by Joseph Trautwein, is held at the Rare Book/Special Collections Reading Room in the Library of Congress.

John Bartlow Martin (August 4, 1915 – January 3, 1987) worked as a police reporter for the *Indianapolis Times* before turning to freelance writing during the 1940s and 1950s. He contributed several murder pieces to *Harper's* and produced many cases for *True Detective*. At his peak, Martin was writing about a million words a year, and critics labeled his work a forerunner to the "new journalism" of such writers as Truman Capote and Norman Mailer. In 1970, Martin joined the faculty of the Medill School of Journalism at Northwestern University as a professor of journalism, becoming professor emeritus in 1980. Martin wrote at least fourteen books, including a biography of presidential contender Adlai Stevenson, published in two volumes, and *Break Down the Walls: American Prisons: Past and Future* (Ballantine, 1954). He was U.S. ambassador to the Dominican Republic under presidents John F. Kennedy and Lyndon Johnson. His collected memoirs, *It Seems Like Only Yesterday: Memoirs of Writing, Presidential Politics, and the Diplomatic Life* (Morrow) was published in 1986. The Papers of John Bartlow Martin, 1900–1986 (bulk 1939–1983), are held by the Library of Congress.

Leroy F. McHugh (May 16, 1890 – May 1975) had been a reporter for the *Chicago Herald-American* for thirty-one years at the time *Chicago Murders* was published. A police reporter, McHugh, who covered more than seven hundred murders in his reporting career, was noted for his aggressive approach to reporting. He used many tricks and deceptions in his work, once posing as a coroner to obtain some privileged information. His biggest scoop resulted in a series of interviews with an escaped swindler in 1952. In his preface to *Chicago Murders*, Sewell Peaslee Wright states, "Buddy" McHugh, as he was known, "was the prototype of the City News Bureau man" in the motion picture "[The] Front Page" (the 1931 United Artists motion picture based on the famous 1928 play by Ben Hecht and Charles MacArthur), adding that McHugh's "presentation of the Dr. Peacock case" in the book "is straight newspaperese . . ."

Craig Rice (pseud. of Georgiana Ann Randolph Walker Craig) (June 5, 1908 – 1957), a one-time crime reporter, was one of the most popular mystery novelists of her time. As Craig Rice she wrote eleven novels and two volumes of short stories and novelettes in the popular John J. Malone series; at least eight other novels; and short stories, radio and television scripts, and screen-plays. As a ghostwriter in the early 1940s, she wrote two murder mysteries with the showgirl-author Gypsy Rose Lee, and another with the actor George Saunders. She appeared on the cover of the January 24, 1946, issue of *Time*, and, for a time, reviewed mysteries for the *Chicago Daily News*. Her non-fiction work, *Forty-five Murders: A Collection of True-Crime Stories*, was published by Simon and Schuster in 1952. Rice edited *Los Angeles Murders* (1947), in the *Regional Murder Series*.

(Charles) Vincent (Emerson) Starrett (October 26, 1886 – January 5, 1974), a leading member of the Chicago Literary Renaissance, wrote or edited at least fifty books, including bibliographies of the works of Stephen Crane, Robert Louis Stevenson, and Ambrose Bierce. He was a Sherlock Holmes scholar, and cofounder, with Christopher Morley, of the Baker Street Irregulars. For twenty-five years Starrett wrote a weekly column, "Books Alive," for the *Chicago Tribune*. He received a Grand Master Award and an Edgar Award from the Mystery Writers of America. The Starrett Collection at Northern Illinois University includes Starrett's novels and bibliographies, essays, po-ems, correspondence, and other material. His papers are also held by the universities of Iowa and Minnesota and the Henry E. Huntington, Lilly, and Newberry libraries.

NOTES ON *CHICAGO MURDERS*

The book *was* included in Duell, Sloan & Pearce's 1945 Spring List in the January 27, 1945, issue of *Publishers' Weekly*, noting publication scheduled for April. In the March 3, 1945, issue of *PW*, *Chicago Murders* shares a full-page advertisement with *Dread Journey* by Dorothy Hughes, another DSP Bloodhound Mystery. Publication of both books was scheduled for June.

REVIEWS

Book Week, June 10, 1945 (p. 15); *Kirkus*, June 1, 1945 (p. 240); *New Republic*, August 13, 1945 (p. 198); *New Yorker*, June 16, 1945 (p. 72); *Saturday Review of Literature*, June 23, 1945 (p. 42); *Weekly Book Review*, June 17, 1945 (p. 19).

SOURCES

Book Review Digest 1945. New York: The H.W. Wilson Company, 1946, p. 794.

Publishers' Weekly, January 27, 1945, p. 320; March 3, 1945, p. 972; and June 9, 1945, p. 2313.

The New Yorker, June 16, 1945, p. 72.

Benét, William Rose. *The Reader's Encyclopedia: An Encyclopedia of World Literature and the Arts*. New York: Thomas Y. Crowell Company, 1948. (Entry on "The Front Page.")

Cole, John Y. *Books in Action: The Armed Services Editions*. Washington: The Center for the Book in the Library of Congress, 1984, p. 78.

Uglow, Jennifer S., comp. and ed. *The Continuum Dictionary of Women's Biography*. New York: Continuum Publishing Company, 1989. (Entry on Gypsy Rose Lee.)

(Martin) *Contemporary Authors Online*, Gale, 2006. Reproduced in Biography Resource Center. Farmington Hills, Mich.: Thomson Gale. 2006. Accessed July 21, 2006.

(McHugh) *Contemporary Authors Online*, Gale, 2006. Reproduced in Biography Resource Center. Farmington Hills, Mich.: Thomson Gale. 2006. Accessed July 21, 2006.

(Rice) *Contemporary Authors Online*, Gale, 2006. Reproduced in Biography Resource Center. Farmington Hills, Mich.: Thomson Gale. 2006. Accessed July 21, 2006.

(Starrett) *Contemporary Authors Online*, Gale, 2006. Reproduced in Biography Resource Center. Farmington Hills, Mich.: Thomson Gale. 2006. Accessed July 21, 2006.

Library of Congress Online Catalog. Entries on Otto Eisenschiml, 1880–1963. Accessed July 31, 2006.

Chicago Murders, biographical sketches on dust jacket.

CLEVELAND MURDERS

Edited by Oliver Weld Bayer[1]

RM4   First edition, first printing (1947) [6]

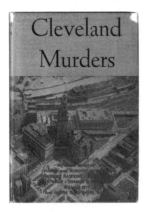

Cleveland I MURDERS I [thin rule] I *by* I
HOWARD   BEAUFAIT   I   CHARLES   and
DOROTHY BODURTHA I LARRY HAWKINS I G.
JACK HEIL I M. R. KELLY I CHARLES J. PATTER-
SON I WILLIAM RITT I *and edited by* I OLIVER
WELD BAYER I [thin rule] I [Bloodhound device]
I NEW YORK I *DUELL, SLOAN AND PEARCE*

COLLATION: 8" x 5½". 128 leaves. [i–vi] [1–2] 3–14
[15–16] 17–40 [41–42] 43–79 [80–82] 83–98 [99–100]
101–136 [137–138] 139–174 [175–176] 177–216
[217–218] 219–249 [250]. Numbers printed in roman in the center at the foot of the page.

CONTENTS: p. [i], half-title:"*Cleveland* I *MURDERS*"; p. [ii], series title:
"*Regional* I *MURDER SERIES* I EDITED BY I MARIE F. RODELL I [thin
rule] I Vol. I New York Murders I Vol. II Chicago Murders I Vol. III Denver
Murders I Vol. IV San Francisco Murders I Vol. V Los Angeles Murders I Vol.
VI Cleveland Murders I Vol. VII Charleston Murders I [Bloodhound device]
I *In Preparation* I DETROIT MURDERS I BOSTON MURDERS"; p. [iii], ti-
tle; p. [iv], copyright page: "Copyright, 1947, by I Duell, Sloan & Pearce, Inc.
I All rights reserved, including the I right to reproduce this book or I portions thereof in any form. I first printing I Printed in the United States of
America"; p. [v], "*CONTENTS*"; p. [vi], blank; p. [1], half-title:"*Cleveland* I
MURDERS"; p. [2], blank; pp. 3–14, "*Preface* [signed Oliver Weld Bayer, followed by a brief biographical sketch of Bayer]"; p. [15], "*1870* I [within a rec-
tangle] The I Galentine-Jones Affair I [below rectangle] by I Larry Hawkins I
[brief biographical sketch of Hawkins]"; p. [16], blank; pp. 17–40, text; p.
[41], "*1917* I [within a rectangle] The Case of I the Careless Killer I [below
rectangle] by I G. Jack Heil I [brief biographical sketch of Heil]"; p. [42],
blank; pp. 43–79, text; p. [80], blank; p. [81], "*1919* I [within a rectangle] The
Kaber Case I [below rectangle] I by ICharles J. Patterson I [brief biographical

1. Oliver Weld Bayer, a joint pseudonym of Leo G. Bayer (September 6, 1908 – December
28, 2004), and his wife, Eleanor (c. 1915– March 14, 1981).

sketch of Patterson]"; p. [82], blank; pp. 83–98, text; p. [99], "*1920* | [within a rectangle] The Kagy Case | [below rectangle] by | Charles and Dorothy Bo-durtha | [brief biographical sketches of the Bodurthas]"; p. [100], blank; pp. 101–136, text; p. [137], "*1923* | [within a rectangle] John Leonard Whitfield: | Sheik and Cop-Killer | [below rectangle] by | M. R. Kelly | [brief biographi-cal sketch of Kelly]"; p. [138], blank; pp. 139–174, text; p. [175], "*1931* | [within a rectangle] The Case of | William E. Potter | [below rectangle] by | Howard Beaufait | [brief biographical sketch of Beaufait]"; p. [176], blank; pp. 177–216, text; p. [217], *1935 – 38* | [within a rectangle] The Head Hunter | of Kingsbury Run | [below rectangle] by | William Ritt | [brief biographical sketch of Ritt]"; p. [218], blank; pp. 219–249, text; p. [250], blank.

BINDING: Dark teal paperboards (close to Pantone 350); medium rust quar-ter cloth (close to Pantone 174) on front, spine, and back, stamped in black. Spine: "[read vertically] Cleveland Murders | [read horizontally] | [Blood-hound device] | DUELL, SLOAN | AND PEARCE". Cream endpapers.

DUST JACKET: (cream paper): Front: "[within a wide medium rose band (close to Pantone 487), which wraps to the spine, in black)] Cleveland | Mur-ders | [black-and-white photograph of downtown Cleveland municipal cen-ter, which wraps to the spine, on which is printed in red (close to Pantone 185)] BY | HOWARD BEAUFAIT | CHARLES and DOROTHY BODURTHA | LAWRENCE HAWKINS · G. JACK HEIL | M.R. KELLY · CHARLES J. PAT-TERSON | WILLIAM RITT | And OLIVER WELD BAYER, Editor". Spine: "[black] Cleveland | Murders | [Bloodhound device] | [red] Duell, Sloan | and | Pearce". Back: White background; printing in black. "[list naming the editor and the seven authors, with a brief biographical sketch of each]". Front flap: "[upper right] $3.00 | CLEVELAND | MURDERS | *by* | Howard Beaufait, Charles and Dorothy | Bodurtha | Lawrence Hawkins, G. Jack | Heil M.R. Kelly, Charles J. Patterson, | William Ritt | *and edited by* | Oliver Weld Bayer | [blurb, including a list of chapter titles] | *A Bloodhound Book* | [publisher's imprint]". Back flap: "REGIONAL MURDER | SERIES | NEW YORK MURDERS | [list of authors and price] | CHICAGO MURDERS | [list of authors and price] | DENVER MURDERS | [list of authors and price] | SAN FRANCISCO MURDERS | [list of authors and price] | LOS ANGE-LES MURDERS | [list of authors and price] | *In Preparation* | CHARLESTON MURDERS | DETROIT MURDERS | BOSTON MURDERS | [publisher's imprint]".

Published at $3.00 on October 9, 1947; number of copies printed unknown. Copyrighted January 19, 1948; deposited October 31, 1947.

The book is listed in "The Weekly Record," October 25, 1947, p. 2114

Note: No evidence found that Duell, Sloan & Pearce reprinted *Cleveland Murders.*

COPIES. CF

REPRINTS AND REPRODUCTIONS

None.

BIOGRAPHIES[2]

Oliver Weld Bayer is a joint pseudonym used by Leo G. Bayer (September 6, 1908 – December 28, 2004) and his wife, Eleanor. Born Eleanor Rosenfeld in 1915, she died on March 14, 1981. Under their joint pseudonym, the couple edited *Cleveland Murders.* They wrote four mystery novels: *Paper Chase* (1943), *No Little Enemy* (1944), *An Eye for an Eye* (1945) and *Brutal Question* (1947), all published by Doubleday, Doran *&* Company. As Eleanor Bayer with L.G. Bayer, they wrote *Dirty Hands Across the Sea*, a novel, (Collins & World, 1952) and *Third Best Sport*, a three-act play produced on Broadway by the Theater Guild in 1958. Leo Bayer, a graduate of Western Reserve University Law School, had a law practice in Cleveland, Ohio, for more than thirty years. After the couple's divorce in 1959, Eleanor married the film director Frank Perry and became a screenwriter. Her work included the films *Diary of a Mad Housewife* (Universal, 1970), *The Man Who Loved Cat Dancing* (MGM, 1973), and eight other screenplays.

Howard Beaufait (October 15, 1904 – November 3, 1976), a graduate of Columbia University, had been a working newspaperman for twenty years when *Cleveland Murders* was published in 1947. Born in Detroit, Beaufait moved to Cleveland Heights, Ohio. He was a reporter for the *Cleveland News*, and, beginning in 1928, he covered the crime scene. During World War II, he was the paper's city editor. He earned an award from the Cleveland Newspaper Guild, Local 1, for his coverage of the Korean War and was president of the Cleveland Newspaper Guild in 1954. When the *News* ceased publication in 1960, he became an executive at the Cleveland Area Heart Society, later returning to journalism and working at the *Lake County News-Herald* and the *Tribune-Review* in Greensburg, Pennsylvania.

Charles and Dorothy Bodurtha were born in Ohio. Dorothy Bodurtha (July 9, 1903 – March 20, 1988) graduated from Wellesley College and earned a master of arts degree from Radcliffe College. She spent a year in London, conducting research on the poet John Keats (1795–1821). Charles Bodurtha (July 14, 1902 – December 1986) graduated from Ohio Wesleyan University

2. Where birth or death dates are not stated, the information was not found.

and attended both Harvard Business School and Harvard Law School. He had practiced law in Cleveland for nearly twenty years when *Cleveland Murders* was published in 1947.

Larry Hawkins, a graduate of the University of Virginia, was a reporter, copyreader, and Sunday magazine feature writer for the *Cleveland Plain Dealer*. He had been a *Plain Dealer* staffer for eighteen years when *Cleveland Murders* was published in 1947. He wrote true detective stories for many popular magazines.

G. Jack Heil (September 29, 1892 – June 15, 1968) was born in Stevens Point, Wisconsin, and spent his boyhood on the North Dakota plains as a sheep-herder. He was a graduate of Marquette University with a major in journalism, and, later, Cleveland Law School. He worked for several newspapers before the United States entered World War I in 1917. During the war, Heil saw service in France with Ohio's famed 37th Division. In 1919, he joined the staff of the *Cleveland Press*, where he covered crime and murders and national news that included political conventions. He left the paper after eight years and began to practice law. During World War II, he worked at the Office of Price Administration and the Federal Housing Administration. When *Cleveland Murders* was published in 1947, Heil had worked for the U.S. government as an investigator for four years.

M.R. Kelly began his writing career as editor of a college newspaper and a prize winner in literary contests. He worked with a little theater group, sold short stories to little magazines, and wrote radio plays, detective and true crime stories, and feature articles. (Between 1912 and 1952, more than six hundred "little magazines" were published in the United States, essentially all of them enabling unknown writers to appear in print.)[3]

Charles J. Patterson (July 26, 1901 – April 28, 1953) was born in Cleveland, Ohio, and graduated from John Carroll University. He attended Columbia University and Cleveland Law School, earning a law degree. He worked at newspapers in Chicago; Baltimore; Norfolk, Virginia; and Bayonne, New Jersey before moving to Cleveland. When *Cleveland Murders* was published in 1947, Patterson had worked as a rewrite man and feature writer on the staff of the *Cleveland Press* for nearly twenty years. During World War II, Patterson was a correspondent for *Yank, The Army Weekly* and the Army newspaper *Stars and Stripes*.

William Ritt (December 29, 1901 – September 1972) had been in the newspaper and newspaper syndicate business for twenty-five years, serving on the

3. Tebbel, John and Mary Ellen Zuckerman. *The Magazine in America: 1741–1990*. New York: Oxford University Press, 1991, p. 216.

editorial staffs of the *Indianapolis Times*, the *Indianapolis Post*, and the *New York World*, when *Cleveland Murders* was published in 1947. He was a writer and editor with the King Features Syndicate. His humor column, "You're Telling Me!" and his science fiction comic strip, "Brick Bradford," were widely syndicated.

NOTES ON *CLEVELAND MURDERS*

The book was included on the Duell, Sloan & Pearce Fall List in the September 27, 1947, issue of *Publishers' Weekly*. *The Saturday Review of Literature* included the book in a section titled "The Criminal Record," the magazine's guide to detective and crime fiction. The book received a "verdict" of "fair," and was described as "another interesting, though unspectacular, chapter in metropolitan American crime."

REVIEWS

Chicago Sun Book Week, October 31, 1947 (n.p.); *Kirkus*, October 15, 1947 (p. 595); *New York Herald Tribune Weekly Book Review*, October 19, 1947 (p. 24); *New Yorker*, October 25, 1947 (p. 136); *San Francisco Chronicle*, October 19, 1947 (p. 27); *Saturday Review of Literature*, November 1, 1947 (p. 45).

SOURCES

Book Review Digest 1947. New York: The H.W. Wilson Company, 1948, p. 53.

Publishers' Weekly, September 27, 1947, p. 1358; and October 25, 1947, p. 2114.

Saturday Review of Literature review, November 1, 1947, p. 45.

Emery, Edwin and Henry Ladd Smith. *The Press and America*. New York: Prentice-Hall, 1954. (Various entries on newspapers.)

Murphy, Bruce, ed. *Benét's Reader's Encyclopedia*, Fourth Edition. New York: HarperCollins, 1996. (Entry on John Keats.)

Tebbel, John and Mary Ellen Zuckerman. *The Magazine in America: 1741–1990*. New York: Oxford University Press, 1991, p. 216, ("little magazines")

(Eleanor Perry, pseud. Oliver Weld Bayer) *Women Filmmakers and Their Films*. St. James Press, 1998. Reproduced in *Biography Resource Center*, Farmington Hills, Mich.: The Gale Group. 2002. Accessed April 18, 2002.

(Eleanor [Rosenfeld Bayer] Perry, pseud. Oliver Weld Bayer) *Contemporary Authors Online*. The Gale Group, 1999. Reproduced in *Biography Resource*

Center. Farmington Hills, Mich.: The Gale Group. 2002. Accessed April 18, 2002.

(Eleanor Perry) *The New York Times* obituary, March 17, 1981.

(Leo G. Bayer, pseud. Oliver Weld Bayer) *The Boston Globe* obituary, January 5, 2005.

(Beaufait) *Encyclopedia of Cleveland History.* http://ech.edu

(Heil) *Cleveland Press* obituary, June 17, 1968.

Cleveland Murders, biographical sketches in the book and on the dust jacket.

(Patterson) Patterson, Jr., Charles J. (son of Charles J. Patterson), telephone interview with CF, July 20, 2008.

DENVER MURDERS

Edited by Lee Casey
August 20, 1889 – January 28, 1951

RM5   First edition, first printing (1946) [3]

Denver I *MURDERS* I [thin rule] I *by* I WILLIAM E. BARRETT I CLYDE BRION DAVIS I BRETT HALLIDAY I RAY HUMPHREYS I GENE LOWALL I FORBES PARKHILL I WILLIAM MacLEOD RAINE I FRANCES WAYNE I *and edited by* I LEE CASEY I [thin rule] I [Bloodhound device] I NEW YORK I *DUELL, SLOAN AND PEARCE*

COLLATION: 8" x 5½". 112 leaves. [i–vi] [1–2] 3–9 [10–12] 13–31 [32–34] 35–55 [56–58] 59–75 [76–78] 79–117 [118–120] 121–136 [137–138] 139–164 [165–166] 167–187 [188–190] 191–217 [218]. Numbers printed in roman in the center at the foot of the page.

CONTENTS: p. [i], half-title: "*Denver* I *MURDERS*"; p. [ii], series title: "*Regional* I *MURDER SERIES* I EDITED BY I MARIE F. RODELL I [thin rule] I

Vol. I NEW YORK MURDERS I Vol. II CHICAGO MURDERS I Vol. III
DENVER MURDERS I [Bloodhound device] I *In Preparation* I LOS ANGE-
LES MURDERS I SAN FRANCISCO MURDERS"; p. [iii], title; p. [iv], copyright page: "Copyright, 1946, by I Duell, Sloan & Pearce I All rights reserved,
including the I right to reproduce this book or I portions thereof in any
form. I first printing I Printed in the United States of America"; p. [v], "*CON-
TENTS*"; p. [vi], blank; p. [1], half-title: "*Denver I MURDERS*"; p. [2], blank;
pp. 3–9, "*Preface* [signed Lee Casey]"; p. [10], blank; p. [11], "[thin rule] I
1860 I *The* I GORDON CASE I *by William MacLeod Raine* I [thin rule]"; p.
[12], blank; pp. 13–31, text; p. [32], blank; p. [33], "[thin rule] I 1901 I *The* I
MAN FROM ROME I *by William E. Barrett* I [thin rule]"; p. [34], blank; pp.
35–55, text; p. [56], blank; p. [57], "[thin rule] I 1911 I GERTRUDE GIBSON
PATTERSON I *by Frances Wayne* I [thin rule]"; p. [58], blank; pp. 59–75, text;
p. [76], blank; p. [77] "[thin rule] I 1911 I MURDER AT THE BROWN
PALACE I *by Brett Halliday* I [thin rule]"; p. [78], blank; pp. 79–117, text; p.
[118], blank; p. [119], "[thin rule] I 1915 I *The* UNITED STATES OF AMER-
ICA I vs. TSE-NE-GAT I *by Forbes Parkhill* I [thin rule]"; p. [120], blank; pp.
121–136, text; p. [137], "[thin rule] 1920 I *The* I SUNDAY GUN MYSTERY I *by
Clyde Brion Davis* I [thin rule]"; p. [138], blank; pp. 139–164, text; p. [165],
"[thin rule] I 1930 I *The* I PEARL O'LOUGHLIN CASE I *by Ray Humphreys*
I [thin rule]"; p. [166], blank; pp. 167–187, text; p. [188], blank; p. [189], "[thin
rule] I 1942 I *The* I SPIDER MAN CASE I *by Gene Lowall* I [thin rule]"; p.
[190], blank; pp. 191–217, text; p. [218], blank.

BINDING: Brick-red cloth (close to Pantone 180), stamped in black. Spine:
"DENVER I MURDERS I [Bloodhound device] I DUELL, SLOAN I AND
PEARCE". Cream endpapers.

DUST JACKET (cream paper): Front carries a black-and-white photograph
of the City of Denver; snow-capped mountains in the background. Front:
"[red, close to Pantone 185)] DENVER I MURDERS I [below photograph,
on a burgundy band (close to Pantone 194), in red] by WILLIAM E. BAR-
RETT · CLYDE BRION DAVIS I BRETT HALLIDAY · RAY HUMPHREYS ·
GENE LOWALL I FORBES PARKHILL · WILLIAM MacLEOD RAINE I
FRANCES WAYNE and edited by LEE CASEY". Spine: "[read vertically] [red
background; printing probably in light red] DENVER MURDERS I [read
horizontally] [Bloodhound device] I DUELL, I SLOAN I AND I PEARCE".
Back: White background; printing in black. "About the editor and authors of
I DENVER MURDERS I [list naming the editor and the eight authors, with
a brief biographical sketch of each]". Front flap: "[upper right] $2.75 I DEN-
VER MURDERS I by WILLIAM E. BARRETT, I CLYDE BRION DAVIS, I
BRETT HALLIDAY, RAY HUMPHREYS, I GENE LOWALL, FORBES

PARKHILL, | WILLIAM MacLEOD RAINE, | FRANCES WAYNE | and ed-
ited by LEE CASEY| [blurb and list of the eight murder accounts in the
book] | *A Bloodhound Book* | [publisher's imprint]". Back flap: "Regional
Murder | Series | NEW YORK MURDERS | [list of authors and quotes from
two reviews] | CHICAGO MURDERS | [list of authors and quotes from two
reviews] | [publisher's imprint]".

Published at $2.75 on April 24, 1946; number of copies printed unknown.
Copyrighted May 10, 1946; deposited April 30, 1946.

The book is listed in "The Weekly Record," April 27, 1946, p. 2350.

Note: No evidence found that Duell, Sloan & Pearce reprinted *Denver Murders*.

COPIES: CF

<h3 style="text-align:center">REPRINTS AND REPRODUCTIONS</h3>

New York: Editions for the Armed Services, No. 1191.

<h3 style="text-align:center">BIOGRAPHIES[1]</h3>

Lee Casey (August 20, 1889 – January 28, 1951), the editor of *Denver Murders*,
worked for five years under Charles Blood at the *Kansas City Star* before
coming to Denver in 1912. In 1915, he left Denver to work at the *Chicago Examiner* (1915–1916), but returned to Denver. When *Denver Murders* was published, Casey was associate editor of the *Rocky Mountain News*. He was
briefly an instructor in English and head of the Journalism Department at
Colorado University. He is a member of the Denver Press Club Hall of Fame,
which honors those who made significant contributions to Colorado journalism. Upon his death, and at his request, Casey's ashes were interred within
the walls of the *Rocky Mountain News* building. In January 2003, in anticipa-
tion of the building's demolition, the ashes were moved to the Olinger Hill
Mortuary and Cemetery in Denver.

William E. Barrett (November 16, 1900 – September 14, 1986) was Southwestern advertising manager for the Westinghouse Company from 1923 until 1929, when he became a freelance writer. He wrote at least twenty books
and more than two hundred short stories. His short stories, articles, essays,
and book reviews were published in Cosmopolitan, Redbook, Saturday
Evening Post, McCall's, Collier's, and other national magazines. He is best
known for the novella *Lilies of the Field* (Doubleday, 1962) and the novel *The*

---

1. Where birth or death dates are not stated, the information was not found.

Left Hand of God (Doubleday, 1951), both of which were made into movies. In 1961 he was awarded an honorary doctorate in literature from Creighton University.

Clyde Brion Davis (May 22, 1894 – July 19, 1962) was a newspaper reporter and editor from 1916 to 1941. During that time, he was in Denver, working at the *Denver Times*, the *Denver Post*, or the *Rocky Mountain News*. He wrote at least twenty books, including *The Anointed* (1937), *The Great American Novel* (1938), both Book-of-the-Month Club selections, and *The Arkansas* (1940), a title in the *Rivers of America* series; all three were published by Farrar & Rinehart. Davis contributed to magazines including *Holiday* and the *Atlantic Monthly*. In 1956, he received a Huntington Hartford fellowship.

Brett Halliday (pseud. of Davis Dresser, July 31, 1904 – February 4, 1977) wrote at least a hundred mystery and Western novels, including the Michael Shayne private eye series. Some were written under his name, David Dresser, others under pen names including Brett Halliday, Asa Baker, Matthew Blood, Kathryn Culver, Don Davis, Hal Debrett, Peter Field, Anthony Scott, and Anderson Wayne. He was founding editor of *Mike Shayne's Mystery Magazine*. In 1953, he received an Edgar Award for criticism from the Mystery Writers of America.

Ray Humphreys was a police reporter and crime expert on the staffs of Denver newspapers. He wrote detective stories, both true and fictional, and a novel, *Hunch* (Loring, 1934). When *Denver Murders* was published in 1946, he had been chief investigator at the Denver District Attorney's office for seventeen years.

Gene Lowall, (September 28, 1905 – March 14, 1975), was city editor of the *Rocky Mountain News* when *Denver Murders* was published in 1946. The October 31, 1949, edition of *Time* reported that Lowall "collects crimes with the passion that other men lavish on postage stamps and Ming vases. A onetime crime reporter himself . . . [Lowall] spends his spare hours reading and writing whodunits. . . ."

Forbes Parkhill (December 31, 1892 – June 19, 1974) was a reporter and news editor at the *Denver Post* from 1913 to 1928. He was later an instructor in journalism and short-story writing at the University of Denver. In the 1940s, he worked as a magazine specialist at the U.S. Department of War, the predecessor of the Department of Defense, and later as a Congressional research assistant. His work, fiction and non-fiction and set in the American West, included four biographies. He received an award for best nonfiction book by a Colorado author from the Colorado Authors League for his 1962 *Last of* *the Indian Wars* (Crowell-Collier). He wrote the screenplays for six MGM films.

William MacLeod Raine (June 22, 1871 – July 25, 1954) was an editorial writer for Denver newspapers and the author of at least eighty Western novels, primarily adventure novels. With Will C. Barnes, he wrote *Cattle* (Doubleday, 1930), a non-fiction work about the cattle industry, that also provides information on western outlaws and feuds. *Cattle*, a standard work widely used by universities, was described by J. Frank Dobie as a "succinct and vivid focusing of much scattered history."[2] In 1959, Raines was posthumously inducted into the Hall of Great Westerners of the National Cowboy and Western Heritage Museum.

Frances (Belford) Wayne (1870 – July 17, 1951) was a member of a pioneer Colorado family. Born in LaPorte, Indiana, she came to Colorado with her parents as an infant. She began her newspaper career with the *Rocky Mountain News* and worked as drama editor of the *Chicago Examiner*. From 1909 to 1946, she was a feature writer for the *Denver Post*, covering birth control, women's rights, drug abuse, and other issues. In 1921, she received a medal of merit from the University of Colorado in recognition of her campaign for the founding of the state medical school and hospital. Her marriage to John Anthony Wayne was brief. She maintained the Wayne surname throughout her life.

NOTES ON *DENVER MURDERS*

The book was included in the Duell, Sloan & Pearce 1946 Spring List, with a planned publication of April. It was published on April 24, 1946. The April 27, 1946, issue of *Publishers' Weekly* carried a full-page advertisement for the book, reading in part, "The success of the first two volumes of the series (New York Murders and Chicago Murders) has attested not only to the spirit of local pride in each of those cities, but to the wide-spread and growing audience for true crime."

Denver Murders was issued as an Armed Services Edition (No. 1191), joining *Chicago Murders* as a true-crime book distributed to military personnel.

REVIEWS

Kirkus, May 1, 1946 (p. 219); *New York Times Book Review*, May 6, 1946 (p. 26); *New Yorker*, April 27, 1946 (p. 92); *Saturday Review of Literature*, May 4, 1946 (p. 44); *Weekly Book Review*, April 28, 1946 (p. 33).

2. Dobie, J. Frank. *Guide to Life and Literature of the Southwest* (1981), p. 114.

SOURCES

Book Review Digest 1946. New York: The H.W. Wilson Company, 1947, p. 133.

Publishers' Weekly, January 26, 1946, (Duell, Sloan and Pearce Spring List) p. 412; and April 27, 1946, p. 2252 and p. 2350.

The New York Times Book Review, May 5, 1946, p. 26.

Adams, Ramon F., comp. *Six–Guns and Saddle Leather.* Norman: University of Oklahoma Press, (rev. ed.) 1969.

Dobie, J. Frank. *Guide to Life and Literature of the Southwest.* Dallas: Southern Methodist University Press, eighth printing, 1981.

(Barrett) *Contemporary Authors Online,* Gale, 2006. Reproduced in Biography Resource Center. Farmington Hills, Mich.: Thomson Gale. 2006. Accessed July 21, 2006.

(Casey) *The New York Times* obituary, January 30, 1951, p. 25; *Rocky Mountain News* obituary, January 29, 1951; *Denver Post* obituary, January 29, 1951; *Rocky Mountain News,* August 10, 2006, article on relocation of Lee Casey's ashes in www.westword.com. Accessed June 30, 2008.

(Davis) *Contemporary Authors Online,* Gale, 2006. Reproduced in Biography Resource Center. Farmington Hills, Mich.: Thomson Gale. 2006. Accessed July 21, 2006.

(Brett Halliday, pseud. of Davis Dresser) *Contemporary Authors Online,* Gale, 2006. Reproduced in Biography Resource Center. Farmington Hills, Mich.: Thomson Gale. 2006. Accessed July 21, 2006.

(Parkhill) *Contemporary Authors Online,* Gale, 2006. Reproduced in Biography Resource Center. Farmington Hills, Mich.: Thomson Gale. 2006. Accessed July 21, 2006.

(Raine) Merriman, C.D. Biographical sketch of Raine in www.online-literature.com/william-raine. Accessed July 22, 2006.

(Wayne) Bluemel, Elinor. *One Hundred Years of Colorado Women.* n.p., 1973, pp. 85–87.

(Wayne) Susie Whiteford, Reference Librarian, AskColorado Representative, Denver Public Library, Denver, Colorado. E-mail message to CF, August 17, 2006.

Denver Murders, biographical sketches on dust jacket.

DETROIT MURDERS

Edited by Alvin C. Hamer
c. 1891–May 4, 1950

RM6   First edition, first printing (1948) [8]

Detroit | *MURDERS* | [thin rule] | *by* | PATRICIA BRONTË | ELIZABETH COULSON | CHARLES G. GIVENS | CHARLES T. HAUN | ROYCE HOWES | PATRICK S. McDOUGALL | ANNA MARY WELLS | *and* | ALVIN C. HAMER, *editor* | [thin rule] | [Bloodhound device] | NEW YORK | *DUELL, SLOAN AND PEARCE*

COLLATION: 8" x 5½". 112 leaves. [i–vi] 1–6 [7–8] 9–25 [26–28] 29–58 [59–60] 61–88 [89–90] 91–115 [116–118] 119–134 [135–136] 137–155 [156–158] 159–176 [177–178] 179–193 [194–196] 197–218. Numbers printed in roman in headline at the outer margin of the page, except for pp. 1, 9, 29, 61, 91, 119, 137, 159, 179, and 197, on which the numbers are printed in the center, at the foot of the page.

CONTENTS: p. [i], half-title:"[within a rectangle] Detroit Murders"; p. [ii], series title: "*Regional* | *MURDER SERIES* | EDITED BY | MARIE F. RODELL | [thin rule] | Vol. I. NEW YORK MURDERS | Vol. II. CHICAGO MURDERS | Vol. III. DENVER MURDERS | Vol. IV. SAN FRANCISCO MURDERS | Vol. V. LOS ANGELES MURDERS | Vol. VI. CLEVELAND MURDERS | Vol. VII. CHARLESTON MURDERS | Vol. VIII. DETROIT MURDERS | [Bloodhound device] | *In Preparation* | BOSTON MURDERS"; p. [iii], title; p. [iv], copyright page: "Copyright, 1948, by | Duell, Sloan & Pearce, Inc. | All rights reserved, including the | right to reproduce this book or | portions thereof in any form. | first printing | Printed in the United States of America"; p. [v], "*CONTENTS*"; p. [vi], blank; pp. 1–6, "*Preface* [signed Alvin C. Hamer]"; p. [7], "*1815* | '*Wilful Murder on the Border*' | [within a rectangle] The Kickapoo Indian Killing | [below rectangle] by | Alvin C. Hamer | [brief biographical sketch of Hamer]"; p. [8], blank; pp. 9–25, text; p. [26], blank; p. [27], "*1889* |'*The Dog in the Night*' | [within a rectangle] The Latimer Case | [below rectangle] by | Anna Mary Wells | [brief biographical sketch of Wells]"; p. [28], blank; pp. 29–58, text; p. [59], "*1927* | '*Murder Domestic*' | [within a rectangle] The Loomis Case | [below rectangle] | by | Charles G. Givens | [brief biographical sketch of Givens]"; p. [60], blank; pp. 61–88, text; p. [89], "*1929* | '*Six Killings and a Cult*' | [within a rectangle] The Evangelista Case | [below the rectangle] by | Royce Howes | [brief biographical sketche of Howes]"; p. [90], blank; pp. 91–115, text; p. [116], blank; p. [117], "*1930* | '*Bloody July*' | [within a rectangle] The Buckley Case | [below rectangle] by | Charles T. Haun | [brief biographical sketch of Haun]"; p. [118], blank; pp. 119–134, text; p. [135], "*1935* | '*Murder of a Big-Shot*' | [within a rectangle] The Dickinson Case | [below rectangle] by | Patrick S. McDougall | [brief biographical sketch of McDougall]"; p. [136], blank; pp. 137–155, text; p. [156], blank; p. [157], "*1936* | '*Night Terror*' | [within a rectangle] The Case of the Black Legion | [below rectangle] by | Charles T. Haun | [brief biographical sketch of Haun]"; p. [158], blank; pp. 159–176, text; p. [177] "*1945* | '*A Man and His Double*' | [within a rectangle] The Beaver Case | [below rectangle] | by | Elizabeth Coulson | [brief biographical sketch of Coulson]"; p. [178], blank; pp. 179–193, text; p. [194], blank; p. [195], "*1945* | '*Strange Woman*' | [within a rectangle] The Lydia Thompson Case | [below rectangle] by | Patricia Brontë | [brief biographical sketch of Brontë]; p. [196], blank; pp. 197–218, text.

BINDING: Orange cloth (close to Pantone 172), stamped in black. Spine: "[read vertically] [in outline] DETROIT MURDERS | [read horizontally] | [Bloodhound device] | DUELL, SLOAN | AND PEARCE". Cream endpapers.

DUST JACKET (white paper): Front and spine carry a navy blue (close to Pantone 295) and grey (close to Pantone 427) photograph of the Detroit skyline, a body of water in the foreground. Front: "[orange (close to Pantone 150, shaded with navy blue] DETROIT | MURDERS | [navy blue] By | Patricia Brontë, Elizabeth Coulson, | Charles G. Givens, Charles T. Haun, | Royce Howes, Patrick S. McDougall, | Anna Mary Wells, *and* Alvin C. | Hamer, editor". Spine: "[read vertically] [orange, shaded with navy blue] DETROIT MURDERS | [read horizontally] [Bloodhound device, in orange and navy blue] | [orange] Duell, | Sloan | and | Pearce". Back: White background; printing in navy blue. "[list naming the editor and the seven authors, with a brief biographical sketch of each]". Front flap: Printing in navy blue. "[upper right] $3.00 | DETROIT MURDERS | *by* | Patricia Brontë, Elizabeth Coulson, | Charles G. Givens, Charles T. Haun, | Royce Howes, Patrick S. McDougall, | Anna Mary Wells, and Alvin C. Hamer, | Editor | [blurb, including a list of chapter titles] | *A Bloodhound Book* | [publisher's imprint]". Back flap: Printing in navy blue. "REGIONAL MURDER | SERIES | NEW YORK

MURDERS | [list of authors and price] | CHICAGO MURDERS | [list of authors and price] | DENVER MURDERS | [list of authors and price] | SAN FRANCISCO MURDERS | [list of authors and price] | LOS ANGELES MURDERS | [list of authors and price] | CLEVELAND MURDERS | [list of authors and price] | CHARLESTON MURDERS | [list of authors and price] | *In Preparation* | BOSTON MURDERS | [publisher's imprint]".

Published at $3.00 on April 21, 1948; number of copies printed unknown. Copyrighted June 2, 1948; deposited June 1, 1948.

The book is listed in "The Weekly Record," April 24, 1948, p. 1839.

Note: No evidence found that Duell, Sloan & Pearce reprinted *Detroit Murders*.

COPIES: CF

REPRINTS AND REPRODUCTIONS

None.

BIOGRAPHIES[1]

Alvin C. Hamer, (c. 1891–May 4, 1950), editor of *Detroit Murders* and the author of a chapter in the book, earned a master of arts degree from the University of California and then worked at the *Los Angeles Record*, *Los Angeles Express*, and *Los Angeles Times*. In 1925, he moved to Detroit. In 1948, when *Detroit Murders* was published, Hamer and his wife, Edna, were the proprietors of a bookshop in Detroit, Hamer's Book Service, which specialized in rare books, with emphasis on Detroit and Wayne County. The Hamers were also the proprietors of a publishing house, Alved of Detroit. They produced an evening radio program, "Our Town, Detroit in History," broadcast twice weekly. In 1948, after settling into new quarters in the Buhl Building in Detroit, they started a series of Sunday broadcasts, "Book Breakfast with the Hamers."

Patricia Brontë, the daughter of an itinerant newspaperman, covered fires, riots, kidnappings, and murders while on the staffs of the *St. Paul Pioneer Press* and *Dispatch*, the *Miami News*, the *Atlanta Constitution*, the New York newspaper *PM*, and the *Detroit Free Press*. She enjoyed a brief career as a nightclub singer and worked as a screenwriter in Hollywood.

Elizabeth Coulson, a journalist, worked for the *Daily Oklahoman* and the *Oklahoma City Times*. She was an instructor in creative writing at Oklahoma City University. In 1943, she joined the staff of the *Detroit Free Press*, leaving

1. Where birth or death dates are not stated, the information was not found.

in 1946 and moving to San Diego, California, where she became a freelance writer. Her stories appeared in popular magazines, including *Collier's* and *Coronet.*

Charles G. Givens (1899? – September 27, 1964) was born in Dayton, Tennessee. A journalist and novelist, he lived in Chattanooga and worked at the *Chattanooga Times*; in Memphis at the *Memphis Commercial Appeal*; and in Oklahoma City, at the *Oklahoman.* He also worked in New York at the *Mirror*, *Morning Telegraph*, and *Herald Tribune*; and at the *Kansas City Journal*; *Chicago American*; *Boston Advertiser*; and the *Detroit Free Press* and *Detroit Times.* He wrote at least a hundred and fifty short stories for pulp fiction magazines and short stories for popular magazines. His five mystery novels, all published by Bobbs-Merrill, were *The Rose Petal Murders* (1935), *The Jig-Time Murders* (1936), *All Cats Are Gray* (1937), *The Doctor's Pills Are Stardust* (1938), and *The Devil Takes a Hill Town* (1939). *The Devil Takes a Hill Town* was adapted into a Broadway play in 1946.

Charles T. Haun (1907 – December 1, 2000) was born on a farm in Corunna, Michigan, where he attended public schools. He was a graduate of the University of Detroit. A lifetime journalist, he worked on the staffs of several newspapers before joining the *Detroit Free Press* in 1934. Over the next forty-three years there, he worked first as a police reporter; then a rewrite man; then assistant city editor; and then night city editor, a post he held for ten years before moving to the photo department. In 1961, he was named Picture Editor of the Year by the National Press Photographers Association. He was night city editor of the *Free Press* when he wrote the "Bloody July" and "Night Terror" chapters of *Detroit Murders.* He retired in 1977.

Royce Howes (January 3, 1901 – March 18, 1973) worked on the editorial staff of the *Detroit Free Press* from 1927 to 1943 and from 1946 to 1966. During World War II, he served in the Army (1942–1946), rising to the rank of lieutenant colonel and receiving a Bronze Star. At the *Free Press* he was an editorial writer and columnist, then an associate editor, and finally editorial director (1961–1966). In 1955, he won a Pulitzer prize and the National Headliners Award, both for editorial writing. He was an instructor in journalism at Wayne State University from 1931 to 1941. From 1935 to 1953, he wrote eight mystery novels, *Edgar A. Guest* (Reilly & Lee, 1953) a biography, and short stories for popular magazines.

Patrick S. McDougall (January 16, 1906 – August 17, 1955), a graduate of Notre Dame, was an instructor in journalism at Mercy College in Detroit. For seventeen years, he was a police reporter and staff writer for the *Detroit Free Press.* At the time *Detroit Murders* was published in 1948, he had been associate editor of the *Michigan Police Journal* for ten years. McDougall's articles were published in popular magazines, including the *Saturday Evening Post.*

Anna Mary Wells (October 22, 1906 –), a 1926 graduate of Mount Holyoke College, earned a master of arts degree from Southern Methodist University in 1927. She was an instructor in English at Texas Christian University (1926–1927) and at New York University (1928–1931) and a part-time instructor in English at Wayne University (now Wayne State University) in Detroit from 1942 to 1953. She worked briefly as a reporter for the *Asbury Park* (New Jersey) *Press* before becoming professor of English at Rutgers University in 1954. She wrote five mystery novels and two works of non-fiction, *Dear Preceptor: The Life and Times of Thomas Wentworth Higginson* (Houghton, 1963) and *Miss Marks and Miss Wooley* (Houghton, 1978). She contributed to the *New Yorker, Harper's, Atlantic Monthly, Family Circle, Woman's Day,* and other magazines.

NOTES ON *DETROIT MURDERS*

The book was included on the Duell, Sloan & Pearce Spring List in the January 31, 1948, issue of *Publishers' Weekly*, with a planned April publication date.

REVIEWS

Kirkus, April 1, 1948 (p. 183); *New York Herald Tribune Weekly Book Review*, May 2, 1948 (p. 9); *New Yorker*, April 24, 1948 (p. 111); *San Francisco Chronicle*, April 5, 1948 (p. 18).

SOURCES

Book Review Digest 1948. New York: The H.W. Wilson Company, 1949, p. 351.

Publishers' Weekly, June 14, 1947, p. 2958; January 31, 1948 (Duell, Sloan and Pearce Spring List) p. 395; March 27, 1948, pp. 1471–1472; and April 24, 1948, p. 1839.

(Givens) *The New York Times* obituary, September 29, 1964.

(Hamer) *Publishers' Weekly.* June 14, 1947, p. 2958 and March 27, 1948, pp. 1471–1472.

(Hamer) *New York Times* obituary, May 6, 1950.

(Haun) *Detroit Free Press* obituary, December 6, 2000.

(Howes) *Contemporary Authors Online*, Gale, 2006. Reproduced in Biography Resource Center. Farmington Hills, Mich.: Thomson Gale. 2006. Accessed July 21, 2006.

(McDougall) (Notre Dame University) *The Scholastic*, February 10, 1933, Vol. 66, Issue 15, p. 14)

(McDougall) *Detroit Free Press* obituary, August 18, 1955, p. 10.

(Wells) *Contemporary Authors Online*, Gale, 2006. Reproduced in Biography Resource Center. Farmington Hills, Mich.: Thomson Gale. 2006. Accessed July 21, 2006.

Detroit Murders, biographical sketches in the book and on the dust jacket.

LOS ANGELES MURDERS

Edited by Craig Rice
June 5, 1908 – August 28, 1957

RM7   First edition, first printing (1947) [5]

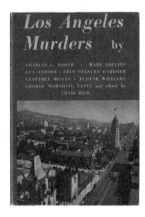

Los Angeles | MURDERS | [thin rule] | *by* | CHARLES G. BOOTH | MARY COLLINS | GUY ENDORE | ERLE STANLEY GARDNER | GEOFFREY HOMES | EUGENE D. WILLIAMS | GEORGE WORTHING YATES | *and edited by* | CRAIG RICE | [thin rule] | [Bloodhound device] | NEW YORK | *DUELL, SLOAN AND PEARCE*

COLLATION: 8" x 5½". 128 leaves. [i–vi] [1–2] 3–9 [10–12] 13–42 [43–44] 45–81 [82–84] 85–119 [120–122] 123–153 [154–156] 157–175 [176–178] 179–198 [199–200] 201–249 [250]. Numbers printed in roman in the center at the foot of the page.

CONTENTS: p. [i], half-title:"*Los Angeles | MURDERS*"; p. [ii], series title: "*Regional | MURDER SERIES* | EDITED BY | MARIE F. RODELL | [thin rule] | Vol. I NEW YORK MURDERS | Vol. II CHICAGO MURDERS | Vol. III DENVER MURDERS | Vol. IV SAN FRANCISCO MURDERS | Vol. V LOS ANGELES MURDERS | [Bloodhound device] | *In Preparation* |

CLEVELAND MURDERS | DETROIT MURDERS | CHARLESTON MUR-DERS | BOSTON MURDERS"; p. [iii], title; p. [iv], copyright page: "Copyright, 1947, by | Duell, Sloan & Pearce, Inc. | All rights reserved, including the | right to reproduce this book or | portions thereof in any form. | first printing | Printed in the United States of America"; p. [v], "*CONTENTS*"; p. [vi], blank; p. [1], half-title:"*Los Angeles* | *MURDERS*"; p. [2], blank; pp. 3–9, "*Preface* [signed Craig Rice, followed by a brief biographical sketch of Rice]"; p. [10], blank; p. [11], "*1921* | [within a rectangle] Madalynne Obenchain | [below rectangle] by | Mary Collins | [brief biographical sketch of Collins]"; p. [12], blank; pp. 13–42, text; p. [43], "*1922* | [within a rectangle] Clara Phillips | [below rectangle] by | George Worthing Yates | [brief biographical sketch of Yates]"; p. [44], blank; pp. 45–81, text; p. [82], blank; p. [83], "*1922* | [within a rectangle] William Desmond Taylor | [below rectangle] | by | Erle Stanley Gardner | [brief biographical sketch of Gardner]"; p. [84], [three-paragraph note advising that the author and publishers 'have tried to compile a running résumé and condensation of newspaper articles' on the William Desmond Taylor case, and concluding, 'What appears herein, therefore, does not purport to be a statement of what happened, but merely a statement of what appeared in the public press and is presented in the hope that this résumé of the case will, perhaps, lead to its eventual solution.']; pp. 85–119, text; p. [120], blank; p. [121], "*1922* | [within a rectangle] The 'Walburger' Case | [below the rectangle] by | Guy Endore | [brief biographical sketch of Endore]"; p. [122], blank; pp. 123–153, text; p. [154], blank; p. [155], "*1931* | [within a rectangle] Winnie Ruth Judd | [below rectangle] by | Geoffrey Homes | [brief biographical sketch of Homes]"; p. [156], blank; pp. 157–175, text; p. [176], blank; p. [177], "*1936* | | [within a rectangle] The Rattlesnake Murder | [below rectangle] by | Eugene D. Williams | [brief biographical sketch of Williams]"; p. [178], blank; pp. 179–198, text; p. [199], "*1944* | [within a rectangle] The Strange Case of Louise Peete | [below rectangle] by | Charles G. Booth | [brief biographical sketch of Booth]"; p. [200], blank; pp. 201–249, text; p. [250], blank.

BINDING: Medium tan (close to Pantone 722), stamped in burgundy (close to Pantone 187). Spine: "[read vertically] Los Angeles Murders | [read horizontally] | [Bloodhound device] | DUELL SLOAN | AND PEARCE". Cream endpapers.

DUST JACKET (white paper): Front and spine have a red background (close to Pantone 186). Front: "[white] *Los Angeles* | *Murders* by | CHARLES G. BOOTH · MARY COLLINS | GUY ENDORE · ERLE STANLEY GARDNER | GEOFFREY HOMES · EUGENE WILLIAMS | GEORGE WORTHING YATES and edited by | CRAIG RICE | [bottom half of cover carries a black-

and-white photo of the City of Los Angeles]". Spine: "[read vertically, in black] *Los Angeles* | *Murders* | [read horizontally] [Bloodhound device] | Duell, Sloan | and Pearce", Back: White background; printing in black. "[list naming the editor and the seven authors, with a brief biographical note on each]". Front flap: "[upper right] $3.00 | LOS ANGELES | MURDERS | by Charles G. Booth, Mary Collins, | Guy Endore, Erle Stanley Gardner, | Geoffrey Homes, George Worthing | Yates and edited by Craig Rice.[1] | [blurb] | *A Bloodhound Book* | [publisher's imprint]". Back flap: "REGIONAL MURDER | SERIES | NEW YORK MURDERS | [list of authors and price] | CHICAGO MURDERS | [list of authors and price] | DENVER MURDERS | [list of authors and price] | SAN FRANCISCO MURDERS | [list of authors and price] | *In Preparation* | DETROIT MURDERS | CHARLESTON MURDERS | CLEVELAND MURDERS | BOSTON MURDERS | [publisher's imprint]".

Published at $3.00 on June 11, 1947; number of copies printed unknown. Copyrighted July 8, 1947; deposited June 21, 1947.

The book is listed in "The Weekly Record," June 14, 1947, p. 2971.

Note: No evidence found that Duell, Sloan & Pearce reprinted *Los Angeles Murders*.

COPIES: CF

REPRINTS AND REPRODUCTIONS

New York: Editions for the Armed Services, No. 1313, 1947.

BIOGRAPHIES[2]

Craig Rice (June 5, 1908 – August 28, 1957), editor of *Los Angeles Murders*, a former crime reporter, was one of the most popular mystery novelists of her time. For a fuller biography, see the entry in *Chicago Murders*.

Charles G. Booth (February 12, 1896 – May 22, 1949) was a screenwriter and author. His book *Mr. Angel Comes Aboard* (Doubleday, 1944) was made into the 1945 film *Johnny Angel;* he wrote the screenplay for the film. In 1946, Booth won an Academy Award for his original screenplay, *The House on 92nd Street.*

1. The name of Eugene D. Williams, author of *The Rattlesnake Murder*, a chapter in the book, is missing from this listing.
2. Where birth or death dates are not stated, the information was not found.

Mary Collins (1908 –) wrote six mystery novels, *The Fog Comes* (1941), *Dead Center* (1942), *Only the Good* (1942), *The Sister of Cain* (1943), *Death Warmed Over* (1947), and *Dog Eat Dog* (1949); all were published by C. Scribner's Sons.

Guy Endore (July 4, 1900 – February 12, 1970) wrote at least a dozen books, many of them in the horror genre, and nine screenplays. His book *The Werewolf of Paris* (Farrar & Rinehart, 1933), adapted as the film *The Curse of the Werewolf* in 1961, was described as "the werewolf novel, just as *Dracula* is *the* vampire novel."[3] In 1945, Endore was nominated for an Oscar for his screenplay, *G.I. Joe.* Endore's *King of Paris* (Simon & Schuster, 1956) was a Book-of-the-Month Club selection.

Erle Stanley Gardner (July 27, 1889 – March 11, 1970), an experienced lawyer, created Perry Mason, the defense lawyer who appeared in scores of his novels. Gardner's stories also featured the "Doug Selby," Terry Clane, and Grampa Wiggins series. Two hundred million copies of his books were sold, and Gardner has been ranked as the best-selling American author. He was an editor and consultant to the "Perry Mason" television series, which ran in prime time from 1957 to 1966, and is said to have earned fifteen million dollars from the series.[4] Gardner received an Edgar Award in 1953 for *The Court of Last Resort*, and a Grand Master Award in 1961.

Geoffrey Homes (pseud. of Daniel Mainwaring) (July 22, 1902 – January 31, 1977) wrote the novel *One Against the Earth* (Long & Smith, 1933) under his own name and twelve mystery novels written as Geoffrey Homes. After *Build My Gallows High* (Morrow, 1946) was bought by RKO, he worked as Geoffrey Homes, writing the screenplays of thirty-six films for RKO, Paramount, MGM, Universal Studios, Allied Artists, Warner Bros., and United Artists during the 1950s and 1960s. Among his best-known screenplays are *The Phoenix City Story* (Allied Artists, 1955) and *Invasion of the Body Snatchers* (Allied Artists, 1956).

Eugene D. Williams (January 13, 1891 – January 23, 1972), was a graduate of the University of Southern California law school. He worked in the office of the district attorney of Los Angeles and as special assistant to the U.S. attorney general in Los Angeles. When *Los Angeles Murders* was published in 1947, Williams was a special prosecutor for the War Department in Tokyo. During the war crimes trials there, he and his colleagues successfully prosecuted Japanese Premier Hideki Tojo and twenty-five other defendants.

---

3. *St. James Guide to Horror, Ghost and Gothic Writers* (St. James Press, 1998.)
4. "Erle Stanley Gardner," Contemporary Authors Online, Gale, 2006, p.3.

George Worthing Yates (August 14, 1901 – June 6, 1975), a screenwriter, wrote mystery novels and teleplays. He wrote the screenplay for the 1927 film, *Lightning Lariats*. The film was based on his 1927 story, *The Cowboy and the King*. He wrote four mystery novels, *The Body that Came by Post* (1937), *The Body That Wasn't Uncle* (1939), *If a Body* (1941), and *There Was a Crooked Man* (1936), all published by W. Morrow & Company:

NOTES ON *LOS ANGELES MURDERS*

The book was advertised in the April 19, 1947, issue of *Publishers' Weekly*, with a planned publication date of June 13, 1947.

REVIEWS

Chicago Sun Book Week, June 15, 1947 (p. 4); *Kirkus*, May 1, 1947 (p. 255); *New Republic*, July 7, 1947 (p. 28); *New York Herald Tribune Weekly Book Review*, July 6, 1947 (p. 10); *New York Times Book Review*, August 3, 1947 (p. 6); *New Yorker*, June 14, 1947 (p. 100); *San Francisco Chronicle*, June 15, 1947 (p. 19); *Saturday Review of Literature*, July 5, 1947 (p. 34.).

SOURCES

Book Review Digest 1947. New York: The H.W. Wilson Company, 1948, p. 750.

Publishers' Weekly, April 19, 1947, p. 2082; and June 14, 1948, p. 2971.

The New York Times Book Review, August 3, 1947, p. 6.

(Endore) Contemporary Authors Online, Gale, 2006. Reproduced in Biography Resource Center. Farmington Hills, Mich.: Thomson Gale. 2006. Accessed July 21, 2006.

(Gardner) Contemporary Authors Online, Gale, 2006. Reproduced in Biography Resource Center. Farmington Hills, Mich.: Thomson Gale. 2006. Accessed July 21, 2006.

Los Angeles Murders, biographical sketches on dust jacket of book (for biographies).

NEW YORK MURDERS

Edited by Ted Collins
1900 – May 27, 1964

RM8   First edition, first printing (1944) [1]

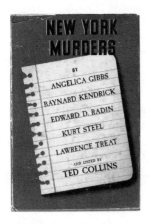

New York | *MURDERS* | [thin rule] | *by* | ANGEL-
ICA GIBBS | BAYNARD KENDRICK | EDWARD
D. RADIN | KURT STEEL | LAWRENCE TREAT
| *and edited by* | *TED COLLINS* | [thin rule] |
[Bloodhound device] | NEW YORK | *DUELL,*
SLOAN AND PEARCE

COLLATION: 8" x 5½". 128 leaves. [i–viii] ix–xiv
[1–2] 3–44 [45–46] 47–59 [60–62] 63–84 [85–86]
87–108 [109–110] 111–141 [142–144] 145–180
[181–182] 183–214 [215–216] 217–242. Numbers
printed in roman in headline at the outer margin
of the type page, except for pp. ix, 3, 47, 63, 87, 111,
145, 183, 217, and 239, on which the numbers are
printed in the center at the foot of the page.

CONTENTS: p. [i], half-title: "*New York* | *MURDERS*"; p. [ii], series title:
"*Regional* | *MURDER SERIES* | EDITED BY | MARIE F. RODELL | [thin
rule] | VOLUME ONE | NEW YORK MURDERS | [Bloodhound device] | *In*
Preparation | SAN FRANCISCO MURDERS | CHICAGO MURDERS"; p.
[iii], title; p. [iv], copyright page: "Copyright, 1944, by | Duell, Sloan &
Pearce, Inc. | All rights reserved, including the | right to reproduce this book
or | portions thereof in any form. | first edition | WAR EDITION | Produced
in accordance with | paper conservation orders of | the War Production
Board. | Printed in the United States of America"; p. [v], "*ACKNOWLEDG-*
MENTS"; p. [vi], blank; p. [vii], "*TABLE OF CONTENTS*"; p. [viii], blank;
pp. ix–xiv, "PREFACE [signed Ted Collins]"; p. [1], "1 | [thin rule] | 1860 |
The | WALTON-MATTHEWS CASE | *by Kurt Steel* | [thin rule]"; p. [2],
blank; pp. 3–44, text; p. [45], "2 | [thin rule] | 1873 | *The* | RYAN MURDERS |
Reprinted from Thomas Byrnes' | *'Professional Criminals of America'* | *Pub-*
lished in 1886 | [thin rule]"; p. [46], blank; pp. 47–59, text; p. [60], blank; p.
[61], "3 | [thin rule] | 1891 | *The* | RUTTINGER-WRIGHT CASE | *by Lawrence*
Treat | [thin rule]"; p. [62], blank; pp. 63–84, text; p. [85], "4 | [thin rule] |

1898 | *The* | DOLLY REYNOLDS CASE | *by Baynard Kendrick* | [thin rule] |
[nine-line Editor's Note]"; p. [86], blank; pp. 87–108, text; p. [109], "5 | [thin
rule] 1900 | KATHRYN SCHARN | *by Lawrence Treat* | [thin rule]"; p. [110],
blank; pp. 111–141, text; p. [142], blank; p. [143], "6 | [thin rule] | 1919 | *The* |
WILKINS CASE | *by Angelica Gibbs* | [thin rule]"; p. [144], blank; pp. 145–180,
text; p. [181], "7 | [thin rule] 1937 | *The* | PERRY-PALM CASE | *by Edward D.
Radin* | [thin rule]"; p. [182], blank; pp. 183–214, text; p. [215], ""[thin rule] |
A CALENDAR | OF | NEW YORK MURDERS | [thin rule]"; p. [216], blank;
pp. 217–238, text; pp. 239–242, "Bibliography".

BINDING: Light-blue cloth (close to Pantone 645), stamped in dark blue
(close to Pantone 648). Spine: "NEW | YORK | MURDERS | [decoration] |
[Bloodhound device] | DUELL SLOAN | AND PEARCE". Cream endpapers.

DUST JACKET (cream paper): Front and spine have a blue background
(close to Pantone 314). Front: "[black, shaded with white] NEW YORK |
MURDERS | [printed on a photo of a piece of blue-lined white notebook
paper torn from a spiral binder, in black] BY | ANGELICA GIBBS | BAY-
NARD KENDRICK | EDWARD D. RADIN | KURT STEEL | LAWRENCE
TREAT | AND EDITED BY | TED COLLINS". Spine: "[read vertically]
[black, shaded with white] NEW YORK MURDERS | [read horizontally]
[Bloodhound device] | DUELL, SLOAN | AND PEARCE". Back: White back-
ground; printing in black, except where noted. "[blue] About the Editor and
the Authors of | NEW YORK MURDERS | [black] [six short paragraphs
providing biographical sketches of the editor and the five contributors to
the book] | [thin blue rule] | [black] [publisher's imprint]". Front flap: "[up-
per right] $2.75 | [blue] NEW YORK | MURDERS | [black] by ANGELICA
GIBBS, | BAYNARD KENDRICK, | EDWARD D. RADIN, KURT STEEL, |
LAWRENCE TREAT | and TED COLLINS, Editor | [blurb] | [blue] *A Blood-
hound Mystery* | [black] [publisher's imprint]". Back flap: "*Coming* | [blue]
SAN FRANCISCO MURDERS | [black] by Anthony Boucher | H.H. Holmes
| Oscar Lewis | Alfred Meyers | Lenore Glen Offord | *and* Joseph Henry Jack-
son, | *Editor* | $2.75 | [blue] CHICAGO MURDERS | [black] by Elizabeth
Bullock | Nellise Child | Otto Eisenschiml | John Bartlow Martin | Craig Rice
| Vincent Starrett | *and* Sewell Peaslee Wright, | *Editor* | $2.75 | *Bloodhound
Mysteries* | [blue] [publisher's imprint]".

Published at $2.75 on October 27, 1944; number of copies printed unknown.
Copyrighted February 21, 1945; deposited December 2, 1944.

The book is listed in "The Weekly Record," October 28, 1944, p. 1772.

Note: Duell, Sloan & Pearce published at least three printings of *New York
Murders*.

COPIES: CF

REPRINTS AND REPRODUCTIONS

None.

BIOGRAPHIES[1]

Ted Collins (Joseph M. Collins) (1900 – May 27, 1964), the editor of *New York Murders*, was known to millions of radio listeners as the business manager, producer, and, at times, announcer of the singer Kate Smith's radio and television programs. Smith and Collins worked together for thirty years. His sixty-year stage, radio, and television career included more than fifteen thousand broadcasts. During World War I, Collins served in the Navy, later attending Fordham University.

Angelica Gibbs (**Canfield**), a reviewer and author, was a frequent contributor to the *New Yorker* from 1940 into the early 1950s. Her work also appeared in *Life*, *McCall's*, and other magazines. She wrote *Murder Between Drinks*, a mystery novel published by W. Morrow & Company in 1932.

Baynard Kendrick (April 8, 1894 – March 22, 1977). A co-founder and first president of the Mystery Writers of America, Kendrick wrote the Duncan Maclain series. The twelve series titles were serialized in the *New York Daily News*, *Redbook*, and *American Magazine*. Kendrick wrote nine novels, seven of them crime novels, two of these under the pseudonym Richard Hayward. From 1961 to 1964, he wrote a column, "Florida's Fabulous Past," in the *Tampa Sunday Tribune*. During World War II, Kendrick was a consultant to a U.S. Army convalescent hospital for blinded veterans. For this service, he received a plaque bestowed by General Omar N. Bradley.

Edward D. Radin (April 28, 1909 – March 28, 1966) was a newspaper reporter, specializing in crime reporting and murder trials. His first book, *Twelve Against the Law* (Duell, Sloan & Pearce, 1946), won the first Edgar Allan Poe Award from the Mystery Writers of America. In 1941, Radin abandoned journalism and became a full-time writer for major periodicals, including *Collier's*, the *Saturday Evening Post*, and *Esquire*. He is best known for his book, *Lizzie Borden: The Untold Story* (Simon & Schuster, 1961), which argued that Borden was innocent and introduced the family maid as a suspect in the famous murders.

Kurt Steel (pseudonym of Rudolph Hornady Kagey) (1905 – May 3, 1946). As Kurt Steel, he created the detective Hank Hyer and wrote short stories

1. Where birth or death dates are not stated, the information was not found.

and books. His novels included *The Imposter* (Harcourt, 1942), *Judas, Inc.* (Little, Brown, 1939), and *Ambush House* (Harcourt, 1943), the last two written as Rudolph Kagey. He also wrote on philosophy and logic; was secretary of the Authors Guild; was an instructor in philosophy and director of the evening division of New York University; and was director of public education for the New York World's Fair in 1939.

Lawrence Treat (December 21, 1903 – January 7, 1998) was born Lawrence Arthur Goldstone. He changed his name in 1940. Treat wrote fifteen mystery novels, three hundred short stories, and the series *Crime and Puzzlement*, in which solving the crime is presented as a challenging game, followed by the solution. In the *St. James Guide to Crime and Mystery Writers*, George N. Dove describes Treat as "a pioneer in police procedural fiction." Treat was a founding member of the Mystery Writers of America. He received Edgar Awards in 1965 and 1978.

NOTES ON *NEW YORK MURDERS*

Although the Duell, Sloan & Pearce announcement of the series in the February 26, 1944, issue of *Publishers' Weekly* named *San Francisco Murders* as the first series title, *New York Murders* became the first.

The book was included in the "DS&P Preview of Bestsellers" in the June 10, 1944, issue of *PW*. The book was later promoted in a full-page advertisement in the September 2, 1944, *PW*, noting, "Ted Collins and his five distinguished collaborators have here presented seven New York murders hitherto inexplicably given little or no attention."

REVIEWS

Book Week, November 5, 1944 (p. 9); *Kirkus*, October 1, 1944 (p. 461); *New Republic*, November 6, 1944 (p. 606); *New York Times Book Review*, January 7, 1945 (p. 7); *New Yorker*, November 4, 1944 (p. 87); *Weekly Book Review*, October 29, 1944 (p. 18).

SOURCES

Book Review Digest 1944. New York: The H.W. Wilson Company, 1945, p. 151.

Publishers' Weekly, February 26, 1944, p. 960; June 10, 1944, p. 2148; September 2, 1944, p. 798; and October 28, 1944, p. 1772.

The New York Times Book Review, January 7, 1945, p. 7.

(Collins) *The New York Times* obituary, May 28, 1964, p. 37.

(Kagey) Benét, William Rose. *The Reader's Encyclopedia: An Encyclopedia of World Literature and the Arts.* New York: Thomas Y. Crowell Company, 1948. (Entry on Rudolph Kagey; pseud. Kurt Steel.)

(Kendrick) *Contemporary Authors Online,* Gale, 2006. Reproduced in Biography Resource Center. Farmington Hills, Mich.: Thomson Gale. 2006. Accessed July 21, 2006.

(Radin) *Contemporary Authors Online,* Gale, 2006. Reproduced in Biography Resource Center. Farmington Hills, Mich.: Thomson Gale. 2006. Accessed July 21, 2006.

(Treat) *Contemporary Authors Online,* Gale, 2006. Reproduced in Biography Resource Center. Farmington Hills, Mich.: Thomson Gale. 2006. Accessed July 21, 2006.

New York Murders, biographical sketches on dust jacket.

SAN FRANCISCO MURDERS

Edited by Joseph Henry Jackson
July 21, 1894 – July 15, 1955

RM9   First edition, first printing (1947) [4]

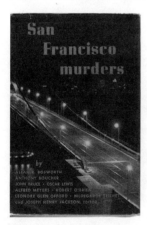

San Francisco I *MURDERS* I [thin rule] I *by* I AL-LAN R. BOSWORTH I ANTHONY BOUCHER I JOHN BRUCE I OSCAR LEWIS I ALFRED MEYERS I ROBERT O'BRIEN I LENORE GLEN OF-FORD I HILDEGARDE TEILHET I *and* I JOSEPH HENRY JACKSON, *editor* I [thin rule] I NEW YORK I *DUELL, SLOAN AND PEARCE*

COLLATION: 8" x 5½". 160 leaves. [i–vi] 1–14 [15–16] 17–47 [48–50] 51–72 [73–74] 75–117 [118–120] 121–147 [148–150] 151–171 [172–174] 175–209 [210–212] 213–242 [243–244] 245–278 [279–280] 281–298 [299–300] 301–314. Numbers printed in roman in the center at the foot of the page.

CONTENTS: p. [i], blank; p. [ii], series title: "*Regional* | *MURDER SERIES* | EDITED BY | MARIE F. RODELL | [thin rule] | Vol. I NEW YORK MURDERS | Vol. II CHICAGO MURDERS | Vol. III DENVER MURDERS | Vol. IV SAN FRANCISCO MURDERS | Vol. V LOS ANGELES MURDERS | [Bloodhound device] | *In Preparation* | CLEVELAND MURDERS | DETROIT MURDERS | CHARLESTON MURDERS"; p. [iii], title; p. [iv], copyright page: "Copyright, 1947, by | Duell, Sloan & Pearce | All rights reserved, including the | right to reproduce this book or | portions thereof in any form. | first printing | Printed in the United States of America"; p. [v], "*CONTENTS*"; p. [vi], blank; pp. 1–14, "*Preface* [signed Joseph Henry Jackson, Berkeley, California, December, 1946]"; p. [15], "*1870* | *'Wolves in the Fold'* | [within a rectangle] The Case of | Laura D. Fair | [below rectangle] by | Robert O'Brien | [brief biographical sketch of O'Brien]"; p. [16], blank; pp. 17–47, text; p. [48], blank; p. [49], "*1885* | *'The Phosphorescent Bride'* | [within a rectangle] The Case of | Dr. J. Milton Bowers | [below rectangle] by | Oscar Lewis | [brief biographical sketch of Lewis]"; p. [50], blank; pp. 51–72, text; p. [73], "*1895* | *'The Demon in the Belfry'* | [within a rectangle] The Case of | Theodore Durrant | [the first of a two column description] I -The Facts | by Hildegarde Teilhet | [brief biographical sketch of Teilhet] | [the second column] II-The Legends | by Anthony Boucher | [brief biographical sketch of Boucher]"; p. [74], blank; pp. 75–117, text; p. [118], blank; p. [119], "*1898* | *'The Gifts of Cordelia'* | [within a rectangle] The Case of | Cordelia Botkin | [below the rectangle] by | Lenore Glen Offord | [brief biographical sketch of Offord]"; p. [120], blank; pp. 121–147, text; p. [148], blank; p. [149], "*1902* | *'Tenderloin'* | [within a rectangle] The Murder of | Nora Fuller | [below rectangle] by | Alfred Meyers | [brief biographical sketch of Meyers]"; p. [150], blank; pp. 151–171, text; p. [172], blank; p. [173], "*1906* | *'Other than a Good One'* | [within a rectangle] The Case of | Emma LeDoux | [below rectangle] by | Joseph Henry Jackson | [brief biographical sketch of Jackson]"; p. [174], blank; pp. 175–209, text; p. [210], blank; p. [211], *1921* | *'The Flapjack Murder'* | [within a rectangle] The Murder of | Father Patrick E. Heslin | [below rectangle] by | John Bruce | [brief biographical sketch of Bruce]"; p. [212], blank; pp. 213–242, text; p. [243], "*1925* | *'Eleven Days' Wonder'* | [within a rectangle] The Case of | Charles Henry Schwartz | [below rectangle] by | Lenore Glen Offord | [brief biographical sketch of Offord]"; p. [244], blank; pp. 245–278, text; [p. 279]," *1930* | *'Boss-Missy'* | [within a rectangle] The Murder of | Rosetta Baker | [below rectangle] | by | Alfred Meyers | [brief biographical sketch of Meyers]"; p. [280], blank; pp. 281–298, text; p. [299], "*1936* | *'The Laughing Killer of* | *the Woodside Glens'* | [within a rectangle] The Case of | Jerome Braun von Selz | [below rectangle] by | Allan R. Bosworth | [brief biographical sketch of Bosworth]"; p. [300], blank; pp. 301–314, text.

BINDING: Gray cloth (close to Pantone 429), stamped in burgundy (close to Pantone 187). Spine: "[read vertically] San Francisco Murders | [read horizontally] | [Bloodhound device] | DUELL SLOAN | AND PEARCE". Cream endpapers.

DUST JACKET (cream paper): Front and spine carry a black-and-white photograph of the Golden Gate Bridge at night. Front: "[orange, close to Pantone 151)] San | Francisco | murders | [lower left] by | ALLAN R. BOSWORTH | ANTHONY BOUCHER | JOHN BRUCE · OSCAR LEWIS | ALFRED MEYERS · ROBERT O'BRIEN | LENORE GLEN OFFORD · HILDEGARD TEILHET | and JOSEPH HENRY JACKSON, EDITOR". Spine: "[read vertically, in orange] San Francisco murders | [read horizontally] [black and white] [Bloodhound device] | [orange] DUELL, | SLOAN | AND | PEARCE". Back: White background; printing in black. "[list naming the editor and the eight authors, with a brief biographical sketch of each]". Front flap: "[upper right] $2.75 | SAN FRANCISCO | MURDERS | by Allan R. Bosworth, Anthony | Boucher, John Bruce, Oscar Lewis, | Alfred Meyers, Robert O'Brien, | Lenore Glen Offord, Hildegarde | Teilhet and Joseph Henry Jackson, | editor. | [blurb, listing the ten murders recounted in the book] | *A Bloodhound Book* | [publisher's imprint]". Back flap: "REGIONAL MURDER | SERIES | NEW YORK MURDERS | [list of authors and price] | CHICAGO MURDERS | [list of authors and price] | DENVER MURDERS | [list of authors and price] | *In Preparation* | LOS ANGELES MURDERS | CLEVELAND MURDERS | CHARLESTON MURDERS | DETROIT MURDERS | BOSTON MURDERS | [publisher's imprint]".

Published at $2.75 on May 21, 1947;[1] number of copies printed unknown. Copyrighted June 25, 1947; deposited May 22, 1947.

The book is listed in "The Weekly Record," May 24, 1947, p. 2632.

Note: No evidence found that Duell, Sloan and Pearce reprinted *San Francisco Murders.*

COPIES: CF

REPRINTS AND REPRODUCTIONS

New York: Bantam Books, 1948. Paperback. Published at $.25.

---

1. A Duell, Sloan & Pearce advertisement in *Publishers' Weekly*, April 19, 1947, p. 2082, notes a May 23, 1947, publication date. May 21, 1947 is taken from copyright information in the Library of Congress.

BIOGRAPHIES[2]

Joseph Henry Jackson (July 21, 1894 – July 15, 1955), was editor of *San Francisco Murders* and the author of a chapter in the book. Jackson was a literary critic and editor, strongly identified with California, especially San Francisco. In 1920, after serving in the U.S. Army in World War I, he joined the staff of *Sunset Magazine* as associate editor, becoming editor in chief in 1926. In 1930, he became literary editor of the *San Francisco Chronicle*, a position he held for twenty-five years, editing a Sunday book page and writing a daily column, "Notes of a Bookman,"that was also carried by the *Los Angeles Times*. Jackson's weekly half-hour radio program, *Bookman's Notebook*, began locally in 1924 and was later broadcast nationally by NBC. The program continued until 1943. Jackson wrote books with California themes, including California mining towns and stage robbers, and *My San Francisco: An Appreciation* (Crowell, 1953). He edited several crime anthologies, including *The Portable Murder Book* (Viking, 1945).

Allan R. Bosworth (October 29, 1901 – July 18, 1986) was a police reporter, copy editor, picture editor, or news editor at California newspapers. When *San Francisco Murders* was published in 1947, he was a columnist at the *San Francisco Chronicle*. He served as an officer in the Navy in World War II and in the occupation of Japan, and retired as a captain in 1960, becoming a freelance writer. He wrote seventeen novels and at least six hundred short stories, a hundred of them in popular magazines, the others in pulp magazines, most with a western or nautical theme.

Anthony Boucher (pseud. of William Anthony Parker White) (August 21, 1911 – 1968) wrote five novels under his own name, including *The Case of the Baker Street Irregulars* (Simon & Schuster, 1940), and two as H.H. Holmes. Boucher was mystery reviewer for the *San Francisco Chronicle*, the *Chicago Sun-Times*, the *New York Herald Tribune*, and the *New York Times Book Review*, writing eight hundred and fifty weekly review columns and winning three Edgar Awards. In the mid 1940s, he wrote the plots of at least a hundred radio episodes of "The Adventures of Ellery Queen." The Bouchercon, named in his honor and self-described as "the world's leading mystery event," conducts an annual world mystery convention.

John Roberts Bruce (June 22, 1895 –) was a San Francisco crime reporter and editor. From 1930 to 1936, his column, "Skylines," ran in the *San Francisco Call*. Bruce was city editor of the *San Francisco Chronicle* when *San Francisco Murders* was published in 1947. He was the author of *Gaudy Cen-*

2. Where birth or death dates are not stated, the information was not found.

tury: The Story of San Francisco's Hundred Years of Robust Journalism (Random House, 1948).

Oscar Lewis (May 5, 1893 – July 11, 1992) was an author and historian who wrote at least twenty-five books, principally works of Western history and biography. The Book Club of California presents the Oscar Lewis Awards each year for significant contributions to Western history, fine printing, and the book arts. For a fuller biography of Oscar Lewis, see the entry for *High Sierra Country* in the *American Folkways Series* section.

Alfred Meyers (August 11, 1906 –) was born in Oregon. In 1922 and 1923, he attended the University of Oregon. He transferred to Notre Dame University and earned a bachelor of arts degree in 1926 and a master of arts degree in 1928, later teaching English there. He wrote the detective novel *Murder Ends the Song* (Reynal & Hitchcock, 1941) and a play, *The Sun Shall Set*. Meyers was assistant editor at the San Francisco office of Doubleday & Co. when *San Francisco Murders* was published in 1947 and, in 1949, manager of the new book department at Macy's San Francisco store.

Robert O'Brien (March 21, 1911 – August 15, 2004) was a journalist whose newspaper career began in 1934 in Goldsboro, North Carolina, and continued in Vermont and Rhode Island before he joined the staff of the *San Francisco Chronicle*. He was a columnist there from 1939 to 1953. *This Is San Francisco: A Classic Portrait of the City* (Whittlesey House, 1948), a collection of his *Chronicle* columns, was reprinted in paperback in 1994. His book *California Called Them* (McGraw-Hill, 1951), is a history of Northern California's Gold Rush towns.

Lenore Glen Offord (October 24, 1905 – April 24, 1991) wrote or was co-author of a dozen novels, including six mysteries published by Duell, Sloan & Pearce. Her last book, *A Boucher Portrait: Anthony Boucher as Seen by His Friends and Colleagues* (1968), was a tribute to her fellow crime writer, Anthony Boucher, the 1951 president of the Mystery Writers of America. From 1950 to 1982, Offord was mystery book critic at the *San Francisco Chronicle*. In 1951, she received an Edgar Award for her criticism. In 1963, the Baker Street Irregulars honored her with a titular investiture as "The Old Russian Woman."

Hildegard (Tolman) Teilhet (November 22, 1905 – January 24, 1999) with her husband, Darwin LeOra Teilhet, wrote the last three of the four "Baron von Kaz" mystery novels. Baron Franz Maximilian Karagoz und von Kaz is the detective featured in the four novels. The Teilhets co-wrote *Skwee-Gee* (Doubleday, 1940), a children's book. She was the author of five novels, *The*

Double Agent (Doubleday, 1945), *The Assassins* (Doubleday, 1946), *The Terri-fied Society* (Doubleday, 1947),*The Rim of Terror* (Coward-McCann, 1950), and *A Private Undertaking* (Coward McCann, 1952).

NOTES ON *SAN FRANCISCO MURDERS*

The book was first advertised in the 1945 Duell, Sloan & Pearce Spring List in the January 27, 1945, issue of *Publishers' Weekly*, with a planned pub-lication in May, but publication was delayed for nearly two years. The pub-lisher again advertised the book in its April 19, 1947, ad in *PW*, with a planned publication date of May 23, 1947. The book's copyright certificate is dated May 21, 1947.

REVIEWS

Chicago Sun Book Week, June 15, 1947 (p. 4); Kirkus, May 1, 1947 (p. 254); *New Republic,* May 26, 1947 (p. 29); *New York Herald Tribune Weekly Book Review,* June 1, 1947 (p. 9); *New York Times Book Review,* August 3, 1947 (p. 6); *New Yorker,* May 24, 1947 (p. 108); *San Francisco Chronicle,* May 25, 1947 (p. 19); *Saturday Review of Literature,* May 24, 1947 (p. 32).

SOURCES

Book Review Digest 1947. New York: The H.W. Wilson Company, 1948, p. 457.

Publishers' Weekly, January 27, 1945, (Duell, Sloan and Pearce Spring List) p. 320; April 19, 1947, p. 2082; May 24, 1947, p. 2632.

The New York Times Book Review, August 3, 1947, p. 6.

(Bosworth) *Contemporary Authors Online,* Gale, 2006. Reproduced in Biog-raphy Resource Center. Farmington Hills, Mich.: Thomson Gale. 2006. Ac-cessed July 21, 2006.

(Boucher) Nolan, William F. "Who was Anthony Boucher?" Undated biog-raphical essay found through Internet search, July, 2006.

(Bruce) *Who's Who in the West.* Chicago, Ill.: A.N. Marquis Co., 1954.

(Jackson) *Dictionary of American Biography, Supplement 5: 1951–1955.* Repro-duced in Biography Resource Center. Farmington Hills, Mich.: Thomson Gale. 2006. Accessed August 3, 2006.

(Lewis) *Contemporary Authors Online,* Gale, 2006. Reproduced in Biography Resource Center. Farmington Hills, Mich.: Thomson Gale. 2006. Accessed July 21, 2006.

(Meyers) *Who's Who on the Pacific Coast.* Chicago, Ill.: A.N. Marquis Co., 1949.

(O'Brien) www.chroniclebooks.com. *This is San Francisco.* Brief biography of O'Brien included with advertisement for the book.

(Offord) *Contemporary Authors Online*, Gale, 2006. Reproduced in Biography Resource Center. Farmington Hills, Mich.: Thomson Gale. 2006. Accessed July 21, 2006.

(Teilhet) [Darwin Teilhet] *Contemporary Authors Online*, Gale, 2006. Reproduced in Biography Resource Center. Farmington Hills, Mich.: Thomson Gale. 2006. Accessed July 21, 2006.

Dillon, Richard H., writer & historian. Letter to CF, August 15, 2006. Valued information regarding the contributors to *San Francisco Murders.*

San Francisco Murders, biographical sketches on dust jacket.

American Customs Series
1946–1949

The Vanguard Press, Inc.
Publisher

1946
It's An Old New England Custom

1947
It's An Old Pennsylvania Custom

1948
It's An Old California Custom
It's An Old New Orleans Custom

1949
It's An Old State of Maine Custom
It's An Old Cape Cod Custom
It's an Old Wild West Custom

AMERICAN CUSTOMS SERIES

Introduction and Publishing History

IN September 1946, *It's an Old New England Custom* by Edwin Valentine Mitchell, the first title in the American Customs Series, was a few weeks away from publication by Vanguard Press when James Henle, Vanguard's president, wrote to Mitchell, asking if he would "mind" if Vanguard took the title of the book as the "basis for other books on other parts of the country." Henle continued, "I think I can predict with some assurance – at least our experience with the American Mountain Series tends to bear this out – that if we published :"It's an Old Carolina Custom" or "It's an Old Kentucky Custom" next year, such a book will almost inevitably re-stimulate the sale of your own title. How does this seem to you, and, incidentally, is there any other part of the country on which you feel inspired to write?" *It's an Old New England Custom* was published on October 3, 1946.

In his reply to Henle, Mitchell wrote, "I think the idea of a series on the regional customs of America is excellent and it is certainly quite all right with me. I have always favored series anyway. Had I known the New England item was to be the first one I should have adhered more strictly to the title and covered more ground. Sometime, if it strikes you favorably, I would like to tackle New York." Mitchell eventually wrote four of the seven books in the Customs series, but the series does not include a book on New York customs.

One series title was published in 1947: *It's an Old Pennsylvania Custom* by Edwin Valentine Mitchell on November 3. Vanguard had begun promoting the book well before then. Henle had written to Mitchell in May, reporting, "we are stirring up a tremendous amount of advance interest – especially in Philadelphia – in *It's an Old Pennsylvania Custom*," adding that the firm had arranged "autographing parties" for Mitchell in Philadelphia and Lancaster and planned to arrange for Mitchell to speak at a *Philadelphia Inquirer* luncheon. Just prior to its publication, advance sales of the book were nearly three thousand copies.

Two series titles were published in 1948: *It's an Old California Custom* by Lee Shippey on January 6, 1948 and *It's an Old New Orleans Custom* by Lura Robinson on October 21. Vanguard had planned to publish Shippey's book in late 1948 or early 1949 in conjunction with the centenary of the California Gold Rush of 1849. Shippey completed the manuscript in the summer of

1947 and suggested the book be published in January 1948, noting that the discovery of gold in California occurred in January 1848 and that "scores of cities and towns in the Mother Lode Country" would begin celebrating centennials in January. His suggestion was accepted by Vanguard.

At the suggestion of the publisher, Lura Robinson's book included some characteristic New Orleans recipes, which, it turned out, helped with sales. At the time, Mitchell was working on two titles in the series, one on Maine, the other on Cape Cod, and Henle suggested that Mitchell include recipes in them. Mitchell accepted the suggestion, and both books contained recipes for local specialities.

Three series titles were published in 1949: *It's an Old Cape Cod Custom* by Edwin Valentine Mitchell *on May 11*, *It's an Old State of Maine Custom*, also by Mitchell, on June 29, and *It's an Old Wild West Custom* by Duncan Emrich, on September 17.

Advance sales of *It's an Old Cape Cod Custom* were nearly two thousand and four hundred copies.

Early advertisements for the *Maine* book used the title "*It's an Old Maine Custom*," generating the observation from a book seller in New England that no one in Maine would say "I'm a Maine man," but rather would say "I'm a State of Maine man." The suggestion was made to Henle to title the book *It's an Old State of Maine Custom*. Henle reported this to Mitchell, who agreed.

Vanguard gave *It's an Old Wild West Custom*, the seventh and final title in the series, a "special" publication date, September 17, for an Author's Day celebration in Virginia City, Nevada, where four authors, residents of the city, would participate in book-signing appearances at various saloons in the city.

Vanguard ceased publication of the American Customs Series after having published seven titles, documenting the "old customs" of three states, California, Maine, and Pennsylvania; two regions, New England and the Wild West; a city, New Orleans; and Cape Cod. *It's an Old California Custom* appears to have had the largest printing in the series, with first and second printings totaling fifteen thousand. Three titles in the series, *New England*, *Pennsylvania*, and *Maine*, were reprinted, *Maine* in paperback. *It's an Old Wild West Custom* was published in a British printing.

If measured by the publication dates of the first and last titles, the series was three years old when it ended. Sales of the books, as might have been expected, seem to have been weak in states, regions, or cities other than those that were the subject of a given title.

IT'S AN OLD CALIFORNIA CUSTOM

Lee Shippey
February 26, 1884 – December 30, 1969

AC1   First edition, first printing (1948) [3]

It's an Old | California Custom | LEE SHIPPEY | [early California illustration (from The Bettman Archive) of a bearded gold miner, pickaxe in hand, at his feet a spade and a pan with perhaps some pieces of gold at its edge] | THE VAN-GUARD PRESS, INC. · NEW YORK

COLLATION: 8" x 5½". 152 leaves. [i–x] [1–2] 3–292 [293–294]. Numbers printed in roman within brackets in the center at the foot of the page.

CONTENTS: p. [i], half-title: "IT'S AN OLD | CALIFORNIA CUSTOM"; p. [ii], blank; p. [iii], title; p. [iv], copyright page: "Copyright, 1948, by Lee Shippey | Published simultaneously in Canada by the Copp Clark Company, Ltd. | No portion of this book may be reprinted in any form without the written | permission of the publisher, except by a reviewer who wishes to quote brief | passages in connection with a review for a newspaper or magazine. | The early California illustrations on the title page and on pages 27, 201, | and 265 are from The Bettman Archive; those on pages 49, 157, and 185 | are reproduced from Clarence P. Hornung's *Handbook of Early American* | *Advertising Art;* those on pages 68 and 134 are from Culver Service; the | illustration on page 248 was adapted from a drawing by Charles Nahl in *Old* | *Block's Sketch Book.* | Designed by Stefan Salter | Manufactured in the United States of America by H. Wolff, | New York, N.Y."; p. [v], dedication: *"TO MY HELPSPEND | my companion in ten thousand happy adventures, vicarious | and personal—vicarious in the good books we have read to- | gether, actual in the many trips we have taken together in | quest of human interest. She is my comrade in nearly all I | read and write, and she read aloud all or part of nearly a | hundred books while I took notes for this one.";* p. [vi], blank; p. [vii], "AC-KNOWLEDGMENTS [signed L.S.]"; p. [viii], blank; p. [ix], "CONTENTS"; p. [x], blank; p. [1], half-title: "IT'S AN OLD | CALIFORNIA CUSTOM"; p. [2], blank; pp. 3–292, text; pp. [293–294], blank.

ILLUSTRATIONS: Small illustrations appear on pp. 3, 27, 49, 68, 88, 112, 134, 157, 171, 185, 201, 220, 248, 265, and 276.

BINDING: Blue-gray cloth (close to Pantone 442); stamped in yellow (close to Pantone 120). Front: Outline of the illustration of the gold miner, which is also found on the title page. Spine: "LEE | SHIPPEY | [read vertically] It's an Old California Custom | [read horizontally] VANGUARD". Cream endpapers.

DUST JACKET (white paper): Front and spine have a dark blue background (close to Pantone 294). Within a yellow, one-inch wide rectangular frame (close to Pantone 128), are eighteen illustrations in dark blue relating to the early days of California, for example, a stage coach, a railroad locomotive, a grizzly bear, a gold miner. Within the yellow frame, in the upper left corner, in yellow, is the illustration of the gold miner also found on the title page and on the front of the binding; to his right, in white, "It's an | Old | California | Custom | Lee Shippey". Spine: "[white] It's | an | Old | California | Custom | by | Lee | Shippey | [at bottom] Vanguard". Back: White background; printing in dark blue. "[upper left] [photograph of Lee Shippey in shirt sleeves, talking on a telephone] [to the right of the photograph] Wherein the Author Confesses | It Was Love at First Sight | [three-paragraph, first-person quotation in which Shippey recounts his love of California and of his job as a newspaper columnist[1]] | (For Other Titles in the American Custom [sic] Series, see back flap) | The Vanguard Press, Inc., 424 Madison Ave., New York 17, N.Y.". Front flap: All printing in dark blue. "[blurb] | It's an Old California Custom: | [list of fifteen California customs corresponding to the fifteen chapters of the book] | This is the latest volume in the Amer- | ican Customs Series begun in It's an Old | New England Custom and It's an Old | Pennsylvania Custom. | With contemporary illustrations | [lower right] $3.00". Back flap: "Other Titles in | THE AMERICAN CUSTOMS SERIES | It's An Old New England Custom | by EDWIN VALENTINE MITCHELL | [blurb, followed by quotes from two reviews] | It's An Old Pennsylvania Custom | by EDWIN VALENTINE MITCHELL | [quotes from two reviews] | Each volume illustrated with contemporary cuts | At all bookstores | $3.00 | [publisher's imprint]."

Published at $3.00 on January 6, 1948; 10,000 copies printed. Copyrighted January 6, 1948; deposited January 5, 1948.

The book is listed in "The Weekly Record," January 24, 1948, p. 347.

1. The quotations are taken from a 1947 letter from Shippey to his editor at Vanguard, James Henle. The letter begins, "Maybe those needing biographical material can get enough from this:" and continues for two typewritten pages.

Note: Vanguard published at least two printings of *It's An Old California Custom.* The first printing, of ten thousand copies, which quickly sold out, was followed by a second printing of five thousand copies.

CITED: *Guns* 2007

COPIES: CF

REPRINTS AND REPRODUCTIONS

Reproduced on microfilm. Berkeley, Calif.: University of California, Library Photographic Service, 1989. 1 reel, 35 mm.

BIOGRAPHY

(Henry) Lee Shippey was born on February 26, 1884, in Memphis, Tennessee, the son of William Francis and Elizabeth Kerr (Freleigh) Shippey. When the elder Shippey died, the family moved to Kansas City, Missouri. Shippey was known throughout his life as Lee.

Shippey worked his way through high school in Kansas City, graduating at age 20. After his graduation, he worked as a proofreader's assistant or a proofreader at several Kansas City newspapers. In his early twenties, he lost his sight, suffering total blindness for about four months. Although he regained some limited vision, he remained legally blind for life.

Shippey had earlier submitted some short, light-hearted pieces to the *Kansas City Star*, work he assumed had been rejected. During the illness of one of its regular columnists, the paper published some of this material. Shippey's sister read one of his humor columns to him as he lay in bed, completely blind, assuring him that she was reading from the actual newspaper, not spoofing him. For the rest of his life, he remembered this as the dream of his life come true, the most thrilling incident he would ever experience. During his convalescence, he was hired as a regular columnist for the paper, at first dictating columns from his sickbed, almost always composing humorous pieces.[2]

During this time, Shippey bought a small-town newspaper, the Higginsville (Missouri) *Jeffersonian*. He worked as the paper's owner, editor, and publisher, but, pressed for money, also wrote feature stories for the *St. Louis Post-Dispatch*, the *St. Louis Republic*, the *Kansas City Star*, and *Collier's* magazine.

With the U.S. entry into World War I, Shippey sold the *Jeffersonian*, returned to Kansas City, and attempted to enlist, first in the Navy and then in the Army, but was refused, given his defective vision. After some maneuver-

2. Miller, Max. "Lee Shippey, Writer." *San Diego Magazine*, September, 1966, p.115.

ing, he became a war correspondent for the *Kansas City Star*, serving in Europe in 1918 and 1919.

While in France, Shippey met Madeleine Babin. After Shippey and his first wife were divorced, he and Madeleine were married. The couple had a daughter, Sylvia, and four sons, Henry, Charles, John, and Frank.

In 1921 and 1922, Shippey edited an English-language newspaper, the *Tampico* (Mexico) *Press*. Back in the United States, the family settled in Del Mar, California. Shippey worked as a freelance writer until 1927, when he began to work for the *Los Angeles Times*. His daily column, "The Lee Side o' L.A.," ran from 1927 to 1950. During these years, he also wrote the columns "Martian Observer," "Joshua Little," "How It Looks to Mars," and "Needles-Eye View," and a weekly column, "The Seymour Family," a humorous look at American families. Through the late 1960s, he contributed such columns as "Surfside o' Del Mar," "Southwest Corner," "Lee Shippey Says," and "Lee Shippey Asks" to the *San Diego Union* and *Del Mar Surfcomber*.

Although Shippey was known as the dean of Southern California columnists, he was also an accomplished poet and novelist and was active in several professional writers' organizations. He wrote nine books, two of which, *The Great American Family* (Houghton, 1938) and *It's an Old California Custom*, were adapted by others into stage plays.

Lee Shippey died in Encinitas, California, on December 30, 1969, at age 85.[3]

PAPERS: Lee Shippey's papers are held by the Mandeville Special Collections Library, University of California, San Diego, La Jolla, California.

NOTES ON *IT'S AN OLD CALIFORNIA CUSTOM*

In a February, 13, 1947, letter to Lee Shippey, James Henle, president of Vanguard Press, said Shippey's name had been mentioned "in connection" with a book Vanguard was planning, to be called *It's An Old California Custom*. After receiving Shippey's expression of interest in his February 17 reply, Henle responded on February 19, noting Vanguard's success in publishing *It's an Old New England Custom* and adding, "Your name was suggested to me by one of our Pacific Coast representatives . . . as 'the ideal man to write this book.'" Vanguard planned to publish the book in conjunction with the centenary of the California Gold Rush, probably late in 1948 or early in 1949, and Henle's letter proposed a deadline of March 1, 1948, for Shippey's manuscript.

On March 11, Henle wrote to Shippey, informing him that he had been chosen to write the California book and noting that the contract would

3. Some sources say 86.

be sent to him in the next few days. With his March 17 letter to Henle, Shippey returned the signed contract, noting "I am delighted with this assignment . . . All my 20 years as columnist on this newspaper [the *Los Angeles Times*] I have taken great interest in the subject and have made friends of many of the persons best qualified to give accurate information on various phases of the subject."

The contract called for the manuscript to be delivered on or before March 1, 1948. Shippey was to receive an advance of five hundred dollars, half upon signing the contract and half upon delivery of the completed manuscript, and royalties of 10 percent of the retail list price of the book on the first five thousand copies sold and 15 percent on all copies sold thereafter. He finished the manuscript in the summer of 1947, well ahead of deadline.

In a July 31, 1947, letter to Henle, Shippey suggested the book be brought out in January, 1948, noting, "Marshall[4] found the nugget heard around the world in January, 1848, and scores of cities and towns in the Mother Lode country will be celebrating centennials between that date and 1854 and there would be news value in presenting the book on a historic date." The book was published on January 6, 1948.

The book was included in Vanguard's 1948 Spring List. By March, the first printing of ten thousand copies had sold out, and the second printing, five thousand copies, was nearly sold out. There is no evidence of a third printing, even though the book was enjoying such strong sales, especially in California. The book was among the "*Candidates for the Best Seller List*" in the March 20, 1948, issue of *Publishers' Weekly*. A few weeks later, *PW* reported the book was a best seller in nonfiction in California.

In November 1950, Vanguard sold some copies of the book at a reduced price, but, by mid-1951, had resumed selling the book at the publication price of three dollars.

REVIEWS

Booklist, February 15, 1948 (p. 215); *Chicago Sun*, January 28, 1948 (n.p.); *Christian Science Monitor*, February 26, 1948 (p. 14); *Kirkus*, December 15, 1947 (p. 687); *Library Journal*, January 15, 1948 (p. 121); *New York Times Book Review*, February 15, 1948 (p. 10); *San Francisco Chronicle*, January 29, 1948 (p. 16); *Wisconsin Library Bulletin*, April 1948 (p. 81).

4. James Wilson Marshall (1810–1885), 19th century discoverer of gold in California.

SELECTED WRITINGS BY LEE SHIPPEY

Personal Glimpses of Famous Folks (Sierra Madre, Calif.; Sierra Madre Press, 1929); *Folks You Should Know* (Sierra Madre, Calif.: Sierra Madre Press, 1930); *Where Nothing Ever Happens* (Boston: Houghton, 1935); *The Girl Who Wanted Experience* (Boston: Houghton, 1937); (with Herbert Floercky) *California Progress* (Sacramento: California State Department of Education, 1936); *The Great American Family* (Boston: Houghton, 1938); *If We Only Had Money* (Boston: Houghton, 1939); ***It's an Old California Custom*** (New York: Vanguard, 1948); *The Los Angeles Book* (Boston: Houghton, 1950); (autobiography) *Luckiest Man Alive* (Los Angeles: Westernlore Press, 1959)

Two of Shippey's books: *The Great American Family* ("The Great American Family: A Comedy") and *It's an Old California Custom* were adapted into plays by others.

SOURCES

Book Review Digest, 1948. New York: The H.W. Wilson Company, 1949, pp. 767–768.

Publishers' Weekly, October 4, 1947, p. 1802; January, 24, 1948, p. 347; January, 31, 1948, p. 513; March 20, 1948, p., 1409; and April 10, 1948, p. 1652.

The New York Times Book Review, February 15, 1948, p. 10.

Miller, Max. "Lee Shippey, Writer." *San Diego Magazine*, September 1966, p. 96.

Wheeler, Tom. "'*The Luckiest Man Alive*', Lee Shippey." *The San Dieguito Citizen*, January 25, 1968, p. A3.

Evening Tribune (San Diego) obituary, December 31, 1969, p. B-8.

The New York Times obituary, January 1, 1970, p. 23.

Publishers' Weekly obituary, February 9, 1970, p. 64.

Who Was Who in America. Volume V, 1969–1973. Chicago: Marquis Who's Who, 1973, p. 659.

Kurutz, Gary F. *The California Gold Rush.* San Francisco: The Book Club of California, 1997.

Contemporary Authors Online, Gale, 2003. Reproduced in *Biography Resource Center*. Farmington Hills, Mich.: The Gale Group. 2003. Accessed February 6, 2003.

Claassen, Lynda Corey. Director, Mandeville Special Collections Library, University of California, San Diego. E-mail message to CF, March 27, 2003.

Mandeville Special Collections Library, University of California, San Diego. Lee Shippey Papers, 1915–1970, Series 3, Writings. Box 3, Folder 1.

Vanguard Press Archives. Box 156. "Lee Shippey 1947–1948" and "Shippey Publicity." Columbia University Rare Book and Manuscript Library. New York, New York. Accessed June, 2003.

IT'S AN OLD CAPE COD CUSTOM

Edwin Valentine Mitchell
April 24, 1890 – November 26, 1960

AC2   First edition, first printing (1949) [5]

It's an Old I Cape Cod Custom I [illustration of a surfaced whale emitting two waterspouts] I by EDWIN VALENTINE MITCHELL I *Author of "It's an Old New England Custom,"* etc. I THE VAN-GUARD PRESS, INC. · NEW YORK

COLLATION: 8" x 5½". 124 leaves. [i–vi] [1–2] 3–242. Numbers printed in roman in headline at the outer margin of the type page, except for pp. 3, 16, 43, 72, 94, 114, 132, 150, 166, 181, 194, 206, and 219, on which the numbers are printed in the center at the foot of the page.

CONTENTS: p. [i], half-title: "IT'S AN OLD I CAPE COD CUSTOM"; p. [ii], blank; p. [iii], title; p. [iv], copyright page: "Copyright, 1949, by Edwin Valentine Mitchell I Published simultaneously in Canada by I the Copp Clark Company, Ltd. I No portion of this book may be reprinted in any form without the written I permission of the publisher, except by a reviewer who wishes to quote brief I passages in connection with a review to be included in a newspaper or I magazine. I Manufactured in the United States of America I by H. Wolff, New York, N.Y.[1]"; p. [v], "CON-

1. No designer is named for this book, which has a cleaner, more modern look than earlier books in the series, all of which were designed by Stefan Salter.

TENTS"; p. [vi], blank; p. [1], half-title: "IT'S AN OLD | CAPE COD CUS-
TOM"; p. [2], blank; pp. 3–242, text.

ILLUSTRATIONS: Small illustrations appear on pp. 3, 16, 43, 72, 94, 114, 132,
150, 166, 181, 194, 206, and 219.

BINDING: Blue-gray cloth (close to Pantone 443); stamped in burgundy
(close to Pantone 187). Front: Stamped in the center is an illustration of a
surfaced whale emitting two waterspouts; this is also found on the title page.
Spine: "EDWIN | VALENTINE | MITCHELL | [read vertically] It's an Old
Cape Cod Custom | [read horizontally] VANGUARD". Cream endpapers.
Top edges orange.

DUST JACKET (white paper): Front and spine have a black background.
"[within an inch-wide medium-tan rectangular frame (close to Pantone
472), with black-and-white sea shells decorating the frame] [upper left, on
an irregular medium tan background, in black and white] [illustration of a
young man leaning against a stool in front of a bar; this illustration is not
found in the book] [to the right and below the illustration, in white] It's an
| Old | Cape Cod | Custom | Edwin Valentine Mitchell". Spine: "[white] It's |
an | Old | Cape Cod | Custom | by | Edwin | Valentine | Mitchell | [three
black-and-white sea shells within a medium tan rectangular panel | [at bot-
tom] Vanguard". Back: "*Other Titles in* | THE AMERICAN CUSTOMS SE-
RIES | [list of the four previous series titles and their authors, with quotes
from reviews for each] | *Each volume illustrated with contemporary cuts and
$3.00 at all booksellers* | THE VANGUARD PRESS | 424 Madison Avenue
New York 17, N.Y.". Front flap: "[blurb] | [list of thirteen Cape Cod customs
corresponding to the thirteen chapters of the book] | [lower right] $3.00".
Back flap: "ABOUT THE AUTHOR | [brief biographical sketch of Edwin
Valentine Mitchell]".

Published at $3.00, on May 11, 1949; number of copies printed unknown.[2]
Copyrighted May 19, 1949; deposited May 9, 1949.

The book is listed in "The Weekly Record," May 21, 1949, p. 2107.

Note: No evidence found that Vanguard Press reprinted *It's An Old Cape
Cod Custom.*

COPIES: CF

2. An undated list (ca. 1952) of four titles in the Customs series in an Edwin V. Mitchell
file in the Vanguard Press archives at Columbia University indicates 4,580 copies printed
as of May 4, 1949.

REPRINTS AND REPRODUCTIONS

None.

BIOGRAPHY

Edwin Valentine Mitchell was born in Hartford, Connecticut, on April 24, 1890, the son of Emlyn Valentine and Mary (Clark) Mitchell. Mitchell's father was a grain shipper in New England for more than fifty years.

Mitchell attended public high school in Hartford and, in 1911, graduated from Boston University Law School. His first book, *The Doctor in Court* (Rebman), was published in 1913. He practiced law in Boston until 1914, when he joined the faculty of the University of South Dakota as assistant professor of law, becoming full professor in 1916 and resigning in 1920. The July, 1920, issue of the *South Dakota Alumni Quarterly* reported Mitchell's departure from the university, noting, "He returns to his native city, Hartford, Connecticut, where he will engage in the business of selling books, and eventually he expects to become a publisher."

In the 1920 U.S. Census, the listing for Mitchell's family includes Margaret S., age 29, identified as his wife, and three daughters, Mary, age 3, and Elinor and Elaine, both listed as 2 months old. At the time, the family lived in Clay County, South Dakota, and Mitchell was 29.

In 1921, Mitchell opened a bookshop at 27 Lewis Street in Hartford. In time, the shop, Edwin Valentine Mitchell, Inc., which engaged in book sales and book publishing, became known for its charm and intelligent service. In 1929, James Thrall Soby, author, art collector, and later a director and trustee of the Museum of Modern Art, became a partner in the firm. In 1931, the two business lines of the firm, book selling and book publishing, were separated. Mitchell sold his interest to Soby and entered the publishing business with Dodd, Mead and Company, which acted as his distributor. Two years later he repurchased his interest in the shop, by then named the Lewis Street Bookshop. He restored the name Edwin V. Mitchell, Inc., and Soby remained a director of the company. In 1935, the shop became part of the Brentano's chain. In 1952, the shop was closed.

In 1945, Mitchell joined the Garden City Publishing Company, a subsidiary of Doubleday, as assistant to Van H. Cartmell, editor in chief of the firm. With the publication of *It's an Old New England Custom* in 1946, Mitchell, by then living in New York, had written fifteen books. He would write three more volumes in the *American Customs Series*: *It's an Old Pennsylvania Custom* (1947), *It's an Old Cape Cod Custom*, and *It's an Old State of Maine Custom*, both published in 1949.

In March 1950, The Frontier Press Co. of Buffalo, New York, announced that Mitchell had been appointed editor of The Lincoln Library of Essential Information, a popular condensed encyclopedia founded in 1924. Mitchell was editor of the twenty-first edition, published in 1953.

Mitchell lived the last five years of his life in Connecticut, residing in Farmington with his daughter, Elaine.

Edwin Valentine Mitchell died in Hartford, Connecticut, on November 26, 1960, at age 70.

NOTES ON *IT'S AN OLD CAPE COD CUSTOM*

Although Vanguard Press introduced and advertised the book and *It's an Old State of Maine Custom* together, noting that they were scheduled to be published on May 16, 1949, only *It's an Old Cape Cod Custom* was ready for publication by May. (The copyright certificate notes a May 11, 1949 publication date.) Vanguard's announcements noted that cooperative advertising for the two books would be offered and that postcards for bookshop mailings would be provided. Advance sales of *It's an Old Cape Cod Custom* were nearly two thousand four hundred.

REVIEWS

Booklist, June 15, 1949 (p. 353); *Christian Science Monitor,* July 12, 1949 (p. 14); *Kirkus,* May 1, 1949 (p. 244); *Library Journal,* May 15, 1949 (p. 816); *New York Herald Tribune Weekly Book Review,* July 3, 1949 (p. 9); *New York Times Book Review,* June 19, 1949 (p. 8); *San Francisco Chronicle,* July 3, 1949 (p. 17); *Saturday Review of Literature,* June 18, 1949 (p. 37); *Springfield Republican,* July 3, 1949 (p. 8B).

SELECTED WRITINGS BY EDWIN VALENTINE MITCHELL

The Doctor in Court (New York: Rebman, 1913); *Hospitals and the Law* (New York: Rebman, 1915); *Morocco Bound: Adrift Among Books* (New York: Farrar & Rinehart, 1929); *The Art of Authorship* (New York: Loring & Massey, 1935); (ed.) *The Art of Chess Playing* (New York: Mussey, 1936); *The Horse & Buggy Age in New England* (New York: Coward-McCann, 1937); *American Village* (New York: Stackpole Sons, 1938); *Maine Summer* (New York: Coward-McCann, 1939); *Anchor to Windward* (New York: Coward-McCann, 1940); (comp.) *An Encyclopedia of American Politics* (Garden City, N.Y.: Doubleday, 1946); ***It's an Old New England Custom*** (New York: Vanguard, 1946); ***It's an Old Pennsylvania Custom*** (New York: Vanguard, 1947); (comp. and author of foreword) *Great Fishing Stories* (Garden City, N.Y.: Garden City Publishing, 1948); *The Pleasures of Walking* (New York: Vanguard, 1948); *Yankee Folk*

(New York: Vanguard, 1948); *It's an Old Cape Cod Custom* (New York: Vanguard, 1949); *It's an Old State of Maine Custom* (New York: Vanguard, 1949); (ed.) *The Perma Week-end Companion* (New York: Permabooks, 1950); *The Romance of New England Antiques* (New York: Current Books, 1950).

SOURCES

South Dakota Alumni Quarterly, Vol. 10, No. 3, October 1914, p. 73; and Vol. 16, No. 2, July 1920, p. 80.

U.S. Federal Census, 1920 and 1930.

Hartford Courant, various clippings, 1931–1946, n.d., n.p.

Book Review Digest 1949. New York: The H.W. Wilson Company, 1950, p. 644.

The New York Times Book Review, June 19, 1949 , p. 8.

Publishers' Weekly, January 22, 1949, p. 245; January 29, 1949, pp. 460 and 568; February 5, 1949, pp. 814–815; and May 21, 1949, p. 2107.

Vanguard Press Archives. Box 104. "Edwin Valentine Mitchell 1948–1949". Columbia University Rare Book and Manuscript Library.

Hartford Courant (obituaries), November 28 and 29, 1960, n.p.

Burke, W.J., and Will D. Howe. *American Authors and Books: 1640 to the Present Day*. New York: Crown Publishers, Inc., 1962, p. 499.

IT'S AN OLD STATE OF MAINE CUSTOM

Edwin Valentine Mitchell
April 24, 1890 – November 26, 1960

AC3   First edition, first printing (1949) [6]

It's an Old | State of Maine Custom | [illustration of a two-masted sailing ship, buildings and hills in the background] | EDWIN VALENTINE MITCHELL | *Author of "It's an Old New England Custom," etc.* | THE VANGUARD PRESS, INC. · NEW YORK

COLLATION: 8" x 5½". 128 leaves. [i–viii] [1–2] 3–248. Numbers printed in roman in headline at the outer margin of the type page, except for pp. 3, 44, 80, 92, 103, 115, 129, 146, 162, 183, 204, 225, and 235, on which the numbers are printed in the center at the foot of the page.

CONTENTS: p. [i], half-title: "IT'S AN OLD | STATE OF MAINE CUS-TOM"; p. [ii], *"Other Titles in The American Customs Series* | [thin rule] | [list of five titles] | *In preparation:* | IT'S AN OLD WILD WEST CUSTOM | *by Duncan Emrich"*; p. [iii], title; p. [iv], copyright page: "Copyright, 1949, by Edwin Valentine Mitchell | Published simultaneously in Canada by the | Copp Clark Company, Ltd., Toronto, Canada | No portion of this book may be reprinted in any form without the written | permission of the publisher, except by a reviewer who wishes to quote brief | passages in connection with a review for a newspaper or magazine. | Manufactured in the United States of America | by H. Wolff, New York, N.Y."; p. [v], dedication: *"To Bob and Anna Addams"*; p. [vi], "ACKNOWLEDGMENTS [signed E.V.M.]"; p. [vii], "CONTENTS"; p. [viii], blank; p. [1], half-title: "IT'S AN OLD | STATE OF MAINE CUSTOM"; p. [2], blank; pp. 3–248, text.

ILLUSTRATIONS: Small illustrations appear on pp. 3, 44, 80, 92, 103, 115, 129, 146, 162, 183, 204, 225, and 235.

BINDING: Dark teal cloth (close to Pantone 329); stamped in black. Front: Stamped in the center is an illustration of lighthouse at the edge of a rocky shore. Spine: "EDWIN | VALENTINE | MITCHELL | [read vertically] It's an

Old State of Maine Custom | [read horizontally] VANGUARD". Cream end-papers. Top edges stained dark teal.

DUST JACKET (cream paper): Front and spine have a forest-green background, close to Pantone 343. "[within a one-half inch wide white rectangular frame, with forest-green pine trees printed on the frame] [upper left, in black] [illustration of a fisherman in a small boat retrieving a lobster trap; this illustration is also found on p. 204 of the text] [to the right and below the illustration, in white] It's an | Old | State of Maine | Custom | Edwin Valentine Mitchell". Spine: "[white] It's | an | Old | State of | Maine | Custom | by | Edwin | Valentine | Mitchell | [six forest-green pine trees within a white rectangular panel | [at bottom] Vanguard". Back: "*Other Titles in* | THE AMERICAN CUSTOMS SERIES | [list of five titles and their authors, with quotes from reviews for each] | *Each volume illustrated with contemporary cuts and $3.00 at all booksellers* | THE VANGUARD PRESS, INC. | 424 Madison Avenue New York 17, N.Y.". Front flap: "[blurb] | *It's an Old State of Maine Custom:* | [list of thirteen Maine customs corresponding to the thirteen chapters of the book] | [lower right] $3.00". Back flap: "[brief biographical sketch of Edwin Valentine Mitchell]".

Published at $3.00, on June 29, 1949;[1] number of copies printed unknown.[2] Copyrighted June 28, 1949; deposited June 20, 1949.

The book is listed in "The Weekly Record," July 2, 1949, p. 89.

Note: No evidence found that Vanguard Press reprinted *It's an Old State of Maine Custom.*

COPIES: CF

REPRINTS AND REPRODUCTIONS

Thorndike, Maine: Thorndike Press, 1978. Paperback ($4.95) and hardback.

Reproduced on microfilm. Harvard social studies textbooks preservation microfilm project; 02704. Cambridge, Mass.: Harvard University Library Photographic Services, 1996. 1 reel; 35 mm.

BIOGRAPHY

For a biography of Edwin Valentine Mitchell, see *It's an Old Cape Cod Custom.*

1. The copyright certificate notes a publication date of June 24, 1949.
2. An undated list (ca. 1952) of four titles in the Customs series in an Edwin V. Mitchell file in the Vanguard Press archives at Columbia University indicates 4,789 copies printed as of June 15, 1949.

NOTES ON *IT'S AN OLD STATE OF MAINE CUSTOM*

The book and *It's an Old Cape Cod Custom*, the fifth volume in the series, were scheduled to be published on May 16, 1949. Early advertisements for the book used the title "*It's an Old Maine Custom.*" In a February 2, 1949, letter to Mitchell, James Henle, president of Vanguard Press, reported, "Arthur Dragon of the Old Corner [Bookstore] suggests that you call your Maine book "It's an Old State of Maine Custom." He says that is the phrase used up there — that someone doesn't say 'I'm a Maine man,' but 'I'm a State of Maine man.'" In his February 7 reply, Mitchell said, "Any suggestion Mr. Dragon of the Old Corner has to make about a book is worth heeding and I am all for calling the book 'It's An Old State of Maine Custom,'"adding that he would tender his thanks in the foreword. The book has no foreword, but "Arthur Dragon of the Old Corner Bookstore, Boston" is among those whose help is cited in the Acknowledgments.

When Henle forwarded the galleys of *Cape Cod* to Mitchell on February 25, 1949, he noted that he hoped reading them would not "interfere with the Maine book but will rather inspire you anew." On March 2, Mitchell replied, "You'll get the Maine book all right. I'll pull the remaining chapters together as speedily as possible. I keep running into things which I think should be included, or at least checked. . . . I wish I could gauge a job of writing better. Believe me I think you are a marvel of patience and controlled temper and I hope you are rewarded."

Increasingly concerned about Mitchell's completion of the manuscript of the Maine book and sales to wholesalers, on March 17 Henle wrote to Mitchell, "In the unlikely event . . . that I do not commit hari kari on your doorstep, I'd like a set of carbons (so far as you have them) for the buyer at the Portland branch of the News Co. . . . Even if the carbons aren't complete, it's better than nothing at all."

In a May 16, 1949, letter to Mitchell, Henle, referring to advance sales of nearly two thousand four hundred copies of Mitchell's Cape Cod book, wrote, "My guess is that unless things turn very bad between now and June 29, when we are going to publish "It's an Old State of Maine Custom" the advance on the book will be somewhat higher."

Vanguard had introduced and advertised both books together, scheduling them for publication on May 16, 1949, and noting that cooperative advertising would be offered and that postcards for bookshop mailings would be provided. *Cape Cod* met the scheduled May 16 publishing date. The *Maine* book was not published until June 29.

REVIEWS

Booklist, November 1, 1949 (p. 81); *Christian Science Monitor,* July 12, 1949 (p. 14); *Kirkus,* June 1, 1949 (p. 286); *Library Journal,* July 1949 (p. 1027); *New York Herald Tribune Book Review,* November 27, 1949 (p. 8); *New York Times Book Review,* October 16, 1949 (p. 10); *San Francisco Chronicle,* July 31, 1949 (p. 14); *Saturday Review of Literature,* August 13, 1949 (p. 33).

SELECTED WRITINGS BY EDWIN VALENTINE MITCHELL

For a list of selected writings by Edwin Valentine Mitchell, see *It's an Old Cape Cod Custom.*

SOURCES

Book Review Digest 1948. New York: The H.W. Wilson Company, 1949, p. 645.

The New York Times Book Review, October 16, 1949 , p. 10.

Publishers' Weekly, January 22, 1949, p. 245; January 29, 1949, p. 460 and p. 568; February 5, 1949, pp. 814–815; and July 2, 1949, p. 89.

Vanguard Press Archives. Box 104. "Edwin Valentine Mitchell 1948–1949" Columbia University Rare Book and Manuscripts Library.

IT'S AN OLD NEW ENGLAND CUSTOM

Edwin Valentine Mitchell
April 24, 1890 – November 26, 1960

AC4   First edition, first printing (1946) [1]

It's an Old | New England Custom | [illustration of a bearded hunter in a thicket, armed with a long gun and eyeing a flock of turkeys near a tumbledown rail fence] | EDWIN VALENTINE MITCHELL | THE VANGUARD PRESS, INC. · NEW YORK

COLLATION: 8" x 5½". 144 leaves. [i–x] [1–2] 3–277 [278]. Numbers printed in roman within brackets in the center at the foot of the page.

CONTENTS: p. [i], half-title: "IT'S AN OLD | NEW ENGLAND CUSTOM"; p. [ii], blank; p. [iii], title; p. [iv], copyright page: "Copyright, 1946, by Edwin Valentine Mitchell | Published simultaneously in Canada by the | Copp Clark Company, Ltd. | No portion of this book may be reprinted in any form without the written | permission of the publisher, except by a reviewer who wishes to quote brief | passages in connection with a review for a newspaper or magazine. | Designed by Stefan Salter | Manufactured in the United States of America by H. Wolff, | New York, N.Y."; p. [v], dedication: *"To Jean Mitchell Boyd"*; p. [vi], blank; p. [vii], "CONTENTS"; p. [viii], blank; p. [ix], "FOREWORD [signed E.V.M.]"; p. [x], blank; p. [1], half-title: "IT'S AN OLD | NEW ENGLAND CUSTOM"; p. [2], blank; pp. 3–277, text; p. [278], blank.

ILLUSTRATIONS: Small illustrations appear on pp. 3, 23, 36, 51, 65, 75, 94, 110, 132, 151, 169, 198, 215, and 253.

BINDING: Dark rose cloth (close to Pantone 493), stamped in black. Front: Stamped in the center is an illustration of a Colonial gentleman, a package under his right arm and, dangling from his left hand, a paper of some kind. Spine: "EDWIN | VALENTINE | MITCHELL | [read vertically] It's an Old New England Custom | [read horizontally] VANGUARD". Cream endpapers.

DUST JACKET (white paper): Front and spine have a burgundy background (close to Pantone 194). Superimposed on a cream, inch-wide rectangular frame are twenty-eight illustrations in black; above each illustration, in capital letters, is a single word, e.g., "TREE;" below each illustration is a drawing of the corresponding object, plant, or animal. Within the cream frame, in the upper left corner, in black, is the illustration found on the front cover of the binding. To the gentleman's right, in white, "It's an | Old | New England | Custom | Edwin Valentine Mitchell". Spine: "[black] It's | an | Old | New | England | Custom | by | Edwin | Valentine | Mitchell | [four, one-inch cream squares with thin black borders; inside each is an illustration in black and the identifying word above the drawing] | [at bottom] Vanguard". Back: White background; all printing in black. "It's an Old New England Custom . . . | [fourteen-entry list corresponding to the fourteen chapters of the book] | and, we may add, to read good books like this one | by EDWIN VALEN- TINE MITCHELL | [decoration] THE VANGUARD PRESS | 424 Madison Avenue New York 17, N.Y.". Front flap: "[brief quotes from two reviews: the *Philadelphia Inquirer* and the *Boston Post*] | [blurb] | [lower right] $2.75". Back flap: "EDWIN VALENTINE | MITCHELL | [brief biographical sketch] | [publisher's imprint]".

Published at $2.75, on October 3, 1946;[1] number of copies printed unknown. Copyrighted October 30, 1946; deposited September 20, 1946.

The book is listed in "The Weekly Record," October 5, 1946, p. 2021.

Note: Vanguard Press published at least two printings of *It's An Old New England Custom.*

COPIES: CF

REPRINTS AND REPRODUCTIONS

"Which Dover?" Excerpts from p. 227 of the chapter "To Adopt Peculiar Place Names" and p. 145 of the chapter "To Excel in Epitaphs" of *It's an Old New England Custom* appear in *A Treasury of New England Folklore: The Stories, Legends, Tall Tales, Traditions, Ballads and Songs of the Yankee People.* Revised Edition. Edited by B.A. Botkin. New York: Bonanza Books, 1965, pp. 247 and 594.

New York: Bonanza Books. Reprinted at least three times.

---

1. The Library of Congress copyright certificate bears a publication date of October 3, 1946. The Vanguard Press 1946 Fall List announcement in Publishers' Weekly noted that the book had been published in September.

Reproduced on microfilm. Ann Arbor, Mich.: University Microfilms International. 1 reel; 35 mm.

BIOGRAPHY

For a biography of Edwin Valentine Mitchell, see *It's an Old Cape Cod Custom.*

NOTES ON *IT'S AN OLD NEW ENGLAND CUSTOM*

On July 31, 1946, more than a month before the book went on sale, James Henle, president of Vanguard Press, wrote to Mitchell asking if he would "mind" if Vanguard took the title of the book as "the basis for other books on other parts of the country," adding, "I think I can predict with some assurance — at least our experience with the American Mountain Series tends to bear this out — that if we published "It's an Old Carolina Custom" or "It's an Old Kentucky Custom" next year, such a book will almost inevitably restimulate the sale of your own title." Henle closed his letter with the question, "How does this seem to you, and, incidentally, is there any other part of the country on which you feel inspired to write?"

On August 6, Mitchell replied, "I think the idea of a series on the regional customs of America is excellent and it is certainly quite all right with me. I have always favored series anyway. Had I known the New England item was to be the first one I should have adhered more strictly to the title and covered more ground. Sometime, if it strikes you favorably, I would like to tackle New York."

On August 8, Henle replied, "Thanks very much for your letter of August 6. I'm glad you like the idea of a series. And don't feel any regret about "It's an Old New England Custom." I think it's precisely right as it is, and will be an excellent introductory volume. We certainly won't assign New York to anyone else. . . ." Although Mitchell eventually wrote three other titles in the Customs series, the series does not include a title on New York customs.

The book was included in the Vanguard Fall List in the October 5, 1946, issue of *Publishers' Weekly.* Noting the book's publication in September, the advertisement described it as an "enchanting book on New England customs for anyone who has no more than stepped on New England soil and an essential family album for every New Englander."

The November 23, 1946, issue of *Publishers' Weekly* reported that Vanguard considered the book an ideal Christmas gift, noting. "a second printing was ordered a few days after publication, to take care of the reorders which began to come in from all parts of the country. One of the large jobbers has reordered the book four times. Although the heaviest sale has been made in New England, especially around Boston and Hartford, where the author once owned the well-known Edwin Valentine Mitchell bookshop and engaged in publishing activities, the book's appeal is not by any means limited to the New England area. Promotion of the book has included national advertising in New York Sunday supplements and New England newspapers, imprinted postcards, and display posters. The book was recently featured in an attractive display in the Park Avenue window of Dutton's bookstore."

REVIEWS

Booklist, November 1, 1946 (p. 68); *Christian Science Monitor,* November 30, 1946 (p. 14); *Kirkus,* October 1, 1946 (p. 517); *New York Times Book Review,* October 13, 1946 (p. 10); *Weekly Book Review,* October 6, 1946 (p. 2); *Wisconsin Library Bulletin,* December 1946 (p. 165).

SELECTED WRITINGS BY EDWIN VALENTINE MITCHELL

For a list of selected writings by Edwin Valentine Mitchell, see *It's an Old Cape Cod Custom.*

SOURCES

Book Review Digest, 1946. New York: The H.W. Wilson Company, 1947, p. 579.

The New York Times Book Review, October 13, 1946, p. 10.

Tebbel, John and Mary Ellen Zuckerman. *The Magazine in America: 1741–1990.* New York: Oxford University Press, 1991.

Van Balen, John. University of South Dakota, I.D. Weeks Library. Fax to CF, with attachments, February 10, 2003.

Weedman, Sylvia, The Bostonian Society, Boston, Mass. E-mail message to CF, March 5, 2003.

Vanguard Press Archives. Box 104, "Edwin Valentine Mitchell 1946–1947." Columbia University Rare Book and Manuscript Library.

Arcari, Ann J., Farmington Room, Farmington Public Library, Farmington, Connecticut. September 12, 2003, memorandum with attachments; press clippings from *Hartford Courant.*

IT'S AN OLD NEW ORLEANS CUSTOM

Lura Robinson
June 6, 1908 – March 8, 1990

AC5   First edition, first printing (1948) [4]

It's an Old | New Orleans Custom | BY LURA ROBINSON | [illustration of a horse-drawn parade float, a seated person and a dog beneath a palm tree at the upper rear and various animals cavorting on the lower, forward portion of the float] | NEW YORK | THE VANGUARD PRESS, INC.

COLLATION: 8" x 5½". 168 leaves. [i–xii] [1–2] 3–322 [323–324]. Numbers printed in roman in headline at the outer margin of the type page, except for pp. 3, 22, 44, 76, 103, 131, 159, 177, 196, 228, 240, 269, 284, and 303, on which the numbers are printed in the center at the foot of the page.

CONTENTS: p. [i], half-title: "IT'S AN OLD | NEW ORLEANS CUSTOM"; p. [ii], blank; p. [iii], title; p. [iv], copyright page: "Copyright, 1948, by Lura Robinson | Published simultaneously in Canada by the Copp Clark Company, Ltd. | No portion of this book may be reprinted in any form without the written | permission of the publisher, except by a reviewer who wishes to quote | brief passages in connection with a review for a newspaper or magazine. | For their permission to reprint in this volume excerpts from the sources | named, the author wishes to thank the following: | Henry Holt and Company, Inc., New York: *Forty Years a Gambler | on the Mississippi* by George Devol. Copyright, 1926 | The Times-Picayune Publishing Company, New Orleans: *Original | Picayune Creole Cook Book*. Copyright, 1936. | The Louisiana State Museum, New Orleans, La., for the flags shown | on page 3 (taken from *Glamorous Louisiana Under Ten Flags)*. | Designed by Stefan Salter | Manufactured in the United States of America by H. Wolff, | New York, N.Y."; p. [v], dedication: *"For* | EVELYN STEELE"[1]; p. [vi], blank; p.

1. The director of Vocational Guidance Research, New York, where Robinson worked and was the co-author or editor of non-fiction books.

[vii], "*Everyone in this good city* | *enjoys the full right to* | *pursue his own inclinations* | *in all reasonable and,* | *oftentimes, unreasonable ways.*' | The *Daily Picayune* | New Orleans, Louisiana | March 5, 1851 | '*To all men whose desire* | *only is to be rich and live a* | *short life but a merry one, I* | *have no hesitation in recommending* | *New Orleans.*' | *Sketches of America* | by Henry Bradshaw Fearon | London, 1819"; p. [viii], blank; pp. [ix–x], "ACKNOWLEDGMENTS [signed L.R.]"; p. [xi], "CONTENTS"; p. [xii], blank; p. [1], half-title: "IT'S AN OLD | NEW ORLEANS CUSTOM"; p. [2], blank; pp. 3–322, text; pp. [323–324], blank.

ILLUSTRATIONS: Small illustrations appear on pp. 3, 22, 44, 76, 103, 131, 159, 177, 196, 228, 240, 269, 284, 303 and 322.

BINDING: Dark teal cloth (close to Pantone 329); stamped in black. Front: Stamped in the center is an illustration of two jesters. Spine: "LURA | ROBINSON | [read vertically] It's an Old New Orleans Custom | [read horizontally] VANGUARD". Cream endpapers. Top edges stained dark teal.

DUST JACKET (white paper): Front and spine have a burgundy background (close to Pantone 249). "[within a cream rectangle framed by dark teal ornamental devices] [upper left, in purple] [two jesters (also stamped on the front of the binding)] [to their right, in dark teal] It's an | Old | New Orleans | Custom | Lura Robinson". Spine: "[white] It's | an | Old | New | Orleans | Custom | by | Lura | Robinson | [a single jester] | [at bottom] Vanguard". Back: Printing in dark teal. "*Other Titles in* | THE AMERICAN CUSTOMS SERIES | [list of the three previous titles and their authors, with quotes from reviews for each] | *Each volume illustrated with contemporary cuts and $3.00 at all booksellers* | THE VANGUARD PRESS, INC. | 424 Madison Avenue New York 17, N.Y.". Front flap: "[blurb] | In some of the fascinating chapters, you will | find that *It's an New Orleans Custom:*[2] | [list of fourteen New Orleans customs corresponding to the fourteen chapters of the book] | *With contemporary illustrations* | [lower right] $3.00". Back flap: "[blurb and four autobiographical paragraphs following 'The author tells us:']".

Published at $3.00 on October 21, 1948:[3] number of copies printed unknown.[4] Copyrighted and deposited October 18, 1948.

The book is listed in "The Weekly Record," June 18, 1949, p. 2484.

2. The word "Old" is missing from this line of print.
3. Vanguard had scheduled the publication of the book for October 14, 1948, but, owing to a truckers' strike in New York City, publication was delayed until October 21. The copyright certificate notes a publication date of October 18, 1948.
4. An undated list (ca. 1952) of four titles in the *Customs* series in an Edwin V. Mitchell file in the Vanguard Press archives at Columbia University indicates 3,117 copies printed as of October 2, 1948.

Note: No evidence found that Vanguard Press reprinted *It's An Old New Orleans Custom.*

COPIES. CF

REPRINTS AND REPRODUCTIONS

New York: Bonanza Books. Reprinted at least two times.

BIOGRAPHY

Lura L. Robinson was born in New Orleans, Louisiana, on June 6, 1908, the daughter of James L. and Otilla Robinson. The 1930 Census reports that Robinson's father was a "special officer with the steam railroad."

In an undated autobiographical typescript furnished to Vanguard by Robinson and adapted by Vanguard for use on the back flap of the dust jacket of *It's an Old New Orleans Custom,* Robinson reported that she had lived for a number of years in the Pontalba Buildings in New Orleans. Built by the Baroness de Pontalba in 1849 and said to be the oldest apartment houses in the United States, the buildings flank Jackson Square, with the Mississippi on one side and the St. Louis Cathedral (1794) and the Cabildo, the 1795 Spanish courthouse, on the other. Robinson noted, "It was here that I first felt the fascination of the city's history, and I believe almost anyone would in that atmosphere — for all the early history of New Orleans centered about that spot, the old Place d'Armes."

Robinson lived in New Orleans until 1943, when she moved to New York to work with Vocational Guidance Research in Flushing, Long Island, where she was the co-author or editor of non-fiction books in the field of vocational guidance. She later worked as a customer relations assistant at the Bayside National Bank in Flushing, New York.

A feature story by Cheri Chandler in the February 8, 1950, edition of the *New Orleans Item* reported that Robinson had returned to New Orleans from New York, having been "trampled in her last subway." A brief report on Robinson in the April 30, 1950, *New Orleans Times-Picayune Magazine* noted that she was "now writing fiction for teenagers," but no evidence of such work has been found.

Lura Robinson died on March 8, 1990, at age 81.

NOTES ON *IT'S AN OLD NEW ORLEANS CUSTOM*

In a February 17, 1947, letter to James Henle, president of Vanguard Press, returning her signed contract with Vanguard, Robinson expressed her gratitude for the opportunity to write the book. "New Orleans lends itself admirably to the 'It's An Old Custom' treatment," she wrote, adding, "(Its people, you know, would not exchange one of the old customs for a dozen shiny new factories-a fact that causes moaning among economists.) More, this framework gives the scope needed to include much delightful material that has not been touched in other books about the city."

Henle wrote to Robinson on March 23, 1948, commenting on the first draft of her manuscript and providing a number of detailed suggestions for its improvement. Robinson reworked and resubmitted the manuscript. In his letter of May 24, 1948, Henle wrote, "I think you have done a swell job . . . the manuscript now seems to me almost perfect, except for details . . . nothing vital."

A copy of the dust jacket was sent to Robinson in late September, 1948. She expressed her pleasure with the design, "particularly the dots on the trousers," a reference to the jesters' costumes on the front of the jacket. She politely noted the omission of the word "Old" from the book's title on the front flap, an error Vanguard had missed that survived the book's publication.

The book was included in the Vanguard 1948 Fall List, with a projected publication date of October 14. In May 1948, Vanguard had reported that *It's an Old New Orleans Custom* would be among the dummies of ten Vanguard books scheduled for publication in September or later that would be exhibited at the ABA Convention Exhibit of Books at the Palmer House in Chicago.

As noted, the book was scheduled to be published on October 14, 1948, but, because of delayed delivery from the printer owing to a truckers' strike in New York, publication did not occur until October 21.

In 1950, disappointed with the book's sales, Vanguard decided to remainder the book, maintaining a stock which could later be sold at full price, with the hope that lower-price sales would generate new interest in the book.

REVIEWS

Booklist, December 1, 1948 (p. 119); *Christian Science Monitor,* December 6, 1948 (p. 18); *Kirkus,* September 15, 1948 (p. 495); *Library Journal,* October 15, 1948 (p. 1509); *New York Herald Tribune Weekly Book Review,* October 24, 1948 (p. 20); *New York Times Book Review,* November 14, 1948 (p. 55); *San Francisco Chronicle,* November 28, 1948 (p. 10).

SELECTED WRITINGS BY LURA ROBINSON

(with Dorée Smedley) *Careers for Women in Real Estate and in Life Insurance* (New York: Dutton, 1945); (project editor) *Outdoor Jobs for Men* (by Vocational Guidance Research) (New York: Vanguard, 1947); *500 Postwar Jobs for Men* (Garden City, N.Y.: Doubleday, Doran, 1945); *It's an Old New Orleans Custom* (New York: Vanguard, 1948).

SOURCES

U.S. Bureau of the Census. 1930 Federal Census records.

New Orleans City Guide. American Guide Series. Boston: Houghton Mifflin Company, 1938.

Book Review Digest, 1948. New York: The H.W. Wilson Company, 1949, p. 705.

Publishers' Weekly, May 15, 1948, pp. 2075–2077; September 25, 1948, p. 1320; and June 18, 1949, p. 2484.

The New York Times Book Review, November 14, 1948, p. 55.

New Orleans Item, February 8, 1950, p. 19.

New Orleans Times-Picayune Magazine, April 30, 1950, p. 12.

Everard, Wayne. Archivist, New Orleans City Archives, Louisiana Division, New Orleans Public Library. E-mail message to CF, February 12, 2003, and copies of various newspaper articles.

Vanguard Press Archives. Box 146. "Lura Robinson" and "Lura Robinson Pub." Columbia University Rare Book and Manuscript Library. Accessed June 2003.

IT'S AN OLD PENNSYLVANIA CUSTOM

Edwin Valentine Mitchell
April 24, 1890 – November 26, 1960

AC6   First edition, first printing (1947) [2]

It's an Old | Pennsylvania Custom | [illustration of a large, spreading tree in the foreground; a city in the background] | EDWIN VALENTINE MITCHELL | *Author of "It's an Old New England Custom"* | THE VANGUARD PRESS, INC. · NEW YORK

COLLATION: 8" x 5½". 136 leaves. [i–x] [1–2] 3–261 [262]. Numbers printed in roman within brackets in the center at the foot of the page.

CONTENTS: p. [i], half-title: "IT'S AN OLD | PENNSYLVANIA CUSTOM"; p. [ii], blank; p. [iii], title; p. [iv], copyright page: "Copyright, 1947, by Edwin Valentine Mitchell | Published simultaneously in Canada by the | Copp Clark Company, Ltd. | No portion of this book may be reprinted in any form without the written | permission of the publisher, except by reviewer who wishes to quote brief | passages in connection with a review to be included in a newspaper or | magazine. | Designed by Stefan Salter | Manufactured in the United States of America by H. Wolff, | New York, N. Y."; p. [v], dedication: *"For Terry*[1] | [floral decoration]"; p. [vi], blank; p. [vii], "AC-KNOWLEDGMENTS [signed E.V.M.] | [small illustration of a bird and flowers]"; p. [viii], blank; p. [ix], "CONTENTS"; p. [x], blank; p. [1], half-title: "IT'S AN OLD | PENNSYLVANIA CUSTOM"; p. [2], blank; pp. 3–[262], text.

ILLUSTRATIONS: Small illustrations appear on pp. 3, 22, 35, 64, 79, 93, 107, 127, 143, 160, 174, 185, 196, 208, and 222.

BINDING: Medium cream cloth; stamped in dark green, close to Pantone 349. Front: Stamped in the center is an illustration of a lady in a print dress and a gentleman in fancy dress, each wearing a high hat (also found on p. 185 of the text, illustrating the chapter "To Observe Strange Customs of Courtship and Marriage')". Spine: "EDWIN | VALENTINE | MITCHELL |

1. Mitchell's wife.

[read vertically] It's an Old Pennsylvania Custom | [read horizontally] VAN-GUARD". Cream endpapers. Top edges stained dark green.

DUST JACKET (medium tan paper, close to Pantone 726): Front: "[within a U-shaped frame of flowers and leaves in orange and dark green] [illustration in dark green, (close to Pantone 349) and orange (close to Pantone 173) of the lady and gentleman depicted on the front of the binding and on p.185 of the text] [to the right and below the illustration, in dark green] It's an | Old | Pennsylvania | Custom | [orange] Edwin Valentine Mitchell | [dark green] author of "It's an Old New England Custom". Spine: "[dark green] It's | an | Old | Pennsylvania | Custom | [orange] by | Edwin | Valentine | Mitchell | [at bottom] Vanguard". Back: Printing in dark green. "ALSO BY EDWIN VALENTINE MITCHELL | It's an Old New England Custom | [quotes from four reviews] | $3.00 *at all bookstores* | THE VANGUARD PRESS, INC. | 424 Madison Avenue New York 17, N.Y.". Front flap: "[blurb] | *It's an Old Pennsylvania Custom:* | [fifteen-entry list corresponding to the fifteen chapters of the book] | *With contemporary illustrations* | [lower right] $3.00". Back flap: "EDWIN VALENTINE | MITCHELL | [brief biographical sketch] | [lower left corner] [diagonal dotted line].[2]

Published at $3.00 on November 3, 1947; number of copies printed unknown. Copyrighted November 20, 1947; deposited November 13, 1947.

The book is listed in "The Weekly Record," November 29, 1947, p. 2491.

Note: No evidence found that Vanguard Press reprinted *It's An Old Pennsylvania Custom.*

CITED: *Bibliography of Pennsylvania History* [1631] and [9163]

COPIES: CF

REPRINTS AND REPRODUCTIONS

New York: Bonanza Books, n.d.

BIOGRAPHY

For a biography of Edwin Valentine Mitchell, see *It's an Old Cape Cod Custom.*

NOTES ON *IT'S AN OLD PENNSYLVANIA CUSTOM*

In a May 16, 1947, letter to Mitchell, James Henle, president of Vanguard Press, reported "we are stirring up a tremendous amount of advance inter-

2. The copy described here is clipped just below this line. The dust jackets of various other Vanguard Press books, however, have the book's title, the publisher's name, and the price printed on the diagonal, below the dotted line.

est-especially in Philadelphia- in "It's an Old Pennsylvania Custom." Perhaps some of your scouts have told you about the excellent display we had at the A.B.A. book browse." After noting that he had already arranged "autographing parties" in Philadelphia and Lancaster and planned to arrange for Mitchell to speak at a *Philadelphia Inquirer* luncheon, Henle concluded his letter by observing that Vanguard is in a "hell of a sweat" for Mitchell's manuscript.

In an October 20 letter, Henle informed Mitchell that the "latest" and "absolutely definite" date for publication of the book would be November 10. With advance sales of nearly three thousand three hundred, the book was published on November 10. (The copyright certificate notes a publication date of November 3, 1947, the date used for this entry.)

It's an Old Pennsylvania Custom was included in the 1947 Vanguard Press Fall List, with projected publication in October. The book was advertised in the November 9, 1947 issue of *The New York Times Book Review*.

REVIEWS

Kirkus, October 1, 1947 (p. 566); *Library Journal,* November 1, 1947 (p. 1538); *New York Herald Tribune Weekly Book Review,* November 30, 1947 (p. 18).

SELECTED WRITINGS BY EDWIN VALENTINE MITCHELL

For a list of selected writings by Edwin Valentine Mitchell, see *It's an Old Cape Cod Custom.*

SOURCES

Book Review Digest 1947. New York: The H.W. Wilson Company, 1948, p. 638.

Publishers' Weekly, September 27, 1947, p. 1478; and November 29, 1947, p. 2491.

Library Journal, November 1, 1947, p. 1538.

The New York Times Book Review, November 9, 1947, p. 46 (advertisement).

Wilkinson, Norman B., comp. *Bibliography of Pennsylvania History.* Second Edition of Writings on Pennsylvania History: A Bibliography. Harrisburg: Pennsylvania Historical and Museum Commission, 1957.

Vanguard Press Archives. Box 104. "Edwin Valentine Mitchell 1946–1947." Columbia University Rare Book and Manuscript Library.

IT'S AN OLD WILD WEST CUSTOM

Duncan Emrich
April 11, 1908 – August 23, 1977

AC7   First edition, first printing (1949) [7]

It's an Old | Wild West Custom | [illustration of a cowboy on horseback riding up a flight of stairs, in a gun duel with a person below and to his right] | DUNCAN EMRICH | THE VAN-GUARD PRESS, INC. · NEW YORK

COLLATION: 8" x 5½". 164 leaves. [i–vi] vii–ix [x] xi [xii] xiii–xiv [1–2] 3–313 [314]. Numbers printed in roman in headline at the outer margin of the type page, except for pp. vii, xi, xiii, 3, 14, 27, 37, 43, 50, 65, 80, 96, 110, 129, 147, 162, 174, 186, 200, 213, 227, 242, 256, 269, 282, and 296, on which the numbers are printed in the center at the foot of the page.

CONTENTS: p. [i], half-title: "IT'S AN OLD | WILD WEST CUSTOM"; p. [ii], "*Other Titles in The American Customs Series* | [thin rule] | [list of six titles]"; p. [iii], title; p. [iv], copyright page: "Copyright, 1949, by Duncan Emrich | Published simultaneously in Canada by the | Copp Clark Company, Ltd., Toronto, Canada | No portion of this book may be reprinted in any form without the written | permission of the publisher, except by a reviewer who wishes to quote brief | passages in connection with a review for a newspaper or magazine. | The author acknowledges generous permission to use copyrighted material | from: | *Copper Camp,* by the Federal Writers' Project, published by Hastings | House, Publishers, Inc. | *Arizona State Guide,* by the Federal Writers' Project, published by Hast- | ings House, Publishers, Inc. | *Memories of Old Montana,* by Con Price, published by Trail's End Pub- | lishing Co., Inc. | Manufactured in the United States of America | by H. Wolff, New York, N.Y."; p. [v], dedication: "*To My* Wife | MARION VALLAT EMRICH | *and Other Western Characters*"; p. [vi], blank; pp. vii–ix, AC-KNOWLEDGMENTS"; p. [x], blank; p. xi, "CONTENTS"; p. [xii], blank; pp. xiii–xiv, "PREFACE [signed D.E.]"; p. [1], half-title: "IT'S AN OLD | WILD WEST CUSTOM"; p. [2], blank; pp. 3–313, text; p. [314], blank.

ILLUSTRATIONS: Small illustrations appear on pp. 3, 14, 27, 37, 43, 50, 65, 80, 96, 110, 129, 147, 162, 174, 186, 200, 213, 218, 219, 223, 224, 225, 227, 242, 256, 269, 282, 296, and 313.

BINDING: Orange cloth (close to Pantone 166); stamped in black. Front: Stamped in the center is a portion of the illustration on p. 162, a bearded man holding a bottle below his chin and against his chest. Spine: "DUN-CAN | EMRICH | [read vertically] It's an Old Wild West Custom | [read horizontally] VANGUARD". Cream endpapers. Top edges stained blue-gray.

DUST JACKET (cream paper): Front and spine have a medium rust background, close to Pantone 471. "[within a black rectangular frame decorated with medium rust cattle brands] [upper left, in black] [illustration of a crowded saloon scene; a group of men, one of them on the back of a burro, playing cards; the bartender in the background pouring a drink; the illustration is also found on p. 80 for the chapter "To Buck the Tiger"] [printed on and below the illustration, in white] It's an | Old | Wild West | Custom | Duncan Emrich". Spine: "[white] It's | an | Old | Wild | West | Custom | by | Duncan | Emrich | [three cattle brands in medium rust within a black rectangular panel | [at bottom, in white] Vanguard". Back: "*Who shot Maggie in the freckle,* | *Who shot Maggie on the Divide,* | *Who shot Maggie near Gold Hill* |*And ran away to hide?* | Who indeed? Especially as: | *Maggie was my boyhood sweetheart,* | *She loved me in the town on the hill,* | *And she never showed her freckle* | *to anyone but me, her Bill.* [to the right of the foregoing verses is a black and white photograph of Duncan Emrich by Lucien B. Wright | [five-paragraph blurb consisting principally of biographical information on the author] THE VANGUARD PRESS, INC. | 424 Madison Avenue New York 17, N.Y.". Front flap: "[blurb] | *It's an Old Wild West Custom:* | [list of thirteen Wild West customs corresponding to selected chapters of the book] | *etc., etc.* | [blurb] | [lower right] $3.00". Back flap: "*Other Titles in* | THE AMER-ICAN CUSTOMS SERIES | [list of the previous six titles and their authors, with quotes from selected reviews] | *Each volume illustrated* | *with contemporary cuts and* | *$3.00 at all booksellers*".

Published at $3.00, on September 19, 1949;[1] number of copies printed unknown. Copyrighted September 12, 1949; deposited September 6, 1949.

The book is listed in "The Weekly Record, " September 24, 1949, p. 1527.

Note: No evidence found that Vanguard Press reprinted *It's An Old Wild West Custom.*

1. There was a special publication date for the book on September 17, 1949, in Virginia City, Nevada. (The copyright certificate notes a publication date of September 6, 1949.)

CITED: *Guns* 679; *Herd* 766; Paher 563

COPIES: CF

REPRINTS AND REPRODUCTIONS

Kingswood, Surrey (England): World's Work, 1951.

BIOGRAPHY

Duncan Emrich was born on April 11, 1908, in Mardin, Turkey, the son of Richard Stanley Merrill and Jeannette (Wallace) Emrich. His parents were missionaries.

In his early years, Emrich worked as a cattle ranch hand, living in Colorado and Arizona. He attended Brown University, receiving the Hicks Prize in English and the Preston Gurney Literary Prize, and earning a bachelor of arts degree in 1932. In 1933, he earned a master of arts degree from Columbia University and, in 1934, a doctorate in letters from the University of Madrid. At Harvard, Emrich was a Shattuck Scholar (1935–1936) and an Edward Austin fellow (1936–1937), earning a doctorate in 1937.

From 1937 to 1940, Emrich was an instructor in English literature at Columbia University. From 1940 to 1942, he was assistant professor of English at the University of Denver.

During World War II, Emrich served in the Army (1942–1945), first in military intelligence and later, with the rank of major, as the official American historian at the headquarters of General Dwight D. Eisenhower, Supreme Commander of the Allied Expeditionary Forces in Europe. In June, 1945, he received the Croix de Guerre from the Provisional French Government.

In October, 1945, after his military service, Emrich was named Chief of the Archive of American Folk Song in the Music Division of the Library of Congress. From 1946 until 1955, he was chief of the library's folklore section. In 1948, he was the U.S. representative at the International Folk Music Council in London and at the International Folklore Conference in Paris. He received a Guggenheim Fellowship in 1949. During these years, he also served as a Fulbright lecturer on American civilization at universities in Rome, Naples, Messina, and Palermo.

Emrich married Sally Richardson Selden on November 20, 1955.

Emrich joined the Department of State in 1955 and over the next ten years worked in U.S. embassies and consulates in Greece, India, and West Africa. From 1966 to 1969, he was a desk officer for the former French West African countries at the U.S. Information Agency. In 1969, he became a professor of folklore at American University.

Emrich wrote or compiled books on folklore, both juveniles and adult, and contributed to folklore quarterlies and *Country Gentleman, Saturday Review of Literature, Reader's Digest, American Heritage,* and other periodicals. Under the pseudonym Blackie Macdonald he contributed articles to *Police Gazette.*

Duncan Emrich died in Washington, D.C., on August 23, 1977, at age 69.

NOTES ON *IT'S AN OLD WILD WEST CUSTOM*

Although Duncan Emrich wrote the book while serving as chief of the folklore section of the Library of Congress and living in Washington, he noted in a May, 1949, letter to James Henle, president of Vanguard Press, that his legal residence had been Virginia City, Nevada, for the preceding ten years. The back of the book's dust jacket identifies him as a legal resident of Virginia City.

In an exchange of letters between Emrich and Henle in the months prior to the book's publication in September 1949, Emrich took a personal interest in the art work for the dust jacket, suggesting, for example, that the cover depict a main-street scene in a Western town. In reply, Henle stated that Vanguard was planning to use a saloon and burro scene for the chief jacket illustration and that it would not be possible to use the street scene Emrich had suggested.

Emrich had also suggested using gold-pans, shovels, spurs, six-shooters, and the like for the border of the dust jacket. Henle noted that the "mining motif" had been used on the jacket of *It's An Old California Custom,* and asked that Emrich supply instead a selection of eight or ten cattle brands. The final jacket designs uses sixteen cattle brands and the saloon and burro scene.

The book was scheduled for publication on September 19, but Vanguard gave it a special publication date, September 17, for a promotion by Compton's Book Store of Reno, Nevada. Compton's mounted an Author's Day celebration in Virginia City featuring book-signing sessions in various saloons by four authors who lived in the city at the time, Lucius Beebe, Charles Clegg, Walter Van Tilburg Clark, and Duncan Emrich.

Capitalizing on Emrich's enthusiastic descriptions of the property and practices of Harolds Club, the famous Reno, Nevada, casino, in the book's eighth chapter, "To Buck the Tiger," the club published and distributed a brochure which reprints most of pages 90–95 of that chapter. The brochure included a picture and a brief biographical sketch of Emrich and advised that the book was on sale at the club's newsstand. Emrich was no stranger to Nevada society. His book, *Who Shot Maggie in the Freckle and Other Ballads of Virginia City,* which was privately printed in 1940, had by 1949 sold seven thousand copies at the Bucket of Blood Saloon in Virginia City, the only place at which it could be purchased.[2]

According to an April 27, 1951, letter from Henle to Emrich, Emrich was to receive 75 percent of Vanguard's royalties on the British edition of the book published in 1951 by World's Work in Kingswood, Surrey. Henle's letter reports, "To date payments from Britain have been coming through with due regularity."

In a December 2, 1952, letter to Emrich, Henle reported that Vanguard had had an overstock of *It's An Old Wild West Custom* which they had been compelled to sell at a remainder price, noting, "We still have ample stock for some time to come."

REVIEWS

Booklist, October 15, 1949 (p. 62); *Kirkus,* August 15, 1949 (p. 449); *Library Journal,* September 15, 1949 (p. 1316) and October 15, 1949 (p. 1563); *New York Herald Tribune Weekly Book Review,* October 9, 1949 (p. 16); *New York Times Book Review,* October 23, 1949 (p. 31); *San Francisco Chronicle,* September 19, 1949 (p. 18); *Saturday Review of Literature,* October 22, 1949 (p. 23).

SELECTED WRITINGS BY DUNCAN EMRICH

Juveniles:
The Cowboy's Own Brand Book (New York: Crowell, 1954); (comp.) *The Nonsense Book of Riddles, Rhymes, Tongue Twisters, Puzzles and Jokes from American Folklore* (New York: Four Winds Press, 1970); (comp.) *The Book of Wishes and Wishmaking* (New York: American Heritage Press, 1971); (comp.) *The Hodgepodge Book: An Almanac of American Folklore, Containing All Manner of Curious, Interesting, and Out-of-the-Way Information Drawn from American Folklore, and Not to Be Found Anywhere Else in the World; As Well as Jokes, Conundrums, Riddles, Puzzles, and Other Matter Designed to Amuse and Entertain – All of It Most Instructive and Delightful* (New York: Four Winds Press, 1972); *The Whim-Wham Book* (New York: Four Winds Press, 1975); *Riddles & Jokes & Foolish Facts* (Scholastic Paperbacks, 1976).

Adult:
Who Shot Maggie in the Freckle and Other Ballads of Virginia City (Privately printed, 1940); *Casey Jones, and Other Ballads of the Mining West* (Denver: W. H. Kistler Stationery Co., 1942); *It's an Old Wild West Custom* (New York:

2. Emrich letter to Henle, May 31, 1949.

Vanguard, 1949); *Comstock Bonanza: Western Americana of J. Ross Browne, Mark Twain, Sam Davis, Bret Harte, James W. Gally, Dan de Quille, Joseph T. Goodman [and] Fred Hart* (New York: Vanguard, 1950); (editor with Charles Clegg) *The Lucius Beebe Reader* (New York: Doubleday, 1967); *The Folklore of Love and Courtship: The Charms and Divinations, Superstitions and Beliefs, Signs and Prospects of Love, Sweet Love* (New York: American Heritage Press, 1970); *The Folklore of Weddings and Marriage: The Traditional Beliefs, Customs, Superstitions, Charms, and Omens of Marriage and Marriage Ceremonies* (New York: American Heritage Press, 1970); *Folklore on the American Land* (Boston: Little, Brown, 1972); *American Folk Poetry: An Anthology* (Boston: Little, Brown, 1974).

Contributor to *Western Folklore Quarterly, Southern Folklore Quarterly, Country Gentleman, Saturday Review of Literature, The New York Times Magazine, Reader's Digest, Library of Congress Quarterly, Holiday, Moslem World, American Heritage,* and other periodicals. Contributor of articles, under the pseudonym Blackie Macdonald, to *Police Gazette.*

In 1970 and 1971, *The Nonsense Book of Riddles, Rhymes, Tongue Twisters, Puzzles and Jokes from American Folklore,* compiled by Emrich, received a number of awards: a Library of Congress children's book award (1970); Best Book of the Year by *School Library Journal* (1970); an American Library Association Notable Book award (1970); Top Honor Book of the Chicago Book Clinic (1971); Children's Book of the Year by the Child Study Association of America (1971); and the Lewis Carroll Shelf Award (1971). *The Hodgepodge Book* was named an Outstanding Children's Book by the *New York Times Book Review* in 1972.

SOURCES

Book Review Digest 1949, New York: H.W. Wilson Company, 1950, p. 276.

Publishers' Weekly, September 3, 1949, p. 1010 and p. 1070; September 17, 1949, p. 1413 and p. 1421; and September 24, 1949, p. 1527.

The New York Times Book Review, October 23, 1949, p. 31.

Contemporary Authors Online. The Gale Group, 1999. Reproduced in *Biography Resource Center.* Farmington Hills, Mich.: The Gale Group. 2001. Accessed February 8, 2002.

Vanguard Press Archives. Box 40. "Duncan Emrich 1949–1952" and "Duncan Emrich." Columbia University Rare Book and Manuscript Library. Accessed June 2003.